The Canadian Family
in Comparative Perspective

The Canadian Family in Comparative Perspective

LYLE E. LARSON
Associate Professor
Department of Sociology
University of Alberta

Prentice-Hall of Canada, Ltd.
Scarborough, Ontario

PRENTICE-HALL, INC., ENGLEWOOD CLIFFS, NEW JERSEY
PRENTICE-HALL INTERNATIONAL, INC., LONDON
PRENTICE-HALL OF AUSTRALIA, PTY., LTD., SYDNEY
PRENTICE-HALL OF INDIA PVT., LTD., NEW DELHI
PRENTICE-HALL OF JAPAN, INC., TOKYO

ISBN 0-13-112797-7 (cloth)

ISBN 0-13-112805-1 (paper)

Design/Maher & Garbutt Ltd.
Cover photo/Miller Services Limited

4   5   80

PRINTED AND BOUND IN CANADA

To three very special people:
Deanna, Julie, and Mark

Contents

Part III *The Family and Social Change*

Preface

There are many excellent textbooks on the family in society which frequently include discussions of family systems in countries other than the United States. Unfortunately, none of these texts emphasize material on the family in Canadian society. This situation is naturally perplexing, if not exasperating, to students who are interested in the similarities and differences between family theory and research in Canada and in other countries. After studying the available Canadian materials and attempting to provide a view of Canadian families in comparative perspective for more than six years, I have come to believe that a solid Canadian textbook is possible. This book is the result of my efforts.

The rather impassioned defense of *Canadian* family study in several recent publications, which typically concentrates on the search for the differences between Canadians and Americans, has in my view missed the point. The more attractive emphasis would seem to lie in *both the similarities and the differences* between the structures and processes of families in Canada and other societies. This book is offered at this time because Canadians should know what is and is not known about the family in Canadian society and how Canadian families compare to families in other cultures.

I have chosen to emphasize Canadian resource materials wherever viable in describing and illustrating the fundamental issues in the sociological study of the family. The focus on an introduction to family study, rather than the family in Canada exclusively, means that non-Canadian materials are also utilized throughout the book. It is not yet reasonable to produce an integrated and substantive textbook with Canadian resource material alone. In addition, a comparative approach seems most applicable to introductory family courses.

If there is a bias in this book it has been toward underscoring the value of: (a) comparative family study between cultures and within cultures — Canada, in particular; and (b) the salience of the struggle of the family between remaining largely unchanged from generation to generation and becoming something quite different.

In my view, first-year students of the family should be exposed to a broad-based overview of family theory and research (comparative, institutional, social psychological and change perspectives). Sociology and family studies departments are increasingly able to offer advanced level family courses, permitting a more comprehensive, survey-type introductory course. Accordingly, this book provides insight into intrafamily interpersonal relationships, family-community exchanges at the sub-cultural level, family-society exchanges at the macrosociological level in several societies, anthropological perspectives on the similarities and differences among families in differing societies, and the dynamics of family stability and change. Each topic is addressed as concisely and accurately as possible. The book provides a useful analytical context for detailed study of any one or more of these themes. Accordingly, textbooks or books of readings which emphasize complementary themes may be readily adopted. Although nearly 60 percent of the book is based on Canadian content, instructors may well adopt collateral materials which deal exclusively with Canadian studies.

The Canadian Family in Comparative Perspective includes twenty-one papers, six of which were specifically prepared for publication in this book. I am grateful to the publishers and authors of each of the other papers for permitting me to reprint their materials. I particularly appreciate the special contributions of Professors Colette Carisse, Charles Hobart, Warren Kalbach, Wayne McVey, Karl Peter, Joan Ryan, and Jean Veevers. The considered and detailed comments of those who reviewed the manuscript are also appreciated. Though I alone am responsible for what has been written here, the manuscript is the benefactor of many helpful suggestions. I am also indebted to the editorial skills of Carol Beatty of Prentice-Hall in the production phase of the manuscript. Prentice-Hall has been a patient and solid supporter during all stages of writing and production. I am pleased that I may express my appreciation to these many able resources.

Lyle E. Larson

Part One

The Study of the Family

1

Introduction

The ancient trinity of father, mother, and child has survived more vicissitudes than any other human relationship. It is the bedrock underlying all other family structures. Although more elaborate family patterns can be broken from without or may even collapse of their own weight, the rock remains. In the Götterdämmerung which overwise science and overfoolish statesmanship are preparing for us, the last man will spend his last hours searching for his wife and child.

Ralph Linton, "The Natural History of the Family", The Family: Its Function and Destiny, *rev. ed., Ruth N. Anshen, ed. (New York: Harper and Row, 1959), p. 52.*

Each new generation smiles with amusement at the courtship patterns of the preceding generation, and each new generation of parents looks with some consternation on the innovations introduced by its children. In this way, intergenerational change calls attention to itself so that our interests are focused on the differences . . . The similarity from one generation to the next is ignored because it consists of everything that both generations take for granted. Yet, studies of attitudes and behavior covering all the generations of the century show only relatively minor changes in basic patterns between contiguous generations. Each generation introduces some new twist on an old theme. . . . in nearly everything basic to the heterosexual relationships of American society, the present generation appears not to have changed as profoundly from its parents as both generations would like to believe.

J. Richard Udry, The Social Context of Marriage, *2nd ed. (New York: J.B. Lippincott, 1971), p. 21.*

The increasing pace of social change has . . . serious implications for family life. The problem is experienced most directly in the feeling that one generation's knowledge and perspectives are irrelevant for the next. The central problem of socialization today is not how society can ensure that the culture and skills of the older generation will be passed on to the children, but rather, how the burden of obsolescent knowledge can be kept from interfering with necessary changes. How can children be taught in a way that will not close their minds against further knowledge? How, in short, can human beings remain childlike all their lives in their curiosity and openness to new experience?

From Arlene S. Skolnick and Jerome H. Skolnick, Family in Transition: Rethinking Marriage, Sexuality, Child Rearing, and Family Organization, *p. 27. Copyright © 1971, by Little, Brown and Company (Inc.). Reprinted by permission.*

Even casual observation of Canadian society provides positive evidence that the ways of males and females are both organized and systematic. Most dwellings are occupied by at least one mating couple who have made pledges of permanence and affection, and who typically are in the process of rearing their offspring. Few people, whatever their marital status, are able to escape the pervasive influence of their own families, past or present, or the implications of our couple- and family-oriented society in their everyday relationships. Canada is not alone. This basic theme, with minor variations, is prevalent in most societies of the world.

Why study the family?

There are many ways of defining and organizing human phenomena. People in Canada are distributed among various racial and ethnic categories and they live in different places. Some still live in the country but most now live in cities, some North of the railroad tracks, others South. People are organized into different occupational strata, participate in many different kinds of voluntary and involuntary associations, have multivariate beliefs and values, and control and are controlled by others. They are frequently motivated to conform to the wishes of others, and sometimes motivated to resist and perhaps rebel against societal structures and processes perceived to be outdated and inappropriate. Each of these ways of categorizing and interpreting the organized processes of man provides insight into the dynamics of becoming and being Canadian. The fact alone that these structures and processes *exist* in Canadian society commands the attention of the social scientist. To acknowledge that heterosexual love and sexual relationships, marriage, child rearing, and parent-child and kinship ties are an integral part of human activity is reason enough for study. Marriage and family ties are part of social reality.

A second reason for the study of the family concerns the influence of the family on human nature. The linkages between the values, motivations, and personality of an individual and the procedures and processes of socialization within his family are well documented, although their implications may not always be clear. In many respects, the family is both the cradle and the citadel of what we are.

The exchange between the family and the community is also significant. For example, Karl Peter, in his paper prepared for this book, examines the struggle between family rights and collective duties among the Hutterites through history. The family is commonly thought of as a conserving force in changing societies; it is imperative, therefore, in any consideration of social change to identify and interpret the dynamics of the transactions between the family and society. This latter issue is of particular importance in understanding the increasing interest in (and probable practice of) alternative marriage and family life styles in Canadian society.

There are many other reasons for family study. Persons anticipating marriage and/or the rearing of children, typically a lifelong enterprise, will profit from insight into the interactions and transactions of family members. First, most who marry know little of what to expect. Many tend to idealize marriage as a kind of permanent euphoria providing the ultimate personal satisfaction. Others marry expecting little, but not knowing what else to do with themselves. In consequence, marriage is often an amateur production in which the actors are forced to ad-lib with the cues they have acquired in previous experience and from the situations they face as a couple. Second, evidence of the impact of parental attitudes and behavior on many aspects of human development, including self conception, conscience formation, motivation, creativity, intelligence, personality, delinquency, mental pathology, and related phenomena, cannot be ignored. Persons responsible for the nurture of children should be aware of the significance of their actions.

Work roles in our society, in contrast to marriage and parenthood roles, usually require training. A teacher, for example, is specifically trained to teach. When the training is completed, the candidate typically receives a certificate or degree to indicate exposure to a body of knowledge and qualification above a minimum level. Qualification for marriage and parenthood roles, however, requires no knowledge and no proof of a capacity to show empathy to a proposed spouse or offspring. All that is generally required is a licence, good blood, a few hours to think about it, a few "I do's" in front of witnesses — and a couple can establish a marriage residence and bear and rear children in relative privacy. Of course neither teacher training nor family training can ensure the practice of the principles acquired, but at least there are more than cues to apply in each situation; hopefully, knowledge is power. In some respects, the family is the most natural place to learn the processes of child development, sexual development and interaction, and the nature of marriage and family relationships. Experience, however, isn't always the best teacher due to inaccurate learning, maladjustment, and the distortion of reality. Furthermore, whatever is learned is more often caught than taught.

The social service professions continually have contact with individuals who have marital and family bonds. Patients, parolees, counselors, clients, and the handicapped, among others, have families. Practitioners should be aware of the characteristics and importance of these relationships. Therapy is, in fact, becoming increasingly oriented toward the *family* rather than the individual.

Ways of understanding the family

Perhaps the most prominent way of understanding the family is through personal experience. Interaction with our parents, siblings, spouses and children gives us a potentially unique point of view toward the family. This approach (which may be thought of as a form of theory, because our experiences guide our relationships with others) is based on the evidence we have collected, however positive or negative. Our perceptions of other families and our preferences toward family life styles cannot be easily separated from our experience.

Our experience also includes exposure to the ideas of others. Sex, marriage, and family life are frequent topics of informal discussion. The media also present their images of family reality, varying from news accounts of what the "experts" are saying, to the experiential wisdom of the columnist, to the tragedy and euphoria of the soap opera.

These experiences often provide the basis for our assistance to other people. Some people have become part of a volunteer corps of individual and group family life educators concerned about enhancing the quality of marriage and family life. Others who work with people have been trained in social work, counseling, or psychological theory but seldom have specific training in family theory and research. Accordingly, insights gained through personal experience play an important role.

Other methods of understanding the family involve analytical description, generalization, explanation, and research. Both personal experience and theory and research offer insight into family life; this book will emphasize the contributions of the latter approach, for three reasons. First, personal experience tends to distort one's view of other families. Persons who have had negative experiences will probably expect to see negative attributes in other families. Experiential analysts often lack perspective. Second, one's own experiences frequently provide a limited view of family reality. Knowing something of the patterns and practices of families in other parts of Canada, as well as in other cultures, leads to new understanding and insights. Third, family members frequently blame each other for family problems. An appreciation of the location of a given family in its social context often leads to very different conclusions.

Scholarship, even so, can be influenced by the values of the scholar. Although objectivity is the password among social scientists, it is sometimes difficult to ignore one's own family experience in conducting research on the structure and process of marriage and family life. Through simple neglect, de-emphasis, or value-oriented preferences, family scholars may overlook many basic questions. The student of science must always be both open-minded and skeptical.

Conceptual issues in family study

Introductory textbooks typically describe the family and discuss research findings in detail. The basic questions underlying family research (questions that led the researcher to search for answers) are seldom discussed. Hypotheses are sometimes included, but the more primitive questions are ignored. The term "analytical issues" refers to fundamental questions about the nature of social reality.

Analytical issues

For the child, these questions typically reflect inquiry into the unknown. For the researcher, they more often reflect an inquiry into how social reality is organized and patterned. The questions are basically of three types: what is (sometimes who is); how is it this way — this question concerns the conditions under which it is this way (such as when and where); and why is it this way. The illustration below provides an example of each type of question.

 a. *What* is marriage?
 b. *How* do people become married? Do people get married in different ways? What kinds of conditions affect how people marry? Do people marry for different reasons?
 c. *Why* do people become married?

The first is the most primitive and deals with description. Answers to questions of this kind are not always clearcut. The meaning of marriage, for example, varies in different societies. The second question seeks clarification of those factors which facilitate more accurate description, providing ways of helping us better understand marriage. The third question is most concerned with explanation and is the most difficult of the three; it is also the most interesting.

A series of unordered analytical questions are presented below to illustrate certain of the types of issues to be addressed in this book. The first set deals primarily with the relationships between the family and society. The second set emphasizes those questions most appropriate to the social psychological study of the family.

Selected questions on the family and society

 1. What are the similarities and differences in courtship, mate choice, and marriage entry procedures and processes cross-culturally and sub-culturally? Why do these patterns and practices exist? What conditions influence persistence and change in

these patterns and practices?

2. What are the similarities and differences in marital role definitions, marital adjustment and satisfaction, sexual relationships, childbirth, the socialization of the young, and exchanges among kin and between kin and the community cross-culturally and sub-culturally? Specifically, do these patterns and practices vary among families and marriages of different types, such as nuclear, extended, monogamous, polygynous, polyandrous, communal and group marriages?[1] What conditions influence persistence and change in these patterns and practices?

3. Are mating, marriage, and family patterns within specific societies interconnected? In what ways do these linkages resist or facilitate persistence and change? Why are family alternatives prevalent in some societies and absent in others?

Selected questions on the social psychology of the family

1. What are the similarities and differences between marriage relationships and unmarried heterosexual relationships? Do homosexual and heterosexual relationships differ? Do married couples interact differently after they have children? Does marital interaction differ in the presence and absence of children?

2. What are the similarities and differences between family relationships and relationships in other small groups? What is the influence of emotional ties on family organization? Do family relationships in large families differ from those in small families? Do family relationships vary by the age of parents and the age and sex of children?

3. How do parent-child relationships differ from adult-child, teacher-student, and parent-adolescent relationships? What is the influence of different age and sex compositions on parent-child relationships? What are the similarities and differences between sibling relationships and other interpersonal relationships?

4. What is the short range and long range effect of different family structures and variant parenting procedures and processes on human development (children, adolescents, parents)? What is the influence of different values and life styles on human development?

5. In what ways do social characteristics such as social class, ethnicity, race, occupation, income and ecological conditions influence marriage and family relationships and socialization processes?

Each of the above questions, as well as many others which are not identified or could be derived, can be explored relative to families in Canada. More detailed consideration of these and related questions is provided in each chapter.

1 These terms are defined in Chapter three.

Conceptual frameworks

The various ways in which these questions are considered by family sociologists may be referred to as *conceptual frameworks*. A conceptual framework is a set of interrelated concepts and assumptions about aspects of human phenomena. It may be thought of as a classification or taxonomous device to organize social data. In collecting information about human culture and behavior, the researcher classifies it into categories to help him understand it.

Perhaps a simple analogy will be helpful. The postman receives mail, classifies it, and delivers the mail in a systematic manner. How well he classifies the mail before he begins his route will have much to do with the efficiency of his delivery. Classifying the letters alphabetically or by block would be inefficient. If the letters are organized by house number, in sequence, moving up and down each street and moving from east to west within the route, the mail will be delivered much more quickly. Some postmen, however, have other types of delivery (or, to put it another way, different kinds of problems with which to deal). For example, the postman who delivers mail to a large number of business establishments and several highrise apartment buildings will need to develop a different classification system, particularly if certain companies require preferred service.

Similarly, conceptual frameworks not only reflect various ways of identifying, classifying, and interpreting the same phenomena; they also deal with different kinds of problems. A good example is reflected in the characteristic approaches of psychology and sociology. Sometimes different language is used to explain the same thing; in other cases the issues under consideration are of a different order.

Conceptual frameworks are important for several reasons. For our purposes, two can be identified. First, they narrow the scope of analysis to more manageable limits. By focusing, as with a microscope, on a small unit of analysis much can be learned about the phenomena which one would miss utilizing a more comprehensive perspective. Second, conceptual frameworks provide helpful and efficient building blocks in the development of theory. By developing and testing hypotheses about specific aspects of the family and eventually linking those findings which have been verified, (or found to be mostly true), the likelihood of more comprehensive explanations of family phenomena is enhanced.

We will briefly discuss five conceptual frameworks commonly used by family sociologists: the structural-functional, institutional, symbolic interaction, developmental and systems approaches.[2]

2 A useful discussion of eleven different conceptual frameworks in family study can be found in Ivan Nye and Felix Berardo, *Emerging Conceptual Frameworks in Family Analysis*, 1966.

Sociological approaches There are two approaches commonly thought of as sociological: the structural-functional and the institutional. Social scientists who use the *structural-functional* approach[3] see the parts of society as basically "interdependent". That is, for example, the family and the economic sector of society depend on each other in order to survive. Each of these parts is said to perform a function or contribution for each other and for the whole society. The contributions of basic family activities, such as creating an equitable division of labor among family members, to the survival of the family and to the care of individuals within families are also emphasized in this approach.

Perhaps the most basic assumption or belief of this approach is that certain minimum requirements must be met in order for society to survive. These are called "functional prerequisites". The typical list of these includes:

a) Reproduction of children to replace dying members — this is usually accomplished by the family.
b) Production and distribution of goods (e.g., food) and services — typically carried out by the economic system.
c) Provision for coping with conflict and maintaining order — generally accomplished by government.
d) Socialization or training of children in the skills and values of the society — generally provided by some kind of formal education.
e) Ways of coping with emotional problems, harmonizing the needs of individuals with the needs of society, and helping individuals maintain a sense of purpose — typically carried out by religious or scientific organizations.
f) Ways of coping with physical disease — usually done by medical care institutions.

In some societies the family may be responsible for all of these functional prerequisites; in others, the family (depending on how it is defined) may not be responsible for any of them. The family (the meaning of this term in comparative perspective is considered in Chapter three) is generally seen as a universal part of societies because it appears to be responsible for at least one of the functional prerequisites — reproduction. Structural-functionalism also emphasizes that the survival of each family is dependent on the successful fulfillment of functional requirements similar to those of the society as a whole. In this sense, each family is a kind of miniature society. Of course there are many flaws in this way of looking at the family in society, just as there are flaws in every approach. For example, easy divorce might not be functional for society, but it may be very helpful to some individuals. Even so, structural-

3 A more detailed treatment of the structural-functionalist approach may be found in Chapter three in Nye and Berardo (1966) and in Chapter two in Christensen (1964). A recently revised book by Bell and Vogel (1968) illustrates the applications of the approach to family study.

functionalism has had a significant influence on family study and remains the predominant approach to comparative family analysis.

The *institutional* approach[4] is concerned with the origin, stability of, and change in the family over time. It is assumed that families evolve or change as society changes, but that change is very slow. People who use this approach for the most part simply describe what families were like in history and what the modal (most common) family is like in different societies. This approach is not widely used by sociologists anymore, but much of what we have learned about the family has grown out of this kind of information.

Social psychological approaches There are several conceptual frameworks that deal with what people think and do *within* families. The three most common approaches will be discussed briefly.

The *developmental* framework[5] emphasizes the importance of the expectations of others in what people do. Family members are said to occupy positions such as "husband-father". Accordingly, much of what husbands and fathers do is strongly related to what society, their families, and their spouses expect them to do. Being a husband, for example, also involves more specific roles, such as being a "social partner" to one's spouse. It should be clear that expectations (or *norms*, as they are called) make up roles and roles make up positions. This framework, applied to social psychological relationships over time, results in the use of such concepts as positional career, role sequence, and norm sequence.

The developmental approach assumes that individual, dyad (e.g., mother-father relationship) and family (all members of a family) development is related to the norms that apply to the differing stages in the life cycle. Families with teenage children, for example, are expected to behave differently than families with preschool children because the norms are different. In addition, certain sets of norms (referred to as "developmental tasks") arise at several points or periods during the life cycle. If the individual or family is unable to fulfill these expectations, normal

4 A more detailed treatment of the institutional approach may be found in Chapter four in Nye and Berardo (1966) and in Chapter three in Christensen (1964). Several classic books reflect different aspects of the institutional perspective: the cyclical view of the family in history (Zimmerman, 1947); the typological view of the changing family (Burgess, Locke, and Thomes, 1963); an evolutionary view (Morgan, 1877); and the changing functions of the family (Ogburn and Nimkoff, 1955).

5 The basic references for further study of the developmental approach include Hill and Hansen (1960), Hill and Rodgers (1964), and Rowe (1966). Duvall (1971) and recently, Rodgers (1973) have written family textbooks utilizing this approach, among others. It may be noted that the structural-functional approach also deals with expectations and their influence on behavior. However, the level of conceptual development has had a more sociological than social psychological focus.

development is retarded and the relationships are expected to become unstable. If a *husband*, for example, fails to behave according to the expectations for a *father*, the father-mother dyad will be in jeopardy, as will the continued development of the husband into the future roles he is expected to assume.

This approach is important to the social psychological study of families in other cultures. Family and kin norms are typically very clear and family members are expected to behave accordingly. The behavior of family members in Western society however, though systematically influenced by norms, appears to deviate more frequently from the script.[6]

The *symbolic interaction* approach[7] emphasizes both expectations and behavior. The concepts utilized in this framework deal with symbols (including language, gestures, and other cues), variant perceptions, the capacity of the individual to receive and evaluate stimuli and response, the self concept, self-esteem, and internal family processes such as role playing, status relationships, communication problems, decision making, and socialization.

The general assumptions of this approach deal with the necessity of learning symbols in order to interact with others; a person's capacity to interpret and manipulate both stimuli and response, i.e., people are *not* robots as in extreme Skinnerian theory; and the belief that when two or more people interact they create a unit of study very different from the cumulative attributes of the individuals involved. Reinterpreting these assumptions and applying them to the family suggests the following general assumption.

> When family members interact, they interpret the situation and variously consider the consequences of their actions for themselves and their interaction partners.

Accordingly, a husband interacting with his wife will consider the various expectations appropriate to the situation (his own, those of his wife), the consequences of different courses of action in view of his own wishes and those he perceives his wife to hold, and then proceed to act in terms of the conclusions he has drawn. His actions indicate to his wife the results of his thoughts. An excellent summary of this particular approach to the *dynamics* of interaction can be found in McCall and Simmons (1966).

In a comparative perspective, symbolic interaction theory is most applicable to

---

6 Although behavior is frequently related to expectations, there is evidence that much of marriage and family behavior is of an "ad-lib" variety. Family members have variant definitions of the norms, and situational cognitions affect bargaining and negotiation processes.

7 The basic references for further study of this framework include Hill and Hansen (1960), Rose (1962), Stryker (1964) and Schvaneveldt (1966).

family study in cultures where spousal and parent-child relationships involve negotiation and bargaining, or, in a more primitive sense, a clarification of role responsibilities. Unfortunately, few attempts have been made to explore the applications of this approach in other cultures.

The symbolic interaction approach has had a considerable impact on family study. However, many of its tenets are difficult to measure and the concepts are most appropriate to timebound and dyadic analysis.

The *systems* approach, although not yet systematically applied to family study, was first developed in 1950 by Von Bertalanffy to emphasize the importance of an organic view of biological organization, in contrast to the then common practice of dividing living organisms into parts and partial processes. The application of the systems approach to the complex and dynamic properties of society is seen by many as a breakthrough in sociological theory.

In general, the approach emphasizes the characteristics of subsystem (e.g., the husband-wife relationship) and system (e.g., the whole family unit) behavior over time. The different ways in which behavior at one point in time is connected to behavior at other points in time are emphasized. The issues considered, for example, might include how behaviors are sequenced and interconnected, and whether there are recurring cycles or identifiable phases of development in behavior. The typical concerns of systems theorists can be divided into two schools of thought: the *closed* and the *open*.

The closed systems approach is heavily based on social psychiatry. In addition, the study of family meals and rituals to help gain insight into what families are like as *whole* units (Bossard and Boll, 1966) and the study of a family as a psychosocial unit by psychologists (Hess and Handel, 1959; Handel, 1972) has had a significant impact on this approach to family study. Generally, closed systems theorists emphasize the struggle of a family in maintaining relationships much the same way over time — there are pressures toward "equilibrium". Lennard and Bernstein (1969) argue that disturbances or problems that exceed certain limits cause disintegration of the family. They also suggest that there are certain minimum inputs of information and affection, and that expectations, behaviors, and goals tend to converge among family members over time. Accordingly, the typical response of a closed system to an "intrusion" would be the weakening of the strength of the unit.

The open systems approach, in contrast, is primarily concerned with the ways in which families adjust and change in response to "intrusions". Instead of avoiding information or contacts that might undermine stability, "open" families solicit information and experiences that will enhance the opportunities for individual and family growth and development. The open systems perspective is based primarily on the work of Buckley (1967; 1968) and Parsons (1951). Several recent papers have attempted to apply this perspective directly to the family (Carisse, 1972; Black, 1972; Straus, 1972; Black and Broderick, 1972).

At this point, assumptions and concepts applicable to both systems views of the family require further development. However, the focus on behavior over time and the characteristics of the family as a whole unit are important in the social psychological study of the family.

Ideas and concepts will be recognized throughout this book which may be put into one or more of these five conceptual frameworks or boxes. You may find it helpful as you read to keep these approaches in mind. However, it is also important to try to put what you read together in ways that make sense to you. As you do so, you will gain greater insight into what the family is and how it operates in Canada and elsewhere.

The family and change

The conceptual approaches discussed above, with the exception of open systems theory, tend to emphasize the relative resistance of families to change. In the functionalist approach, a radical alteration in the system of interdependence between the family and society would likely be seen as dysfunctional. To permit a mating couple in Canada to bear and rear children without legal obligations either to each other or to their children, for example, would be seen as a step toward a decline in the motivation to marry and the protection of individual rights. It may well be, however, that this event is an adaptive response to the characteristics of Canadian society.

The institutional approach, while directly concerned with family change, tends to emphasize the conserving role of tradition. Change occurs slowly because current family patterns have evolved from less efficient ways of meeting the needs of people. While changes in tradition will occur, these changes will typically lag behind other sectors such as technology (Ogburn and Nimkoff, 1955). Radical changes, as a result of a significant intrusion into the life of man, are seen to have temporary effects. It is regularly suggested that "modern" family experiments are not new and have been tried before. Although there is no evidence to question these assumptions, the de-emphasis on what the family is becoming provides a selective view of the family and change.

The developmental approach is primarily concerned with the changes in the normative system as family members move through their marital and familial careers. While these are clearcut changes for individuals, they more accurately reflect family *processes* from a societal perspective. Conceptually, this approach is an attractive way of exploring the seeds of change within family systems, e.g., forming a group marriage with close friends. To my knowledge, however, little theoretical attention has been given to questions of this type.

The systems frame of reference is concerned with the processes of adaptation, reorganization, and elaboration (becoming more complex) (Buckley, 1967). As indicated earlier, this perspective has not been systematically applied in family study. Even so, the implications for understanding the processes of family change are clear. The family can change without destroying itself or the society of which it is a part. Of course, various types of family systems respond differently to inputs (e.g., information, additional leisure time, crisis events) as suggested in recent papers by Larson (1973) and Carisse (1972). The significant advantage of the open systems view of family process is that it permits analysis of radical alterations (such as a change from conjugal to group marriage).

Whether the family is disintegrating or remaining strong, maintaining its present form and function or changing, and changing slowly or rapidly are controversial issues among family sociologists. Most would likely agree with the comments of Udry (1971) at the beginning of this chapter: a certain amount of change is inevitable as the family adjusts to the changing demands of society, but for the most part, the similarities from generation to generation far exceed the differences. An increasing minority of family sociologists, however, believe that the significance of family change has been underemphasized and are actively publishing books and anthologies (apparently widely used) exclusively devoted to innovative and renovative mating, marital and familial practices.[8] The Skolnicks' recent book (1971) is an excellent example of a scholarly emphasis on family change. Their basic point is aptly illustrated in the excerpt at the beginning of the chapter: social change is occurring rapidly and the family sociologist would do well to rethink marriage, sexuality, child rearing, and family organization in view of these changes. They offer evidence of widespread changes in these basic dimensions of life. The debate cannot really be resolved. Statistical "facts" and logical arguments are utilized by both sides — stability versus change — in defense of their respective positions. The "conservative" arguments and facts include, but are not limited to:

a) the consistent increase, or at least stabilization, of the marriage rate, living together arrangements notwithstanding;

b) the unusual success of marriage in modern society, in that more than 90 percent will

8 An extensive bibliography of these publications, and those reflecting other points of view, is provided at the end of the book (see, for example, Libby and Whitehurst, 1973; the O'Neills, 1972; the Constantines, 1973).

live with their first *or* second spouse until death do them part;

c) the enormous preference, in spite of pressures to the contrary, of most people for traditional marital (monogamy) and family (nuclear) patterns; and

d) family changes now being widely discussed are not new but are rather a recurrent feature of history — inevitable self-regulatory mechanisms will restore and/or maintain practices as they are because they have been found to be the most efficient.

The more "liberal" arguments and facts include, but are not limited to:

a) the rapidly increasing divorce rate — two out of three in California, in spite of increased levels of education and the stabilizing age at marriage;

b) the apparent change in attitudes toward premarital sexuality, unmarried living together arrangements, the meaning of marriage (credence to the possibility of divorce rather than commitment to permanence), the nature of love, and the viability of alternative marital and family life styles;

c) the rapidly increasing participation in premarital intercourse by females, living together arrangements, and group marriages and communes — the high failure rate is merely symptomatic of the problems of change; and

d) the open violation of norms without guilt concomitant with favorable publicity weakens tradition and ultimately undermines support for the status quo.

It is obvious that both the conservative and the liberal position can be supported. Indeed, it is suggested that current family realities, in Canada or elsewhere, cannot be understood or explained without a discussion of family stability and family change.

In essence, this book attempts to illustrate and document a rather basic assumption: marriage and family patterns are directly related to the sociocultural context in which they occur. These patterns, whether in the Trobriand Islands or in Canada, have both a history and a future. Any analysis of family stability and change must include historical processes and trends relative to both family patterns and sociocultural context, and the relationships between the family and society in the present. Matters related to culture complexity, technological development and innovation, urbanism, affluence, global village concerns and opportunities, work and leisure roles, environment, mass communication, changing systems of ethics and values, geographical and social mobility, heterogeneity, and the overlap and/or conflict of institutional functions, among others, have a bearing on marriage and family relationships.

Any one of the alternative ways of understanding the family outlined above might be utilized in the preparation of a textbook. In my view, the use of a single frame of reference is inappropriate for an *introduction* to family study. This book takes an eclectic view of marriage and the family, with particular focus on structural-functionalism, social change, and social psychology (in general rather than in terms of specific approaches) in comparative perspective. Comparisons are made at many different levels including intrafamily, interfamily, family-community and family-society, both sub-culturally (in terms of ethnicity and social class) and cross-culturally. Although all of these levels will not be systematically analyzed, their consideration constitutes the general frame of reference in which comparisons will be made.

SUMMARY

Most people in Canada are intimately connected to some family unit, whether by birth or marital status. This reality, along with evidence of the influence of the family on human development and the need to prepare for family roles, is indicative of the importance of family theory and research.

The ways of understanding the family vary markedly. Our experiences within families and our contact with the ideas of others about families provide useful insights into family life. However, our experience often provides a selective and inaccurate view of the family. It is assumed in this book that knowledge of families other than our own in Canada and elsewhere, the ideas of family theorists, and evidence from research can help to reduce the gaps in our understanding. Even so, the family scholar and student alike should exercise critical judgement in assessing what social scientists believe they *know* about the family in Canada and other societies.

Family study first involves asking questions about the role of the family in society, its relationships to other institutions, differences in family patterns both cross-culturally and sub-culturally, and the characteristics of interpersonal relationships within families. These levels of family analysis are addressed somewhat differently by various theorists. Structural-functionalists emphasize the interdependence between the family and society. The institutional approach, in contrast, deals with the origin, stability and change of the family over time. Change is assumed to occur very slowly. The social psychological approaches to family study deal with microsociological questions. Three were discussed in this chapter, including the developmental, symbolic interaction, and systems approaches. The expectations associated with being a family member over time are emphasized in the developmental approach. The interactional perspective deals with the interpretation and evaluation of the consequences of actions, both for one's self and those with whom one is interacting. The most recent approach, systems theory, is concerned with the family as a *whole* group and the sequences of family behaviors over time. Each of these perspectives offer complementary insights into family persistence and change within and among societies. This book is designed to *introduce* the student to the diverse, but profitable, ways in which the family is studied by family theorists and researchers.

The next chapter deals directly with the relative importance and unique characteristics of family analysis in Canada. The emphasis in this chapter is on comparative issues in defining the characteristics of Canadian society and Canadians, and the relative impact of these differences on the study of the family.

Chapter three provides an overview of marriage and the family cross-culturally and sub-culturally. The first section identifies the primary and secondary forms of marriage and families, and discusses the interconnections of these forms with other aspects of society. Consideration is given to the dynamics of persistence and change. The second section discusses the implications of social class and ethnicity in Canada, and summarizes what is known about sub-cultural family structures and processes in Canada. The two articles concern the universality of the family and a description of the demographic characteristics of the family in Canada.

The remainder of the book is divided into two parts. The first, titled Comparative Family Organization and Interaction, includes twelve articles organized into Chapters four through seven. Each chapter contains a general introduction to the topic, and a critical introduction is provided for each article. The same format is followed in Part III, The Family and Social Change.

The dilemma of a society in its attempts to control mate selection processes is discussed in Chapter four. The cross-cultural significance of courtship, the development of heterosexual love, the characteristics of premarital sexual activity, and the socio-legal aspects of marriage entry in Canada are also discussed. A classic article by William Goode on the various ways in which heterosexual love is controlled, a recent study of sexual attitudes and behavior among English and French Canadians, and a study of the development of love in courtship are included. The introductions to the Goode and Hobart articles discuss related Canadian studies.

Marriage as an institution in East and West is discussed in Chapter five. The analytical issues in the study of marriage relative to sex role differentiation, the changing roles of men and women, marital adjustment, and sexual exchange are identified. Recent Canadian research on women, divorce, and remarriage is summarized. Articles are included on French and English Canadian intermarriage, the interconnection between marital satisfaction and economic opportunity, and the ways in which married couples get involved in swinging.

Chapter six focuses on parent and child relationships and socialization issues in comparative perspective. The articles selected in this section include a commissioned paper on family socialization among the Squamish Indians in British Columbia, a provocative observational study of the maternal care of infants in Japan and the United States, and a comparative study of child rearing in England and the United States.

The relationships between the nuclear family and kinship units are explained in Chapter seven. Canadian material on kinship interaction is considered in some detail. The two articles include discussions of kinship patterns among French Canadians and among lower-middle class families in Toronto.

The controversy over the supposed impact of industrialization (more recently thought of as modernization) on marriage and family life is discussed in Chapter eight. Changes in marriage and family structure and process over the past fifty years in Canada are summarized. Articles by Murray Straus, Karl Peter and Charles Hobart illustrate the issues in the interplay between the family and the community and/or society of which it is a part.

The final chapter examines the identity crisis of the contemporary family and assesses its search for a future. Emerging sexual and mating variations of the monogamous model and the increasing development of alternative marriage and family forms are considered in some detail. Theoretical issues concerning the entry into alternative life styles and their relative stability are emphasized. The articles selected for this section of the book consider the characteristics of successful women, childless marriage, a model which illustrates and explains alternative marriage behavior patterns, and the future of marriage and the family. A comprehensive bibliography emphasizing Canadian references appears at the end of the book.

2

The study of the family in Canada

With some societies (e.g. Britain, France, or China) the definition of what a society is, is largely contained within its own boundaries. Other societies may impinge from time to time, and the country itself may take over other territories with important consequences for its own internal development. But, by and large, it is possible to say that certain institutions and processes are unique to that country. Canada did not make itself — it was made by others. When we talk about family patterns in Canada we are talking about English or Scots or American or French or Ukrainian family patterns; and yet not entirely. The subsequent development of imported institutions makes the character of these different from those of their country of origin. The problem is to be able to specify the interconnecting structures, values and time sequences which give these institutions their specifically Canadian meaning.

D.I. Davies and Kathleen Herman, Social Space: Canadian Perspectives *(Toronto: New Press, 1971), p. vii.*

The major concern of this chapter is to examine the differences and similarities between Canadian and American society. There are two reasons for emphasizing comparisons between Canada and the United States. First, it appears that the primary referent point for Canadian identity lies in the differences between Canada and the United States, rather than in Canada's differences from other societies (Wrong, 1955; Lipset, 1964). These concerns have become particularly apparent in recent years. Second, most of the family theory and research discussed in the average Canadian classroom was written in the United States and is based on data collected in the United States. Until sufficient Canadian data is available, this practice cannot be avoided. This fact alone, however, suggests that a Canadian textbook on the family should articulate, but not exaggerate, the differences and similarities between the United States and Canada if and where they exist.

The implications of these comparisons for the study of the family in Canada are indicated. However, the implications drawn, while they will appear reasonable, should be thought of as only suggestive and exploratory.

The first section of this chapter discusses the significance of certain general issues, including Canadian values (such as nationalism) and Canadian social structure (e.g., pluralism and dualism), in explaining family structure and process. The second section compares certain basic demographic patterns in the United States and

Canada, including the use of space, various vital statistics, marital and family status, and the employment of married women.[1]

Social structure and value patterns

Comparisons between societies are easy to make, but their validity is difficult to demonstrate. Perhaps the most important concern is what Stolte-Heiskanen (1972) calls "contextual analysis". Intracountry variations are typically widespread, although averages will frequently hide much of this variation. In addition, the reasons for the occurrence of certain phenomena in one country may be different from those in another country. These reasons are seldom adequately known or articulated in comparative research.

A second concern, however, is particularly appropriate to comparisons between the United States and Canada. It is reasonable to expect observers to be biased in favor of their own country; recent literature has tended to de-emphasize or reject differences which seem on balance to be "unfavorable" to Canada and emphasize, if not exaggerate, differences which seem favorable to Canada.

Pluralism and dualism

It has been commonly assumed that Canada is distinguished from the United States by the existence and encouragement of multi-culturalism in Canada. A recently published reader on the Canadian family, for example, focuses on the diversity of family patterns by ethnicity and urban-rural status (Ishwaran, 1971). A guest American family sociologist, in commenting on the articles included in the Ishwaran reader, concluded that one of the major themes of Canadian family systems is "the dominance of ethnicity and its function in providing a measure of stability and means for maintenance of variant family forms in pluralistic Canadian society" (Sussman, 1971). In a more general and romantic sense, Canada is described as a cultural free port where no single ideology or vision predominates, with "ethnic

1 Comprehensive census materials for Canada (1971), the United Kingdom (1971) and the United States (1970), as well as comparable vital statistics relating to marriage and the family were to be analyzed and compared, in a way similar to that of an earlier monograph (Larson, 1971b). However, most of this material is not yet available in published form. Furthermore, there were so many problems with definitions and measures in these countries that valid comparisons in several areas could not be made.

islands and cultural archipelagos . . . [and] . . . ghettos of the unpasteurized and unhomogenized'' (Kilbourn, 1970: xvi). Ossenberg (1967) argues that Canada is a pluralistic society, unlike the United States, because of the relative absence of assimilation and the persistence of pronounced, if not permanently divisive, separate and autonomous institutionalized ethnic groups.[2] A study of nuptiality and fertility in 1871 by Tepperman (1974) concludes that regional and provincial variations across Canada can be explained by variations in ethnic composition. It is suggested that these patterns remained unchanged and led to ethnic distinctiveness and the development of the vertical mosaic in Canadian society. The impact of ethnic variability on Canadian social structure is most clearly seen in the classic work of Porter (1965).

The single most important question, however, is whether Canada is in fact more pluralistic than the United States. The U.S. also has numerous native and immigrant groups. Negroes, Mexican-Americans, Indians, Japanese-Americans, the Amish and Hutterite peoples, and many others have been shown to retain distinctive life styles and family patterns in the U.S. (Greeley, 1974; Laumann, 1973). In addition, one cannot analyze the U.S. without considering regional differences such as Appalachia, or North-South. Assimilation (''becoming more like majority groups'') occurs for some groups (for example the Italians — see Lalli, 1969) and not for others. Similar patterns of assimilation occur in Canada (Ukrainian Canadians are discussed later in this book). Porter himself (1967:38) suggests the ''homogenization of Canadian society . . . [such that] . . . the differences between . . . [even] . . . the English-speaking and the French-speaking in Canada will lessen greatly as French Canada becomes more industrialized''. Horowitz candidly states that the rejection of the melting pot hypothesis for Canada represents:

> exaggeration of the cultural uniformity of the United States and exaggeration of the cultural diversity of English Canada. Ethnic segregation does not necessarily preserve genuine cultural diversity. The forces of assimilation can and do operate as powerfully on the segregated immigrant groups of Canada as they do on the less segregated immigrant groups of the United States. In both countries, cultural diversity and

---

2 Van den Berghe suggests that ''a society is pluralistic to the extent that it is structurally segmented and culturally diverse. In more operational terms, pluralism is characterized by the relative absence of value consensus; the relative rigidity and clarity of group definition; the relative presence of conflict, or, at least, of lack of integration and complementarity between various parts of the social system; the segmentary and specific character of relationships, and the relative existence of sheer institutional duplication between the various segments of the society.'' (From Pierre L. Van den Berghe, ''Toward a Sociology of Africa,'' *Social Forces* 43, October, 1964, p. 12. Reprinted by permission.)

assimilation coexist. . . . In Canada, however, assimilation has not levelled the barriers of social segregation — it has not eroded ethnicity as a criterion for assignment of social status — to the same extent as in the United States.[3]

In other words, both ethnic diversity and processes of homogenization are endemic in both societies. In Canada, however, ethnicity appears to be a more significant criterion of achievement and status than in the U.S. This is perhaps one of the most important points in *The Vertical Mosaic* (Porter, 1965). In the United States, in contrast, social class appears to be more salient than ethnicity in achievement and status matters. There are, even so, qualifications to these themes. Color and race clearly modify the effects of class in the United States. Native groups in Canada, as well as certain immigrant groups, face greater opposition than others, particularly if of the wrong social class. On balance, it would seem that pluralism is an apt description of both the United States and Canada. The differences within Canada are far more important than the differences (which, in fact, are yet to be demonstrated) between Canada and the United States.

There is, however, less ambiguity concerning the significance of dualism in Canadian society. There is no complement to the French-English pattern of coexistence in American society.[4] As Ossenberg (1967) demonstrates, the French-English Canadian relationship is the clearest example of pluralism. There are conflicting ideologies, life styles, histories, family patterns, and commitments. Wrong (1955) has argued that the differences between the French and English are far greater than those between the English and the Americans. Among other things, Wrong has emphasized the strong relationship between family ties and religious commandments among French Canadians: condemnation of divorce and birth control; the emphasis on motherhood, procreation, familism, and kinship ties; and the importance of religion in education. More recent research seems to support his thesis (cf. Moreux, 1971).

The importance of dualism in understanding the family system in Canada lies in the relative visibility and proportionate maintenance of competing life styles — "two cultures within a culture". French Canadians represent nearly 29 percent of the population (1971 Census), have never been in the position of an ethnic *minority* as have other native and ethnic groups in both the United States and Canada, and

---

3 Gad Horowitz, "Mosaics and Identity", *Canadian Dimension* 3 (January–February 1966), pp. 17–19. Reprinted by permission.

4 Some have argued that the black-white caste distinction in the U.S. is at least as important as French-English dualism in Canada. However, this distinction is largely one of class rather than ethnicity.

have distinct institutionalized traditions and practices emanating from a distinct historical pattern. The longstanding and unambiguous Canadian support for cultural diversity has unquestionably given unique credibility to dualism in Canadian culture. In any discussion of Canadian nationalism, compared to American nationalistic patterns, a distinction must be made between the Canadian and the French Canadian identity.

There is no necessary reason or evidence, however, to overemphasize Canadian *pluralism* in comparisons with American society. Cultural diversity is an essential insight into both societies.

Values

Value comparisons between Canada and the United States are also frequently made by scholars on both "sides of the border". Dennis Wrong (a Canadian) has described Canadian society, compared to the United States, as more conservative, more authoritarian, more acceptant of class differences and informal social controls, and as preferring more ritual and ceremony in politics. Law is said to be associated with liberty and democracy among Canadians, and with freedom of business enterprise and individual economic development among Americans. Canadians are said to venerate parliament while Americans have more reverence for their constitution. There is also said to be more support for governmental involvement in the economic sphere (e.g., transportation, energy) in Canada (Wrong, 1955). Lipset (an American) and Naegele (a Canadian) both emphasize the "middle status" of Canadians compared to England and the United States. Canadians are described as somewhat more *ascriptive* (emphasis on inherited qualities rather than abilities), *elite* (stress on status), *particularistic* (treated according to status or personal qualities rather than equality before the law), and *diffuse* (treatment on the basis of group membership rather than position within a group) than Americans but less so than citizens of Great Britain (Lipset, 1968; Naegele, 1961). A study by Fearn (1973) attempts to assess certain of these assumptions and concludes that there is some support for certain value differences, but on the whole, the evidence is either contradictory or imprecise. Even so, the study is not an adequate test of national character and much of the literature seems relatively consistent — there are value differences between Canadians and Americans.[5] To the extent that values such as conservatism, greater

5 Comparisons which attempt to discover those implicit or explicit ways in which most Canadians (or Americans) are alike generally attempt to represent the *average* profile of the society. Obviously such comparisons do an injustice to the heterogeneity of a society — particularly where multi-culturalism is emphasized as in Canada and the United States.

respect for authority, and ascription *in fact* characterize Canadian culture, the socialization of children in families would likely be more traditionalistic (kinship oriented, lower divorce rates, fewer employed married women) than in the United States.

One of the more commonly accepted arguments, however, is that the Canadian emphasis on ethnicity has militated against the development of a Canadian identity, that is, blocked the society from acquiring nationalistic values (Porter, 1965). Horowitz (1966b) believes that this factor, more than any other, distinguishes Canada from the United States. Ethnic *assimilation* in the United States is seen to facilitate the development of an American identity which *supplements* ethnic identity. Ethnic groups desire recognition as *American* Mexicans. Ethnic groups in Canada, however, do not develop as strong a sense of national commitment. In this sense, ethnic groups desire recognition as *Ukrainian* Canadians.

It would seem, nonetheless, that these arguments are no longer valid. Nationalism is emerging as a significant force in Canadian life. As Lipset (1968) pointed out, Canadians are the oldest anti-Americans (since the Loyalist exit from the States during the independence struggles of the Americans). While much of the current nationalism appears to be a continuation of the anti-American tradition, the reasons have changed to concerns about foreign control and independence, and there is increasing evidence in the popular media of a *pro-Canadian identity*. These patterns are seen in the training of the young in both family and educational settings. Ethnicity does not seem to be a significant block to these developments. However, we really don't know how widespread pro-Canadianism is. Ethnicity in the United States, in contrast, now seems to be moving in the opposite direction — away from nationalism, witness *Mexican* Americans and "Black is beautiful". Whether these trends are distinct remains to be substantiated.

In summary, Canadian dualism appears to be the most significant difference between Canadian and American society. Assumptions that pluralism and values also constitute important differences remain to be demonstrated. As Lipset (1968) stresses, the similarities between Canada and the United States are far more evident than the differences. These similarities are even more evident in comparing English Canadians with Americans. Even so, there is considerable need for substantive research on whether "asserted" differences *and* similarities do in fact exist, and if they do, whether they have a significant impact on understanding marriage and family patterns in the two societies. The rest of the chapter turns to demographic comparisons between the United States and Canada. Census materials and vital statistics are a useful source of information on marriage and family patterns.

Selected demographic patterns

Tables 2.1 to 2.5 present comparative data for Canada and the United States on the use of space, selected vital statistics, marital status, and the employment of women. The implications for understanding the family in Canada are drawn wherever possible.

However, there are several good reasons for interpreting the data cautiously. First, the data represents an average of all variables (regional, provincial-state, racial, ethnic, religious, class) into societal totals. Second, strictly speaking, it is very difficult to compare census materials from the two countries because the census definitions (this is the most serious problem), population bases for calculations, availability of data, and the years in which the data was obtained vary (Canada, for example, conducted its last census in 1971 while the United States did so in 1970). Every effort has been made to obtain comparable data. At times, however, this has been impossible; in such instances the different baselines are noted and the implications suggested. Third, a large-scale research project is required before the comparisons presented in this chapter can be adequately understood and explained. The data presented should be thought of as a primitive comparison of selected demographic issues.[6]

Use of space

It is self-evident that Canadians have more geographical space than Americans. Table 2.1 shows that there are only 6.1 persons per square mile in Canada compared to 56.2 persons per square mile in the United States. There are more than ten times as many houses and families per square mile in the States. Canadians also have slightly more families per household in urban areas. Space is greater in rural areas and the differences between the societies are greatest in the rural areas. Canadian households, however, on the average have more persons and family size tends to be larger in both urban and rural areas. Again, societal differences are greatest in the rural areas. About 76 percent of Canadians live in urban areas compared to about 73 percent of Americans.

Canadians do have more space to use once they leave their households. However, they will need to drive some distance to unsettled and unused areas (some 88 percent of Canada's land space is unsettled and unused for economic gain — see Gajda, 1960). The number of persons per square mile in *used* areas (defined as ecumene by

---

6 Applicable census definitions for the U.S. and Canada are provided at the end of this chapter.

Gajda) is only 49.1 — still less than the number of persons per square land mile in the United States.

Table 2.1   The Use of Space, Canada and The United States, 1970-71

	Canada	United States
Rates		
Persons per square mile	6.1	56.2
Houses per square mile	1.7	19.0
Families per square mile	1.4	14.1
Families per household	.82	.80
Urban	.81	.78
Rural	.86	.86
Persons per household[a]	3.5	3.0
Urban	3.4	3.0
Rural	3.9	3.3
Persons per family[a]	3.7	3.6
Urban	3.6	3.5
Rural	4.1	3.7
Average number of persons per room	1.51	1.69
Urban	1.53	1.64
Rural	1.43	1.75
Frequencies on which rates are based		
Total land square miles	3,560,238	3,615,122
Total population	21,568,315	203,211,926
Urban population	16,410,785	149,324,930
Rural population	5,157,525	53,886,996
Total housing units	6,041,302	63,445,192
Urban	4,743,279	47,567,372
Rural	1,298,023	15,877,820
Total family units	4,933,450	50,968,827
Urban	3,820,320	37,334,825
Rural	1,113,125	13,634,002

The data is based on the actual frequencies provided in the census materials of each country. Otherwise, the official statistics provided would not be comparable. Data for this table was drawn from the 1970 Census of Housing, Part I, United States Summary, Detailed Housing Characteristics, HC (1)-B1; Volume I, Housing Characteristics for States, Cities and Counties; and the U.S. Summary, General Population Characteristics, PC (1)-B1. Canadian data was obtained from Statistics Canada Cat. Nos. 93-712, 93-714, and 93-730.

[a] Drawn from official statistics rather than calculated on the basis of the housing units by the number of persons. The average number of persons per household is smaller than the average number of persons per family because households also include single persons who are not living with families. The definition of household does not include collective households ("group quarters" in the U.S.) such as institutions. See end of chapter for census definitions.

There is little research on the significance of space to family and socialization patterns but there is considerable agreement on the importance of space. All people are reared in geographical space, and all action and interaction is anchored in space. In general, the child has little control over the kind of space he inhabits — its size, shape, texture, quality, use, location, and relationship to other spaces. Space may be relatively open (ease of passage and visibility, movable walls, unlocked doors, unlocked buildings, high ceilings, large windows, large rooms) or relatively closed. Impressionistic arguments would suggest that the development and maintenance of a distinct identity depends on being treated as distinct from others, a circumstance which becomes increasingly difficult as population density increases (Inkles, 1968). Do people reared in small spaces (500 square feet) tend to seek small spaces or do they seek large spaces? Do people reared on the prairies feel hemmed in in the city? Do people reared in the Atlantic provinces near the ocean feel confined in the Canadian Rockies? Do people reared in dense populations become more impersonal and formal in their relations with others? Do people reared in a country like Canada (with more space than the United States) tend to be more individualistic? more flexible? These are important questions that need good answers. If we were able to provide them, we might find that childhood and family relations in Canada are influenced by the amount of space available and occupied.

Vital statistics

Table 2.2 provides comparative data on vital statistics since 1960. Birth rates have been nearly the same since 1968. Illegitimate births to 1968 are slightly higher in the U.S. but they appear to have increased more rapidly in the U.S. to 1971. Marriage rates are consistently lower in Canada but have been generally increasing in both the U.S. and Canada. The higher marriage rates in the U.S. likely reflect the higher number, proportionately, of remarriages. It is clear that the divorce rates in the United States are two to three times as high as in Canada. If states are compared to provinces, this difference remains. The state of Washington, for example, had a divorce rate of 410 (per 100,000 population) in 1965 as compared to a divorce rate of 109 in the province of British Columbia. The divorce laws in Canada were quite restrictive until 1968, and so the difference in rates is partly related to the law. Further, divorce rates are not indicators of marital breakdown. Marital breakdown may be as high in Canada. Even so, the rates are indicative of a greater propensity for legally ending a marriage in the U.S.

The mean age, in Canada, and the median age, in the United States, of males and females at first marriage are also presented in table 2.2. The differences are large

Table 2.2   General Vital Statistics, Canada and The United States, 1960—1973

| | Birth Rates[a] | | Illegitimate[b] births | | Marriage rates[a] | | Divorce rates[c] | | Age at first marriage[d] | | | |
| | | | | | | | | | Males | | Females | |
	Can.	U.S.	Can.	U.S.	Can.	U.S.	Can.	U.S.	Can.	U.S.	Can.	U.S.
1960	26.8	23.7	4.3	5.3	7.3	8.5	39	220	25.8	22.8	23.0	20.3
1965	21.3	19.4	6.7	7.7	7.4	9.3	46	250	25.3	22.8	22.6	20.6
1968	17.6	17.5	9.0	9.7	8.3	10.4	55	290	25.0		22.6	
1969	17.6	17.7	9.2	10.0	8.7	10.6	124	320	25.0	23.2	22.7	20.8
1970	17.5	18.2	9.6	10.6	8.8	10.7	140	350	24.9	23.2	22.7	20.8
1971	17.0	17.3	9.0	11.2	8.8	10.6	137	370	24.9	23.1	22.6	20.9
1972	15.7	15.6	9.0	12.3	9.2	10.9	148	400	24.8	23.3	22.6	20.9
1973	15.8	15.0	9.0		9.0	10.9	166	440	24.9		22.4	

All rates from 1970 onward are provisional. Data is based on the Statistical Abstract of the United States, 1973 edition, and the Monthly Vital Statistics Report. Canadian vital statistics are drawn from Statistics Canada Cat. No. 84-201 for 1972 and 1973 and from Statistics Canada Cat. No. 84-201 for 1968-1971.

a per 1,000 population.
b percent of all live births.
c per 100,000 population.
d Canadian data provides the *mean* age at first marriage whereas U.S. data uses the *median* age.

enough, the unequal statistic notwithstanding, to suggest that (a) the age at marriage for both males and females is increasing in the U.S. and decreasing in Canada; and (b) both Canadian males and females tend to marry somewhat older than do their American counterparts. A recent study of the mean age of brides at first marriage (Légaré, 1974), found that the mean age difference between Canadian and U.S. brides was 1.1 years in 1920-1924 and .8 years in 1955-1959. The modal (most common or highest number) age at first marriage for brides has always been twenty to twenty-one years of age in Canada and eighteen to nineteen years of age in the United States.

In general, these statistical differences are indicative of more traditional marriage patterns in Canada: fewer divorces, fewer remarriages, and fewer young marriages. There are significant variations across Canada, as between Alberta and Quebec (just as there are significant variations in the U.S., as between California and Utah), but on the whole the differences between the U.S. and Canada remain. The use of the term "traditional" is of course interpretable in many ways. It may mean that the family system is more stable, more rational, and more familistic. Or, in contrast, traditionalism might be thought of as less flexible, more conservative, and more backward.

Marital status

Table 2.3 compares the marital status of the urban and rural population in Canada and the United States. The population base in Canada includes persons over the age of fifteen; the population baseline in the U.S. is fourteen years of age. These differences must be considered in interpreting the data. The percentage of the population that is single is greater in Canada for both males and females (more so for males) than in the United States, even though the population baseline is one year older. This provides clear support for the differences in age at first marriage identified above. It is interesting that Canada has a larger percentage of unmarried males and females in rural areas whereas the United States has fewer single people in rural areas. This difference would indicate that the age at marriage varies in urban and rural areas, and that singles are more inclined to move to the city in the U.S. than in Canada. There are no notable differences in the percentage married. However, there are more married males in rural areas in the United States and *fewer* married males in Canadian rural areas than in urban areas. These differences, it appears, are strongly related to the differences in the percentage of widowed and divorced males and females. There are slightly fewer widowed males and slightly more widowed females in Canada compared to the United States. Similarly, there are nearly three times as many divorced males and females in the U.S. This data indicates that widowed males are somewhat more likely to marry, and widowed females somewhat less likely to marry, in Canada. The percentage of persons in the divorced status is indicative of the lower divorce rates in Canada.

Table 2.3   Marital Status, Canada and the United States, 1970—1971

Marital Status	CANADA			UNITED STATES		
	Total	Urban	Rural	Total	Urban	Rural
Males[a]						
Single	31.6	30.7	34.4	28.6	29.1	27.1
Married[b]	64.9	65.8	62.1	64.2	63.3	66.6
Widowed	2.5	2.4	2.8	2.9	2.9	3.0
Divorced	1.0	1.1	.7	2.7	3.0	2.1
Separated[b]				1.5	1.7	1.1
Totals	(7,531,890)	(5,730,805)	(1,801,080)	(71,492,364)	(52,335,766)	(19,156,598)
Females[a]						
Single	25.0	25.4	23.3	22.4	23.2	20.0
Married[b]	63.9	62.8	67.8	59.0	56.8	65.4
Widowed	9.8	10.2	8.4	12.4	12.8	11.1
Divorced	1.3	1.5	.5	3.9	4.5	2.2
Separated[b]				2.3	2.6	1.3
Totals	(7,655,525)	(6,032,165)	(1,623,365)	(77,914,869)	(58,394,587)	(19,520,282)

Data based on U.S. Summary, General Population Characteristics, PC (1)-B1 and Statistics Canada Cat. No. 92-717.

[a] In Canada, the population base is 15 years of age for both males and females. The population base in the United States is 14 years of age.

[b] In Canada, separated spouses are classified as married.

Parenthood status

Households in which both the husband and wife are present are the predominant household form in both Canada and the United States (see table 2.4). The spread between urban and rural areas is greater in the States (4.9 percent compared to .6 percent in Canada). This distinction is further illustrated in mother-only households. Nearly twice as many households, proportionately, are headed by mothers alone in the United States and this difference is most pronounced in urban areas. There are no important differences in urban and rural areas relative to father-only households, but there are, proportionately, more than twice as many such households in the U.S. as in Canada. There are slightly more father-only households in rural than in urban areas in Canada. A comparison of negro and white households in the U.S. revealed that 68 percent of the negro population lived in husband-wife families and 28 percent were in households headed by mothers alone, compared to 88 and 9 percent, respectively, among white households. Accordingly, while the differences between Canada and the United States are reduced somewhat by controlling for race, the essential magnitude of the differences remains.

Table 2.4   Parenthood Status, Canada and The United States, 1970—71 (in percentages)

Family Type	CANADA			UNITED STATES		
	Totals	Urban	Rural	Totals	Urban	Rural
Husband-wife families[a]	93.6	93.7	94.3	86.5	85.1	90.0
Mother-only	5.1	5.1	4.2	10.8	12.1	7.2
Father-only	1.3	1.2	1.5	2.8	2.8	2.8
	(4,904,030)	(3,916,510)	(1,148,275)	(50,968,827)	(37,334,825)	(13,634,002)

Data based on U.S. Summary, General Population Characteristics, PC (1)–B1 and Statistics Canada Cat. Nos. 93-712 and 93-714.

[a] Includes families without children.

Family size

Several studies have compared Canadian and American data on the average number of children in families.[7] Légaré (1974), for example, analyzed 1960 census data on family size for first marriage cohorts. He found that between 1920 and 1950 the average family in the United States had 2.5 children. The Canadian family, in contrast, varied from an average of 2.91 children in 1920 to 2.5 children in 1950. Légaré also found that the decrease in family size over these thirty years was predominantly due to a reduction in the number of families with more than three children. The most marked decrease occurred among families with six children or

7 Family size reported in table 2.1 is based on all families; accordingly the data will differ as the data reported in this section is limited to *first* marriages of women.

more. Because of their later mean age at first marriage, Canadians in general have more children in a shorter period of time than their American counterparts.

The evidence also suggests that Canadians want more children. The 1960 Gallup poll (Gallup, 1972) found that the ideal mean family size in Canada was 4.2 children compared to 3.6 children in the United States. Nearly 70 percent of the Canadians gave an answer of four or more children compared to 50 percent among Americans. Both the ideal family size and the difference between Canadians and Americans, however, have been decreasing in more recent times. In 1970, 33 percent of the Canadian respondents gave four or more children as the ideal family size, compared to 23 percent of the American respondents in 1971 (as reported in Boyd, 1974). Boyd (1974) suggests that the difference may be decreasing even more in the middle 1970s and that it may reflect the different types of questions asked. Even so, it seems clear that there *have been* rather significant differences in ideal family size between Canadians and Americans.

Childlessness, to be discussed in some detail in Chapter nine, also reflects differ- ent patterns between the two countries. Légaré (1974) reports that childless mar- riages have represented about 11 percent of all marriages in Canada since 1920, while in the United States, they have varied from more than 18 percent to about 13 percent of all marriages. Among wives twenty-two to forty-four years of age, nearly 20 percent of American and 15 percent of Canadian first marriages were childless.

Women in the labor force

The final comparison between the United States and Canada concerns the proportion of women in the labor force by age, marital status, and age of children. This data is presented in table 2.5. It should be noted that these comparisons are limited in two respects. First, the United States uses a female population base of sixteen years of age and older, while the publications of the Canadian Department of Labor Women's Bureau are based on females fourteen years of age and older. Second, there is not any up-to-date data on working *mothers* in Canada.[8] The latest available data, published by the Women's Bureau (1970c), is based on working motherhood in 1967.

As can be seen in table 2.5, there are substantive differences between the United States and Canada. Fifty-two percent of all women over the age of sixteen were employed full- or part-time in the United States compared to 37 percent of all women over the age of fourteen in Canada. This difference is partly a function of the

8 Canadian census data on the female labor force is based on those fifteen years of age and older. See note, table 2.5.

Table 2.5   Women in The Labor Force, Canada and The United States, 1971—72

Women in labor force	CANADA		UNITED STATES	
	1971	1972	1971	1972
Percent of all women employed[a]	36.5	37.1	53.4	52.0
by age: 14-19[b]	31.1	32.0	57.8	58.8
20-24	59.9	60.5	72.4	75.0
25-34	40.7	43.2	55.0	57.2
35-44	41.1	42.2	58.2	58.6
Employment of women by marital status[c]				
Single	48.3	48.9	52.7	54.9
Married	33.0	33.9	40.8	41.5
Other (Divorced and widowed)	28.3	28.3	35.7	37.2
Divorced			70.4	70.1
Widowed			25.7	26.8
Percent employed married women:[c]				1973
by children 6-17			49.4	50.2 50.1
by children under 6			29.6	30.1 32.7
		1967 Data		
by children 6-14[d]	28.0		45.0	
by children under 6	19.0		26.5	

[a] Canada, 14 years and over; United States, 16 years and over. Employment includes both full-time and part-time employment.

[b] U.S. data includes women between the ages of 16-19 alone.

[c] Data on working mothers is not available in Canada since the study by the Women's Bureau (1970c) using 1967 data.

[d] The age of children for the U.S. is 6-17 years rather than 6-14 years.

The data presented in the table is based on studies and estimates rather than official census data. The U.S. data is drawn from Waldman and Gover (1972) and Hayghe (1974). The Canadian data is drawn from publications of the Women's Bureau (1974).

Aside from the comparisons in the table, Canadian census data on the 1971 labor force is now available (Statistics Canada Cat. No. 94-785). This data is based on women 15 years of age and older and is therefore more comparable to the U.S. data. The data by marital status and age is presented below.

Table 2.5 cont'd.

	Canada 1971	U.S. 1971
Total women in labor force	39.9%	53.4%
Single women	53.5%	52.7%
Married women	37.0%	40.8%
Widowed/Divorced	26.6%	35.7%
15-19 years old	37.0%	57.8%
20-24 years old	62.8%	72.4%
25-34 years old	44.5%	55.0%
35-44 years old	43.9%	58.2%

differing population base of women. However, the difference remains highly significant even when age is controlled. Nearly 15 percent more women between the ages of twenty and twenty-four were employed in the U.S., and this difference persists in each of the other age cohorts reported. Looking at marital status in particular, though the differences aren't as marked it is clear that more American women, regardless of marital status, were employed. In 1972, for example, about 42 percent of American married women were employed, compared to 34 percent in Canada. Data available for the States indicates that more than 70 percent of divorced women were employed.

The third section of table 2.5 presents data on working mothers. Recent data is only available from the United States. Nearly 50 percent of employed married women had children between the ages of six and seventeen. These statistics changed very little between 1971 and 1973. Less than 30 percent of married and employed women had children under the age of six. Evidence from historical data (since 1960) indicates that the proportion of married women in the labor force with children under six years of age is continuing to increase. In order to compare working motherhood in Canada and the United States, data is presented for 1967, as more recent data is not available in Canada. Among married employed women, 19 percent in Canada and 26 percent in America have children under the age of six. It is estimated that the differences would be similar for mothers with children between six and seventeen. (The percentage for Canada is based on children between the ages of six and fourteen.) Given the change in the United States between 1967 and 1973, it is likely that the current percentage of employed married women in Canada with children six to fourteen would be about 33 percent, and about 25 percent for mothers with children under six years of age.

The comparisons between the United States and Canada relative to women in the labor force provide further evidence of a somewhat more traditional family system in Canada in a process of change.

SUMMARY

This chapter has attempted to explore certain of the similarities and differences between Canada and the United States. The evidence is not clear but does suggest that certain assumptions about differences may not be valid and certain assumptions about similarities may have been accepted too quickly. The single most important structural difference is Canadian dualism. There is no obvious complement to this pattern in the United States. It has been argued, however, that pluralism is a structural feature of both societies. As a societal principle, pluralism provides support to the existence and persistence of many marriage and family patterns. Race, ethnicity, social class, religion, and region, among other attributes of heterogeneous societies, offer important insights into understanding and explaining the family in both Canada and the United States. It has also been suggested that the similarities in values would appear to exceed any differences between the two countries, the various "assertions" notwithstanding.

The statistical data on Canada and the United States suggests that Canadians have more space, fewer divorces — though marital dissatisfaction may be equally as high — fewer remarriages, fewer young marriages, fewer divorced persons and single-parent families, and fewer single and married women and mothers in the labor force than do Americans. In general, it would seem that these patterns are indicative of a more traditional and conservative family system. As suggested by the analysis of patterns within Canadian society in subsequent chapters, these patterns vary widely across Canada and are in a process of change.

Whether the differences observed between Canada and the United States are important can only be established by explaining them. Further research comparing the values and practices of Canadians and Americans is essential. In addition, current census materials contain a wealth of additional information. A large scale demographic study of these materials will lead to a clearer picture of the relative influence of the many pluralistic factors identified above on both the similarities and differences between the U.S. and Canada.

The most important assignment, however, is to establish what we do and do not know about the family in Canada. The remaining chapters attempt to offer some insight into these questions.

Canadian Census Definitions*

Household

For census purposes, a household consists of a person or group of persons occupying one dwelling. It usually consists of a family group with or without lodgers, employees, etc. However, it may consist of two or more families sharing a dwelling, of a group of unrelated persons or of one person living alone. Every person is a member of some household and there is a one-to-one relationship between households and occupied dwellings except in the case of certain special households, such as those of military and diplomatic personnel stationed overseas, from which no housing information was collected.

The census classifies households into two main groups: (1) the household which consists of one person or a small group of persons occupying an ordinary dwelling, usually spoken of as a private household, and (2) the "collective" type household which includes hotels, large lodging-houses of 10 or more lodgers, institutions, hospitals, or military camps, lumber camps and other establishments of a similar nature. Unless otherwise specified, these "collective" type households are excluded from household reports.

Dwelling

A dwelling is a structurally separate set of living quarters with a private entrance from outside or from a common hallway or stairway inside the building; i.e., the entrance must not be through someone else's living quarters.

Household head

For census purposes, every household must have a head. This is the husband if both husband and wife are present, the parent (regardless of age or dependency) if living with unmarried children, or any member of a group sharing a dwelling equally. The household head may or may not be the family head as well. A person occupying a dwelling alone is always reported as the head.

*Source: Statistics Canada.

Type of household

Refers to the basic division of households into family and non-family households. The term FAMILY HOUSEHOLD refers to a household containing at least one census family. ONE-FAMILY HOUSEHOLD refers to a single census family occupying one dwelling. The family may be that of the household head or one living as a related, lodging or other type of family with a household head who is a non-family person. A TWO-OR-MORE-FAMILY HOUSEHOLD is one in which two or more census families occupy the same dwelling. One family may be that of the household head, or the household head may be a non-family person with whom two or more census families are residing.

The term NON-FAMILY HOUSEHOLD refers to one person living alone in a dwelling or a group of persons, occupying one dwelling, who do not constitute a census family.

Family

A census family consists of a husband and wife (with or without children who have never been married, regardless of age) or a parent with one or more children never married, living in the same dwelling. A family may consist, also, of a man or woman living with a guardianship child or ward under 21 years for whom no pay was received.

Family head

The term family head refers to the husband in a husband-wife family or the parent in a one-parent family.

United States Census Definitions*

Household

A household includes all the persons who occupy a group of rooms or a single room which constitutes a housing unit. A group of rooms or single room is regarded as a

*Source: Appendix B, U.S. Summary, General Population Characteristics, PC (1) — B1.

housing unit when it is occupied as separate living quarters, that is, when the occupants do not live and eat with any other persons in the structure, and when there is either (1) direct access from the outside of the building or through a common hall or (2) complete kitchen facilities for the exclusive use of the occupants of the household.

Relationship to head of household

Five categories of relationship to head of household are recognized. More detailed categories of relationship appear in subsequent reports.

1. *Head of household* One person in each household is designated as the "head," that is, the person who is regarded as the head by the members of the household. However, if a married woman living with her husband was reported as the head, her husband was considered the head for the purpose of simplifying the tabulations.

Two types of household head are distinguished — the head of a family and a primary individual. A family head is a household head living with one or more persons related to him by blood, marriage, or adoption. A primary individual is a household head living alone or with nonrelatives only.

2. *Wife of head* A woman married to and living with a household head, including women in common-law marriages as well as women in formal marriages. The number of women in this category may not always be the same as the number of "husband-wife households" and the number of "husband-wife families," because of minor differences in the weighting of the data.

3. *Child of head* A son, daughter, stepchild, or adopted child of the head of the household of which he is a member, regardless of the child's age or marital status. The category excludes sons-in-law and daughters-in-law. (See definition of "own child" below.)

4. *Other relative of head* All persons related to the head of the household by blood, marriage, or adoption but not included in any specific relationship categories shown in the particular table.

5. *Not related to head* All persons in the household not related to the head by blood, marriage, or adoption. Roomers, boarders, lodgers, partners, resident employees, wards, and foster children are included in this category.

Group quarters

All persons in living arrangements other than households are classified by the Bureau of the Census as living in group quarters. Persons living in group quarters are shown in this report as either inmate of institution or resident of other group quarters.

Family and subfamily

According to 1970 census definitions, a family consists of a household head and one or more other persons living in the same household who are related to the head by blood, marriage, or adoption; all persons in a household who are related to the head are regarded as members of his (her) family. A ''husband-wife family'' is a family in which the head and his wife are enumerated as members of the same household. Not all households contain families, because a household may be composed of a group of unrelated persons or one person living alone. The mean size of family is derived by dividing the number of persons in families by the total number of families.

A subfamily is a married couple with or without children, or one parent with one or more single children under 18 years old, living in a household and related to, but not including, the head of the household or his wife. The most common example of a subfamily is a young married couple sharing the home of the husband's or wife's parents. Members of a subfamily are also included among the members of a family. The number of subfamilies, therefore, is not included in the number of families.

3

An overview of comparative family organization

In all known societies, almost everyone lives his life enmeshed in a network of family rights and obligations called role relations. A person is made aware of his role relations through a long period of socialization during his childhood, a process in which he learns how others in his family expect him to behave, and in which he himself comes to feel this is both the right and the desirable way to act. . . . The strategic significance of the family is to be found in its mediating function in the larger society. It links the individual to the larger social structure. . . . Only if individuals are motivated to serve the needs of the society will it be able to survive. . . . What is needed is a set of social forces that responds to the individual whenever he does well or poorly. . . . The family, by surrounding the individual through much of his social life, can furnish that set of forces. . . . The family . . . is made up of individuals, but it is also part of the larger social network. Thus we are all under the constant supervision of our kin, who feel free to criticize, suggest, order, cajole, praise, or threaten, so that we will carry out our role obligations. . . . Men who have achieved high position usually find that even as adults they will respond to their parents' criticisms, are still angered or hurt by a brother's scorn.

William J. Goode, The Family *(Englewood Cliffs, New Jersey: Prentice-Hall, 1964), pp. 1-3.*

The family is not the same everywhere; what many Canadians think of as the family doesn't exist in some societies of the world. Within the kibbutzim of Israel, for example, parents and their offspring live separately (Spiro, 1965). Among the Nayar of the South Malabar coast of India, the family is typically composed of brothers and sisters, their maternal uncles, and the offspring of the females within the group. Fathers are not part of the family unit, do not live with the family, and are commonly thought of as "lovers" (Mencher, 1965). Siwai men of high status in the Solomon Islands often have several wives (Oliver, 1955). In one of the basic forms of the Marquesan Islands family, one woman lives with two men (Otterbein, 1968).

Family patterns also differ *within* Canada. Socio-cultural factors such as social status, ethnicity, religion, and race are important in understanding the various family patterns in Canada. French Canadian families, for example, maintain strong kinship ties and religious traditions (Garigue, 1962). Premarital virginity, conjugal fidelity, and fecundity (large families) are expected of French Canadian women (Moreux, 1971). Due to conditions associated with culture contact and technological change, the Athapaskan Indian family is primarily composed of an unmarried mother and her offspring (Cruikshank, 1971). The Hutterite family unit lives in a collective and cooperative community of people related by marriage or descent (Peter, 1971). Recent evidence suggests that the traditional Netsilik and Iglulik Eskimos formed large composite family units (father, his spouse, his sons and their spouses, and offspring) during the winter months (Damas, 1971).

These patterns illustrate both cross-cultural and sub-cultural diversity. There are also similarities in family patterns the world over, between and within societies.[1] Goode, in the introductory statement, suggests that two of these similarities include the socialization of children and the pervasiveness of kinship influence. However, the ways in which children are socialized and kin groups behave vary widely.

This chapter provides an overview of family structure and process in comparative perspective.[2] The uniformities in marriage and family patterns, various types of marriage and kinship ties, and an overview of sub-cultural patterns within Canadian society are considered. Two articles chosen to illustrate selected aspects of these issues are included.

Cross-cultural family patterns

Problems in the definition of the family

To most Canadians the family means a married couple and their children. Some Canadians, however, would not hesitate to include their grandparents and other relatives when they use the term "family". In contrast, many Tibetans would think of the family as several brothers living together with one wife and their children (Peter, 1965). The Nayar child may well think of the family as one's siblings, mother, her sisters and brothers, and perhaps one's grandmother and her sisters and brothers (Mencher, 1965). Thus it is difficult to define the family adequately.

The Reiss article (1965) included in this chapter is concerned with certain of these definitional problems. Though his analysis is not exhaustive and tends to oversimp-

1 No one knows how many societies there are in the world. Murdock (1967) estimates that there may be as many as 4,000, varying in size from less than 400 members to over 750 million. The Kaingang society, according to Jules Henry (1964) has a population of less than 150 persons.
2 Comparative analysis is subject to many qualifications. First, variability within a society is ignored. Ethnographic reports and research studies within many preliterate societies typically only discuss the dominant patterns. Second, the findings aren't, strictly speaking, comparable because though practices are the same, they may have different meanings for different societies. Accordingly, discussions of the comparisons among societies should be thought of as descriptive rather than explanatory. Interested students may wish to consult an excellent article on this subject by Stolte-Heiskanen (1972).

lify the problem, the conclusions are helpful. It is impossible to specify *who* will always be part of the family unit and how many persons of differing generations will be present. Instead, it is argued that the family is composed of persons related by blood or kinship ties who are expected, within a particular society, to be primarily responsible for the emotional care of dependent children. The most important dimension in the definition is that the unit, whatever the positions and roles which make it up, is expected by its society to be predominantly responsible for the nurturant care of small children. The predominant pattern in all cultures is a group of relatives taking care of their children. This definition does not include married persons without children; i.e., a married couple is a form of marriage, not a family. Marriage is defined as a publicly recognized enduring relationship between two or more persons, including at least one member of the opposite sex.

Marriage and family forms

Many societies contain more than one form of marriage and frequently contain several family forms, though one or more of these will usually predominate. In Canada, for example, the nuclear family (parents and children) is the basic and predominant family form, but there are many family units which contain three generations. Similarly, while monogamy (marriage between one man and one woman) is the only acceptable legal form of marriage in Canada, some Canadians are living in homosexual marriages, group marriages (two or more women and men living together), and various types of communes (differing combinations of men, women, and children). Although marriage and family alternatives are not as evident in studies of preliterate and non-Western societies, it would be inappropriate to assume that variations do not exist in most societies. We may think of societies as containing both primary and secondary marriage and family forms, although it will not be possible to systematically discuss the latter.[3]

Marriage forms Three basic forms of marriage were found to exist in the "World Ethnographic Sample" of societies (Murdock, 1957): monogamy, polygyny, and polyandry. Monogamy (one man and one woman) exists in every society, is the predominant marital form in most societies, and is the preferred form of marriage in about 24 percent of the 554 societies in Murdock's sample. Polygyny (one man and two or more wives) is preferred, but only practised by a minority of people, within 415 societies (75 percent). Polyandry (one woman and two or more husbands) is the

---

3 Little evidence is available on the variability within many of the cultures of the world. Ethnographic studies generally emphasize the modal, or predominant, family patterns and tend to ignore or de-emphasize the alternative patterns.

predominant form of marriage in four societies.[4]

Polyandrous marriage appears to be of two kinds. The Toda household, for example, is made up of several brothers and their common wife (Rivers, 1906). This pattern is referred to as fraternal polyandry. Marquesans, in contrast, have predominantly non-fraternal households (the husbands are unrelated). Otterbein (1968) reports three types of polyandrous households among the Marquesans: (a) a woman marries two men at the same time; (b) a man marries a married woman and the couple moves in with him; and (c) a married man marries a married woman and the latter couple moves in with the first couple. The last form is an example of group marriage. Stephens (1963) notes three basic features of polyandrous systems. First, female infanticide is practised in at least two of the four societies, resulting in an unequal sex ratio — more males than females. Second, group marriage and polyandrous marriage appear to occur together. When female infanticide is not practised systematically, unmarried sisters or unrelated women are added to the household. In addition, higher status males have more freedom than lower status males in marrying an already married woman — the fringe benefit being her husband. Third, there is an economic advantage for brothers and unrelated men in becoming affiliated with a polyandrous household. An acceptable social status and legitimate sexual access is achieved for the junior husband, while the senior husband acquires employees.

Polygyny is considerably more complicated to describe because of the large number of societies which practise this form of multiple marriage, and the variable patterns among them. The most widespread pattern is sororal polygyny, in which the wives are sisters. The evidence suggests that there are fewer problems in this form of polygyny: less sexual jealousy and fewer disagreements. Sororal co-wives typically live in the same house with their common spouse. In Murdock's sample (1957), forty-seven societies were characterized by non-sororal polygyny. Each wife had her own house, referred to as "mother-child households", in all but three of these societies. In non-sororal societies, the husband is usually expected to rotate among the households. In both sororal and non-sororal polygynous societies, co-wives apparently have clearly defined equal rights — particularly with reference to sexual privileges (Stephens, 1963). The senior wife is generally also accorded special authority over junior wives.

As might be expected, polygyny is related to having the necessary resources and

---

4 Scholars do not agree completely on the number of polyandrous societies. Stephens (1963) discusses several additional societies in which polyandry is both accepted and practised. The Nayar, defined as polyandrous by Murdock (1957), are used as an example of a family unit without fathers or husbands by another author (Reiss, 1965). In fact, polyandry is practised in many societies. Recent evidence on Eskimo marriage patterns in Canada suggests that polyandry is still practised, for example, among the Eskimos of Churchill, Manitoba (Vranas and Stephens, 1971).

status to obtain and provide for several wives. The wealthy and politically powerful men, typically somewhat older than their wives, are in a better position to form a polygynous household.

Social scientists in Western society generally agree that both polyandry and polygyny are relatively less adaptable marital forms for the majority of people within a society, because monogamy clearly maximizes the opportunity of *each* individual to marry, if they desire to do so. However, polygamous marital forms do seem to work well when they are not widespread within a society, or when the sex ratio is unbalanced.

Family forms The smallest and most basic kinship unit the world over is the *nuclear family* (parents and their children). The nuclear family is the basic building block of, and primary means of maintaining, the kinship system. The nuclear family is not universal (cf. Reiss, 1965) and is certainly not the predominant family form in *all* societies. Among the Nayar of India, for example, it is reported that some 30 percent of family units are nuclear families (as reported in Schultz, 1972:26). In Murdock's study of 192 societies (1949), about 50 percent contained the nuclear family exclusively. The remaining half of the societies contained some form of *extended family* (nuclear family plus one or more additional relatives related by blood).

Family systems vary in composition and size. The *stem family* (Humphreys, 1965) is perhaps the smallest extended family form, consisting of three generations. It typically includes a father's eldest son, the son's spouse and his children. In the rural Irish family, remaining sons are given cash settlements as the one selected by the father moves into his father's household and takes possession of property rights. The *lineal family* also contains three generations but includes two or more sons, their spouses, and families. The largest, and quite uncommon, family form is the *fully extended family* (Murdock, 1957). This family consists of two or more male siblings in the senior generation, with their spouses, and two or more of each of their sons and their spouses and children. The traditional joint Indian family (Gore, 1965) consists of two or more male siblings, their wives, and children. The *joint family* shares a common household and treasury. In reality, the joint family is part of a life cycle, beginning as an extended family when the sons marry. After the father dies, the true joint family begins and remains in existence until the youngest sons marry. At this point in the cycle, this rather large joint family splits into several extended families (the stem family). In Calcutta in 1960, approximately half of the family units were nuclear and the other half were either extended or joint families.

It may be noted in conclusion that both nuclear and extended families may be either monogamous or polygamous (i.e., polyandrous or polygynous). Murdock (1965) reported that about half of those societies defined as being predominantly nuclear family oriented were also polygamous.

Kinship regulations

All of us are related by blood to thousands of people whom we will never know.[5] Whom one considers a relative, however, is typically socially defined and reflects on the somewhat arbitrary cutting lines of a given society. In some societies, everyone is not only related but is able to classify and identify distant relatives with accuracy. Kinship terminology for the average Canadian seldom goes beyond one's first cousin. All societies recognize certain categories of kinsmen and ignore others.

It will be helpful to first illustrate the complexity of kinship ties. Figure 3.1 diagrams three different levels of kinship analysis (based on distinctions developed by Radcliffe-Brown, 1941). As can be seen, there are 7 different *categories* of primary relatives for ego, 24 categories of secondary relatives, and 124 categories of tertiary relatives. In common language, the parental uncle's son would be ego's first cousin; in this case, ego's father's brother's son. In all, there are 155 different categories of relatives. If one can conceptualize the probability of several persons occupying each category (e.g., four primary sons and three primary daughters), it will readily be seen that the average Canadian "knows of" a lot of relatives. The addition of polyandrous or polygynous families to the diagram would add approximately 36 categories of relatives.

Kinship has a pervasive influence on the life of society as well as the individual. In this sense, kinship may be thought of as a social system which defines appropriate and inappropriate life choices and activities including: who, when, and how many one may marry; where a married couple will live and for how long; who will be accountable to whom; the responsibilities of each family member; the right to inherit property and related possessions; and a myriad of sexual regulations relating to incest, illegitimacy, nonmarital sexuality, adultery, and the prohibition of sexual intercourse during various events and time periods. The relative rigidity or flexibility of these regulations, as well as the way in which they are enforced, varies as widely as the form or content of the regulations from society to society. In order to understand the family system in comparative context, it is essential to recognize the basic fact that kinship patterns are systematic rather than random.

Descent Rules of descent usually represent the basic identity of an individual in society: his name, who his relatives are, and his attendant rights and duties. There are four basic types of descent. *Patrilineal* descent means that a child is assigned the

---

5 Persons adopted at birth remain "a relative" of an unknown parentage and accordingly a large kinship structure *and*, through legal assignment, also become a relative of a second kinship system. In addition, each of us gain thousands of relatives via marriage or the marriages of our kin. Ties acquired through marriage are referred to as affinal kinship ties.

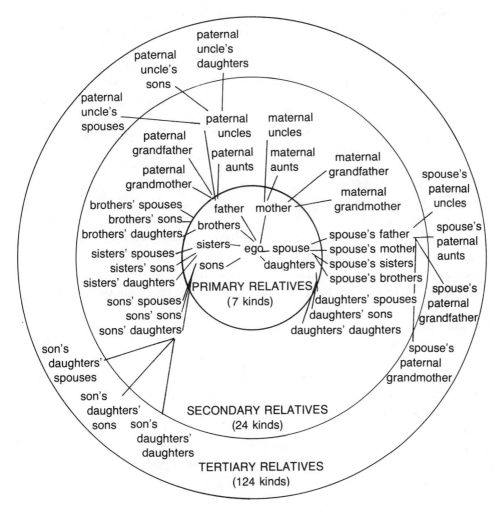

Figure 3-1 Diagram of maximum number of kinds of primary, secondary, and tertiary relatives.

name of kin related through the male line and so the rights and duties are defined by his father, grandfather, and their male siblings. In the "World Ethnographic Sample", 43 percent of the 560 societies were patrilineal (N=239). The next most prevalent form is referred to as *bilateral descent*. In societies in which bilateral lineage is practised, the kinship systems of both the husband and wife have basically equal influence and significance to the married couple. Though it is uncommon for the married couple to retain both kin names upon marriage (typically the male's kin name is used), each spouse has legitimate access to possessions inherited from the other's kinship group. Canada is an example of a bilateral descent form. There are 214 societies with bilateral descent (38 percent). Societies in which the husband comes under the authority of his wife's family have what is referred to as a *matrilineal descent* system. Matrilineage, however, does not mean that the female members of the kinship structure exercise the authority. Instead, authority is invested in the brothers of one's wife and in her maternal uncles. Eighty societies are matrilineal (14 percent). *Bilineal descent*, sometimes referred to as double descent, may be thought of as a conditional lineage system. In this case, inheritance rights and kinship duties are different within a society depending on one's social status or other related factors, such as whether one is a son or daughter. The most common practice, however, is to assign a child at birth to the father's patrilineal group *and* the mother's matrilineal kin group. Less than 5 percent of societies are bilineal (N=27).

Residence Norms of residence are concerned with who will live with whom and for how long. Table 3.1 summarizes the various types of residence patterns and the frequency with which they occur. The relationships between residence and descent norms are also illustrated.

The majority of societies have *patrilocal* residence norms (55.9 percent). In these societies, the bride leaves her own kinship group and she and her husband either occupy the same dwelling as her husband's parents or they live in the same community. The second most common residence pattern, though considerably less prevalent, involves the movement of the husband from his kinship group to the immediate locality of his wife's kinship group. This practice is referred to as *matrilocal* residence. In fifty-nine societies (10.5 percent), the marriage begins in or near the residence of the bride's family and after a designated period of time, usually one year, this marital unit moves in with or near the groom's family. This pattern is defined as *matripatrilocal* residence. It is interesting to note that bride service (working for a period of time for the bride's family in payment of the bride price) is commonly practised in matripatrilocal societies. Brief definitions of the other forms of residence norms are provided below.

> Bilocal — a conditional residence pattern in which one chooses to live with or near the parents of either spouse; social status is the primary determinant of intra-societal variation.
> Neolocal — the marital unit maintains a separate residence from either kinship group; the norms specify the importance of separate residence.
> Duolocal — the husband and wife live in separate residences, typically side by side, and apart from both kinship groups.

Avunculocal — the marital unit lives with or near the maternal uncle of the groom.
Matrineolocal — the initial residence is with the bride's family. After a designated
    period of time the couple establish a separate residence apart from both kin groups.

Canadian society has a predominantly neolocal pattern. However, many married couples remain in the same city and sometimes in the same neighborhood in which they were reared. Kalbach and McVey (1971) report that 2.3 percent of married couples in Canada were not maintaining their own household in 1966. Among lower class families with tight finances it is not uncommon for a matrineolocal pattern to be practised. Sub-cultural patterns also vary widely. The Hutterites, for example, practise patrilocal residence rules, as do several different Eskimo subcultures.

As can be seen from table 3.1, the duolocal pattern is unique. Three of the four societies are matrilineal. Co-residence is a disadvantage in these cultures because of widespread regulations concerning deference; where women are expected to kneel or stop all work when their husbands enter the room, for example, it is an advantage to live separately.

There are several obvious relationships between descent and residence illustrated in table 3.1. First, nearly all patrilineal societies also have patrilocal residence patterns. The remainder are primarily matripatrilocal. Second, nearly half of the matrilineal societies are also matrilocal (47.5 percent). The remaining matrilineal

Table 3.1   The Relationship between Residence and Descent Norms

Residence norms	Descent norms									
	Patrilineal		Bilateral		Matrilineal		Bilineal		Total	
	N	%	N	%	N	%	N	%	N	%
Patrilocal	(202)	84.5	(74)	34.6	(14)	17.5	(23)	85.2	(313)	55.9
Matrilocal	(3)	1.3	(43)	20.0	(38)	47.5	(1)	3.7	(85)	15.2
Bilocal	(1)	0.4	(29)	13.6	(0)	0.0	(0)	0.0	(30)	5.4
Neolocal	(1)	0.4	(24)	11.2	(2)	2.5	(0)	0.0	(27)	4.8
Duolocal	(1)	0.4	(0)	0.0	(3)	3.8	(0)	0.0	(4)	0.7
Avunculocal	(0)	0.0	(1)	0.4	(12)	15.0	(0)	0.0	(13)	2.3
Matripatrilocal	(28)	11.7	(28)	13.1	(2)	2.5	(1)	3.7	(59)	10.5
Matrineolocal	(0)	0.0	(5)	2.3	(0)	0.0	(0)	0.0	(5)	0.9
Other	(3)	1.3	(10)	4.7	(9)	11.2	(2)	7.4	(24)	4.3
Total	(239)	42.7	(214)	38.2	(80)	14.3	(27)	4.8	(560)	100.0

Based on an adaptation of data provided in the "World Ethnographic Sample" (Murdock, 1957).

societies are either patrilocal or avunculocal. The avunculocal pattern would appear to be a clear example of accommodation of the matrilineal kinship group to the kinship group of the groom. Third, the bilateral lineage pattern appears to be generally unrelated to the residence pattern; the differences by residence are relatively small. Fourth, societies which reflect double lineage regulations appear to also practise patrilocal residence patterns.

Comportment The relationships within and between kinship groups between spouses, siblings, and parents and children have been extensively discussed by Stephens (1963) and are frequently considered in ethnographic descriptions of specific cultures. These relationships offer some insight into the social psychological patterns of pre-industrial societies.

Many societies have ritualistic ways of expressing the social inequality of males and females and age versus youth. These patterns are commonly referred to as *deference* rules. The principles of respect, submissiveness, and obedience are reflected in bowing, kneeling, hand kissing, speech etiquette, mealtime etiquette, body elevation rules, being quiet unless spoken to, and social distance practices in public. Extreme deference practices are common in the rural areas of the Middle East and India. Stephens found that deference is typically required by younger persons to older persons and by women to men. Deference emphasizes the subordinate and inferior role of women and younger men to defined authority. *Avoidance* rules, in contrast, assume a relatively equal social status between the avoiders. Avoidance is most common between affinal kin such as a man and his mother-in-law or a man and his daughter-in-law. Among the Baganda of Africa, for example, a man and his mother-in-law can't touch each other, can't look at each other, and can't eat together or converse alone (Mair, 1934). Avoidance rules within one's own kinship group are typically between brothers and sisters and likely reflect a fear of, or control of, incestuous sexual relationships. *Joking* patterns frequently exist in societies in which there are avoidance regulations. Joking refers to roughhousing, sarcasm, belittling, and sexual horseplay (Stephens, 1963:92). Joking typically does not occur within one's primary family. If there are avoidance rules between a man and his mother-in-law, the man may joke with his brother-in-law. Similarly, avoidance between a boy and his sister is frequently associated with acceptable joking between the boy and his father's sisters.

Comportment patterns tend to be formalized in many pre-industrial societies. It would be inappropriate, however, to assume that similar kinds of expectations are absent in Canada. A sixteen-year-old son, for example, should not kiss his father on the lips but a five-year-old son may. In contrast, a sixteen-year-old daughter apparently has greater freedom, in that she may kiss both her mother and father on the lips without undue concern from the neighbors. Similarly, there are times when children are to be seen but not heard. Men are expected to defer to women when there is only one empty seat on the bus. These patterns and many others are pervasive in Canadian culture. Regulations concerning the choice of mate and the nature of courtship will be discussed in Chapter four.

Sexual regulations

Few societies are silent concerning sexual activities. There is no society which regards *all* sexual activities as an absolutely private affair and of no concern to others. The Kaingang tribe perhaps comes the closest to non-regulation but even here marriages are not permitted between brothers and sisters and adultery is "believed" to be inappropriate, even though most of the members have frequent adulterous affairs (Henry, 1964). The Trobrianders permit parent-child incestuous affairs, but sexual regulations after marriage are uniquely rigid (Malinowski, 1927). The following is a brief cross-cultural discussion of various types of sexual regulation.

Incest Incest refers to the prohibition of sexual intercourse with close relatives. Which relatives are taboo, however, varies from society to society. Where incest taboos exist, as they do in nearly all societies, the taboo is most evident within the nuclear family. But no society stops with the nuclear family. To quote Leslie (1973:54): "there is no one kinsman, or class of kin, outside the nuclear family who is not an acceptable sex partner in some society." There is perhaps no other so-called sexual aberration that ensures more aversion and disgust.[6] Incest rules are typically reflected in whom one is permitted to marry. In the U.S. for example, thirty of the fifty states do not permit marriage between first cousins, whereas in the remaining states as well as throughout Canada marriage is permitted between first cousins (Farber, 1973:25; Chapman, 1968:5). Incest rules as they apply to marriage or incestuous intercourse, however, are not universal. Incest, whether approved or not, is practised in every society including Canada. One can assume that incest is far more widespread than the statistical evidence suggests.

6 The explanations for the near-universality of incest taboos are speculative and questionable. A summary of the basic arguments is available in Aberle et al., 1963. Generally, it is assumed that incest taboos are necessary to prevent sexual rivalry and role confusion in the nuclear family. It is apparent that some children, but certainly not all, learn to be disinterested in sex with siblings and parents.

Illegitimacy The birth of children outside of wedlock or to other inappropriate sexual partners (such as the celibate, or crosscaste partners) results in the labeling of the children as illegitimate, and to some extent reflects on the mother (in our society referred to as the unwed mother), in most societies of the world. Most societies cope with the problem of illegitimacy by tolerating the practice and hoping that things will improve (Rodman, 1966). In some societies, however, illegitimacy is not a social problem but merely one of definition. In some of the Caribbean countries, where illegitimacy rates are as high as 60 percent, unmarried girls are given a home by a sister's husband. Children born to them are defined as illegitimate even though born into and accepted within a family household. Both the Eskimo (Vranas and Stephens, 1971) and the kibbutzniks in Israel (Spiro, 1965) apparently accept the illegitimate child into the household without hesitation, treating him in the same way as a legitimate child. The illegitimacy rate among Indians in Alberta was more than 46 percent in 1968 (Alberta Department of Health, 1968), but this is a function of a high incidence of common-law marriage and the welfare practices of the federal government. The general response of most societies, however, is to activate "emergency" procedures to help solve the identity and inheritance problems of the illegitimate child.

Premarital sexual regulation In a study of 158 societies, Murdock (1965) found that about 70 percent permitted premarital intercourse, either conditionally or without reservation. In a related study (Stephens, 1963) similar results were obtained. Premarital intercourse was forbidden in forty-four societies in Murdock's sample and in six societies in Stephens's sample. The restrictions were typically directed toward women rather than men; the double standard appears to be prevalent in restrictive societies. Although Canada would be classified as a society which values premarital chastity, recent evidence suggests that about half of the unmarried college students (both males and females) have experienced sexual intercourse (Hobart, 1972). Virginity is required among the Bedouins of Cyrenaica (Peters, 1965); if a man discovers that his wife's hymen is already broken, a crucial test of the marriage ceremony, he will likely refuse to marry her. Even so, unmarried men occasionally have sexual relations with married women. The Trobriand Islanders, in contrast, permit almost any form of sexual exchange among children. Most children's games involve genital play, coitus, and songs related to sexual organs and activities. There are no inexperienced males and females at marriage. Yet sexual restrictions tend to increase with age, and after marriage, are considerably more restrictive than those in most societies of the world (Malinowski, 1927).

Extramarital sexual regulation Adultery is proscribed in the majority of the societies of the world, but the evidence suggests that the rules aren't always observed. Murdock (1965) found that 81 percent of the societies in his sample had rules against adultery. Ford and Beach (1951) found adultery regulations in 61 percent of the 139 societies in their sample. In sixty-nine of these eighty-five societies, however, there were no rules concerning male extramarital activity. Stephens (1963), in his study of thirty-eight societies, likewise found rules in twenty-six societies but males were exempted in eighteen of them. It appears that the double standard is even more evident after marriage than prior to marriage.

Occasional sexual taboos The major remaining area of sexual regulation concerns time periods in the marriage career during which the spouses are not permitted to have sexual intercourse. Occasional sexual taboos, as they are called by Stephens (1963), typically include pregnancy, menstruation, and post partum taboos (varying from one to four years). In addition to these, the Trobrianders also prohibit sexual intercourse for one year when a couple are first married (Malinowski, 1927). Stephens (1962), in a study of 100 societies, found evidence of post partum taboos in half the societies and menstruation taboos in nearly all of them.

Sub-cultural family patterns in Canada

The preceding discussion has emphasized the significant role of kinship in the identity and destiny of the individual in the majority of the societies of the world. It has also been suggested that kinship regulations, though less visible, exist in Canada. The purpose of this part of the chapter is to continue the comparative analysis of marriage and family patterns but to focus on the uniformities and variabilities *within* Canada.

Intrasocietal variation is not uncommon in the developing nations of the world. India, for example, has 15 major languages, 23 major tribal dialects, 720 minor dialects, 7 predominant religions, and a myriad of differing caste groups (Gore, 1965). Though scholars frequently use the terms American family, Japanese family, and Canadian family (as I have done for the sake of convenience), there is little justification for these labels in complex, heterogeneous societies which permit, if not encourage, multiple value systems, divergent normative proscriptions and prescriptions, and the relative autonomy of individuals. While certain patterns, such as monogamy, a separate residence for each nuclear family, legal marriage, and the right to divorce if necessary, are common to most Canadians, the range of variation *within* Canadian society, if native peoples are included, is nearly as broad as the range of cross-cultural variations. Based on a review of census materials and research in Canada to 1964, Elkin (1964:31) concluded:

> There is no one Canadian family. With its distinctive geography and history, Canada is much too heterogeneous to have one or ten or twenty distinctive family types. As the geographical setting, social class, religious, ethnic, occupational, and other groupings vary, so too do our families.

The vertical mosaic

The concept "vertical mosaic" was developed by Porter (1965) to describe the multicultural status patterns in Canadian society. It is, of course, an axiom of society that people are unequally educated and have different jobs, incomes and religious values. However, as Porter has demonstrated, these standard dimensions of society are not equally distributed in Canada, but are systematically linked to a hierarchical system of social status. Ethnicity[7] is closely related to many social indicators. Certain of these patterns are illustrated in table 3.2.

The largest proportion of the population is composed of English and French Canadians (73.3 percent). The remainder of the population is distributed among over thirty-four ethnic groups; six of the largest of these are included in the table. As can be seen, the German group is the third largest in Canada (6.1 percent). Jews and Italians live predominantly in urban areas (99 and 97 percent, respectively), whereas the native Indians live predominantly in rural areas. Both Germans and Scandinavians are less urban than the Canadian average.

There is also systematic variation in the type of occupation held by ethnic group. Jews, for example, are considerably over-represented (in fact, the highest proportion) in white-collar occupations (managerial, teaching, medicine, clerical, and sales). In these same occupations, English and French Canadians are over-represented compared to the Canadian average, while the other ethnic groups are under-represented. In contrast, English and Jewish Canadians, compared to the Canadian average, are less involved in service, farming, machining and construction occupations. Italian Canadians are most involved in service, machining and construction related jobs. A distinct minority of Italians are in farming. German, Ukrainian and Scandinavian ethnic groups are the most active in agriculture. Native Indians are most involved in service and construction related activities. In a study by Blishen (1958), a status index of occupations in Canada was developed. Occupa-

---

7 Ethnicity is determined in the 1971 Census by the response to the following question: "To what ethnic or cultural group did you or your ancestor (on the male side) belong on coming to this continent?"

tions were classified into social class categories varying from class I (highest status) to class VII (lowest status). Though dated, this study provides a more accurate description of the distribution of various ethnic groups into the occupational hierarchy. The results are presented in table 3.2. Jewish Canadians are clearly over-represented in the upper classes (38.6 percent, compared to a Canadian average of 11.6 percent) and under-represented in the lower classes (23.8 percent, compared to a Canadian average of 40.9 percent). French and Scandinavian Canadians are slightly over-represented in the middle classes, whereas native Indian Canadians are markedly over-represented in the lower classes (84.6 percent as compared to the Canadian average of 40.9 percent).

To the extent that occupation is an important indicator of social status, the selective access of various ethnic groups to the occupational structure of Canadian society has significant consequences for family patterns. The education, occupation and income of fathers, for example, has been shown to significantly influence children's academic achievement and educational problems (Card et al., 1966; Farley, 1969; Hughes, 1968; Locke, 1969) and educational and occupational aspirations (Siemens and Jackson, 1965; Breton and Macdonald, 1971; Forcese and Siemens, 1965).

Educational attainment does indeed vary substantially among ethnic groups. Nearly 80 percent of the native Indian population, twenty years of age or older, have only completed elementary school compared to about 26 percent of the English Canadians. Similarly, 74 percent of the Italians stopped their education after elementary school. Only the English Canadians are above the national average in the completion of high school and university training. Germans, English, and Scandinavians have apparently pursued post-secondary education more actively than other ethnic groups.

Table 3.2 also provides information on the type of religion adhered to or favored by ethnic group. Religion, it is suggested, represents an indicator of the types of constraints and priorities by which individuals, and more particularly the family, order their style of life. Ethnic groups which adhere to one particular religious position will likely be more resistant to assimilation, while those groups who are spread out, or have many religious orientations, will likely be less significant as an ethnic force in the vertical mosaic sense. As might be expected, French and Italian Canadians are over 90 percent Roman Catholic. Though not reported, Jews are predominantly Jewish in faith (93 percent) and Ukrainians are predominantly Greek Orthodox or Ukrainian Catholic (52 percent). The data also indicates that Germans tend to be Roman Catholic or Lutheran; native Indians, due to the efforts of missionaries, are typically Anglican or Roman Catholic (78 percent); Scandinavians are predominantly Lutheran or United (60 percent). English Canadians appear to be the most spread-out group.

Table 3.2   Multiculturalism: Occupation, Educational Attainment, Religion, and Marital Status by Ethnicity, 1971 (in percentages)

	Canada	English	French	German	Indian	Italian	Jewish	Scandi-navian	Ukrai-nian
				Ethnic Group					
Population[a]									
Total Population	21,568,310	9,624,120	6,180,120	1,317,200	295,215	730,830	296,945	384,790	580,660
Percent of Total	—	44.6	28.7	6.1	1.3	3.4	1.4	1.8	2.7
Percent Urban	76.2	75.9	75.9	68.8	30.7	96.6	98.8	68.3	75.0
Occupation[b]									
Managerial-Administrative	4.3	5.2	3.7	3.6	1.5	1.8	10.7	3.8	2.9
Teaching	4.1	4.3	4.5	3.6	1.6	1.6	5.2	4.0	3.5
Medicine	3.8	4.1	3.6	3.5	2.2	1.1	4.9	3.7	3.0
Clerical	15.9	18.5	14.7	13.4	6.9	9.7	18.8	13.7	14.8
Sales	9.5	10.4	8.7	8.7	2.7	6.7	24.2	9.1	8.4
Service	11.2	10.6	11.2	10.6	12.4	13.0	4.9	10.7	12.9
Farming	5.9	5.4	4.4	12.5	5.9	1.8	.4	12.6	11.6
Machining-Production	10.2	8.3	11.0	11.0	6.6	20.8	7.0	7.2	9.6
Construction	6.5	5.6	6.9	7.9	9.8	15.3	1.7	8.0	6.5
Occupational Class[c]									
Class I & II	11.6	13.1	10.1	9.8	1.3	8.2	38.6	10.2	6.4
Class III, IV, V	47.5	53.0	40.1	48.9	14.1	37.9	37.6	49.8	47.2
Class VI & VII	40.9	33.9	49.8	41.3	84.6	53.9	23.8	40.0	46.4

Educational Attainment[d]									
Elementary	36.8	26.2	49.5	47.0	79.5	74.0	*	45.7	54.8
Secondary	36.0	42.5	29.0	25.7	15.0	16.0	*	29.8	27.3
Post-Secondary	15.4	17.5	12.8	18.7	3.8	5.7	*	16.0	9.9
University	11.8	13.8	8.7	8.6	1.7	4.3	*	8.3	8.0
Religion[e]									
Anglican	11.8	22.5	.9	5.4	22.3	1.2	.6	8.4	4.6
Baptist	3.1	5.1	.6	4.3	1.4	.3	.1	2.7	1.4
Lutheran	3.3	1.3	.2	24.5	.3	.3	.2	33.4	1.8
Pentecostal	1.0	1.5	.1	1.7	2.1	.5	—	2.1	1.0
Presbyterian	4.0	7.7	.3	2.3	1.2	.4	.1	2.6	1.3
Roman Catholic	46.2	20.7	94.0	25.7	55.6	93.0	1.1	8.2	15.3
United	17.5	30.8	1.9	15.8	10.4	1.9	—	26.9	13.9
No Religion	4.3	5.4	1.1	5.6	2.7	1.3	3.3	8.5	5.1
Marital Status[f]									
Single	49.4	47.9	53.6	45.8	64.5	48.4	41.8	44.5	43.8
Married	45.2	45.7	42.3	49.2	31.7	48.5	51.0	49.4	49.9
Widowed	4.5	5.3	3.7	4.0	3.3	2.7	5.8	4.7	5.0
Divorced	.9	1.1	.4	1.1	.5	.4	1.4	1.3	1.2

[a] Data obtained from Statistics Canada Catalog No. 92-723.
[b] Data obtained from Perspective Canada, Table 13.24, pp. 279-280. Categories are loosely defined, including persons involved in "related" occupations, e.g., medicine and related.
[c] Adapted from Blishen (1958).
[d] Based on percent attaining the educational level among persons 20 years of age or older. Data obtained from Perspective Canada, Table 13.23, p. 278.
[e] Census figures do not measure church membership or indicate the degree of affiliation with a particular religious body, but rather indicate the religion to which each person stated he or she belonged, adhered, or favored. Data obtained from Statistics Canada Catalog No. 92-735.
[f] Data obtained from Statistics Canada Catalog No. 92-734.
*Not available.

Marital status varies by ethnic group as well. The most apparent difference is among native Indians. Nearly 65 percent are single and less than 32 percent are married. This pattern is indicative of a larger number of children under the age of fifteen (45 percent, compared to the national average of 29.6 percent) and a higher level of unwed parenthood than among other ethnic groups. Jews, in contrast, have the lowest number of single persons (41.8 percent) and the highest number of persons married (51 percent). Accordingly, there are considerably fewer children under the age of fifteen (20 percent). The proportion of people who are divorced is smallest among French and Italian Canadians and largest among the Jews.

Social status or ethnicity alone, however, does not explain marriage and family patterns adequately in Canada. French Canadians of differing social status maintain strong kinship ties (Garigue, 1962; Piddington, 1971), whereas kinship relationships among English Canadians vary systematically by social status (Seeley, Sim and Loosley, 1956; Pineo, 1968; Irving, 1972). Similarly, while intermarriage has increased rapidly among Ukrainians and Italians as the family has achieved higher levels of social status (Hobart et al., 1963; Hobart, 1966), family ties and intramarriage are as strong as ever among Jewish families, though structural and authority patterns have changed (Latowsky, 1971; Schlesinger, 1971d). These examples illustrate the significance of the vertical mosaic in Canada. Ethnicity and social status must both be considered in interpreting the structure and process of family life in Canada.

Family patterns

There have been numerous studies of the marriage and family patterns of specific ethnic groups in Canada.[8] Many of these studies, however, have not been concerned with the family system per se, and much of the data is out of date. Although considerable research is yet to be done, there is sufficient evidence to discuss certain

8 For those interested in reading more extensively, selected references are provided for fifteen different ethnic groups. Books and articles dealing with *general* patterns are identified. The ethnic groups and selected references are as follows: *Chinese* (Davison, 1952), *Doukhobors* (Lewis, 1952), *Dutch* (Ishwaran, 1971b, 1971c), *English* (Seeley, Sim and Loosley, 1956; Irving, 1972), *Eskimos* (Jenness, 1922; Vallee, 1967; Damas, 1971; Vranas and Stephens, 1971; Honigmann and Honigmann, 1971), *French* (Garigue, 1962; Piddington, 1961; Moreux, 1971), *Hungarians* (Kosa, 1957), *Hutterites* (Hostettler and Huntington, 1967; Peter, 1967, 1971, 1975), *Indians* (Jenness, 1935; Dunning, 1959a, 1959b; Hatt, 1969; Rohner and Rohner, 1970; Cruikshank, 1971; Ryan, 1975), *Italians* (Hobart, 1966; Richmond, 1967a, 1967b); *Japanese* (Maykovich, 1971a), *Jews* (Latowsky, 1971; Schlesinger, 1971d), *Lebanese Muslim* (Barclay, 1971), *Negroes* (Tysko, 1959), and *Ukrainians* (Hobart, 1963).

basic aspects of family life in several subcultures. Family patterns among English, French, Eskimo, and Indian Canadians are briefly discussed in this chapter. *General* relationships are emphasized, as specific findings will be considered for these and other ethnic groups in subsequent chapters.

English Canadian family In 1971, English Canadians accounted for about 45 percent of the Canadian population. The Atlantic provinces are predominantly English (Newfoundland 94 percent, Prince Edward Island 82 percent, Nova Scotia 77 percent). New Brunswick, Ontario and British Columbia are about 58 percent English.

English Canadian families are perhaps the most diverse of all ethnic groups. Collectively, the present evidence suggests three fairly distinct family patterns: a middle to upper-middle class family with traditional and idealistic values and practices; a lower-middle, working class kin-oriented family; and an emergent, more liberal pattern of attitudes and behaviors which *may* represent a family system "in the making". The last pattern is more ambiguous than the others for two reasons: (a) it is based primarily on the attitudes and behaviors of married and unmarried college and university students; and (b) the studies illustrate the dilemma of change — there is support for both the old and the new. There are likely other family patterns among English Canadians which have not yet been studied; this analysis is of necessity limited to the research available. This limitation should be kept in mind in the discussion of Canadian family patterns throughout the book.

In an out-of-date study (Seeley, Sim and Loosley, 1956), the middle and upper-middle class family was described in ideal-typical terms. A marital unit is established by two persons from unrelated and often unacquainted families on the basis of "love". Companionship is emphasized in the relationship, and it is expected that sexual relations will be both exclusive and satisfying. The woman's role is to be a good wife and mother and an active participant in the life of the community. Among other things, she is responsible for developing and maintaining an appropriate life style relative to the imagery of household appointments. The man's role is primarily to be a successful provider, a good father to his children, responsible for major economic decisions, and ritually responsible for household tasks requiring physical strength. This family maintains only minimum ties with kin, and is frequently isolated both geographically and socially from both sets of parents. Where kin relationships occur, they are largely limited to ritual occasions. The wife is responsible for letter writing, card and gift sending, and telephoning activities. Close friends often become substitute kin and are called "uncle" or "aunt". The average family has two children, who are raised permissively but expected to develop "responsible" attitudes and behaviors. A child properly trained will be an individual, capable of making decisions and managing an allowance. Even so, parents and children will frequently have differing attitudes because of relative isolation from the traditions of the kin group and the emphasis on individuality.

If there is a "melting pot" in Canada, this pattern probably represents the most typical family. The third generation Ukrainian and Italian families, for example, could both be said to approximate this family style.

However, modifications to this ideal-typical family profile may be required. As indicated in Chapter two, nearly 34 percent of all Canadian married women are employed. This may involve changes in the roles of husband and wife described above. Further research is needed.

A more recent study (Irving, 1972) focused on the significance of kinship exchange among lower-middle, working class families. Almost 75 percent of these family units were found to visit and telephone their parents weekly. One third of the families spent more time with relatives than they did with friends. Over half the families had lived with parents at some time during their marriage. Helping patterns in the form of financial aid, care during illness, and emotional support were found to be widespread. Kinship exchange was more frequent and satisfying between married couples and the wife's parents; conflict, where it existed, was most pronounced between wives and their mothers-in-law. When husbands visited their own parents, they typically did so alone. This study offers strong evidence of active kinship ties, most often matrifocal in practice.

Similar results concerning kin ties were obtained in a study of middle and lower-middle class English Canadians in a Montreal suburb (Osterreich, 1965). An earlier study of the working class family also found evidence of active kinship exchange. In this study, however, the patterns of visiting and help were primarily patrifocal (Pineo, 1968).

Several recent studies of college students in different parts of Canada have attempted to assess mate selection preferences (Wakil, 1973), attitudes toward marriage (Hobart, 1972), attitudes toward parenthood (Hobart, 1973), sexual attitudes and behavior (Hobart, 1972; Mann, 1967), and attitudes toward and practice of trial marriage (Hobart, 1973).[9] Collectively, these papers appear to document both the persistence of middle class Anglo-Saxon traditions and the emergence of considerably more liberal attitudes and behaviors. Given the assumption that college students are potential marital partners and community leaders, their views and behaviors may be indicative of future family patterns. The Saskatchewan study (Wakil, 1973) suggests that potential marrieds value honest, understanding, pleasant, mature marital partners who will be loyal in marriage. They tend to idealize families with three

---

9 The specific findings of these studies are discussed in some detail in Chapter four.

to four children, even though the Canadian average is two children. Similarly, Whitehurst (1973) found that about 88 percent of his sample of students believed that monogamy would continue as the predominant marital form. Trade school students in Alberta and Ontario tend to hold traditional attitudes toward marital and parenthood roles. For example, the male is seen to be the primary breadwinner and disciplinarian while the female's primary responsibility is motherhood. Only half of the trade school students thought that a couple should divorce if the partners are no longer compatible (Hobart, 1973). University students, in contrast, were generally found to have more liberal attitudes than trade school students (Hobart, 1972, 1973). Attitudes toward child rearing, divorce, employment among women, authority and education were in most respects considerably more egalitarian.

The most apparent, and for our purposes most important, differences were those between males and females. Female students, on nearly every important indicator, were significantly more egalitarian in their orientations toward marriage and parenthood. These attitudes would seem to indicate significant changes in the wife-mother role. Hobart has also found that nearly half the university students in Ontario and Alberta (male and female) have experienced sexual intercourse. Furthermore, nearly 60 percent of his sample are favorable to trial marriage and some 50 percent know of at least one couple living together. In the Whitehurst study of 300 Ontario universtiy students in Toronto (1973), nearly 60 percent believed that they were capable of both love and ongoing sexual relations with several persons at one time. Over half of the students anticipated a different marital and sexual life style than their parents. Nearly 20 percent were willing to try group marriage.

The changes in female role definitions and sexual attitudes and behaviors seem to offer credence to an emergent marriage and family life style among English Canadians. Whether the conflict between traditional and emergent patterns will resolve itself, or facilitate the persistence of the traditional English family and development of an alternative emergent English family, as assumed, remains to be seen.

French Canadian family In 1971, French Canadians represented about 29 percent of the Canadian population. About 79 percent of the population of Quebec is of French origin; in the remaining provinces, the proportion varies from 37 percent in New Brunswick to 3 percent in Newfoundland. There are few French Canadians in the western provinces, varying from 4 percent in British Columbia to 9 percent in Manitoba.

Because of the high proportion of French Canadians in the province of Quebec, a comparison of certain vital statistics between Quebec and Canada as a whole offers insight into the French Canadian marriage and family system. Table 3.3 illustrates several important differences. The birth rate in Quebec is the lowest of all the provinces (varying from 13.8 to 31.9 in the Northwest Territories). The marriage rate, with the exception of the Northwest Territories, is also the lowest in Canada (it varies from 5.9 to 10.3). Even so, Quebec has more persons per household and more persons per family, in both rural and urban areas, than Canada as a whole. There are approximately one third as many divorced families in rural Quebec and one half as many divorced families in urban Quebec as in Canada. Quebec also has one of the lowest divorce rates in Canada.[10] It is important to emphasize, however, that the divorce rate in Quebec has increased more than 13 times since the change in the divorce act in 1968, whereas the divorce rate in Ontario has increased only 2½ times.

Table 3.3 Selected Vital Statistics, Quebec and Canada, 1971

Vital statistics	Quebec	Canada
Percent urban population divorced	.48	.94
Percent rural population divorced	.14	.41
Live birth rate[a]	13.8	15.5
Age specific fertility rate[b]		
15-19	17.5	37.2
20-24	93.3	117.7
25-29	124.7	131.6
Marriage rate[a]	8.5	9.0
Divorce rate[c]	133.1	166.1
Average persons per household	3.7	3.5
Average persons per family	3.9	3.7
Urban	3.8	3.6
Rural	4.5	4.1

Data obtained from Statistics Canada Catalog No. 84-201 for 1973 and Statistics Canada Catalog Nos. 92-717, 93-702, and 93-714.
[a] Per 1000 population.
[b] Birth rate per 1000 total women.
[c] Per 100,000 population.

As has been suggested elsewhere (Elkin, 1964; Ishwaran, 1971a), the widespread data on the French Canadian family appears to present a confusing and selective view. Little is known about rural/urban, religious/non-religious, social class and

10 Newfoundland, Prince Edward Island, New Brunswick and the Northwest Territories have lower divorce rates (varying from 41.4 in Newfoundland to 110.5 in the Northwest Territories).

white-collar/blue-collar differences in marriage and family patterns. As with the English Canadian family, there is evidence of both persistence and change. Three main characteristics of the predominant French Canadian family system have been suggested (Ishwaran, 1971a): the family is basically (a) matricentric (mother centered); (b) kinship oriented, i.e., the nuclear family is regulated by kin ties; and (c) family activities are largely defined by religious traditions.

The significant role of kinship in French Canadian life is apparent. In contrast to several other ethnic groups in Canada, kinship regulations remain important in the city; kinship contacts with parents and siblings were found to be frequent (Garigue, 1956).[11] A more recent study in a Montreal suburb (Moreux, 1971) also found that contacts with relatives were frequent, as well as obligatory. The French family is characterized by a rigid division of labor between the sexes. The male is primarily an authority figure and involved very little in the education of children. The female, in contrast, is responsible for the welfare of the family and the care of the children (Garigue, 1962). The salient role of the woman in the French Canadian family is seen in the expectation that she will be a virgin when she marries, will be loyal to her husband, and will bear him a large number of children (Moreux, 1971). The emphasis placed on the importance of individualism by other Canadians takes a different form in French Canadians, according to Wrong (1955:12):

> The individualism with which French Canadians are often credited is really an individualism of families rather than single persons, for the kinship group tends to be the center of the French Canadian's universe.

Though the above evidence suggests a rather tightly knit, mother-centered, father-dominated, and kin-oriented family, there is no clear agreement. Elkin (1968:103) reports on several studies of professional families in which egalitarianism and companionship in the marriage relationship is pronounced. Parent-adolescent conflict and communication problems are reported in other studies (Elkin, 1964:111).

There is also some evidence of change. In a study of values among innovative women in Quebec, attitudes toward many aspects of the woman's role and marriage and family life were found to be quite different from the traditional view. Self-fulfillment in motherhood is rejected or de-emphasized in preference to fulfilling experiences with others in work-roles and related non-family roles (Carisse, 1972, 1976). In another study of attitudes toward marriage based on student responses at

---

11 Garigue's work has been strongly criticized by Rioux (1959) without any research evidence. Indeed, the evidence generally supports Garigue's work (e.g., Moreux, 1971).

the University of Montreal, French Canadian women were found to be "pioneers in advocating egalitarian and permissive orientations," compared to both English men and women and French men (Hobart, 1972:192). Relative to sexual activities, 47 percent of French Canadian men and 23 percent of French Canadian women advocated premarital intercourse with affection (Hobart, 1972). Participation rates were similar.

Based on the research evidence available, it would appear that there is definitely more than one French Canadian family. The traditional mother-centered and kin-oriented family, heavily influenced by religious traditions, is undoubtedly the predominant family form in both rural and urban Quebec. It is also probable that this family system crosses social class lines, although this has not been clearly documented.

A second, less visible, type of family can be inferred from the data available. There is evidence of a professional family with democratic and egalitarian intrafamily relationships. The college student survey provides clear support for egalitarian attitudes toward marriage roles; maternal employment is also accepted with little hesitation. Similarly, the Carisse study illustrates a commitment among innovative women to marital equality and parent-child democracy. These patterns, however, must be seen in the context of an apparent double standard in sexual attitudes and behavior among the students. If such a family exists, it is clearly distinct from the matricentric family and might be thought of as marriage-centric. It is closer in many respects to the emergent English Canadian family than to the common ideal-typical, middle-class family system. Before we can be sure of these suggestions, of course, further research is needed.

Canadian Eskimo families Of some 17,000 Eskimos living in Canada, about 70 percent live in the Northwest Territories and 22 percent in Arctic Quebec. Thirteen hundred Eskimos live in Labrador. Less than .1 percent of the Canadian population is Eskimo.

Historically, there were vast variations in Eskimo family patterns; Damas (1971) discusses no less than seventeen different Eskimo groups. Until recently, the most distinctive features of Eskimo society were their nomadic life style and different living patterns in winter and summer. Eskimos tended to live in snowhouses during the winter (frequently composite snowhouses accommodating more than one family) and in tents during the summer, moving to new fishing and hunting areas.

Kinship patterns varied widely,[12] with the Copper Eskimos perhaps the most

12 Most of this discussion is based on the recent paper by Damas (1971). Appropriate references for further study are identified in the Damas paper.

variable of the Eskimo groups. Many lived in composite snowhouses during the winter months, although single dwellings were also common, and frequently occupied by two nuclear families. Patrilocal ties among nuclear units sharing accommodation were common. Damas concluded, nevertheless, that kin ties were modest and that the nuclear family was the predominant household form. The Netsilik and Iglulik Eskimos, however, are assumed to have basically been extended families with strong kinship ties. Composite snowhouses connected to a common entrance were shared by nuclear families with patrilineal and patrilocal ties. The father and his younger married son typically occupied the rearmost snowhouse, while the others were occupied by older married sons. The authority pattern was patriarchal, the oldest male being thought of as the leader. Younger brothers were expected to obey older brothers and younger cousins, older cousins. Males and females ate separately. The Caribou, Baffin Island, and Hudson Bay Eskimos are described as following a similar pattern.

Among the Eskimos on the coast of Labrador, most older men had two or more wives, and the household form was typically a polygynous joint family. The Angmagsalik and Mackenzie Eskimos are said to have used one large household to accommodate an entire village of some thirty people. Matripatrilocal residence patterns were apparently practised by the Eskimos in the St. Lawrence Island area and the Nunivak and Chugach Eskimos in Alaska.

In the Akudlik neighborhood near Churchill, Manitoba, Vranas and Stephens (1971) report an example of polyandry. The males live in adjacent houses which the female shares equally. One family includes eleven children, and neither the children nor the mother are able to distinguish which of the two houses is "home". Names are assigned primarily on the basis of appearance and the judgment of the mother. Sleeping arrangements varied between households. Other related patterns were also observed in this community. Children are desired and so illegitimate children are accepted into the household. Even so, extra-marital activity causes strife. As among the Athapaskan Indians, cross-racial adultery nearly always involved an Eskimo female and a non-Eskimo male.

The role of kinship in Eskimo communities is emphasized in nearly all materials available on Eskimo culture. As Ferguson (1971) suggested, the kinship unit forms a community *band*, typically composed of the original parents of two or more sons and their spouses and children (similar to the classical extended family outlined earlier in this chapter). The band constituted more than a kinship group, in that it was also a cooperating economic unit and a political group under the leadership of the family head (Ferguson, 1971:19).

Although the extended family continues to be an important force in Eskimo society, there is evidence that the nuclear family is becoming the basic household unit in both winter and summer (Damas, 1971).

Indian Canadian families In 1971, there were 295,215 native Indians in Canada including some 60,000 Métis (mixed Indian and white ancestry). Registered Indians (257,619) are organized into 565 legal bands varying in size from 100 to over 8000 members. A "band" constitutes a group of Indians having in common lands or funds held in trust for them by the government. Most Indians live on 700 reserves, out of some 2200 reserves involving nearly six million acres. About 21 percent of the total Indian population lives in Ontario and 18 percent in British Columbia. The prairie provinces each contain about 15 percent of the Indians. At present, the Indian population is increasing at about twice the rate of the rest of the Canadian population. Since 1961 there has been an active movement of Indians from rural to urban areas. The Indian population in Calgary, Alberta increased 576 percent between 1961 and 1971, for example, compared to about 328 percent in Edmonton and 357 percent in Winnipeg, Manitoba. Although housing has improved considerably since 1963, census data for 1971 shows that nearly 60 percent of Indian homes contained four rooms or less, only about 30 percent contained running water, 20 percent had indoor toilets and baths, and about 20 percent had telephones. In 1951, nearly 83 percent of Indians listed their first spoken language as Indian. In 1971, in contrast, 54 percent listed Indian as the mother tongue and 41 percent listed English. Only 4 percent listed French.[13]

Indian family traditions vary widely. Contemporary Indian family patterns also vary. We will briefly discuss the traditions of two Indian groups, the Blackfoot family of Alberta (Langevin, 1970) and the Kwakiutl Indians of British Columbia (Rohner and Rohner, 1970). Contemporary family patterns among the Athapaskan Indians in the Northwest Territories are also considered (Cruikshank, 1971).

The traditional Blackfoot Indian family was predominantly patrilineal and patrilocal. Other residence patterns, though less common, were also practised. Monogamy was the predominant form of marriage; however, polygyny was practised, particularly among the more prestigious members of the Blackfoot community. The "sits-beside-me" wife was the husband's primary companion and senior wife, with special privileges, in the household. Multiple wives were typically sisters. Polygyny became acceptable because of a surplus of marriageable women as a result of war. Marriage generally occurred by arrangement, or a form of brokerage service, and involved a bride price. The double standard operated both before and

---

13. This section is based on data provided in *Perspective Canada* (Statistics Canada, 1974), pp. 237-253.

during marriage; women were expected to be chaste upon marriage and faithful after marriage. Adultery was commonly avenged. Adulterous wives sometimes had the end of their nose cut off to mark them for life. The division of labor between spouses was standard: the men were hunters, and the women were responsible for the household. Children were reared to have good manners and to respect their elders.[14]

Traditional Kwakiutl kinship organization also involved patrilocal household residence; the new marital unit typically lived in the groom's father's house as part of an extended family. In contrast to the Blackfoot Indians, however, the Kwakiutl placed a high value on historical rank, related to a complex stratification system. Therefore both the residence and lineage system are technically defined as ambilineal and ambilocal. Residence and lineage requirements were determined by the claims to rank of the groom. Even so, the *practice* was patrilineal and patrilocal. The "potlatch" ceremony was the center of the ranking system of social organization. The potlatch constituted a "public display and distribution of property in the context of one individual or group claiming certain hereditary rights or privileges vis-à-vis another group" (Rohner and Rohner, 1970:95). The basic feature of this ceremony was the display, in front of witnesses, of the transmission of hereditary privileges according to rank. Potlatch ceremonies occurred at critical events, including birth, puberty, marriage, and death.

Contemporary patterns have changed markedly. No one in the village under the age of thirty-five had had their marriage arranged. Sixty percent of those above the age of thirty-five had had arranged marriages. Potlatch is still practised, though more informally and symbolically, after Indians are legally married according to Canadian law. Residence and lineage rules are no longer evident and the nuclear family is predominant. Village members want children; illegitimate children are generally accepted. Socialization emphasizes traditional sex roles: boys acquire fishing skills and girls learn housekeeping roles, primarily by observation. Appropriate behavior is reinforced and inappropriate behavior is punished. Teenage boys and girls do not mix publicly unless they are courting. Once courting gets serious, sleeping together is not uncommon; however, "sleeping around" is not acceptable. Though common-law relationships exist, couples are expected to marry and "get their own house" (Rohner and Rohner, 1970: 74).

Socialization patterns among Indians in most of Canada reflect many basic problems compared to socialization of non-Indians. A recent study by Hawthorn (1967) illustrates the significance of these differences. Detailed results are summarized in table 3.4 below.

---

14 This analysis is based on a carefully researched term paper by an undergraduate student in one of my classes. He utilized a large selection of historical documents and interviewed a number of older Blackfoot Indians. The paper has not been published (Langevin, 1970).

Table 3.4   Characteristics of Indian and Non-Indian Socialization

	Indian	Non-Indian
Housing:	Generally over-crowded; child sleeps with siblings in same bed; little or no privacy; scarcity of furniture; sometimes dirty house; often unattractive, unpainted and uncared for.	Seldom crowded; child may share room but not bed; possibility for privacy; furniture adequate, usually clean; house usually painted and attractive.
Food:	Generally inadequate for good nutrition and often inadequate in amount; lack of diversity and poorly prepared; meals when hungry rather than scheduled and communal; school lunches often lacking.	Sometimes inadequate for good nutrition but seldom is child hungry; usually diverse and adequately prepared by adult; always scheduled and usually social; school lunches available and adequate.
Clothing:	Generally insufficient and in poor condition; often unclean or unironed; often hand-me-downs and obtained from poor quality bargain sales.	Usually adequate and in good condition; always washed and ironed; some hand-me-downs but in good condition and usually of good quality.
Objects:	Few toys; sometimes T.V.; seldom books or magazines available for child to read; sometimes records available; seldom any use of scissors, crayons and paste in making objects for play; meagre household furniture and objects usable for variety of experiences.	Often over-abundance of toys; usually child has own books, records and access to those of adults; considerable use of paste, scissors, crayons for constructing play objects; child uses own or household items such as eggbeaters.

From data provided in H. Hawthorn, ed., *A Survey of the Contemporary Indians of Canada*, Volume II. (Ottawa: Indian Affairs Branch, 1967), pp. 110-114. Reproduced by permission of Information Canada.

	Indian	Non-Indian
Attitudes toward child:	At age of mobility child is considered a person and left relatively free to create and explore his own environment. He develops a sense of independence and autonomy. He has limited stimulation and feedback from adults.	Child is watched and controlled by parents and remains dependent on them throughout childhood. He is not autonomous and has little opportunity to become independent. He has constant interaction and feedback from adults around him.
Parental Interest in Learning:	Parents have little background in formal education and are not oriented to, nor do they have time to teach their children specific skills. Little time is spent on teaching the child to walk and talk; some time may be spent in encouraging child to imitate father or mother in activities related to life on the reserve.	Parents have usually completed high school and are oriented toward preparing the child for school. Time is taken to teach children skills which will help them in school. Time is spent urging child to walk early and to talk early and correctly. Time is taken to expose child to a variety of stimuli through expeditions, shopping and visiting.
Verbal Practice and Development:	Conversations between children and adults limited; questions often answered in monosyllables; custom sometimes demands silence from children in presence of adults; English spoken by adults often inaccurate and limited vocabulary. Some children have the opportunity to hear stories and folk tales which have colourful imagery and language. No one reads to the child.	Conversations often unlimited; detailed answers given as often as monosyllabic replies; child's speech and labelling may be corrected consistently. English spoken by parents usually correct and diverse; child is read to often and has books of his own.

Table 3.4 cont'd.

	Indian	Non-Indian
Sanctions for Learning:	Child is permitted to do things which interest him when he is ready. Seldom is he rewarded or punished for specific learning attempts, although he receives approval when he does the task correctly after trial-and-error learning. Time is not a factor; he can take all morning to get dressed if he needs it. If child attempts a task and can't complete it, he is not urged to stay with it.	Child is urged to try things which are considered appropriate for him to know, whether he has expressed interest or not. He is rewarded for trying whether he learns task or not. Time is a factor: "see how fast you can dress yourself." Emphasis is placed on trying and on completing tasks undertaken.
Routines for Learning:	Routines are flexible and often non-existent. Meals are served on demand; bedtimes vary with sleepiness and family activity. Life is adult-centred and child is fitted in.	Routines are rigid. Meals served regularly and bedtimes are stringently adhered to. Life is more child- than adult-centred in sense that child's bedtime would not be disrupted for adult activities.
Discipline:	Discipline is primarily protective and loose. Seldom is child punished. Age-graded behavioral expectations are minimal in early childhood; as child grows older, he is ridiculed if he fails to meet expectations but he has plenty of leeway. The concept of autonomy allows him his own decisions.	Discipline is relatively over-protective and rigid. Age-graded behaviour is demanded; few decisions are permitted, routines are controlled by adults; punishment is meted out for failure to comply with adult demands.

	Indian	Non-Indian
Economic Involvement of Children:	Children often involved in economic routines and pursuits of parents which sometimes mean frequent mobility for seasonal labour, babysitting while mother works, helping on fishboats, and with fruit picking. Illness of mother often means older siblings care for whole family; economic level of reserve may involve children in wood and water-hauling and similar tasks.	Economic pursuits of parents seldom involve children; patterns tend to be stable and regular; mobility is low and participation of child in maintaining economic level is virtually nil; chores seldom disrupt routines of child; illness of mother and help with household chores usually handled by importing an adult.
General Family Patterns:	Often unstable and father may be absent for long periods of time; in some cases, there is a great deal of conflict and disruption within the home; drunken periods may mean children are left on their own for days at a time; care of children tends to diminish with periods of drinking.	Usually stable and father is usually at home more consistently than he is absent. Many homes have conflict but in most cases, there is an attempt to keep outbursts to a minimum and hidden from children. Children virtually never left on their own.

A recent study by Cruikshank (1971) provides insight into the dynamics of the matrifocal Athapaskan Indian family in the Canadian north. The available marriage statistics for the ten bands studied indicate that less than half of the Indian men and women over the age of twenty-one are married. Among the unmarried women, 55 percent are unmarried mothers living with their children. Cruikshank emphasizes the significance of the intrusion of the white man into the culture of the Athapaskan

Indian. Indian men are forced to compete with non-Indians for both jobs and Indian women. An Indian man, however, is at a disadvantage because he is not an asset to the Indian woman. Her survival is possible without a husband: economic opportunities are available for untrained women, and the woman is more mobile because of her familiarity and interaction with the white man's ways. If the Indian woman chooses to marry a white man she must forfeit her Indian status and her treaty rights. Accordingly, the law and economic opportunities work together in maintaining a matrifocal, common-law family system.

Like English Canadian, French Canadian and Eskimo families, Indian family life can only be understood in the context in which it is found. This theme is fundamental to family analysis in every society.

SUMMARY

This chapter has provided a concise survey of cross-cultural family patterns and sub-cultural family patterns within Canada.

All societies contain readily visible and predominant institutions which may be referred to as marriages and families. Marriage is defined as a publicly recognized enduring relationship between two or more persons, including at least one member of the opposite sex. The family is composed of persons related by blood or kinship ties who are expected, within a particular society, to be primarily responsible for the emotional care of dependent children.

Three predominant forms of marriage were identified and described. Monogamy, the most prevalent form of marriage, involves the marriage of one man and one woman. Polygyny, the most preferred form of marriage, involves one man and two or more wives. Polyandry, thought to exist in only four societies, involves the marriage of one woman and two or more husbands. It is generally assumed that monogamy is the most practised form of marriage because the opportunity for each individual to marry is maximized. Family forms also vary in composition and size. The smallest and most basic kinship unit is the nuclear family (parents and their offspring). Larger, or extended families, are of many forms but there are four basic ones. The stem family typically includes a father's eldest son, the son's spouse and their children. The lineal family includes two or more sons, their spouses, and children. The fully extended family consists of two or more male siblings in the senior generation, with their spouses, and two or more of each of their sons and their spouses and children. The joint family is simply two nuclear families, in which the husbands are brothers, sharing a common household.

Kinship is a pervasive influence in society and in the life of the individual. In most societies of the world, one's kin group is actively involved in defining appropriate life choices and activities. Residence rules deal with where a married couple will live (with or apart from the bride or groom's family) and for how long. Rules related to descent generally deal with whom, when, and how many one may marry, who will be accountable to whom, the responsibilities of each family member, and the rights and duties related to possessions. Comportment regulations deal with what is "proper" in everyday activities. The relative rigidity or flexibility of these regulations, as well as the way in which they are enforced, varies as widely as the form or content of the regulations from society to society.

Few societies regard sexual activities as a private affair; rather, they typically establish several regulations which "should not" be broken. Incest refers to the prohibition of sexual intercourse with close relatives, usually within the nuclear family, but no society limits incest rules to the nuclear family alone. Children born outside of wedlock are thought of as illegitimate and, in most societies, are treated as a problem to be resolved through special means. Premarital sexual intercourse is permitted in the majority of the world's societies. Where permitted, however, there are usually other reasons for marriage that have been institutionalized. Adultery is proscribed in the majority of cultures but there tends to be a marked discrepancy between values and practice. Occasional sexual taboos exist in many tribal societies and typically regulate the amount of sexual intercourse during pregnancy, menstruation, and during the post partum period.

Just as there are cross-cultural similarities and differences in marriage and family patterns, kinship and sexual regulations, there are also sub-cultural variations within Canada. Indeed, intrasocietal variation is nearly as apparent as cross-cultural variation. Canada, in particular, is characterized correctly as the "vertical mosaic". As Porter (1965) has demonstrated, education, occupation, and income are not equally distributed in Canada, but instead are systematically linked to a hierarchical system of social status related to ethnicity and social class. Jews, English and French Canadians, for example, tend to be over-represented in white-collar occupations, compared to the national average, while most of the other thirty-three ethnic groups are under-represented. Italian Canadians, for example, are most involved in service, machining and construction related occupations. German, Ukrainian and Scandinavian ethnic groups are clearly the most active in agriculture and related activities. With regard to status, Jews are distinctly over-represented in the upper social classes and native Indians in the lower classes.

Four different family systems were discussed in some detail: the English, French, Eskimo, and Indian. Generally, current evidence suggests that there are at least three types of English Canadian family: a middle to upper-middle class family with traditional and idealistic values and practices; a lower-middle, working class kin-oriented family; and an emergent, more liberal pattern of attitudes and behaviors which seem to represent a family system "in the making". The predominant French Canadian family appears to be mother centered, kinship oriented, and strongly influenced by religious traditions. Though less apparent, there is also evidence of a professional family with democratic and egalitarian intrafamily relationships in the French culture. This family seems to be marriage centered, less kinship oriented, and more influenced by cultural and scientific traditions than by religion. Little information is available on the contemporary Eskimo family. The most apparent distinguishing feature of contemporary Eskimo family life is their nomadic life style and different living patterns in winter and summer. The extended family, quite common historically, has been largely replaced by the nuclear family. Historically speaking, there were many different types of Eskimo families. Life styles were typically related to geographical location and relative isolation from other Eskimo groups. Family patterns among the native Indians also vary markedly relative to particular tribal customs, geographical location, and the degree of adaptation to the culture of the white man. Both the traditional Blackfoot and Kwakiutl Indian families are described as patrilocal and patrilineal. Contemporary Indian life, however, reflects problems in the socialization of children and satisfactory marriage and family life largely due to status, educational and legal inequities.

The significance of change has been de-emphasized in this chapter. In fact, world changes are increasingly apparent. Though societies are responding differently and some pre-industrial societies still seem unaffected, the influence of industrialization, urbanization, and culture contact need to be considered. These matters are discussed through the remainder of the book and in chapters eight and nine, in particular.

The universality of the family:
a conceptual analysis

Most textbooks assume that the family is universal. With varying evidence, the family is said to exist in every society in all times and all places. Murdock (1949), in his book *Social Structure*, concluded that the nuclear family is essential to the maintenance of society and universally performs four essential functions: the reproduction and socialization of children, and the provision of legitimate sexual relations and economic cooperation between spouses.

This argument has been called into question, for different reasons, by several scholars (e.g., Schneider and Gough, 1961). In this paper, Reiss raises two basic questions: (a) are all four of these functions performed by the family in *all* societies? and (b) is the nuclear family always primarily responsible for one or more of these functions? He examines several societies with atypical family systems and demonstrates that three of Murdock's functions (sexual relations, reproduction, and economic cooperation) are not performed by the family. Each of these societal exceptions, however, is found to contain a kin-related primary group responsible for the nurturance of children. Accordingly, Reiss offers a universal definition of the family: the family is "a small kinship structure group with the key function of nurturant socialization of the new-born". The remainder of the paper attempts to demonstrate that the nurturant care of children is a functional prerequisite to the maintenance of society. The evidence offered is threefold: (a) there are no cross-cultural exceptions; (b) studies of monkeys emphasize the need for mothering; and (c) the demonstrated impact of maternal deprivation on human infants.

The most obvious flaw in the Reiss argument lies in his assumption that the family, as defined, is *universal*. As Weigert and Thomas (1971) pointed out, this part of the argument suggests that the family is both trans-spatial and trans-temporal. That is, this type of family has always been and will always be in every society. Test tube technology, adoption, sperm banks, ova transplantations, and even the preservation of conception material after the donors are dead are already on the horizon. Even to assume that every human infant needs a minimum of physiological and emotional nourishment in order to survive and reproduce as an emotionally stable individual, does not *require* a specification of who or what persons or objects are necessary to perform these tasks. It is not inconceivable that future technology will produce an efficient and satisfying mechanical alternative to mothering. The minimally necessary "family structure" according to the radical definition of Weigert and Thomas (1971: 193) is "one self (or more) and the infant". The proper task of the sociologist is not to prove that a particular type of family has been or will always be necessary, but instead to document and analyze the types of families that exist and the various functions that they perform (Weigert and Thomas, 1971: 194). In this perspective, the Reiss definition of the family and its essential function should be thought of as a *conditional universal*.

The universality of the family: a conceptual analysis

Ira L. Reiss

During the last few decades, a revived interest in the question of the universality of the family has occurred. One key reason for this was the 1949 publication of George Peter Murdock's book *Social Structure*.[1] In that book, Murdock postulated that the nuclear family was universal and that it had four essential functions which it always and everywhere fulfilled. These four functions were: (1) socialization, (2) economic cooperation, (3) reproduction, and (4) sexual relations. Even in polygamous and extended family systems, the nuclear families within these larger family types were viewed as separate entities which each performed these four functions.

The simplicity and specificity of Murdock's position makes it an excellent starting point for an investigation of the universal functions of the human family. Since Murdock's position has gained support in many quarters, it should be examined carefully.[2] Brief comments on Murdock's position appear in the literature, and some authors, such as Levy and Fallers, have

elaborated their opposition.[3] The present paper attempts to go somewhat further, not only in testing Murdock's notion but in proposing and giving evidence for a substitute position. However, it should be clear that Murdock's position is being used merely as an illustration; our main concern is with delineating what, if anything, is universal about the human family.

The four functions of the nuclear family are "functional prerequisites" of human society, to use David Aberle's terms from his classic article on the topic.[4] This means that these functions must somehow occur for human society to exist. If the nuclear family everywhere fulfills these functions, it follows that this family should be a "structural prerequisite" of human society, i.e., a universally necessary part of society.[5] The basic question being investigated is not whether these four functions are functional prerequisites of human society — almost all social scientists would accept this — but whether these four functions are necessarily carried out by the nuclear family. If these functions

Ira L. Reiss, Ph.D., is Professor of Sociology and Director of the Family Studies Center, University of Minnesota, St. Paul.

From *Journal of Marriage and the Family*, 27 (November, 1965), pp. 443-453. Copyright 1965 by National Council on Family Relations. Reprinted by permission.

are not everywhere carried out by the nuclear family, then are there any functional prerequisites of society which the nuclear family or any family form does fulfill? Is the family a universal institution in the sense that it always fulfills some functional prerequisite of society? Also, what, if any, are the universal structural features of the family? These are the ultimate questions of importance that this examination of Murdock's position is moving toward.

Murdock's contention that the nuclear family is a structural prerequisite of human society since it fulfills four functional prerequisites of human society is relatively easy to test. If a structure is essential, then finding one society where the structure does not exist or where one or more of the four functions are not fulfilled by this structure is sufficient to refute the theory. Thus, a crucial test could best be made by focusing on societies with rather atypical family systems to see whether the nuclear family was present and was fulfilling these four functions. The more typical family systems will also be discussed. A proper test can be made by using only groups which are societies. This limitation is necessary so as not to test Murdock unfairly with such subsocietal groups as celibate priests. For purposes of this paper, the author accepts the definition of society developed by Aberle and his associates:

A society is a group of human beings sharing a self-sufficient system of action which is capable of existing longer than the life-span of an individual, the group being recruited at least in part by the sexual reproduction of the members.[6]

A test of Murdock's thesis

One of the cultures chosen for the test of Murdock's thesis is from his own original sample of 250 cultures — the Nayar of the Malabar Coast of India. In his book, Murdock rejected Ralph Linton's view that the Nayar lacked the nuclear family.[7] Since that time, the work of Kathleen Gough has supported Linton's position, and Murdock has accordingly changed his own position.[8] In letters to the author dated April 3, 1963 and January 20, 1964, Murdock took the position that the Nayar are merely the old Warrior Caste of the Kerala Society and thus not a total society and are more comparable to a celibate group of priests. No such doubt about the societal status of the Nayar can be found in his book. Murdock rejects the Nayar only after he is forced to admit that they lack the nuclear family. In terms of the definition of society adopted above, the Nayar seem to be a society even if they, like many other societies, do have close connections with other groups.

The matrilineage is particularly strong among the Nayar, and a mother with the help of her matrilineage brings up her children. Her husband and "lovers" do not assist her in the raising of her children. Her brother typically assists her when male assistance is needed. Assistance from the linked lineages where most of her lovers come from also substitutes for the weak husband role. Since many Nayar women change lovers rather frequently, there may not even be any very stable male-female relation present. The male is frequently away fighting. The male makes it physiologically possible for the female to have offspring, but he is not an essential part of the family unit that will raise his biological children. In this sense, sex and reproduction are somewhat external to the family unit among the Nayar. Very little in the way of economic cooperation between husband and wife occurs. Thus, virtually all of Murdock's functions are outside of the nuclear family. However, it should be noted that the socialization of offspring function is present in the maternal extended family system. Here, then, is a society that seems to lack the nuclear family and, of necessity, therefore, the four functions of this unit. Even if we accept Gough's view that the "lovers" are husbands and that there really is a form of group marriage, it is still apparent that the separate husband-wife-child units formed by such a group marriage do not here comprise separately functioning nuclear families.

One does not have to rely on just the Nayar as a test of Murdock. Harold E. Driver, in his study of North American Indians, concludes that in matrilocal extended family systems with matrilineal descent, the husband role and the nuclear family are often insignificant.[9] It therefore seems that the relative absence of the nuclear family in the Nayar is approached particularly in other similar matrilineal societies. Thus, the Nayar do not seem to be so unique. They apparently demonstrate a type of family system that is common in lesser degree.

A somewhat similar situation seems to occur in many parts of the Caribbean. Judith Blake described a matrifocal family structure in which the husband and father roles are quite often absent or seriously modified.[10] Sexual relations are often performed with transitory males who have little relation to the raising of the resultant offspring. Thus, in Jamaica one can also question whether the nuclear family exists and performs the four functions Murdock ascribed to it. Socialization of offspring is often performed by the mother's family without any husband, common law or legal, being present. Naturally, if the husband is absent, the economic cooperation between husband and wife cannot

occur. Also, if the male involved is not the husband but a short-term partner, sex and reproduction are also occurring outside the nuclear family.

The above societies are all "mother-centered" systems. A family system which is not mother-centered is the Israeli Kibbutz family system as described by Melford Spiro.[11] Here the husband and wife live together in a communal agricultural society. The children are raised communally and do not live with their parents. Although the Kibbutzim are only a small part of the total Israeli culture, they have a distinct culture and can be considered a separate society by the Aberle definition cited above. They have been in existence since 1909 and thus have shown that they can survive for several generations and that they have a self-sufficient system of action. The function which is most clearly missing in the Kibbutz family is that of economic cooperation between husband and wife. In this communal society, almost all work is done for the total Kibbutz, and the rewards are relatively equally distributed regardless of whether one is married or not. There is practically no division of labor between husbands and wives as such. Meals are eaten communally, and residence is in one room which requires little in the way of housekeeping.

Here, too, Murdock denies that this is a real exception and, in the letters to the author referred to above, contends that the Kibbutzim could not be considered a society. Murdock's objection notwithstanding, a group which has existed for over half a century and has developed a self-sufficient system of action covering all major aspects of existence indeed seems to be a society by almost all definitions. There is nothing in the experience of the Kibbutzim that makes it difficult to conceive of such groups existing in many regions of the world or, for that matter, existing by themselves in a world devoid of other people. They are analogous to some of the Indian groups living in American society in the sense that they have a coherent way of life that differs considerably from the dominant culture. Thus, they are not the same as an average community which is merely a part of the dominant culture.

Melford Spiro concludes that Murdock's nuclear family is not present in the Kibbutz he and his wife studied. He suggests several alterations in Murdock's definition which would be required to make it better fit the Kibbutz. The alterations are rather drastic and would still not fit the Nayar and other cultures discussed above.[12]

There are other societies that are less extreme but which still create some difficulty with Murdock's definition of the nuclear family. Malinowski, in his study of the Trobriand Islanders, reports that except for perhaps nurturant socialization, the mother's brother rather than the father is the male who teaches the offspring much of the necessary way of life of the group.[13] Such a situation is certainly common in a matrilineal society, and it does place limits on the socialization function of the nuclear family *per se*. Further, one must at least qualify the economic function in the Trobriand case. The mother's brother here takes a large share of the economic burden and supplies his sister's family with half the food they require. The rigidity of Murdock's definition in light of such instances is apparent. These examples also make it reasonable that other societies may well exist which carry a little further such modifications of the nuclear family. For example, we find such more extreme societies when we look at the Nayar and the Kibbutz.

Some writers, like Nicholas Timasheff, have argued that the Russian experience with the family evidences the universality of the nuclear family.[14] While it is true that the Communists in Russia failed to abolish as much of the old family system as they wanted to, it does not follow that this demonstrates the impossibility of abolishing the family.[15] In point of fact, the family system of the Israeli Kibbutz is virtually identical with the system the Russian Communists desired, and thus we must admit that it is possible for at least some groups to achieve such a system. Also, the Communists did not want to do away with the family *in toto*. Rather, they wanted to do away with the patriarchal aspects of the family, to have marriage based on love, easy divorce, and communal upbringing of children. They ceased in much of this effort during the 1930's when a falling birth rate, rising delinquency and divorce rates, and the depression caused them to question the wisdom of their endeavors. However, it has never been demonstrated that these symptoms were consequences of the efforts to change the family. They may well have simply been results of a rapidly changing social order that would have occurred regardless of the family program. Therefore, the Russian experience is really not evidence pro or con Murdock's position.

The Chinese society deserves some brief mention here. Marion Levy contends that this is an exception to Murdock's thesis because in the extended Chinese family, the nuclear family was a rather unimportant unit, and it was the patrilineal extended family which performed the key functions of which Murdock speaks.[16] Regarding present day

Communist China, it should be noted that the popular reports to the effect that the Chinese Communes either aimed at or actually did do away with the nuclear family are not supported by evidence. The best information indicates that the Chinese Communists never intended to do away with the nuclear family as such; rather, what they wanted was the typical communist family system which the Israeli Kibbutzim possess.[17] The Communists in China did not intend to do away with the identification of a child with a particular set of parents or vice-versa. If the Israeli Kibbutz is any indication, it would seem that a communal upbringing system goes quite well with a strong emphasis on affectionate ties between parent and child.[18] However, it is well to note that the type of communal family system toward which the Chinese are striving and have to some extent already achieved, clashes with Murdock's conception of the nuclear family and its functions in just the same way as the Kibbutz family does.

Overall, it appears that a reasonable man looking at the evidence presented above would conclude that Murdock's position is seriously in doubt. As Levy and Fallers have said, Murdock's approach is too simplistic in viewing a particular structure such as the nuclear family as always, in all cultural contexts, having the same four functions.[19] Robert Merton has said that such a view of a very specific structure as indispensable involves the erroneous ''postulate of indispensability.''[20] Certainly it seems rather rash to say that one very specific social structure such as the nuclear family will always have the same consequences regardless of the context in which it is placed. Surely this is not true of specific structures in other institutions such as the political, religi-

ous, or economic. The consequences of a particular social structure vary with the socio-cultural context of that structure. Accordingly, a democratic bicameral legislative structure in a new African nation will function differently than in America; the Reform Jewish Denomination has different consequences in Israel than in America; government control of the economy functions differently in England than in Russia.

The remarkable thing about the family institution is that in so many diverse contexts, one can find such similar structures and functions. To this extent, Murdock has made his point and has demonstrated that the nuclear family with these four functions is a surprisingly common social fact. But this is quite different from demonstrating that this is always the case or necessarily the case. It should be perfectly clear that the author feels Murdock's work has contributed greatly to the advancement of our knowledge of the family. Murdock is used here because he is the best known proponent of the view being examined, not because he should be particularly criticized.

A safer approach to take toward the family is to look for functional prerequisites of society which the family fulfills and search for the full range of structures which may fulfill these functional prerequisites. At this stage of our knowledge, it seems more valuable to talk of the whole range of family structures and to seek for a common function that is performed and that may be essential to human society. What we need now is a broad, basic, parsimonious definition that would have utility in both single and cross-cultural comparisons.[21] We have a good deal of empirical data on family systems and a variety of definitions — it is time we strove for a universal definition that would clarify the essential features of this institution and help us locate the family in any cultural setting.

Looking over the four functions that Murdock associates with the nuclear family, one sees that three of them can be found to be absent in some cultures. The Nayar perhaps best illustrate the possibility of placing sex and reproduction outside the nuclear family. Also, it certainly seems within the realm of possibility that a "Brave New World" type of society could operate by scientifically mating sperm and egg and presenting married couples with state-produced offspring of certain types when they desired children.[22] Furthermore, the raising of children by other than their biological parents is widespread in many societies where adoption and rearing by friends and relatives is common.[23] Thus, it seems that sex and reproduction may not be inexorably tied to the nuclear family.[24]

The third function of Murdock's which seems possible to take out of the nuclear family is that of economic cooperation. The Kibbutz is the prime example of this. Furthermore, it seems that many other communal-type societies approximate the situation in the Kibbutz.

The fourth function is that of socialization. Many aspects of this function have been taken away from the family in various societies. For example, the Kibbutz parents, according to Spiro, are not so heavily involved in the inculcation of values or the disciplinary and caretaking aspects of socialization. Nevertheless, the Kibbutz parents are heavily involved in nurturant socialization, i.e., the giving of positive emotional response to infants and young children. A recent book by Stephens also reports a seemingly universal presence of nurturance of infants.[25] It should be emphasized that this paper uses "nurturance" to mean not the physical, but the emotional care of the infant. Clearly, the two are not fully separable. This use of the term nurturant is similar to what is meant by "expressive" role.[26] Interestingly enough, in the Kibbutz both the mother and father are equally involved in giving their children nurturant socialization. All of the societies referred to above have a family institution with the function of nurturant socialization of children. This was true even for the extreme case of the Nayar.

The conception of the family institution being developed here has in common with some other family definitions an emphasis on socialization of offspring. The difference is that all other functions have been ruled out as unessential and that only the nurturant type of socialization is the universal function of the family institution. This paper presents empirical evidence to support its contention. It is important to be more specific than were Levy and Fallers regarding the type of socialization the family achieves since all societies have socialization occurring outside the family as well as within. It should be noted that this author, unlike Murdock, is talking of *any* form of family institution and not just the nuclear family.

As far as a universal structure of the family to fulfill the function of nurturant socialization is concerned, it seems possible to set only very broad limits, and even these involve some speculation. First, it may be said that the structure of the family will always be that of a primary group. Basically, this position rests on the assumption that nurturant socialization is a process which cannot be adequately carried out in an impersonal setting and which thus requires a primary type of relation.[27] The author would not specify the biological mother as the socializer or even a female, or even more than one person or the age of the person. If one is trying to state what the family must be like in a minimal sense in any society — what its universally required structure and function is — one cannot be too specific. However, we can go one step farther in specifying the structure of the family group we are defining. The family is here viewed as an institution, as an integrated set of norms and relationships which are socially defined and internalized by the members of a society. In every society in the world, the institutional structure which contains the roles related to the nurturant function is a small kinship structured group.[28] Thus, we can say that the primary group which fulfills the nurturant function is a kinship structure. Kinship refers to descent — it involves rights of possession among those who are kin. It is a genealogical reckoning, and people with real or fictive biological connections are kin.[29]

This specification of structure helps to distinguish from the family institution those non-kin primary groups that may in a few instances perform nurturant functions. For example, a nurse-child relation or a governess-child relation could, if carried far enough, involve the bulk of nurturant socialization for that child. But such a relationship would be a quasi-family at best, for it clearly is not part of the kinship structure. There are no rights of "possession" given to the nurse or the child in such cases, and there is no socially accepted, institutionalized, system of child-rearing involving nurses and children. In addition, such supervisory help usually assumes more of a caretaking and disciplinary aspect, with the parents themselves still maintaining the nurturant relation.

Talcott Parsons has argued, in agreement with the author's position, that on a societal level, only kinship groups can perform the socialization function.[30] He believes that socialization in a kin group predisposes the child to assume marital and parental roles himself when he matures and affords a needed stable setting for socialization. Clearly other groups may at times perform part of the nurturant function. No institution in human society has an exclusive franchise on its characteristic function. However, no society exists in which any group other than a kinship group performs the dominant share of the nurturant function. Even in the Israeli Kibbutz with communal upbringing, it is the parents who dominate in this area.

Should a society develop wherein nonkin primary groups became the predominant means of raising children, the author would argue that these nonkin groups would tend to evolve in the direction of becoming kin groups. The primary quality of the adult-child relation would encourage the notion of descent and possession. Kin groups would evolve as roles and statuses in the nonkin system became defined in terms of accepted male-female and adult-child relationships and thereby became institutionalized. Once these nonkin groups had institutionalized their sex roles and adult-child (descent) roles, we would in effect have a kinship-type system, for kinship results from the recognition of a social relationship between "parents" and children. It seems that there would be much pressure toward institutionalization of roles in any primary group child-rearing system, if for no other reason than clarity and efficiency. The failure of any one generation to supply adequate role models and adequate nurturance means that the next generation will not know these skills, and persistence of such a society is questionable. The importance of this task makes institutionalization quite likely and kinship groups quite essential. To avoid kinship groups, it seems that children would have to be nurtured in a formal secondary group setting. The author will present evidence below for his belief that the raising of children in a secondary group setting is unworkable.

In summation then, following is the universal definition of the family institution: *The family institution is a small kinship structured group with the key function of nurturant socialization of the newborn*. How many years such nurturant socialization must last is hard to specify. There are numerous societies in which children six or seven years old are given a good deal of responsibility in terms of care of other children and other tasks. It seems that childhood in the West has been greatly extended to older ages in recent centuries.[31] The proposed definition focuses on what are assumed to be the structural and functional prerequisites of society which the family institution fulfills. The precise structure of the kinship group can vary quite radically among societies, and even within one society it may well be that more than one small kinship group will be involved in nurturant socialization. The definition seeks to avoid the "error" of positing the indispensability of any *particular* family form by this approach. Rather, it says that any type of kinship group can achieve this function and that the limitation is merely that it be a kinship group. This degree of specification helps one delimit and identify the institution which one is describing. Some writ-

ers have spelled out more specifically the key structural forms in this area.[32] Adams has posited two key dyads: the maternal dyad and the conjugal dyad. When these two join, a nuclear family is formed, but these dyads are, Adams believes, more fundamental than the nuclear family.

There are always other functions besides nurturant socialization performed by the kinship group. Murdock's four functions are certainly quite frequently performed by some type of family group, although often not by the nuclear family. In addition, there are some linkages between the family kinship group and a larger kinship system. But this is not the place to pursue these interconnections. Instead, an examination follows of evidence relevant to this proposed universal definition of the family institution.

Evidence on revised conception

The evidence to be examined here relates to the question of whether the definition proposed actually fits all human family institutions. Three types of evidence are relevant to test the universality of the proposed definition of the family. The first source of evidence comes from a cross-cultural examination such as that of this article. All of the cultures that were discussed were fulfilling the proposed functional prerequisite of nurturant socialization, and they all had some sort of small kinship group structure to accomplish nurturant socialization. The author also examined numerous reports on other cultures and found no exception to the proposed definition. Of course, other functions of these family groups were present in all instances, but no other specific universally present functions appeared. However, the author hesitates to say that these data confirm his position because it is quite possible that such a cross-cultural examination will reveal some function or structure to be universally *present* but still not universally *required*. Rather, it could merely be universally present by chance or because it is difficult but not impossible to do away with. As an example of this, one may cite the incest taboo. The evidence recently presented by Russell Middleton on incest among commoners in Ptolemaic Egypt throws doubt on the thesis that incest taboos are functional prerequisites of human society.[33] We need some concept of functional "importance," for surely the incest taboo has great functional importance even if it is not a prerequisite of society. The same may be true of the functional importance of Murdock's view of the nuclear family.

If being universally present is but a necessary and not a sufficient condition for a functional prerequisite of society, then it is important to present other evidence. One source of such evidence lies in the studies of rhesus monkeys done by Harry Harlow.[34] Harlow separated monkeys from their natural mothers and raised them with surrogate "cloth" and "wire" mother dolls. In some trials, the wire mother surrogate was equipped with milk while the cloth mother was not. Even so, the monkeys preferred the cloth mother to the wire mother in several ways. The monkeys showed their preference by running more to the cloth mother when threatened and by exerting themselves more to press a lever to see her. Thus, it seemed that the monkeys "loved" the cloth mother more than the wire mother. This was supposedly due to the softer contact and comfort afforded by the cloth mother. One might

speculatively argue that the contact desire of the monkeys is indicative of at least a passive, rudimentary nurturance need. Yerkes has also reported similar "needs" in his study of chimpanzees.[35]

Further investigation of these monkeys revealed some important findings. The monkeys raised by the surrogate mothers became emotionally disturbed and were unable to relate to other monkeys or to have sexual relations. This result was produced irreversibly in about six months. One could interpret this to mean that the surrogate mothers, both cloth and wire, were inadequate in that they gave no emotional response to the infant monkeys. Although contact with the cloth mother seemed important, response seemingly was even more important. Those laboratory-raised females who did become pregnant became very ineffective mothers and were lacking in ability to give nurturance.

Harlow found that when monkeys were raised without mothers but with siblings present, the results were quite different. To date, these monkeys have shown emotional stability and sexual competence. In growing up, they clung to each other just as the other monkeys had clung to the cloth mother, but in addition they were able to obtain the type of emotional response or nurturance from each other which they needed.

Harlow's evidence on monkeys is surely not conclusive evidence for the thesis that nurturant socialization is a fundamental prerequisite of human society. There is need for much more precise testing and evidence on both human and non-human groups. Despite the fact that human beings and monkeys are both primates, there is quite a bit of difference in human and monkey infants. For one thing, the human infant is far more helpless and far less aware of its environment during the first few months of its life. Thus, it is doubtful if placing a group of helpless, relatively unaware human infants together would produce the same results as occurred when monkeys were raised with siblings. The human infant requires someone older and more aware of the environment to be present. In a very real sense, it seems that the existence of human society is testimony to the concern of humans for each other. Unless older humans care for the newborn, the society will cease to exist. Every adult member of society is alive only because some other member of society took the time and effort to raise him. One may argue that this care need be only minimal and of a physical nature, e.g., food, clothing, and shelter. The author believes that such minimal care is insufficient for societal survival and will try to present additional evidence here to bear this out.

One type of evidence that is relevant concerns the effect of maternal separation or institutional upbringing on human infants. To afford a precise test, we should look for a situation in which nurturant socialization was quite low or absent. Although the Kibbutzim have institutional upbringing, the Kibbutz parents and children are very much emotionally attached to each other. In fact, both the mother and father have expressive roles in the Kibbutz family, and there is a strong emphasis on parent-child relations of a nurturant sort in the few hours a day the family is together.

A better place to look would be at studies of children who were raised in formal institutions or who were in other ways separated from their mothers. Leon J. Yarrow has recently published an excellent summary of over one hundred such studies.[36] For over 50 years now, there have been reports support-

ing the view that maternal separation has deleterious effects on the child. The first such reports came from pediatricians pointing out physical and psychological deterioration in hospitalized infants. In 1951, Bowlby reviewed the literature in this area for the World Health Organization and arrived at similar conclusions.[37] More recent and careful studies have made us aware of the importance of distinguishing the effects of maternal separation from the effects of institutionalization. Certainly the type of institutional care afforded the child is quite important. Further, the previous relation of the child with the mother before institutionalization and the age of the child are important variables. In addition, one must look at the length of time separation endured and whether there were reunions with the mother at a later date. Yarrow's view is that while there is this tendency toward disturbance in mother separation, the occurrence can best be understood when we learn more about the precise conditions under which it occurs and cease to think of it as inevitable under any conditions. In this regard, recent evidence shows that children separated from mothers with whom they had poor relationships displayed less disturbance than other children. Further, infants who were provided with adequate mother-substitutes of a personal sort showed much less severe reactions. In line with the findings on the Kibbutz, children who were in an all-day nursery gave no evidence of serious disturbance.

Many studies in the area of institutionalization show the importance of the structural characteristics of the institutional environment. When care is impersonal and inadequate, there is evidence of language retardation, impairment of motor functions, and limited emotional responses toward other people and objects.[38] Interestingly, the same types of characteristics are found among children living in deprived family environments.[39] One of the key factors in avoiding such negative results is the presence of a stable mother-figure in the institution for the child. Individualized care and attention seem to be capable of reversing or preventing the impairments mentioned. Without such care, there is evidence that ability to form close interpersonal relations later in life is greatly weakened.[40] As Yarrow concludes in his review of this area:

It is clear from the studies on institutionalization that permanent intellectual and personality damage may be avoided if following separation there is a substitute mother-figure who develops a personalized relationship with the child and who responds sensitively to his individualized needs.[41]

The evidence in this area indicates that some sort of emotionally nurturant relationship between the child in the first few years of life and some other individual is rather vital in the child's development. Disease and death rates have been reported to rise sharply in children deprived of nurturance. The author is not rash enough to take this evidence as conclusive support for his contention that nurturant socialization is a functional prerequisite of human society which the family performs. Nevertheless, he does believe that this evidence lends some support to this thesis and throws doubt on the survival of a society that rears its children without nurturance. In addition, it seems to support the position that some sort of kin-type group relationship is the structural prerequisite of the nurturant function. Indeed, it seemed that the closer the institution approximated a stable, personal kinship type of relationship of the

child and a nurse, the more successful it was in achieving emotional nurturance and avoiding impairments of functions.

Summary and Conclusions

A check of several cultures revealed that the four nuclear family functions that Murdock states are universally present were often missing. The nuclear family itself seems either absent or unimportant in some cultures. An alternate definition of the family in terms of one functional prerequisite of human society and in terms of a broad structural prerequisite was put forth. The family was defined as a small kinship structured group with the key function of nurturant socialization of the newborn. The nurturant function directly supports the personality system and enables the individual to become a contributing member of society. Thus, by making adult role performance possible, nurturant socialization becomes a functional prerequisite of society.

Three sources of evidence were examined: (1) cross-cultural data, (2) studies of other primates, and (3) studies of effects on children of maternal separation. Although the evidence did tend to fit with and support the universality of the new definition, it must be noted that much more support is needed before any firm conclusion can be reached.

There is both a structural and a functional part to the definition. It is theoretically possible that a society could bring up its entire newborn population in a formal institutional setting and give them nurturance through mechanical devices that would reassure the child, afford contact, and perhaps even verbally respond to the child. In such a case, the family as defined here would cease to exist, and an alternate structure for fulfilling the functional requirement of nurturant socialization would be established. Although it is dubious whether humans could ever tolerate or achieve such a means of bringing up their children, this logical possibility must be recognized. In fact, since the evidence is not conclusive, one would also have to say that it is possible that a society could bring up its offspring without nurturance, and in such a case also, the family institution as defined here would cease to exist. The author has argued against this possibility by contending that nurturance of the newborn is a functional prerequisite of human society and therefore could never be done away with. However, despite a strong conviction to the contrary, he must also admit that this position may be in error and that it is possible that the family as defined here is not a universally required institution. There are those, like Barrington Moore, Jr., who feel that it is largely a middle-class sentimentality that makes social scientists believe that the family is universal.[42] It is certainly crucial to test further the universality of both the structural and functional parts of this definition and their interrelation.

The definition proposed seems to fit the existing data somewhat more closely than Murdock's definition. It also has the advantage of simplicity. It affords one a definition that can be used in comparative studies of human society. Further, it helps make one aware of the possibilities of change in a society or an institution if we know which functions and structures can or cannot be done away with. In this way, we come closer to the knowledge of what Goldenweiser called the "limited possibilities" of human society.[43] If nurturance in kin groups is a functional and structural prerequisite of soci-

ety, we have deepened our knowledge of the nature of human society for we can see how, despite our constant warfare with each other, our conflicts and internal strife, each human society persists only so long as it meets the minimal nurturant requirements of its new members. This is not to deny the functions of social conflict that Coser and others have pointed out, but merely to assert the importance of nurturance.[44]

In terms of substantive theory, such a definition as the one proposed can be of considerable utility. If one views the marital institution, as Malinowski, Gough, Davis, Radcliffe-Brown, and others did, as having the key function of legitimization of offspring, then the tie between the marital and family institution becomes clear.[45] The marital institution affords a social definition of who is eligible to perform the nurturant function of the family institution. However, it is conceivable that a family system could exist without a marital system. This could be done by the state scientifically producing and distributing infants or, as Blake believes occurs in Jamaica, by the absence of socially acceptable marriage for most people until childbirth is over.[46]

There may be other universally required functions of the family institution. Dorothy Blitsten suggests universal family contributions to the social order.[47] Kingsley Davis posits several universal functions, such as social placement, which are worth investigating further.[48]

One major value of the approach of this paper is that it has the potentiality of contributing to our ability to deal cross-culturally with the family. Surely it is useful to theory building to ascertain the essential or more essential features of an institution. Such work enables us to locate, identify, and compare this institution in various cultural settings and to discover its fundamental characteristics. In this respect, Murdock has contributed to the search for a cross-cultural view of the family by his work in this area, even though the author has taken issue with some of his conclusions. It should be clear that this "universal, cross-cultural" approach is not at all presented as the only approach to an understanding of the family. Rather, it is viewed as but one essential approach. Research dealing with important but not universal functions is just as vital, as is empirical work within one culture.

Also of crucial importance is the relation of the family institution to the general kinship structure. It does seem that every society has other people linked by affinal or consanguineal ties to the nurturant person or persons. It remains for these aspects to be further tested. The family typologies now in existence are adequate to cover the proposed definition of the family, although a new typology built around the nurturant function and the type of kin who perform it could be quite useful.

The interrelations of the marital, family, and courtship institutions with such institutions as the political, economic, and religious in terms of both important and essential functions and structures is another vital avenue of exploration. One way that such exploration can be made is in terms of what, if any, are the functional and structural prerequisites of these institutions and how they interrelate. It is hoped that such comparative research and theory may be aided by a universal definition of the family such as that proposed in this paper.

NOTES

1 George P. Murdock, *Social Structure*, New York: Macmillan, 1949.
2 Many of the textbooks in the family field fail to really cope with this issue and either ignore the question or accept a position arbitrarily. The Census definition also ignores this issue: "A group of two persons or more related by blood, marriage, or adoption and residing together." The recently published *Dictionary of the Social Sciences*, ed. by Julius Gould and William Kolb, Glencoe, Ill.: Free Press, 1964, defines the nuclear family as universal. See pp. 257-259. Parsons, Biles, Bell and Vogel are among those who also seem to accept Murdock's position. See: Talcott Parsons and Robert P. Biles, *Family, Socialization and Interaction Process*, Glencoe, Ill.: Free Press, 1955; Talcott Parsons, "The Incest Taboo in Relation to Social Structure and the Socialization of the Child," *British Journal of Sociology*, 5 (January 1954), pp. 101-117; *A Modern Introduction to the Family*, ed. by Norman Bell and Ezra Vogel, Glencoe, Ill.: Free Press, 1960.

3 Marion J. Levy, Jr. and L. A. Fallers, "The Family: Some Comparative Considerations," *American Anthropologist*, 61 (August 1959), pp. 647-651.
4 David F. Aberle et al., "The Functional Prerequisites of a Society," *Ethics*, 60 (January 1950), pp. 100-111.
5 *Ibid.*
6 *Ibid.*, p. 101.
7 Murdock, *op. cit.*, p. 3.
8 For a brief account of the Nayar, see: E. Kathleen Gough, "Is the Family Universal: The Nayar Case," pp. 76-92 in *A Modern Introduction to the Family*, *op. cit.* It is interesting to note that Bell and Vogel, in their preface to Gough's article on the Nayar, contend that she supports Murdock's position on the universality of the nuclear family. In point of fact, Gough on page 64 rejects Murdock and actually deals primarily with the marital and not the family institution. See also: *Matrilineal Kinship*, ed. by David M. Schneider and Kathleen Gough, Berkeley: U. of California Press, 1961, Chaps. 6 and 7. A. R. Radcliffe-Brown was one of the first to

note that the Nayar lacked the nuclear family. See his: *African Systems of Kinship and Marriage*, New York: Oxford U. Press, 1959, p. 73.

9 Harold H. Driver, *Indians of North America*, Chicago: U. of Chicago Press, 1961, pp. 291-292.

10 Judith Blake, *Family Structure in Jamaica*, Glencoe, Ill.: Free Press, 1961. Whether Jamaicans actually prefer to marry and have a more typical family system is a controversial point.

11 Melford E. Spiro, *Kibbutz: Venture in Utopia*, Cambridge, Mass.: Harvard U. Press, 1956: and Melford E. Spiro, *Children of the Kibbutz*, Cambridge, Mass.: Harvard U. Press, 1955.

12 Spiro suggests that "reference residence" be used in place of actual common residence. The Kibbutz children do speak of their parents' room as "home." He suggests further that responsibility for education and economic cooperation be substituted for the actual doing of these functions by the parents. The parents could be viewed as responsible for the education of their children, but since nothing changes in economic terms when one marries it is difficult to understand just what Spiro means by responsibility for economic cooperation being part of the family. Spiro also would alter Murdock's definition of marriage so as to make emotional intimacy the key element.

13 Bronislaw Malinowski, *The Sexual Life of Savages in North-Western Melanesia*, New York: Harvest Books, 1929.

14 Nicholas S. Timasheff, "The Attempt to Abolish the Family in Russia," pp. 55-63 in Bell and Vogel, *op. cit.*

15 Timasheff refers to the family as "that pillar of society." But nothing in the way of convincing evidence is presented to support this view. The argument is largely that since disorganization followed the attempt to do away with the family, it was a result of that attempt. This may well be an example of a *post hoc ergo propter hoc* fallacy. Also, it should be noted that the love-based union of parents that the early communists wanted might well be called a family, and thus that the very title of Timasheff's article implies a

rather narrow image of the family. For a recent account of the Soviet family see: David and Vera Mace, *The Soviet Family*, New York: Doubleday, 1963; and Ray Rause et al., *How the Soviet System Works*, Cambridge, Mass.: Harvard U. Press, 1959.

16 Levy and Fallers, *op. cit.*, pp. 649-650.

17 Felix Greene, *Awakened China*, New York: Doubleday, 1961, esp. pp. 142-144. Philip Jones and Thomas Poleman, "Communes and the Agricultural Crisis in Communist China," *Food Research Institute Studies*, 3 (February 1962), pp. 1-22. Maurice Freedman, "The Family in China, Past and Present," *Pacific Affairs*, 34 (Winter 1961-2), pp. 323-336.

18 Spiro, *op. cit.*

19 Levy and Fallers, *op. cit.*

20 Robert K. Merton, *Social Theory and Social Structure*, Glencoe, Ill.: Free Press, 1957, p. 32.

21 Zelditch attempted to see if the husband-wife roles would be differentiated in the same way in all cultures, with males being instrumental and females expressive. He found general support, but some exceptions were noted, particularly in societies wherein the nuclear family was embedded in a larger kinship system. Morris Zelditch, Jr., "Role Differentiation in the Nuclear Family: A Comparative Study," in Parsons and Bales, *op. cit.* The Kibbutz would represent another exception since both mother and father play expressive roles in relation to their offspring.

22 Aldous Huxley, *Brave New World*, New York: Harper & Bros., 1950.

23 See: *Six Cultural Studies in Child Rearing*, ed. by Beatrice B. Whiting, New York: John Wiley, 1963. Margaret Mead reports exchange of children in *Coming of Age in Samoa*, New York: Mentor Books, 1949. Similar customs in Puerto Rico are reported in David Landy, *Tropical Childhood*, Chapel Hill: U. of North Carolina Press, 1959.

24 Robert Winch, in his recent textbook, defines the family as a nuclear family with the basic function of "the replacement of dying members." In line with the present author's arguments, it seems that the actual biological production of infants can be removed from the family. In fact, Winch agrees that the Nayar

lack the family as he defined it because they lack a permanent father role in the nuclear family. See: *The Modern Family*, New York: Holt, 1963, pp. 16, 31, and 730.

25 William N. Stephens, *The Family in Cross Cultural Perspective*, New York: Holt, Rinehart & Winston, 1963, p. 357. Stephens discusses the universality of the family in this book but does not take a definite position on the issue. See Chapter 1.

26 Zelditch, *op. cit.*, pp. 307-353.

27 The key importance of primary groups was long ago pointed out by Charles Horton Cooley, *Social Organization*, New York: Scribners, 1929.

28 The structural definition is similar to Levy and Fallers, *op. cit.*

29 Radcliffe-Brown, *op. cit.*

30 Parsons, *op. cit.*

31 Phillippe Aries, *Centuries of Childhood*, New York: Alfred A. Knopf, 1962.

32 Richard N. Adams, "An Inquiry into the Nature of the Family," pp. 30-49 in *Essays in the Science of Culture in Honor of Leslie A. White*, ed. by Gertrude E. Dole and Robert L. Carneiro, New York: Thomas Y. Crowell, 1960.

33 Russell Middleton, "Brother-Sister and Father-Daughter Marriage in Ancient Egypt," *American Sociological Review*, 27 (October 1962), pp. 603-611.

34 See the following articles, all by Harry P. Harlow: "The Nature of Love," *American Psychologist*, 13 (December 1958), pp. 673-685; "The Heterosexual Affection System in Monkeys," *American Psychologist*, 17 (January 1962), pp. 1-9; (with Margaret K. Harlow), "Social Deprivation in Monkeys," *Scientific American*, 206 (November 1962), pp. 1-10.

35 Robert M. Yerkes, *Chimpanzees*, New Haven: Yale U. Press, 1953, esp. pp. 43, 68, 257-258; and Robert M. Yerkes and Ada W. Yerkes, *The Great Apes*, New Haven: Yale U. Press, 1929, passim.

36 Leon J. Yarrow, "Separation from Parents During Early Childhood," pp. 89-136 in *Review of Child Development*, ed. by Martin L. Hoffman and Lois W. Hoffman, New York: Russell Gage Foundation, 1961, Vol. 1.

37 John Bowlby, *Maternal Care and Mental Health*, Geneva: World Health Organization, 1931.

38 Yarrow, *op. cit.*, p. 100.

39 *Ibid., pp. 101-102.*

40 *Ibid.*, p. 106.

41 *Ibid.*, pp. 124-125.

42 Barrington Moore, Jr., *Political Power and Social Theory*, Cambridge, Mass.: Harvard U. Press, 1958, Chap. 5.

43 Alexander A. Goldenweiser, *History, Psychology, and Culture*, New York: Alfred A. Knopf, 1933, esp. pp. 45-49.

44 Lewis Coser, *The Functions of Social Conflict*, Glencoe, Ill.: Free Press, 1956.

45 See Gough, *op. cit.*: Kingsley Davis, "Illegitimacy and the Social Structure," *American Journal of Sociology*, 43 (September 1939), pp. 213-233; A. R. Radcliffe-Brown, *op. cit.*, p. 3. The structure of the marital institution is not specified in terms of number or sex, for there are cultures in which two women may marry and raise a family. See: B. E. Evans Pritchard, *Kinship and Marriage Among the Nuer*, London: Oxford U. Press, 1951, pp. 108-109. It is well to note here that Murdock stressed a somewhat different view of marriage. He focused on sexual and economic functions, and the woman-woman marriage found in the Nuer would not fit this definition. Morris Zelditch recently has used this legitimacy function as the key aspect of his definition of the family rather than marriage. Such a usage would, it seems, confuse the traditional distinction between these two institutions. See: p. 682 in *Handbook of Modern Sociology*, ed. by Robert Faris, New York: Rand-McNally, 1964.

46 Blake, *op. cit.*

47 Dorothy R. Blitsten, *The World of the Family*, New York: Random House, 1963, esp. Chap. 1.

48 Kingsley Davis, *Human Society*, New York: Macmillan, 1950, p. 395. Davis lists reproduction, maintenance, placement, and socialization of the young as universal family functions. Social placement is the only function that differs from Murdock's list. One could conceive of this function as part of the marital rather than the family institution.

The Canadian family:
a demographic profile

At this point, the most readily available and most accurate knowledge of the family in Canada comes from census and vital statistics sources. Although this information cannot provide clear indications of the relationships within families, it does offer insight into the *form* and *distribution* of marriage and family patterns.

Demographic analysis seldom asks *why* families differ in structure and distribution, choosing instead to ask *how*. Do divorced families have fewer children? Do divorced families rent rather than own their dwellings? Do divorced families have lower incomes? Do divorced families have certain ethnic or religious characteristics? Do young families tend to live in apartments? Do young families tend to live in cities? These are the type of queries that can be answered with census data. Answers to these questions can guide the structure and distribution of housing and the formation of policy for meeting the needs of people or altering social disparities, or simply provide insight into the organization of society.

The paper by Kalbach and McVey doesn't attempt to answer all of these questions but rather presents a basic demographic profile of selected aspects of the characteristics of family heads, types of family living arrangements, housing, family size, and demographic trends for Canada *as a whole*.

It is of interest to briefly discuss selected vital statistics and census data in terms of provincial variations. Table 3.5 presents selected data on natural increase, marriage and divorce rates, family size, family types, and household occupancy for each of the provinces.

The rate of natural increase (the number of births exceeding the number of deaths in any given year) decreased in all provinces between 1970 and 1973. There was a net increase in all of the Atlantic provinces between 1970 and 1971 but this trend reversed in 1972 and by 1973 was well below the 1970 rate. For Canada as a whole, the marriage rate continued to increase to 1972 (9.2) leveling off at 9.0 for 1973. The marriage rate appears to have reached its highest point in 1972 for most of the provinces as well. The highest marriage rate occurred in the Yukon (10.3) and the lowest in the Northwest Territories (5.9). The most apparent variation among the provinces is in the divorce rate. Between 1970 and 1973, the divorce rate increased 112 percent in the Northwest Territories, 66 percent in Quebec, and more than 40 percent in Newfoundland, Nova Scotia and New Brunswick. The divorce rate in Prince Edward Island, in contrast, decreased more than 20 percent, the only province to do so. Most of the provinces experienced a temporary decrease in the

Table 3.5 Summary of Selected Vital Statistics and 1971 Census Data, by Provinces

	Canada	Newfound-land	Prince Edward Island	Nova Scotia	New Bruns-wick	Quebec	Ontario	Manitoba	Saskat-chewan	Alberta	British Columbia	Yukon	Northwest Territories[a]
Vital Statistics:													
Natural increase[b]													
1970	10.2	17.9	8.6	9.5	10.5	8.6	10.3	10.6	9.6	13.7	9.3	20.1	32.8
1971	9.5	18.4	9.8	9.6	11.4	8.0	9.5	10.1	9.3	12.3	7.9	21.8	30.4
1972	8.5	17.9	8.5	8.3	10.6	6.8	8.5	9.2	8.6	11.2	7.4	18.3	26.9
1973	8.1	15.7	7.5	7.9	9.7	6.8	8.0	8.8	7.9	11.0	7.0	15.7	25.3
Marriage rate[c]													
1970	8.8	8.6	8.3	8.7	9.1	8.3	9.1	9.2	7.8	9.6	9.4	11.8	7.2
1971	8.9	9.0	8.6	8.7	9.7	8.2	9.0	9.2	8.4	9.6	9.3	9.0	7.2
1972	9.2	9.6	9.0	9.2	10.0	8.9	9.2	9.3	8.6	9.9	9.2	9.5	7.1
1973	9.0	9.3	8.8	9.0	9.8	8.5	9.1	9.2	8.6	9.7	9.2	10.3	5.9
Divorce rate[d]													
1970	139.8	27.1	59.1	105.2	61.6	80.9	164.9	125.5	92.6	236.4	240.2	241.2	51.5
1971	137.6	28.7	54.5	91.4	76.1	86.3	158.5	140.1	88.1	224.6	225.5	261.1	71.4
1972	148.4	33.3	57.5	116.6	72.5	106.2	168.6	142.6	90.3	228.1	224.3	247.4	100.0
1973	166.1	41.4	47.0	155.2	88.0	133.1	173.6	162.3	97.7	263.5	245.7	300.0	110.5
Census Data:													
Persons per family[e]													
urban	3.6	4.3	3.9	3.7	3.8	3.8	3.5	3.5	3.6	3.6	3.4	4.0	
rural	4.1	4.6	4.1	3.9	4.2	4.5	3.9	4.0	3.9	4.1	3.7	4.8	
Families — own household[f]													
urban	96.7	92.7	95.0	95.2	95.0	97.3	96.0	97.4	98.1	97.9	97.0	97.3	
rural	96.3	91.7	94.3	94.6	94.0	96.4	97.0	96.4	97.7	96.7	97.1	93.6	
Relatives in household[g]													
urban	71.0	88.0	82.0	81.0	81.0	76.5	68.6	68.8	67.6	65.2	64.0	59.4	
rural	80.0	93.4	93.0	87.6	89.9	87.3	81.0	60.8	70.0	58.5	66.3	76.7	
One family household[h]	96.8	92.1	95.0	95.0	95.1	97.3	96.2	97.6	98.2	98.0	97.3	96.0	
Both parents home	88.5	84.9	86.6	86.4	87.0	88.1	88.6	89.0	90.4	89.9	89.1	86.5	
One parent home	8.3	7.2	8.4	8.6	8.2	9.2	7.7	8.5	7.8	8.1	8.2	9.5	
Two family households	2.4	6.5	3.8	3.6	3.7	2.1	2.8	1.8	1.2	1.4	2.0	3.3	

Based on Statistics Canada. Cat. Nos. 84-201 for 1973, 93-703 and 93-714.

[a] The Yukon and N.W.T. are merged in the census data. [b] Net increase in persons per 1000 population after births and deaths are compared. [c] Per 1000 population. [d] Per 100,000 population. [e] Average number of persons per family. Definitions of all census terms are provided at the end of Chapter two. [f] Percent of families maintaining own household. (cf. Census definitions.) [g] Percent of families *not* maintaining own household who have *related* persons living in the household. [h] Percentages do not equal 100 because of rounding error and exclusion of families without related household head.

number of divorces per 100,000 population in either 1971 or 1972. Four provinces consistently increased during the four-year period: Newfoundland, Quebec, Manitoba and the Northwest Territories. In 1973, the divorce rate was nearly twice the national average in the Yukon (300 compared to 166) and 1½ times as high in Alberta and British Columbia. Comparatively speaking, Newfoundland and Prince Edward Island have an extremely low number of divorces each year. Indeed, the divorce rate is considerably below the national average in all the Atlantic provinces except Nova Scotia, and in Saskatchewan.

The remainder of the table illustrates differences for urban and rural areas for each of the provinces for type and size of family. The urban family contains consistently fewer persons than the rural family regardless of the province. The urban-rural difference is most marked in the Northwest Territories (+.8) and Quebec (+.7). Northern Canada and Newfoundland have the largest families in both rural and urban areas. British Columbia has the smallest number of persons per family in both rural and urban areas. There are few differences among the provinces concerning the proportion of Canadian family units that maintain their own household. Further, the differences are typically minor between urban and rural areas. Saskatchewan appears to have the highest percentage of families maintaining their own household (98.1 percent) and Newfoundland the lowest (92.7 percent). These patterns hold in both urban and rural areas. There is greater variability, however, in who shares the household among families not maintaining a separate household. Census data identifies persons as being related or unrelated (e.g., lodgers). It would appear that as one moves from east to west the percentage of relatives sharing households with urban residents decreases (from 88 percent relatives in Newfoundland to 64 percent with related household members in British Columbia). There are definitely more non-related household members in the western provinces. In general, these patterns are similar in rural areas. With the exception of Manitoba and Alberta, there are typically more relatives in the household in rural than in urban areas.

Newfoundland has the highest percentage of two or more families in a household (6.5 percent), Saskatchewan the lowest (1.2 percent). One-parent households are most evident in Quebec (9.2 percent) and least prevalent in Newfoundland (7.2 percent).

The demographic patterns described above illustrate the variability in family patterns across Canada. These differences are important in understanding what it means to be a member of a family unit in Canada.

The Canadian family:
a demographic profile

Warren E. Kalbach and Wayne W. McVey, Jr.

Nuclear families consisting of parents and their unmarried children living together in the same dwelling as a family constitute the basic social unit of Canadian society. As of June 1, 1971, the census of Canada revealed that 87.4 percent of the total population, or 18,852,110 persons, were living in such family groups while the balance, or 12.6 percent, was reported as either living alone or in non-family groups.[1]

While the number of families has continued to increase over the years in keeping with Canada's continuing population growth, the average size of the family has remained relatively constant since World War II. In 1941, the average family size was 3.9 persons, and while the average declined to 3.7 persons in 1951, it again reached 3.9 in 1961 and 1966 and returned to 3.7 in 1971. In view of post-war increases in both fertility and immigration, as well as the dramatic decline subsequent to 1971 in fertility rates, this relative constancy in family size may seem somewhat surprising. However, one must keep in mind that family size is not only a function of its fertility and mortality experience, but also of the rates of family and non-family group formation. When the population living in families increases more rapidly than the total population, as it did between 1941 and 1971, other compensatory forces, e.g., an increase in the formation of new family units, must operate to keep family size relatively constant. In this case, census data for Canada show consistent and significant increases in the proportion married for the population fifteen years of age and older.[2]

Characteristics of family heads:
marital status and sex

The traditional patterns of marriage and male dominance continue to persist in the family statistics for Canada. In the 1971 Census, 94 percent of all family heads were married and 93 percent of all families had male heads. The proportion of family heads either divorced or never married has been quite small, but the movement towards some liberalization of divorce laws is reflected in the increase in the proportion of divorced family heads from 0.3 to slightly over 1 percent between 1951 and 1971. Since the proportion of family heads who were never married also increased slightly, family heads who were widowed had to decline relative to the other statuses. This is reflected in the proportion of widowed heads, which drop-

*Warren E. Kalbach, Ph.D., is Professor of Sociology, University of Toronto, Ontario.
Wayne W. McVey, Ph.D., is Professor of Sociology, University of Alberta, Edmonton.*

This paper was specially written for this book.

ped to 4.4 percent in 1971, from 6.6 percent in 1951.

The number of females reported as family heads has been increasing, with the total reaching 378,000 in 1971. However, the number of male family heads has increased almost at a similar rate and the proportion with female heads has remained relatively constant near 7 percent between 1956 and 1971. As might be expected, the 1971 Census revealed that approximately 49 percent of the women became heads of families through the death of their spouse. Because of the greater likelihood of death among males with advancing age, the proportion increases rapidly with increasing age.[3] An additional 32 percent were family heads because their husbands were not present in the home, and the remaining 19 percent were heads because of divorce, or because they had assumed the responsibility of being family head for a variety of reasons even though they had never married. In contrast to the increasing importance of mortality of spouse with age, the proportion who are heads because of the absence of their husbands, or because of divorce, or for other reasons, declines rapidly with age as husbands rejoin their families or these women remarry or marry for the first time.

Age of husbands and wives

Approximately one half of all family heads were under forty-five years of age in 1971. Relatively few family heads were under the age of twenty-five or sixty-five years of age and over — 6.4 and 11.8 percent, respectively. Changes in the age distribution of family heads would tend to reflect shifts in the ages at which people marry. For example, a period of prosperity could produce both a significant decline in the age at marriage, and an increase in the marriage rate, which would tend to lower the average age of family heads. Conversely, a recession could produce the opposite effect, as would similar disruptive events, e.g., war or periods of rapid social change and political unrest.

In Canada, the average age at marriage for all bridegrooms declined from 28.9 years in 1941 to 27.3 years in 1971. Considering only those marrying for the first time during this period, the decline was somewhat more rapid — from 27.6 to 24.9 years. Accompanying this decline in age at marriage was a simultaneous decline in the age difference between brides and grooms. As early as 1921, the age difference for all brides and grooms was 4.4 years; however by 1941, the difference had declined to 3.8 years, and by 1971 to 2.5 years. For those marrying for the first time, the same trend prevailed, with the gap narrowing from 3.2 years in 1941 to 2.3 years in 1971.

While the age differential is still significant, the preference of males for younger women, or of women for older men, appears to be diminishing. This is illustrated more clearly through an examination of the 1961 Census data for husbands showing the proportion of wives in the same or different age group, by age of husband. The proportion of male family heads with wives in the same five-year age group was highest, with 76.9 percent, for those under twenty years of age, and declined steadily with increasing age of husband, reaching a minimum of 27.7 percent for the sixty-five to sixty-nine year age group. The trend reverses only for those seventy years of age and older, where 50 percent had wives in the same age group as themselves. Remarriage among older males might provide the explanation for this singular exception. It just may be that a strong preference for younger women is simply not sufficient in the face of decreasing opportunities to socially interact with them, and the increasingly accessible numbers of widows to be found in their own social groups and in retirement communities.

The relative number of husbands with older wives never exceeded 10 percent, with the one interesting exception for those males under twenty years of age. The young male who wishes to marry would tend to find considerable opposition to his marrying very young girls, and since those of his own age tend to marry older men, his greatest opportunity would appear to be with older women. This predicament would contribute to the very high proportion marrying within the same general age group, as well as the relatively high proportion of males under twenty years (23 percent) with wives in an older age group.

A similar type of "marriage squeeze" can be produced for females as a result of rapid increases in the birth rate, such as occurred during the immediate post-war period in Canada. Since the female birth cohorts for 1946 and 1947 were much larger than the preceding male cohorts of 1944 and 1945 from which they would traditionally select their husbands, there was an imbalance of numbers creating a shortage of males in the ideal age group, for those attempting to follow the traditional path to the altar. The alternative for those unable to find husbands somewhat older than themselves was to find prospective mates of their own age or younger. The fact that the proportion of the population married increased significantly during this period would suggest that women tended to adjust this traditional preference to the available manpower rather than remain

unmarried. It should be kept in mind, however, that the age difference between brides and grooms had been declining before the arrival of the post-war baby boom cohorts on the marriage market; thus, the demographically produced marriage squeeze may have served only to accelerate an existing trend.

Ethnicity of husbands and wives

The continuing predominance of the British and French origin groups in the Canadian population is a well established fact. In 1971, those of British origin constituted approximately 45 percent; the French, 29 percent; and the remaining 26 percent of the population was comprised of a variety of ethnic and racial groups from numerous European, Asian, and other countries. As would be expected, this dominance is also evident in the characteristics of family heads.

It is a generally accepted fact that the British origin group has maintained its dominance in numbers through the years by means of immigration, while the French have maintained their relative numbers through high levels of fertility. However, with heavy post–World War II immigration by other ethnic groups and the declining fertility of the French Canadian, the historically dominant position of these two "founding" groups may experience considerable erosion.

One factor with a considerable potential for ameliorating the impact of continuing large scale immigration from non-British and non-French sources, would be ethnic intermarriage between the established resident population and the new immigrants. However, the amount of intermarriage, as revealed in census statistics, involving husbands of either British or French origin has not been very great. For the British, 81 percent of all male family heads had wives of similar origin, while 86 percent of French family heads had wives of French origin.

Several origin groups reflect higher rates of endogamous marriage, e.g., Jewish with 91 percent, and native Indian and Eskimo with 92 percent, but most other origins show considerably lower rates. Males of Scandinavian origin show the lowest degree of endogamous marriage, with only 27 percent having Scandinavian wives at the time of the 1971 Census.

The age and marital status of arriving immigrants, as well as the effects of residential propinquity and the relative sizes of the various ethnic populations, are crucial factors affecting opportunities for intermarriage. These need to be taken into consideration in order to derive valid generalizations concerning the propensity of Canada's various ethnic populations to intermarry. Even so, using more refined measures and controlling for as many of these other influences as is possible in statistical analysis still produces much the same result. Controlling for the effect of variations in size and examining only the families with native-born heads still shows the Jews, native-born Indians and Eskimos, French, Asians, and British to be most endogamous, and the Scandinavians the least.

Initial settlement patterns and the extent and nature of subsequent internal migration also appear to be significant factors in explaining the propensity of some ethnic groups to intermarry. Native Indians and Eskimos, for example, provide an extreme case, illustrating how continuing physical and social isolation operates to restrict opportunities for interaction and intermarriage. The Jewish population provides another good example,

as they constituted only 1 percent of the total population in 1971. Their strong ethnic and religious identity, combined with a very high degree of residential segregation in urban areas, combine to produce the lowest index of intermarriage for any origin group. Of course, one must not overlook the importance of socio-economic differences in further hindering interaction between the various groups.

In general, members of most ethnic origin populations exhibit a greater degree of endogamy if they remain within their areas of original settlement. The cultural influences operating on those of rural origin tend to weaken considerably through rural-urban migration and adaptation to the urban environment. Populations such as the Ukrainians and Dutch, who leave their ethnic rural strongholds, decrease their own chances of marrying someone of similar ethnic background. Not only does the supply of eligible males of other origins increase, but group constraints are weakened while opportunities for expanding one's social contacts are greatly enhanced. While the nature of the internal migration differs, the same process affects the marriage behavior of Jewish origin males who settle in non-urban areas, and those of French origin who move to urban areas outside of Quebec. Each of these two groups exhibit atypically high rates of intermarriage with individuals of different ethnic origin backgrounds.

Because of the significance of religion in ethnic differences, some comment on religious endogamy is relevant here. Accumulation of evidence concerning the extent of religious endogamy in mate selection has contributed to the increasing attacks on the validity of the "melting pot" theory of cultural assimilation in North American society. Its validity would also be questionable for Canada, considering that in 1972, 61 percent of all Canadians getting married that year married within their own faith.[4]

As in the case of ethnic origins, considerable variation in religious endogamy exists from one religious affiliation to another. The high proportion of brides having the same religious affiliation as grooms, at the time of marriage, between 1959 and 1961, for Jews (89 percent) and Roman Catholics (88 percent) suggests the importance of religion as a factor in the high ethnic endogamy exhibited by family heads of Jewish and French origins in addition to more general social and cultural considerations and such contingencies as residential propinquity. In the census, the Mennonites (which include Hutterites) had the third highest proportion of endogamous marriages (76 percent), followed by Greek Orthodox (64 percent) and United Church (62 percent). The lowest proportions found marrying within their own faith were found for Presbyterians and Christian Scientists with 37 and 28 percent, respectively.[5]

One problem with religious data on brides and grooms at time of marriage is that such indications may not reveal the actual religious background of the individuals concerned, and perhaps contribute to an overestimate of the real degree of religious homogamy reflected in marriage statistics. The ease with which persons can, and do, change their religious affiliation at the time of marriage in the interest of religious and marital harmony can introduce a serious bias into the data. A comparison of the 1941 census data on religious characteristics of married persons with marriage statistics of the preceding decade showed greater similarity in religious affiliations of husbands and wives in the census than at the time of marriage.[6]

The significance of a large proportion of interdenominational marriages in Canadian society for its future religious composition would be difficult to assess on the basis of census data alone. The overall trend in Canada is towards a Catholic majority, and subsequent censuses will provide more clues to the process by which this has been brought about. The data will reflect the effect of religious conversions of spouses and subsequent socialization of their children, but these effects will be difficult to separate from the contributions of fertility, mortality, and net migration, if all of these, like fertility, are also shown to vary with religious affiliation.

Education of husbands and wives

In 1961, there was little difference between the educational attainment of family heads and the total male population fifteen years of age and over. Slightly less than half of each group did not have any secondary education. On the other hand, for those with some university or degree, there was a slightly larger percentage of family heads (8.1 percent) than among all males fifteen years of age and older (7.5 percent).

An examination of the educational attainment of husbands, vis-à-vis their wives, quickly reveals that education along with ethnic origin and religion plays a significant part in delimiting the appropriate boundaries within which mate selection may occur. It is no accident that as the educational attainment of the husband increases, so does that of his wife, so that husbands and wives tend to have approximately the same educational backgrounds. In addition, the wives of those husbands who had less than two years of secondary schooling generally had achieved higher educational levels. For husbands with more schooling, the wives tended to have less, e.g., in 1961, of those husbands with four or five years of secondary schooling, 44 percent had wives with similar levels of schooling, 6 percent had some post-secondary schooling, while 50 percent had less than four years. Generally, it would seem that men have tended to marry women with less education. This presents little difficulty at the upper educational levels where the number of men tends to exceed the number of women. However, at the lower end of the scale, where men also tend to outnumber women, this presents something of a problem to the extent that educational superiority on the part of the male is a necessary component of the traditional concept of the dominant male and husband. Obviously, some men had to marry women with more education than themselves. To take the extreme case, of the 47,449 heads of families who reported no schooling (1961), only 38 percent had wives with no schooling, 55 percent had wives with elementary schooling only, while the remaining 7 percent had to contend with wives who had some secondary education or more.

The consequences of similarity in educational background are not limited to marital interactional patterns and personal life styles of the parents alone. The probabilities of the children achieving some post-secondary education are directly related to the educational attainment of the family head. For example, the 1961 census also showed that the proportion of children between fifteen and nineteen years of age still attending school was positively related to the level of education achieved by the family head. This is also true for the nineteen to twenty-four year olds, the ones most likely to be attending college or university. Of those in the latter age group whose fathers had less than five years of elementary education, only 8.5 percent were still in school compared to 63.7 percent of those whose fathers had a university degree.

Of course, many immigrant fathers, with little or no formal education, have worked very hard to provide their children with opportunities for higher education. While this has certainly been possible in Canada, the data attest to its difficulty. Certainly it cannot be achieved without considerable social and economic cost to the family. In this respect, further research is needed to determine more precisely the effect of educational upgrading of the second generation on the maintenance of ethnic identity and support for ethnic and religious constraints in courtship and mate selection.

Labor force status and income

Labor force status and income of family members are several of the more basic determinants of a family's social status and life style. However, neither is constant throughout the age range associated with general labor force participation. The extent of labor force participation varies significantly with age and differs markedly for men and women. Similarly, the earning patterns vary with age, and for family heads reach maximum levels in the latter part of the middle age range (forty-five to fifty-four years), generally declining thereafter. The adequacy of income at any one time is, of course, quite relative not only to the particular life cycle stage, but to family size and one's life style expectations as well.

While the demarcation of the poverty line with reference to family income must always be somewhat arbitrary, there would be little argument that the 781,000 families who were reported in the Survey of Consumer Finances for 1971 as earning less than $4,000 were experiencing some hardship. Certainly they were enjoying fewer amenities than those families with incomes closer to the estimated national average of $9,347.

Two of the more interesting labor force trends, having special relevance for discussions of the Canadian family are (1) the decline in male participation since 1911; and (2) the consistent increase in female participation. Between 1951 and 1971, the decline in male participation was evident for most categories of marital status within the population fifteen years of age and over. On the other hand, increases in female participation were greatest for married women, with only slight increases indicated for the widowed and divorced. Participation for single females actually declined during this period. By 1971, approximately 87 percent of all married males and one third of all married women were in the labor force. For the latter, participation declines during the years of maximum fertility, peaks again between the ages of forty-five and fifty-five years, and then steadily declines with advancing years.

The increase in participation in the labor force by married women may, in part, be due to the increase in non-economic motives for women seeking more meaningful and challenging roles in society. On the other hand, the need for additional income to meet family needs beyond that provided by the family head is also apparent. Since World War II, the employment opportunities for females have expanded considerably, particularly in

the sales and service sectors. This, combined with the fact that women, generally, are better educated and can be employed at a lower wage level than males in comparable job categories, provides the employer with an unusually attractive combination – quality labor at a cheap cost.[7] In 1961, the husband alone was employed in approximately two of every three husband-wife families. In one out of every twenty families, the wife as well as the husband was employed. Greater participation by wives living in urban areas is consistent with the greater employment opportunities to be found for women in these areas.[8]

While the reasons for wives working may be numerous and complex, the economic need is clearly revealed through a comparison of the earnings of family heads with working and non-working wives. Average earnings for all husbands with working wives were $3,867 in 1961, compared to $4,303 for those whose wives were not in the labor force. Furthermore, the earnings of family heads with working wives were consistently lower for every age level. This discrepancy tends to increase with increasing age of family head, suggesting that the need for additional income becomes more pressing in the latter stages of the family life cycle.

An examination of the sources of family income, by age of family head, where there are multiple contributors is also revealing. In Podoluk's analysis of incomes in Canada, it is revealed that wives under twenty-five years of age make the maximum contribution (19 percent of the reported family income), and that this contribution declines steadily reaching minimum levels for family heads between thirty-five and sixty-five years of age. Thereafter it rises again, reaching a maximum of 17.9 percent when heads of families reach seventy years of age and over. Another interesting aspect of family income is the rapid increase in contributions made by unmarried children with increasing age of family head. Their contribution increases from a negligible 0.1 percent for young family heads (twenty-five to thirty-four years of age), to 15.2 percent for heads fifty-five to sixty-four years of age, and then declines only slightly to 14.7 percent for family heads seventy years and older.[9]

In the past, unmarried children have been the most important source of supplementary income, but Podoluk's analysis has shown that wives have now taken over this role. As she points out, this appears to be less a matter of choice than necessity as the extended schooling required of children, combined with earlier marriage and larger proportions getting married, puts more pressure on the wife to meet family financial needs.[10]

Something of an exception, but perhaps only in a matter of degree, might be found in the case of post-war immigrant families. In these families total family earnings exceed the earnings of family heads by a considerably greater margin than is the case for families with native-born heads. This could reflect the generally lower incomes of recent immigrants during their initial period of adjustment, and their greater need for help from all family members during their early attempts to become established in their new country.[11]

Types of family living arrangements

A family's particular living arrangement is related to the marital status and sex of the family head, and to social and economic circumstances. The 1966 Census provides adequate illustration of this, and does not appear to be inconsistent with early, but partial, releases of the 1971 Census data. Of the four and one-half million families reported in 1966, exactly 96 percent were maintaining their own households. Only 3 percent were living with related families, and 1 percent were lodging-type families consisting of unrelated individuals. Considering only those families with husband and wife present, almost 97 percent maintained their own households, but among families with only one parent, the percentage ranged from 54 to 93 percent. For heads of families who had never married, 70 percent of the females maintained their own households compared to just 55 percent for male heads.

Death of one spouse does not tend to reduce the proportion maintaining separate households to a significant degree. Broken homes have fewer independent households, the percentage being 80 percent for divorced females and 78 percent for divorced males. Understandable is the fact that divorced females appear to be more independent in this respect than wives who are family heads in the absence of their husbands. The transitory nature of the latter situation would seem to invite more temporary solutions, such as moving in with one's relatives.

With respect to the other major factors, age and income, sharing was greatest for family heads under twenty-five years (17.8 percent), and declined with increasing age. The same inverse relationship held for income, and when the family head was under twenty-five years of age, 33.5 percent of those earning under $2,000 shared households with others. Interestingly, as earnings increased, it is the younger family head who is most likely to share a household rather than maintain his own. As will be seen in the following section, the ability to establish an independent household may depend to a large degree upon the nature and variety of the housing supply. Housing suitable for families in differing circumstances and at different points in their life cycles is a relatively recent development in the housing market.

Housing the Canadian family

As previously noted, the one-family household, i.e., one family occupying either a single dwelling unit or structurally separate living quarters, is the most common housing arrangement found in Canada. While the number of family households has continued to grow, increasing by 63 percent between 1951 and 1971, the number of non-family households has increase by 188 percent in the same period. The increase in the latter type of household has been occasioned by the increasing numbers of divorced, widowed, and separated individuals in society, plus a greater interest in and the means to live by oneself or with other unrelated individuals, for example, sharing apartments with friends, or in the extreme form, cooperative living ventures exemplified by the urban commune.

The fact that the greatest increases in family households have been for those with family heads under thirty-five years, and for non-family heads under thirty-five and sixty-five years and older, has considerable significance for the type of housing most in demand, and most likely to be constructed in the immediate future. Considering these growth trends in light of the rural to urban movement of population, as well as the increasing scarcity and value of land in the large urban centres, provides part of the explanation for the high-rise building boom which has become so visible on Canada's urban skyline.

With the gradual decline in the proportion of single detached housing among Canada's total housing supply from 85 percent in 1921 to 60 percent in 1971, and the relatively more rapid expansion of apartment dwellings from 2 to 28 percent during the same period, new options are opening for the one-family household at various stages in its life cycle. The traditional preference reflected in the dominant position of single detached dwellings across Canada made no provision for changes in the size of the family or consequent changes in space needs. In the past, the problem was often solved by having the young married couple, or the divorced daughter, move in with their parents. Similarly, the aging parents might live with their children when they could no longer manage in the large, old family home. Clearly, the availability of small and medium-size apartments near the amenities of urban centers provides a partial answer for these specialized housing needs.

The single detached and attached units of the expanding suburbs, on the other hand, will continue to cater to the needs of the family during its child-rearing stage. Yet even here, the new apartment blocks, town houses, and garden courts may prove increasingly popular for the more mobile families. The increasing attraction of condominiums will provide a continuing opportunity for home ownership, while tailoring housing more specifically to individual or family requirements. Home ownership still remains a dominant force in Canada, with almost two thirds of all dwellings being owner-occupied. The emergence of a new trend in tenure may be seen in the increase of tenant-occupied dwellings from 34 to almost 40 percent between 1951 and 1971. Of course, the trend would be much more apparent if only occupied dwellings in the larger urban centres were considered, as the apartment is primarily an urban housing form. Data on building permits issued between 1950 and 1971 lend further evidence to this shift in preference. Permits for single family dwelling units more than doubled, but decreased proportionately from 76 to 37 percent of annual housing construction. Apartment starts, on the other hand, increased from approximately 7 to 54 percent during the same period.[12]

As the number and variety of housing options increase for the Canadian, it would seem logical to expect changes in attitudes towards appropriate housing to coincide with various stages in the life cycle. The simple fact is that the typical single detached dwelling, which has held the spotlight for so long as the ideal mode of accommodation, is the typical housing type only for a limited number of years. Greater mobility in the future will require some modification of our traditional notions of home ownership and financing. Both notions are still geared to the "one family — one house in a lifetime" attitude more appropriate for traditional rural societies experiencing a minimum of social change. Certainly, if the emerging housing market is increasingly characterized by a variety of housing types and styles to meet the many stages and contingencies of individual and family life cycles, some revision in our procedures for home financing will be necessary.

Variations in family size

Fertility is the basic factor affecting family size; however, one must keep in mind the important distinction made between "completed fertility" and the "size of families" at any given point in time. The former refers to the total number of live births that a woman has during her childbearing years, while the latter includes as children only those offspring twenty-four years of age and younger still unmarried and living at home at the time of a particular census. The determinants of completed fertility for specific birth cohorts of women are very important for the understanding of fertility behavior in a population, while the family size is an important variable of the family life cycle.

Fertility

The most popular and widely reported measure of fertility is the crude birth rate. From 1921 to the Depression year of 1937, the crude birth rate experienced an overall decline from 29.3 to 20.1 (births per 1,000 population). Thereafter, it rose gradually to 24.3 in 1945, then increased dramatically during the post-war years to a high of 28.9 in 1947. Between 1953 and 1957, the birth rate remained slightly above 28.0, then declined with increasing rapidity until in 1971 it had fallen to 16.8. The post-war "baby boom" had collapsed and the crude birth rate provided few explanations.

The increase in marriages following the end of World War II, and the making up for children that married couples would normally have had during the war years, are two of the factors given considerable credit for the post-war fertility increases. In addition, the post-war economic boom and continuing rise in standards of living encouraged the trend towards earlier marriage, with the average age for males (marrying for the first time) dropping from 27.1 years in 1946 to 24.9 years in 1971. For females, the corresponding figures were 24.1 and 22.6 years, respectively.

An examination of more refined measures of fertility for specific age groups shows that the birth rates increased more rapidly for the females in the youngest age groups, i.e., those 15 – 19, 20 – 24, and 25 – 29 years of age, while the older age groups experienced little change or actual decline, as was the case for those forty years of age and over. During the latter part of the 1950s, the total fertility rate reached its post-war peak and then the trend for all age groups turned downward. Henripin and Légaré, in their concise analysis of recent fertility trends, concluded that the rise in fertility up to 1959 could be explained almost entirely in terms of an increase in the proportion of married women during this period, and to a lesser extent to an actual increase in marital fertility.[13]

As for the drastic fertility decline subsequent to 1959, this appears to be the consequence of a decline in marital fertility. How much of the decline reflects a postponement of births, or a decline in completed fertility is more difficult to say. Henripin and Légaré indicate that changes in the timing and spacing of children may be the primary explanation. An analysis of vital statistics data for 1959 and 1967 does reveal that the average interval between first and second births increased from 2.45 to 2.52 years; between second and third births, from 2.36 to 2.61 years; and, between third and fourth births, from 1.81 to 2.08 years. Intervals between higher order births showed progressively smaller increases, suggesting that only those with smaller families who are most likely to practise birth control are altering the timing of their births to any significant degree.

While Henripin and Légaré suggest that the size of the Canadian family may again be declining,[14] the data on cumulative fertility is not sufficiently current to permit any accurate isolation of the specific cohort of women who have decided to have smaller families. Until a cohort has aged beyond the childbearing years, it is not possible to calculate its average completed fertility. The only certainty to be derived from the 1961 Census is that the long-term decline in family size, i.e., completed fertility, stopped with the cohort of urban women who were 45 – 49 years of age in 1961, and the 50 – 54-year-old rural non-farm women. Completed fertility for these two groups was 2.7 and 3.9, respectively. No reversal was apparent in the case of rural farm women. Among urban women, the 40 – 44-year-olds had already surpassed the fertility levels of their immediate predecessors, and the 35 – 39-year-olds had already achieved comparable levels. However, which of the younger cohorts will be responsible for the new downturn in completed fertility, detected by Henripin and Légaré, can only be determined by careful analysis of the 1971 and subsequent censuses.

Average number of children per family

The average number of children has followed the trend in family size very closely. Between 1941 and 1951, the number of children declined from 1.9 to 1.7 (compared to 3.9 and 3.7 for family size). The average number of children increased to 1.9 in 1961, remained at that level in 1966, and decreased once again to 1.7 in 1971. Rural-urban differentials in fertility are reflected in these data for 1966, with rural farm families showing an average of 2.4 in contrast to 2.2 for rural non-farm, and 1.7 for urban families.

Analysis of regional variations show eastern Canada with the highest average number of children per family and western areas with the lowest. More specifically, Newfoundland, with 2.6 children per family, had the highest overall average, while both Ontario and British Columbia had the lowest with just 1.7. Looking at both rural-urban and regional differences simultaneously, one finds the highest rural-farm average of 3.5 children in Quebec, and Newfoundland reflects the highest averages for rural non-farm and urban areas. While the average numbers are down slightly in 1971, the same regional contrasts continue to hold.

It should be noted that variations in the average number of children per family reflect more than changes in fertility behavior, as the trends for the two do not always correspond. The reduction in average number of children between 1941 and 1951, in the face of rapidly increasing fertility, would be partially explained by the larger increase in new families during the immediate post-war period which would necessarily have relatively few children. Thus, average family size and number of children would reflect the rate of family formation, as well as other factors, e.g., variation in age at marriage, differences in family life cycle, increases in divorce and separation, and longevity, as indicated in the increasing proportion of families with older heads.

Post-war fluctuations in fertility are also visible in the data showing composition of families by number of children. For example, the fairly consistent decline in fertility of older women, i.e., those thirty-five years of age and over since 1931, is exhibited in the proportionate decline of families with six or more children from 6.8 percent in 1941 to 3.4 percent in 1971. On the other hand, the post-war increase in fertility up to the late 1950s, and subsequent decline for each of the younger age groups produced (1) declines in the proportions of families with either none or one child (from 31.2 to 30.5 percent for childless families, and from 23.6 to 20.6 percent for one-child families); and (2) increases in proportions of families with two to five children. Since 1951, the largest proportionate increases occurred in families with three and four children. However, a leveling off or decline in the proportion of families with four and five children, at home, in the early 1970s would be consistent with present analyses. The 1971 data do, in fact, show a slight decline from 11.4 to 10.9 per cent in families with this number of children.

Family size differentials: nativity

Any of the factors associated with fertility differentials are clearly relevant for explaining differences in family size, e.g., the consistently higher cumulative fertility of native-born vs. foreign-born women at all age levels,[15] as well as the generally accepted rural-urban differences. In addition, because of the crucial importance of the family life cycle for variations in the number of children living at home, the age of the family head is of considerable importance and would be reflected in any comparison of groups where a significant age difference occurs, as in comparisons involving pre-war immigrant family heads. Thus, while average family size tends to increase with length of residence for post-war immigrants, it drops significantly for pre-war immigrant families who have resided in Canada for a much longer period of time. Thus, families with native-born heads, with an average of 3.8 persons per family in 1971, had the largest families, post-war immigrant heads the next largest, with approximately 3.5, and pre-war immigrants the smallest with 2.8 persons. The same relationship also tends to hold with respect to the number of children under twenty-five years of age living at home.

Ethnic origin of family head

Variations by ethnicity of family heads reflect the association between ethnic, religious, educational, and locational factors. The three ethnic origin groups with the largest average size in 1961 (native Indians and Eskimos, 5.1; French, 4.4; and Netherlands, 4.1), each rank high for somewhat different reasons. The native Indians and Eskimos show the high fertility of poorly educated, low income minority groups living on marginal lands, while the French reflect levels consistent with their religious, rural, and educational backgrounds. Those of Netherlands origin are still predominantly rural-farm families.

The smallest families are found for heads of families with Jewish and Hungarian origins, with 3.4 and 3.3 persons per family, respectively. Both groups, in contrast to those mentioned above, are highly educated, heavily professional in occupational composition, and concentrated in urban areas, all of which have been established as correlates of lower fertility. In the case of families with Hungarian heads, many of whom fled their country during the revolt of the late 1950s, it is possible that many did not bring their entire families with them. If this, in fact, did occur, the average of 3.3 persons might well be an underestimate of their true family size while accurately representing their families in Canada at the time of the 1961 census.

Demographic trends, family life cycle, and life style

The various stages of the family life cycle are closely linked to and affected by levels of mortality, fertility, and migratory patterns characteristic of a given society. These in turn are affected by changing technology, social and economic conditions, and expectations. Every family experiences a typical sequence of events starting with courtship, marriage, childbearing, the departure of children from home, and the final stage of dissolution as one and then the other of the original couple dies. Not all families follow the same sequence or exhibit the same timing, while some stages are omitted entirely through the absence of child-bearing, or premature death. The timing and duration of the various stages are clearly influenced by the religious and cultural characteristics of the family, as well as the prevailing social, political, and economic climates.

The long-term trend of a declining mortality, and the relatively more rapid decline for women in recent decades have had considerable significance for changes in the family life cycle. Husbands and wives can expect an increasing period of time together after their last child has left home, while the wife can look forward to an increasing period of widowhood. The deeply-ingrained attitude that marriage was to be for a lifetime had a firm demographic basis in the past, when life expectancy was relatively low. Now, the extended period of the post-childbearing stage, combined with earlier retirement from employment, is changing the nature of marriage in the later years and is creating problems which have never had to be faced before. Perhaps the nature of the marital bond is not sufficiently strong to withstand drastic change in the later years of marriage or perhaps couples are not being prepared well enough through the socialization process to adapt to longer duration in marriage. If not, an increase in divorce, remarriage, and perhaps a return to the labor force in an occupation more suitable for older age groups may be expected. The contrasting nature of the early, middle, and late stages of the family life cycle have led some to speculate that perhaps serial monogamy — with a minimum of three marriages — might very well be the ideal solution to the problems created by an increasingly complex and changing family in the post-industrial world.

The introduction of more effective contraceptive technology, e.g., the pill, gives women interested in the planning of their families much greater control over the timing and spacing of their children. It is quite possible that this greater control will permit earlier marriage or non-marital cohabitation, and a longer period of time when both partners can participate in the labor force before having children and entering the childbearing stage. It may also facilitate the earlier return of the wife to the labor force by eliminating the higher order births that have represented planning and contraceptive failures in the past, after the desired family size had already been attained.

The increasing participation of females, and especially married females, in the labor force, which is expected to continue into the future, can only take place as attitudes towards early and uncontrolled reproductive behavior change. The downward extension of schooling into the pre-school years, establishment of day care centers for children, and the drive towards equality for women in employment will drastically alter the role-status relationships within the family and life styles for increasing numbers of families. Furthermore, increasing divorce and separation will intensify the pressure on women to re-enter the labor force in order to maintain their economic independence and care for their children.

The philosophy of continuing education, plus a general upgrading of educational attainment within the population may also affect husband-wife relationships, and by extending the period of family dependence for children will tend to shift greater responsibility to the wife to provide supplementary income. Continuing adult education and job retraining, necessitated by technological change in business and industry, may contribute to an incompatibility of interests and place additional stress on the marital relationship at a time when the childbearing responsibilities have been fulfilled and the parents have been freed from this traditional function.

In short, almost every major demographic trend has involved and affected the family in the past and will continue to be among the prime movers of future change. While some of the changes which have been discussed are obvious, insofar as their general consequences are concerned, only time will tell what the more specific effects will be for the individual and the family in the near future.

NOTES

Unless specifically noted to the contrary, all statistics incorporated in this article have been taken from official census publications released by Statistics Canada (formerly Dominion Bureau of Statistics). Materials from the 1971 census are used wherever possible.

1 Non-family groups include either related or unrelated persons living together, but not meeting the *census* criteria for ''families''. Examples of unrelated persons would be lodgers, employees, persons living in hotels and inmates of institutions.

2 Percent males married (fifteen years of age and older) increased from 55.2 to 64.9 percent between 1941 and 1971, with a similar increase for females. See *1971 Census of Canada, Population, Marital Status*, Bulletin 1.2-5, April, 1973 and Kalbach, W. E., and W. W. McVey, Jr., *The Demographic Bases of Canadian Society*, (Toronto: McGraw-Hill Co. of Canada, Ltd., 1971), Table 11:7, p. 277.

3 See the discussion of mortality in Kalbach and McVey, *op. cit.*, pp. 44-54 for an elaboration of trends and differentials in Canada.

4 Statistics Canada, *Vital Statistics, 1972*, Vol. II (Ottawa: Information Canada, 1974), table 14, pp. 82-83.

5 Dominion Bureau of Statistics, *1961 Census of Canada*, Bulletin 7.1-11 (Ottawa: The Queen's Printer, 1965), Table XII.

6 Census Division, Dominion Bureau of Statistics, "Some Characteristics of Husbands and Wives Indicated in the Census and Vital Statistics," Reference Paper No. 10, 1950, Ottawa.

7 Ostry, Sylvia, "Labor Force Participation and Childbearing Status," in *Demography and Educational Planning*, edited by B. Macleod, Monograph Series No. 7, (Toronto: The Ontario Institute for Studies in Education, 1970), pp. 143-156.

8 See Kalbach, W. E., and W. W. McVey, Jr., *op. cit*, pp. 289-292; also, Kalbach, W. E., *Impact of Immigration on Canada's Population* (Ottawa: The Queen's Printer, 1970), pp. 323-330.

9 Podoluk, J. R., *Income of Canadians* (Ottawa: The Queen's Printer, 1968). Table 6:11.

10 *Ibid*, pp. 123-150.

11 Kalbach, W. E., *op. cit*, Table 5.42, and pp. 326-330.

12 Kalbach, W. E., and W. W. McVey, Jr., *op. cit*, Fig. 13-5, p. 330.

13 Henripin, J., and J. Légaré, "Recent Trends in Canadian Fertility," *Canadian Review of Sociology and Anthropology*, 8(2), 1971, pp. 117-118.

14 *Ibid*.

15 Henripin, J., *Trends and Factors of Fertility in Canada*, Census Monograph of 1961, Statistics Canada, Ottawa, 1972.

Part Two

Comparative Family Organization and Interaction

4

Courtship and mate choice

All societies recognize that there are occasional violent emotional attachments between persons of opposite sex, but our present . . . culture is practically the only one which has attempted to capitalize these and make them the basis for marriage. Most groups regard them as unfortunate and point out the victims of such attachments as horrible examples. Their rarity in most societies suggests that they are psychological abnormalities to which our own culture has attached an extraordinary value just as other cultures have attached extreme values to other abnormalities.

Ralph Linton, The Study of Man, © *1936, Renewed 1964, p.*
175. By permission of Prentice-Hall Inc.,
Englewood Cliffs, N.J.

From the romantic point of view marriages are "made in heaven." People are "destined" to marry each other, brought together by "fate," "mysteriously attracted to each other," and marry even if families, friends, and their own minds demur. It does not occur to romanticists that marriage partners need qualifications to be suitable to each other. Choosing a mate sounds too cold and calculating, evoking images of impersonal checklists fed into a heartless computer. . . . In practice more couples are thrown together by accident than by either the magic of romance or the strategy of intelligence.

Robert Blood, Jr., Marriage, *2nd ed. (New York: Free Press, 1969), p. 36.*
Copyright © 1969 by The Free Press, a division of the Macmillan
Company. Copyright © 1962 by The Free Press of Glencoe.
Copyright 1955 by The Free Press, a corporation.

The introductory statements by Linton and Blood both reflect on the relative importance of heterosexual love in the choice of a mate. Linton argues that most cultures see romantic love as an evil force which tends to undermine the fabric of society. In a paper presented later in this chapter, Goode (1959) suggests that societies have developed various ways of controlling the development of love relationships. Blood, in contrast, suggests that the romantic ideal of love is over-valued and rare in Western society, and that most people come to "love" as an accident of age and social status.

Cross-cultural and sub-cultural variations in premarital mating and mate choice activities are widespread. This chapter emphasizes the centrality of the ways of becoming married to understanding the nature of a society, and discusses the characteristics of love and sex exchanges in courtship and the socio-cultural and socio-legal significance of the marital event.

Becoming married in cultural context

The choice of a mate, in view of the typical regulations and ceremonies involved, might be thought of as the cornerstone of the kinship system in most societies of the world. Encapsulated in the activities leading up to marriage and, in particular, the marriage event itself, are the basic features of kinship ideology, regulation, and practice. In another sense, culture itself is most explicitly illustrated by the ways of becoming married. It is little wonder that society has a substantial stake in marriage procedures.

The concern of society in the ways in which its members become married might be thought of as a continuum from maximum to minimum interest.[1] A conceptual model developed by Farber (1964), though somewhat different in perspective, is helpful in illustrating the characteristics of each end of the continuum. *Maximum societal interest* is represented by an emphasis on maintaining an identical system of values, beliefs, and practices over time. Each generation is expected to differ in no essential way from preceding generations. Children are socialized to be duplicates of their parents when they reach adulthood. The kinship system is not an initiator of change but a conserver of custom and tradition. In order to ensure the orderly replacement of culture by successive generations, Farber argues that at least three controls are necessary:

1. the allocation of authority and responsibility for judging and directing replacement to an individual or group outside the nuclear family;
2. the restriction of marriage to individuals who come from families with identical norms and values — to avoid familiarity with alternative values, contact between persons with different cultural backgrounds would also be restricted; and
3. in view of the time-linked bases for replacement, authority would necessarily be determined by age and experience rather than skill.

Under these conditions, an individual would have little control over whom he marries or the rearing of his offspring. Change and inappropriate values would be actively resisted.

Minimum societal interest reflects an absence of social regulations about whom or when one marries and how long one remains married. Each individual, whether unmarried or married, is theoretically available as a potential mate at any time.

---

1 The idea that ''society'' intrudes itself into the life space of individuals in a sense personalizes an abstract sociological construct. Even so, any group, regardless of size, concerned about its own stability and destiny will have an interest in the training of its new members (Inkles, 1968).

Marriage is not expected to last beyond the commitment of the individuals concerned. Marriage is a personal matter, and so mate choice is based on the desirability of the persons involved; marriage is maintained only if the desirability of one's spouse is greater than that of the available alternatives. In such societies, controls would be less visible and less direct: protection of individual rights, implicit segregation of people into similar social categories (age, education, occupation, residential area), and inculcation of ''responsible'' values.

The ''interests'' of societies vary systematically along this continuum. The potential conflict between individual autonomy (the right to determine one's own destiny) and orderly replacement of culture is resolved in different ways in different societies. It appears that most societies emphasize orderly replacement. The traditional joint Indian family (Gore, 1965), for example, required that the wife make all the adjustments, the husband take the family's side in every dispute, and that the family culture be perpetuated over generations. Accordingly, marriage involved three basic principles:

1. The marriage was arranged by elders; the couple had nothing to do with it. The selection involved *all* elders to ensure family acceptance. Marriage by arrangement prevented the possibility of prior loyalties, commitments or affection between the husband and wife which would lead to an emphasis on the conjugal relationship. A successful ''arrangement'' reinforced a kinship rather than conjugal identity.
2. The girl was chosen from another kinship system within the same caste group. This ensured a basic similarity in the values and practices of the two kinship groups and also reduced the likelihood of conflict between the wife and her husband's family.
3. Marriage took place prior to the puberty of the girl. Child marriage enabled the husband's kinship group to rear the wife in the appropriate rules and customs, and also permitted her some latitude in learning how to adjust to authority. The family was able to overlook minor aberrations from the rules in a child, while reinforcing change in the appropriate direction.

As Goode (1959) argues, child marriage is an efficient way of controlling the emergence of love-emotions because love between the sexes is rare prior to puberty. In addition, the young child has few resources available to oppose the marriage. A related form of control is infant betrothal, which means the elders decide who will marry whom when the child is born. According to a somewhat out-of-date film on Eskimos, *Angotee – A Story of an Eskimo Boy* (National Film Board of Canada, 1953), infant bethrothal was not uncommon in Eskimo tradition. The general principle of arranged marriage, regardless of when it occurs, is designed to reinforce the kinship rather than the conjugal bond. It is also commonly assumed that this technique is an efficient way of facilitating marital satisfaction and reducing marital disorganization (Kurian, 1961).

The controls described above are the most visible means in which society is involved in the ways of becoming married. In these situations, the choice of a mate is a matter to be settled between the kinship groups, not the individuals themselves. Choice of a mate is limited in at least two other basic ways: the eligible persons to whom one is exposed, and the socialized predispositions of the chooser toward potential mates. The opportunity to interact with a field of eligibles is severely restricted in some societies. Because of social isolation of the young from inappropriate potential spouses, the adolescent is forced to choose from among those available. As Goode points out (1959), this practice is most common in civilized societies among upper-class families who send their children to private schools and prohibit dating until mid-adolescence. Mate choice, although an individual decision, occurs within an approved social matrix.

Intramarriage rates are quite high among several religious and ethnic groups in Canada.[2] Most Hutterites, for example, marry Hutterites. Due to their relative insulation (protection from outside influence) and isolation (minimal contact with outsiders), Hutterite youth do not interact with non-Hutterite youth. Inter-colony celebrations or activities related to regular exchanges between colonies form the basis for most dating activity. Although the Hutterite youth is free to choose a mate, formal approval must be obtained from both sets of parents (Peter, 1971).

Similarly, Heer (1962) found that religious intramarriage varied from about 93 percent among Jews to 88 percent among Protestants in Canada in 1957.[3] More recent evidence suggests that intramarriage has decreased for many religious groups. About 76 percent of Jews still intramarry (Larson, 1971b). Mate choice is a function of selective exposure to certain types of persons *and* one's values (in this case, ethnic and religious values) predispose one to choose persons with similar values. In addition, the impact of socio-structural factors on access to potential mates cannot be overemphasized. The average person interacts with a highly select and relatively small number of people. Because of the age-segregation system of the school, associations are limited to one's own age cohort. Most women marry men their own age or slightly older. Similarly, because of residential segregation (whether directed or an artifact of intracity mobility), the average person interacts with people from families with similar occupational, educational, and income levels. These factors, combined with race, ethnicity, religion, and the particular personality characteristics of an individual, severely limit the number of eligible persons from among whom

2 Intramarriage and intermarriage are frequently referred to as endogamous and exogamous marriage, respectively. The terms refer to whether marriage occurs within one's social group or outside it.

3 Heer also demonstrated that intermarriage rates have consistently increased since 1922 for Canada as a whole and all provinces. Quebec, however, has changed the least.

one chooses a spouse.

Goode (1959) identifies one other area of societal control in becoming married. Several societies conceive of marriage as the beginning of a unique and sacred relationship. Love and/or sexual experiences which undermine the sanctity of marriage, as defined by a society, must be controlled. Accordingly, some societies supervise the courtship of engaged couples. Couples are not allowed to be alone together. Unchaperoned dates are seen as dangerous. For example, in a study of University of Puerto Rico students, randomly drawn, Hill (1955) found that 82 percent of the men and 74 percent of the women had never had an unchaperoned date. Although Canadian courtship is unsupervised, there is good reason to suspect that many couples "supervise" their own courting behavior because of their socialized predispositions concerning appropriate courtship activities.

The regulation of the marital event itself is also an indication of societal interest in becoming married. Though these controls are less visible than kinship control, Canadian marriage laws clearly reflect our society's interest in the commitment and seriousness of the parties wishing to marry.[4] The marriage licence is designed to ensure legal protection for both parties. The average waiting period of three days after the licence is obtained and before marriage, as well as the residence requirement, typically fifteen days, before a licence can be obtained, are intended to ensure a serious commitment to marriage. Quebec law is most explicit on this issue. Applicants must have lived in Quebec for six months and must post an $800 bond (a deposit) in order to obtain a marriage licence. Similarly, persons wishing a licence must fulfill several minimum requirements. These include evidence that the presentors aren't already married, do not have blood or affinal ties closer than first cousin, are not mentally ill or defective or under the influence of drugs or alcohol, and in several provinces, medical evidence that they do not have a social disease. In addition, persons under the age of eighteen are required to have parental consent to marry. Finally, the marital event itself must be solemnized in either a religious or civil ceremony in front of at least two witnesses in addition to the couple and the officiator. This ceremony is the clearest indication of the *public* nature of marriage. In a sense, this mutual action is a public statement of a removal of spouse options and an affirmation of monogamous commitment.

It is questionable whether these laws do ensure a serious commitment to marriage. In fact, waiting periods, blood tests, licences, and so forth are merely modest hurdles that most couples can overcome with extraordinary ease. These regulations are considerably less difficult than issues such as finding a place to live or deciding which ring to buy or whether to buy one at all. In a sense, the *public* nature of the

4 Most of this section is based on Chapman (1968). Students interested in the legal requirements for marriage and the provincial variations will find this book an excellent guide.

marriage event is a significant force against marriage; those who are willing to remove spouse options voluntarily are probably those who have a serious commitment. It would seem that in this society as well as others, the marital event itself is the most vivid indicator of commitment.

Courtship and mate choice in cultural context

The opportunity for premarital "activities", whatever their scope, is typically found in cultures which permit individuals, rather than parents or elders, to choose mates. The dating, love, and sexual experiences of couples, however, vary widely both cross-culturally and sub-culturally. After a history of coital experiences with many members of the opposite sex, the Trobriander male begins courtship by inviting a girl to sleep with him in his Bachelor's house (Malinowski, 1929). They are only together at night and the relationship remains exclusive until a decision is made to marry or to break up. If they break up, a second trial marriage is initiated, and others if necessary, until the "right" mate is found. When the decision to marry is finally made, the couple appear in public together for the first time. When the average Canadian boy or girl is beginning to take an active interest in the opposite sex, the male adolescent in the kibbutz is being assigned a bedroom which he will share with another boy and two girls (Spiro, 1965). Informal dating among the Hutterites begins between the ages of sixteen and eighteen and varies in length from three to five years. Serious dating involves the exchange of photographs. "Going steady" couples see each other infrequently but exchange letters regularly. The actual engagement and marriage of the couple takes place within a one-week time period (Peter, 1971).

Courtship generally involves several stages, which vary in number and definition. The courtship sequence typically includes at least these four stages: playing the field or dating around; selective dating (dating only a limited number of persons); going steady (dating one person exclusively); and engagement (the couple have decided to marry). Each dating stage involves a different set of expectations concerning appropriate male-female behavior (as defined by the couple themselves, their families, and the larger society). Puerto Rico is said to have seven stages of involvement, each of which involves specific expectations, beginning with a deliberate attempt by girls to attract the attention of boys by going where they are and dressing in obvious ways (Hill, 1955).

Data on courtship in the United States offers clear evidence of several courtship characteristics. First, sexual intimacy consistently increases with dating stage. Females, in particular, become more permissive in their sexual activities with their partners as their affection deepens. Males, in contrast, appear to decrease the amount and scope of their sexual activities as they become more emotionally involved with one female (Ehrmann, 1959; Reiss, 1967). Second, emotional intimacy, empathy (the capacity to take the role of the other), and agreement appear to increase with length and stage of courtship (Kirkpatrick and Hobart, 1954; Heiss, 1962; Murstein, 1972) to the time of engagement. In fact, it is more likely that areas of disagreement are de-emphasized and increasingly forgotten as one moves into more intimate courtship levels. The preceding characteristics appear to be applicable to most courting couples. Even so, the particular way in which courtship affects each individual and courting couple varies widely. The personality and perceptual skills, the reasons for dating (e.g., pleasure, mate choice, status-seeking, socialization), and the degree of commitment of each partner have an influence on the individual's development and change during courtship. Because two individuals involved in courtship are seldom the same, the ways in which they change as a couple also vary (Bolton, 1961; Lewis, 1973).

The conceptualization of courtship in terms of stages, however, isn't always directly applicable to the courtship experiences of couples in Western society. Many persons pass through a series of courtship involvements, each of which reflects both sexual and emotional intimacy at relatively intense levels. Farber (1964) argues that these experiences prepare the individual for permanent availability as a potential spouse even after marriage. Such an individual has the resilience to "switch" emotional commitments, as do people who experience multiple divorces. Similarly, some Canadians now participate in living together arrangements which frequently begin at the "going steady" stage. Further research needs to be carried out on the characteristics of multiple courtship involvements and alternative courting forms (e.g., trial marriage) in order to assess the impact of courtship stage on premarital attitudes and behaviors.

Whatever the scope of courtship intimacy, courting persons in Canada are expected, after a reasonable "trial and error" period, to choose a mate with whom they believe themselves to be "in love" and, on the basis of this love-commitment principle, eventually marry. It is believed that they marry this one because they are more "attracted" to this specific person than to any other. As Farber (1964) suggests, it appears that the key dimension of both love-relationships and love-marriages is the high *desirability*, in the individual's perspective, of one's mate.[5]

A Canadian replication of a study on the importance of romanticism in the choice of a mate (Theodorson, 1965), demonstrated that Canadian students appear to be at

---

5 According to Farber (1964), "desirable" persons might be thought to have a pleasing personality, interpersonal competence, and an attractive appearance. Physical characteristics appear to be an important part of the romantic language system.

least as romance oriented as their American counterparts.[6] In the original study, romanticism was defined in terms of the importance attached to physical attractiveness in mate choice and for wives after marriage, companionship in marriage, and marriage as a partnership. Americans were found to value romanticism nearly twice as much as Chinese students in Singapore. Burmese and Indian students, in that order, valued romanticism the least. Although the Wakil study (1973) found that students rank a pleasant personality, consideration, and understanding substantially above good looks (the latter ranked eleventh in the attributes of an ideal mate), it might also be argued that these attributes form part of a common attitudinal set toward desirability or attractiveness in the opposite sex.

If desirability is the key dimension in both love-relationships and love-marriages, then the more "desirable" persons are in a better competitive position in Western society, and will likely be objects of more widespread and intense interest. Similarly, the less desirable will be at a competitive disadvantage, and therefore will likely be less selective choosers and tend to marry earlier. It would seem that the significant role of "looking and acting just right" in Canadian dating and marriage activity cannot be over-emphasized in comparing Canadian culture with other societies.

SUMMARY

This chapter has shown the significance of societal controls in the choice of a mate, and the systematic patterns of courtship, where permitted, as individuals attempt to choose a mate for themselves. The interests of society are reflected in the practices of child marriage, infant marriage, controlled exposure to appropriate eligible mates, the supervision of courtship activity, age and social status segregation of societal members, and a socialization system designed to predispose persons to appropriate types of mates. Courtship, in many societies of the world, is an institutionalized device to enable persons to learn to relate to the opposite sex (socialization), to obtain entertainment and pleasure, and to choose an appropriate mate based on the love-relationship principle. It is suggested that the emphasis on love is significantly related to appearance in Canadian culture, and thus courtship should be seen as a competitive process in which there are both winners and losers.

The remainder of the chapter deals more explicitly with certain of the matters

---

6 The replication was conducted as part of laboratory exercises in an introductory sociology class at the University of Alberta. Some 500 students participated in the experiment in 1969. The results are unpublished.

discussed above. The first paper is concerned with the interests of society in the development of love and the mate choice process. Goode's definition of heterosexual love is critically assessed and an alternative, more realistic, definition is offered. Premarital sexual behavior and the development of love (positive affect) are discussed in some detail in the article by Hobart on sexual permissiveness and the article by Larson on heterosexual love. Relevant data collected in Canada is summarized.

The theoretical importance of love

In this paper, Professor Goode examines definitions of love in various societies. He suggests that heterosexual love is a universal psychological potential (a capacity inherent in every infant at birth). The primary contribution of this paper is its discussion of the ways in which different societies control the emergence and expression of love feelings between males and females. Societies which assign priority to kinship ties over conjugal ties may practise infant or child marriage or limit interactional opportunities to appropriate persons. In contrast, societies which permit individual mate choice are said to either supervise courting activity to maintain the exclusivity of marriage as the only acceptable male-female relationship *or* to encourage the development of love roles while indirectly regulating love ties through socio-structural limitations and implicit social pressures. This paper effectively illustrates the difference between "natural" heterosexual love and the acquisition of culturally appropriate "love roles".

The most effective societal control of love is not openly acknowledged. Through a quite deliberate process of socialization by parents, one's peer group and sexual subculture, as well as the mass media (advertising, music, theatre), the *romantic* and *double standard* love roles become part of the male and female symbolic and behavioral patterns (Udry, 1971: 58—181). A recent study of male and female attitudes toward attractiveness, and the linkages of these attitudes to parental and subcultural influences, conducted among junior high school students in Alberta and Saskatchewan found that male orientations were predominantly in terms of physical attributes (e.g., shape) and female orientations in terms of appearance (e.g., dress) (Berg, 1973). Similarly, the socialization process also predisposes one toward certain kinds of love orientations in view of the values toward the opposite sex that one has acquired. If one strongly believes in chastity, for example, this value will have a significant influence (control) on the ways in which one's love feelings will be expressed.

A weakness of this paper, in my view, is the definition of love which Goode provides. He defines love as a "strong emotional attachment, a cathexis, between adolescents or adults of opposite sexes, with at least the components of sex desire and tenderness". Although this definition effectively avoids the common conceptual mistake of specifying the kind of motivation essential to love, it errs in several respects. These concerns are carefully discussed in the article on heterosexual love.

The theoretical importance of love

William J. Goode

Because love often determines the intensity of an attraction[1] toward or away from an intimate relationship with another person, it can become one element in a decision or action.[2] Nevertheless, serious sociological attention has only infrequently been given to love. Moreover, analyses of love generally have been confined to mate choice in the Western world, while the structural importance of love has been for the most part ignored. The present paper views love in a broad perspective, focusing on the structural patterns by which societies keep in check the potentially disruptive effect of love relationships on mate choice and stratification systems.

Types of literature on love

For obvious reasons, the printed material on love is immense. For our present purposes, it may be classified as follows:

1. Poetic, humanistic, literary, erotic, pornographic: By far the largest body of all literature on love views it as a sweeping ex-

perience. The poet arouses our sympathy and empathy. The essayist enjoys, and asks the reader to enjoy, the interplay of people in love. The storyteller — Boccaccio, Chaucer, Dante — pulls back the curtain of human souls and lets the reader watch the intimate lives of others caught in an emotion we all know. Others — Vatsyayana, Ovid, William IX Count of Poitiers and Duke of Aquitaine, Marie de France, Andreas Capellanus — have written how-to-do-it books, that is, how to conduct oneself in love relations, to persuade others to succumb to one's love wishes, or to excite and satisfy one's sex partner.[3]

2. Marital counseling: Many modern sociologists have commented on the importance of romantic love in America and its lesser importance in other societies, and have disparaged it as a poor basis for marriage, or as immaturity. Perhaps the best known of these arguments are those of Ernest R. Mowrer, Ernest W. Burgess, Mabel A. Elliott, Andrew G. Truxal, Francis E. Merrill, and Ernest R. Groves.[4] The antithesis of romantic love, in such analyses, is

William J. Goode, Ph.D., is Professor of Sociology, Columbia University, New York.

From *American Sociological Review*, 24 (February, 1959), pp. 38-47. Reprinted with permission of the author and the American Sociological Association.

"conjugal" love; the love between a settled, domestic couple.

A few sociologists, remaining within this same evaluative context, have instead claimed that love also has salutary effects in our society. Thus, for example, William L. Kolb[5] has tried to demonstrate that the marital counselors who attack romantic love are really attacking some fundamental values of our larger society, such as individualism, freedom, and personality growth. Beigel[6] has argued that if the female is sexually repressed, only the psychotherapist or love can help her overcome her inhibitions. He claims further that one influence of love in our society is that it extenuates illicit sexual relations; he goes on to assert: "Seen in proper perspective, [love] has not only done no harm as a prerequisite to marriage, but it has mitigated the impact that a too-fast-moving and unorganized conversion to new socioeconomic constellations has had upon our whole culture and it has saved monogamous marriage from complete disorganization."

In addition, there is widespread comment among marriage analysts, that in a rootless society, with few common bases for companionship, romantic love holds a couple together long enough to allow them to begin marriage. That is, it functions to attract people powerfully together, and to hold them through the difficult first months of the marriage, when their different backgrounds would otherwise make an adjustment troublesome.

3. Although the writers cited above concede the structural importance of love implicitly, since they are arguing that it is either harmful or helpful to various values and goals of our society, a third group has given explicit if unsystematic attention to its structural importance. Here, most of the available propositions point to the functions of love, but a few deal with the conditions under which love relationships occur. They include:

(1) An implicit or assumed descriptive proposition is that love as a common prelude to and basis of marriage is rare, perhaps to be found as a pattern only in the United States.

(2) Most explanations of the conditions which create love are psychological, stemming from Freud's notion that love is "aim-inhibited sex."[7] This idea is expressed, for example, by Waller who says that love is an idealized passion which develops from the frustration of sex.[8] This proposition, although rather crudely stated and incorrect as a general explanation, is widely accepted.

(3) Of course, a predisposition to love is created by the socialization experience. Thus some textbooks on the family devote extended discussion to the ways in which our society socializes for love. The child, for example, is told that he or she will grow up to fall in love with someone, and early attempts are made to pair the child with children of the opposite sex. There is much joshing of children about falling in love; myths and stories about love and courtship are heard by children; and so on.

(4) A further proposition (the source of which I have not been able to locate) is that, in a society in which a very close attachment between parent and child prevails, a love complex is necessary in order to motivate the child to free him from his attachment to his parents.

(5) Love is also described as one final or crystallizing element in the decision to

marry, which is otherwise structured by factors such as class, ethnic origin, religion, education, and residence.

(6) Parsons has suggested three factors which "underlie the prominence of the romantic context in our culture": (a) the youth culture frees the individual from family attachments, thus permitting him to fall in love; (b) love is a substitute for the interlocking of kinship roles found in other societies, and thus motivates the individual to conform to proper marital role behavior; and (c) the structural isolation of the family so frees the married partners' affective inclinations that they are able to love one another.[9]

(7) Robert F. Winch has developed a theory of "complementary needs" which essentially states that the underlying dynamic in the process of falling in love is an interaction between (a) the perceived psychological attributes of one individual and (b) the complementary psychological attributes of the person falling in love, such that the needs of the latter are felt to be met by the perceived attributes of the former and vice versa. These needs are derived from Murray's list of personality characteristics. Winch thus does not attempt to solve the problem of why our society has a love complex, but how it is that specific individuals fall in love with each other rather than with someone else.[10]

(8) Winch and others have also analyzed the effect of love upon various institutions or social patterns: Love themes are prominently displayed in the media of entertainment and communication, in consumption patterns, and so on.[11]

4. Finally, there is the cross-cultural work of anthropologists, who in the main have ig-nored love as a factor of importance in kinship patterns. The implicit understanding seems to be that love as a pattern is found only in the United States, although of course individual cases of love are sometimes recorded. The term "love" is practically never found in indexes of anthropological monographs on specific societies or in general anthropology textbooks. It is perhaps not an exaggeration to say that Lowie's comment of a generation ago would still be accepted by a substantial number of anthropologists:

But of love among savages? . . . Passion, of course, is taken for granted; affection, which many travelers vouch for, might be conceded; but Love? Well, the romantic sentiment occurs in simpler conditions, as with us — in fiction. . . . So Love exists for the savage as it does for ourselves — in adolescence, in fiction, among the poetically minded.[12]

A still more skeptical opinion is Linton's scathing sneer:

All societies recognize that there are occasional violent, emotional attachments between persons of opposite sex, but our present American culture is practically the only one which has attempted to capitalize these, and make them the basis for marriage. . . . The hero of the modern American movie is always a romantic lover, just as the hero of the old Arab epic is always an epileptic. A cynic may suspect that in any ordinary population the percentage of individuals with a capacity for romantic love of the Hollywood type was about as large as that of persons able to throw genuine epileptic fits.[13]

In Murdock's book on kinship and marriage, there is almost no mention, if any, of love.[14] Should we therefore conclude that, cross-culturally, love is not important, and thus cannot be of great importance structurally? If there is only one significant case, perhaps it is safe to view love as generally unimportant in social structure and to concentrate rather on the nature and functions of romantic love within the Western societies in which love is obviously prevalent. As brought out below, however, many anthropologists have in fact described love *patterns*. And one of them, Max Gluckman,[15] has recently subsumed a wide range of observations under the broad principle that love relationships between husband and wife estrange the couple from their kin, who therefore try in various ways to undermine that love. This principle is applicable to many more societies (for example, China and India) than Gluckman himself discusses.

The problem and its conceptual clarification

The preceding propositions (except those denying that love is distributed widely) can be grouped under two main questions: What are the consequences of romantic love in the United States? How is the emotion of love aroused or created in our society? The present paper deals with the first question. For theoretical purposes both questions must be reformulated, however, since they implicitly refer only to our peculiar system of romantic love. Thus: (1) In what ways do various love patterns fit into the social structure, especially into the systems of mate choice and stratification? (2) What are the structural conditions under which a range of love patterns occurs in various societies? These are overlapping questions, but their starting point and assumptions are different. The first assumes that love relationships are a universal psycho-social possibility, and that different social systems make different adjustments to their potential disruptiveness. The second does not take love for granted, and supposes rather that such relationships will be rare unless certain structural factors are present. Since in both cases the analysis need not depend upon the correctness of the assumption, the problem may be chosen arbitrarily. Let us begin with the first.[16]

We face at once the problem of defining "love." Here, love is defined as a strong emotional attachment, a cathexis, between adolescents or adults of opposite sexes, with at least the components of sex desire and tenderness. Verbal definitions of this emotional relationship are notoriously open to attack; this one is not more likely to satisfy critics than others. Agreement is made difficult by value judgments: one critic would exclude anything but "true" love, another casts out "infatuation," another objects to "puppy love," while others would separate sex desire from love because sex presumably is degrading. Nevertheless, most of us have had the experience of love, just as we have been greedy, or melancholy, or moved by hate (defining "true" hate seems not to be a problem). The experience can be referred to without great ambiguity, and a refined measure of various degrees of intensity or purity of love is unnecessary for the aims of the present analysis.

Since love may be related in diverse ways to the social structure, it is necessary to forego the dichotomy of "romantic love — no romantic love" in favor of a continuum or range between polar types. At one pole, a strong love attraction is socially viewed as a laughable or tragic aberration; at the other, it is mildly shameful to marry without being in love with one's intended spouse. This is a gradation from negative sanction to positive approval, ranging at the same time from low or almost non-existent institutionalization of love to high institutionalization.

The urban middle classes of contemporary Western society, especially in United States, are found toward the latter pole. Japan and China, in spite of the important movement toward European patterns, fall toward the pole of low institutionalization. Village and urban India is farther toward the center, for there the ideal relationship has been one which at least generated love after marriage, and sometimes after bethrothal, in contrast with the mere respect owed between Japanese and Chinese spouses.[17] Greece after Alexander, Rome of the Empire, and perhaps the later period of the Roman Republic as well, are near the center, but somewhat toward the pole of institutionalization, for love matches appear to have increased in frequency — a trend denounced by moralists.[18]

This conceptual continuum helps to clarify our problem and to interpret the propositions reviewed above. Thus it may be noted, first, that individual love relationships may occur even in societies in which love is viewed as irrelevant to mate choice and excluded from the decision to marry. As Linton conceded, some violent love attachments may be found in any society. In our own, the Song of Solomon, Jacob's love of Rachel, and Michal's love for David are classic tales. The Mahabharata, the great Indian epic, includes love themes. Romantic love appears early in Japanese literature, and the use of Mt. Fuji as a locale for the suicide of star-crossed lovers is not a myth invented by editors of tabloids. There is the familiar tragic Chinese story to be found on the traditional "willow-plate," with its lovers transformed into doves. And so it goes — individual love relationship seems to occur everywhere. But this fact does not change the position of a society on the continuum.

Second, reading both Linton's and Lowie's comments in this new conceptual context reduces their theoretical importance, for they are both merely saying that people do not *live by* the romantic complex, here or anywhere else. Some few couples in love will brave social pressures, physical dangers, or the gods themselves, but nowhere is this usual. Violent, self-sufficient love is not common anywhere. In this respect, of course, the United States is not set apart from other systems.

Third, we can separate a *love pattern* from the romantic love *complex*. Under the former, love is a permissible, expected prelude to marriage, and a usual element of courtship — thus, at about the center of the continuum, but toward the pole of institutionalization. The romantic love complex (one pole of the continuum) includes, in addition, an ideological prescription that falling in love is a highly desirable basis of courtship and marriage; love is strongly institutionalized.[19] In contemporary United States, many individuals would even claim that entering marriage without being in love requires some such rationalization as asserting that one is too old for such romances or that one must "think of practical matters like money." To be sure, both anthropologists and sociologists often exaggerate the American commitment to romance;[20] nevertheless, a behavioral and value complex of this type is found here.

But this complex is rare. Perhaps only the following cultures possess the romantic love value complex: modern urban United States, Northwestern Europe, Polynesia, and the

European nobility of the eleventh and twelfth centuries.[21] Certainly, it is to be found in no other major civilization. On the other hand, the love *pattern*, which views love as a basis for the final decision to marry, may be relatively common.

Why love must be controlled

Since strong love attachments apparently can occur in any society and since (as we shall show) love is frequently a basis for and prelude to marriage, it must be controlled or channeled in some way. More specifically, the stratification and lineage patterns would be weakened greatly if love's potentially disruptive effects were not kept in check. The importance of this situation may be seen most clearly by considering one of the major functions of the family, status placement, which in every society links the structures of stratification, kinship lines, and mate choice. (To show how the very similar comments which have been made about sex are not quite correct would take us too far afield; in any event, to the extent that they are correct, the succeeding analysis applies equally to the control of sex.)

Both the child's placement in the social structure and choice of mates are socially important because both placement and choice link two kinship lines together. Courtship or mate choice, therefore, cannot be ignored by either family or society. To permit random mating would mean radical change in the existing social structure. If the family as a unit of society is important, then mate choice is too.

Kinfolk or immediate family can disregard the question of who marries whom, only if a marriage is not seen as a link between kin lines, only if no property, power, lineage honor, totemic relationships, and the like are believed to flow from the kin lines through the spouses to their offspring. Universally, however, these are believed to follow kin lines. Mate choice thus has consequences for the social structure. But love may affect mate choice. Both mate choice and love, therefore, are too important to be left to children.

The control of love

Since considerable energy and resources may be required to push youngsters who are in love into proper role behavior, love must be controlled *before* it appears. Love relationships must either be kept to a small number or they must be so directed that they do not run counter to the approved kinship linkages. There are only a few institutional patterns by which this control is achieved.

1. Certainly the simplest, and perhaps the most widely used, structural pattern for coping with this problem is child marriage. If the child is betrothed, married, or both before he has had any opportunity to interact intimately as an adolescent with other children, then he has no resources with which to oppose the marriage. He cannot earn a living, he is physically weak, and is socially dominated by his elders. Moreover, strong love attachments occur only rarely before puberty. An example of this pattern was to be found in India, where the young bride went to live with her husband in a marriage which was not physically consummated until much later, within his father's household.[22]

2. Often, child marriage is linked with a second structural pattern, in which the kinship rules define rather closely a class of

eligible future spouses. The marriage is determined by birth within narrow limits. Here, the major decision, which is made by elders, is *when* the marriage is to occur. Thus, among the Murngin, *galle*, the father's sister's child, is scheduled to marry *due*, the mother's brother's child.[23] In the case of the ''four-class'' double-descent system, each individual is a member of *both* a matri-moiety and a patri-moiety and must marry someone who belongs to neither; the four classes are (1) ego's own class, (2) those whose matri-moiety is the same as ego's but whose patri-moiety is different, (3) those who are in ego's patri-moiety but not in his matri-moiety, and (4) those who are in neither of ego's moieties, that is, who are in the cell diagonally from his own.[24] Problems arise at times under these systems if the appropriate kinship cell — for example, parallel cousin or cross-cousin — is empty.[25] But nowhere, apparently, is the definition so rigid as to exclude some choice and, therefore, some dickering, wrangling, and haggling between the elders of the two families.

3. A society can prevent widespread development of adolescent love relationships by socially isolating young people from potential mates, whether eligible or ineligible as spouses. Under such a pattern, elders can arrange the marriages of either children or adolescents with little likelihood that their plans will be disrupted by love attachments. Obviously, this arrangement cannot operate effectively in most primitive societies, where youngsters see one another rather frequently.[26]

Not only is this pattern more common in civilizations than in primitive societies, but is found more frequently in the upper social strata. *Social* segregation is difficult unless it is supported by physical segregation — the harem of Islam, the zenana of India[27] — or by a large household system with individuals whose duty it is to supervise nubile girls. Social segregation is thus expensive. Perhaps the best known example of simple social segregation was found in China, where youthful marriages took place between young people who had not previously met because they lived in different villages; they could not marry fellow-villagers since ideally almost all inhabitants belonged to the same *tsu*.[28]

It should be emphasized that the primary function of physical or social isolation in these cases is to minimize informal or intimate social interaction. Limited social contacts of a highly ritualized or formal type in the presence of elders, as in Japan, have a similar, if less extreme, result.[29]

4. A fourth type of pattern seems to exist, although it is not clear cut; and specific cases shade off toward types three and five. Here, there is close supervision by duennas or close relatives, but not actual social segregation. A high value is placed on female chastity (which perhaps is the case in every major civilization until its ''decadence'') viewed either as the product of self-restraint, as among the seventeenth-century Puritans, or as a marketable commodity. Thus love as play is not developed; marriage is supposed to be considered by the young as a duty and a possible family alliance. This pattern falls between types three and five because love is permitted before marriage, but only between eligibles. Ideally, it occurs only between a betrothed couple, and, except as marital love, there is no encouragement for it to appear at all. Family elders largely make the specific choice of mate, whether or not intermediaries carry out the arrangements. In the preliminary stages youngsters engage in

courtship under supervision, with the understanding that this will permit the development of affection prior to marriage.

I do not believe that the empirical data show where this pattern is prevalent, outside of Western civilization. The West is a special case, because of its peculiar relationship to Christianity, in which from its earliest days in Rome there has been a complex tension between asceticism and love. This type of limited love marked French, English, and Italian upper-class family life from the eleventh to the fourteenth centuries, as well as seventeenth-century Puritanism in England and New England.[30]

5. The fifth type of pattern permits or actually encourages love relationships, and love is a commonly expected element in mate choice. Choice in this system is *formally* free. In their teens youngsters begin their love play, with or without consummating sexual intercourse, within a group of peers. They may at times choose love partners whom they and others do not consider suitable spouses. Gradually, however, their range of choice is narrowed and eventually their affections center on one individual. This person is likely to be more eligible as a mate according to general social norms, and as judged by peers and parents, than the average individual with whom the youngster formerly indulged in love play.

For reasons that are not yet clear, this pattern is nearly always associated with a strong development of an adolescent peer-group system, although the latter may occur without the love pattern. One source of social control, then, is the individual's own teenage companions, who persistently rate the present and probable future accomplishments of each individual.[31]

Another source of control lies with the parents of both boy and girl. In our society, parents threaten, cajole, wheedle, bribe, and persuade their children to "go with the right people," during both the early love play and later courtship phases.[32] Primarily, they seek to control love relationships by influencing the informal social contacts of their children: moving to appropriate neighborhoods and schools, giving parties and helping to make out invitation lists, by making their children aware that certain individuals have ineligibility traits (race, religion, manners, tastes, clothing, and so on). Since youngsters fall in love with those with whom they associate, control over informal relationships also controls substantially the focus of affection. The results of such control are well known and are documented in the more than one hundred studies of homogamy in this country: most marriages take place between couples in the same class, religious, racial, and educational levels.

As Robert Wikman has shown in a generally unfamiliar (in the United States) but superb investigation, this pattern was found among eighteenth-century Swedish farmer adolescents, was widely distributed in other Germanic areas, and extends in time from the nineteenth century back to almost certainly the late Middle Ages.[33] In these cases, sexual intercourse was taken for granted, social contact was closely supervised by the peer group, and final consent to marriage was withheld or granted by the parents who owned the land.

Such cases are not confined to Western society. Polynesia exhibits a similar pattern, with some variation from society to society, the best known examples of which are perhaps Mead's Manu'ans and Firth's Tikopia.[34] Probably the most familiar Melanesian cases are the Trobriands and

Dobu,[35] where the systems resemble those of the Kiwai Papuans of the Trans-Fly and the Siuai Papuans of the Solomon Islands.[36] Linton found this pattern among the Tanala.[37] Although Radcliffe-Brown holds that the pattern is not common in Africa, it is clearly found among the Nuer, the Kgatla (Tswana-speaking), and the Bavenda (here, without sanctioned sexual intercourse).[38]

A more complete classification, making use of the distinctions suggested in this paper, would show, I believe, that a large minority of known societies exhibit this pattern. I would suggest, moreover, that such a study would reveal that the degree to which love is a usual, expected prelude to marriage is correlated with (1) the degree of free choice of mate permitted in the society and (2) the degree to which husband-wife solidarity is the strategic solidarity of the kinship structure.[39]

Love control and class

These socio-structural explanations of how love is controlled lead to a subsidiary but important hypothesis: From one society to another, and from one *class* to another within the same society, the socio-structural importance of maintaining kinship lines according to rule will be rated differently by the families within them. Consequently, the degree to which control over mate choice, and therefore over the prevalence of a love pattern among adolescents, will also vary. Since, within any stratified society, this concern with the maintenance of intact and acceptable kin lines will be greater in the upper strata, it follows that noble or upper strata will maintain stricter control over love and courtship behavior than lower strata. The

two correlations suggested in the preceding paragraph also apply: husband-wife solidarity is less strategic relative to clan solidarity in the upper than in the lower strata, and there is less free choice of mate.

Thus it is that, although in Polynesia generally most youngsters indulged in considerable love play, princesses were supervised strictly.[40] Similarly, in China, lower-class youngsters often met their spouses before marriage.[41] In our own society, the "upper upper" class maintains much greater control than the lower strata over the informal social contacts of their nubile young. Even among the Dobu, where there are few controls and little stratification, differences in control exist at the extremes: a child betrothal may be arranged between outstanding gardening families, who try to prevent their youngsters from being entangled with wastrel families.[42] In answer to my query about this pattern among the Nuer, Evans-Pritchard writes:

You are probably right that a wealthy man has more control over his son's affairs than a poor man. A man with several wives has a more authoritarian position in his home. Also, a man with many cattle is in a position to permit or refuse a son to marry, whereas a lad whose father is poor may have to depend on the support of kinsmen. In general, I would say that a Nuer father is not interested in the personal side of things. His son is free to marry any girl he likes and the father does not consider the selection to be his affair until the point is reached when cattle have to be discussed.[43]

The upper strata have much more at stake in the maintenance of the social structure and thus are more strongly motivated to control the courtship and marriage decisions of their young. Correspondingly, their young have much more to lose than lower-strata youth, so that upper-strata elders *can* wield more power.

Conclusion

In this analysis I have attempted to show the integration of love with various types of social structures. As against considerable contemporary opinion among both sociologists and anthropologists, I suggest that love is a universal psychological potential, which is controlled by a range of five structural patterns, all of which are attempts to see to it that youngsters do not make entirely free choices of their future spouses. Only if kin lines are unimportant, and this condition is found in no society as a whole, will entirely free choice be permitted. Some structural arrangements seek to prevent entirely the outbreak of love, while others harness it. Since the kin lines of the upper strata are of greater social importance to them than those of lower strata are to the lower-strata members, the former exercise a more effective control over this choice. Even where there is almost a formally free choice of mate — and I have suggested that this pattern is widespread, to be found among a substantial segment of the earth's societies — this choice is guided by peer group and parents toward a mate who will be acceptable to the kin and friend groupings. The theoretical importance of love is thus to be seen in the socio-structural patterns which are developed to keep it from disrupting existing social arrangements.

NOTES

1   On the psychological level, the motivational power of both love and sex is intensified by this curious fact (which I have not seen remarked on elsewhere): Love is the most projective of emotions, as sex is the most projective of drives; only with great difficulty can the attracted person believe that the object of his love or passion does not and will not reciprocate the feeling at all. Thus, the person may carry his action quite far, before accepting a rejection as genuine.

2   I have treated decision analysis extensively in an unpublished paper by that title.

3   Vatsyayana, *The Kama Sutra,* Delhi: Rajkamal, 1948; Ovid, "The Loves," and "Remedies of Love," in *The Art of Love*, Cambridge, Mass.: Harvard University Press, 1939; Andreas Capellanus, *The Art of Courtly Love*, translated by John J. Parry, New York: Columbia University Press, 1941; Paul Tuffrau, editor, *Marie de France: Les Lais de Marie de France*, Paris L'edition d'art, 1925; see also Julian Harris, *Marie de France*, New York: Institute of French Studies, 1930, esp. Chapter 3. All authors but the first *also* had the goal of writing literature.

4   Ernest R. Mowrer, *Family Disorganization*, Chicago: The University of Chicago Press, 1927, pp. 158-165; Ernest W. Burgess and Harvey J. Locke, *The Family*, New York: American Book, 1953, pp. 436-437; Mabel A. Elliott and Francis E. Merrill, *Social Disorganization*, New York: Harper, 1950, pp. 366-384; Andrew G. Truxal and Francis E. Merrill, *The Family in American Culture*, New York: Prentice-Hall, 1947, pp. 120-124, 507-509; Ernest R. Groves and Gladys Hoagland Groves, *The Contemporary American Family*, Philadelphia: Lippincott, 1947, pp. 321-324.

5   William L. Kolb, "Sociologically Established Norms and Democratic Values," *Social Forces*, 26 (May, 1948), pp. 451-456.

6   Hugo G. Beigel, "Romantic Love," *American Sociological Review*, 16 (June, 1951), pp. 326-334.

7   Sigmund Freud, *Group Psychology and the Analysis of the Ego*, London: Hogarth, 1922, p. 72.

8   Willard Waller, *The Family*, New York: Dryden, 1938, pp. 189-192.

9   Talcott Parsons, *Essays in Sociological Theory*, Glencoe, Ill.: Free Press, 1949, pp. 187-189.

10   Robert F. Winch, *Mate Selection*, New York: Harper, 1958.

11   See, e.g., Robert F. Winch, *The Modern Family*, New York: Holt, 1952, Chapter 14.

12   Robert H. Lowie, "Sex and Marriage," in John F. McDermott, editor, *The Sex Problem in Modern Society*, New York: Modern Library, 1931, p. 146.

13   Ralph Linton, *The Study of Man*, New York: Appleton-Century, 1936, p. 175.

14   George Peter Murdock, *Social Structure*, New York: Macmillan, 1949.

15   Max Gluckman, *Custom and Conflict in Africa*, Oxford: Basil Blackwell, 1955, Chapter 3.

16   I hope to deal with the second problem in another paper.

17   Tribal India, of course, is too heterogeneous to place in any one position on such a continuum. The question would have to be answered for each tribe. Obviously it is of less importance here whether China and Japan, in recent decades, have moved "two points over" toward the opposite pole of high approval of love relationships as a basis for marriage than that both systems as classically described viewed love as generally a tragedy; and love was supposed to be irrelevant to marriage, i.e., non-institutionalized. The continuum permits us to place a system at some position, once we have the descriptive data.

18   See Ludwig Friedländer, *Roman Life and Manners under the Early Empire* (Seventh Edition), translated by A. Magnus, New York: Dutton, 1908, Vol. 1, Chapter 5, "The Position of Women."

19   For a discussion of the relation between behavior patterns and the process of institutionalization, see my *After Divorce*, Glencoe, Ill.: Free Press, 1956, Chapter 15.

20   See Ernest W. Burgess and Paul W. Wallin, *Engagement and Marriage*, Philadelphia: Lippincott, 1953, Chapter 7, for the extent to which even the engaged are not blind to the defects of their beloveds. No one has ascertained the degree to which various age and sex groups in our society actually believe in some form of the ideology. Similarly, Margaret Mead in *Coming of Age in Samoa*, New York: Modern Library, 1953, rates Manu'an love as shallow, and though these Samoans give much attention to love-making, she asserts that they laughed with incredulous contempt at Romeo and Juliet (pp. 155-156). Though the individual sufferer showed jealousy and anger, the Manu'ans believed that a new love would quickly cure a betrayed lover (pp. 105-108). It is possible that Mead failed to understand the shallowness of love in our own society: Romantic love is, "in our civilization, inextricably bound up with ideas of monogamy, exclusiveness, jealousy, and undeviating fidelity" (p. 105). But these are ideas and ideology; *behavior* is rather different.

21   I am preparing an analysis of this case. The relation of "courtly love" to social structure is complicated.

22   Frieda M. Das, *Purdah*, New York: Vanguard, 1932; Kingsley Davis, *The Population of India and Pakistan*, Princeton: Princeton University Press, 1951, p. 112. There was a widespread custom of taking one's bride from a village other than one's own.

23   W. Lloyd Warner, *Black Civilization*, New York: Harper, 1937, pp. 82-84. They may also become "sweethearts" at puberty; see pp. 86-89.

24   See Murdock, *op. cit.*, pp. 53 ff. *et passim* for discussions of double-descent.

25   One adjustment in Australia was for the individuals to leave the tribe for a while, usually eloping, and then to return "reborn" under a different and now appropriate kinship designation. In any event, these marital prescriptions did not prevent love entirely. As Malinowski shows in his early summary of the Australian family systems, although every one of the tribes used the technique of infant betrothal (and close prescription of mate), no tribe was free of elopements, between either the unmarried or the married, and the "motive of sexual love" was always to be found in marriages

by elopement. B. Malinowski, *The Family Among the Australian Aborigines*, London: University of London Press, 1913, p. 83.

26   This pattern was apparently achieved in Manus, where on first menstruation the girl was removed from her playmates and kept at "home" — on stilts over a lagoon — under the close supervision of elders. The Manus were prudish, and love occurred rarely or never. Margaret Mead, *Growing Up in New Guinea*, in *From the South Seas*, New York: Morrow, 1939, pp. 163-166, 208.

27   See Das, *op. cit.*

28   For the activities of the *tsu*, see Hsien Chin Hu, *The Common Descent Group in China and Its Functions*, New York: Viking Fund Studies in Anthropology, 10 (1948). For the marriage process, see Marion J. Levy, *The Family Revolution in Modern China*, Cambridge: Harvard University Press, 1949, pp. 87-107. See also Olga Lang, *Chinese Family and Society*, New Haven: Yale University Press, 1946, for comparisons between the old and new systems. In one-half of 62 villages in Ting Hsien Experimental District in Hopei, the largest clan included 50 per cent of the families; in 25 per cent of the villages, the two largest clans held over 90 per cent of the families; I am indebted to Robert M. Marsh who has been carrying out a study of Ching mobility partly under my direction for this reference: F. C. H. Lee, *Ting Hsien. She-hui K'ai-K'uang t'iao-ch'a*, Peiping: Chunghua p'ing-min Chiao-yu ts'u-chin hui, 1932, p. 54. See also Sidney Gamble, *Ting Hsien: A North China Rural Community*, New York: International Secretariat of the Institute of Pacific Relations, 1954.

29   For Japan, see Shidzué Ishimoto, *Facing Two Ways*, New York: Farrar and Rinehart, 1935, Chapters 6, 8; John F. Embree, *Suye Mura*, Chicago: University of Chicago Press, 1950, Chapters 3, 6.

30   I do not mean, of course, to restrict this pattern to these times and places, but I am more certain of these. For the Puritans, see Edmund S. Morgan, *The Puritan Family*, Boston: Public Library, 1944. For the somewhat different practices in New York,

see Charles E. Ironside, *The Family in Colonial New York*, New York: Columbia University Press, 1942. See also: A. Abram, *English Life and Manners in the Later Middle Ages*, New York: Dutton, 1913, Chapters 4, 10; Emily J. Putnam, *The Lady*, New York: Sturgis and Walton, 1910, Chapter 4; James Gairdner, editor, *The Paston Letters*, 1422-1509, 4 vols., London: Arber, 1872-1875; Eileen Power, "The Position of Women," in C. G. Crump and E. F. Jacobs, editors, *The Legacy of the Middle Ages*, Oxford: Clarendon, 1926, pp. 414-416.

31   For those who believe that the young in the United States are totally deluded by love, or believe that love outranks every other consideration, see: Ernest W. Burgess and Paul W. Wallin, *Engagement and Marriage*, Philadelphia: Lippincott, 1953, pp. 217-238. Note Karl Robert V. Wikman, *Die Einleitung der Ehe. Acta Academiae Aboensis (Humaniora)*, 11 (1937), pp. 127 ff. Not only are reputations known because of close association among peers, but songs and poetry are sometimes composed about the girl or boy. Cf., for the Tikopia, Raymond Firth, *We the Tikopia*, New York: American Book, 1936, pp. 468 ff.; for the Siuai, Douglas L. Oliver, *Solomon Island Society*, Cambridge: Harvard University Press, 1955, pp. 146 ff. The Manu'ans made love in groups of three or four couples; cf. Mead, *Coming of Age in Samoa, op. cit.*, p. 92.

32   Marvin B. Sussman, "Parental Participation in Mate Selection and Its Effects Upon Family Continuity," *Social Forces*, 32 (October, 1953), pp. 76-81.

33   Wikman, *op. cit.*

34   Mead, *Coming of Age in Samoa*, pp. 97-108; and Firth, *op. cit.*, pp. 520 ff.

35   Thus Malinowski notes in his "Introduction" to Reo F. Fortune's *The Sorcerers of Dobu*, London: Routledge, 1932, p. xxiii, that the Dobu have similar patterns, the same type of courtship by trial and error, with a gradually tightening union.

36   Gunnar Landtman, *Kiwai Papuans of the Trans-Fly*, London: Macmillan, 1927, pp.

243 ff.; Oliver, *op. cit.*, pp. 153 ff.

37   The pattern apparently existed among the Marquesans as well, but since Linton never published a complete description of this Polynesian society, I omit it here. His fullest analysis, cluttered with secondary interpretations, is in Abram Kardiner, *Psychological Frontiers of Society*, New York: Columbia University Press, 1945. For the Tanala, see Ralph Linton, *The Tanala*, Chicago: Field Museum, 1933, pp. 300-303.

38   Thus, Radcliffe-Brown: "The African does not think of marriage as a union based on romantic love, although beauty as well as character and health are sought in the choice of a wife," in his "Introduction" to A. R. Radcliffe-Brown and W. C. Daryll Ford, editors, *African Systems of Kinship and Marriage*, London: Oxford University Press, 1950, p. 46. For the Nuer, see E. E. Evans-Pritchard, *Kinship and Marriage Among the Nuer*, Oxford: Clarendon, 1951, pp. 49-58. For the Kgatla see I. Schapera, *Married Life in an African Tribe*, New York: Sheridan, 1941, pp. 55 ff. For the Bavenda, although the report seems incomplete, see Hugh A. Stayt, *The Bavenda*, London: Oxford University Press, 1931, pp. 111 ff., 145 ff., 154.

39   The second correlation is developed from Marion J. Levy, *The Family Revolution in China*, Cambridge, Harvard University Press, 1949, p. 179. Levy's formulation ties "romantic love" to that solidarity, and is of little use because there is only one case, the Western culture complex. As he states it, it is almost so by definition.

40   E.g., Mead, *Coming of Age in Samoa*, pp. 79, 92, 97-109. Cf. also Firth, *op. cit.*, pp. 520 ff.

41   Although one must be cautious about China, this inference seems to be allowable from such comments as the following: "But the old men of China did not succeed in eliminating love from the life of the young women. . . . Poor and middle-class families could not afford to keep men and women in separate quarters, and Chinese also met their cousins. . . . Girls . . . sometimes even served customers in their parents' shops." Olga Lang, *op. cit.*, p. 33. According to Fried, farm girls would work in the fields, and farm girls of ten years and older were sent to the market to sell produce. They were also sent to towns and cities as servants. The peasant or pauper woman was not confined to the home and its immediate environs. Morton H. Fried, *Fabric of Chinese Society*, New York: Praeger, 1953, pp. 59-60. Also, Levy (*op. cit.*, p. 111): "Among peasant girls and among servant girls in gentry households some premarital experience was not uncommon, though certainly frowned upon. The methods of preventing such contact were isolation and chaperonage, both of which, in the 'traditional' picture, were more likely to break down in the two cases named than elsewhere."

42   Fortune, *op. cit.*, p. 30.

43   Personal letter, dated January 9, 1958. However, the Nuer father can still refuse if he believes the demands of the girl's people are unreasonable. In turn, the girl can cajole her parents to demand less.

Toward a conceptual model of heterosexual love

This paper was first written in 1966 in an attempt to apply exchange theory to heterosexual love, both to the development of love feelings prior to marriage and to the nature of love feelings in marriage. The literature review and the results of the exploratory study which provided essential support for the model are deleted from the revised edition of the model which appears here. The reader is encouraged to evaluate these ideas critically in seeking to define and describe love in Canadian society.

Toward a conceptual model of heterosexual love

Lyle E. Larson

Introduction

Love is central to human experience, even though its character and expression vary widely from culture to culture. Few scholars would argue the assertions that people in Western society marry for love; that love plays an important part in male-female relationships; or that male-female relationships are basic to on-going human affairs. However, little is known about the nature, expression, or development of heterosexual love. Even though love is profusely written about — from poetic and mythological narrative to academic and pseudo-empirical treatises — there is little empirical literature on the subject. The basic assumption of this paper is that love can be identified empirically.

This paper attempts to present a conceptual model of the nature and expression of heterosexual love, whether unmarried or married. Though the model in many respects is little more than a point of view, it has a sound basis in previous and current theory and research.

Two general questions are asked about heterosexual love in our society: (1) What is the essential nature of the heterosexual love relationship; and (2) To what source(s) may be traced the development and persistence of heterosexual love. Each of these questions is dealt with in turn below.[1]

Nature of heterosexual love in Western society

Definition of love. The first problem is to define "heterosexual love". Goode's (1959) definition of love is probably the most widely accepted. He defines love as a "strong emotional attachment, a cathexis, between adolescents or adults of opposite sexes, with at least the components of sex desire and tenderness". Although this definition effectively avoids the common conceptual mistake of specifying the kind of motivation essential to love, it errs in several respects.[2] In the first place, it implicitly suggests that love is a one-dimensional feeling with a single standard of expectation ("a *strong* emotional attachment"). In reality, love is not the ultimate result of a process. It is, rather, a *process* of interpersonal positive affect regulated by a range of expectations varying from weak to strong.

Secondly, the concept of "cathexis" implies the *concentration of psychic energy on one person*. It would seem that if love varies from weak to strong for a given couple or between individuals, this concept of love is certainly not widely characteristic of lovers. Furthermore, it is widely believed that people are capable of loving several people at the same time (Whitehurst, 1973). The key is not whether they can, however, but whether they are willing to.

Third, while tenderness is typically a part of a positive heterosexual love relationship, loving relationships aren't always tender. They are sometimes "rough" by choice. A lover also occasionally finds it necessary to be "unloving" in order to help his partner in the long run. The central issue is that the partners *mutually perceive* the affect to be positive. Finally, "sex desire", while usually part of heterosexual love, is not always present. There is both cross-class evidence (Green, 1941; Miller, 1953) and cross-cultural evidence (Gough, 1952; Stephens, 1963) to the effect that love and sex *can* be separate. As Udry suggests (1971), "for people who are *not* taught that sex and love must go together they do not."

A more appropriate definition of love should permit a range of emotional involvement, multiple loving, the possible absence of sex and tenderness, and emphasize *perceived* mutual positive feelings. While both persons in a heterosexual relationship may not love each other, in order for heterosexual love to exist in a relationship, at least one person must perceive that it is mutual, however wrong he or she may be. In this tradition, heterosexual love might be defined as the perception of mutual positive affect.

It may be emphasized that love and liking are not the same. Liking is intellectual rather than emotional. Liking or disliking tends to be based on dispositions toward others based on some rationale. Love, in contrast, is not an intellectual concept but an emotional concept. It is not necessarily based on reason. Typically, loving and liking go together. However it can readily be seen, for example, that it is possible to love one's mother even though one doesn't like what she believes in. Similarly, Jane may love Robert even though she doesn't like his irreligious behavior. Hate, in contrast, is an emotion and can be defined as "negative affect". Hate and love need not be reasonable but are nonetheless difficult to maintain when one's partner has contradictory emotions; i.e., it is difficult to hate someone who loves you and it is difficult to love someone who hates you.

The nature of what positive affect *ought* to be in our society is widely discussed in the literature, but there is neglect of what positive affect *is*. Whether love should be long-suffering and gentle, or passionate and demanding, are questions which need not be considered in this paper. Instead, the central quest is to determine the salient characteristics of heterosexual love without reference to their functional or dysfunctional value.

Love is learned. Since love attachments, in various forms, can occur in any society, and since the love-sex configuration is equally divergent from society to society, it is well to ask the source of Western patterns. It is clear that cross-cultural variations do not lend support to a simple biological or psychological explanation. In fact, one must concede that whatever innate inclinations toward love and sex exist are repressed (if not erased), ignored, allowed to develop, supported, or even nurtured by the role performance demands of the social system. Hence, the patterns of love and sex expression in our society are largely a result of past and current socialization — the learning of social roles. Acknowledgement of the fundamentals of socialization will help clarify the nature of the transmission and maintenance of Western love and sex values and patterns of behavior.

It can be seen that the organizational and normative structures of our society are systematized influences on the individual throughout his life cycle. The persons (individual family members, particular teachers, friends or other significant others) and groups (family, peers, organizations) with which the individual has or has had contact are important sources of power and support, resource and sanction, and role-models. These impingent forces regulate the role-learning process. In addition, these primary units mediate or filter the effects of organizations or a normative system with which the individual is not directly involved (cf. Larson, 1969).

Thus, the child, endowed with the proclivity for love and sex, need not rely on these urges alone. They are nurtured and manipulated by formal and informal means. Mothers and fathers are married because they are in love; they show physical affection because they are in love; they have John and Sue, their children, because they are in love; older brother, Mike, acts so funny because

he is in love. Through these sources of influence, among others, the child comes to conceive of no viable alternative to similar patterns.

In addition, the youngster is besieged by love songs, movies, television shows, and commercials which tell the story of falling in love and what one does when one loves. These stimuli, together with the value-system acquired from those the child counts most important, serve to provide the growing child with a fairly clear idea of the limitations placed on the field of eligibles, when love can legitimately occur, what to expect when it occurs, and what to do when it occurs. Udry (1966) succinctly says:

By mid-adolescence, whatever psychological proclivity for love there is in human beings has been powerfully reinforced and elaborated into a compelling set of expectations to use the emotional responses one has rehearsed and stored in readiness. The adolescent in American Society should have developed an overpowering need to fall in love, and he usually does (pp. 181-182).

Past socialization, however, does not stand as the lone predictor of current love behavior. Socialization is a life-long process. The confrontation with differing value systems, the type of situation, and social pressure from family or peers, facilitate change in attitudes toward love as well as in heterosexual love behavior. Thus, because our culture upholds an increase in love involvement with dating, a relationship may be expected between dating stage and attitudes toward love, attitudes toward dating partner, and the intensity of emotional involvement.

By far the most significant single element in the nature of love and sex expression in our society, however, is the development of sex-roles. Every facet of heterosexual love, love orientation, development of love, sexual behavior, the relationship of sex to love, appears to be intensely connected to one's learned sex-role. Sex-role socialization appears to have profound importance through, and including, the early stages of dating in adolescence. In the higher stages of love development sex differences appear to be outweighed by the socialization for love process. Soon after the marriage however, sex-role expectation appears to return as a crucial explanatory variable in heterosexual love behavior.

Sex-role is strongly related to the widely used concepts of femininity and masculinity. These are not idle passwords in our society. They denote distinctive value systems: the compliant, passive, and dependent female; the independent, aggressive, and self-assertive male. These identities are assigned arbitrarily at infancy and thereafter nurtured by both parents and peers.

Early in the child's career, generally soon after entering school, the sexes enter a prolonged period of "culture-class" segregation during which the traits that characterize male and female love and sex behavior in adolescence and early adulthood are developed (Didato and Kennedy, 1956). Groups are held together by rewards for obedient role performance and punishment for role failure. Although the formalized character of this segregation has declined, the implicit content of the expectations remain.

The young male's goals are achieving independence, learning emotional control, and experiencing sexual conquest. In a very real sense these characteristics comprise the male personality organization. In addition, the male acquires status through a display of sexual knowledge, a command of sexual language, and sexual escapades (Ehrmann, 1959). Sex is seen as a physical act, divorced from emotional involvement. One does not achieve status among one's peers by simply dating the most sought-after girl so much as by seducing her (Kirkendall, 1961).

The young female, however, is concerned with social activity, popularity, and attractiveness. While males master a vocabulary about sex, young females learn the jargon of clothes and fashion. Males gloat over their sexual accomplishments; girls hide their sexual activities or attempt to justify them as expressions of love (Ehrmann, 1959). While boys attempt to take from a relationship, girls debate how much to give to the relationship.[3]

In sum, it may be seen that heterosexual love in our society is often the behavioral expression of the normative expectations for the sex-role the individual occupies. Furthermore, the orientation toward heterosexual love and the manner and character of the development of love are connected inherently to the identification with one's learned sex-role and numerous "socialization for love" experiences. Whatever the psychological or biological impulse felt by the individual in heterosexual contact, and the subsequent established relationship, it seems that they are regulated not only by expectations but also by the learned responses to specific stimuli.

Love is multidimensional. Heterosexual love does not have a single character. The content of positive affect, on the contrary, varies from individual to individual. That which draws two persons of the opposite sex together may be nothing more than sexual convenience for some; for others it may be companionship. The particular value orientation a person holds concerning heterosexual love reflects the general value system through which and by which the person conducts his daily affairs. Although previously learned and altered by the situation itself (as discussed above), the individual's attitudes do have an influence on his relationships with the opposite sex. Three basic heterosexual love orientations may be identified as having systematic and long-range effects on heterosexual relationships: the *sexual* (''I will love her as long as she gives me what I need''); the *companion* (''I will love her as long as she loves me''); and the *altruist* (''I will love her even if she stops loving me''). These are, of course, ideal types. Evidence of the prevalence of sexual and companion orientations toward love is widely available. While the altruist concept is not normally considered part of a heterosexual relationship, its possibility makes logical sense. All heterosexual positive affect undoubtedly contains elements of each orientation. However, it may be expected that persons having a basic sexual orientation to heterosexual love will demonstrate a higher intensity on this dimension than on the other two. A similar expectation may be held for the companion and altruist orientations as well.

Persons espousing a *sexual* perspective of heterosexual love see sex as the most important element in human expression. For them, love can neither exist nor persist without sex.[4] Love continues as long as the individual's sexual needs are being gratified. It is expected, also, that this dimension is applicable to those who look to love as a means of self-gratification and who need fulfillment, sexual or not.

Those espousing a *companion* perspective of heterosexual love, however, recognize the value and importance of sex but rate it secondary to such factors as togetherness, friendship, communication, and happiness. The emphasis is on mutuality and agreement — one will continue to love as long as one is loved in return. This view of love is quite similar to the Greek concept of ''filial'' love, which means loving those who love you. The importance of companionship is emphasized in Western marriage to a considerably greater extent than in cultures in which kinship systems have greater importance than the conjugal unit. In fact, most find a *weak* companionship bond just cause for ending the relationship.

The third type of orientation has been called *altruistic*. Its character is different from either the sexual or companion orientation, in that love is given without expecting love in return. Although altruistic love has an object similar to that of the other two types of love, it need not be reciprocal or mutual. The true altruist is other-centered. He will love, even though it is costly to himself, in preference to seeing others rewarded.

Though this orientation may be held by those having a sexual or companion orientation, its fullest expression is found when sexual and companion needs are unmet, yet the relationship endures because of positive affect. Altruism is similar to the Greek love concept of ''agape''. Agape finds its fullest expression in difficult and costly situations: ''Love your enemies . . . do good to them that hate you . . .'' (Matthew 5:44). The humanistic perspective of loving those who do not return that love (in contrast to those who hate or destroy in return), however, is probably closer to the concept used in this typology.

Love is interpersonal. Heterosexual love is also an interpersonal rather than an intrapersonal process. The ''absence makes the heart grow fonder'' theory does not generally work for the average person. Love is a relational concept. It develops, persists, or breaks down within an interpersonal relationship. Persons in love whose relationship is severed by distance, for whatever reason, generally may be expected to build new relationships through simple contact with new members of the opposite sex.[5]

There are, of course, exceptions to this rule. Individuals who have difficulty mixing with others of the opposite sex (the bashful) will continue to find their existence in their ''love'' in spite of distance. It may also be expected that conditions such as marginality, alienation, or ideological commitment (e.g., strong religious commitment) will facilitate the maintenance of previous or present positive affect, even through spatial separation. The length of time separated will, of course, be an important factor. In terms of a developmental model, couples who have established an interdependent relationship either through habit or need fulfillment, will find it more difficult to be separated or to establish new relationships. Furthermore, love may persist, even in the partner's absence, because of perceived expectations, social pressure from a group or person with whom the person identifies, or by internalization of the expectations so completely that the person cannot conceive of any alternative.

Love is developmental. The most central characteristic of heterosexual love is that it is developmental. Time and frequency of contact increase the degree of positive affect to a mutually satisfactory stage. The particular stage or intensity of positive affect reached will depend largely on what the individuals expect in their relationship. The time required to achieve mutual expectations will vary widely from couple to couple. For some, an evening may be sufficient; for others several years may be necessary. Though the stages may run together for some, and be considerably spread out for others, they are clearly identifiable.

Figure 1 presents the character of heterosexual love development. Within the limits imposed by the socio-cultural structure, heterosexual contacts are made. These contacts may be *expedient* (e.g., a clerk-customer relationship or teacher-student relationship); *accidental* (e.g., conversation while waiting for the stoplight to change); or *planned* (e.g., varying from a blind date to an overt contact). What most often follows the heterosexual contact may be called the process of *estimation*. This refers to the sometimes unconscious activity of mutual assessment in which the individuals determine the relative value of continuing, repeating, or ending the contact. The *rewards* (the qualities of the opposite sex partner and the relative benefits derivable from establishing a relationship) are compared with the *costs* (the value of other rewards given up) to determine the degree of profit or loss. Attraction, or the beginning of positive affect, will occur when the *outcome* (the profit and loss statement) is above the minimum level of expected reward from a heterosexual relationship, often referred to as ''the comparison level''.[6] The type of reward expected and the minimum level of expectations will, of course, depend on an individual's orientation toward heterosexual love, past experience in comparable relationships, his judgment as to what others like himself are receiving, and his motivation in seeking to establish a heterosexual relationship.

The life-long interpersonal process referred to as *bargaining* often occurs with the

Figure 1 Development of Heterosexual Positive Affect

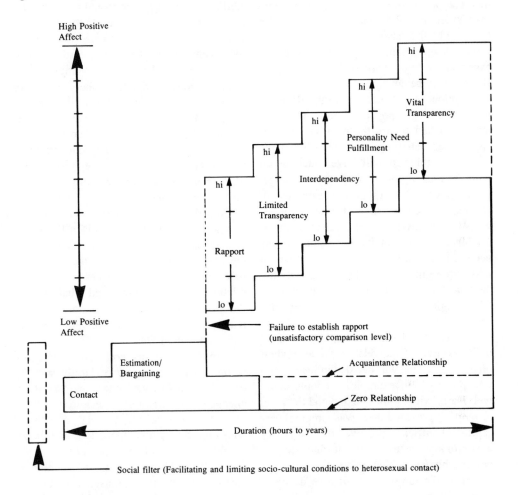

Social filter (Facilitating and limiting socio-cultural conditions to heterosexual contact)

process of estimation or shortly thereafter, though it recurs repeatedly in the early stages of non-marital love and seems to be a central feature of marital interaction. Its later expression is strongly connected to the character of its initial establishment. There are two essential functions of bargaining: (1) to emphasize the rewards and minimize the costs of the relationship; and (2) to determine the acceptable guidelines for the conduct of the relationship. Often the person having the greatest degree of outcome in terms of the comparison level will be in the best bargaining position. Whether the individuals involved will be able to establish rapport and thus enter the first stage (the first step in the staircase, see figure 1) in the development of heterosexual love will depend largely on the comparison level for alternatives (whether this relationship obtains a greater profit ratio than other available relationships) and the outcome of the bargaining process.[7]

The development of *rapport* ("I feel at ease when with my partner") with the opposite sex may be conceived as a developmental emotional task[8] essential to the development of stronger positive affect. This step must be taken before the next step can be approached. The degree or intensity of the rapport established will have much to do with the relative intensity of the next stage. Thus, if only low rapport is established, progress to the next stage, if it occurs at all, will be at a low level. Rapport may not be established immediately. For some, it may occur during the initial contact; for others it may require many contacts. (Continual contacts without rapport can only occur when the potential rewards outweigh the comparison level.)

A couple need not climb the "staircase" to be assured of the relative value of their relationship. That was decided in the estimation process. For example, a couple could well marry without moving beyond the level of rapport, provided there was a mutual perception of sufficient positive affect to justify a continuous relationship. It may be expected, however, that relationships established on the lower levels of love development will be more readily susceptible to "greener grass on the other side of the fence". It is questionable whether rapport is sufficient to establish exclusive relationships at all. Thus, it may be expected that "multiple loves" will occur considerably more often among those in the lower stages than among those in the higher stages of love development.

The exchange model of interpersonal attractions would suggest two basic possibilities: a change in costs and rewards; or a change in comparison level. In the first case, costs and rewards may change through (a) past exchanges which shift reward-cost values of current behaviors, (b) changes in the characteristics of dyad members occurring through training, education, or other experiences, (c) changes in external circumstances that introduce new rewards and costs or modify the values of old ones, (d) sequential factors in the relation itself, or (e) associations with other behaviors having different reward-cost values.

Even though the costs-rewards ratio may remain the same, the comparison level may change through the everyday experience of the reward-cost ratio within the dyad, the perception of the experiences of others in relations like one's own, and what each of the participants estimates he might legitimately expect in alternative relations (Secord and Backman, 1974).

Ivan Nye and his colleagues have developed a partial theory of family stability based on many of the same principles of exchange theory. Stability is seen to be a function of positive affect, internal or external constraint felt against disruption, and the attractiveness of alternative roles (Nye, et al., 1966). It would seem that these general explanations for stable relationships are applicable to all forms of heterosexual interaction. It might also be emphasized that multiple love is not always incompatible with higher levels of love *as long as it is mutually acceptable.*

Infatuation is not part of this model. Infatuation is nothing more or less than heterosexual positive affect occurring before it is supposed to, with someone that it is not supposed to, or occurring with someone previous to the current relationship which is conceived to involve "real" positive affect. Kephart (1967) recently explored the incidence of romantic experiences among males and females. It appears that infatuation is sufficient positive affect to consider the relationship important. Kephart's treatment fits nicely into a model in which a series of "infatuations" may be considered sequential loves, while simultaneous "infatuations" may be considered multiple loves.

The second major stage in the development of love has been labeled *limited transparency* ("I feel free to tell my partner things I would not generally tell anyone else") rather than self-revelation, as used by Reiss (1960) to avoid the idea of self-discovery. The emphasis of this stage is upon the progressive revealing of one's aspirations, plans, and problems normally not shared with others. This stage represents the beginning of a commitment to an exclusive relationship. This period is crucial in determining whether positive affect will continue to develop or whether it will stabilize or decline.

The development of *mutual dependencies* ("I feel incomplete when I am not with my partner" or "Nothing seems to go right when we miss a date") or interdependent habit systems is the third stage. A natural step in the process of coming to depend on the satisfactions derived from the relationship, the forming of a habit is perhaps the most important element in the stability of heterosexual love. Relationships which provide continual reward, once acquired, are difficult to give up. In the absence of similar alternatives, loneliness and frustration naturally result. Nonetheless, habits can be broken through separation or overt effort. It is more difficult, however, to transfer allegiance at this stage in the development of love than at previous stages. It may be emphasized that these are not simply habits of being together (like every afternoon for coffee) but the habit of feeling rapport and sharing some intimate aspects of one's self.

The fourth stage in the increasing intensity of positive affect is *fulfillment of personality needs* ("My partner seems to be strongest in areas in which I am weak"). Whether these are real needs, or whether they are simply believed to be real by the individuals involved (the latter seems more realistic), is inconsequential when one considers the fact that most people perceive that certain needs are fulfilled by heterosexual love. The ideas of self-actualization, self-awareness, self-revelation, and the recognition of the contribution of one's lover to the relationship are central to this conception of need fulfillment.

The final stage is referred to as *vital transparency* ("I find it easy and natural to be *totally* honest and open with my partner"). In contrast to limited transparency, in which the emphasis is upon getting to know one another better, vital transparency is used to convey the idea of total openness. It is characterized by a mutual willingness to engage in total self-exposure with the mutual assurance of complete trust and acceptance. The term *vital* is used to denote the excitement and vibrancy of a relationship of mutual interest and effort, in preference to the term "total", used to describe a relationship in which there is no privacy or privilege of separate pursuit.[9]

The measurement of the character of heterosexual love development may be further facilitated by the perceived *quality* (attraction, enjoyment, acceptance) of the relationship and the degree of *commitment* (emotional involvement, importance, dependence) to one's opposite sex partner. It may be expected that the relative quality of the relationship will be established rather early in the development of love, whereas commitment may be expected to occur in the more advanced stages of love development.

There are several issues relating to the staircase model of the development of love which may now be discussed. First, it is apparent that the heterosexual orientations (sexual, companion, altruist), or the motivations in continuing a particular relationship (status-seeking, recreation, socialization, or courtship),[10] or even the steps on the staircase may not be the same for the individuals within the dyad. The question of possible disparity (or lack of mutuality) in heterosexual love orientations, motivations in dating, or in stages of love development in a heterosexual relationship is a perplexing question. It is apparent in the model of love development presented that mutuality is essential. Nonetheless, there is little doubt that a person may deceive, take undue advantage, and betray confidences in a heterosexual relationship. It may be expected, of course, that when individual A considers his relationship more important with individual B than individual B does with individual A that B is in a better position to control the relationship; B may thus more readily deceive and take advantage of A than A of B — see Skipper and Nass, 1966. The nature of the relationship established will depend on the related processes of estimation and bargaining. If A perceives the comparison level of outcome to be substantial enough in the beginning, A will tolerate greater disparities. Thus, the greater the control of B over A the greater the degree of disparity accepted by A and, concomitantly, where A feels positive affect toward B the lower the awareness of the disparity. In terms of the conceptual model of heterosexual love presented in this paper, relationships besieged with disparities will be neither exclusive nor durable, even though marriage may occur. The greater the disparity in level of love development, the greater the distress and frustration of the deceived. It would seem justifiable to assert that little is known about the characteristics of the individual described above as A who would forego mutuality, if necessary, just to maintain the relationship.

It may also be suggested, however, that not all disparities should be defined as enduring or stressful. Disparities may be expected to fluctuate from day to day because of the relative instability of emotions. Emotions may "bounce" from love to hate, for example, when a girl catches her boyfriend flirting with another girl. Orientations toward love (sexual, companion, altruist) may also vary. Sexual orientations may well be the predominant "operational" approach to love in one situation, even though the more basic and typical orientation is companionship. Similarly, the motivations for being together vary within individuals in different situations. With regard to the staircase of love itself, there is no reason to assume that both individuals will always interact at the same level. It would not be uncommon for individuals to experience what might be dubbed the "up the down staircase phenomenon". Reaching a particular step in love development only means that this aspect of love interaction is now part of the interactional repertoire. Until this stage of interaction becomes a regularized feature of the interaction, there will be much walking up and down the steps. Certain situations will return one individual to a lower stage (such as rapport) while the partner may remain at the limited transparency stage. Other situations will encourage the couple to try higher steps in the development of their relationship. In this sense, love is dynamic, involving experimentation with different aspects of intimacy, retreat and hesitancy, attempts to disclose to and to obtain disclosure from one's partner, checking and double checking meanings, determining costs and rewards for sharing and withholding, and reviewing the value and implications of differences in orientation, motivation, and stage of development with respect to changing emotions.

The relationship of the staircase of love development to sexual behavior may be readily seen. Any form of sexual expression (touching to coitus) may occur as part of any stage of love development, providing the attitudes toward its expression are mutually favorable. Sexual exchange, it may be emphasized, need not require rapport or any degree of positive affect. It requires only mutual willingness. The prostitute-customer relationship, for example, need not involve more than *expedient* heterosexual contact. As long as a couple "estimate" their sexual experience to be rewarding, sexual intercourse may readily occur. However, given the pronounced evidence that sexual sharing is an act of interpersonal communication, it may be expected that sexual experience will be considerably more satisfying at the higher levels of love development (cf. Masters and Johnson, 1975).

Summary

The major assumptions of this approach to heterosexual love are summarized below.

1. Heterosexual love is defined as the mutual perception of positive affect between persons of the opposite sex.
2. Heterosexual love behavior in Western society is frequently an expression of the expectations others hold as to how a person must, ought to, ought not to, or must not behave in particular situations.
3. The degree of positive affect considered sufficient to establish an enduring relationship varies widely from couple to couple.
4. The sexual, companion, and altruist orientations toward heterosexual love have a distinctive influence on the character of heterosexual relationships.
5. Heterosexual love is an interpersonal rather than an intrapersonal process. It develops, is sustained, or breaks down within an interpersonal relationship.
6. The development of heterosexual love is an ordered, step-by-step and cumulative process — herein referred to as the "staircase of heterosexual love". The stages of love development are: rapport, limited transparency, mutual dependency, personality need fulfillment, and vital transparency.

NOTES

1 This analysis is limited to Western society. The model does not deal specifically with such questions as: Is love found in all societies? How is love controlled in various societies? What kinds of conditions facilitate the development of certain patterns of love while hindering others? An excellent discussion of the ways in which love patterns fit into other cultures as well as a defense of the hypothesis that love is a universal psychological potential may be obtained in Goode (1959). This model focuses, instead, on the character and expression of heterosexual love. As the structural

limitations and supports, its class variations, etc., are not explored in this paper, the model may be considered more socio-psychological than sociological. It may also be noted that this conceptual attempt, in terms of current theoretical terminology, may be best classified as a "frame of reference". Although a number of concepts are defined and certain of the relationships among the concepts are suggested, considerable work remains to be done. For a discussion of conceptual frameworks in relation to theory see Hill and Hansen (1960).

2 It may be noted that Goode took pains to point out that his definition of love would not be above criticism. Furthermore, as he points out, the purpose of his definition was not to eliminate conceptual ambiguity. Unfortunately, however, the definition has been widely used as if it were conceptually pure. Consequently, it is necessary to attempt to eliminate the ambiguity and develop a more widely usable definition of heterosexual love. It is apparent in Goode's article that love is seen as a continuum and an interpersonal process. The anachronism lies in the fact that the discussion and analysis of love followed a path almost totally unrelated to the definition of the concept given. It would seem that there ought to have been considerable correspondence between the concept and its usage.

3 Much of the discussion concerning the development of sex roles is based on several excellent chapters on this topic in the recently published text by Udry (1974).

4 The erotic dimension of hetero-human relationships has been widely exploited for commercial gain. In advertising, for example, "sexy sell" seems to be the secret to an increase in sales. Crestwood Advertising, Inc. credits a sultry woman's coy phrase "Had any lately?" to have been instrumental in a 48 percent increase in the sales of Chateau Martin champagne, vermouth and wine (Time, 1966). There is little doubt that advertising, the press, theatre, etc., have an important influence on one's conception of love.

5 This paper does not deal with the numerous social, as well as interpersonal, factors such as age, race, social class, education and religion which limit the field of eligibles. These factors determine, to a large extent, the heterosexual patterns of choice by limiting the opportunity for interaction and defining the appropriate value-system. Heterosexual love operates within the limits imposed by socio-cultural structure. Love relationships which transcend these limits may be readily explained by the degree of normative variance and the social-psychological process of identification.

6 The exchange theory of interpersonal attraction seems to explain effectively the initial stages of heterosexual contact and the facilitation of the beginning of positive affect. For an excellent, concise statement of this model see: Paul F. Secord and Carl W. Backman, *Social Psychology,* (New York: McGraw-Hill Book Co., 1974), 204-233.

7 The discussion of the developmental stages of heterosexual love is based in part on a conceptual model presented by Ira Reiss (1960). The model has been expanded and revised, however, to include aspects of exchange and development theory and amplified so as to place the model in perspective with other aspects of heterosexual love. The notion of circularity ("the wheel theory"), while plausible, does not have as much explanatory power as the notion that the stages are cumulative. Thus, the intensity of each stage may be expected to be higher than the previous stage, provided of course that there is an increase in the level of positive affect. For example, persons having a high degree of mutual interdependency may be expected to have a greater degree of rapport than persons with a low degree of interdependency or with a high degree of limited transparency.

8 The concept of developmental task refers to a task in the life cycle of the individual which must be mastered in order to successfully proceed or develop normally. The concept is commonly used to denote a set of roles which must be adopted in order to continue development from infancy to adulthood. See: Roy H. Rogers, *Family Interaction and Transaction: The Developmental Approach* (Englewood Cliffs, N.J.: Prentice-Hall, 1973).

9 The difference between total and vital

relationships was developed in the research of Cuber and Harnoff, 1963.

10 Skipper and Nass (1966) defined the basic motivations in dating as: recreation — source of entertainment and immediate enjoyment, e.g., a boy may date an attractive girl because he desires sexual experience with her; socialization — to get to know the opposite sex, learn to adjust, and to develop appropriate techniques of heterosexual interaction, e.g., a boy may date a girl in order to learn something about women; status-seeking — dating to raise one's status and prestige level within one's own group, e.g., a girl may date a wealthy boy just to be seen with him in his expensive sports car; and courtship — to select a future mate, e.g., a girl may be dating a boy because she views him as a potential husband. Where disparity in dating purpose occurs, Skipper and Nass predict conflict and distress.

REFERENCES

Beigel, H. G., "Romantic Love", *American Sociological Review*, 16 (3, June, 1951), pp. 326-334.

Bell, R. R. and L. Blumberg, "Courtship Stage and Intimacy Attitudes", *The Family Life Coordinator*, 8 (3, March, 1960), pp. 61-63.

Broderick, C. B. and S. E. Flowler, "New Patterns of Relationships Between the Sexes Among Pre-adolescents", *Marriage and Family Living*, 23 (1, February, 1961), pp. 27-30.

Burchinal, Lee G., "The Premarital Dyad and Love Involvement", in Harold T. Christensen (ed.), *Handbook of Marriage and the Family*, Chicago, Rand McNally and Company, 1964, pp. 623-674.

Cavan, Ruth Shonle, "Dating in College", in Ruth Shonle Cavan, (ed.), *Marriage and Family in the Modern World*, Second Ed., New York: Thomas Y. Crowell, 1965, pp. 124-134.

Cuber, John F. and Peggy B. Harroff, "The More Total View: Relationships Among Men and Women of the Upper Middle Class", *Marriage and Family Living*, 25 (2, May, 1963), pp. 140-145.

Didato, S. V. and T. M. Kennedy, "Masculinity-femininity and Personal Values", *Psychological Reports*, 2, (1956), pp. 231-250.

Ehrmann, W., *Premarital Dating Behavior*, New York: Holt, 1959.

Ehrmann, W., "Marital and Nonmarital Sexual Behavior", in Harold T. Christensen (ed.), *Handbook of Marriage and the Family*, Chicago: Rand McNally, 1964, pp. 585-622.

Ellis, Albert, "A Study of Human Love Relationships", *Journal of Genetic Psychology*, 75 (1, September, 1949), pp. 61-77.

Goode, William J., "The Theoretical Importance of Love", *American Sociological Review*, 24 (1, February, 1959), pp. 38-47.

Gough, E. Kathleen, "Changing Kinship Usages in the Setting of Political and Economic Change Among the Nayars of Malabar", *Journal of the Royal Anthropological Institute*, 82 (1, 1952), pp. 71-88.

Green, Arnold W., "The 'Cult of Personality' and Sexual Relations", *Psychiatry*, 4 (3, August, 1941), pp. 343-348.

Greenfield, Sidney M., "Love and Marriage in Modern America: A Functional Analysis", *The Sociological Quarterly*, 6 (3, Summer, 1965), pp. 361-377.

Hill, R. and D. A. Hansen, "The Identification of Conceptual Frameworks Utilized in Family Study", *Marriage and Family Living*, 22 (4, November, 1960), pp. 299-311.

Homans, George C., *The Human Group*, New York: Harcourt, Brace, 1950.

Kanin, Eugene J., "An Examination of Sexual Aggression as a Response to Sexual Frustration", *Journal of Marriage and the Family*, 29 (3, August, 1967), pp. 428-433.

Kephart, William M., "Some Correlates of Romantic Love", *Journal of Marriage and the Family*, 29 (3, August, 1967), pp. 470-474.

Kinsey, A.C., W. B. Pomeroy, C. E. Martin, and P. H. Gebhard, *Sexual Behavior in the Human Female*, Philadelphia: Saunders, 1953.

Kirkendall, L. A., *Premarital Intercourse and Interpersonal Relationships*, New York: Julian Press, 1961.

Kirkpatrick, C., and T. Caplow, "Emotional Trends in the Courtship Experience of College Students as Expressed by Graphs with Some Observations on Methodological Implications", *American Sociological Review,* 10 (5, October, 1945), pp. 619-626.

Kirkpatrick, C., and C. Hobart, "Disagreement, Disagreement Estimate and Nonempathic Imputations for Intimacy Groups Varying from Favorite Date to Married", *American Sociological Review*, 19 (1, February, 1954), pp. 10-20.

Kirkpatrick, C., and E.J. Kanin, "Male Sex Aggression on a University Campus", *American Sociological Review,* 22 (1, February, 1951), pp. 52-58.

Kolb, W. L., "Family Sociology, Marriage Education and the Romantic Complex", *Social Forces,* 29 (1, October, 1950) pp. 65-72.

Komarovsky, Mirra, "Functional Analysis of Sex Roles", in Marvin B. Sussman, (ed.), *Sourcebook in Marriage and the Family,* Boston: Houghton Mifflin, 1963, pp. 125-132.

Lowrie, S. H., "Factors Involved in the Frequency of Dating", *Marriage and Family Living*, 18 (1, February, 1956), pp. 46-51.

Masters, William H., and Virginia Johnson, *The Pleasure Bond*, Boston: Little, Brown & Co., 1975.

Mead, Margaret, "Introduction", in A. M. Krich, (ed.), *Women: The Variety and Meaning of Their Sexual Experience,* New York: Dell Publishing, 1953, pp. 9-24.

Miller, Walter B., "Lower-class Culture as a Generating Milieu of Gang Delinquency", *Journal of Social Issues,* 14 (3, July, 1958), pp. 5-19.

Nye, F. Ivan, Lynn White, and James Frideres, "A Partial Theory of Family Stability," Paper presented at the National Council on Family Relations meeting, October, 1966.

Poffenberger, Thomas, "Three Papers on Going Steady", *The Family Life Coordinator*, 13 (1, January, 1964), pp. 7-13.

Price, Alfred J. and Gordon Shipman, "Attitudes of College Students Toward Premarital Sex Experience", *The Family Life Coordinator*, 6 (4, January, 1958), pp. 57-60.

Reiss, Ira L., "Toward a Sociology of the Heterosexual Love Relationship", *Marriage and Family Living,* 22 (2, May, 1960), pp. 139-145.

Reiss, Ira L., "The Scaling of Premarital Sexual Permissiveness", *Journal of Marriage and the Family*, 26 (2, May, 1964), pp. 188-198.

Rodgers, Roy H., *Family Interaction and Transaction: The Developmental Approach,* Englewood Cliffs, N.J.: Prentice-Hall, 1973.

Secord, Paul F., and Carl W. Backman, *Social Psychology*, rev. ed., New York: McGraw-Hill, 1974.

Skipper, James K., and Gilbert Nass, "Dating Behavior: A Framework for Analysis and an Illustration", *Journal of Marriage and the Family,* 28 (4, November, 1966), pp. 412-420.

Stephens, William N., *The Family in Cross-Cultural Perspective,* New York: Holt, Rinehart, and Winston, 1963.

Stratton, John R., and Stephen P. Spitzer, "Sexual Permissiveness and Self-evaluation: A Question of Substance and a Question of Method", *Journal of Marriage and the Family,* 29 (3, August, 1967), pp. 434-446.

Symonds, Perceival M., *The Dynamics of Human Adjustment,* New York: Appleton-Century, 1946.

Time, "Advertising — King Leer", (May 6, 1966), p. 99.

Udry, J. Richard, *The Social Context of Marriage,* New York: J. B. Lippincott, 1966.

Vernon, G. M., and R. L. Stewart, "Empathy as a Process in the Dating Situation", *American Sociological Review,* 22 (1, February, 1957), pp. 48-52.

Stewart, R. L., and G. M. Vernon, "Four Correlations of Empathy in the Dating Situation", *Sociology and Social Research,* 43 (1959), pp. 279-285.

Yang, Martin C., *A Chinese Village: Taitou, Shantung Province,* New York: Columbia University Press, 1945.

Sexual permissiveness in young English and French Canadians

This paper is one of several published (and yet to be published) papers on a study of 700 English-speaking and 404 French-speaking trade school and university students. The data was collected in 1968 in a large exploratory study of the attitudes and behaviors of students regarding courtship and marriage. This particular paper presents the findings on the students' attitudes toward and experience of various premarital sexual intimacies. The findings are compared with United States data (Reiss, 1967) and two other Canadian studies (Mann, 1967; 1970). Comparisons are also made between two trade schools (Alberta and Montreal) and three universities (Alberta, Waterloo and Montreal).

The data provides a comprehensive portrait of the sexual attitudes and behaviors of French-speaking and English-speaking Canadians. Most English-speaking students advocated or approved premarital intercourse for both men and women who were engaged or in love. French-speaking students also shared these standards, though to a significantly lesser extent. Actual coital experience varied little among males in the various samples, including the studies of Mann in Canada and Reiss in the USA. However, evidence is offered that female sexual experience reflects a marked increase compared to all preceding research. English-speaking females apparently are experiencing premarital sexual intercourse considerably more often than French-speaking females.

Hobart's article also attempts to discover which background factors (e.g., religion, social class) might help us to understand why young people hold certain sexual attitudes, and why they participate in premarital sexual behaviors. Because of the complexity of this analysis in his paper, this section is not reprinted. However, the procedures he used and the findings he obtained may be briefly summarized.

Professor Hobart was interested in determining how much influence *each* factor has on sexual attitudes and behaviors, holding other factors constant. This technique is commonly referred to as multiple regression analysis. The question might go something like this: "Does religion explain more of what young people think than social class, how many people they have dated, or whether they are in college or trade school?" In fact, Hobart used fifteen such factors and asked a similar kind of question for *each* factor, holding the other fourteen factors constant each time. In general, Hobart found that sexual intimacy *attitudes* were best explained by the conventionality factor (perceived similarity to the sex standards of parents and friends) among English-speaking Canadians, and by the religiosity factor among French-speaking Canadians. Intimacy *behavior* among both English and French students is primarily related to those variables concerned with relationships (e.g., courtship involvement) rather than norms.

This paper is difficult to critically assess for several reasons. First, it is based on exploratory findings and is primarily oriented toward providing information on the attitudes and behaviors of Canadian young people. There is little question that these objectives are achieved. Second, because of the exploratory nature of the study, little attention is given to relevant theoretical issues. Though the roles of religious values and interpersonal relationships are identified, and the findings illustrate significant changes in the courting attitudes and behaviors of females, these matters are not considered in terms of their overall implications for a theory of premarital sexual permissiveness or emergent sexual standards. It is obvious that changes in courting attitudes and behaviors reflect changes in the practices of Canadian young people ("these data point to the erosion of the grip of old morality"). Given the supposed linkage of premarital activities to the eventual choice of a mate in cross-cultural context, it is well to inquire of the theoretical implications of courting and mating for its own sake in a society which clings to the belief that the ultimate expression of the love-relationship principle is marriage.

In two other papers, Hobart considers standards of sexual morality and trial marriage attitudes and experience. In the first of these papers (Hobart, 1974a; 1974c), it was found that there are four different moral standards. The abstinence standard (no sex until marriage) was the most widespread, represented by 40 percent; the love standard (sexual permissiveness with affection) was accepted by about 40 percent of French and 30 percent of English students; the double standard (no sex for females until marriage but premarital sex is acceptable for males) was preferred by 16 percent of the English sample; and the fun standard (sex if desired without affection) was accepted by 12 percent of the English sample. Support for the last two standards was considerably lower among French students. Behavioral standards were basically similar.

In both language samples, abstinence adherents were younger, rural, lower class, religious, romantic, and inexperienced in drinking, sex, and courtship. Love standard adherents were older, higher class, irreligious, unromantic, egalitarian, university students, and experienced in drinking, courtship, and sex. Double standard adherents were older, irreligious, sexually experienced drinkers, but they came from rural, non-egalitarian family backgrounds. Fewer men professed the abstinence standard than behaviorally conformed to it, whereas women more often professed it but deviated from it. The reverse was found for the love standard: more men advocated the love standard than practised it, and more women rejected the love standard than practised it.

Hobart also found expected characteristics among students with different belief-behavior patterns. The regretful non-virgins (those who advocated abstinence but had experienced intercourse) were typically female trade school students from poor homes, who related warmly to parents, were devout, inexperienced in drinking, and who usually had sexual intercourse with their first love, frequently after drinking and under pressure from their partner. In general, the evidence presented suggests that female sexual behavior is related to the abstinence standard and its derivatives, whereas male sexual behavior reflects the double standard and its derivatives.

The paper dealing with trial marriage (Hobart, 1974b), based on the same sample of students in Ontario, Quebec, and Alberta, found that nearly half the students were opposed to trial marriage. Approximately one fourth of the sample thought it might be a good idea and the remaining 25 percent were either tolerant or indifferent. There were few differences between the attitudes of men and women. Less than half the students knew of anyone living in a trial marriage and only 5 percent (thirty-eight individuals) indicated that they had tried trial marriage. Comparable research by Mann (1967, 1970) is briefly reviewed in Professor Hobart's article which follows.

Sexual permissiveness in young English and French Canadians

Charles W. Hobart

This paper reports on a factorial study of sexual permissiveness in attitude and behavior among samples of English and French Canadian students.

The decade of the 1960s has been a period of unprecedented change in many aspects of the context of permissiveness in sexual behavior in Canada. At the biological level, the increasing availability of the birth control pill, even at the junior high school level according to one informant, has freed increasing numbers from the fear of accidental pregnancy. At the mass media level, there has been a new realism and a new frankness in presentation of sexual involvement issues — scenes portraying nudity and increasingly explicit sexual intimacy are frequent in films, for example. Press reports suggest that casual public nudity is commonplace at hippie gatherings and rock festivals, and that wife swapping is becoming more common in suburbia. At a more "scientific" level, nude therapy is promoted and practiced to free people from "hangups," and couple members are "wired" to permit recording a range of data while they go through routines of foreplay and sexual intercourse under the recording eye of the camera, so that science may learn more about human sexual responsiveness. Advertising today makes use of

Charles W. Hobart, Ph.D., is Professor of Sociology, University of Alberta, Edmonton. From *Journal of Marriage and the Family*, 34 (May, 1972), pp. 292-297, 302-303.

photographs found only in "girlie" magazines a decade ago, and sex education books are illustrated with photographs of intercourse ("more than 200 candid sex act illustrations in full color . . .") available only from shady peddlers in seaports a few years ago. The line between old-fashioned pornography, and advertising, science, and education seems to be becoming increasingly blurred.

The present study was undertaken to attempt to discover the impact of these developments on the attitudes and behaviors of young people in French and English Canada. Such studies have been done in the United States, and recently Mann has published data for very adequate student samples drawn at two universities in Ontario (Mann, 1967, 1970) as well as some for less adequate data from two other campuses (Mann, 1968). Comparative reference will be made to these studies in the course of this paper. There appears to be no published Canadian data, however, on nonuniversity samples; no comparative data for English- and French-speaking Canadian subjects, no rigorous analytic studies of the contribution of various background factors to variations in permissiveness in terms of attitude or behavior. The design of this study was contrived to cover these gaps. This is a study of attitudes and behavior among trade school and university students in Edmonton, Waterloo, and Montreal.

The sample

The anglophone university samples were drawn by randomly sampling third and fourth year students at the Universities of Alberta and Waterloo. First and second year students were excluded since we wanted members to have had ample opportunity to emancipate themselves from the moral influences of home and community. Of the 726 students drawn in the first sample and a later resample, 558 were contactable and eligible (under 27 years of age, of European or North American ancestry, and not belonging to a religious order). Of these, 497, or 89 per cent, returned usable questionnaires.

At the Alberta trade school it was necessary to include first and second year students in the sample because there were few third and no fourth year students enrolled. Accordingly all of the second and third year, and a random sample of first year students were selected to be contacted. Of the 298 students drawn in the first sample and a later resample, 253 were contactable and eligible, and of these, 203, or 80.2 per cent, returned usable questionnaires. The main reason for the lower rate of return from trade school students was that a larger proportion of them — 26 per cent as compared with 7 per cent of Alberta university students — could only be contacted by mail, and many of them were in apprenticeship positions away from Edmonton.

These students were contacted by telephone or by mail and asked to participate in a study of changing orientations to courtship and marriage. They were asked to come to a conveniently situated room on campus to fill out a questionnaire. Upon arrival they were given a questionnaire and seated at widely spaced desks to assure privacy. When a respondent had completed the questionnaire he placed it in a plain envelope and returned it to the assistant, and was then asked to cross his name off the appointment list. Those missing an appointment were telephoned again that same evening and asked to set a new appointment time.

The French Canadian data were collected by a research assistant at the University of

Montreal and a trade school in the same city. Here questionnaires were delivered to the residences of the randomly selected university sample members, and returned through the mail. In the trade school they were administered in selected classes.

The rate of return at the University of Montreal was very much lower than at the anglophone schools. One hundred and sixty-two questionnaires were returned by 370 students who received them, giving a rate of return of 43.8 per cent. One important reason for this was that questionnaires were unfortunately mailed out to a resampling of Montreal students only shortly before the lengthy mail strike of the summer of 1968 and apparently many, knowing that the questionnaire could not be immediately mailed back, simply did not bother to fill it out. At any rate, only 27 out of the 100-person resample returned their questionnaires. No data are available on what proportions of students in the Montreal trade school classes were absent when the questionnaire was filled out, or refused to fill it out. Returns were actually received from 242 trade school students.

It is clear that while the English samples are adequately representative of the student populations from which they were drawn, this is not true of the French Canadian samples. No claims of representativeness are made; the French data are included for their suggestive value only. We may add, however, that where sample members receive sex permissiveness questionnaires and a sizable proportion fail to return them, evidence from other studies shows that it is the more permissive who return the schedules, and the more conservative who fail to. Given that this study shows that more traditional, less secularized influences are more powerfully predictive for the French than for the English

Canadian sample members, it would appear that the selectivity bias of the former sample tends to minimize actual differences which exist between the two populations.

A comparison of some characteristics of the anglophone and francophone samples is found in Table 1.

The questionnaire

Several sections of the lengthy questionnaire are relevant to this paper: those dealing with attitudes toward various types of premarital sexual behavior, and with the background and prior social experience of the respondent. The major index of attitudes used was the Reiss Premarital Sexual Permissiveness Scale (Reiss, 1967: 21-22). In addition various other attitude questions relating to premarital sexual intimacy, some from Reiss (1967), some from Mann (1967), and some original, were used. The Reiss Scale is a 24-item Gutman Scale which probes subjects' attitudes on (1) what degrees of physical intimacy (2) are appropriate to men, and to women, given (3) different degrees of courtship and/or emotional involvement. Sample items include:

"I believe that petting is acceptable for the male before marriage when he is not particularly affectionate toward his partner."

"I believe that full sexual relations is acceptable for the female before marriage when she is in love."

Most of the items dealing with subjects' own sexual experiences had been used in earlier studies by Ehrmann (1960) and Mann (1967). These dealt with kinds of intimacies experienced, age at first experience, number of partners with whom he (she) was experienced, number of partners per kind of experience, and the courtship and/or emotional

Table 1. Selected Characteristics of Subjects Studied for English- and French-Speaking Canadian Samples

Characteristic	English		French	
TOTAL	*N=700*	*%**	*N=404*	*%*
Sex — Male Respondents	336	48.0	205	50.7
Age — Aged 20 or less	209	29.8	279	69.0
— Aged 22 or more	142	20.3	41	10.2
Siblings — none or one only	219	31.3	79	19.6
— 4 or more	184	26.3	192	47.4
Born outside Canada	85	12.1	5	1.2
Generation in Canada — first or second	206	29.6	61	15.1
Has ever lived on a farm	266	38.3	159	39.2
Lived in one place all their lives	235	33.7	203	50.7
Lived in 5 or more different places	112	16.0	39	8.7
Lived longest in a city over 80,000	258	37.0	168	44.6
Occupation of father — farmer	115	16.8	33	8.8
— manual worker	187	27.4	171	42.9
Education of father — some university	86	12.4	38	9.4
Education of mother — some university	39	5.5	5	1.2
Mother never worked	375	54.2	311	78.5
Respondents' parents living together	602	86.0	344	85.1
Average marks in high school less than 66%	287	41.6	70	17.8
Roman Catholic affiliation	137	20.6	386	98.0
Attend church 4 or more times/month	161	23.1	220	54.8
Rated self "not very" or "not at all religious"	322	46.4	167	41.6
Income no more than $5000	141	20.8	132	35.2
Income over $11,000	147	21.6	53	14.1
Male respondents own a car	165	58.1	23	12.0
Now engaged or married	111	16.0	13	3.2
Ever engaged or married	190	27.2	27	6.7
Live at home with family	201	32.7	255	66.2
Could entertain opposite sex friend alone anytime at all	145	23.8	88	22.8
Self rating as "quite" or "fairly attractive"	291	41.7	108	27.8

*Percentages are proportion of those answering the question.

relationships of the respondent with these partners.

Many background items were also included in the questionnaire to provide information on the antecedents of variations in attitude and experience. These included generation of Canadian residence, areas of residence, amount of physical mobility the respondent had experienced, occupation and amount of education of the respondent's parents, denominational membership and dev-

outness of the respondent and his parents, his grades in school, his attitudes toward his parents, self ratings of his attractiveness, his success in attainment of his goals, his perception of the clarity of sexual norms, his current living arrangements, opportunities for entertaining opposite sex members alone, etc. Scales found in the questionnaire included a romantic love scale devised by Reiss (1967), a Protestant Ethic scale designed to measure the respondent's commitment to work production values vs. leisure values (Johnson, n.d.), and items from Dean's Alienation Scale (Dean, 1961).

A first draft was pretested on 200 students in a university class, and some deletions and rewordings were made on the basis of the responses received, but none were necessary for items of the Reiss Sexual Permissiveness Scale. After the data collection was completed, a scaleogram analysis was made of the responses to the Reiss Permissiveness Scale to see whether the responses from Canadian sample members to these items met the criteria of Gutman scale, and it was found that they did. The coefficient of reproducibility for the Male Permissiveness scale was .934 and for the Female Permissiveness scale it was .938 for the anglophone sample, and .905 and .908 respectively for the francophone sample. The Romantic Love items did not scale, however; the coefficient of reproducibility being .833 and .628 for the two samples.

It was originally anticipated that the French language questionnaire would be a verbatim translation of the English original. However, unauthorized changes and deletions were made by the research assistant. These will be noted as relevant.

The findings

In this section are the descriptive findings, consisting of the incidences, attitudes toward, and experience of various forms of premarital intimacy.

Attitudes toward premarital intimacies

In Tables 2 through 5 are found summaries of the male and female permissiveness attitudes of those members of the anglophone and francophone samples who responded to the Reiss Sexual Permissiveness Scale. Since we are primarily interested in the cross-cultural and the analytic aspects of this study we will comment on these tables only briefly.[1]

The data show that both the male and the female francophone students are distinctly less permissive than the male and female anglophone students. Twenty-six per cent of the former, as compared with 8 per cent of the latter, feel that premarital petting is never acceptable for men, while 30 as compared with 11 per cent feel that it is never acceptable for females. At the other extreme the discrepancies were much smaller. Forty-six per cent of the anglophone compared with 35 per cent of the francophone sample members feel that premarital intercourse is never permissible for men and 49 per cent of the former as compared with 44 per cent of the latter feel that such intercourse is never permissible for females.

Students in the Montreal sample, like those in the anglophone sample, are willing to grant more freedom of sexual expression to men than to women. The data are contradictory on the question of which ethnic group has a stronger commitment to the double standard. The French-speaking more often than the English-speaking respondents said they believed in more freedom of sexual expression for males than for females, the proportions being 38 per cent and 34 per cent. However, a higher proportion of the latter (28 per cent) than of the former (20 per cent) had higher sexual *permissiveness scores* for males than for females, thus giving clear indication of a double-standard orientation.

In the French-, as in the English-speaking sample the female component was consistently less permissive than the male compo-

Table 2. Attitudes of Anglophone Sample Members Towards Various Forms of Sexual Permissiveness for Males by School and Sex, with Comparison Data from Reiss

Agree With Attitudes	Total Sample			Reiss White College Students[4]	Reiss White Student Sample			U. of A.			Alberta Trade School			U. of W.		
	TOTAL	M	F		TOTAL[1]	M[2]	F[3]	TOTAL	M	F	TOTAL	M	F	TOTAL	M	F
1. No petting	8%	6%	10%	11%	15%	8%	17%	8%	7%	10%	8%	8%	9%	6%	3%	9%
2. Pet acceptable when engaged or in love	92	94	90	89	85	92	83	92	93	90	92	92	91	94	97	91
3. Pet if feel strong affection	80	86	74	75	67	79[a]	56	80	87[a]	73	83	86	81	77	82	72
4. Pet even though not particularly affectionate toward partner	45	63[a]	29	37	34	—	—	49	68[a]	30	42	65[a]	21	43	53[a]	34
5. Intercourse only if engaged or in love	59	67[b]	52	51	52	69[a]	42	64	71[a]	57	50	59[b]	41	62	67	59
6. Intercourse if feel strong affection toward partner	44	52[b]	37	47	37	54[a]	25	49	58[a]	41	36	44[b]	28	45	50	40
7. Intercourse though not particularly affectionate toward partner	25	38[a]	13	22	21	31	13	30	44[a]	17	20	33[a]	9	21	32[a]	11
Number of Respondents	681	329	352	452	811	405	434	296	145	151	198	97	101	187	87	100

[1] Reiss, *op. cit.*, p. 29.
[2] *Ibid.*, p. 225
[3] *Ibid.*
[4] *Ibid.*, p. 23

[a] signifies male-female differences are significant at .01 level.
[b] signifies male-female differences are significant at .05 level.
— signifies data not available.

Table 3. Attitudes of Anglophone Sample Members Towards Various Forms of Sexual Permissiveness for Females by School and Sex, with Comparison Data from Reiss

Agree With Attitudes	Total Sample			Reiss White College Students[4]	Reiss White Student Sample			U. of A.			Alberta Trade School			U. of W.		
	TOTAL	M	F		TOTAL	M[2]	F[3]	TOTAL	M	F	TOTAL	M	F	TOTAL	M	F
1. No petting	11%	9%	12%	13%	18%	8%	23%	11%	9%	13%	11%	11%	11%	9%	6%	12%
2. Pet acceptable when engaged or in love	89	91	88	87	82	92[b]	77	89	91	87	89	89	89	91	94	88
3. Pet if feel strong affection	76	82[b]	69	67	57	70[a]	46	75	83[b]	67	78	79	76	75	83[b]	67
4. Pet even though not particularly affectionate toward partner	30	45[a]	17	20	18	—	—	34	52[a]	17	29	43[a]	15	27	38[a]	17
5. Intercourse only if engaged or in love	56	66[b]	47	44	44	64[a]	32	61	71[b]	52	46	58[a]	35	59	66[b]	53
6. Intercourse if feel strong affection toward partner	37	49[a]	26	26	27	42[a]	14	43	54[a]	32	27	39[a]	15	40	49[b]	31
7. Intercourse though not particularly affectionate toward partner	13	24[a]	4	14	11	19[b]	4	18	30[a]	6	10	21[a]	0	10	17[b]	4
Number of Respondents	681	329	352	444	811	405	434	296	145	151	198	97	101	187	87	100

[1] Reiss, *op. cit.*, p. 29
[2] *Ibid.*, p. 225
[3] *Ibid.*
[4] *Ibid.*, p. 33

[a] signifies male-female differences are significant at the .01 level.
[b] signifies male-female differences are significant at the .05 level.
— signifies data not available.

Table 4.   Attitudes of Francophone Sample Members Towards Various Forms of Sexual Permissiveness for Males by School and Sex, with Comparison Data from English Sample

Permissiveness Indices	Total French Sample			Total English Sample			University of Montreal			Trade School		
	Total	M	F	Total	M	F	Total	M	F	Total	M	F
1. Premarital petting is never acceptable	26%	20%	31%	8%	6%	10%	15%	12%	18%	32%	27%	36%
2. Petting acceptable only when engaged or in love	74	80	69	92	94	90	85	88	82	68	73	64
3. Pet if feel strong affection toward partner	58	70[a]	45	80	86	74	60	67	53	57	72[a]	42
4. Pet even though not particularly affectionate toward partner	15	23[b]	8	45	63[a]	29	20	26	13	12	19[b]	5
5. Intercourse only if engaged or in love	54	60	47	59	67[b]	52	65	71	59	46	51	42
6. Intercourse if feel strong affection	37	49[a]	24	44	52[b]	37	40	49[a]	28	35	48[a]	22
7. Intercourse though not particularly affectionate toward partner	14	22[b]	6	25	38[a]	13	16	23[b]	8	12	19[b]	5
8. No premarital intercourse	46	40	53	41	37	48	35	29	41	54	49	58
Numbers of respondents	377	190	187	681	329	352	179	92	87	198	98	100
Believes in more freedom of sex expression for males than females	38	43	33	34	35	32	24	24	25	48	58[a]	36
Higher permissiveness score for males than females	20	19	22	28	27	28	20	16	25	20	20	20
Higher non-affection permissiveness score for males than females	13	17	10	28	31	24	12.5	12	13	13	20[b]	7
Number of respondents	399	203	196	697	335	362	160	86	74	239	117	122

*Note school information not available for 32 respondents.
a signifies difference between males and females are significant of .01 level.
b signifies difference between males and females are significant of .05 level.

nent. Generally the differences between the permissiveness of men and women were smaller in the latter than in the former sample, except in terms of attitudes toward petting and intercourse where the couple members are not particularly affectionate toward each other. Here, whereas both male and female francophone subjects tended infrequently to approve of such behavior, in the anglophone sample larger proportions of men approved of such behavior, while only small proportions of women approved. Thus for these four items — two on the male and two on the female permissiveness scales — the male-female differentials were larger for the English- than for the French-speaking samples.

Premarital sexual experience

In Tables 6 and 7 are found the proportions of English- and French-speaking respondents who have experienced various forms of premarital sexual behavior, by school subsample and by sex. The data appear to show that the francophone sample members are generally less sexually experienced than are the anglophone sample members. Unfortunately in this section the relevant questions were not translated literally from English to French; thus the contrasts between the two samples must be taken as only generally suggestive. The implication of the data is, however, that the francophone sample members were less experienced in petting, and

Table 5.   Attitudes of Francophone Sample Members Towards Various Forms of Sexual Permissiveness for Females by School and Sex, with Comparison Data from English Sample

Permissiveness Indices	Total French Sample			Total English Sample			University of Montreal			Trade School		
	Total	M	F	Total	M	F	Total	M	F	Total	M	F
1. Premarital petting is never acceptable	30%	24%[b]	37%	11%	9%	12%	20%	16%	24%	36%	30%	42%
2. Premarital petting is acceptable only when engaged or in love	70	76[b]	63	89	91	88	80	84	76	64	70	58
3. Pet if feel strong affection for partner	51	66[a]	36	76	82[b]	69	57	64[b]	49	48	67[a]	29
4. Pet even though not particularly affectionate toward partner	9	14	4	30	45[a]	17	13	17	9	7	12	2
5. Intercourse only if engaged or in love	51	60[b]	42	56	66[b]	47	62	70[b]	53	43	50[b]	35
6. Intercourse if feel strong affection for partner	33	45[a]	20	37	49[a]	26	36	47[a]	23	32	44[a]	19
7. Intercourse though not particularly affectionate toward partner	7	13	1	13	24[a]	4	8	15[a]	0	6	10[b]	2
8. No premarital intercourse	49	40[b]	58	44	34[b]	53	38	30[b]	47	57	50[b]	65
Premarital sex is good	77	72	82	44	50	38	80	81	79	74	64[b]	83
Premarital sex is definitely good	37	48[a]	28	11	16	7						
Number of respondents	399	203	196	697	335	362	160	86	74	239	117	122

*Note school information not available for 32 respondents.

[a] signifies difference between males and females are significant of .01 level.

[b] signifies difference between males and females are significant of .05 level.

Table 6. Incidence of Various Sexual Experiences with Information on Relationship to Partners for Anglophone Sample Members with Comparison Data from Mann

SEXUAL ACTIVITIES	Mann's York Sample[1]		Mann's Western Sample[2]			Total Sample			U. of A.			U. of W.			Alberta Trade School		
	M	F	M	F	Total	Total	M	F	Total	M	F	Total	M	F	Total	M	F
1. Has never petted	13%	7%	15%	23%	8%	9%	8%	9%	12%	6%	9%	6%	12%	6%	5%	7%	
2. Has ever petted	87	93	85	77	92	91	92	91	88	94	91	94	88	94	95	93	
3. Has petted but not gone past above belt petting	10	15	24	31	12	10	14	12	10	13	12	12	13	12	6	17	
4. Has gone past above but not below belt petting	23	40	27	31	25	21	30	25	18[b]	31	33	30	36	36	32	41	
5. Total experienced in below belt petting	73	77	62[a]	46	80	82	78	79	77	81	79	83	74	82	88	76	
6. Respondent was in love with all partners	—	—	—	—	43	27[a]	59	41	25[a]	55	47	31[a]	63	43	27[a]	60	
7. Respondent was going steady with all partners	—	—	—	—	35	21[a]	48	33	21[a]	43	36	26[a]	47	36	16[a]	56	
8. Experienced mutual petting below the belt	—	—	—	—	63	67	59	62	66	57	69	73	65	59	64	54	
9. Has experienced intercourse	50	37	35[b]	15	50	56[b]	44	55	60	50	46	53	40	46	56[a]	37	
10. Respondent was in love with all intercourse partners	—	—	—	—	50	34[a]	70	47	33[a]	64	59	45[a]	75	46	24[a]	77	

[1] Mann, 1970, 164

[2] Mann, 1967, 28

[a] signifies differences between males and females are significant at .01 level.

[b] signifies differences between males and females are significant at .05 level.

— no data available.

Table 7. Incidence of Various Sexual Experiences with Information on Relationship to Partners for Francophone Sample Members by School and Sex, with Comparison from English Sample

	Total French Sample			Total English Sample			University of Montreal			Quebec Trade School		
	Total	M	F	Total	M	F	Total	M	F	Total	M	F
1. Has never petted	33%	20%	47%	8%	9%	8%	40%	31%b	50%	28%	11%	46%
2. Has ever petted	67	88a	53	92	91	92	60	69b	50	72	89a	54
3. Has experienced above but not below belt petting	20	17	23	25	21	30	23	18	28	18	17	20
4. Has petted, but not gone past petting	60	72a	48	80	82	78	50	56	42	68	84a	51
5. Respondent was in love with all partners in 4	38	29a	51	43	27a	59	31	26	40	39	30a	56
6. Has experienced intercourse	47	63a	30	50	56	44	37	51a	22	54	72a	36
7. Respondent was in love with all intercourse partners	46	38a	56	50	34a	70	50	40a	75	44	38a	58
Number of cases	369	194	177	699	336	363	152	84	70	217	110	107

[a] signifies differences between males and females are statistically significant at .01 level.
[b] signifies differences between males and females are statistically significant at .05 level.

the women in this sample were less experienced in intercourse, than the anglophone sample members. French-speaking men reported more intercourse experience than English-speaking men, however.

The data for the school samples show that among the francophones, the trade school students are distinctly more sexually experienced than the university students, and this is equally true for both the male and the female components of these samples. This is precisely the reverse of the situation in the anglophone sample where it was the trade school students who were least experienced.

Are there differences between the French- and the English-speaking samples in proportions sharing intimacies with loved and unloved partners? The data in the tables suggest generally that there are no such differences between the total samples or between the male and the female components of the two samples. There is a slight tendency for more of the trade school students to report that they were in love with those with whom they petted than university students in the fran-

cophone sample. However these differences are not substantial.

Discussion

There are a number of points of interest in the descriptive and the analytic findings of this study. In terms of the former, our data suggest distinct tendencies toward the emergence of a "new morality" in two specific ways. The first is that a majority of the anglophone subjects advocated premarital intercourse for women, and three-fifths advocated it for men, when couple members were engaged or in love. A clear majority of the francophone students advocated these same standards. Thus a new morality is apparent — *new* in its advocacy of greater sex permissiveness, *morality* in its tendency to restrict intimacy privileges to those who are emotionally involved or committed to each other.

The second point is the massive increase in reported intercourse experience by the women, and particularly among the English-speaking university students. The rates of intercourse experience we found among male members of our sample are generally comparable with those found in a number of studies made in North America during the last 15 or 20 years. However these studies have also reported low premarital intercourse rates for women. The rate of 44 per cent found among the English-speaking women (and 46 per cent among the female anglophone university students) is remarkably high. However it is supported by Mann's findings that 37 per cent of all York female students (including first and second, as well as third and fourth year students) reported intercourse experience. (Mann, 1970, 164). These data point to erosion of the grip of the old morality at its most tenacious point perhaps — the expectation of premarital virginity among women. That this cannot be an artifact of sampling error is adequately demonstrated by the high response rate to the questionnaire. It should be noted that this intercourse-experience rate was significantly lower (30 per cent) for French-speaking women. What the significance of this is cannot be said because of the very low rate of return from the francophone university sample and also because the latter sample was significantly younger than the English-speaking sample. Thus whether or not the premarital intercourse rate now differs between comparable groups of English- and French-speaking female students cannot be said on the basis of our data.

Turning to the analytic aspects of the study, we find that the permissiveness criteria were very well predicted for both the French and the English language data. However the variance in the *attitude* indices for the French-speaking subjects was best predicted by the religiosity factor. For the ang-

lophone data it was the conventionality factor which best predicted the variance in these indices. For the intimacy *behavior* index, the relationship factors were much more powerful predictors than the normative factors for both samples. Further, the relationship and sex identity factors were more powerful predictors of the behavior criterion for the English-speaking than they were for the French-speaking subjects.

What can be the explanation of this predictive pattern? An answer is suggested by the hypothesis of differential secularization of issues which at one time were more exclusively religiously defined, in two contrasting cultures. There are significant differences on sexual permissiveness issues between French and English speaking respondents and between male and female respondents: the latter are more emancipated than the former, and within each cultural group the male adherents are more emancipated than are the females from identification with the traditional moral perspectives.

Furthermore, in terms of sex differences, data reported here and elsewhere[2] show clearly that both English- and French-speaking female respondents are more concerned with courtship interaction in terms of the marriage which may result — a traditional concern. Men on the other hand are more committed than women to increasing sex permissiveness in courtship interaction.

A gradient of change appears to describe these variations in attitudes toward courtship interaction found across Canada today. Among French-speaking students the traditional conceptions of acceptable levels of premarital sexual behavior are sanctioned by the Church, while among more secularized English-speaking students such conceptions are increasingly sanctioned only by conceptions of conventional morality. Within each linguistic group, women are more conservative in acceptance of a new morality, in abandoning the double standard, and in their continuing orientation to marriage, rather than love, than are men. Among the anglophone respondents moreover, the traditional moral norms show a strong tendency to yield as intense emotional relationships with opposite sex members provide both the motivation and the rationalization to violate traditional moral standards.

These data point to the greater weakness of conventionality, as contrasted with religiosity, in inhibiting intimate behavior under conditions of high courtship involvement. If we assume that secularization and early dating are trends which are going to be felt increasingly by Roman Catholics in French Canada, the nature of future developments is clear. Other changes now taking place will further speed these develop-

ments. We have in mind (1) the increasing availability of birth control pills, and very soon, of more effective and less troublesome birth control procedures, such as shots that provide dependable contraception for a month or more. (2) The changes now taking place most dramatically in the Roman Catholic Church, especially in rebellion against its discipline, but in other churches as well, will also work to this end, as will (3) the spread of a "death of God" theology which raises the question of whether traditional moral conceptions were in fact *divinely* ordained. (4) The increasing physical mobility of young people, and the opportunities which increasing availability of automotive transportation provides them with for easy escape from surveillance, will further facilitate their own well-rationalized interest in increasing permissiveness of conduct.

NOTES

1   A more detailed discussion of the intra-group differences for the English Canadian Data is found in Hobart, C. W. "Sexual Permissiveness in Young Canadians, A Factorial Study"

forthcoming.
2   C. W. Hobart, "Trial Marriage in Canada, A Study of Attitudes and Experience," forthcoming.

REFERENCES

Dean, Dwight G.
  1961 "Alienation, its meaning and measurement." *American Sociological Review* 26:753-758.
Ehrmann, Winston
  1960 *Premarital Dating Behavior*. New York: Bantam Books.
Fletcher, Joseph
  1066 *The New Morality*. Philadelphia: Westminster Press.
Johnson, Benton
  n.d. The Comparative Value Project. United States Government, National Institute of Mental Health, Grant No. 4309-R1.
Mann, W.E.
  1967 "Canadian trends in premarital behavior," Bulletin, The Council for Social

Service No. 198.
  1968 "Non-conformist sexual behavior on the Canadian campus." Pp. 300-309 in W. E. Mann (ed.), *Deviant Behavior in Canada*. Toronto: Social Science Publishers.
  1970 "Sex at York University." Pp. 158-174 in W. E. Mann (ed.), *The Underside of Toronto*. Toronto: McClelland and Stewart.
Reiss, Ira L.
  1967 *The Social Context of Premarital Sexual Experience*. New York: Holt, Rinehart and Winston.
Smigel, E. O. and R. Seidon
  1968 "Decline and fall of the double standard." Pp. 6-17 in Annals of the American Academy of Political and Social Science.

5

Marriage relationships

There is no other god on earth for a woman than her husband. The most excellent of all the good works that she can do is to seek to please him by manifesting perfect obedience to him. Therein should lie her sole rule of life. . . . Be her husband deformed, aged, infirm, offensive in his manner; let him also be choleric, debauched, immoral, a drunkard, a gambler; let him frequent places of ill-repute, live in open sin with other women, have no affection whatever for his home; let him rave like a lunatic; let him love without honour; let him be blind, deaf, dumb or crippled, in a word, let his defects be what they may, let his wickedness be what it may, a wife should always look upon him as her god, should lavish on him all her attention and care, paying no heed whatsoever to his character and giving him no cause whatsoever for his displeasure. . . . A wife must eat only after her husband has had his fill. If the latter fasts, she shall fast, too; if he touch not food, she shall not touch it; if he be in affliction she shall be so, too; if he be cheerful he shall share his joy. . . . If he sing she must be in ecstasy; if he dance she must look at him with delight; if he speak of learned things she must listen to him with admiration. In his presence, indeed, she ought always to be cheerful, and never show signs of sadness or discontent.

J.A. Dubois, Hindu Manners, Customs, and Ceremonies, *trans. Henry K. Beauchamp, 3rd ed., 1906, pp. 344-349. By permission of The Clarendon Press, Oxford.*

It is one thing to say, and for that matter to believe, that men and women are equal, that a husband and wife should therefore share the responsibilities of family life, while each has the freedom to develop an independent full-time career. It is a far more difficult matter to effect that equality, for the inflexible demands of the occupational world and the traditional patterns of male and female roles in family life present formidable barriers to the couple with two careers. More important than the theoretical principle of equality in marriage is the question of what actually happens in the day-to-day life of the two-career family. What happens when the wife receives a better job in another city and the husband is not inclined to move? What happens when the babysitter suddenly cannot come and both partners have appointments?

Lynda Lytle Holmstrom, The Two-Career Family *(Cambridge, Mass.: Schenkman Publishing Company, 1972), back cover.*

The relationships between husbands and wives in every society are systematically defined by role expectations. These expectations regulate and stabilize marital activities in the interest of both the society and the individual. The nature and rigidity of these expectations, however, vary widely. Societal or kinship interest may reflect unambiguous requirements concerning what married couples must and must not do, or more simply, emphasize the values of marriage and goals such as intimacy and companionship. Husbands and wives may enter marriage "trained" to behave in certain ways and to expect appropriate responses from their spouses. Socialization *within* marriage, in contrast, is common in Western society. In this case, couples, given their own unique socialization experiences prior to marriage, "make" their own roles through negotiation (Aldous, 1972). The agreements a married couple reach concerning matters such as who is accountable to whom (authority) and who will do what (division of labor) become the expectations that will regulate their behaviors.

Many societies conceive the conjugal and parental bonds as opposing forces: the greater the solidarity of the husband-wife bond, the weaker the parent-child bond. The traditional Indian family, for example, practised both arranged and child marriage to protect the interests of the joint family structure. The husband-wife relationship was defined in formalistic terms and the husband was expected to take the side of the kinship group in any dispute (Gore, 1965). Perhaps the clearest example of the supposed dangers of the conjugal bond is found among the Bedouins (Peters, 1965). Marriage is seen as a violent split from the ties of the father-son relationship, and so the father "pretends" that his sons are not married for many years after the "marriage ceremony that didn't occur" has occurred. The sons' tents are tied to the tent of their father and the sons continue to eat with their father as if nothing had changed.

The actual expectations of how husbands are to relate to their wives and wives to their husbands also vary widely. The excerpt from *Hindu Manners, Customs and Ceremonies* quoted at the beginning of this chapter, taken literally illustrates the extreme deference that wives are expected to reflect in many cultures. In these societies, wives have many duties and few rights while husbands have many rights but few duties. The opposite extreme, deference of husbands to wives, doesn't appear to exist. The clearest approximation to role equality between husbands and wives appears to be the Western dual-career marriage, in which sex role expectations are egalitarian and flexible. As Holmstrom (1972) points out, however, role equality in marriage is largely an ideal and difficult to achieve because of the organization of society relative to the roles of males and females and the socialization of the sexes.

Even though role expectations have a systematic influence on the behavior of married couples in every society, what married couples actually do in the privacy of their own households doesn't always correspond to these expectations. Much of Western marital activity may well be ad-lib, reflecting trial and error attempts to cope with unanticipated events or situations. In general, it will be seen that Eastern marriage relationships tend to reflect normative ideals (Mace and Mace, 1960), while Western marriage is characterized by role ambiguities and unanticipated behaviors (Farber, 1964).

Marital status and function

In every society most people marry. Among the Trobriand Islanders, for example, all persons of mature age were married, with the exception of albinos and the sickly, who were not permitted to marry (Malinowski, 1927). Most Canadians eventually marry, and all evidence suggests that the marriage rate is continuing to increase (Kalbach and McVey, 1971). But the reasons for marriage differ from society to society.

Western observers might expect Trobrianders not to marry because of the opportunity for unrestricted sexual access without marriage, a required one-year abstinence from sex for the first year of marriage and for two years after the birth of each child, and the prohibition of adultery. Yet Trobrianders marry. According to Malinowski (1927), a Trobriander does not obtain the status of adult until marriage. Bachelors are not permitted to have their own houses and are debarred from many privileges. In addition, unmarried men want children, who can only be acquired after marriage.[1] Married men also regularly receive food from their wife's relatives. In general, married Trobrianders have many social and economic advantages, compared to the unmarried. If a wife leaves her husband he will do everything in his power to get her to return; if a divorce occurs, remarriage takes place as quickly as possible.

The reasons why Canadians marry are less obvious. There is no requirement to marry, nor for divorced and widowed persons to remarry. The social and economic advantages of married persons, compared to singles, are modest. The legitimation of sexual access, thought to be a widespread function of marriage by Stephens (1963) and certainly a basic principle in most of the major religious traditions, continues to have a measurable influence on the desire to marry. However as Hobart (1973) has demonstrated, sexual relationships are increasingly common among unmarried Canadian youth. It would seem that Canadians, like their Trobriand counterparts, marry because they value marriage.

Because of their socialization experiences and the organization of their respective societies, most people hope for marriage and have high anticipations of the satisfactions it will provide. It is in this respect, however, that societies vary dramatically: the expectations for marriage are culturally defined. Stephens (1963) reports that in

1 Trobrianders are said to believe that sexual intercourse is unrelated to the conception of children. Married women are said to conceive spirit-infants, who when placed on the woman's forehead are washed to the womb by the blood of the mother. Accordingly, a man cannot have a child unless he marries. Even though premarital intercourse is widespread, childbirth seldom occurs outside of marriage. There is no definitive explanation for this seeming biological exception. Malinowski (1927), after considering many possible explanations, concluded that ꞓ to semen due to regular contact during childhood. The ꞓ marriage purportedly breaks down the resistance.

many societies husbands and wives do not even live together (e.g., mother-child households), sleep together (because of sexual taboos), eat together, go places together, own property together, address each other by personal names, or show affection in public. Mace and Mace (1960) in their study of Eastern marriage, conclude that husbands and wives do not talk together about their innermost feelings. Intimate communication occurs between relatives, not within the conjugal relationship. Disagreement is said not to occur, because disagreement between spouses is inappropriate.

Western marriage, in contrast, is specifically designed to satisfy the emotional and social needs of individuals (Parsons and Bales, 1955). Research findings emphasize the satisfactions gained from marriage, rather than the adaptation of the conjugal unit to the expectations of society or the kinship group. Both husbands and wives generally expect to achieve the ultimate in personal fulfillment and love-intimacy, to be companions in both private and public places, to share personal problems with each other, and to experience satisfaction in their sexual relationship. The following quote from an eighteen-year-old Canadian girl effectively illustrates these assumptions (Schlesinger, 1972:20).

> Marriage to me symbolizes compatibility with my husband, enjoyment of sexual relations, love and concern for each other, social acceptance for both of us, and a moderate income to cover the rising cost of living. Through him I would know and experience happiness, a desire to live and love, and above all a sense of security and belonging.

In a recent study of Saskatchewan students (Wakil, 1973), these ideal-typical principles of what marriage offers the aspirant are even more evident. Selected rankings and the percentage supporting the preferred mate characteristic for urban males and females are presented below.

Males
  1. Faithful, loyal (97%)
  3. Considerate, understanding (93%)
  4. Emotionally mature (91%)
  5. Sexually responsive, not
     inhibited (90%)
  6. Pleasant personality and
     disposition (91%)
  7. Dependable, honest (89%)
  8. Tolerant (89%)
  10. Intelligent (82%)
  13. Attractive, good looking (80%)

Females
  1. Dependable, honest (98%)
  2. Faithful, loyal (98%)
  3. Considerate, understanding (96%)
  3. Emotionally mature (96%)
  6. Pleasant personality and
     disposition (94%)
  7. Tolerant (91%)
  7. Intelligent (91%)
  9. Sexually responsive, not
     inhibited (90%)
  22. Attractive, good looking (68%)

The patterns identified above illustrate the basic similarities in the orientations of males and females toward marriage (in some ways, the list is similar to what one might say about "friends"). The greater interest of males in the attractiveness of their spouse and the lesser concern about intelligence, compared to females, is evidence of the persistence of certain differences in sex roles. These dimensions of Canadian marriage are further considered in the article by Hobart (1972) appearing later in this chapter.

Marital role equality

Studies of role relationships in small groups, regardless of sex distribution, have concluded that every group has, at least, a task or instrumental leader (the person who is oriented to goals and getting things done) and an emotional-expressive leader (the person who helps people feel good and reduces tension). Recent evidence suggests that husbands and wives *both* perform instrumental and expressive tasks, though the domains and purposes may differ (Scanzoni, 1970; McIntire, Nass, and Dreyer, 1972). Role relationships involve expectations that are reciprocal: a husband's duties are his wife's rights and his rights are his wife's duties (Gouldner, 1960). Conceptualized in this way, marriage involves instrumental and expressive rights and duties for both husbands and wives. This model, adapted from Scanzoni (1970), is illustrated below.

Figure 5-1 Husband-Wife Role Reciprocity

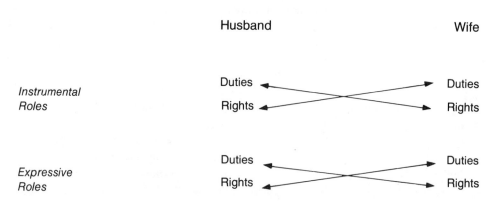

The reciprocal rights and duties of the marriage relationship provide a basis for a discussion of the distribution of sex-role responsibilities. The duties of the husband and the rights of the wife are not necessarily reciprocal in all societies. Based on the

reciprocity principle, Scanzoni (1972) has identified four types of marital role relationships: wife as property, wife as complement, wife as junior partner, and wife as
equal partner. The first type, wife as property, represents a marriage with little
reciprocity between husband and wife. The wife as equal partner is a marriage in
which the duties and rights are equal. Each of these types is briefly discussed below.

In the *wife as property* marriage, the husband has few expressive duties and his
wife has few expressive and instrumental rights. While the husband is obligated to
provide for his spouse, his wife is expected to defer to his authority, manage his
possessions, rear his children, and fulfill his sexual demands. Such a wife can expect
only minimal affection, and she has little control over the provisions and protection
her husband provides. His duties are defined either by the society or the kinship
system. The evidence in cross-cultural family research indicates that many preliterate and Eastern marriages approximate this patriarchal model (Stephens, 1963; Mace
and Mace, 1960). Stephens, for example, found a near-universal division of labor
standard in the marriages he studied. Non-family activities were nearly always
performed by men, only rarely by women. Child care and housekeeping activities
were nearly always performed by women, only rarely by men. Task segregation
(little sharing of activities) was the most common pattern; where overlap occurred, it
involved the wife helping the husband with "his" tasks.[2] In addition, men were
allocated privileges that women did not receive. Because of the double standard, the
practise of deference in respect to the husband's authority, and the exercise of power
by the husband in decision-making and tension control, a wife had little say. Sex
role segregation and male-dominated marital privilege is also illustrated in studies of
lower social status families in many societies, including Western society.
Rainwater's (1964) discussion of marital sexuality in Mexico, Puerto Rico, England, and the United States (based on a survey of several studies of poverty-stricken
families) concluded that the basic norm of marriage is "sex is a man's pleasure and a
woman's duty". Men apparently do not share in household responsibilities, provide
only a minimum of affection, but expect a great deal from their wives. Sex role bias
is most apparent in the wife as property marriage. In this case, one's rights and
duties are exclusively a function of one's sex, rather than skills, training, or experience.

In the second marriage type, the most common in Western society, the role of the
wife is *complementary*. In this marriage, the expressive rights and duties of both
husbands and wives are shared equally. Companionship and intimacy are reciprocal
rights and duties. There is a slight decrease in the husband's instrumental rights,

---

2 In some societies these roles are apparently reversed (Murdock, 1957).

compared to the norms of the chattel relationship, and the wife has the right to expect him to help her with her responsibilities. The overlap in the division of labor, sharing of authority, and the exercise of power will be modest. The basic norm is complementation, not equality or ownership.

Marriages in which the wife is employed outside the household are defined by Scanzoni as *wife as junior partner* marriages. Although the instrumental duties-rights ratio changes somewhat, the majority of working women typically assume an additional job — the work role. The wife's domestic instrumental duties decline somewhat, in that she is less obliged to defer to her husband's wishes and participates more actively in authority roles (her instrumental rights increase). It is rare, however, that she will achieve more than junior partner status because she continues to be primarily responsible for domestic tasks.

Scanzoni's model (1972) is heavily based on the superordinate status of the provider role and the subordinate status of all non-provider roles in the marital system. Accordingly, a wife can only achieve marital role equality if she is able to achieve a *societal* role equal or greater in status than that of her husband. In this type of marriage, defined as the *wife as equal partner marriage*, the duties and rights of a husband and wife are identical and equal in reciprocity because both fulfill provider roles of equal importance.

Because complementary or junior partner roles are of lesser societal importance, Scanzoni defines these marriages as inequitable. Domestic work roles, however, are not inherently inferior to provider work roles. Status differentials are as culturally defined as sex roles. Therefore, if domestic and provider roles were defined as equally important by both society and marital partners, sex-role bias could be reinterpreted as sex-role respect. Both domestic and provider work roles must be performed; the fact that one sex more often performs one role is not discriminatory unless the roles are of unequal status. The reciprocal rights and duties of a husband and wife could be equal in the complementary and junior partner status roles if the provider and domestic roles were defined as equal.

Volumes of research on role relationships in Western marriage (including marriage in the United States and Canada) reflect the principles of either the complementary or junior partner marriage types. Marriages in which the wife is unemployed tend to emphasize companionship (similar rights and duties in the expressive domain), a traditional division of labor with some sharing of activities, and the predominant role of the husband in authority and power relationships (though most married couples "say" that they more or less make decisions together — egalitarianism). The employed wife, however, appears to be somewhat more involved in decision-making activities and somewhat less responsible for household and child care responsibilities (cf. Blood and Wolfe, 1960; Scanzoni, 1970).

A recent study of English protestant families in Montreal (Westley and Epstein, 1969) found that most husbands and wives shared in activities involving the care of children. However, the majority of household tasks were carried out by women and the economic tasks by men. About 42 percent of the marriages were found to have a "balanced" division of labor. In these marriages, the husband exclusively performed 20 percent of the total domestic load, the wife about 60 percent, and the couple shared about 20 percent of the tasks. Nearly one third of the marriages "shared" more tasks than they performed separately. The sharing, however, was predominantly in the child care domain, rather than in the traditional areas such as housekeeping and economic affairs. Somewhat less than 16 percent of the sample were defined as traditional, i.e., the husband did not participate in household activities and seldom shared any tasks with his spouse. With regard to the distribution of privilege (authority and power), one third of the marriages were defined as egalitarian, 27 percent as husband-led, 25 percent as husband-dominant, and 15 percent as wife-dominant.[3] In a more sophisticated study of power among 336 families in the Toronto area (Turk and Bell, 1972), on a measure of "reported power" it was found that 42 percent of the marriages were egalitarian, 22 percent were husband-dominant, and 28 percent were dominated by the wife.

The Canadian Women's Bureau (1969) reports that the majority of Canadian wives work because they need the money, not for self-fulfillment. The typical working mother has a job, not a career. The results of a recent study of working mothers (Women's Bureau, 1970c) found that: one in five mothers are working, comprising about 25 percent of the total female labor force; 50 percent of working mothers have children under six years of age; 75 percent of working mothers have one or two children under the age of fourteen; 63 percent of working mothers work thirty-five or more hours a week; and 63 percent of working mothers are employed in clerical, sales, and service occupations. The impact of the working wife on marital role equality, however, appears to be minimal. Elkin reports one master's thesis at the University of Montreal (Guilbault, Lacharite and Lafontaine, 1956) which concludes that both the husband and children increase their involvement in household chores. Research in the United States (Nye and Hoffman, 1963) also reveals increased sharing of household activities and greater participation by working wives in decisions. However, there is no evidence in these studies or in any research project to date that all family activities are equally and randomly shared. A husband and wife may "help" each other but they do not systematically share in all tasks. Even in studies of dual-career marriage, marital role equality has seldom been found (Holmstrom, 1972; Rapoport and Rapoport, 1971).

3 The distribution of power was defined in this study in terms of discipline, conflict resolution, decision making, and responses to questions concerning "who" dominated.

Marriage as process

Marriage in most societies can be explained if one knows the expectations of the society or kinship group for the roles of husband and wife. In this sense, what married persons *do* differs in no essential respect from what they are expected to do. Potential marrieds enter marriage trained to adopt their appropriate roles. Appropriate behaviors will be reinforced by one's spouse and kinship group.

In Western societies, in contrast, most people enter marriage with high anticipations of what it has to offer. These ideals are seldom realized, though the reasons vary for different subcultures. In blue-collar marriage, for example, Komarovsky (1964) found that conjugal roles were learned after marriage. The wife, typically unhappy with the way her husband treated her, sought counsel from her mother. Her mother reinforced the rightful dominance of the husband and the importance of his sexual rights and her sexual duties. The husband, in contrast, sought counsel from his buddies concerning the "high" expectations of his wife. His buddies reinforced his dominant role. Though primarily learned after marriage (they were certainly "exposed" to these role patterns in their own families), blue-collar marital behavior eventually comes to reflect the way it is and is supposed to be. In this sense, blue-collar marital interaction focuses on the acceptance of defined rights and duties.

Marriage in the middle class, however, typically reflects role ambiguity, conflicting expectations, and the need to establish a mutually acceptable normative system. Marital behavior is often of an ad-lib variety, with the husband and wife, through trial and error, discovering their partner's likes and dislikes, values, attitudes, personality, self conceptions and evaluations, and commitments. Of the many theoretical approaches to this variety of marital behavior, two may be briefly mentioned here.

The developmental approach (Rodgers, 1973) assumes that each married couple must resolve certain basic developmental tasks (sometimes referred to as predicaments or dilemmas) in order to maintain the marriage. These tasks involve the making of roles (reaching agreements) which will regulate and clarify marital behavior for both the husband and wife. It is assumed that agreement needs to be reached in several basic role domains, including who is accountable to whom and who will do what (authority and division of labor); the nature and frequency of relationships with outsiders (friends, kin and community); and the articulation of marital versus parental needs and priorities.[4] Successful role making in these re-

---

4 The number of developmental tasks commonly specified varies. The three presented here are intended to be illustrative rather than exhaustive. Duvall (1971), for example, specifies eight to ten developmental tasks for the husband, wife, and couple for eight differing stages of the marital and family life cycle.

spects results in the predictability of marital response by both spouses, as well as by the researcher, and leads to marital interaction which can be largely explained by the expectations the partners hold for each other.

Conflict (Sprey, 1969) and bargaining or negotiation approaches (Bernard, 1964) focus on the ways in which partners maneuver and manipulate each other in order to maximize self gain without excessive loss to their partners.[5] These approaches recognize the importance of agreements, but emphasize their dynamic and fragile nature. Agreements are continually revised in the light of renegotiations and changing conditions and situations which the couple cannot anticipate, e.g., the developmental changes in themselves or their children. These approaches, as well as others such as systems theory, offer insight into the nature of marriage relationships in Western society.

Divorce and remarriage

Stephens (1963) reports that all societies provide a way out of marriages in which the stress and strain becomes intolerable. The form of out, however, varies widely. For example, Quebec permitted only annulment (a return to single status, as if the marriage had never occurred) or separation (without permission to remarry) until 1968. Divorce became possible with the Canada-wide change in the Divorce Act in 1968. Grounds for ending a marriage also vary widely, from mere incompatability (including casual excuses such as ''she didn't like me'') to severe forms of physical cruelty. Generally speaking, divorce law, whether in preliterate or complex societies, is based on the assumption that one party is guilty and the other is innocent. In Western society, this means that the innocent spouse must file suit against the guilty spouse.[6] It may be emphasized that divorce is seldom a painless event — it is a difficult, if not traumatic, experience for most people. Divorced persons tend to remarry as soon as possible in most societies.

Three recent studies of divorce and remarriage in Canada are briefly summarized below. In a demographic study of divorce rates Roberts and Krishnan (1972), using a per 1000 married female population fifteen years old and over and age-specific divorce rates, found that Alberta, followed by British Columbia and Ontario, had the highest divorce rate in Canada. Newfoundland, followed by Quebec, had the lowest divorce rate. Between 1968 and 1969, as a result of the change in the divorce laws,

5 These approaches are strongly related to exchange theory and symbolic interactionism (see Chapter one).

6 Students interested in the Canadian laws concerning marriage and divorce may wish to consult a book by Chapman (1968) which summarizes the applicable regulations.

the divorce rate increased the least in Nova Scotia and Alberta and the most in Quebec and Newfoundland. Roberts and Krishnan also found that Catholicism and poverty help explain low divorce rates. Youth culture, percent population urban, and percent of women in the labor force did not appear to have a significant impact on divorce rates.

Between 1950 and 1964, an average of 13 percent of all marriages in Canada were remarriages (Scheslinger, 1970). This study also found that bachelors tended to marry divorced women rather than widows. Divorced men tended to marry single women more often than either widows or divorced women. Divorced women tended to remarry at the age of thirty-five compared to the age of thirty-eight for divorced men. Widowed brides married, on the average, at the age of fifty while widowers married at the average age of fifty-six. The length of time divorced or widowed before marriage was found to vary by sex and marital status in a related study (Kuzel and Krishnan, 1973). Males, compared to females, and widowed, compared to divorced, were found to remarry more quickly. These differences are summarized in table 5-1.

It was also found that the probability of remarriage for males, whether divorced or widowed, is high to the age of forty. For females, in contrast, the probability is 60 percent or better to the age of thirty. After these ages, the probability of remarriage declines rapidly. The study also reports that the chances of remarriage, between 1961 and 1966, have increased more for males than females and more for persons thirty-five years of age than for those younger than thirty.

Table 5-1.   Length of time before remarriage

| Age | Divorced | | Widowed | |
	Male	Female	Male	Female
20	3.6 yrs	10.7 yrs	6.1 yrs	8.5 yrs
25	3.5	18.5	4.6	14.6
30	8.5	24.3	6.3	21.0
40	19.7	29.5	11.2	26.0
50	22.1	26.7	14.3	24.7
60	18.2	19.3	14.2	18.7
70	9.7	9.9	9.1	9.9

Based on data reported in Kuzel and Krishnan, 1973.

SUMMARY

This chapter has briefly discussed comparative marital status and function, marital role equality, marital process, and divorce and remarriage.

In every society most people will marry. Typically, the status of single persons is considerably lower than that of marrieds, and subject to various forms of legal and social penalties. Most people are socialized to value marriage, though the kinds of satisfaction actually obtained vary from merely acquiring an acceptable adult status to the fulfillment of the emotional and social needs of individuals.

Appropriate marital roles are usually culturally defined. Though marriage involves instrumental and expressive rights and duties for both husbands and wives, these expectations are seldom reciprocal. Indeed, the most common pattern in most societies is the *wife as property* marriage, in which the husband has few expressive duties and his wife has few expressive and instrumental rights. The *wife as complement* marriage, most common in Western society, involves equal expressive rights and duties but the wife has marked instrumental rights. In the *wife as junior partner* marriage, the wife is generally employed outside the home and accordingly acquires more instrumental duties and rights. Complete reciprocity is obtained when the wife's career is of equal status with that of her husband. This is referred to as the *wife as equal partner* marriage. Marriage roles in Western society have emphasized the reciprocal rights and duties of companionship and intimacy but have maintained many of the traditional conceptions concerning the division of labor. Married couples who relate well in the expressive domain "help" each other in the instrumental area and frequently think they "decide things" together. However, marital role equality remains an ideal that is seldom realized. The acceptance of marital inequities is rapidly decreasing among married women in Western society (see, for example, Stephenson, 1973).

While the role of cultural expectations for marriage is significant in most societies, Western marriage is frequently characterized by either role-making activities or regularized negotiation and bargaining to achieve satisfactory relationships. Role making leads to the establishment of normative guidelines to regulate marital behavior, while agreements in more dynamic marriages tend to be more fragile and transitory.

All societies apparently provide ways of ending marriage when it becomes intolerable. A divorce action generally assumes that one party is innocent and the other guilty. Though it is a traumatic experience, most divorced persons try again.

In the remainder of this chapter four articles, three of which are based on Canadian data, are presented and briefly discussed to illustrate several basic issues, including variant expectations for marriage (Hobart); the impact of cultural background on marriage roles (Carisse); the interconnections between marital satisfaction and expectations (Scanzoni); and a study of mate swapping and decision making (Henshel).

Orientations to marriage among young Canadians

This study considers the attitudes of Canadian students toward marriage. The sample is the same as the one used in the study of sexual permissiveness, and similar techniques were utilized. Accordingly, information on the sample and the analysis procedures (multiple regression analysis) has been deleted. The orientations were measured with respect to egalitarianism in marriage roles, social activities, female employment, education, and role alternatives for wives. In general, English students were found to have more egalitarian attitudes concerning marital relationships, except toward female employment. In this case, French women were distinctly more egalitarian in their views. The spread between male and female responses toward marriage was generally minimal among English Canadians but quite large among French Canadians. In several respects, French men were found to be the most traditional and French women the most liberal.

The search for explanations for these findings was not very fruitful. Religion and sex identity explained the greatest proportion of the variation among French-speaking students. The background characteristics of English Canadians, however, appeared to offer little insight into their orientations toward marriage.

Several other studies in Canada have assessed attitudes toward marriage. Whitehurst and Plant (1971), in comparing the attitudes of a sample of Canadian and American students toward marriage, found that Canadian youths were significantly more discontented with conventional marriage forms and more willing to consider alternative forms of marriage. Canadians made consistently more negative comments about marriage and were typically more concerned about inequalities in marital roles. In a more recent study, Whitehurst (1973a) found that only 12 percent of a sample of 300 students thought monogamy was a dying institution. Some 20 percent, however, were willing to try group marriage, 60 percent considered multiple loving possible and over half of the students expected to have a different life style than their parents. In another as yet unpublished paper, Whitehurst compared the responses of 143 U.S. students and 125 students in Ontario. The data was obtained in the spring of 1973. High expectations for marriage characterized the responses of both samples; however, Canadian respondents were more inclined to support spousal openness and flexibility, less optimistic about a satisfactory adjustment in marriage, more interested in non-conventional marriage, and less concerned about physical attributes in the ideal mate. These findings must be taken as only suggestive of possible trends in attitudes toward marriage. There is no evidence that these samples are representative of American and Canadian viewpoints. The current findings in various studies of marital attitudes (Hobart, Mann, Whitehurst, Wakil) are somewhat inconsistent. The differences may be a function of methodological technique, the location in which the studies were conducted, an inadequate conceptualization of the problems, or countless other factors. Further research is needed to clarify the persistence of certain value-frames and the extent to which these values are changing.

Orientations to marriage among young Canadians

Charles W. Hobart

Future historians must surely identify the twentieth century as the period during which women gained a slow but increasingly complete emancipation from the second class status that had been their lot in North America. At the turn of the century they were disfranchised; their property rights and their freedom of access to gainful employment were inferior to those of men.[1] Their sexual freedom, too, was inferior, as the well-known double standard and some of the Kinsey research clearly testify (Kinsey, *et al*, 1948, 1953). By 1971 there were many indications that these restrictions had been significantly mitigated (Hobart, 1971).

The major developments of this century are quickly outlined. The employment op-portunities accompanying World War I reinforced women's sense of the limitations of their traditional status and their ambitions for a changed future, thus strengthening the suffragette demands that gained the franchise for women in 1918 in Canada,[2] and in 1920 in the United States.[3]

If the Crash of 1929 and the Great Depression that followed closed factories in every major centre and drove women back into the home, it drove men — up to 26 per cent of the male work force in Canada at the height of the Depression[4] — into the streets, making them unable to provide for their families. Thus the justification for masculine dominance of the family based on economic support was broken as never before, particularly

Charles W. Hobart, Ph.D., is Professor of Sociology, University of Alberta, Edmonton.

From *Journal of Comparative Family Studies*, 3 (Autumn, 1972), pp. 171-182, 191-193. Reprinted by permission of the author and the publisher.

so as some wives were able to get work and support their families when their husbands could not.

World War II was more desperately fought than was the First World War; accordingly the needs for female labor on the farm, in the factory, and in the armed forces as well was greater. Thus its emancipating effect was correspondingly great, and this effect has been prolonged in attenuated form to the present day, particularly in the United States. A nostalgic demand to return to "normalcy" after the war — including returning women to the home — was soon terminated by the Cold War, the Berlin Crisis, and wars in Korea and Viet Nam. These influences were of course weaker in Canada because Canada was less involved in these wars and also because massive immigration after the war brought millions of men and women here who had more conservative traditional conceptions of sex roles than most native-born Canadians.[5] But this conservatism was powerfully counteracted in English speaking Canada at least, by the heavy impact of American Mass Media.[6] Thus it appears that the egalitarianism pressures which have been building in the United States since about 1950 have been communicated with almost undiminished power to Canada, though the socio-economic conditions here are not so urgently conducive.

Several recent studies have investigated changes in allocation of role responsibilities in American married couples (Hobart, 1958, 1960; Blood and Wolfe, 1960). Such research has rarely been done in Canada and the few studies that exist are severely limited in scope. Thus this study was designed, just at the time when concern for women's liberation was becoming urgent, to discover what changes are taking place in young Canadians' conceptions of appropriate division of responsibilities between husbands and wives. The issue is important because the opportunities Canadian women have to play a bigger part in public life depends on their being relieved of at least some of their traditional duties.

Specifically the research was designed to answer the following questions: is there evidence of a shift towards more egalitarian definition of marital roles? and if so, is it more pronounced in certain areas of married life? What influences make for more traditional or egalitarian orientations? What is the influence of coming from a family in which the mother worked, of urban vs. rural background, of education, social class and other social background factors on marital role conceptions?

The questionnaire

Several sections of the lengthy questionnaire are relevant to this paper; those dealing with marriage role expectations, child rearing procedures, and the background and prior social experience of the respondent. Sixty-seven questions about the marriage role obligations of husbands and wives were selected from the Hobart Marital Role Expectation (Hobart, 1956) and the Dunn Marriage Role Expectation Inventories (Dunn, 1960) and were scored according to the technique suggested by Dunn. Sample items included:

"In my marriage I expect that if there is a difference of opinion the husband will decide where to live."
"In my marriage I expect that if the wife prefers a career to having children, the husband will accept that decision and cooperate."

Sample members responded to these items using six point Likert type response categories.

Many background items were also included in the questionnaire to provide information on the antecedents of variations in attitude. These included generation of Canadian residence, areas of residence, amount of physical mobility the respondent had experienced, occupation and amount of education of the respondent's parents, denominational membership and devoutness of the respondent and his parents, his grades in school, his attitudes toward his parents, self rating of his attractiveness, his success in attainment of his goals, his perception of the clarity of sexual norms, his current living arrangements, opportunities for entertaining opposite sex members alone, etc. Scales found in the questionnaire included a Protestant Ethic Scale designed to measure the respondent's commitment to work production values vs. leisure values, (Johnson, n.d.) and items from Dean's Alienation Scale (Dean, 1961).

A first draft was pretested on 200 students in a university class, and some deletions and rewordings were made on the basis of the responses received. It was originally anticipated that the French language questionnaire would be a verbatim translation of the English original. However, unauthorized changes and deletions were made by the research assistant. These will be noted as relevant.

The findings: English Canadian data

In this section are found the descriptive findings, consisting of attitudes toward various traditionalism — egalitarianism and role of the wife issues for the English and French language samples.

Traditionalism – egalitarianism

The 67 marital role conception items are about equally divided between those dealing with the role of the husband and the wife and between items reflecting a traditional definition of roles and those reflecting an egalitarian definition of roles. The items relate to seven areas: personal characteristics, education, social participation, care of children, homemaking, employment and support, and authority. They are scored so as to give subscores for each of these seven areas, and a total score which is reflective of the overall traditionalism or egalitarianism of the respondent.

In this section we shall present information on the personal characteristics, education, and social participation subscores and on the total score, for the total sample and the school subsamples, by sex of respondent. Since there are no norms available for any of the Dunn Inventory scores we cannot determine whether our sample members are distinctively traditional or egalitarian in their orientation, but we can make comparisons between subsamples of our total sample. The relevant data are found in Table 1 which shows the distribution of the various Dunn Inventory scores for the total and the school subsamples, by sex. Higher scores signify more egalitarian, and lower scores signify more traditional orientations.

The data show that for the three subscores as well as for the total score, the female sample members were consistently significantly more egalitarian than the male sample members. In regard to the personal characteristics of husbands and wives subscore the university samples were more egalitarian than the trade school sample, and this was true of the male and female components of

Table I   Personal Characteristics, Education, and Social Participation Sub-Scores, and Total Role Scores for English Sample Members, by School and Sex

		Total Sample			U. of A.			U. of W.			Trade School		
		Total	M	F	Total	M	F	Total	M	F	Total	M	F
Personal Characteristic Sub-Score*	43+	40%	32%[a]	48%	45%	37%[a]	53%	41%	30%[a]	51%	32%	24%[b]	38%
Education Sub-Score*	26+	36	30[a]	42	41	38	44	35	28[b]	41	31	20[a]	40
Social Participation Sub-Score*	40+	35	24[a]	46	39	25[a]	53	35	24[a]	47	29	23[a]	36
Total Role Score*	260+	29	19[a]	38	31	25[b]	38	34	17[a]	49	21	12[a]	29
Number of Cases (no less than)		662	319	342	279	147	132	177	87	90	189	90	99

*   Higher score signifies more egalitarian orientation

[a] — signifies that differences between males and females are significant at the 1% level of confidence

[b] — signifies that differences between males and females are significant at the 5% level of confidence

each as well. By contrast, for the education area, the differences between the school samples were due solely to the differences between the male sample members, while the differences between the universities and the trade school in regard to the social participation scores were due to differences between the female members of the samples.

These data suggest some inferences about recency of impact of the egalitarian orientation in various areas. Two assumptions must be made, both largely substantiated by our data: (1) that women tend to accept egalitarianism before men do, and (2) that university students tend to accept egalitarianism before trade school students do. Granted these assumptions, it appears that egalitarianism is more completely accepted in the education area than in the other

two, since all the female samples show the same high level of acceptance, and since the University of Alberta males show about the same level of acceptance as do the females. The social participation area appears most resistant to the impact of egalitarianism, since all the male samples are at the same low level of acceptance of an egalitarian orientation here, and since there are sizable differences between the female samples with some reflecting little acceptance of egalitarianism. The personal characteristics area falls between these two, since the two female university samples show high egalitarianism tendencies, but the trade school female sample does not, and the male samples have significantly lower scores than the female samples.

Table II   Indices Relating to Attitudes toward the Role of the Wife, for English Sample Members, by School and by Sex

		Total Sample			U. of A.			U. of W.			Trade School		
		Total	M	F	Total	M	F	Total	M	F	Total	M	F
Household management sub-score*	36+	30%	33%	28%	32%	34%	30%	30%	29%	32%	27%	32%[b]	22%
Authority sub-score*	42+	40	33[a]	46	39	35	42	44	35[a]	53	37	28[a]	45
Employment and support sub-score*	33+	22	16[b]	27	26	18[b]	33	28	18[a]	37	11	10	12
Wife's role-housewife & mother only		20	26[b]	15	16	21	11	18	23	13	29	36[b]	23
Wife's role-employed only after children in high school		37	31[b]	42	39	33[b]	45	37	32[b]	42	34	27[b]	40
Not willing for wife to work after we have children		58	60	55	51	55	47	50	51	50	75	77	72
Wife take better job? Yes, definitely		28	39[a]	18	29	38[a]	21	25	42[a]	11	28	38[a]	20
Numbers of Cases (no less than)		662	319	342	279	147	132	177	87	90	189	90	99

*   Higher score signifies more egalitarian orientation.
[a] — signifies that differences between males and females are significant at the 1% level of confidence
[b] — signifies that differences between males and females are significant at the 5% level of confidence

The role of the wife

Information on the expected role of the wife includes three area scores from the Dunn Inventory — the household responsibility, authority, and employment and support areas — and several other questionnaire items dealing with issues relating to employment of the wife. These data are summarized in Table II for the total and the school samples, by sex of respondent.

The data show only one significant difference among the sex and school subsample comparisons, involving the household management area. The authority area, and employment and support area data show that women were generally significantly less traditional than were the men. School comparisons show that trade school women are less egalitarian than those in university, in regard to the employment and support area.

Responses to the first single item indicator were as follows:

"In my marriage I want the wife to be:
(1) housewife and mother to our children only (18 per cent)
(2) employed, but only after the children are in high school (37 per cent)
(3) able to pursue a work career, with children taken care of by babysitters as necessary (10 per cent)
(4) primarily a career woman who has babies only if they will not handicap her career, and maybe childless (2 per cent)
(5) I don't know, I'm quite confused (33 per cent)

Men responded (1) significantly more often than women, and women responded (2), (3) or (4) more often than men.

In response to the question, "How do you feel about the wife's working following your marriage?" 58% said they were not willing for the wife to work after children came. Trade school students were significantly less willing for mothers to work than either of the two university samples, but there were not differences between men and women.

A final question relevant to the role of housewife asked:

"What decision would you press for if in your marriage the wife had the opportunity to take a higher ranking or higher paying job than the husband's job? Why?"

About two thirds of the sample members said the wife ought to take the job, 37 per cent qualifying their affirmative answers ('yes, if we needed the money'). Eleven per cent qualified their negative answers ('no, unless we were desperate') and 22 per cent said the wife definitely should not take the job. Significantly more men than women in all of the samples gave definite affirmative answers. There were no differences between the school samples.

The reasons given by respondents (too detailed to enumerate here) show that women were more likely to be defensive in approaching the issue posed by the question, while men were more likely to be expensive. Women significantly more often said the wife could take the job only if the money was badly needed, or said the wife should not take the job because she should not threaten the husband. Men significantly more often said women should be equal or should have a chance to exercise their capabilities.

Again it is possible to rank these areas in terms of differential impact of egalitarianism. More general egalitarianism is found in the authority area — where women in all three schools were significantly more egalitarian than their male classmates, and there were no differences between women at different schools — than in the employment and support area, where only university women were significantly more egalitarian than their male classmates, and technical school were less egalitarian than university women. The authority area thus falls in the same middle egalitarianism range as the personal characteristics area, while the employment and support area falls in the same low egalitarianism range as the social participation area.

However, the household management shows a second different pattern, similar to the pattern of responses to the single item questioning whether the wife should take a better job than her husband. For the latter, men at all three schools made more egalitarian responses than their female classmates, and for the former, only the technical school men made more egalitarian responses than female students, while there were no differences between the men. We infer that areas demonstrating the *first* pattern are areas where men feel threatened by egalitarianism, whereas the *second* pattern is characteristic of areas where women feel threatened or defensive. It is plausible that women might feel defensive about men taking responsibility in the household management area; or threatened by their anticipation of a husband's response should they take a better job than his.

Responses of French Canadian sample members

In making the French translation, the French-Canadian research assistant, without authorization, reduced response alternatives of the Marital Role Expectation Inventory and of the Shobin Parent Attitude Survey from six to four. This change makes no difference in comparing proportions of students in the two samples who agree or disagree with various items. However, the scores for various scales and subscales of the Marital Role Expectation Inventory and the Shobin Parent Attitude Survey differ. Responses in the English language schedule were scored by weighing the six response alternatives in sequence from one to six. For the French language schedules "entirely in agreement" was scored as 1, "partially in agreement" as 3, "partially in disagreement" as 4, and "entirely in disagreement" as 6, or the reverse, depending on whether the item as stated was pro-egalitarian or pro-traditionalism.[7] These two scoring procedures may not be commensurable, and this should be borne in mind when comparisons between French and English samples are tentatively made.

Traditionalism – egalitarianism

The data in Table III suggest that the English sample members may be more egalitarian in their conceptions of marital roles than the French sample members. On all three of the subscores, as well as for the total score, the French sample scored lower than the English. The differential between these two was particularly large for the education subscore, where 55 percent of the English as compared with 41 percent of the French sample members scored under 23, as well as for the total score.

The data show that male French students were consistently less egalitarian in their orientations than the female students on all three subscores and that trade school students were consistently less egalitarian than the university students, for all areas. However, the spread in egalitarianism between the male and the female students was less wide among the university than among the trade school students.

Given the same assumptions as were made with the English language data, it is again possible to rank these areas in terms of differential impact of egalitarianism on them. The pattern is the reverse of that found for the English data, since the education area reflects the least spread of egalitarianism, among the French speaking students, and the personal characteristics and social participation areas reflect more egalitarianism, though neither to the extent of the education area among the English speaking respondents.

Table III   Personal Characteristics, Education and Social Participation Sub-Scores and Total Role Scores for French Sample Members, by School and by Sex with Comparison Data for English Sample

	Total French Sample			Total English Sample			University of*** Montreal			Trade School		
	Total	M	F	Total	M	F	Total	M	F	Total	M	F
Personal Characteristics Score* Under 39	56%	67%a	46%	28%	35%a	21%	32%	34%	28%	72%	88%a	56%
Education Score* Under 23	41	55a	27	32	39a	25	18	26b	10	57	75a	39
Social Participation Score* Under 34	39	52a	25	25	30a	20	22	26	18	50	70a	30
Total Role Score* Under 240	49	65a	32	43	51a	35	31	44a	16	60	78a	40
Numbers of Cases	376	185	191	662	319	342	158	74	84	218	111	107

* Higher score signifies more egalitarian orientation.

*** School information not available for 32 respondents.

a Signifies that differences between males and females are significant at the 1% level of confidence.

b Signifies that differences between males and females are significant at the 5% level of confidence.

The role of the wife

In interesting contrast to the pattern of French-English sample contrasts seen in the previous section, the data in Table IV suggest that in defining the wife's role the French sample was generally more egalitarian than the English sample. French Canadian women were more egalitarian than men, and university students more egalitarian than trade school students on all subscores.

Responses to the first single item indicator were as follows:

"In my marriage I want the wife to be:
(1) Housewife and mother to our children only (17 per cent)
(2) Employed at productive and interesting work, but only after the children are in high school (34 per cent)
(3) Able to pursue a work career under any conditions (23 per cent)
(4) I don't know (26 per cent)

These data show little commitment to the traditional conception of the wife as housewife and mother, since only one in six chose this limited role. Men were five times as likely as women to choose this response, as the data in Table IV show, and women twice as often as men felt a woman should be able to pursue a career under any conditions.

The second question asked "How do you feel about the wife's working following your marriage?" The responses were as follows:

(1) I would approve of her working only before we have children (39 percent)

Table IV   Indices Relating to Attitudes Toward the Role of the Wife, for French Sample Members, by School and by Sex, with Comparison Data from English Sample

	Total French Sample			Total English Sample			University of*** Montreal			Trade School		
	Total	M	F	Total	M	F	Total	M	F	Total	M	F
Household Score* Under 31	31%	33%	28%	36%	35%	37%	21%	24%	18%	38%	42%	35%
Authority Score* Under 38	35	52a	18	36	40a	31	23	33a	11	44	67a	21
Employment and Support Score* Under 27	28	38a	17	42	48a	37	20	30a	8	33	42b	22
Wife's Role-Housewife and Mother Only	17	29a	5	20	26b	15	6.4	11.5a	0.0	24	40a	6
Wife's Role Employed only after children in high school	34	29a	39	37	31b	47	34	33	34	32	26a	40
Not Sure About What the Wife's Role Should Be	26	28a	23	31	33	30	28	33	21	25	25	25
Wife's Role — A Career Under Any Conditions	23	14	33	12	10	13						
Not willing For Wife to Work After We Have Children	59	56	61	58	60	55	39	41	36	70	65	76
Wife Should be Free to Choose Whether or not to Take a Better Job Than Her Husband's Yes Definitely	47	47	48	28	39a	18	56	55	58	43	42	43
Would let Wife Choose Whether or Not She Worked	22	40	4	9	17	1						
Numbers of Cases	371	191	180	662	319	342	158	85	73	213	106	107

* High score signifies more egalitarian orientation
*** School information not available for 32 respondents
a Signifies that differences between males and females are significant at the 1% level of confidence.
b Signifies that differences between males and females are significant at the 5% of level confidence.

(2) I would not approve of her working under any circumstances (4 per cent)

(3) I would approve under any circumstances (7 per cent)

(4) I would approve if we needed the money (16 per cent)

(5) I would leave my wife free to choose (22 per cent)

(6) I would leave my husband free to choose (4 per cent)

(7) Others (9 per cent)

The responses also show a rather liberal orientation to the question of the wife's working. The women very much more often than the men said they would approve of the wife's working under any circumstances, if they needed the money while the men much more often said they would leave the decision to the wife. (See Table IV.)

The last question asked: "If the wife had the opportunity to take a position which was more important and more remunerative than that of the husband, the latter should let the wife make her own decision." An overwhelming 77 per cent of the respondents agreed with this statement, 47 per cent agreeing "entirely." The responses of men and women were similar.

The information reviewed in this section suggests that the attitude of French Canadian students toward the role that the wife should play in marriage may be more emancipated than that of English speaking students. One cannot be sure because of differences in scoring procedures. But this does not mean that there is consensus between French Canadian young men and women. On all the indicators the women were found to have a more egalitarian orientation than men.

These areas may also be ranked in terms of the differential impact of egalitarianism that the respondents' scores reflect. The rankings of the employment and authority areas are the same as for the English speaking respondents, with the former reflecting less egalitarianism than the latter. However instead of presenting quite a different pattern of differential egalitarianism, as the household management area did for the English data, the pattern for the French speaking respondents is the same as the employment area. That is, instead of seeming less accepting than men of the suggestion that they should share household chores with men, as were the English language women, the French language women were more accept-

ing of egalitarianism than the men in this as in other areas.

Conclusions from analysis of English and French Canadian data

The indices of orientation to marriage used in the present study related to marital interaction and responsibility in terms of egalitarianism, with special reference to personal characteristics, social life, significance of education and role alternatives of the wife. It is not possible to make statements about the relative egalitarianism or permissiveness of the sample as a whole since adequate comparison data from other groups are not available. Comparisons between French and English members of the sample are tentatively made because of differences in the wording and some of the response categories used in the two questionnaires. One of the most fruitful uses of the data is to test the ability of various independent variables to predict variance in the criterion items, thus identifying differences in attitude forming influences between some of the subsamples studies on the criterion.

The available data suggest some interesting contrasts between the French and the English-language samples. In terms of general egalitarianism, the data suggest that the English sample was distinctly more egalitarian. However, on several items relating to the conditions of employment of the wife, the English were less egalitarian than the French speaking respondents. For almost all the items, the male-female sex differences were larger for the French than for the English samples, since the women in both samples were consistently more egalitarian than the men and the English speaking men were more egalitarian, generally, than their

French counterparts.

We cannot conclude that one language group is consistently more egalitarian in its orientation toward marriage than the other. The English speaking sample members were the more egalitarian in areas concerned with personal characteristics of marriage partners, social life and education expectations. In the area of the wife's role, including her authority, housework and gainful employment, the French speaking respondents were more egalitarian. However, this was entirely a result of the high egalitarianism of the women. The French men were more traditional than were the English speaking men.

Thus in several areas, French Canadian women are pioneers in advocating egalitarian and permissive orientations, in comparison with English speaking respondents, while French Canadian men are the most traditional of all.

We have found evidence of the differential impact of egalitarianism in different marital role areas, as follows. Among English speaking respondents the impact of egalitarianism was most strongly seen in the education area, and least seen in the social participation and employment areas, with the personal characteristics and authority areas in between. In addition to these areas reflecting male conservativism, the household management was found to reflect female conservativism, with men making more egalitarian responses than women, among the English respondents. Among French speaking respondents there was no area reflecting as much egalitarianism as the education area among the English, where only trade school men were significantly less egalitarian than other sex-school categories. However the personal characteristics, social participation, and authority areas had response patterns suggesting medium egalitarianism, and the education, household management, and employment and support area scores suggest low spread of egalitarianism. No area was found reflecting female conservativism, among the French respondents, comparable to the household management area for the English speaking respondents.

One of the most interesting findings of this study is the magnitude of the difference in the explainable variance in the indicators of these marital role issues. In general at least 18 or 20 percent of the variance for most items was explained by the predictive factors in the French data, but no more than 7 to 10 percent of the variance was explained for these items in the English data. These data indicate that there are much more powerfully entrenched definitions of orthodox orientations in the French Canadian culture than in the Anglo-Canadian culture. Wide variations in the responses of Anglo-Canadian students were found but it is not possible to predict these variations on the basis of knowledge of their background characteristics. Thus background characteristics do not identify subcultures that define orthodoxies related to marital role expectations.

The pattern of predictive relationships for the French sample data is in marked contrast. Of the 12 indicators considered in this study, in 8 cases for the French data the variance predicted in the criterion by the predictive variables exceeded 19 percent, while this was true for none of the indicators for the English data. The reason for this much higher degree of predictability of the French student responses in these areas is easily seen. For seven of the twelve items the sex identity factor was the most powerful predictor and for two it was the second most powerful. For two items the religious factor was the most powerful predictor and for five it was the second most powerful. Thus for these areas there are very substantial differences between the men and women in the French student sample, and crucial issues in these areas are still significantly morally (religiously) defined for a substantial minority.

Two aspects of these data suggest that the revolution in sex roles in marriage is more advanced among the English than among the French speaking students. First, among the English, religiosity is little predictive of attitudes on relevant issues; thus traditional moral definitions of these issues have broken down. Second, during the early stages of a feminist revolt one would expect sizable differences between male and female perspectives among *avant garde* elements of the population, such as students. These differences are in fact found in the French but not in the English speaking sample members, generally speaking, suggesting that the "revolution" is sufficiently advanced among the latter for it to have affected men as well as women.

However, this is an oversimplified picture since (1) the French sample members tended to have more egalitarian attitudes toward employment of the wife than did the English members, and (2) the French women students had more egalitarian attitudes in many areas than the English women. The reasons for these findings are not clear. Perhaps the first may be explained by larger differences on value issues between the French and English Canadian cultures. A reason for the second point may be that during any period of conflict the attitudes of the two sides tend to polarize, with each taking a more extreme position.

NOTES

1 This is shown by certain provincial and federal laws in force prior to 1900, see, British Columbia, e.g. (Married Women's Property Act, R. S. B. C., 1888, 51 Vic., c. 80; Dower Act, R. S. B. C., 1897, 60 Vic, c. 63); Alberta, e.g. (Property and Civil Rights Act, Ord., 1884, 47 Vic., no. 26; Married Women's Real Estate Act, Ord., 1886, 49 Vic., no. 6; Personal Property of Married Women, R. S. O., 1889, 52 Vic., no. 16, 1898, c. 47); Ontario, e.g. (An Act Respecting Certain Separate Rights of Property of Married Women, C. S. U. C., 1859, 22 Vic., c. 73; *Ontario Statutes Annotations*, R. S. O., *1960* (Toronto: Canada Law Bank Co., 1961) p. 378, citing "Married Women's Real Estate Act," C. S. U. C. 1859, c. 85; Property Act of Married Women, R. S. O., 1887, 50 Vic., c. 132, Dower Act, c. 133, Married Woman's Real Estate Act, c. 134); New Brunswick, e.g. (Married Woman's Property Act, S. N. B., 1896, 58 Vic., c. 24); Newfoundland, e.g. (Married Woman's Property Act, R. S. N., 1883); Nova Scotia, e.g. (Married Woman's Property Act, 1898, 52 Vic., c. 22, Dower Act, c. 23); Prince Edward Island, e.g. (Married Woman's Property Act, 1896, Journ. P. E. I.). This may also be inferred from amendments to the above laws, and passage of later statutes pertaining to the property rights of women. For the statutes passed after 1900, see, British Columbia, e.g. (Married Woman's Property Act, S. B. C., 1915, 5 Geo. V, c. 41, as amended; Mother's Pension Act, S. B. C., 1920, 10-11 Geo. V, c. 61); Alberta, e.g. (Henrietta Muir Edwards, ed., *Legal Status of Women of Alberta As Shown by Extracts from Dominion and Provincial Laws* (2nd ed; Edmonton: Issued by Attorney General, 1921), p. 26, citing "Dower Act", S. A., 917, p. 28, citing "Personal Property Act", C. O., 1911, c. 47, sec. 1, no. 20 of 1890; "Real Estate Act", S. A., 1906, c. 9, sec. 10; "Intestate Succession Act", S. A., 1920, sec. 3 (a)(c), c.

19, S. A., 1906; p. 31, citing "Married Woman's Relief Act", S. A., c. 19, 1910, as amended; p. 72, citing "Dominion Lands Act", S. C., 1908, c. 20; An Act Respecting the Transfer and Descent of Land, 1906, S. A., c. 19, 1922, c. 10); Saskatchewan, e.g. (Married Woman's Property Act, 1907, S. S., 7 Ed III, c. 18); Manitoba, e.g. (Married Woman's Property Act, 1913, 3 Geo. V, c. 123; Devolution of Estates Act, c. 48; Ontario, e.g. (Property Rights of Married Women, R. S. O., 1914, 9 Ed. VII, c. 149, as amended; Dower Act, 1914, S. O., 9 Ed. VII, c. 39); Quebec, e.g. (Property Rights of Married Women, C. C. Q. S., 1931, art. 986, 1954, art. 986, as amended; Women's Property Rights, Q. S., 1909, 9 Ed. VII, c. 30; Woman's Contract Rights, C. C. Q. S., 4 Ed. VII, art 1301, as amended); New Brunswick, e.g. (Act Respecting Dower, C. S. N. B., 1903, 6 Vic., c. 77): Newfoundland, e.g. (Property Rights of Married Women Act, R. S. N., 1952, c. 143, as amended); Prince Edward Island, e.g. (Married Woman's Property Act, 1903, 3 Ed. VII, c. 9).

2 Elections Act, S. C., 1918, 8-9 Geo. V. c. 20. This Act amended sec. 62 (p) of the Wartime Election Act, S. C., 1917, 7-8 Geo. V. c. 39, which limited the franchise to women having close relatives in the armed forces.

3 U. S. const. amend, XIX, sec. 177 (1920). *August 26, 1920 May 24, 1918.*

4 Canada, Department of Trade and Commerce, *The Canada Yearbook,* 1940 (Ottawa: King's Printer, 1940), subsections 1, 2, and 4 pp. 750, 751, and 759; see also Canada, Department of Labour, *The Labour Gazette,* 1934 (Ottawa: King's Printer, 1934) XXXIV, 49-65.

5 Immigration figures cited in Canada, Department of Manpower and Immigration, *Immigration Statistics: Canadian Immigration Division,* 1967 (Ottawa: King's Printer, 1967)

p. 4, show that during the years 1951 to 1960, 1,521,679 people entered Canada. This represented 10.8% of the total population in 1951. The years of peak immigration were 1957 and 1953, when 282,164 and 168,868 people entered respectively. (1967 when 222,876 people entered; 1966 when 194,743 entered).

6 The most recent figures on television content reported by the Committee on Broadcasting, *Report of the Committee on Broadcasting,* Robert M. Fowler, chairman (Ottawa: Queen's Printer, 1965), pp. 32-36, show that in a study of television programs shown from 6:00 p.m. to midnight in four typical Canadian cities during March, 1964, 51% to 78% of all programs available to viewers were of American origin. The proportion of American programs broadcast by Canadian stations is limited to the Canadian Broadcasting Act (S. C., 1958, 7 Eliz. II, c. 22) ruling, that 55% of daily television program content must be Canadian produced. However, on the average, 54% of Canadian homes can receive American television programs directly from U. S. stations. The most recent information on magazine distribution available here is found in the *Report of the Royal Commission on Publications to the Governor General in Council,* M. Grattan O'Leary, chairman (Ottawa: Queen's Printer, 1961), p. 36, which used borrowed figures reported in the A. B. C. Publisher's Statements, *Audit Bureau of Circulation New Bulletin,* June 30, 1960, to estimate that 75% of the consumer magazines sold in Canada in the month of June, 1960 were of American origin.

7 If responses were equally distributed across all six categories for the English Canadian respondents and across all four categories for the French Canadian respondents, these scoring procedures would give identical total scores.

REFERENCES

Blood, Robert O. Jr. and Donald M. Wolfe, 1960. *Husbands and Wives,* New York: Free Press of Glencoe.

Dean, Dwight G., 1961. "Alienation: Its Meaning and Measurement", *American Sociological Review*, Vol. 26, pp. 753-758.

Dunn, Marie S., 1960. "Marriage Role Expectations of Adolescents", *Marriage and Family Living,* Vol. 22, p. 100.

Hobart, Charles W., 1956. "Disagreement and

Non-Empathy During Courtship'', *Marriage and Family Living*, Vol. 18, pp. 317-322.

Hobart, Charles W., 1958. ''Disillusionment in Marriage and Romanticism'', *Marriage and Family Living,* Vol. 20, pp. 156-162.

Hobart, Charles W., 1960. ''Attitude Changes During Courtship and Marriage'', *Marriage and Family Living,* Vol. 22, pp. 352-359.

Hobart, Charles W., 1971. ''Sexual Permissiveness in Young English and French Canadians'', Forthcoming in the Journal of Marriage and the Family.

Johnson, Benton, n. d. ''The Comparative Value Project'', National Institute of Mental Health, Grant No. 4309-R1. United States Government.

Kinsey, A. C., W. B. Pomery, and C. E. Martin, 1948. Sexual Behaviour in the Human Male, Philadelphia: Saunders.

Kinsey, A. C., W. B. Pomery, C. E. Martin and P. H. Gebhard, 1953. Sexual Behaviour in the Human Female. Philadelphia: Saunders.

Cultural orientations in marriages between French and English Canadians

As seen in Chapter four, maximum societal interest in the choice of a marital partner typically leads to endogamous marriage patterns. Through this technique among others, the replacement and duplication of culture is ensured. Exogamous marriage, in contrast, appears to undermine the persistence of tradition and facilitate either the emergence of new cultural forms (the merger of two cultures creates a different pattern) or the assimilation of one cultural form into another. Cultural assimilation is the more common process, particularly when a minority group is exposed to the dominant influences of the majority group. The Lebanese Muslim family in Canada, for example, appears to have lost most of its unique characteristics because of the influence of Canadian custom and law (Barclay, 1971).

The paper by Carisse assesses the implications of intermarriage between French and English Canadians. The paper is of considerable interest, given the assumption that Canada is not a melting pot but a stronghold of both pluralism and dualism. If indeed bilingualism and biculturalism are possible, the most obvious test of this ideal is in the French-English marriage. On the assumption that French and English spouses are bi-ethnic equals (dualism), Carisse explores several behavioral areas where bicultural differences might be expected. One would expect a system of tradeoffs and bargains which approximate equality for the behavioral preferences of both the French and English spouse. In fact, the English Canadian culture dominates most cultural aspects of the marriage, especially if the male is English.

While this study appears to document the significance of intermarriage for the demise of dualism in Canadian culture, it must be recognized that persons who marry outside their own ethnic group are *less committed* to their ethnic values than those who don't intermarry. Therefore evidence of decreased bilingual and bicultural activities is to be expected. Bicultural bargaining activities will not be as intensive because the commitment to cultural alternatives is modest (Bernard, 1964). Religious intermarriage, for example, typically occurs among persons who are neither active in nor committed to their particular religious dogma. This study also appears to offer credence to the emergence of a new cultural form: a family oriented to the community and actively involved in kin relations (from the French Canadian culture) combined with the predominant characteristics of the English Canadian culture. In this sense, there appears to be some evidence that dualism works, though not as well for French as for English Canadians.

Cultural orientations in marriages between French and English Canadians

Colette Carisse

Research problems

The timeliness of marriage studies between Canadians of English and French origins does *not* stem from the numerical importance of this phenomenon which actually only represented in 1962 about five per cent of marriages by French Canadians and twenty per cent by English Canadians in Montreal (see Table 1).[1] Small in number, these marriages have always been considered social deviance, threatening the survival of the French Canadian group. Both traditional and recent novels present these unions as treason by the French Canadian to his race and to the language of his ancestors.[2]

In American studies, inter-ethnic marriage is most often envisaged as a step in the assimilation process of a minority in the American melting pot. This approach is not appropriate to a study in Quebec because both groups belong to the culture of a majority group, defined as such whether Quebec or Canada is taken as the totality. From the demographic point of view, there are two majority groups in Canada: French Canadians in the province of Quebec, and English Canadians in the whole of Canada.

In Montreal, where the research was carried out, the two ethnic groups form the basis of two distinct communities which have, however, numerous links in various spheres of social organization. Since two different cultural systems could be referred to in defin-

Colette Carisse, Ph.D., is Associate Professor, Department of Sociology, University of Montreal, Quebec.
From Jean L. Elliott, ed., *Immigrant Groups* (Scarborough: Prentice-Hall of Canada, Ltd., 1971), pp. 191-206. Originally published as "Orientations culturelles dans les mariages entre Canadiens français et Canadiens anglais" in *Sociologie et Sociétés, 1, No. 1, (May, 1969).* Reprinted by permission of the author, Prentice-Hall of Canada, Ltd., and L'Université de Montréal.

Table 1   Percentage Distribution of Marriages by the Ethnicity of the Spouse for Montreal, 1951 and 1962

| | | | | | *Ethnicity of Spouse* | | | |
| | | | *1951* | | | | *1962* | | |
Ethnic group		*N*	*French*	*English*	*Other*	*N*	*French*	*English*	*Other*
French:									
	Male	7818	93.6	3.7	2.6	7367	92.9	4.3	2.6
	Female	7995	92.7	3.8	3.4	7735	88.5	5.0	6.4
English:									
	Male	1417	14.7	74.9	10.4	1258	21.9	64.9	13.1
	Female	1375	12.4	76.5	9.0	1286	17.9	63.3	18.8

SOURCE: Yvon Lacoste, *Une étude des statistiques des mariages interethniques à Montreal pour les années 1951 et 1962*, M.A. Thesis, Department of Sociology, University of Montreal, 1966.

ing many common activities, we posit that the present arrangement is in the nature of a compromise. The initial question of interest to this study is the following: in a situation known to require compromise, which cultural elements will be given up or retained by each ethnic group? It is from this perspective that we have studied bi-ethnic marriages. Marriage is a face-to-face social relation which crystallizes individual choices, choices which must be made if a marriage is to persist.

This study analyzes the cultural orientation of spouses, i.e., their choices when confronted with the two cultural systems which, as a result of marriage are accessible to them. It is our hypothesis that these choices are not distributed at random, but rather that their distribution will reveal the "strong" and "weak" points of each culture.

Research Design

From the marriage registers in Montreal, we obtained the names of French/English couples married in 1951. At the time of the study, these couples had been married approximately fifteen years. We were able to

trace fifty-nine couples where the husband is English and the wife French, and fifty-seven couples where the husband is French and the wife English. Each spouse was interviewed individually. Thus the population totalled 232 respondents.

We wanted to be able to measure the losses and gains of each ethnic group engaged in the accommodation process. Operationally we measured the individual's choices in terms of the two cultural poles — French and English — with respect to the following areas of behaviour:

a) Community structures: neighbourhood, school, church;

b) Social network: relatives, friends, voluntary associations;

c) Mass media: television, newspaper, magazines;

d) Family interaction: language used by spouses when communicating among themselves and with children, and language used by children when communicating among themselves and with parents.[3]

Since the subjects are considered as members of ethnic *groups*, we are not concerned with studying the acculturation or assimilation of *individuals*. The ethnic group *per se* is the unit of analysis in this comparative study. For each of twelve categories of social behaviour, we established the proportion of individuals who, at the time of the study, were functioning in their own cultural system, and inversely, the proportion of those who have adopted their spouse's culture. By ordering the results for each behavior on a give and take continuum, we hope to reveal the aspects of a culture which an ethnic group is willing to relinquish, and contrarily, the areas which each group tends to retain. In this manner we will attempt to establish the "strong" and "weak" points of each culture.

Our hypothesis is that there is a process of exchange (Lévi-Strauss) or bargaining (Goode, Homans) taking place between the two ethnic groups. Accordingly, one concedes on a particular point in order to win on another. This hypothesis postulates that the two cultures are different in the sense that their valued areas are not the same. The hypothesis will be confirmed if there is a strong, negative correlation between that which is relinquished by each of the two groups.

Cultural orientation

Indices attempting to measure cultural orientation were constructed as ordinal scales. Totally English or totally French orientations were considered as polar opposites. The results are summarized in Table 2.

Table 2   Proportion of Spouses in Bi-Ethnic Marriages Who Are Oriented to Their Culture of Origin, by Ethnicity and Sex of Spouse

Areas of behaviour	English spouse	French spouse	Husband	Wife	Husband English	Husband French	Wife English	Wife French
Community:								
Neighbourhood	23	77	54	47	27	82	18	73
Language of religion	36	53	54	35	44	65	28	42
School	44	56	56	44	49	63	37	49
Social network:								
Visits by friends	50	52	59	43	60	59	40	46
Voluntary associations	86	26	63	45	87	39	83	7
Ties with relatives	46	63	47	61	39	55	53	70
Mass media:								
T.V.	86	28	63	51	93	32	78	24
Newspapers	75	36	61	50	77	45	73	27
Magazines	94	13	55	53	93	16	95	11
Language of use:[a]								
Family in general	61	51	64	48	71	51	51	46
With spouse	63	36	55	44	66	60	60	29
With sons	68	49	64	54	74	69	69	45
With daughters	68	51	62	56	74	59	59	52
Total	116	116	116	116	59	57	57	59

[a] This is a composite measure of the language used by each member with each one of the others.

The data have been dichotomized: proportion of subjects studied which favoured somewhat or totally the culture of origin, and inversely, proportion of the respondents who are oriented toward the culture of their spouse (this latter percentage can be calculated by deducting from one hundred per cent the percentages in Table 2). Thus, with respect to the *dominant language* index, one sees by referring to Table 2A, that sixty-one per cent of the English spouses use their mother tongue in family interaction as opposed to fifty-one per cent of the French spouses. The data are reported by also taking into consideration the sex of the spouse. One notices that husbands use their mother tongue more frequently than wives, and the breakdown of data by sex and ethnic group indicates that this tendency is more pronounced for English husbands than French husbands. One is able to analyze each index in a similar fashion.

Table 2A   Proportion of English Canadians and French Canadians, Husbands and Wives, Who Use Their Mother Tongue in Conjugal Relationships[a]

	Ethnic group		
Sex	English	French	Total
Husband	71%	56%	64%
Wife	51	46	48
Total	61	51	N=232

[a] Figures are from Table 2 above.

The difference between the percentages indicates (a) the ethnic group more likely to maintain its cultural orientation, and (b) which spouse, husband or wife, uses the mother tongue to a greater extent. In Table 2A we see the English group ten per cent ahead of the French group with respect to language retention and male spouses sixteen per cent more likely than female spouses to retain their mother tongue. When the same calculations are made for each behavioural item, we not only are able to ascertain which ethnic group tends to conserve its culture of origin, but also the intensity with which it is conserved relative to the other ethnic group. It is this differential which is used in Table 3, where behavioural items are ordered from the most marked orientation toward the English culture to the most marked orientation to the French culture. Two important conclusions may be reached by reading Table 3 in conjunction with Table 2.

1. In an interaction situation which poses a choice between the French and English culture, the English ethnic group tends to conserve its own culture more than the French group. This first conclusion, however, must be qualified by the following:

2. The behavioural areas which the English and French cling to tend to be different. In fact the items may be grouped into three distinct life sectors:

   a) areas in which adherence to the French culture is evident: home, kin, religion, school, friends;

   b) areas in which adherence to the English culture is evident: magazines, associations, television, and newspapers;

   c) intermediate areas: language in the home, for example, where English predominates but in a restrictive manner.

In behavioural items in which the French culture prevails (see "a" above), it appears

Table 3   Difference in the Proportion of English and French Spouses Who Choose Their Culture of Origin in Different Behavioural Areas

Area of behaviour	Percentage difference[a]	Subgroup control[b]
English +		
Magazines	61	Both spouses
Associations	60	Both spouses
T.V.	58	Both spouses
Newspapers	39	Both spouses
Language spoken to spouse	27	Both spouses
Language spoken to sons	19	Both spouses
Language spoken to daughters	11	Both spouses
Dominant language	10	Both spouses
French +		
Visits by friends	2	Wives only
School	12	Both spouses
Religion	17	Both spouses
Ties with relatives	17	Both spouses
Neighbourhood	54	Both spouses

a For each item, the difference is calculated from the percentage for each sub-group "English" and "French," as reported in Table 2. For the example used in Table 2A, dominant language, the difference is 10%, as can be read in the present table.

b Indicates whether predominance exists for respondents of both sexes when compared separately, i.e., English husbands with French husbands, English wives with French wives.

that the indices point to one underlying factor: community structure, the traditional bastion of French-Canadian culture, which has as its basis primary face-to-face relations. The traditional society has always relied upon a close-knit kin group attending church and school in an homogeneous community. It tends to be these values which French-Canadian spouses refuse to relinquish even when they inhabit an urban milieu, as is the case with the couples studied here.

On the other hand, the English (see "b" above) are not likely to abandon their mass media and voluntary associations representing perhaps the modern element of the society (one would be tempted to say access to power).[4]

At the beginning of this study, we put forth the hypothesis that the choices made between the French and English culture were not randomly distributed, but reveal "strong" and "weak" aspects of each culture. Our data tend to confirm our main hypothesis. French culture is anchored in the community; English culture is centred upon secondary relationships and mass media, important elements of industrial life and power.

As a corollary to this fact, one could say that there is a process of exchange taking place with respect to what each culture is willing to give up or refuses to give up. The *marchandage* (bargaining) follows the strong and weak points of each of the two cultures. One concedes to the other in areas of value in order that one might be the beneficiary of concessions in areas of even greater value.

This conclusion follows from an analysis of Table 4 which rank orders behavioural items by adherence accorded them, ranging from the item where each of the sub-groups concedes the least (rank 1) to the item where one concedes the most (rank 13). The area of behaviour which comprises the largest proportion of spouses having retained their own culture is the area where the group gives up the least; therefore, by inference, the behavioural area which he values the most. The rank order of adherence to cultural items was established for each sub-group — male/English (ME), male/French (MF), female/English (FE), female/French (FF) — and for each ethnic group and sex. If this correlation was weak or even positive, this would be because there are predominant cultural areas which are bound to a supra-ethnic value system, let us say Canadian or North American — areas so highly valued by both cultures that neither spouse in either system is willing to relinquish. On the contrary, a negative correlation means that that which is valued the most highly by one group is the least valued by the other group and accommodation can thus take place in the form of an exchange. We found a rank order correlation which is strong and negative when comparing the following groups: French and English (r = −.923), French men and English men (r = −.816), and French women and English women (r = −.847).

In order to pursue this analysis further, it would be interesting to have behavioural comparisons by social class. One can formulate the hypothesis that the middle class individual will be more strongly oriented toward the English culture than the lower class individual. For the middle class person in Montreal, the orientation towards the English culture would mean an identification with the power structure of the business and industrial world which, in fact, is controlled by ''Anglo-Saxon'' money — be it British,

Canadian, or American. Analysis by social class has been made with respect to adherence to the following cultural items: language, voluntary associations, kin relationships, friends, and newspapers. We have divided the individuals into two occupational categories important from the sociological point of view: (a) workers and the very small businessmen, and (b) professionals, administrators, and entrepreneurs, normally possessing a certain amount of autonomy and liberty in decision-making. Differences in cultural orientation by social class as measured by occupation are in the direction of our hypothesis; there is a more marked orientation towards the English culture, the higher the social class of the individual. The exception occurs with respect to relationships with kin; the ties are stronger with the French-Canadian family when the family is of a relatively high social status. However, the differences are appreciable and statistically significant only in six of the eighteen possibilities: the language in the family used by

Table 4   Cultural Orientation of Bi-Ethnic Marriages, Rank Ordered by Ethnicity and Sex[a]

Behaviour area	English	French	English Husband	French Husband	English Wife	French Wife	Male	Female
Magazines	1	13	1.5	13	1	12	10.5	4
Associations	2.5	12	3	11	2	13	4.5	9
T.V.	2.5	11	1.5	12	3	11	4.5	5
Newspapers	4	9.5	4	9	4	10	7	6
Language spoken to sons	5.5	8	5.5	7	5	8	2.5	3
Language spoken to daughters	5.5	6	5.5	8	7	3	6	2
Language spoken to spouse	7	9.5	9	10	6	9	10.5	10.5
Language spoken to family	8	6	7	5	9	6.5	2.5	7
Visits of friends	9	5	10	4	10	6.5	8	12
Language of religion	10	3	8	2	12	5	1	13
Ties with relatives	11	2	12	6	8	2	13	1
School	12	4	11	3	11	4	9	10.5
Neighbourhood	13	1	13	1	13	1	12	8

[a] Rank 1 = least willing to compromise in this area.
  Rank 13 = most willing to compromise in this area.

Table 5 Proportion of Bi-Ethnic Marriages Oriented to Culture of Origin, by Ethnicity, Sex and Social Status of Spouse[a]

Sex	Husbands				Wives			
Ethnicity	English		French		English		French	
Behaviour:								
Social Status	+	−	+	−	+	−	+	−
Dominant language	78	66	46	65	77	35**	27	62**
Associations	100*	75*	34	55	85	80	6	15
Friends' visits[b]	62	44	48	75*	52	25*	38	56
Newspapers	88	66	23	59**	86	62	8	44*
Ties with relatives	32	42	64	48	41	61	80	61
Total[c]	27	32	22	34	22	34	27	32

a Significance level: * = .05; ** = .01.
b The same measure is applicable to both spouses; therefore, this measure of orientation is reciprocal.
c Social status was not determined for one marriage involving a French-Canadian husband and his English-Canadian wife.

wives of both ethnic groups, membership retention in English associations by English men, friendships with English friends by couples where the husband is French, and newspapers read by the French group of both sexes. With the data at our disposal, one can say that our hypothesis is partially confirmed; when there is a significant difference in behaviour by social class, this difference favours, weakly in some cases, but without exception, the English culture.[5]

So far our analysis has been a comparison of the French and English ethnic groups. Let us now consider the sex of the spouse. The research question becomes the following: when an accommodation is required, is it the husband or the wife (regardless of ethnic group) who wins or loses in the game of cultural bargaining? The data distributed on a continuum *man wins/female wins* (Table 6) furnishes an obvious answer. The wife, whether she is French or English, wins only on a single point, that of visits to her relatives more often than her spouse's relatives. This confirms the well known fact that the women are agents of cohesion and communication within the kinship group. In all other areas, choice tends to be in keeping with the ethnic group of the husband. This mode of marital adjustment which favours the male to the detriment of the female explains the masculine preponderance in the choice of the culture to be transmitted to children of a bi-ethnic marriage.[6] One can deduce, from these observations, that the combination *husband English/wife French* will tend to result in the eventual assimilation of the French woman. Indeed, the English male is in a doubly strong position — by sex and ethnic group. In the combination *husband French/wife English*, the female

Table 6 Difference in the Proportion of Husbands and Wives Who Choose their Culture of Origin by Behaviour Areas

Behaviour area	Percentage Difference[a]	Subgroup Control[b]
Husband +		
Religion	19	English & French
Associations	18	English & French
Friends' visits	16	English & French
Language (total)	16	English & French
Television	12	English & French
School	12	English & French
Newspapers	11	English & French
Language with spouse	11	English & French
Language with sons	10	English & French
Neighbourhood	7	English & French
Language with daughters	6	English only
Magazines	2	French only
Wife +		
Ties with relatives	14	English & French

a For each item, the difference is calculated from the percentage of both subgroups "husband" and "wife" as reported in Table 2.
b Indicates whether predominance exists for respondents of both ethnic groups, when compared separately.

gains because of her ethnic group and the male gains because of his sex. From our limited data, it appears that this conjugal situation contains fewer conflicts.[7]

Biculturalism

We now know the answer to the question formulated at the beginning of this study, i.e., in an interaction situation between two persons from different ethnic groups, which culture, which community, is privileged? One could conceive that the ideal solution does not consist of privileging one or the other culture, but rather of functioning simultaneously or alternately (depending on the case) in the two communities and cultures. Thus one can make use equally of French and English in the family situation, looking at French and English television, receiving French and English friends, reading French and English newspapers, etc. Let us see the concrete implications of this proposal.

In the preceding section, we described the dominance of one culture over another when dichotomizing our measures. In order to measure biculturalism, we isolated the central category of the distribution, cases where only one culture is strongly privileged, being thus isolated at the two opposing poles of the scale. Table 7 gives the proportion of the cases which are situated inside the central category, that is, bicultural behaviour. The following facts are elicited by reading this table:

1. In general, behaviour is not predominantly bicultural in any of the specific areas. In fact, if one looks in the total column of Table 7, there is not a single

percentage which includes over fifty per cent of the cases.

2. The proportion of spouses who refer to both cultures is appreciable (from thirty-three to fifty per cent of the subjects interviewed) in the following areas: social relations with friends and relatives, television, and magazines.

3. Bicultural behaviour is rare (less than thirty-three per cent of the cases) when it is a question of residential area, language of one's religion, voluntary associations, newspapers, and the language used in one's general family life.

4. In the four sub-groups (ME, MF, FE, FF), a majority of French spouses opt for

Table 7   Proportion of Spouses Who Ascribe to Both Cultures

| Behaviour Area | Husband | | Wife | | Total |
	English %	French %	English %	French %	%
Community structures:[a]					
Neighbourhood	32	28	20	33	27
Language of religion	13	5	5	5	8
Social network:					
Friends' visits	42	39	32	50	41
Associations	42	34	26	25	32
Relatives	47	52	39	42	45
Mass media:					
T.V.	40	45	40	32	41
Newspapers	23	16	20	30	22
Magazines	32	39	46	60	45
Dominant language in home[b]	34	30	25	34	30

[a] We have eliminated the choice of school from this section. Actually an adequate measure of biculturalism would be applicable to cases, where, in the family, one would find one or more of the children who attend a French school, *and* one or more who attends an English School. The tabulation of the data by child, and not by family, does not permit us to apply this measure.

[b] We could not use language spoken with spouse, sons, and daughters, because the form of the question which offered four choices: always English, often English, often French, always French. The addition of the two central categories would give a measure which over-estimates bilingualism. Contrarily, the measure for the whole of the relationships is an index which corrects for this bias.

cultural behaviour in three areas: visits with relatives (MF), magazines (FF), and ties with friends (FF). This last fact leads us to a point which is of particular importance to the French Canadian. The incidence of bicultural behaviour measured at the individual behaviour level must be interpreted carefully when two individuals of different cultures are members of the same interaction system. When bicultural behaviour is present have we in actuality an example of cultural forces in equilibrium or disguised assimilation? Let us take by way of illustration the language used in the home.

One would be tempted to see bilingualism or the use of two languages as a symbol of compromise and good cultural and marital rapport; it is necessary to look more closely at such an interpretation. Thus, the French woman who uses both languages is not in a compromise situation if her husband uses English almost exclusively. In such a situation, the use of two languages could just as well be a step in an acculturation process. To investigate this problem, it is necessary to study the behaviour of each respondent, taking into account the behaviour of the spouse. Since each individual is able to give priority to English and French or use both languages, we have a total of nine logical possibilities for compromise between English and French spouses, as one may see from the following schema:

Language used by English spouse	Language used by French spouse		
	English	Both languages	French
English	1	2	3
Both languages	4	5	6
French	7	8	9

These nine possibilities may be reduced to three categories:

a) English spouse dominates   1, 2, 4 Cases

b) Equitable compromise   3, 5, 7 Cases

c) French spouse dominates   6, 8, 9 Cases

Viewed in an interaction context, the data takes on a new dimension. With respect to the above example, the true compromise solution in which each individual loses and gains equally (''b'' above) exists in only twenty-one per cent of the cases. For four couples out of five, then, the linguistic accommodation is made to the cultural detriment of one of the spouses.

The behavioural items studied in this research have been analyzed in this perspective; the results are presented in Table 8.

Until this point we have based our conclusions on the comparisons of sub-groups of our population: English *vs* French, men *vs* women. The analysis of behaviour on the level of interaction allows us to introduce into the discussion certain additional elements.

1. We found that equitable compromise is rare (first column of Table 8). As may be recalled, in an equilibrium situation, no one wins in the compromise game because the two spouses win or lose equally.

2. Whenever spouses reach an equitable compromise, it often tends to be a bicultural solution (case 5 of the above typology). Indeed, cultural isolation in which each is loyal to his own culture (case 3 above) is difficult to realize in an actual

Table 8   Percentage Distribution of Modes of Accommodation Between Spouses of Different Ethnicity, by Behaviour Area

Behaviour area[a]	Compromise	French spouse dominates	English spouse dominates	Gain between English and French
Friends' visits	31	35	25	F + 10
Ties with relatives	29	42	29	F + 13
Magazines	24	6	70	E + 64
Associations	22	17	61	E + 44
Dominant language in home	21	32	46	E + 16
T.V.	16	15	69	E + 55
Newspapers	13	22	64	E + 42
Neighborhood	13	69	17	F + 52
Language of religion	12	49	39	F + 10

[a] Ordered by the importance of the compromise as a type of accommodation.

interaction situation. And, of course, the extreme courtesy where each refers to the other's culture (case 7 above) is a logical possibility which may seldom occur empirically.

3. In all areas of behaviour compromise at *the level of interaction* (Table 8) is less frequent than bicultural behaviour which was measured as individual behaviour (Table 7). One can therefore formulate the hypothesis that when one spouse refers to two cultures we have a disguised assimilation process in the direction of the ethnic group of the uni-cultural spouse. Disguised assimilation is more common for the female than the male, and also more common for the French spouse.

4. Compromise is most generally the case in the area of social relationships with friends and parents.[8]

5. The data is in agreement on both levels of analysis — individual and interactional. Compromise tends to occur to the detriment of one of the two cultures. If one compares them with respect to the balance sheet of gains and losses, in the areas in which one culture predominates, there is agreement between Table 8 and Table 3. The French spouse yields when it is a matter of buying magazines and newspapers, choosing television programs or voluntary associations; there are also relatively more families in which the English language is used more. Likewise the French spouse's influence dominates with respect to social ties, friends and parents, the choice of a church and neighbourhood. Nevertheless, at this dyadic level of analysis, one notices a slipping toward the English pole. The English spouse wins relatively more often in areas where his culture predominates and the French spouse relatively less often.

The cold statistical analysis presented in this article tends to neglect the human element which is a part of the compromise game, the daily victories and defeats. The general norm in a society is ethnocentrism: in numerous activities undertaken by the couple, ethnic differences may raise choices which are conflicting. The observed situation is the result of a long process of adjustment during the course of almost fifteen years of married life. Young married people when interviewed in the pilot study before this research, often expressed the hope of seeing their household function on a bilingual basis. The data in this present study suggest that this hope is naive and the great majority of them will be disappointed. We established the fact that the accommodation tends to be to the advantage of one culture and to the detriment of the other. But that is not the whole picture; the winner changes according to the area of behaviour. At the level of relations between ethnic groups, which is the principal object of this research, the English cultural orientation predominates in modern areas centered around power. A French cultural orientation remains strong in the area of community life. In a recent conference on "le socialisme au Québec" several participants pointed out that precisely this strong traditional value placed upon community life might be able to serve as the basis for a reform of the political structure.[9]

NOTES

1 Yvon Lacoste, "Une étude des statistiques des mariages interethniques à Montréal pour les anneés 1951 et 1962", (M.A. Thesis, Department of Sociology, University of Montreal, 1966). This work presents the rate of exogamy for different ethnic groups in Montreal, taking into account sex, age, religion, and occupation.

2 Cultural resistance to such unions is so strong that when they occur the road of those who dare to violate the barriers is often unhappy. In *les Anciens Canadiens* (1890, Philippe Aubert de Gaspé), Blanche d'Haberville refuses, immediately after the Conquest, to marry her childhood friend, an Anglais who wishes to become Canadian. *"Il y a maintenant entre nous un gouffre que je ne franchirai jamais."* Her lover has become the conquerer and she refuses *"allumer le flambeau de l'hyménée aux cendres fumantes de [sa] malheureuse patrie."* In *le Nom dans le bronze* (1932, Michelle Le Normand), all traditional values are pressed upon Marguerite by her friends and relatives; she gives up her lover, Stephen, Anglo-Saxon and Protestant. She renounces him in the name of her religion and language. *"Nous ne nous ressemblons pas, nos deux races s'opposent." "Ton bonheur aurait été à la merci des conflits politiques, scolaires, que sais-je?"*, her brother said to her approving her break. In *le Calvair de Monique* (1953, Geneviève de Francheville), the marriage takes place, but from the title may be glimpsed the disastrous consequences of this union. The spouse is Protestant and English, but the difficulties are caused especially by the religious difference. It is suggested that religion and language are indissoluble ties. Ultimate proof: the son of Monique will himself marry an English Protestant female. The recent novel of Jacques Godbout, *le Couteau sur la table* (1964) is more complex. The French Canadian here kills his English mistress who left him in order to return to a higher social class existence, after sharing with him a bohemian life.

3 The majority of the information is related to the parents. However, we know who the children's friends are, the television programs they watch, the language used in the religion, and the language used in the home. It is therefore possible to discern the phenomenon of cultural transmission, for the inquiry contains also information about the parents of the spouses. The results will be presented in a subsequent study.

4 It is necessary to underline here a methodological aspect: the items used in the study are only indicators of an underlying reality; thus if one multiplied the items concerned with primary relations, one would

show, by the addition of the indicators, the predominance of the French culture. Inversely, if one multiplied the indicators of secondary relations, one would show the strength of the English culture. In fact, within each life sector, indices strongly correlate with one another.

5 It must be stressed that there was difficulty in measuring differences in social class behaviour because of the occupational distribution of male spouses. Actually, spouses in bi-ethnic marriages find themselves to a large extent in the group of small businessmen and skilled workers where they are greatly over represented in relation to the total population. We do not have sufficient cases in the extreme categories (high or low class) to see if differences are statistically significant. However, the dichotomy we used is justifiable from the conceptual point of view, but still we compare cases that are not widely distributed on a social class scale. We would need a higher number of cases to control systematically for social class.

6 The results of cultural transmission in bi-ethnic marriages are not presented in this article.

7 One can see confirmation of this hypothesis from the fact that when the same question was posed to the couple M French/F English, the answers are far more in accordance than when the couple is M English/F French. In the first case, the answers are almost always identical; in the second case, one notes more often a variation in the valuation of reality perceived and described by the spouses who were questioned.

8 We have reported elsewhere the ties which exist between the compromise of spouses within the familial framework and in their relation to the social network. Cf. *Revue français de sociologie*, Vol. 7, No. 4, (October-December, 1966). pp. 472-484.

9 Jacques Dofny, "Le socialisme au Québec: une hypothèse sérieuse," and Pierre Maheu, "Vers une Culture québécois responsable," *Socialisme*, 67, 12-13, (April-May-June, 1967), pp. 28-33 and 55-58.

Toward a theory of conjugal cohesion in modern society

This article consists of parts of Chapters one and eight (pp. 16–22, 183–191) from Scanzoni's recent book, *Opportunity and the Family* (1970). It summarizes the theoretical assumptions and findings of a classic study of 916 randomly drawn households in the city of Indianapolis, Indiana. Only one spouse was interviewed in each household, and the final sample consisted of 497 wives and 419 husbands. The social status of respondents varied from lower working class to lower upper class.

This work is of unusual importance for several reasons. First, it rightly calls into question the traditional importance of social class distinctions in studies of marital relationships. Recent studies of social class in relation to marriage have tended to show insignificant or inconclusive differences. This study relocates the status issue relative to the *realistic* opportunity structure available to an employee. For example, a ditch digger has an opportunity range varying from pushing a shovel to organizing and planning digging operations; a university teacher has an opportunity range varying from assistant professor to professor. How much both the ditch digger and the university teacher achieve within their respective range of opportunity compared to their peers becomes the measure of social status. Second, this study directly confronts the relationship between marriage and the society of which it is a part. It demonstrates the important linkages of marital interaction and satisfaction to the organization and philosophy of the Western economic system. Third, the study demonstrates the significance of spousal expectations in the determination of satisfying marital relationships. While one's expectations may differ from those in other societies of the world, their importance to the realities of marital success and satisfaction is the same in all societies. Though the study may overemphasize the role of the husband in his attempts to efficiently "provide" for his wife and family, it clearly underlines the important role of expectations in marital process.

This study tends to underemphasize the role of the career wife and the impact of this increasing phenomenon on the reciprocal rights and duties of husbands and wives. In a later book Scanzoni (1972) argues that equal partner status marriages (in which the wife is pursuing a career of equal importance to that of her spouse) are structured to make the provider role interchangeable. In this sense, instrumental duties and rights become almost exclusively occupation oriented and the wife's achievement within her range of occupational opportunity (her duty) becomes her husband's right. It is likely, however, that this interpretation over-simplifies the dual career marriage. Husbands will probably not perceive their spouse's career as their right in most of the marriages of this type. Nor will the average career wife see her career as her husband's right. A more likely effect will be the separation or compartmentalization of "external" activities — one's occupational behaviors — from the duties and rights internal to the marriage. The issue might well be defined in terms of the degree to which occupational obligations undermine the mutually accepted system of reciprocity within the marriage.

Toward a theory of conjugal cohesion in modern society

John H. Scanzoni

Husbands and wives, as members of the conjugal unit, do not escape the impact of the pervasive universalistic criteria surrounding definitions of "personal excellence." The question is how and why, and the displacement hypothesis provides us with a start, because it suggests that positive feelings associated with greater achievement and success in the task-oriented dimension "lap over," or are transferred on to, or help account for, positive feelings in the expressive dimension of the conjugal family. Although the displacement hypothesis describes something of the interpersonal processes involved here, it is admittedly vague. Fortunately, it is possible to go beyond it through utilizing a notion that has received increased attention by sociologists in recent years.

Rodman notes that "Heer has introduced exchange theory into the discussion of marital decision-making."[33] The basic idea (a refinement of Blood and Wolfe's earlier notions) is the comparison of resources that the wife might earn within as opposed to outside

the marriage. The more her husband provides within the marriage, therefore, the more likely he is to exercise greater power. Heer himself notes that the implicit bargaining and exchange involved might "seem to violate some of the tenets of the romantic love complex."[34] He is obviously being sensitive to the kinds of critics Edwards is responding to, *i.e.*, those who believe the universalistic and particularistic spheres should be kept separate within the conjugal unit.

The point is that some sociologists see exchange theory as a way of explaining certain aspects of husband-wife interaction. In this case, how the husband performs in the economic system is exchanged for a measure of power within the conjugal unit. Sussman has argued that exchange theory is also useful in understanding the maintenance of the kin network.

Numerous studies . . . [indicate] . . . that individuals engage in reciprocal acts because they expect to be rewarded; *i. e.*, receive some payoff.

John Scanzoni, Ph.D., is Associate Professor, Department of Sociology, University of Indiana.

In the family field, in contrast, there pervades a certain alarm and fearfulness about talking so blatantly, because it is hard to believe that marital partners engage in activities that result in payoffs for themselves. Rather, we like to believe that individuals in a marriage relationship act according to some moral code which requires each partner to be completely "other" oriented. It becomes obvious to the serious student of social behavior that the kinds of interaction and reasons for such interaction which exist in one societal system must exist in all others.[35]

Sussman's cogent argument is quite adequate for those who might argue on ideological grounds per se that exchange theory is not appropriate for study of our family system. But his chief hypothesis is that reciprocity among the kin promotes maintenance of the kin network. What about maintenance of the conjugal unit itself? Gouldner states that the concept of reciprocity "provides new leverage for analysis of the central problems of sociological theory, namely, accounting for stability and instability in social systems."[36] Inasmuch as we are dealing with precisely this issue in terms of the conjugal unit, exchange theory and the notion of reciprocity could conceivably have theoretical application and thus explanatory power for this social system. Gouldner argues that

Reciprocity . . . connotes that *each* party has rights *and* duties . . . it would seem that there can be stable patterns of reciprocity *qua* exchange only insofar as *each* party has both rights and duties. In effect, then, reciprocity has its significance for *role systems* in that it tends to structure *each* role so as to include both rights and duties.[37]

Gouldner's application of reciprocity to stability of social systems goes beyond Parsons' stress that stability is based merely on role conformity, and asks why conformity persists. It persists because processes of reciprocity

. . . mobilize egoistic motivations and channel them into the maintenance of the social system . . . egoism can motivate one party to satisfy the expectations of the other, since by doing so he induces the latter to reciprocate and to satisfy his own. . . . The motivation for reciprocity stems not only from the sheer gratification which Alter receives from Ego but also from Alter's internalization of a specific norm of reciprocity which morally obliges him to give benefits to those from whom he has received them. In this respect, the *norm* of reciprocity is a concrete and special mechanism involved in the maintenance of any stable social system. . . . When one party benefits another, an obligation is generated. The recipient (Y) is now *indebted* to the donor (X) and remains so until he repays.[38]

But as soon as Y pays X the cycle commences all over again, and the reciprocal process goes on indefinitely. What is more, there are "mechanisms which induce people to *remain* socially indebted to each other and which *inhibit* their complete repayment."[39] There exists a "certain amount of ambiguity as to whether indebtedness has been repaid and, over time, generates uncertainty about who is in whose debt."[40] Reciprocity, furthermore, need not be equal either in amount or kind. Reciprocity engenders stability because it sets up a chain of enduring obligations and repayments within a system of roles in which *each* role contains both rights and duties.

The principle of reciprocity as exchange has long been observed within the kinship system in terms of the related issues of incest, illegitimacy, and mate selection. The names of Malinowski, Goode, Lévi-Strauss, Parsons, Kingsley Davis, and Merton are attached to this kind of work. Without attempting to summarize this literature in detail, we can nonetheless make two points: one, the norms governing incest, illegitimacy, and mate selection are essentially rules or expectations pertaining to forms of social exchange; two, as Merton remarks:

This does not at all imply that the exchange is necessarily the result of an explicit utilitarian calculus in which the contractants deliberately weigh the economic and social returns to be gained from the marriage. The event may be experienced by them as simply an affectional relationship, but this *psychic reaction is manifestly structured by the social organization* [italics supplied].[41]

We wish to go one step further and suggest that the exchange principle does not mysteriously vanish upon consummation of the marriage. It may very well continue to be a part of processes within the conjugal unit itself. The application of reciprocity as exchange to the conjugal family is presented graphically in Figure 1. Recalling that it is the husband's occupational role that is articulated with the economic system, and that the status and prestige of the wife and children are dependent on him, we must therefore start the chain of reasoning at Wd. Following the arrows we read:

1. The more positively the husband performs his economic *duties*, the more positively the wife defines her economic *rights* (status, prestige, income [Xr]) as being met.
2. The more (1) is true, the more positively she performs her instrumental household duties ([Xd], washing clothes, preparing meals, and so on, either doing them or seeing they are done), and the more positively the husband defines his instrumental household rights (Wr) being met.

3. The more positively the wife defines her economic rights (Xr) as being met, the more positively she performs her expressive duties (primary relations [Zd]).
4. The more (3) is true, the more the husband defines his expressive rights (Yr) as being met, and the more positively he performs his expressive duties (Yd).
5. *a.* The more (4) is true, the more the wife defines her expressive rights (Zr) being met.
   b. The more (5a) is true, the more motivated the wife is to perform her expressive duties (Zd).
6. The more each spouse defines his expressive and instrumental rights as being met, the more likely each is to experience feelings of gratification ("the sentiment of gratitude joins forces with the sentiment of rectitude and adds a safety-margin in the motivation to conformity"[42]) with each other and with the system or situation in which they find themselves.
7. *a.* The more (6) is true, the more the husband is motivated to continue performance of his economic duties (Wd).
   b. The more (6) is true, the more the shared feelings of solidarity and cohesion, and the greater the motivation to maintain the system, and the greater the stability of the system.

Ultimately, therefore, this chain of propositions rests on the degree to which the husband performs his economic role obligations. In simplified form, we may suggest that the husband in modern society exchanges his status for conjugal solidarity. If we accept as given that expressive satisfactions are the major manifest goals of modern marriage, and the major latent goal is status and economic well-being, then we may say that the latent goal influences the attainment of the manifest goal. Specifically, the greater the degree of the husband's articulation with the economic opportunity system, the more

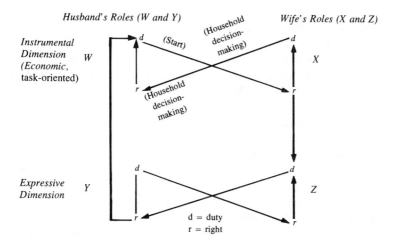

Figure 1 Husband-Wife Role Reciprocity

fully and extensively is the interlocking network of conjugal rights and duties performed in reciprocal fashion. The economic rewards he provides induce motivation in the wife to respond positively to him, and her response in turn gives rise to a continuing cycle of rectitude and gratitude. There are obviously numerous questions that emerge in connection with a model of this sort, and the remaining chapters will attempt to deal with many of them.

One point that should be raised here pertains to secondary husband-wife relations, or what is generally called authority or power relations, or the processes of decision-making. Wr and Xd refer specifically to secondary-type behaviors necessary to every household. These involve decisions regarding who will do what chores, what goods and services and how much of same the family needs, how to discipline the children, and so on. Most studies, for example, including this one (see Chapter Six) find that money is the major source of husband-wife

disagreement.[43] Sometimes the decision-making process does focus on primary-type behaviors, but for analytical purposes it seems best to keep the instrumental and expressive dimensions distinct.

We can fit Heer's analysis into Figure 1 by agreeing with him that the husband exchanges his status with his wife for power in these processes of decision-making. The more she perceives Xr (status and prestige) being met, *the more she is willing to allow her husband to shape the role definitions of Xd.* The more this is true, the greater are the mutual gratifications on the instrumental level, and the more ongoing is the web of reciprocity; hence, the more cohesive is the system.

Moreover, Goode's general notion of psychological displacement, or transfer, is made more specific by its incorporation into the more rigorous and sociological notion of exchange theory. In other words, if there are indeed negative feelings about limited status, these are displaced onto expressive elements because certain duties and rights are not being fulfilled, and because the exchange principle that is inherently part of the norm of reciprocity is being improperly met. In summary, the proposition that marital cohesion increases relative to articulation with the economic opportunity system, is based on the rationale that with increased articulation comes increased fulfillment of reciprocal duties and rights, and that on the basis of this exchange system comes increased gratification and thus cohesion. The processes of reciprocity include not only instrumental rights and duties, as suggested by other sociologists, but expressive rights and duties as well.

Smith and also Greenfield have shown what happens when the husband is unable to gain any meaningful economic articulation of his own, and the wife does. In our society, a theoretically related long-range trend may be toward educated women pursuing individualistic careers to the degree that their status is recognized independently of their husband's. What the actual consequences of this might be for the conjugal family system as we now know it is unclear because the pervasiveness of this trend is speculative at best.

Some clue, however, to shore up our speculation, might be gleaned from the entertainment industry. There wives' careers are often totally distinct from husbands' careers, and when hers is more "successful" than his, divorce is a common occurrence. This is, of course, the extreme illustration of the point to which Parsons speaks regarding husband-wife rivalry in the occupational sector. At present, it seems safe to assume that the vast majority of career women (even the most educated) do not view their pursuits in extreme individualistic terms. If the trend

becomes such that they do, it is obvious that a model like that in Figure 1 will have to be substantially modified.

We shall now try and move down from these rather abstract levels to the conjugal family to see how they help us understand it. But in so doing, we should always be prepared to move back up to the more general level and down again to other substantive areas where these general notions might also have explanatory power. In this fashion is systematic social theory developed. We begin at the cultural level with the dominant values of occupational achievement and material success. For good or ill, these values pervade every segment of our social structure — obviously the economic system, but also the kinship system. It so happens that the conjugal family in our society is the social unit in which achievement and success are displayed and thus "proved."

Efforts to "prove" success do not reflect a Marxian proclivity for gain, but instead the traditional ascetic Protestant notion of worth and respect based on material success. The upshot is that material success, suitably displayed, becomes a major goal of this particular social unit. But in order to consume, resources must be available; and in modern society these are most generally gained via the economic system. It is here that Parsons and others have described the role differentiation that occurs between parts of the conjugal unit. The male assumes the role of chief resource provider, and it is his occupation that provides the most significant linkage of the economic and conjugal systems.

But if one major goal of the modern conjugal unit is the display and proof of success, the other equally important goal is expressive satisfactions. To the degree that both major goals are met, the system will be that much more cohesive. In this regard and in terms of role differentiation, the wife assumes the position of "expressive hub" of the conjugal family. It should be noted that this type of role differentiation and these dual goals apply chiefly to those families located in the lower-working class and above. Within the lower or "lower-lower" class, the extent of the relevancy and pertinence of these types of role expectations and system goals becomes more problematic.[1]

In the role of provider, the husband's duties to his wife include objective rewards of status, prestige, and income, but also subjective rewards in the form of certain powerful feelings toward the economic opportunity system. These consist of allayed feelings of alienation and anomie. Alienation here refers to the feeling that one is currently "cut off" from achievement and success — one is powerless to use means deemed necessary for success, discontent with job rewards, and relatively estranged from the status system. *Anomie* here refers to the feeling that one's future chances for achievement-success are blocked. The husband, in short, is obligated to provide his wife with the feeling that she and the family are not currently "cut off" from the opportunity structure, plus the feeling that she (and her children) are not "blocked" from attainment of *future* success goals as well. At several points we saw that these "subjective" rewards are often more potent in terms of husband-wife interaction than are "objective" rewards.

The duty of the husband to provide objective and subjective rewards corresponds to the wife's right to receive these rewards from him. But as she does receive rewards, this puts her in his debt — she must now reciprocate, she must express her gratitude and show rectitude. She now has a duty to meet her husband's rights. But it is not a duty of unwilling constraint. She is now highly motivated to reciprocate positively. To do so, she fulfills certain expressive duties (primary relations) to meet his expressive rights. Likewise, she has certain instrumental household duties to fulfill that meet his rights in this particular sector as well. But as she performs both kinds of duties, he is then bound to reciprocate in the performance of his expressive duties that correspond to her expressive rights. Concomitantly, he is also bound to continue fulfillment of his economic duties.

The consequences of these ongoing processes are evident on both the structural and social psychological levels. First is the structural effect of interdependence: where there is a high degree of mutual interdependence, there is cohesion — there is order. Chapter One presents a detailed discussion drawn from Gouldner on the linkage of exchange theory to the phenomenon of interdependence and the persistence of social systems. Second is the definition of the situation as "satisfactory" by the principal actors involved. Where economic and expressive goals are being met, and the issue of authority regarding internal tensions is being resolved in legitimate fashion, there also we find cohesion and order. Thus persistence of any social system, including the conjugal unit, is not based solely on either structural or processual elements operating independently of one another. Cohesion is dependent on both structure and process. The assumption made by some that structural interdependence is missing from the modern conjugal unit simply because spouses do not physically labor together on the family farm is misleading. Interdependence based on economic-status factors persists in spite of role differentiation. Role differentiation has made husband-wife interdependence more complex and subtle, but no less present or potent.

Before moving to a consideration of problems for future investigation, it is useful to form our conclusions into a set of propositions. These propositions link the entire study together and provide a springboard for ongoing research. In the interests of parsimony, these propositions are stated in general form. Some of them contain specific modifications that yet do not alter their general sense. These modifications can be noted by consulting the earlier chapters. Moreover, in considering the following generalizations, the reader should recall that our sample tended to exclude those who, for practical purposes, are outside the opportunity structure. Thus, these generalizations apply chiefly to what may be termed the "lower reaches" of the "stable" working class and above.

1. The greater the articulation or integration (at the objective level: systematic increases in occupational prestige, education, income; on the subjective level: systematic reductions in the several dimensions of alienation and anomie) of the conjugal unit into the economic opportunity structure, and thus the greater the level of rewards provided by the husband, the greater the perceived satisfaction with the three major dimensions of husband-wife primary relations, and conversely.
   a. For affiliativeness, generally true for both sexes.
   b. For physical affect, generally true for both sexes, except less so for males in terms of objective indices of economic integration.
   c. For empathy, strongly true for both sexes.
   d. The consequences of perceiving oneself, one's general milieu, the spouse's view of a particular primary relation, and the family life style in positive terms is generally an increase in one's own evaluation of a particular primary relation, in comparison to the consequences of perceiving these four mediating dimensions in negative terms, which generally results in a decrease in one's own evaluation of primary relations.
   e. The longer the marriage, the more negative, in general, is the evaluation of affiliativeness and physical affect.
   f. The longer the marriage, the more positive is the evaluation of empathy.
2. The less the degree of economic opportunity integration, the greater the degree of hostility between husbands and wives, and conversely.
   a. The consequence of a positive self-esteem is to reduce levels of perceived hostility; the consequence of a negative perception of oneself is to increase levels of perceived hostility.
3. a. Among employed wives, the higher the status of her job and the higher the status of her husband, the more positively she evaluates primary relations when compared to nonemployed wives with same husband status.
   b. Among employed wives, the lower the status of her job and the lower the status of her husband, the less positively she evaluates primary relations when compared to nonemployed wives with same husband status.
   c. Among husbands of employed wives, there is less satisfaction with primary relations than among husbands of comparable economic integration with nonemployed wives.
      (1) The major exceptions are husbands with least integration who have employed wives and who show greater satisfaction than comparable husbands with nonemployed wives.
4. a. The less the economic opportunity integration (objective and subjective), the more frequent is the dominance of husbands in conflict resolution.
   b. The greater the economic opportunity

integration, the greater the probability of shared authority between spouses in conflict resolution.

c. The less the economic articulation, the less traditional and the more modern are wives in their beliefs regarding male authority, and conversely.

d. The less the integration, the less legitimate to wives is the dominance of husbands in the resolution of conjugal conflict, and conversely.

e. From the perspective of the wife, employment increases her participation in conflict resolution. From the perspective of the husband, the less his education the more likely he is to perceive wife employment as increasing her participation in conflict resolution, and nonemployment as decreasing it; whereas the greater his education the more likely he is to perceive wife employment as decreasing her participation and nonemployment as increasing it.

f. If the wife is employed, then both husbands and wives from these households generally appear less traditional and more modern in their beliefs regarding male authority. If the wife is not employed, then there is more of a tendency for both sexes to be traditional in outlook.

5. a. The lower the level of economic opportunity integration, the more strongly do parents hold (and presumably try to transmit) for their children passivity values vis-à-vis the opportunity structure, and conversely.

b. The lower the integration, the more strongly do parents hold (and presumably try to transmit) for their children mastery values vis-à-vis the opportunity structure, and conversely.

c. Combining these propositions (5a and 5b), we may say that the lower the level of articulation, the greater is the dissonance or conflict in achievement orientations to which the child is exposed. The higher the

articulation, the greater or more consistent is the "fit" experienced by the child in terms of achievement orientations.

d. The more orderly the milieu is perceived to be by the parent, the less strongly he tends to hold both passivity and mastery-type values, and conversely.

e. There tends to be general perceived consensus between husbands and wives over child-passivity and child-mastery values at each level of economic articulation.

6. Summary

a. Therefore, the greater the degree of material-status rewards provided by the husband, the greater is the degree of perceived satisfaction with primary relations (valued goals) and with authority relations, and thus:

(1) The greater is the degree of husband-wife interdependence.

(2) The greater is the degree of husband-wife feelings of cohesion and solidarity.

b. The greater is the interdependence, and the greater the feelings of cohesion and solidarity, the greater is the probability of system-maintenance, of stability, of order, and the more is dissolution unlikely.

c. Conversely, the less the degree of material-status rewards provided by the husband, the less the degree of perceived satisfaction with primary relations and with authority relations. Therefore:

(1) The less is the degree of husband-wife interdependence.

(2) The less is the degree of feelings of solidarity and cohesion.

(3) The less is the probability of system-maintenance.

Among questions that arise out of these propositions, and one that certainly needs future examination, is the place of psychological variables in husband-wife interaction. For other than self-esteem and anomie, we have not dealt with important psychological factors such as personality needs or personality characteristics, and so on. What we have attempted is a structural combined with a social-psychological analysis of the conjugal family. Principles of reciprocity and exchange between duties and rights of positions and roles provide the vehicle for this "synthesized approach" toward an explanation of conjugal cohesion.

But by no means would this model explain all the variance in husband-wife interaction. Personality factors must account for some of it, and help explain continued attraction for each other and for a desire to maintain the marriage relationship.[2] Future investigation, therefore, should address itself to the systematic isolation of some of these factors. There should also then be an attempt to integrate these psychological variables with the sociological model presented here. Until that time, we lack a full-orbed theory of conjugal cohesion. Specifically, psychological variables would seem excellently suited and perhaps requisite to deviant case analysis. These would include, for instance, dissolution among those with relatively high economic integration, and maintenance of the marriage among the relatively disadvantaged. But deviant case analysis alone is not the only function of psychological variables. We would expect that in all marriages certain personality configurations in their own right play a major role in husband-wife interaction, and thus ultimately in conjugal cohesion.

Some other instances of marriages that deviate from the general model might be due to three variations on the theme of rejection of the "success ethos" and its implications for definitions of personal excellence. First, on religious grounds, a strong case can be made for the deprecation of material gain and status based on the biblical warnings against covetousness. Hence the Catholic stress on the virtue of poverty, and the ascetic Protestant suspicion of conspicuous consumption. Weber notes that John Wesley, for example, advised eighteenth-century Christians to give away most of their newly got gain in order to avoid the inevitable perils that attend thereto.[3]

Therefore, those who today are strongly committed to these kinds of values, and who are perhaps only relatively or even less advantaged, are probably willing to overlook limited economic rewards. Limited means are deemed a "test of faith sent by God." Because the whole economic issue is therefore ultimately in Beneficent Hands, marital primary relations do not have the same relationship to economic rewards that they do in other families. In addition, wives in these kinds of situations are also likely to be very traditional regarding male authority, and thus to grant their husbands genuine deference regardless of the reward levels they may provide.

Then, too, a highly rationalized, intellectual Humanism could have the same consequences. Although Humanists are not often likely to be found among the ranks of the disadvantaged, and thus not put to the "acid test," some of them might hold a "contempt" for the materialism of our society. They might define it as crude, vulgar, and demeaning, and not "worthy" to be linked with interpersonal relations. This type of strong commitment therefore could distinguish these kinds of persons, in terms of actual conjugal behavior, from the masses who may simply hold to vague and general notions of romantic love. For the latter, simply holding to romantic love does not negate the systematic effects of varying levels of economic rewards. But for strongly committed Humanists, such negation might indeed occur. More will be said later regarding romantic love — for now, it suffices to distinguish its consequences from those of a highly refined Humanist philosophy.

Finally, there is that third minority of the population that has "turned off and dropped out." Whether among "hippies" or the "extreme new left," or some lower-class families, or whatever, there may not be clearly stated religious or Humanist values, but simply a feeling that the modern "rat race to success" is absurd. Since for them it lacks meaning, they refuse to be a part of it. This third category may, in some cases, represent the activist extension among the young of Humanist orientations. Theoretically, it is significant to note that in the past there has been an association between rejection of individualistic occupational success and attempts at revisions of conjugal family structure.[4] This was true of the Oneida Community, Communist family experiments, the kibbutzim, and now of certain "Hip communes."

To borrow Goode's terminology, there is a "fit" between the conjugal family form and the modern technological system.[5] As applied here, those people who reject one part of the fit seem to reject the other as well; those who accept one part tend to accept the other also. To the extent that individual occupational achievements are minimized, it seems more possible to experiment with variations in family form. To the extent individual achievement is central, as it is currently in our society, the less possible it seems to be to deviate greatly from the dominant family form. What the actual causal chain may be awaits further investigation, but the fact of this kind of association underlies once again the intrinsic linkage of the economic and kinship systems.

Aside from psychological variables and deviant case analysis, there is the question of limits or thresholds. We have assumed that cohesion varies with degree of interdependence and situational satisfaction, and that dissolution of the conjugal unit takes place when feelings of cohesion and solidarity are diminished beyond a certain point. But when does that point occur? What may be tolerable levels of interdependence and satisfaction for certain couples may be far too low for others. It is at this crucial point that the insights of Thibaut and Kelley can be fruitfully applied. The twin notions of *comparison level* (CL) and particularly *comparison level for alternatives* (CL alt) speaks to the question of thresholds. (See footnote 2, Chapter Two.) CL refers to the "standard by which the person evaluates the rewards and costs of a given relationship in terms of what he feels he 'deserves.' "[6] CL alt is the reference point to decide whether or not to remain in the relationship. "It can be looked at as the lowest level of reward which the individual will accept in order to continue in the relationship."[7]

Thus, future research into the limits of situational satisfaction and interdependence — limits beyond which cohesion and solidarity are quite seriously undermined — ought probably to be conceptualized in terms of CL and especially CL alt. Special attention might be given to those situational and psychological conditions that give rise to varying degrees of CL alt within the framework of similar levels of economic inputs. We have noted again and again the complexity of analyzing the cohesion of any social system, including the conjugal family. The complexity is nowhere more evident than when we attempt to investigate the host of intricate and interrelated factors that might influence CL alt. Yet it would seem that such efforts are called for if progress is to be made in grasping more fully the complex phenomenon of cohesion. Ideally, a longitudinal study in which families are followed over a period of several years would be best suited to determine this kind of issue. The sample might be heavily weighted with those in the blue-collar ranges of the economic structure, in order to gain maximum cases of actual dissolution, and also to take particular note of units that remain intact.

Part of this thresholds question hangs on the relative importance to husbands and wives of the three levels of primary interaction plus legitimate authority. We have inferred a priority of primary relations — especially as the length of the marriage increases. But this priority may vary by factors such as class or education. Likewise, degree of acceptance of an unsatisfactory authority or power situation may vary by certain kinds of variables, perhaps personality factors. At the same time, there may also exist a priority of objective and subjective economic-status rewards. Thus, certain combinations of instrumental factors and expressive elements may link together. First, evidence for such priorities needs to be established. If this is possible, then perhaps a rank ordering of these combinations could be discovered and shown to be related to varying degrees of conjugal cohesion. To carry out such intricate objectives, certain powerful statistical techniques would be useful if the data deserve them. Such techniques are currently available to sociologists, and provided certain assumptions can be met, they could help to attain the objectives just noted and thus enhance considerably our knowledge of structure and process within the conjugal unit.

An enormously complex issue hinges around wife employment. We have assumed that the money she brings into the household is not generally defined by the husband as a reward to which he is indebted to reciprocate either expressively or in terms of authority. Instead, he seems to view it as either a threat (moderate to low status) or as an incursion (higher status). Only do the lowest-status males seem to view it as a reward to which they are motivated to respond positively on the expressive plane. Yet employed higher-status wives evidently do see it as some form of benefit or resource they bring into the family, as a result of which they perceive their husbands ''as if'' they respond more positively.

As suggested in the text, women are probably increasingly coming to view employment behaviors as a right inherent in the role of wife. Husbands, on the other hand, still regard such behaviors more as an option. The actual existence and extent of this strain requires considerable examination. For if over the next generation a growing proportion of wives come to define employment strongly as a right, then it is possible that current established role differentiation could be undercut. Wives of this kind might be less likely to define their husbands as the chief provider on whom their status, prestige, self-worth, and material well-being depend. The long-term consequences for conjugal cohesion of such a major shift in definitions of rights, duties, and options are difficult to foresee without further research. A crucial factor to consider is the degree to which male expectations change in the same direction and at the same pace as those of females. If our data are any indication, the ''ancient war between the sexes'' promises to be waged in this sector for some time to come.

NOTES

33 Hyman Rodman, "Marital Power in France, Greece, Yugoslavia, and the United States," *Journal of Marriage and the Family*, 29 (May 1967), p. 322.

34 David M. Heer, "The Measurement and Bases of Family Power: An Overview," *Marriage and Family Living*, 25 (May 1963), p. 138.

35 Marvin B. Sussman, "Theoretical Bases for an Urban Kinship Network System," unpublished paper read at a meeting of the theory section, National Council on Family Relations, Oct. 29, 1966, Minneapolis, Minn. See also Winch, *op. cit.*, for what is essentially an application of exchange theory to the conjugal family.

36 Alvin W. Gouldner, "The Norm of Reciprocity: A Preliminary Statement." *American Sociological Review*, 25 (April 1960), p. 162.

37 *Ibid.*, p. 169.

38 *Ibid.*, p. 173.

39 *Ibid.*, p. 175.

40 *Ibid.*

41 Robert K. Merton, "Intermarriage and the Social Structure: Fact and Theory," in Ruth L. Coser, ed., *The Family: Its Structure and Functions*, New York: St. Martin's Press, 1964, p. 149. Reprinted from *Psychiatry*, August 1941.

42 Gouldner, *op. cit.*, p. 176.

43 Levinger, *op. cit.* [see bibliography]

1 On the other hand at least two reports found that lower-class Negroes do in fact share dominant values regarding both economic and conjugal roles. But because Negroes at this status level are frustrated in attaining these goals, other kinds of patterns emerge out of the exigencies of their white-dominated situations. See Elliot Liebow, *Tally's Corner*, Boston: Little, Brown and Company, 1967; also Lee Rainwater, "Crucible of Identity: The Negro Lower-class Family," in Gerald Handel, ed., *The Psychosocial Interior of the Family*, Chicago: Aldine Publishing Company, 1967, p. 371.

2 Winch notes that "very little has been found in the way of personality traits that are consistent predictors of marital felicity or stability." But he also points out that to conclude that "personality makes no difference in the marriage relationship . . . seems contrary to common sense." Robert F. Winch, *The Modern Family*, New York: Holt, Rinehart and Winston, Inc., 1963 (rev.), p. 712. Useful steps toward identifying important psychological elements have been taken, for instance, by Susan R. Orden and Norman B. Bradburn, "Dimensions of Marriage Happiness," *American Journal of Sociology*, 73 (May 1968), especially pp. 730-31. See also Gerald Handel, *The Psychological Interior of the Family*, Chicago: Aldine Publishing Company, 1967, especially Chaps. 1 and 23.

3 Max Weber, *The Protestant Ethic and the Spirit of Capitalism*, New York: Charles Scribner's Sons, 1958 edition, pp. 175-76.

4 Gerald R. Leslie, *The Family in Social Context*, New York: Oxford University Press, 1967, p. 150. See also Peter M. Blau and Otis Dudley Duncan, *The American Occupational Structure*, New York: John Wiley and Sons, Inc., 1967, p. 205.

5 William J. Goode, *World Revolution and Family Patterns*, New York: The Free Press, 1963, pp. 13 ff.

6 John W. Thibaut and Harold H. Kelley, *The Social Psychology of Groups*, New York: John Wiley and Sons, Inc., 1959, pp. 21-24. See also Edwin P. Hollander, *Principles and Methods of Social Psychology*, New York: Oxford University Press, 1967, p. 205.

7 Thibaut and Kelley, *op. cit.*

Swinging: a study of decision making in marriage

This paper presents a review of how married couples become involved in swinging (swinging differs from an ''affair'' in that both spouses are involved and participate together without deceit). The data is drawn from a non-random sample of twenty-five swinging couples in the Toronto metropolitan area. The results clearly indicate that swinging is a male-initiated activity, rather than a joint decision. This seems to reaffirm the persistence of the double standard.

The reasons why married couples swing and the relative consequences of doing so are not discussed in this study. There is in fact a wide body of literature on wife-swapping, co-marital sexual sharing, and swinging (see the bibliography at the end of Professor Henshel's article). Recent references include Smith and Smith (1970), Varni (1972), and selected articles in Libby and Whitehurst (1973). Gilmartin and Kusisto's comparative study of one hundred swinging and one hundred non-swinging couples, for example, found that swingers were significantly different in several ways: childhood relations with parents were less gratifying; interaction with kin occurred less frequently and kin were seen as less important; and there was evidence of more psychotherapeutic experience. Swingers and controls, however, were alike in other respects: personal happiness, marital happiness, the extent to which alcoholic beverages were consumed, and degree of personal boredom (Gilmartin and Kusisto, 1973). Whether these differences can be generalized to other swingers, however, is questionable. Swinging appears to be increasing — or at least becoming more visible. A report on sexual activity among some 20,000 readers of *Psychology Today* (Anthanasiou, Shaver and Tavris, 1970) indicates that only about 5 percent of married couples have participated in swapping, but nearly one third said they might.

Extramarital intercourse (the affair) is found to be strongly related to a low degree of sexual satisfaction in marriage among males — not among females — combined with opportunities for involvement and the perceived desire of others for involvement (Johnson, 1970). It seems that the affair, like swinging, is a male-initiated activity — providing further evidence of the persistence of the double standard. Most research continues to show (as did studies by Kinsey, et al., in 1948 and 1953) that extramarital relationships are a significant source of marital conflict, if not violence. Whitehurst (1971), in a study of Canadian court records and clinical cases, found that known unfaithfulness remains a serious problem because of an absence of normative ways of coping and traditional socialization patterns of males and females. The problems notwithstanding, extramarital sex is practised by many married couples. Kinsey estimated that nearly half of all married men and more than 25 percent of all married women have intercourse with someone other than their spouse by the age of forty (Kinsey, et al., 1948, 1953). Similarly, the recent *Psychology Today* survey found that 40 percent of married men and 36 percent of married women have had extramarital sex (Anthanasiou, Shaver, Tavris, 1970). Nearly 80 percent accepted extramarital sex in various circumstances. While actual participation in extramarital sex and swinging is not that high, attitudes toward these practices are important to an understanding of marital process in North American society.

Swinging: a study of decision making in marriage

Anne-Marie Henshel

One very important aspect of the life of married couples, sex, has been generally omitted in studies of decision-making patterns among married couples. Swinging, defined as the pursuit of sexual activities with extramarital partners by both spouses at the same time and usually in the same place (Walshok 1971), can, because of its nonspontaneous character, lend itself to research from the decision-making perspective. While studies of marital decision-making patterns became prevalent more than a decade ago, only in the late 1960s did researchers direct their attention to swinging as a social phenomenon. This new research trend partakes of a more general cultural impetus leading to experimentation with alternate life styles and follows the windfall of the "sexual revolution" of the past decades, a revolution characterized by a diminution of the double standard (Reiss 1967), a wider acceptance of premarital coitus among women, the pill, and a growing interest in sex as a form of leisure and of achievement (Gagnon and Simon 1970).

Measurements of marital decision-making patterns have traditionally involved the eight areas included in Blood and Wolfe's now classic study (1960, p.19): the choice of husband's job, car, life insurance, vacation, housing, wife's working, physician, and food budget. Other researchers have added items regarding child rearing (Smith 1969), family planning (Dyer and Urban 1958), relations with relatives, and choice of friends (Safilios-Rothschild 1969). Most studies on middle-class couples point to a certain equalization of decision making (e.g., Kan-

Anne-Marie Henshel, Ph.D., is Associate Professor, Department of Sociology, York University, Toronto.

From *American Journal of Sociology*, 78 (4, January, 1973) pp. 885–891, published by The University of Chicago Press. Reprinted by permission of the author and The University of Chicago Press.

del and Lesser 1972; Smith 1969; Blood and Wolfe 1960). However, certain researchers have questioned these conclusions. The possible advantage the male retains in this process is being reviewed in light of various structural factors (Gillespie 1971). In addition, methodological shortcomings have been pinpointed in the reappraisal of past studies. Most important for our purposes is the criticism that, in the overall decision-making score, all decisions are given equal weight regardless of their importance for the entire family. It is also pointed out that since some decisions are made less frequently than others, they may alter the absolute power of either spouse. Depending on which decisions a researcher chooses to include, "one could get a completely different picture of the over-all power structure" (Safilios-Rothschild 1969, pp. 297–98).

Swinging has been described as "an outgrowth of the dramatic changes that have taken place in this century in the position of women in American society and, more crucially, changes that have taken place in the conception of female sexuality and female sexual rights" (Denfeld and Gordon 1970, p. 89). Bell (1972) points out that "swinging represents a single standard of sex — that what is right for the man is also right for the woman." Swinging is also seen as benefiting wives as much as and, in certain respects, more than their husbands (Bartell 1971; Smith and Smith 1970). Yet, in spite of these equalitarian trends, researchers note passim that husbands are the usual instigators in the initial involvement in swinging (Palson and Palson 1972; Bell 1972, 1971; Bartell 1971; Smith and Smith 1970). However, a systematic decision-making approach has yet to be applied; the present article is a modest attempt in this direction.

Three questions

Three questions related to the preinvolvement stage of swinging are explored in this pilot study, with the ultimate aim of relating swinging to a more general discussion of marital power. (1) Which of the two spouses first becomes aware of swinging as an activity engaged in by people similar to them? (2) Which of the two spouses first suggests swinging as a likely alternative? (3) Who makes the final decision to swing? In each instance, there are three possible outcomes: the husband, the wife, or the two jointly.

The inclusion of the first question deserves additional explanation. It is very important that swinging be perceived by either or both spouses as an activity accessible to them rather than as an activity restricted to a particular, perhaps deviant, group. The first question, like the second and third, pertains to the relative position of the spouses in society. The spouse who has more access to certain information may have a double advantage; not only will he or she be able to act as the informant to the other and thereby acquire a measure of power but also, in the context of swinging, he or she may distort the information to induce the other into this activity or to avoid involvement.

Method and sample

This research was designed as a pilot study to explore the attitudes and decision-making behavior of women who swing, using a non-structured, open-end questionnaire. The sample was purposely limited to women. While husband-wife response discrepancies have occurred whenever both spouses have been studied regarding decision making

(Safilios-Rothschild 1970, 1969), the answers the women in this sample gave are largely validated by other researchers' work on swinging where both partners had been interviewed and/or observed (Palson and Palson 1972; Bell 1971; Smith and Smith 1970).

The first contact was made through a personal referral; additional names were solicited from each interviewee. Thirty-two names were gathered; three could not be reached and four refused. The final sample of 25 is not random, and, at this point, it is difficult to imagine how randomness could be achieved with swingers. A preset sampling condition was that all the women had to be currently living with the husband they were swinging with. Two exceptions occurred: one couple had ceased swinging two months earlier; and another woman was swinging as a single, with married couples but as the extra female, while the husband was unaware of her activities.

All the women lived in the Toronto metropolitan area. The median and average age was 30, with a range from 23 to 40. Fifteen were full-time housekeepers, nine were employed — four of these part-time only — and one was a student. Occupations included nursing, teaching, and secretarial work. Five had attended only high school, eight had additional training such as nursing, another five had some college, and seven had a baccalaureate. Five couples had no children; the median number for the others was two (average 2.2). The husbands were close to their wives in age, had more education (10 had graduate training), and tended to be semi-professionals, professionals, and executives.

I made initial contact when I arrived at the homes of respondents unannounced. I immediately told them how I had obtained their names and emphasized the confidentiality of the study. I saw the women alone; the usual length of the interview was 2–2.5 hours. While some subjects' answers were probably influenced by their perception of the interview situation, there is ample evidence that the women confided in me as frankly as possible. For instance, while social conventions usually preclude such admissions (Laws 1971, p. 485), most discussed their marital problems. Then, all volunteered unsolicited information, and practically all said that they had enjoyed the interview. Finally at least half switched roles with me at some point during the encounter.

Results

The responses to the three questions are summarized in table 1. The husband is shown to have a definite advantage over his wife by being the first to become aware of swinging as an accessible activity. This advantage is structural; occupational circumstances were the main source of their information. As we proceed through the decision-making process, the wife as the sole or joint initiator plays an ever lesser role. Only three women, including the "lone" swinger, were the first to suggest swinging as a possibility, and five others went through this process jointly with their husbands.[2] Seventeen husbands (68%) made the initial suggestion. Finally, only two women, again including the "lone" swinger, reported having been the one who had made the decision that led to involvement, and seven other wives reported a joint decision. The husbands alone therefore made 59% of *all* the initial decisions, 28% were joint decisions, while only 12% were made by the women.[3]

Table 1   Initiating Agent(s) Toward Involvement in Swinging: Incidence by Stage

Initiating Agent(s)	First to Learn of Swinging (1)	First Suggested It (2)	Reached Final Decision (3)	Total
Husband	11	17	16*	44
Wife	4	3	2	9
Both spouses together	9	5	7	21
No data	1	0	0	1
Total	25	25	25	75

* One of these 15 cases is not clear-cut. Although the scale seemed tipped in favor of the husband, the spouses could have actually reached the decision jointly.

It appears that there was a lapse between the time the couples learned of swinging and the time when they considered it seriously. More time elapsed before the final decision was reached, indicating that decision making as discussed here is multiphasic (Safilios-Rothschild 1970). A third lapse occurred between the decision to swing and the involvement. Unfortunately, while the respondents could recall the threefold decision-making process, they could not recall well enough the duration of various time spans involved. It would be interesting to know whether the process proceeds more quickly when the husband initiates the idea and makes the final decision as, for instance, Goode found for the decision to divorce (1965, p. 145).

Discussion

That husbands have an advantage in decisions about swinging is usually mentioned only casually by researchers; rather, there is a tendency to emphasize that women tend to adapt better to the new sexual freedom than their husbands, that they may obtain more sexual gratification than their husbands, and that swinging may be a more important channel of socialization toward true sexual freedom for them. These advantages are not shrugged off here but are viewed within the implicit and probably unconscious value context in which they were presented. For instance, if sexual freedom and equality is seen as an improvement over the double standard, one may be tempted to conclude that it is "good"; and, if it is such a great improvement for women that it offsets their decision-making disadvantage, we may thereby have an indication that the sexual freedom advantage may be more highly valued than the possible advantage the women could have were they the decision makers (jointly or singly).

Unlike studies of swinging, studies of marital decision making have tended to emphasize who made the decision rather than the comparative advantages to either spouse once the decision had been implemented. For example, if the husband decides to buy a car, the subsequent advantages arising from this decision for the wife are not discussed. It is pertinent that we adopt the same approach here for comparative purposes. Nevertheless, it should be added that, in this study, when the advantages the wives reported having gained from swinging were compared to the disadvantages similarly reported, the latter outweighed the former in 11 cases.[4]

Our data, as well as those mentioned by other researchers, seem to indicate that when we can obtain a measure of decision making with regard to nonspontaneous sex — and sex in general is an important correlate of marital happiness (Burgess and Wallin 1953; Locke 1951) — the egalitarian model does not hold in its entirety.

In spite of expectations of change in the sex structure, males still have a higher status than females; by the same token, they are the ones to confer status on women, both professionally and globally, the latter through marriage.[5] There are also indications that marriage is more important for women's happiness than for men's in our society (Bernard 1971, p. 87). Therefore, applying principles of lesser commitment (e.g., Blau 1964) or of least interest (Waller and Hill 1951, p. 191) for the males, it is not surprising that wives tend to do more of the adjusting in marriage (Blood and Wolfe 1960, p. 23; Rainwater and Weinstein 1960, pp. 68-69; Burgess and Wallin 1953, p. 618). Our data support these related points. In terms of exchange, the wife usually has less power (and decision making is one indicator of power) for she has fewer alternatives outside marriage;[6] she has fewer "commodities" of high *social* value to offer, and she has a higher need for the husband's *social* commodities than he has for hers. Her contributions to the marital relationship are of lower social value (Pitts 1964), thereby requiring that she increase them even if there already was imbalance (Blau 1964). Again, our data substantiate this perspective. In the context of decision making, swinging can be viewed as a male institution, and confirmations of the advent of a "sexual revolution" and of the abolition of the double standard should be reconsidered.

NOTES

2 A joint suggestion means that the matter was discussed jointly even though, in terms of seconds, one of the two spouses may have said it first. This is in contrast to the other cases when one spouse leaps ahead, brings up the suggestion, and there is an obvious psychological discrepancy between the two partners at that time.

3 As the spouses' relative resources have been a topic of importance in discussions on decision making (e.g., Rodman 1967; Heer 1963; Blood and Wolfe 1960), the wife's employment status was taken into consideration and found to be unrelated to the phenomenon under study.

4 The interviewees were asked (1) what they thought swinging had added to their lives and to their marital relationships, (2) to evaluate the problems involved, and (3) to weigh the advantages against the disadvantages.

5 In another study, 30% of 113 Toronto students agreed with the statement that they tended to take unmarried women above 35 less seriously than unmarried men of the same age. This finding surfaced in spite of the fact that many students had tried to adopt a "liberal" attitude. Subsequent classroom discussions more than amply validated the trend.

6 Thibaut and Kelley's (1959) treatment of power in the dyad is highly relevant here.

REFERENCES

Bartell, Gilbert D. 1971. *Group Sex*. New York: Wyden.

Bell, Robert R. 1971. *Social Deviance*. Homewood, Ill.: Dorsey.

———. 1972. Review of *Group Sex*, by Gilbert D. Bartell. *Journal of Marriage and the Family* 34 (February): 193-94.

Bernard, Jessie. 1971. "The Paradox of the Happy Marriage." In *Woman in Sexist Society*, edited by Vivian Gornick and Barbara K. Moran. New York: Basic.

Blau, Peter M. 1964. *Exchange and Power in Social Life*. New York: Wiley.

Blood, Robert O., Jr., and Donald M. Wolfe. 1960. *Husbands and Wives: The Dynamics of Married Living*. New York: Free Press.

Burgess, Ernest W., and Paul Wallin. 1953. *Engagement and Marriage*. Philadelphia: Lippincott.

Denfeld, Duane, and Michael Gordon. 1970. "The Sociology of Mate Swapping: Or the Family That Swings Together Clings Together." *Journal of Sex Research* 6 (May): 85-100.

Dyer, William G., and Dick Urban. 1958. "The Institutionalization of Equalitarian Family Norms." *Marriage and Family Living* 20 (February): 53-58.

Gagnon, John H., and William Simon, eds. 1970. *The Sexual Scene*. Chicago: Transaction.

Gillespie, Dair L. 1971. "Who Has the Power? The Marital Struggle." *Journal of Marriage and the Family* 33 (August): 445-58.

Goode, William J. 1965. *Women in Divorce*. New York: Free Press.

Heer, David M. 1963. "The Measurement and Bases of Family Power: An Overview." *Journal of Marriage and the Family* 25 (May): 133-39.

Kandel, Denise B., and Gerald S. Lesser. 1972. "Marital Decision-Making in American and Danish Urban Families: A Research Note." *Journal of Marriage and the Family* 34 (February): 134-38.

Laws, Judith Long. 1971. "A Feminist Review of Marital Adjustment Literature: The Rape of the Locke." *Journal of Marriage and the*

Family 33 (August): 483-516.

Locke, Harvey J. 1951. *Predicting Adjustment in Marriage: A Comparison of a Divorced and a Happily Married Group*. New York: Holt.

Palson, Charles, and Rebecca Palson. 1972. "Swinging in Wedlock." *Society* 9 (February): 28-37.

Pitts, Jesse R. 1964. "The Structural-Functional Approach." In *Handbook of Marriage and the Family*, edited by Harold T. Christensen. Chicago: Rand McNally.

Rainwater, Lee, and Karol K. Weinstein. 1960. *And the Poor Get Children*. Chicago: Quadrangle.

Reiss, Ira L. 1967. *The Social Context of Premarital Sexual Permissiveness*. New York: Holt, Rinehart & Winston.

Rodman, Hyman. 1967. "Marital Power in France, Greece, Yugoslavia and the United States." *Journal of Marriage and the Family* 29 (May): 320-24.

Safilios-Rothschild, Constantina. 1969. "Family Sociology or Wives' Family Sociology? A Cross-Cultural Examination of Decision Making." *Journal of Marriage and the Family* 31 (May): 290-301.

———. 1970. "The Study of Family Power Structure: A Review 1960-1969." *Journal of Marriage and the Family* 32 (May): 539-52.

Smith, Herbert L. 1969. "Husband-Wife Task Performance and Decision-Making Patterns." In *Perspectives in Marriage and the Family*, edited by J. Ross Eshleman. Boston: Allyn & Bacon.

Smith, James R., and Lynn G. Smith. 1970. "Co-Marital Sex and the Sexual Freedom Movement." *Journal of Sex Research* 6 (May): 131-42.

Thibaut, John W., and Harold H. Kelley. 1959. *The Social Psychology of Groups*. New York: Wiley.

Waller, W. W., and R. Hill. 1951. *Family*. Rev. ed. New York: Holt, Rinehart & Winston.

Walshok, Mary Lindenstein. 1971. "The Emergence of Middle-Class Deviant Subcultures: The Case of Swingers." *Social Problems* 18 (Spring): 488-95.

6

Parent and child relationships

Bringing up a child is an art. Perhaps it always will be, but to let the matter rest there is to give up too soon. The art involves working with an unusual medium, one that has a mind and will of its own, a child who is constantly his own designer. A parent can enter into partnership with the child's process of self-creation, or he can stifle it.

Caroll Davis, Room to Grow: A Study of Parent-Child Relationships
(Toronto: University of Toronto Press, 1966), p. 3.
© *University of Toronto Press, 1966.*

He must pray with humility, cry with faith, and hallucinate with conviction, as far as the Supernatural Providers are concerned; he must learn to make good nets, to locate them well, and to collaborate in the fish dam, as his technology requires; he must trade and haggle with stamina and persistence when engaged in business with his fellow men; and he must learn to master his body's entrances, exits and interior tube ways in such a manner that nature's fluid ways and supply routes will find themselves magically coerced.

Reprinted from Childhood and Society *(Second edition) by Erik H. Erikson (p. 182). By permission of W.W. Norton & Company, Inc. Copyright 1950* © *1963 by W.W. Norton & Company, Inc.*

Although the rearing of children is perhaps the most nearly universal and significant of all family activities, to be a child or parent or sibling means something very different from culture to culture. The quotation from Davis (1966) at the beginning of this chapter is indicative of the importance of independence training and emergence of self in the rearing of Canadian children. The Yurok child (Erikson, 1963), in contrast, is encouraged to become in faith, work, personality, and physical stamina a Yurok — not a self-created person. While Davis explores the processes of emancipation in the rearing of seven Canadian children, Erikson emphasizes the ways in which the Yurok male child becomes the "incarnate" of Yurok culture. A recent comparison of child rearing in the Soviet Union and the United States (Bronfenbrenner, 1970) concluded that Soviet children are consciously reared to put the wishes of others first, and to respect the needs and expectations of their society. American children, in contrast, are reared by their peers and by television sets in a climate of affluent neglect and subtle opposition to adult society. They are, he argues, uniquely antisocial and egocentric compared to Soviet children. In the film *Four Families* (National Film Board of Canada, 1959), Canadian children are described as independent, tough, and private-property conscious, compared to Japanese, French, and Indian children. These values are developed through parental responses to pain, roughhouse activities, feeding and bedtime activities, and the individual ownership of toys. While the film overemphasizes the differences, there is little doubt that the child-rearing perspectives of the Western parent are significantly different from those of parents in many other cultures. Changes have occurred in all four cultures since the film was made; the changes, however, are more modest than one might expect.

Birth and the early care of children

Birth in most preliterate societies is characterized by numerous magical or supernatural beliefs and rites (Stephens, 1963). Postpartum (after birth) sexual taboos are also common. In most of these societies, births seem to occur with only minor difficulty and without serious pain. There is considerably more tactile contact between mother and infant than in our own society; for example, in forty-five of sixty-four societies the nursing infant was found to sleep by its mother's side (Stephens, 1962). In addition, there is considerable body contact between mother and child during the waking hours, including frequent nursing — the breast is commonly used as a pacifier. In the Whiting and Child study of seventy-five societies (1953), the median age of weaning was found to be two and a half years. Though no data is available on birth and postpartum rituals in Canada, the predominant patterns would appear to include extensive prenatal care by skilled physicians, a relatively painful birth controlled by sedatives, minimal contact between baby and family (let alone the mother) for several days after birth, early bottle feeding and propping (compared to extended breast feeding and holding), and early weaning and toilet training. Most Canadian couples probably follow their doctor's recommendations concerning sexual relations before and after the birth.

In contrast to most primitive societies and many Eastern societies, nearly half the Canadian women in one study did not want their child upon learning of their pregnancy (as reported in the Edmonton *Journal*, November, 1973). Even so, most of the 196 women studied wanted their child by the time it was born. This general pattern is evident in most research on parenthood (Le Masters, 1974). There are, however, significant sub-cultural variations on this theme. Ryan (1976), in her study of Squamish Indians, found evidence that producing and rearing children is essential to the male ego and to the woman's sense of worth. Hutterites hope to have ten or more children (Hostetler and Huntington, 1967). In addition, most Canadian studies of attitudes toward parenthood indicate that unmarried college students want to have children, and many desire more than three children (Hobart, 1973; Wakil, 1973). Our current knowledge of birth and early parenthood in Canada, however, appears to be inadequate and inconsistent.

Recent observational studies of infant care in the natural household setting illustrate the continued differences between cultures, even in industrialized societies. A comparative study of Japanese and American middle class families, which is reprinted in this chapter (Caudill and Weinstein, 1970), found that the American baby is more active and vocal than the Japanese baby. The American mother encourages her baby to respond, whereas the Japanese mother quiets and soothes her baby. Whether Canadian infant care patterns are similar to American ones is unknown, but it seems likely that they are.

Parent-child relations

The literature on cross-cultural parent-child relationships is extremely diverse and difficult to compare with the predominant literature on Western parent-child relations. Western literature tends to describe or explain the *effects* of parents on children, while anthropological literature seldom deals with consequences but simply describes, for example, parent-child relations and initiation rites (e.g., Williams, 1969; Jocano, 1969).

Stephens (1963) emphasizes the role of apprenticeship in preliterate societies. All children, by the age of ten and beginning as early as the age of three, are involved "in a clear-cut, specific apprenticeship to the adult occupational role" (p. 386). Girls work at being women; boys typically work at the occupational roles of their fathers. This study, as well as others, offers support for the argument that childhood in these cultures is regulated by clear goals. The young are raised to adopt and practise the values of their society. Adolescence in primitive society is short-lived and tends to be marked by intense competition among age-mates to demonstrate "adultness" through various initiation rites (Gottlieb, Reeves, TenHouten, 1966). Adolescence in Western society reflects the struggle of the adolescent for autonomy and a strong alliance with age-mates who are perceived to help in achieving self-created goals (Gottlieb, Reeves, TenHouten, 1966). It has, of course, been demonstrated that parent-adolescent relationships can also be satisfying and supportive (Larson, 1972a; Kandel and Lesser, 1972).

Recent comparative research on the impact of parents on children provides unambiguous support for the conclusions of Devereux (1970) in his study of twelve-year-old children in England, Germany and the United States. He suggests:

> The evidence from our research strongly supports the view that the same set of variables may be used to account for intra-cultural variability in all three cultural settings. Essentially the same influences which make some children in one culture more responsible, or more adult-oriented, or more autonomous have these same consequences for children in other cultures as well, *wherever the same combination of influences are encountered.*[1] (emphasis supplied)

In general, the research evidence in Japan (Aoi, et al., 1970; Makino, et al., 1970), Thailand (Udyanin and Yamklinfung, 1970), Hong Kong (Shan-Lam, 1970), England, Germany, and the United States (Devereux, 1970; Becker, 1964), Russia (Bronfenbrenner, 1970) and Canada (cf. master's and doctoral theses annotated in Larson, 1971b), among others, suggests that certain combinations of parental support and control tend to be *associated* with certain attitudinal and behavioral characteristics of children. Extreme parental indulgence (excessive warmth and permissiveness) is associated with irresponsible, impulsive, and immature characteristics of children; extreme over-protectiveness (warmth-control) is related to submissive, dependent, over-socialized patterns in children; extreme authoritarianism (hostility-control) is related to aggressive, rebellious, dominating attributes of children; and extreme neglect (hostility-permissiveness) is associated with flighty, anxious, and emotionally starved patterns in children.[2] Children reared with *optimum* levels of support and control (guidance, discipline, punishment, and encouragement of autonomy) tend to have more positive self views, attitudes, and behaviors.

The study by Carroll Davis (1966) clearly demonstrates, among the seven Canadian children she studied in depth, the significance of extremes and optimums in human growth and development. Optimal, in contrast to extreme, parental support and control is most favorable to satisfactory child development. A study of seventy-nine English Canadian families in Montreal (Westley and Epstein, 1969) produced similar findings. The emotional health of children is directly linked to warm, constructive relationships between their parents. Marital couples who balanced sharing of tasks with individual responsibilities were found to have significantly healthier children than those couples who didn't share at all or shared in everything.

However, these studies do not necessarily *prove* that parental behaviors *cause*

---

1 Edward C. Devereux, "Socialization in Cross-Cultural Perspective: Comparative Study of England, Germany, and the United States" in Reuben Hill and Rene Konig, eds., *Families in East and West: Socialization Process and Kinship Ties* (The Hague: Mouton, 1970), p. 105. Reprinted by permission.
2 This discussion is largely based on Devereux (1970).

these responses in children. Parental attitudes and behaviors may be related to or associated with the attitudes and behaviors of children, but the attribution of responsibility to parents is not as simple as it seems. In fact, parent-child relationships are dynamic: parental support and control may also be thought of as responses to supportive or controlling behavioral patterns of their children. If a mother, for example, harshly punishes her child for spilling ink on the new drapes and the child subsequently becomes despondent, doesn't eat dinner and lies awake for several hours after being sent to bed, the mother might well be said to have caused her child's behavior. However, the child might also be said to have caused her mother to be harsh by spilling the ink. If the child had been apologetic and offered to help her mother in response to her mother's harshness, the remaining exchanges of the day might have had different consequences for mother and child alike. Assumptions concerning parental influence, in view of the greater resources, power, and size of the adult, may reasonably be made but are frequently exaggerated.

Two other Canadian studies with relevance to parent-child relations are discussed below. The first deals with attitudes toward parenthood among Canadian young people, and the second explores what is known about one-parent families in Canada.

In Hobart's study (1973) of English- and French-speaking college students, it was found that French Canadians were significantly more egalitarian and permissive in their child-rearing attitudes, but less willing to support the use of birth control, than English Canadians. French Canadians were also less positive toward divorce. Utilizing multiple regression techniques in an attempt to explain these differences in attitudes, Hobart found that rurality and social class were relatively unimportant, but sex role attitudes (masculinity-femininity) and religion accounted for greater variation in the French than in the English sample. Apparently, young French Canadians continue to expect a clear differentiation of mother and father parental roles.

Considerable material has been published on the one-parent family (Canadian Council on Social Development, 1971; Guyatt, 1971; Schlesinger, 1969) and multi-problem family in Canada (Schlesinger, 1971e). The report by Guyatt (1971), largely based on census materials, indicates that one in every twenty-nine families is a single-parent family with all children under the age of eighteen. The majority of single-parent families are headed by widowed females (41 percent) or separated females (31 percent).[3] Single parents were found to have somewhat lower educational levels, lower-status occupations, lower incomes, and to live in less adequate housing. These patterns are considerably more pronounced for single-parent families headed by females than those headed by males. The exploratory study of 112 single-parent families reveals significant problems of adjustment, inadequate social concern, and the need for child-care assistance.

3 Statistics are based on 1966 data.

The family as a small group

While the socialization of children and parent-child relations are basic dimensions of family analysis, it should be remembered that the family is a small group composed of individuals who derive their identity and status from membership in a particular family in a particular culture or subculture. In this sense, the family is a miniature society which may be described in terms of such characteristics as rituals and values, cohesiveness, degree of openness to exchanges with non-family members, and degree of role organization. Most studies of families in other cultures de-emphasize the attributes of individual family members or interactional characteristics in families, describing instead the structure, functions, and processes of families as units. The traditional joint Indian family, for example, is distinguished from the nuclear family by a system of role organization necessitated by the addition of exchanges among cousins, uncles, aunts, and sister-in-laws living in the same household (Gore, 1965; Narain, 1970). The concept of the family as a system enables us to categorize a particular family, for example, as marriage-centric or child-centric. Two studies have demonstrated that these types of family units have very different characteristics in terms of perceptions, goals, and performance (Liebman, 1960; Farber and Jenne, 1963).

Colette Carisse (1972) of the University of Montreal has studied information processing among different types of families. Matrifocal families are suggested to be least open to information, while person-focal families are most open. The patrifocal family is sensitive to information but is more selective than the person-focal family. Her model distinguishes the three types of families relative to eleven family characteristics, such as goals, basic social context, socialization orientation, and communication pattern. Certain of these differences are illustrated below.

Family Type

Characteristic	*Matrifocal*	*Patrifocal*	*Person-focal*
System goal	Group survival	Group project	Individual plans
Communication pattern	Peer oriented	Object oriented	Person oriented
Social context	Home centered	Work and status centered	Commitment centered
Socialization orientation	One model	Alternative models	Self actualization

In a similar paper (Larson, 1973), eight different types of families are identified based on role organization, resources, and family goals, and their probable response to changes in the work week is projected. Both of these studies focus on the systemic characteristics of the family, and emphasize the significance of these characteristics for the response of the family to external and internal inputs.

The study of the family as a small group is a recent development. Perhaps the most valuable contribution to the study of whole families is the work of Handel (1972) on the psychosocial interior of the family. Handel explores the role of the family as a culture and mediator of culture for its members, as a boundary-regulating agency, as a system of interpersonal communication, and as a cohesive or disconnected unit. Children reared in a disqualifying and disaffirming communication system, for example, will have significant environmental support for the development of schizophrenic behavior patterns (Haley, 1959). There is much yet to be learned about the importance of family structure and process in the socialization of children.

SUMMARY

This chapter has briefly reviewed the birth and early care of children, and parent-child and family relations.

The prenatal period and birth in most societies is characterized by institutionalized rituals which symbolize the importance of children. Though there is some evidence of visible opposition to pregnancy and of parental crises associated with the addition of children to the household, particularly in Western society, in general children are highly valued the world over. Patterns of care seem to effectively illustrate the fundamental socialization goals of the society into which the child is born, such as apprenticeship, political support, or individualism.

The relative influence of parents on the attitudes and behaviors of children appears to be strongly related to the variant uses of support and control, regardless of societal context. Parental indulgence, for example, seems to encourage the development of irresponsible and impulsive characteristics in children, while submissive, dependent children appear to have overprotective parents. It is well to emphasize, even so, that parent-child relations are dynamic and interrelated: e.g., supportive parenthood is related to supportive responses of children to parents. In a sense, also, the interpersonal relationships within the family as a whole form a kind of miniature society with system characteristics.

Three articles are included in the remainder of the chapter. The first compares infant care patterns in Japanese and American families. The second paper provides an in-depth analysis of child-rearing patterns in English and American families. The paper by Ryan describes the socialization of the Squamish Indian child in British Columbia.

Maternal care and infant behavior in Japanese and American urban middle class families

In the past, most cross-cultural research involved the simple description of basic family patterns (e.g.. getting married, child rearing and kinship relationships). Recently, however, more sophisticated research methods have been employed, including detailed survey instruments, interviews, and direct observations. The study by Caudill and Weinstein is based on systematic observations of the care of infants in the homes of thirty Japanese and thirty American families with firstborn children three to four months of age. Though the samples were not randomly drawn, they are quite similar in life style.

Several papers have already been published comparing the patterns within these families (Caudill, 1962; Caudill and Scarr, 1962). In general, it was found that Japanese families valued a kind of mutual interdependence or familism, while American families were much more individualistic. Japanese families tended to avoid descriptive phrases such as competition, aggression, or sexuality in preference for phrases such as talking, relaxation, and sleeping. In 86 percent of the Japanese families, the infant slept in the same room as the parents, even though other space was available. In the United States, in contrast, this practice was very rare.

In the study reprinted below, the observational data were collected in four areas related to: (a) the presence or absence of a caretaker (typically the mother); (b) where the baby was, e.g., in arms or lap of caretaker, or elsewhere; (c) what the baby was doing; and (d) what the caretaker was doing with the baby. The findings suggest that the American mother spends less time with her child, but that when she is there, she talks to her child more. The American child is more active, both physically and vocally. It is important to emphasize, as do the authors, that these findings do not indicate that one culture is worse or better than the other. The findings merely indicate the similarities and differences in infant care patterns in these two cultures.

The next step in this research project is now in process. How do certain behavioral patterns interconnect? Is talking by the mother related to vocalization by infants? Are there overall differences in the patterns of behavior between the two cultures? Are there certain behavioral sequences?

This study is unique and provocative for two reasons. First, what families actually *do* to their children is far more important than what they say they do. It is well recognized that parents tend to give socially desirable answers when queried about their treatment of their children. Although it is possible for parents to "put on a front" for the observers, the procedures employed in this study make it next to impossible for parents to do so continually. Thus, this study provides one of the first "inside views" of what family life is like for infants. Second, the study offers insight into important differences in the social psychological dynamics of infant care in two different cultures. As a cross-cultural study, it is pace-setting in both method and the kind of data it provides.

Even so, the results should be interpreted cautiously. In the first place, the sample is relatively small in both societies, and may be unrepresentative of even the urban middle-class family it purports to probe. Generalizations must be limited to the sixty families studied. In addition, observational data is uniquely subject to bias. By creating certain categories of behavior to look for, the observer may not see other behaviors that are equally important in adequately interpreting a family situation. An observer's personal biases may also facilitate a selective view of what behavior actually occurred. Reliability tests were conducted in this study to ascertain the level of agreement between two independent observers of the same behaviors. Agreement, in fact, exceeded 70 percent in twenty-six of the thirty-seven observational categories. The observers did disagree substantially as to whether the baby's actions represented a "cry" or a "protest". This difference, however, is probably unimportant because both are negative actions. The authors do report a significant bias in the number of vocal-to-mother acts. The Japanese observer recorded significantly fewer and the American observer recorded significantly more vocal-to-mother acts than did the senior author. This indicates that one's culture may well influence what one sees. In general, however, observational data is a valuable and under-utilized resource in research.

Maternal care and infant behavior in Japanese and American urban middle class families

William Caudill and Helen Weinstein

This is a preliminary report of an observational study of mothers and infants in their homes in Japan and the United States. The background for this study comes from previous research in Japan which forms, in a sense, a tissue of predictions as to the gen-

Dr. William Caudill and Mrs. Helen Weinstein (both deceased) were with the National Institute of Mental Health in Bethesda, Maryland.
From Reuben Hill and Rene Konig, eds., *Families in East and West: Socialization Process and Kinship Ties* (The Hague: Mouton, 1970), pp. 39, 43-46, 54-65, 69-71. Reprinted by permission.

eral qualities of the relation between mother and baby that we expected to find in the homes in the two countries.

III.   Background characteristics of the sample

It is not the purpose of this section to try to present a summary of all of the information we have on the backgrounds and current settings of our families. Rather, the purpose is to provide only the information necessary for the understanding of the variables used in the analysis of the observations presented here.

Fifteen of the Japanese cases are families in which the father is a 'salary man', and the other 15 cases are families in which the father is engaged in a small independent business. This matter of 'style of life' is an important dimension in Japan today, although this scarcely needs mention to a Japanese audience. For readers from other countries, however, it is useful briefly to characterize the distinction between salary men and workers in small business (see also, Dore, 1958; Vogel, 1963; Plath, 1964; and Caudill, 1964).

At present, in large urban settings in Japan, something over half of all employed persons work in large companies or governmental settings as salary or wage earners. Within this broad way of life, the 'ideal typical' salary man is a graduate of a good university who gets a white-collar job in a large company or with the government and expects to stay in this setting for the remainder of his occupational life with periodic advancement more on the basis of seniority than of merit (although both are necessary). Such a person is not paid very well at the beginning, but he has the security of an assured income, as well as help from the or-

ganization with housing, marriage plans, vacations, and many other fringe benefits. At a higher level executives also participate in this style of life, and at a lower level so do wage earners.

On the other hand, something under half of all employed persons in urban settings in Japan are engaged in a different style of life as independent owners or employees of small business. Typically, these are neighbourhood shops or small manufacturing enterprises, but independent professionals such as physicians in private practice are also included in this style of life. The crux of the matter, regardless of high or low social status, is that the owner or employee of a small business must rely more on his own ability to maintain his financial situation, and he does not have the security of a fixed income that is a major factor in the salary man's style of life.

Twenty of the American cases are families in which the father is employed in a large business or in government, while 10 of the American cases are families in which the father is engaged in a small independent business. The matter of 'style of life' in these terms is apparently of lesser importance in the United States today, although the position taken by Miller and Swanson (1958) would seem to indicate that bureaucratic and entrepreneurial families do show differences in child rearing. Their study, however, has been criticized as to method in the literature.

By sex of infant, there are more males in the Japanese sample (18 Japanese males to 12 females, 15 American males to 15 females). The age in days of the infants is quite close in both samples — a Japanese median of 103 days, and an American median age of 109 days — and a comparison of the rank-ordered distribution of the two samples is not significant.

Japanese mothers in the sample are some-what older on the average at the time of birth of their first child (26,6 years) when com-pared with American mothers (23,7) years. This should be related to the somewhat older average age of the Japanese fathers (29,7 years) compared with the American fathers (26,7 years). These differences are in line with the reality in the middle class in the two cultures concerning the age of marriage and the time of birth of the first child.

There is more breast feeding among the Japanese than among the American cases. Eighteen of the Japanese and only five of the American cases were continuing breast feed-ing at the time of observation. In many of these cases, and particularly in the Japanese sample, this is a combination of breast and bottle feeding, with the breast usually being given early in the morning and late at night and the bottle used during the day. Among the Japanese cases there are more indepen-dent business family mothers (12 cases) than salary man family mothers (6 cases) who were continuing breast feeding at the time of observation.

In terms of the number and composition of household members, the largest group for both cultures (15 Japanese and 25 American cases) consists of husband and wife and new baby — that is, the nuclear family. For the Japanese, those families with additional members (usually the father's parents) are mainly independent small business house-holds, whereas the nuclear families are mainly salary man households.

The type of housing in the two samples is strikingly different in the division between houses and apartments. The Japanese tend to live in houses (22 cases) and the Americans in apartments (21 cases). Despite this, grea-ter floor space and more rooms are available to American families than to Japanese families. One should not, however, conclude from this that greater 'crowding' in the Japanese home leads to greater involvement in interpersonal contacts by necessity rather than choice. People in Japanese families, crowded or not crowded, tend to group to-gether by choice — as, for example, in the sleeping arrangements reported earlier.

In all 30 of the Japanese cases, the mother, father, and infant sleep in the same room. On the other hand, in 17 of the American cases the infant sleeps alone in a separate room, while in 13 cases the infant is in a crib in the parents' bedroom. In these latter cases, the young married couple is liv-ing in an apartment with one bedroom, but without exception, as indicated in the inter-views, each couple plans to move to another dwelling with two bedrooms so that the in-fant can have a separate room by the time he is one year old. As has been seen, this type of physical separation seldom occurs in the Japanese family.

IV.   Method

In the observations in the home on the three-to-four months old infant and his caretakers, we used a time-sampling procedure adapted from that originally developed by Rheingold (1960). An observation (of approximately one second in duration) is made every fif-teenth second in terms of a set of predeter-mined categories concerning the actions of the baby and of the caretaker for a ten-minute period, giving a total of 40 observa-tions per sheet (see chart 1). This is followed by a 'free' period of five minutes during which the observer clarifies (if necessary) the data on his previous sheet, and also keeps track of what is going on in the intervening five minutes by making notes. At the end of five minutes, another ten-minute sheet of 40 observations is begun.

Observations on a case were carried out in the above manner for two-and-a-half hours on each of two days (usually consecutive days, and never separated by more than a few days). Thus, 10 sheets, or 400 observations, are available for each day, resulting in a total of 800 observations per case for the two days. On the first day we made our observations from 9:30 a.m. until noon, and on the second day from 1:30 p.m. until 4:00 p.m.

Throughout the observations, our focus was on the infant, and if the mother (or other caretaker) left the room, the observer stayed with the infant. Initially we told the mother that our interest was in the ordinary daily life of her baby, and we requested that she go about her normal routines including leaving the house if this was her usual activity on the day of the observations. It is important to note that we stressed to the mother that our interest was in the life of the baby, and not in her behavior as a mother.

A focused interview for about an hour was done with the mother following the observations on each day. This covered such topics as the course of her pregnancy, the stay in the hospital, the birth, the subsequent development of the infant, and general background data. One reason for the interview was to gather material on those aspects of the current life of the baby that we were not likely to observe because of the particular hours during which we were in the home.

VI. Preliminary results

Table 2 illustrates the main method used in the analysis of the data in this paper. The frequencies obtained in a category of behavior over the 60 cases are rank ordered, and then the degree of overlap between the ranks assigned to the 30 Japanese and 30 American cases is tested by use of the Mann Whitney U Test.

As can be seen, the degree of overlap is virtually complete between the Japanese and American cases in the category of baby awake. This means that there is no difference in the samples from the two cultures as to the amount of time that the baby is awake (and hence, also, no difference as to the time spent asleep). On the other hand, in the category of baby active, there is almost no overlap between the Japanese and the American cases ($p < .0001$). Most of the Japanese cases are below the median of ranks, and most of the American cases are above. Thus, the Japanese baby is much less active than is the American baby. In the third category in the table, mother talks to baby, the degree of overlap also is small, and it can be seen that the Japanese mother talks significantly ($p < .02$) less to her baby than does the American mother.[1]

The data referred to in the next two tables have been analyzed by the method just described, but because of limitations of space the rank-ordered frequencies for each observation category are not presented. Table 3 gives the median frequency of the rank-ordered distribution for the Japanese and American cases in each observation category, and the level of significance as to the degree of overlap. When a comparison results in a significant difference, the culture in which the behavior occurs more frequently is indicated by a letter code — 'A' for American, and 'J' for Japanese.

From the data in table 3, let us first consider the areas of similarity in the behavior of

Table 2   Illustrative Rank-Ordered Distributions of Observations in Selected Categories for Thirty Japanese and Thirty American Cases.*

Baby awake (60 cases)	Baby active (60 cases)	Mother talks to baby (60 cases)
796	270	276
740	253	**267**
689	243	239
632	207	235
621	174	228
615,615	172	**208**
613	**171**	206
609	164	203
607	160	186
602	**157**	**184**
600,600	154	**183**
588	138	181
580	136	**176**
578	133,133	174
565	123	**164**
563,563	122	**159**
561	120	157
560	119	155
540	117	154
533	108	150
535	**106**	**149**
524	**104**	146
518	96	143,143
512	**95**	141
511	**88,88**	139,139
499	**87,87**	138,138,138
493	82	

*Japanese case frequencies are printed bold (**000**), American case frequencies are not (000). Presence or absence of behavior is a category determined over 800 observations. The Mann-Whitney U Test (two-tailed) was used to determine the probability of independence of the Japanese and American distributions.

Table 2. (*continuation*)

Baby awake (60 cases)	Baby active (60 cases)	Mother talks to baby (60 cases)
	Median of Ranks	
498	81	**132**
469,469,469	79	130
458	**74**	127
457	67	**122**
454	66	111
452	63	**105**
443	61	**102**
425	**59**	95
417	57,57	**87,87**
413	55,55	**82,82**
408	**50**	79
402	**46,46**	74
397	33	**73**
392	**30**	**72**
390	29	**70**
378	27	68
377	**21,21,21,21,21**	67
374	**18**	55
367	**15,15**	53
355	**13**	51
342	**12**	47
326	**10**	39
323		37
320		**29**
310		24
309		12
281		**8**
263		4
s = 0.04	z = 4.56	z = 2.51
p < .97	p < .0001	p < .02
No Diff	A > J	A > J

the infant and caretaker in the two cultures. Infants in both cultures are awake and asleep the same amount of time. They are also drinking milk (either from the breast or the bottle) the same amount of time. The greater intake of food by the American infant is a somewhat specious finding because the feeding of semi-solid food is not usually started in Japan until the fifth month, whereas in America it is begun at about the end of the first month. Though not shown in table 3, when the categories of breast/bottle and food are collapsed into a broader category of *intake of nutritive substances*, the same amount of time is spent in this activity in both cultures. In these similarities, what we are seeing in operation are the biologically rooted needs for sleep and nutrition.

The main area of similarity for caretakers in the two cultures seems to occur in those

Table 3   Median Frequencies of Observation Categories and Probability Values for Comparisons of Rank-Ordered Distributions Among Japanese and American Cases.

Observation category	Median frequencies		Comparison of rank-ordered distributions*	
	Japanese (30 cases)	American (30 cases)	$p<$	Group with higher median frequency
Infant				
Alone	191	352	.002	A
Awake	506	479	n.s.	
Active	48	121	.0001	A
Vocal	17	71	.0001	A
Vocal to mother	4	24	.0001	A
Protest**	47	27	.0001	J
Cry**	3	8	.01	A
Breast/Bottle	65	51	n.s.	
Food	0	14	.0002	A
Finger	47	185	.02	A
Toy	40	61	.03	A
Hand	10	17	.06	A
Other (blanket, etc.)	17	52	.0001	A
Caretaker				
Looks at	243	281	n.s.	
Talks	22	63	n.s.	
Talks to	87	143	.02	A
Arms/Lap	152	134	n.s.	
Pats	38	49	.001	A
Affections	5	6	.06	A
Plays	23	17	n.s.	
Positions	4	23	.0001	A
Rocks	35	6	.005	J
Diapers	24	15	.07	J
Bathes	insufficient data			
Feeds	72	64	n.s.	
Dresses	11	12	n.s.	
Other (wipes mouth, etc.)	15	20	n.s.	

* *Probability determined by use of Mann-Whitney U Test (two-tailed).*
** *Combining Protest and Cry into Negative Sounds, p. < .01, J.*

categories of behavior in which caretaking is required if the minimum needs of the infant are to be met. Thus, there is no difference in the amount of time spent by Japanese or American mothers in the categories of feeds, dresses, and other (wipes mouth, etc.). We feel that the additional categories of looks at and in arms/lap also belong, in part, in this general area of caring for minimum needs because, in the observations, mothers in both cultures are looking at and holding their babies as they give them the breast or bottle. As can be seen in table 3, there is no difference between the cultures in the categories of looks at or in arms/lap.[2]

In two other categories — plays and talks — there is no difference between the cultures in the behavior of the caretaker. These categories do not fall in the general area of caring for the minimal needs of the infant, and represent, therefore, additional areas of similarity in the type of analysis presented in table 3. As will be recalled from the definitions of the categories, plays means playing with the baby, and talks means talking to people other than the baby — directly to neighbors and tradespeople in Japan, and more on the telephone to friends and to the father at his office in America.

Let us turn now to the areas of difference in behavior in the two cultures. These seem to occur as aspects of what might be called the 'style' of the infant in his behavior, and that of the mother in hers. And this is what one would expect — an essential human similarity evident in the two cultures concerning a core area of behavior related to biological needs, coupled with differences in other areas of behavior as a result of cultural pressures in interaction with individual attributes of the infant and the mother. What is particularly interesting is that, despite the considerable individual variation present in the two samples, the cultural differences in 'style' of behavior are so clear for both the infant and the mother.

In the discussion of cultural differences, let us first consider the category of alone. As can be seen, the American infant is much more alone ($p < .002$). This does not mean, however, that he is merely sleeping while his mother is out of the room, because, although not shown in table 3, the American infant is also more awake and alone ($p < .06$) than is the Japanese infant. For the American mother caretaking is largely an 'in' and 'out' affair. When she is in the room, she is usually actively doing something for the infant, and upon finishing this she goes out of the room. The Japanese mother, although not engaged in active caretaking any greater amount of time, is passively present in the room with the infant to a much greater extent, and is, therefore, in a position to respond more quickly to her infant.

For the infant, the differences between the two cultures occur in two major areas of behavior: 1) manipulation of the body and exploration of physical objects in the environment, and 2) vocalization in terms of both positive and negative sounds. We will discuss each of these areas in turn.

As can be seen in table 3, the American infant is engaged in manipulating his body more than the Japanese infant in all three of the categories of active ($p < .0001$), finger ($p < .02$), and hand ($p < .06$). Equally, the American infant is more engaged with physical objects, as represented by the categories of toy ($p < .03$), and other objects ($p < .0001$). The finding for the category of hand may be questionable because of the marginal level of significance, but it is in the same direction as the very clear findings in the other four categories. The American infant, therefore, is more vigorously using his body and also playing more with objects in the environment. In contrast, the Japanese infant seems passive — he spends much more time simply lying awake in his crib or on a *zabuton* (a flat cushion) on the floor.

We are particularly interested in the category of active, and we thought that the greater occurrence of gross bodily movements among the American infants might be related to the difference in temperature in the homes, especially in the winter, in the two cultures.

During the colder months, Japanese infants are wearing more clothing, and are under more covers, than American infants. Fortunately, roughly half of the cases in each culture were observed during the colder months of November through April, while the other half of the cases were observed during the warmer months of May through October. For the American infants, there is no difference between the rank-ordered frequencies of active behavior for the cases observed during the colder and warmer months. For the Japanese infants, however, the cases observed during the warmer months are more active ($p < .04$). Nevertheless, in the cross-cultural comparison of the infants observed only during the warmer months, the American babies are still the more active ($p < .003$). Naturally, then, the American infants are also the more active ($p < .001$) in the comparison of cases observed during the colder months. It appears, therefore, that temperature of the home and heavier clothing make some difference, but not enough to account for the greater activity of the American infant.

The occurrence of behaviour in the category of finger — meaning sucking on fingers, other parts of the body, or on a non-nutritive object such as a pacifier — appears to be related to breast versus bottle feeding in both cultures, although the Japanese infants are in general much lower in any sort of comparison. The clearest data on this question come from the comparison of those mothers who never breast fed versus those mothers who were feeding entirely by breast (no use of the bottle at all) at the time of observation. The nine American infants who were never breast fed have an average of 196 observations in the category of finger, while the four American infants being fed entirely by breast have

an average of 97 observations in the category of finger. Among the Japanese cases, the four infants who were never breast fed have an average of 88 observations in the category of finger, while the six infants being entirely breast fed have an average of 42 observations in the category of finger. Thus, there is roughly twice as much finger sucking by babies who have never been breast fed in both cultures, but the average for the Japanese babies fed entirely by bottle is lower than the average for the American babies fed entirely by breast. It seems unlikely, therefore, that the greater activity of the American infant in the category of finger is due to differences in methods of feeding.

The second area of difference for the infant in the two cultures occurs in the area of vocalization. With regard to positive sounds, the American baby is clearly more vocal ($p < .0001$), and the same direction is indicated in the category of vocal to mother, although this more specific latter category is not reliable. With regard to negative sounds, the Japanese infant is higher in protest ($p < .0001$), while the American infant is higher in cry ($p < .01$). When these two categories are combined, however, the Japanese infant is definitely higher in the broader category of negative sounds ($p < .01$).

With regard particularly to negative sounds, it is our distinct impression that the Japanese mother responds more quickly than the American mother to the vocal signals of her infant, and this question is one which we intend to test empirically in the data as part of further analysis. If this impression is true, it would help to account for the greater amount of protesting relative to crying in Japan as the intervention of the mother would have the effect of cutting off the protests before they developed into cries. The constant repetition in the Japanese home of this sequence of a short burst of protests by the baby followed quickly by a response on the part of the mother would also have the effect of increasing the infant's expectation that things will be done for him by others.[3]

Although not shown directly in table 3, when the four categories of vocal, vocal to mother, protest, and cry are collapsed into a general category of *total vocalization,* the American infant is clearly using his voice more than is the Japanese infant. This fact is important for considering the relative emphasis placed on verbal versus non-verbal (through looking and physical contact) communication in the interaction of infant and mother; and, this fact is also important for its possible relation to later facility in the use of spoken language.

Studies (Arai, *et al,* 1958; Toshima, 1958) carried out at the Tohoku University Medical School on 776 children from Miyagi Prefecture who were less than 36 months of age show that the development of language is slower among Japanese than among American children on the basis of Gesell's norms. For example, concerning the Japanese children, Arai, *et al* (1958, p. 5) say: 'Ce champ du langage est le plus en retard et pose de multiples problèmes. Le retard est très net et souvent l'enfant ne commence pas à bredouiller avant 40 semaines. De 4 à 20 semaines, il n'y a pas de problème . . .' This general finding is in line with the results presented here, and, in addition, our data do show that there is a problem at 12 to 16 weeks (three to four months of age) in that the Japanese infants show less total vocalization than do the American infants. Quite obviously, this is an area for further comparative research.

Turning now to the differences between the two cultures in the caretaker's behavior, we believe that the key categories are talks to and rocks. The American mother is significantly ($p < .02$) talking to her baby more, while the Japanese mother is rocking ($p < .005$) her baby more. Thus, the style of the American mother seems to be in the direction of stimulating her baby to respond by use of her voice, whereas the style of the Japanese mother seems to be more in the direction of soothing and quieting her baby by non-verbal means.

The greater push toward activity by the American mother is also evident in the category of pats ($p < .001$) which is comprised largely of attempts to help the baby to burp. The Japanese mother does not do this very frequently, and if the Japanese baby does burp, this is usually a spontaneous reflex action. And, at least in line with the push toward response and activity, the American mother may be showing more affection (kissing, nuzzling, etc.) to the baby, and positioning the baby more, although neither of these categories is very reliable.

The soothing and quieting approach of the Japanese mother may also be evident in the possibly greater ($p < .07$) attention she pays to the diapering of her baby. Several of the Japanese mothers commented in their interviews that they felt they could sense the baby's need to urinate or defecate, and respond to this need before the diaper became soiled. This belief of the mothers indeed proved to be true in the observations on these cases.

Finally, with regard to differences, behavior in the category of bathing contrasts strongly in Japan and America although we do not have direct observational data on this from our Japanese cases because of the times of day chosen for the observations plus the nature of the bathing situation itself. From the interviews, and from common knowledge, we know that starting approximately at the beginning of the second month of life, the Japanese infant bathes with the mother or another adult in the deep bathtub (*furo*) at home, or they bathe together at the neighborhood public bath (*sento*). Just as in the case of sleeping arrangements discussed in the first section of this paper, the pattern of bathing with an adult family member will continue for a Japanese child until he is six or seven years of age, and often much longer (see Vogel, 1963, pp. 229-232). The American middle class pattern of bathing a child is almost the opposite. The American mother seldom bathes with an infant; rather, she gives a bath to the infant from outside of the tub, and she communicates with the infant verbally and by positioning his body. Moreover, she encourages him to learn quickly to bathe himself.

In summary, then, of the similarities and differences in the behavior of infants and caretakers in the two cultures, the similarities center around a core of minimal needs of the infant — such as sleeping, eating, and being clothed — which must be attended to by the mother. The differences lie more in the style in which behavior is carried out. The American mother leaves her baby more alone, but when she is with him, she talks to him more and encourages him to respond and to be active. And, the American baby is more active in the use of his body, in playing with objects, and in his vocalization. In contrast, the Japanese mother is more constantly with her baby, but her focus is on the reduction of tension — on soothing and quieting. And, the Japanese baby is more passive in his physical behavior, and less communicative verbally.

The Japanese mother will say that she responds quickly to the protesting or crying of her infant because she wants to be a good mother, and also because she does not want the neighbors to complain that she has a noisy baby. While at a certain level of meaning this is undoubtedly true, it is also true that Japanese place less emphasis on clear verbal communication than do Americans. Such communication implies self-assertion, and the separate identity and independence of the person. As indicated at the start of this paper, Japanese values place more weight on self-effacement and the interdependence of people. What is at issue here in terms of the data presented in table 3 is not the question of these values as such, but rather how very well the infants in the two cultures seem to have learned their lessons by the age of three to four months.

Beyond the over-all analysis just presented, we are interested in certain subgroup comparisons, both within and across the two cultures. The first of these concerns the sex of the infant. The comparison by sex of infant within each culture over the observation categories does not reveal any significant findings except in one instance — the American mothers show more affection ($p < .02$) to their male than to their female babies.

The cross-cultural comparison by sex of infant does show significant differences, as would be expected from the results obtained in the over-all analysis. As can be seen in table 4, however, the differences between the male babies in the two cultures are greater than the differences between the female babies. For example, American male babies are considerably more active than their Japanese counterparts, whereas this contrast is less evident for the female babies in the two cultures. This situation is also true in the two other categories (finger and hand) concerned with manipulation of the body, and may be true for the general area of vocalization as well. Under the caretaker's actions, the American mother seems to be showing more affection to her male baby than does the Japanese mother whereas this contrast is not true for the mothers of female babies. The Japanese mother, on the other hand, is rocking her female baby more than is the American mother, but this contrast is not evident for the mothers of male babies.

The second sub-group comparison in which we are particularly interested is that between families in which the father works for a salary or wages and families in which the father is engaged as an owner or employee of a small independent business. In the American sample there are no differences over the categories between families with these two styles of life. In the Japanese sample, however, there are differences, as can be seen in table 4. The infant in the independent business family is alone less (p < .02), awake more (p < .06), and protests more (p < .02). The complementary differences for the caretaker in the independent business family are that she talks to the baby more (p < .04), holds him a greater amount in arms/lap (p < .05), and rocks him more (p < .06).

In Japan, the way of life of the small independent business family is considered more traditional, and the way of life of the salary man family is considered more modern. Thus, in terms of the results just cited, the salary man mother spends less time with her baby, and is less engaged in interaction and non-verbal communication with him through holding and rocking. In these ways she is more like the American mother. And yet the

Table 4
Probability values for comparisons of rank-ordered distributions of observation categories by sex of infant and style of life among Japanese and American cases*.

Observation Category	Japanese-American comparisons by sex of infant				Intra-Japanese comparisons by style of life	
	Male Jpse N = 18 Amer N = 15 p <		Female Jpse N = 12 Amer N = 15 p <		S/W N = 15 Ind N = 15 p <	
Infant						
Alone	.08	A	.007	A	.02	S/W
Awake	n.s.		n.s.		.06	Ind
Active	.0001	A	.06	A	n.s.	
Vocal	.0001	A	.002	A	n.s.	
Vocal to mother	.0001	A	.002	A	n.s.	
Protest	.02	J	.003	J	.02	Ind
Cry	.03	A	n.s.		n.s.	
Breast/Bottle	n.s.		n.s.		n.s.	
Food	insuf. data		insuf. data		insuf. data	
Finger	.02	A	n.s.		n.s.	
Toy	.05	A	n.s.		n.s.	
Hand	.02	A	n.s.		n.s.	
Other (blanket, etc.)	.003	A	.009	A	n.s.	
Caretaker						
Looks at	n.s.		n.s.		n.s.	
Talks	n.s.		n.s.		n.s.	
Talks to	.07	A	.08	A	.04	Ind
Arms/Lap	.08	J	n.s.		.05	Ind
Pats	.07	A	n.s.		n.s.	
Affections	.05	A	n.s.		n.s.	
Plays	n.s.		n.s.		n.s.	
Positions	.0001	A	.0001	A	n.s.	
Rocks	n.s.		.02	J	.06	Ind
Diapers	n.s.		n.s.		n.s.	
Bathes	insuf. data		insuf. data		insuf. data	
Feeds	n.s.		n.s.		n.s.	
Dresses	n.s.		n.s.		n.s.	
Other (wipes mouth, etc.)	.07	A	n.s.		n.s.	

*Probability determined by use of Mann-Whitney U Test (two-tailed).

American mother, like the Japanese independent business mother, talks to her baby a great deal, which the Japanese salary man mother does not do.[4] In her efforts to be modern, the Japanese salary man mother seems to have subtracted from certain more traditional ways of relating to her baby without adding anything. This results in a relative impoverishment of the environment for the infant. In the more qualitative aspects of the observation, there are long hours of time in the salary man homes which go by silently — the mother does housework or sews while the baby lies passively, awake or asleep, on his back and the sunlight makes patterns on the *tatami* in the quiet room. In contrast, in the small independent business homes, the mother chats with her husband's unmarried sister (or other relatives living in the home), the father may return from his shop for lunch, the baby is cared for jointly by several persons, and the passage of time is punctuated by the ending of one bit of neighborhood gossip and the beginning of the next.[5]

Despite these differences, as real as they are, in styles of life in Japan, the major finding in our data still occurs in the comparison of the behavior of the infant and caretaker across the two cultures. The Japanese mother in the salary man family may be more 'modern' than the Japanese mother in the small independent business family, but the behavior of the two types of Japanese mothers, and that of their infants, still is sharply different in many areas from that of the American mother and her infant.

VIII.   Conclusions

As much work remains to be done, definite conclusions are premature, but some major dimensions in the data are clear. There is an area of basic similarity for the infant and caretaker in both cultures centered around the infant's needs for sleep, food, and clothing, and the mother's caring for these needs. Beyond this, however, and in line with our predictions at the beginning of this paper, the greatest contrasts, for both the infant and the mother, are between the two cultures. The American baby is more alone, is more active in the manipulation of his body and in the use of objects and is higher in vocalization. The American mother talks to her baby more, and seems more to encourage him toward response and activity. The Japanese baby is less alone, and is both physically and vocally more quiet. The Japanese mother rocks her baby more, and talks to him less. Her actions seem directed to soothing and quieting the baby rather than encouraging response and activity. These differences between the cultures do not occur as isolated characteristics of behavior, but rather are interwoven in such a way that the general patterning of behavior is different in the two cultures.

In Japan, style of life makes a difference in the behavior of the infant and the caretaker. The baby in the small independent business family is less alone, and more awake and protesting. The mother in the independent business family is talking more to her baby, and is holding and rocking him more. In contrast, the infant in the salary man family seems more quiet and passive, and his mother, in her move toward modernity, seems more to have subtracted from traditional ways of caretaking rather than to have added anything new.

A further major dimension in the data for both Japan and America is the great extent to which the infant has 'learned' to pattern his behavior in terms of the cultural expectations of his mother even by as early an age as three to four months.

Finally, it should be stressed that, in reporting our results, we do not mean to imply that one or the other way of life for the baby and mother — the Japanese or the American — is 'better' or 'worse'. Our emphasis is that the patterns of behavior and emotional expression are different, regardless of whether the carrying out of the details is done well or poorly in individual cases. The differences in the patterning of behavior and emotional expression, repeated day after day in the simple routine of life, lead, we believe, to different psychological and social results as a child grows to be an adult in the two cultures.

NOTES

These same data have been treated in a more extensive fashion, using multi-variate analysis of variance in W. Caudill and H. Weinstein, 'Maternal care and infant behavior in Japan and America', *Psychiatry* 32 (1) 1969, pp. 12-43.

1 The terms 'mother' and 'caretaker' will be used interchangeably from this point on in the paper since the great bulk of caretaking actions are performed by the mother in the observations in both cultures.
2 It should be noted that the grouping we have made here of four categories — looks at and arms/lap with breast/bottle and feeds — rests upon the determination of a significant simultaneous occurrence in the observations of these four categories. As such, this information cannot be derived from table 3, and is part of another type of analysis described later in the section of this paper dealing with further plans for analysis.
3 A fuller discussion of the implications of this situation can be found in Caudill and Doi (1963).
4 The cross-cultural comparison by style of life shows the American salary man mother talking to her baby more than the Japanese salary man mother at the level of p < .01; on the other hand, there is no significant difference in this category between small independent business mothers in the two cultures.
5 In some ways, this is a contrast, viewed in miniature through the flow of events for mother and infant during the daytime hours, between a *yamanote* (the hillsides) and a *shitamachi* (the downtown districts) style of life. The former stems historically from the Tokugawa bureaucrat and *samurai*, and leads to the modern professional man, government official, and white collar or clerical worker. The latter stems from the Tokugawa shopkeeper and craftsman, and leads to the modern independent business man or small factory owner. In the course run by individual families or persons, there are, naturally, crossovers between these two ways of life. See Dore (1958, chap. 2) for a fuller discussion of these distinctions.

REFERENCES

Arai, S., et alii, 'Développement psychomoteur des enfants Japonais', *La Revue de Neuropsychiatrie Infantile et d'Hygiène Mentale de l'Enfance* 6, 1958.
Caudill, W., 'Patterns of emotion in modern Japan', in: R. J. Smith and R. K. Beardsley, eds. *Japanese Culture: Its Development and Characteristics*. Chicago, 1962.
— 'Sibling rank and style of life among Japanese psychiatric patients', in: H. Akimoto, ed. *Proceedings of the Joint Meeting of the Japanese Society of Psychiatry and Neurology and the American Psychiatric Association*. Tokyo, May 1963.
— 'A comparison of sleeping arrangements for infants and children in urban Japanese families', manuscript, available through the author.

Caudill, W.; Doi, L. T., 'Interrelations of psychiatry, culture, and emotion in Japan', in: I. Galdston, ed. *Man's Image in Medicine and Anthropology*. New York, 1963.

Caudill, W.; Plath, D. E., 'Who sleeps by whom? Parent-child involvement in urban Japanese families', *Psychiatry* 29 (4) 1966, pp. 344-366.

Caudill, W.; Scarr, H., 'Japanese value orientations and culture change', *Ethnology* 1, 1962.

Dore, R. P., *City Life in Japan*. London, 1958.

Miller, D. R.; Swanson, G. E., *The Changing American Parent*. New York, 1958.

Oleinick, M.S., 'A retrospective study of early socialization experiences and intrafamilial environment of psychiatric outpatient clinic children and control group children', manuscript, available through author.

Plath, D. W., *The After Hours: Modern Japan and the Search for Enjoyment*. Berkeley, 1964.

Rheingold, H., 'The measurement of maternal care', *Child Development* 31, 1960.

Toshima, K., 'Tōhoku chihō ni okeru nynyoji seishinhattatsu ni kansuru kenkyū, *Nihon Shonika Gakkai Zasshi* 62, 1958.

Vogel, E. F., *Japan's New Middle Class: The Salary Man and His Family in a Tokyo Suburb*. Berkeley, 1963.

Child-rearing in England and the United States: a cross-national comparison

This study provides an excellent illustration of typical research on parental discipline in child rearing. The types of questions used, samples drawn, and analysis techniques employed are standard in the child-rearing literature. This article, more so than many, discusses the implications of the results in considerable detail.

The data may be particularly relevant to Canada because it involves comparisons of child rearing in England and the United States. If, as suggested in Chapter two, Canadian values and practices do fit between those of the United States and England, an interesting profile emerges. Perhaps the most important point that needs to be made is that the similarities are, indeed, more obvious than the differences. There are, however, certain consistent and important differences which should not be ignored. England is described as having greater sex-role segregation in both marital and child roles. English parents are described as less affectionate and supportive, less demanding and controlling, but more punitive, than American parents. Affection in the English family is linked to indulgence, whereas in the American family, affection is linked to discipline. Is the average Canadian parent less involved but more punitive than the average American parent? Is affection more strongly related to indulgence than to discipline in Canadian child rearing compared to American child rearing? No one really knows, unfortunately, but the assumption seems plausible until research evidence demonstrates otherwise.

Though the findings are almost as interesting as the implications, there are several good reasons for being cautious about them. First, the data was collected from 741

English and 968 American *sixth grade* students. Each child answered a questionnaire about the child-rearing practices employed by his parents. There is no evidence that children in the sixth grade are able to accurately describe child-rearing practices in their homes. Would the responses of tenth grade students, for example, be the same? Would fathers and mothers themselves give the same answers as their sixth grade children? Based on increasing evidence of pronounced disagreement within families concerning family relationships (Niemi, 1974; Larson, 1974a), it is unlikely that these responses are more or less accurate than those of other family members. It is clear, however, that it is not acceptable to rely on the responses of the sixth grade child without knowing that the response is representative of the way other family members see child rearing. Second, the authors make clear that the data cannot be termed either representative or typical. Purposive rather than random samples were drawn. Accordingly, generalizations can only be made about the persons who participated in the study. Even so, the authors have done an excellent job of carefully and cautiously reviewing the results, and for the most part, their conclusions seem warranted.

Child-rearing in England and the United States: a cross-national comparison

Edward C. Devereux, Urie Bronfenbrenner, and Robert R. Rodgers

Cross-cultural research, like travel, is a broadening experience, for in learning of other people and other ways we also learn something about ourselves as well. In a foreign land, the visitor encounters alternative arrangements for child-rearing, not as random variants but as institutionalized patterns, and he also sees, or believes he sees, their patterned consequences "writ large" in the behavior of all the children he meets. The shock effect of this experience helps to make him aware, perhaps for the first time, of the tacit assumptions and taken-for-granted values which serve as boundary conditions for child-rearing in his own culture.

American visitors to England have often commented on what they see as "different" in English families and English children. "Good Children or Happy Ones?" wrote an American visitor in the London *Observer* (February 5, 1964) and went on to observe that English children, though admittedly

Edward C. Devereux, Ph.D., and Urie Bronfenbrenner, Ph.D., are Professors and Robert R. Rodgers, Ph.D., is a lecturer and Senior Research Associate in the Department of Child Development and Family Relationships at Cornell University.

From *Journal of Marriage and the Family*, 31 (2 May, 1969), pp. 257-270. Copyright 1969 by National Council on Family Relations. Reprinted by permission.

well mannered, seemed strangely unresponsive, unchildlike, and "repressed." "Americans adore children who are friendly, talkative and 'outgoing'," she wrote. "The English adore children, too, as long as they are quiet, polite, clean, and don't interrupt." She found the relations of parents to children, at least in the upper classes, a bit strained and formal, lacking in spontaneity and warmth; and she described with dismay how the British upper classes pack their children off to boarding schools at a tender age and dread the long holidays. In subsequent weeks, this paper contained floods of letters from the embattled British mums, defending the British system and recalling their pleasure when an hitherto unruly child returned for the school holidays "visibly tamed and improved."

English visitors have also recorded their views about American children and their parents. "American Kids!*%#" exploded a visiting Englishman in the *New York Times* (November 14, 1965) and went on to document the view that American children are undisciplined and rude, and, worst of all, don't know their place, which is to be silent and respectful in the presence of adults until the minimum of civilities are done with, and then to vanish to a separate world of childhood. This time the floods of letters came from outraged American moms, who argued that American children are not undisciplined and rude, but rather spontaneous, spirited, and friendly.

But while this sort of fascinated dialogue has been going on for many years among lay observers, the topic has apparently never been subject to systematic comparative research. American child-rearing practices have been extensively documented,[1] but most of these studies provide no comparative

framework to give perspective on our particular style of deviance. There is also a growing research literature on child rearing in England, much of it rich in descriptive detail, but unfortunately most of these studies do not deal with operationally defined and indexed variables applied to large, cross-sectional samples.[2] And in any event, as with the American research, there is little with an explicit cross-cultural framework to provide the necessary comparative perspective.[3]

The central question thus still remains largely unanswered: just what are the differences in how children are actually raised in England and the United States? How different, in fact, are English mums and American moms, or English fathers and American dads, in their day-to-day practices of rearing their children? In what ways are boys brought up differently from girls in the two countries?

In the present paper, we attempt to answer these questions by comparing the responses given by a sample of children in England with those given by a sample of children in America on a questionnaire designed to produce detailed data, among other things, on their experiences with their parents. While our purpose in this paper is largely descriptive, in fact this report forms a part of a larger ongoing project with a more serious scientific purpose. If families, or nations, differ in their styles, strategies, and goals of child-rearing, the more important question must be: what difference do such differences make for how the children turn out? Our data on child-behavior outcomes for the English and American samples, not yet fully analyzed, will be reported in more detail in a separate paper later.

The present study is designed to parallel

and supplement our own earlier comparative study of child-rearing in Germany and America.[4] In this earlier study, Germany was selected because we thought that its strong family-centered tradition would present some interesting contrasts with the child-centered focus of the American family. England was selected to represent a more adult-centered family tradition.

Methods and procedures

The data for the present study consist entirely of responses made by groups of American and English school children, all in their sixth school year and hence mostly 11 or 12 years old, on a group-administered questionnaire in which they were called upon to report in some detail about the child-rearing practices currently employed in their homes by their fathers and mothers.

The research populations

Subjects for the English sample were all pupils in the top class of primary schools in Surrey, the county which begins just below London and extends some 40 miles southward, through tiers of suburbs to a rural hinterland. With the assistance of school officials, 27 school classes were selected for testing, with the objective of including schools at all levels of socioeconomic status and in a wide range of community settings. Within these 27 school classes there were 894 children who took part in our research procedures. For the present analysis we retain 741 of these, 385 boys and 356 girls, these being all the children from intact families, living at home with both natural parents, and about whom we have full in-

formation.

Subjects for the American sample were all pupils in the sixth grades of elementary schools in Onondaga County in central New York State. This area was selected because it appeared to offer a wide range of variation in socioeconomic status and of urban, suburban, and rural settings roughly corresponding to those included in the English sample. Testing procedures were carried out in 39 school classes. About one-third were taken within the City of Syracuse, the balance from peripheral areas ranging from predominantly industrial communities to more sparsely settled residential suburbs. Because approximately half of the children in this area attend parochial schools, half of the children in this sample were taken from parochial schools; the balance were in public schools.[5] In the 39 classes, there were 1,169 children. Of these, 968 — consisting of 498 boys and 470 girls — are retained in the present analysis, these being all the children living in intact families with their own natural parents and about whom full information was available.

It should be clear that these are both purposive samples, drawn from particular areas within the countries they are here used to represent. We can make no valid claim that they are representative or typical. It may well be that samples drawn from other areas in England or America would yield somewhat different results. However, we have attempted to make each sample cover a wide range of socioeconomic status and of types of neighborhoods and communities and so far as possible, comparable to each other. When both samples are ordered on a measure of socioeconomic status (hereafter SES) based on father's occupation,[6] the distributions are substantially similar and there is no

Table 1 Parent Practice Dimensions and Variables, Item Wordings, and Response Alternatives

Dimensions and Variables	Item Wording and Response Alternatives*
A. Supporting	
1. Nurturance	1. She (he) comforts and helps me when I have troubles.†(A)
	2. She makes me feel I can talk with her about everything. (A)
	3. She makes me feel she is there if I need her. (A)
2. Principled Discipline	4. When she punishes me, she explains why. (A)
	5. When she wants me to do something, she explains why. (A)
3. Instrumental Companionship	6. She helps me with homework or lessons, if there is something I don't understand. (C)
	7. She teaches me things I want to learn. (C)
4. Consistency of Expectation	8. I know what she expects of me and how she wants me to behave. (A)
	9. When I do something she doesn't like, I know exactly what to expect of her. (A)
5. Encouragement of Autonomy	10. She encourages me to try new things on my own. (A)
	11. She lets me make my own plans about things I want to do, even though I might make a few mistakes. (A)
6. Indulgence	12. She lets me off lightly when I do something wrong. (B)
	13. She cannot bring herself to punish me. (B)
B. Demanding	
7. Prescription of Responsibilities	14. She expects me to keep my things in good order. (A)
	15. She expects me to help around the house or yard (Eng.: garden). (C)
8. Achievement Demands	16. She keeps after me (Eng.: keeps on at me) to do well in school. (B)
	17. She keeps after me (Eng.: keeps on at me) to do better than other children. (B)
C. Controlling	
9. Control	18. She wants to know exactly where I am going when I go out. (A)
	19. She expects me to tell her exactly how I spend my pocket money. (A)

significant difference in the means for the two distributions either for boys or girls. The children in the English sample, however, were slightly younger on the average (11.2 years old) than those in the American sample (11.7 years old).

The parent practices questionnaire

The questionnaires employed in the present study were filled out by the children in their regular school classrooms. All instruments were administered by a trained member of our own research staff, who read aloud all instructions and each of the questions. In its present version, the parent-practices questionnaire consisted of 30 items, each descriptive of some specific bit of parental behavior. The entire set, identical except for pronouns, was presented twice, once with respect to the mother, again, after other intervening materials, with respect to the father. Each item was followed by a set of five scaled response alternatives, and the

Table 1 — continued

Dimensions and Variables	Item Wording and Response Alternatives*
C. *Controlling – cont'd.*	
10. Protectiveness	20. She worries that I cannot take care of myself. (B)
	21. She won't let me go places because something might happen to me. (B)
D. *Punishing*	
11. Affective Punishment	22. When I do something she doesn't like, she acts hurt and disappointed. (B)
	23. She punishes me by trying to make me feel guilty and ashamed. (B)
12. Deprivation of Privileges	24. She punishes me by not allowing me to be with my friends. (C)
	25. She punishes me by not letting me use my favorite things for a while. (C)
13. Scolding	26. She nags at me. (C)
	27. She scolds me. (C)
14. Physical Punishment	28. She slaps me. (C)
	29. She spanks me (Eng.: smacks me). (C)
	30. She says she will give me a spanking (Eng.: smacking) if I don't behave better. (C)

Letter in parentheses after each item indicates which of the following response alternatives was used:

(A)	(B)	(C)
1. Never	1. Never	1. Never
2. Only once in a while	2. Only once in a while	2. Only once or twice a year
3. Sometimes	3. Sometimes	3. About once a month
4. Usually	4. Often	4. About once a week
5. Almost always	5. Very often	5. Almost every day

† All items are given here with the female pronouns, as used in the questionnaire concerning mother's behavior. The identical questions with male pronouns were used to inventory father's behavior.

children were instructed to check the response which best described the behavior of this particular parent during the current school year.

The 30 items included in the present inventory are those which have survived from longer batteries used by the authors in earlier studies.[7] They were designed to provide indexes for 14 more general variables which, in our experience, provide a useful system for mapping variations in patterns of parent behavior.[8] It should be clear, however, that these 14 parent-practice variables are not wholly independent of one another. Our experience has indicated that when these variable scores are intercorrelated and factor analyzed they generate a set of more general factorial dimensions, and these appear to be fairly similar both for boys and for girls, whether applied to fathers or mothers.[9] Here we group the 14 variables under four more general dimensions, labeled *Supporting, Demanding, Controlling, and Punishing.*[10] In Table 1 we show the 14 parent practice variables grouped in terms of the broader dimensions with which they tend to cluster, and for each variable, the specific items used to index it. On the questionnaire itself, of course, the items appeared in a random order and there was no reference to the variables they were used to measure.[11]

While we shall talk, rather eliptically, of parent behavior, the reader must bear in mind that our data consist entirely of children's reports as elicited in our questionnaire procedure. Although we have no direct data from the parents themselves in this study, we find some encouragement regarding their validity from two sources. In a separate study by Bronson et al.,[12] data permitting comparisons of both children's and parents' responses with direct observations of actual parent behavior showed generally convergent results. Similarly, in one of our own earlier pilot studies in America, in which a sample of parents rated themselves on the same parent-practice items, the correlations with their children's responses were all positive, even though in some cases rather distressingly low. The direction of the differences, incidentally, most often indicated that parents were more inclined than children to skew their responses toward the norms of social acceptability. There is at least some ground for believing, therefore, that the children's candid accounts may in fact be more valid than those which might be obtained from parent interviews.

Analysis of data

The raw data consist of children's responses on two 30-item questionnaires dealing separately with the behavior of mothers and of fathers. These responses have been summed to produce scores for each parent on 14 par-

ent practice variables, all scores having been given a range from 2 to 10, with the higher scores indicating more of the behavior. Analysis takes the form of a series of analyses of variance in which we have provided tests for relevant differences in parental behavior both within each culture and between the two cultures. Fixed variables are sex of child, sex of parent and culture, and the quantitative variables are the means on the 14 parent practices.[13]

In the tables which follow, we have made all tests separately for each of the 14 parent practice variables, as if these were wholly independent of each other. In fact, this is not the case. The reports on fathers and mothers given by the same children are obviously not wholly independent. There are also patterned intercorrelations among different sets of parent practice variables. Following presentation of the results concerning mean differences on the 14 individual parent practices, we will present a discussion of the correlational patterns among these variables.

Findings concerning cross-national similarities and differences

We may begin by looking for gross patterns of similarities or differences between the cultures, as revealed when the responses from children of both sexes concerning parents of both sexes are pooled. The outcome of this analysis is shown in Table 2.

In some respects the similarity in the accounts of parent behavior given by American and English children is quite striking. This similarity is indicated most clearly in the rank ordering of means, as shown in parentheses in the table. In both countries, prescription of responsibilities comes at the

Table 2 Differences in Ratings of Parental Behavior by American and English Children

Parent Practice Variables	Mean and Rank		Difference Favoring American Sample[a]
	American Sample	English Sample	
A. *Supporting*			
1. Nurturance	8.06 (3)	7.56 (3)	.50**
2. Principled Discipline	7.72 (5)	7.45 (4)	.27**
3. Instrumental Companionship	7.94 (4)	7.83 (2)	.11
4. Consistency of Expectation	8.49 (2)	7.41 (5)	1.08**
5. Encouragement of Autonomy	7.28 (7)	7.23 (6)	.05
6. Indulgence	4.74 (12)	5.50 (11)	−.76**
B. *Demanding*			
7. Prescription of Responsibilities	8.92 (1)	7.91 (1)	1.01**
8. Achievement Demands	7.53 (6)	6.50 (7)	1.03**
C. *Controlling*			
9. Control	6.80 (8)	5.70 (8)	1.10**
10. Protectiveness	5.60 (10)	5.51 (10)	.09
D. *Punishing*			
11. Affective Punishment	5.66 (9)	5.23 (12)	.43**
12. Deprivation of Privileges	4.01 (14)	3.60 (14)	.41**
13. Scolding	5.38 (11)	5.66 (9)	−.28*
14. Physical Punishment	4.28 (13)	5.16 (13)	−.88**

* $p \leqslant .05$
** $p \leqslant .01$

[a]Because of the existence of intercorrelations among some of the variables in this and subsequent tables, these tests of significance are not all fully independent.

head of the list, followed by most of the variables in the supporting cluster. Achievement demands, the controlling variables, indulgence, and finally punishments follow in roughly similar rank positions for both groups. The rank order correlations of means for the 14 variables for the American and English samples is .93, ($p \leqslant .01$). It appears that children in both cultures agree in seeing their parents as being more supporting and demanding than controlling and punishing.

However, there are important differences as well, as evidenced in the third column of Table 2. American children tend to describe their parents as more supporting and also as more demanding and controlling than do English children. From this it would appear that there may be more emotional involvement and psychological pressure between American parents and children than is present in English families. In the realm of punishment, moreover, American parents rely more upon such psychologically oriented techniques as reasoning, revoking privileges, withdrawing affection, showing disappointment, or attempting to make the child feel guilty about his behavior. In contrast, English parents are seen as more inconsistent and indulgent and as more inclined to employ direct forms of punishments such as spankings and scoldings.

Table 3   Patterns of Parental Role Differentiation: American vs. English Samples

Parent Practice Variables	Mean Difference Favoring Mother over Father			American Minus English Differences
	Both Samples (1)	American Sample (2)	English Sample (3)	(4)
A. *Supporting*				
1. Nurturance	.82**	.89**	.73**	.16
2. Principled Discipline	.22**	.24**	.18**	.06
3. Instrumental Companionship	.25**	.42**	.01	.41**
4. Consistency of Expectation	.08*	.11	.05	.06
5. Encouragement of Autonomy	−.12*	−.07	−.18*	.11
6. Indulgence	.25**	.10	.44**	−.34**
B. *Demanding*				
7. Prescription of Responsibilities	.45**	.38**	.54**	−.16*
8. Achievement Demands	.30**	.35**	.23**	.12
C. *Controlling*				
9. Control	.91**	.83	1.01**	−.18
10. Protectiveness	.84**	.69**	1.05**	−.36**
D. *Punishing*				
11. Affective Punishment	.50**	.30	.78**	−.48**
12. Deprivation of Privileges	.25**	.20**	.32**	−.12
13. Scolding	.91**	.69**	1.23**	−.54**
14. Physical Punishment	.41**	.23**	.65**	−.42**

* $p \leqslant .05$
**$p \leqslant .01$

Parental role differentiation

Still other patterns of similarity and difference emerge when we consider separately the roles of mothers and fathers in the two cultures. The results of this analysis are presented in Table 3. Perhaps the most striking finding, though hardly a surprising one, is that children in both cultures report receiving more of virtually every kind of treatment from their mothers than from their fathers. In fact, the only area in which the fathers receive slightly higher scores than the mothers is with respect to the encouragement of autonomy and initiative in their children. Both in England and America, child-rearing is primarily women's work, as everybody knows.

At the same time, the relative importance of the mother versus the father, as reflected by the size of the mean differences, shown in the first three columns of the table, varies markedly for different practices. In both samples, the mother's activity, relative to that of the father, is especially great in the areas of nurturance, control, protectiveness, and to a lesser extent, in nagging and scolding. In other areas, the mean differences are somewhat smaller, indicating that the father begins to approach the mother in degree of activity. Besides encouraging autonomy in children, fathers become relatively more active in maintaining an atmosphere of principled discipline and consistency in the home,

Table 4 Differences in Ratings of Parental Behavior by Boys and Girls: American vs. English Samples

Parent Practice Variables	Mean Differences Favoring Boys over Girls			Cultural Difference
	Both Samples (1)	American Sample (2)	English Sample (3)	Col. 2 minus Col. 3 (4)
A. *Supporting*				
1. Nurturance	−.10	.14	−.43*	.57**
2. Principled Discipline	−.09	.01	−.22	.23
3. Instrumental Companionship	−.09	.08	−.32*	.40*
4. Consistency of Expectation	−.07	−.12	−.02	−.10
5. Encouragement of Autonomy	.13	.20	.04	.16
6. Indulgence	−.10	.04	−.30**	.34*
B. *Demanding*				
7. Prescription of Responsibilities	−.24**	−.18**	−.33**	.15
8. Achievement Demands	.64**	.55**	.78**	−.23
C. *Controlling*				
9. Control	−.23*	−.24	−.22	−.02
10. Protectiveness	−.32**	−.36*	−.28*	−.08
D. *Punishing*				
11. Affective Punishment	.30**	.42**	.14	.28
12. Deprivation of Privileges	.39**	.28**	.52**	−.24
13. Scolding	.29**	.12	.52**	−.40*
14. Physical Punishment	.66**	.40**	1.02**	−.62**

* $p \leqslant .05$
** $p \leqslant .01$

in urging their children toward achievement, and in the use of deprivation of privileges to enforce discipline. Even though he is less active in the day-to-day details of child-rearing, the father may nevertheless play a crucial role as a kind of balance wheel in regulating and moderating family discipline. In all these respects, the patterns of parental role differentiation in England and America appear to be generally similar.

But there are also certain significant differences in the roles of the two parents in England and America, as indicated in the fourth column of the table. Most generally, there is a clear tendency toward greater parental role differentiation in England than in America. This is especially pronounced in the areas of controlling and punishing, in which the mother's activity relative to the father is greater in England than it is in America. The only significant exception to this pattern occurs with the variable of instrumental companionship, that is to say, helping the child with homework, hobbies, etc., in which English fathers play a somewhat more prominent role.

An examination of the separate means for fathers and mothers, not shown in the table, reveals that the direction of cultural difference tends to be the same for both parents; for example, both mothers and fathers in America are seen as more nurturant, consistent, demanding, and controlling than English fathers and mothers, while both English parents are seen as more indulgent and also as more given to the use of physical punishment than their American counterparts.

Similarities and differences in the treatment of boys and girls

Next, let us consider how children of opposite sexes are treated in England and America. The relevant data for this analysis are presented in Table 4. Perhaps the most striking finding here is the similarity in ways in which parents in both cultures handle boys differently from girls. Both in England and America, boys experience significantly more achievement demands and punishments of all kinds, while girls are given more household responsibilities and treated more protectively.

At the same time, there are clear indications that English parents differentiate more in their treatment of boys and girls than do American parents. In the area of support, English girls experience significantly more nurturance, companionship, and indulgence than English boys, whereas in these respects American girls and boys are treated almost alike. And while boys in both countries are punished more than girls, when it comes to spanking and scolding, this difference is far bigger in England than in the United States.

Parental behavior associated jointly with sex of parent and sex of child

Finally, we must ask how these patterns of similarity and difference are affected when we take into account both the sex of the parent and the sex of the child simultaneously. Our data here indicate a tendency in both cultures for parents to differentiate their behavior in relation to the same-sex versus the opposite-sex child. In matters of control and discipline as well as in companionship, for example, fathers are more concerned with sons, while mothers are more concerned with daughters. However, precisely the reverse is true for variables such as indulgence and protectiveness; here fathers receive the higher ratings from daughters and mothers from sons. We may summarize by saying that each parent seems to accept somewhat more responsibility for the discipline, control, and socialization of children of the same sex, while being somewhat more lenient and indulgent with children of the opposite sex. We must report, however, that this tendency for parental role specialization in relation to the sex of the child appears to be somewhat more marked in America than in England.

Similarities and differences in patterns of parent behavior

We have been concerned until now with the 14 parent practice variables as more or less separate entities. In fact, as noted earlier, these variables are not all empirically independent. We now go on to ask what can be learned about the similarities and differences in the patterning of parent behavior in England and America, as revealed by the intercorrelations among these parent variables? The basic data for this analysis consisted of eight 14 × 14 correlation matrixes, representing all the relationships among the parent practices reported by children of each sex for parents of each sex in the two cultures.[14]

As noted before, there were a number of general similarities in patterns of intercorrelation which ran through all eight matrixes. Specifically, the general dimensions which we have labeled supporting, demanding, controlling, and punishing tended to appear as identifiable clusters for all matrixes in both cultures, and in each case included some or all of the variables assigned to them in the preceding tables. In spite of this general similarity, however, there were also a number of instructive differences in the structure of the matrixes for the two cultures.

Let us begin with a look at indulgence, placed with the supporting variables in the tables. In fact, within the English sample there was a fairly extensive network of highly significant correlations between indulgence and all the other variables in the supporting cluster, except with consistency. Within the American sample not a single significant correlation occurred between indulgence and any of the other support variables. In the English sample moreover, indulgence also showed an extensive pattern of highly significant negative correlations with three of the four variables in the punishing cluster. Once again, in the American sample no such negative correlations occurred on any of the matrixes. Evidently emotional support in the English family is colored by an easy-going, permissive attitude and an unwillingness to impose punishments, while punishments tend to be imposed in contexts which are lacking in nurturance, consistency, and principled discipline. Emotional support in America apparently does not imply unreadiness to punish.

Let us next consider the context in which achievement demands and responsibilities are imposed in the two cultures. In the American sample there is a fairly extensive network, consisting of 21 highly significant correlations, linking the demand and supporting variables. For England, only nine such linkages occur. In both countries, demanding was linked with supporting more strongly in reports of fathers' behavior than in those dealing with mothers.

But when we look at the correlations between demanding and punishing, the nature of the relationship is just the other way around. In the English sample, 16 highly significant correlations occur linking demanding and punishing, while the American sample yields only seven such linkages. In both countries affective or guilt-oriented punishments appear to play an especially prominent role in relation to achievement demands. But in England, scoldings and spankings are also linked to achievement demands with six highly significant correlations; the American sample shows not a single correlation between these variables.

Summarizing, we may conclude that American parents show a stronger tendency to impose their demands in a context of reliable emotional support and to rely primarily upon psychological pressures to enforce them. In British families, perhaps since affectional ties are more attenuated, demands are enforced more often by direct punishments.

A similar pattern appears with the variable we have labeled "control." In the American sample this variable also shows strong correlations with supportive parental behavior. There are ten highly significant correlations to this cluster in the American matrixes, as against only four in the English. As with demanding, it is the father's controlling behavior more than the mother's which is most closely linked with strong emotional support.

We should also note in passing that not a single correlation occurs in either culture between "protectiveness" and any of the supporting variables. This fact suggests the possibility that protectiveness may represent a kind of nervous, pathological extension of control. In the factor analyses for the American sample, protectiveness tended to become attached to indulgence, which, at face value, might seem to represent the opposite of control. Whereas the control variable was closely linked with achievement demands and prescription of responsibilities in all matrixes, protectiveness was linked with the demanding variables only for the girls in both cultures. As noted earlier, girls are treated more protectively than boys anyway. Perhaps we may infer that parental treatment of girls contains an element of anxious concern.

Finally, in both cultures there are extensive linkages between the dimensions of controlling and punishing. In the American sample, deprivation of privileges and affective punishments are especially closely tied to the controlling variables. English boys, who seem to get spanked more than anybody, also get spanked in the interests of control and protectiveness, while American boys do not. In fact, in the American family, physical punishment seems to be linked primarily to other forms of punishment, which in turn show more direct linkages with demanding and controlling. This fact suggests that in America, physical punishment may serve as a kind of court of last resort, employed primarily after other methods of discipline have failed, while in England this is evidently not the case.

A note on child-rearing and socioeconomic status

As noted earlier, while both the English and American samples covered a broad range of socioeconomic status, the two samples were reasonably well matched in their distribution across this range, and their means were almost identical. Nevertheless, we have taken the precaution to reexamine the relationships reported above for possible contamination by SES. Without going into detail here, we merely report that the results of this analysis were wholly negative. It appears, therefore, that to the extent that child-rearing patterns vary with socioeconomic status, the nature and directions of variation are substantially similar in both countries. To this we may now add the additional finding that, in both the English and American samples, there was in fact relatively little difference in styles of child-rearing reported by children in different classes. In no instance did any correlation in this set exceed .19, and most were much lower. Within each culture, the direction of these small relationships was similar: in general, higher-socioeconomic-status parents use less physical punishment and impose their disciplines in a context characterized by somewhat more support and consistency. But perhaps the major finding is really the absence of any strong relationship with SES in these samples.

Summary

Before turning to a discussion of their implications, let us attempt to summarize our principal empirical findings. In many important respects English and American styles of child-rearing are pretty much alike. In both, the roles of fathers and mothers are differentiated in a similar way, with the mother being the principal source both of emotional support and of day-to-day discipline and control, and with the father functioning as an occasional companion and helper to the children, especially to boys, as a kind of balance wheel in disciplinary matters to which he brings an element of principle, consistency and authority, and as the occasional agent of punishment. And in both countries, the treatment of boys and girls is differentiated along similar lines, with the boys receiving relatively more pressure and discipline, and with the girls being somewhat more nurtured and protected.

The differences between the two countries in patterns of child-rearing represent relatively minor variations in emphasis on these central themes. In England, the pattern of role differentiation between mothers and fathers is considerably sharper than in America, where the father is relatively more active than in England and where the father's activities more closely parallel those of the mother. And in England, also, the pattern of differentiation between boys and girls is somewhat more marked than in America, where boys and girls are treated more nearly alike.

Even though the absolute differences in levels of parental activity are mostly fairly small, and even though the intercorrelations among variables are mostly low, the direction and pattern of these differences appear to be fairly consistent and meaningful. In comparison with American parents, English parents are described by their children as less affectionate and supportive, as less demanding and controlling, but as more punitive. Affection in the English family becomes linked with indulgence, and perhaps because of this linkage, demands and controls are imposed more inconsistently and enforced more by direct punishments than by reasoned explanations and appeals to the conscience.

In contrast, American parents are seen by their children as more demanding and controlling, but also as more loving and supporting. Perhaps because of this greater emotional involvement between American parents and their children, parents are able to use these affectional ties as their most powerful lever for controlling their children and enforcing their demands. Affection, in the American family, is not linked to indulgence, but rather to firm, consistent discipline. Though spanked and scolded less than his English peers, the American child is nevertheless exposed to considerably more psychological pressure from his parents. Most generally, it appears that parent-child relationships in America are richer, stronger, more salient, and more binding than in England, where they seem somewhat attenuated and strained.

Discussion

Concerning the validity of the findings

For several reasons we must approach the task of putting any interpretation on these findings with caution. First, while our samples are large enough for statistical reliability, each was taken from a single county of the nation it is used to represent. If there are significant regional variations in child-rearing, different sampling areas might have yielded somewhat different results. Second, while there are statistically reliable differences between the two samples, in absolute terms these are mostly fairly small; so perhaps our most substantial finding is really the basic similarity in patterns of child-rearing in both countries. Third, while we have talked only of means, there is obviously extensive variation within each sample on all of our variables. The presence of mean cultural differences should not obscure the more fundamental fact of overlapping ranges for all variables. In a later paper, we shall examine the patterns and consequences of these internal variations in some detail. Here, our awareness of such variations may serve to protect us, and our readers, from talking too glibly of *the* English family or *the* English child. Finally, our data for the present report consist entirely in children's reports of parental behavior. We cannot be certain these reports are objectively valid accounts of what parents really do.

Our findings, however, do seem to provide a reasonably consistent and meaningful picture. We gain some confidence in their validity from their convergence in pattern with those of Barker and Barker concerning adult-child relations in England versus America.[15] The Barkers' sampling areas were quite different from ours: for America they studied a small community in the Midwest; for England, a similar community in a northern county. Moreover, their data stem not from questionnaires or interviews, but rather from direct observation of children interacting with adults or each other in a variety of different settings, in schools, playgrounds, etc. In addition, they gathered data from an analysis of settings involving adults and children in English and American children's books. These two sources of data yielded generally similar results.[16]

For comparison with our own results, derived from different sources, with different methods and from different sections of the two countries, here are the Barkers' conclusions concerning the most significant differences in how adults interact with children in America and England. American adults significantly exceeded English adults in the following ways of relating to children:[17]

1. Exercising routine personal influence (requesting, suggesting).
2. Using adult role authority and competence (teaching, leading, cautioning, guiding).
3. Responding willingly to personal influences of children (answering requests, accepting advice and suggestions).
4. Seeking insight into children's motives and behavior (analyzing, probing, withholding judgment).
5. Expressing affection for children (hugging, kissing, etc.).

English adults exceeded American adults in these other behaviors with children:

1. Using maximal personal influence (bossing, commanding, etc.).
2. Making negative evaluations of children (disapproving, belittling).
3. Threatening to punish or expressing "dangerous" emotions (scolding, expressing exasperation, etc.).
4. Expressing impatience with children (annoyance, anger).
5. Being distant with children (unconcerned, indifferent, unaware).
6. Being baffled by children (confused, uncomprehending).
7. Punishing children (smacking, shaking, denying privileges).

There is evidently a substantial degree of pattern similarity between the adults in the Barkers' research and the parents in our own.

In fact, as noted in a fascinating study by S. M. Lipset, these patterned differences in English and American styles for relating to children have apparently existed for a long, long time. In his survey of British travellers' accounts of American styles of parenting, he quotes from Harriet Martineau, writing in 1837:

[In child-rearing Americans try] to avoid to the utmost the exercise of authority, and to make children friends from the very beginning . . . They watch and guard: they remove stumbling-blocks: they manifest approbation and disapprobation: they express wishes, but at the same time, study the wishes of their little people: they leave as much as possible to natural retribution. . . . The children of America have the advantage of the best possible early discipline; that of activity and self-dependence.[18]

Some Implications of the Findings for Child Behavior

Without assuming that all parents and all children in each country are alike, let us assume that the "averaged" differences in styles of child-rearing for England and America are as we have described them. If so, the intriguing question arises: in what "averaged" way might we expect children in England and America to differ from one another? What difference do these differences make for children?

Since our own data on child behavior in the two cultures are not yet fully analyzed, we must defer most of our answer to this question to a later paper. But having come so far, perhaps we may be indulged in a few speculations.

When we look at the ways in which the cultural differences in styles of child-rearing tend to be patterned, three general tendencies appear, each of which suggests a general hypothesis about the ways in which English and American children might be expected to differ:

1. The American family has less parental role differentiation and is more egalitarian than the English family.
2. American children are treated differently from English children in many of the same ways in which girls are treated differently from boys in both cultures.
3. American children are treated differently from English children in many of the same ways in

which middle-class children are treated differently from working-class children in both cultures.

We may hypothesize, therefore, that American children might be different from English children: (1) in some of the same ways in which children from egalitarian families differ from those whose parents are more differentiated, (2) in some of the same ways in which girls differ from boys in general, and (3) in some of the same ways in which middle-class children differ from working-class children generally.

Let us consider briefly what kinds of child behavior characteristics might be expected from the first of these three types of differentiation. In one of our own previous studies, concerned with variations in parental role differentiation within an American sample,[19] children from egalitarian homes — in which both parents were described as warm, permissive, and undifferentiated — were rated as more spontaneous and outgoing, more cheerful and friendly, better adjusted, more sensitive to the feelings of others, and better able to express their own feelings freely than were children from homes with greater parental role differentiation. However these same children were also rated as somewhat less mature emotionally, as more mischievous, anxious, not very responsible, and not very persistent with their studies. In contrast, children from homes with a more differentiated father figure were reported as higher on leadership, dominance, daring, persistence, and achievement; but also as more selfish, hostile, and insensitive to the feelings of others. In a review of many other studies on this theme, Slater[20] has reported generally convergent results.

To what extent, we must now ask, do these contrasting profiles provide a model for the pattern of differences between American and English children? Some fragmentary evidence relevant to this question is supplied in a study by H. J. Butcher *et al.*,[21] comparing test scores for a large sample of British and American seventh-grade school children: in comparison to the Americans, the English children were found to be less sociable, less sensitive, less conscientious, more assertive, and more tense. Similarly, in the Barkers' study cited above, peer-group relationships among American children were found to be characterized by more friendliness, affection, enjoyment, and mutual understanding than those of English children, whose peer relationships contained significantly more of dominance and compliance.

What should our second general hypothesis lead us to expect? In some respects, the ways in which girls are different from boys parallel those cited above, perhaps because girls, like the children in the more egalitarian families, get a generous dosage of nurturance. Girls are generally thought to excel boys in social sensitivity and emotional expressiveness. But the socialization of girls, as we have seen, also entails a greater dosage of protectiveness and control and more training for routine responsibilities. In most previous studies including some of our own,[22] girls have generally been described as more compliant, docile, obedient, conformist, and responsible than boys. Perhaps because of the linking use of strong emotional support with love-oriented techniques of discipline, which tends to characterize the rearing of girls more than boys, girls also develop an internalized conscience earlier than boys. They tend to identify with adults and their values more readily than boys and to become "rule-enforcers," imposing adult-sponsored standards on others.[23]

How well, we must ask, do these patterns of difference between girls and boys also tend to predict directions of difference between American and English children? Preliminary analyses of some of our own data for the English and American samples suggest that they may fit fairly well. Children in both cultures responded to an instrument we call the "dilemmas test." In this test they were presented with a series of 54 hypothetical situations in which internalized standards of the correct, adult-approved behavior, on such matters as lying, stealing, or cheating, are confronted head-on with strong peer-pressure toward deviance, and the child must indicate "what he would really do." On this paper and pencil test, the results were quite striking. In both countries and on every item, girls were more inclined than boys to skew their answers in the direction of the adult-approved behavior choice; boys in general yielded more readily to pressures from their peers to violate the adult norms. Similarly, in every single situation, American children were more "adult-oriented" than English children. In other situations, girls showed themselves more inclined than boys to engage in rule-enforcing behavior, attempting to dissuade other children from some mischief or informing on them to adults. In these respects also, American children generally responded more like girls than did English children.

Finally, what should our third general hypothesis lead us to expect about the ways in which English and American children might differ? Studies of class differences in child-rearing in America indicate that in the working classes more use is made of physical punishment, and discipline tends to be inconsistent and sporadic, penalties and controls being imposed more for the convenience of the parents than for the welfare of the child.[24] As we have seen, parent practices in England bear some resemblance to this working-class model. Also the goals of child discipline in England, even if solidly middle-class in content, are focused more on the needs and convenience of the adult and his world: the "good child" is clean, quiet, formally polite, does not interrupt nor intrude in adult-centered home activities, especially when company is present, and above all else, does nothing in public places which might annoy other adults and thus humiliate his parents.[25]

For children brought up in the working-class style, we might expect a covert attitude of defiance toward authority and rules; because the rules have been imposed by authority figures towards whom they feel no particular emotional identification, because they have been enforced in arbitrary and inconsistent ways, and because the rules themselves may seem rather arbitrary and superficial. Under these circumstances, we would expect overt conformity in the presence of authority figures, but little commitment to the adult-sponsored rules when the sanctioning authority is absent. Moreover, we would expect relatively little guilt or anxiety concerning non-conformity.

How well do these expectations for working-class children fit the differences between English and American children? In the Barkers' study, cited earlier, the relation of English children to adults was different from that of American children, in being more formally polite and "compliant without enthusiasm" and also in being more distant, resistant, and negative. American children accommodated themselves more easily to adult standards, expressed more affection for adults, but also disagreed and argued with adults more readily than English children. From their analysis of children's books, the Barkers also came up with a most intriguing finding: in the English stories there was relatively less "heterogeneity" in children's behavior in settings in which adults were also present, but a great deal more behavior variability in settings with no adult present; in the American stories, the presence or absence of adults made no difference whatever. The implication would seem to be that for the English children, control of behavior may depend more heavily upon external authority symbols and constraints than upon an internalized feeling of commitment to some standard of conduct. Evidently adults do not appear as authority symbols for American children, who behave in much the same way whether adults are there or not; whatever controls there are come more from within the child himself.

Further data relevant to this theme was reported in a study by H. H. Anderson et al.,[26] in which school children in four countries, including England and the United States, were asked to complete a story involving a late and missing assignment. The responses of the English children in this sample differed from those of the American children in the following ways: English children were more likely to say that the teacher would take the initiative in raising the issue of the missing paper, that the child would lie to the teacher, that the child would not be believed by the teacher, whether he lied or not, and that the teacher would punish the child, whether or not his story was believed. Yet another study, by J. Sarnoff et al.,[27] found significantly higher test anxiety among English than among American school children. All this confirms the impression that, for English children, adult-controlled situations are perceived as especially authority-bounded and stressful.

Finally, in a separately reported study of our own, concerned with values and standards of behavior, as reported in a different section of the questionnaire by some of the same children who participated in the present research, we found that American children differed from English children in placing a generally higher value on most all standards of behavior, and especially upon telling the truth; while English children differed from American children "in assigning a greater importance to a standard of masculinity or strength involving both a stoical boyish ideal and some opposition to adult authority."[28]

Clearly there are certain advantages to both systems of child-rearing, but it is also clear that these advantages are not achieved without cost. No doubt American children really are noisier and perhaps naughtier as well, especially in public places where adults may observe them. But as the American mothers point out, what is taken as bad manners by the foreign visitor may really be mostly an expression of unrepressed childish spontaneity and probably represents no ill will nor desire to offend. In fact, the American child-rearing system seems to produce in children a kind of expansive good will toward fellow creatures, including even adults. We suspect it may also foster a fairly solid commitment to the fundamental values of moral conduct, once they get them straight. Only a few years ago many observers of American families were seriously concerned that the wave of parental permissiveness then so prevalent would result in a generation of wholly undisciplined children. Perhaps the most emphatic result of the present study is the evidence it provides that this wave of permissiveness is now definitely past. American children today appear to get a generous measure of discipline and control, but of a different sort and for a different purpose than that experienced by English children.

The English system evidently does fairly well in achieving the often-stated objective of producing children who are quiet and polite and who do not intrude unwanted upon adults. As fellow passengers in a railroad carriage, most grown-ups would probably much prefer a group of English children to a group of Americans. English children are also more persistent and disciplined in their study habits and not so easily distracted as American children by the need to be a good fellow. Perhaps the experience of resisting authority rather than identifying with it pays dividends in shaping the sort of autonomous, rugged individualism for which the British are justly famous.

Against these gains, if they be that, one must weigh the possible consequences for character of growing up in a world where relationships are so often distant, constrained, and hostile. On this, the perceptive Harriet Martineau, returning from her American travels more than 100 years ago, commented:

I have a strong suspicion that the faults of temper so prevalent where parental authority is strong, and where children are made as insignificant as they can be made, and the excellence of temper in America, are attributable to the different management of childhood in the one article of freedom. There is no doubt that many children are irrecoverably depressed and unnerved for want of being convinced that anybody cares for them.[29]

NOTES

1 See, for example, R. R. Sears, E. Maccoby, and H. Levin, *Patterns of Child Rearing,* Evanston, Ill.: Row, Peterson & Co., 1957; D. R. Miller and G. E. Swanson, *The Changing American Parent,* New York: John Wiley & Sons, 1958; and U. Bronfenbrenner, "The Changing American Child: A Speculative Analysis," in *Educating For Mental Health,* ed. by J. Seidman, New York: Thomas Y. Crowell Co., 1963.

2 For an excellent account of much of this research, see Josephine Klein, *Samples From English Cultures,* London: Routledge & Kegan Paul, 1965, Vol. 2. This work contains an extensive bibliography of relevant research on British child-rearing.

3 We shall comment on a few explicitly comparative studies below, in connection with the discussion of our own findings.

4 E. C. Devereux, U. Bronfenbrenner, and G. Suci, "Patterns of Parent Behavior in the United States of America and the Federal Republic of Germany: A Cross-National Comparison," *International Social Science Journal,* 14:3 (1962), pp. 488-506.

5 Because the English sample consisted almost entirely of native-born white children, school classes with large concentrations of Negroes or foreign-born families were excluded from the American sample.

6 O. D. Duncan, "A Socioeconomic Index for All Occupations," in *Occupations and Social Status,* ed. by A. J. Reiss, New York: Crowell-Collier, 1961, chap. 6, pp. 109-138.

7 Cf. Devereux *et al., op. cit.*

8 Assignment of two or three items to each of these variables was initially made on an a priori basis; however in the set of items here employed, it has also been established in prior studies that the items included in each variable in fact tend to correlate more closely with each other than with any items assigned to other variables, and to cluster together in various factor-analytic procedures. In the present analysis, therefore, we deal only with variable scores obtained by summing the responses to items in each set, rather than with responses to individual items.

9 See M. Siegelman, "Evaluation of Bronfenbrenner's Questionnaire for Children Concerning Parental Behavior," *Child Development,* 36:1 (1963), pp. 163-174.

10 Clusters including some or all of the variables assigned to these four dimensions appeared on all eight matrixes from the present samples, whether for English boys' description of their mothers or of American girls' description of their fathers.

In spite of the existence of extensive intercorrelations among the parent practices variables, we have decided to use these specific variables in preference to more general factor scores in our analyses, because in fact the correlations within clusters are fairly low, and because there are important substantive and theoretical grounds for keeping the individual variables separate. For example, while both "physical punishment" and "affective punishment" appear on the same more general factorial dimension, in fact the correlation between these variables is only .32, leaving ample room for independent variation. And there is good reason to believe that these contrasting styles of punishment may have quite different consequences for children.

11 To mitigate the problem of response sets, the right-to-left or left-to-right direction of the response alternatives was also randomized on the questionnaire, and the questions dealing with fathers were widely separated from those dealing with mothers. Even so the children's reports on mother's and father's behavior all correlate positively, with coefficients ranging from .4 to .6. Some of this non-independence may indeed reflect varying response sets of individual children, some of whom may be more willing than others to check extreme response alternatives; but part of the mother-father correlation almost certainly also reflects empirical reality. If there are significantly differing culturally shaped sets which affect how children in the two samples deal with our questions, then some or all of

our results could be spurious. This, of course, is a major risk and liability of all cross-cultural questionnaire research.

12 W. C. Bronson, E. S. Katten, and N. Livson, "Patterns of Authority and Affection in Two Generations," *Journal of Abnormal and Social Psychology,* 58 (1959), pp. 143-152.

13 Because all testing was done in school classrooms, and because we are aware that within each culture patterns of child behavior and perhaps also of parent behavior vary significantly from one classroom to another, we have employed the mean of classroom means within each culture as the appropriate error term. In effect, this design insists that any difference claimed as a difference between the two cultures must clearly override the within-culture differences attributable to classroom effects.

Even though the two samples are fairly well matched on SES and only slightly different in age composition, we have nevertheless carried out a subsidary covariance analysis in which all of the findings reported below have been systematically examined for any possible effects of age and SES.

14 We also had available for each of these matrixes three rotated factor-analytic solutions, for three, four, and eight factors, respectively. Space precludes any attempt to set forth all of these materials in tabular form here. Instead we shall attempt to summarize the principal outcomes, commenting on the main similarities and differences within and between clusters for the two samples. Among the 1,456 correlation coefficients which comprised the eight matrixes, there were 277 which attained levels of .18 or better (p ≤ .001). It is these which provide the basis for the trends here described.

15 R. G. and L. S. Barker, "Social Actions in the Behavior Streams of American and English Children," in *The Stream of Behavior,* ed. by R. G. Barker, New York: Appleton-Century-Crofts, 1963.

16 Pointedly, the Barkers speak of adult-child relations, rather than of parent-child relations. In the study reported, they apparently did not attempt observations inside the home, though some were made of children playing in yards

beside their homes. Although some of the adults observed with children may indeed have been their parents, evidently other adults are included as well, such as teachers, playground supervisors, and so on.

17 Barker and Barker, *op. cit., pp.* 156-158.

18 Quoted in S. M. Lipset, "A Changing American Character?" in *Culture and Social Character,* ed. by S. M. Lipset and L. Lowenthal, New York: Free Press of Glencoe, 1961, p. 153.

19 U. Bronfenbrenner and E. C. Devereux, "Family Authority and Adolescent Behavior," *Proceedings of the Sixteenth International Congress of Psychology,* Bonn, Germany, 1961.

20 P. E. Slater, "Parental Role Differentiation," *American Journal of Sociology,* 67:3 (1961), pp. 296-311.

21 H. J. Butcher, M. Ainsworth, and J. E. Nesbitt, "A Comparison of British and American Children," *British Journal of Educational Psychology,* 33:3 (1963), pp. 278-285.

22 U. Bronfenbrenner, "Toward a Theoretical Model for the Analysis of Parent-Child Relationships in a Social Context," in *Parental Attitudes and Child Behavior,* ed. by J. D. Glidewell, Springfield, Ill.: Charles C. Thomas Co., 1961; and U. Bronfenbrenner, "Some Familial Antecedents of Responsibility and Leadership in Adolescents," in *Leadership and Interpersonal Behavior,* ed. by L. Petrullo and B. L. Bass, New York: Holt, Rinehart & Winston, 1961, pp. 239-272.

23 On these points, see in particular Sears, Maccoby, and Levin, *op. cit.,* and E. E. Maccoby, "The Taking of Adult Roles in Middle Childhood," *Journal of Abnormal and Social Psychology,* 63 (1961), pp. 493-503.

24 On these points, see M. L. Kohn, "Social Class and the Exercise of Parental Authority," *American Sociological Review,* 24 (1959), pp. 352-366; and M. L. Kohn, "Social Class and Parental Values," in *Readings in Child Development and Personality,* ed. by P. H. Mussen, J. J. Conger, and J. Kagan, New York: Harper,

Row, 1965, pp. 345-365.

25 These themes were stressed again and again in the letters to the editor of the London *Observer* during our period of field work in England.

26 H. H. and G. L. Anderson, I. H. Cohen, and F. A. Nott, "Image of Teacher by Adolescent Children in Four Countries: Germany, Mexico, England and the United States," *Journal of Social Psychology,* 50 (1959), pp. 47-55.

27 J. Sarnoff, F. Lighthall, R. Waite, K. Davidson, and A. Sarason, "A Cross-Cultural Study of Anxiety Among American and English School Children," *Journal of Educational Psychology,* 49 (1958), pp. 129-136.

28 Robert R. Rodgers, Urie Bronfenbrenner, and Edward C. Devereux, "Standards of Social Behavior Among School Children in Four Cultures," *International Journal of Psychology,* 3:1 (1968), pp. 31-41, 40.

29 Quoted in Lipset, *op. cit.,* p. 155.

The Squamish family: a setting for daily socialization

This article is based on Ryan's research among Squamish Indians for her doctoral dissertation. She describes the Squamish philosophy of child rearing in some detail, relative to contact with white children, self-determination, sex-typing, the role of siblings and fathers, the systematic relationships with members of the extended kin, and the process of schooling. The socialization of the male child is emphasized, with comparisons of the traditional family ("old elite") to the more modern family ("new elite"). A brief description of the differences for the socialization of females is included.

This paper is based on data obtained through participant observation and should be thought of as descriptive rather than explanatory research. This technique offers useful insights into family activities and their meanings to family participants which are frequently missed or de-emphasized in questionnaire or interview studies. It would have been preferable, however, to have combined the participant method with several of the more conventional measurement techniques to gain a more comprehensive picture of the Squamish family system. Standardized instruments administered to several family members, the use of experimental games to assess family processes, and a comparison with several white families might have increased the value of this study.

The paper does, however, offer important insights into Squamish socialization and permits comparisons with other studies carried out in a similar way. Lewis's research into Doukhobor childhood (1952), for example, reflects a very different socialization pattern. The Doukhobor child is reared in a climate which emphasizes "controlled, submissive, obedient behavior". Whether the differences between Squamish childhood and white childhood are as great as Ryan suggests remains to be seen.

The Squamish family: a setting for daily socialization

Joan Ryan

The Squamish Indians occupy reserves on the North Shore of the British Columbia Mainland and in the area up Howe Sound. I collected the information on socialization between 1968 and 1970. During this time, I was in several homes and attended all major Squamish social gatherings as well as ritual ones. Since that time, my daughters and I have continued our association with the Squamish people.[1]

In this report, I present the Squamish theories of socialization and describe their application in two family situations: the old and the new elite. The extended family behaviors described are a composite drawn from several family studies. They are "real" since they reflect the actual daily socialization practices and philosophies now in effect on a Squamish reserve. They are analytic and abstracted representations to the extent that they polarize and become rigid in their reification. The similarities among Squamish families are greater than any differences. Old and new elite groups overlap as well as polarize at many points in time.

I use the Squamish definition of family throughout this paper, i.e., the domestic group comprised of members tracing a rela-

tionship to a common ancestor. As well, most of the concepts presented are drawn from Squamish usage and information.

General Squamish beliefs associated with socialization

Most Squamish families share the belief that children should be highly nurtured in infancy. The nurturance can be provided by an adult and by siblings. Young girls often become "mothers" before puberty through being the primary caretaker of a younger sibling. By the time they produce their own children, they are highly competent to care for them. Nurturance takes the form of constant attention, feeding on demand, acquiescing to the natural rhythm of the child as far as weaning and toilet training are concerned. In order to obtain such care, the child needs to be where the adults are. He is mobile at an early age, therefore, being taken by an adult to a gathering, shopping, to do laundry. Siblings take him to the corner store, the baseball game, and to many of their other activities. In this way, the rhythm of adult and older sibling activities is also

Joan Ryan, Ph.D., is Associate Professor, Department of Anthropology, University of Calgary, Alberta.

This paper was specially written for this book.

maintained. If it is not possible to take the child to such activities, the grand-mother, an aunt or another relative will be asked to care for him over a short period. Members of that household will treat him to the same attention that he receives at home. Such care is optimal emotionally.

Squamish people share the belief that children should be left free to develop in their own ways, restricted only by minimal safety features. This concept of autonomy is made explicit in many ways within the culture. Individuals are viewed as ultimately responsible for their own affairs. If they make bad decisions, they are to be pitied, not condemned. In the same way, if the child must learn by doing things the wrong way, he will be allowed to make his mistakes and learn from them. The autonomy which young children have helps mature them and enables them to be much more independent and innovative than their white counterparts. Such autonomy also brings the child into conflict with the school personnel who find it difficult to accept that attendance and other matters are the child's decisions, not parental ones.

Disciplinary philosophies are also shared by many Squamish. The stated ideal behavior is that no parent should discipline a child harshly, either verbally or physically. Few Squamish mothers hit their children or scream at them. When such behavior does occur, it is noted as unusual and generally is reflective of some family crisis. Generally, children are spoken to quietly and firmly. The adage that speaking in a quiet voice forces someone to listen is well illustrated on Squamish reserves. Verbal control is prevalent but not abusive. Children are teased about silly behavior, talked about at length for serious infractions, and talked to about

undesirable behavior observed in other children. Great importance is placed on the value of not giving other people the chance to gossip. Children learn early that some of their behavior can shame the name of the family. Such knowledge places full responsibility on the child himself but it also has the positive effect of leaving him free from continuous harping and imposed controls. Occasionally, verbal controls are stated in projective terms. Children are warned that certain behavior may provoke a deceased relative who will haunt the child or rebuke him in some way from the spirit world. Use of projective agents is not general, but for the few, it is real and effective.

Most Squamish people share a body of expectations about what constitutes good behavior. Such ideals are articulated through the concepts of class and status and the appropriateness of any given behavior at any given time for an individual perceived in certain categories. What is appropriate for one household, therefore, is not necessarily seen as appropriate for another. However, the means of arriving at such a decision are shared, i.e., "acceptability" is attached to roles, names and family corporate status.

The focus of Squamish socialization is not physical development or early resolution of developmental tasks. The focus is on the development of more abstract qualities needed to become a good Squamish person. Such expectations evolve around concepts of honesty, reliability, respect, kindness, generosity and similar characteristics which involve concern with others rather than oneself. The process is reciprocal, however, for a child who learns these things early is treated in a like manner early and receives a great deal of satisfaction from the positive verbal statements as well as the reciprocal services he receives.

Squamish people generally prefer children to form their peer groups on the reserve. Peer groups are made up of siblings and cousins. Few children have friends outside the reserve setting or outside their extended families.[2] The term "friend" usually refers to a relative of the same sex with whom the child has a particularly warm relationship. The impact of peers in socializing each other should not be underestimated but the effect is usually one of reinforcement since nuclear groups within the extended family tend to share the same values, perspectives and behavior. Thus a child who is a member of one nuclear household is defined as a member of an extended family; he uses the other households as his own; his peers are relatives and they all share the basically similar social atmosphere, restrictions, and privileges. Young parents look to their siblings to reinforce their ideas about ideal socialization, and to deal with some of the problems which arise in one household but which can be resolved while visiting in another. Models, as well as processes, are shared in this way.

In Squamish society, a generally-held belief is that children are primarily the "property" of women. Women are essentially responsible for their socialization. This belief is reflected in the relative lack of contact that males have with children in the first few years of their lives. Men do not share responsibilities for the care of small children. They spend little time with them until they are old enough to talk, walk, and to participate in some degree with the father in some of his activities. In contrast, male siblings do care for their younger siblings but this service tends to drop off as the older boy ages. Generally, an older boy will only care for a younger boy, and after twelve years of age males consider demands for such services as unreasonable. On the other hand, children are also viewed as the "property" of the extended family. This means that it is acceptable to the parents, and to the child, if a relative of any degree comments positively or negatively on the behavior of the child. Such comments reflect the consensus that children are members of a corporate domestic group, any branch of which can be enhanced or shamed by the behavior of any single member.

Finally, in general, Squamish people believe in the continuity of the socialization process. Therefore, socialization can cover a broad spectrum of time, of agents, and of ends. In contrast to the popular white, middle class socialization model which views socialization as terminal somewhere in early adulthood, the Squamish feel that any person can learn different behavior as children or adults which will effectively determine their life situation. They view things as task-oriented and, as well, content-ordered. The ritual socialization which is a tertiary process for some Squamish adults is a good example of such concepts and behavior. Even if a person is not involved in something as dramatic as becoming a spirit dancer, he can still always learn ways to become a "better" Squamish person. It is to this concept of being a "good" Squamish that all roles, behavior and evaluations attach.

Methods

The information presented in this paper is drawn from observations of a variety of Squamish families. I have placed the families on a continuum using a variety of economic and social criteria such as income and involvement in the smokehouse. I have clustered the families at each end and drawn from them gross models of typical families on the reserve. One cluster constitutes an extended family composed of nine households. The family consists of three senior men (brothers) and their progeny (sons and daughters) who are currently resident on the reserve as family heads. Their progeny are also included and they constitute the parents and children (two generations) whose socialization practices were observed. All homes were visited over a period of months, but intensive interviews were carried out over a twelve-month period in several households. I can see no significant disparities in information or interpretation. Therefore, I draw generalizations from these nine households which apply equally to other Squamish families. In the same way, the information gathered in the intensive contacts with the three families mentioned does not differ significantly from that of the other six. Therefore, I use data from all nine households to form the composite family discussed below as the new-elite family.

I gathered information and compiled it in the same way for the old elite family. I have selected an extended family for discussion which consists of three households. The family consists of senior parents, their adult son and daughter and their progeny.

The Squamish people often refer to a person as "important". This term is used in a variety of ways by different people. The people who are elected to Council are "important" when they are acting in that capacity. This means the individual draws power from his position and that both his role and his access to political power enhance his status in the community *as long as he behaves in ways defined to be appropriate to his role and status*. People who have favors or jobs or cash to give away are important to know and important to the family who depends on them for such benefits. A man also adds to his importance if he has a position of note in the white world, i.e., as a union executive, or as a director of a club. Money (and its obvious expenditures), political power and position, and a demonstrated ability to deal with the white world constitute the criteria attached to being part of the "new elite". Since success at each of these things produces visible results, people are able to evaluate the degree to which a family is elite. The term includes the ascription of a superior status to those families which meet the criteria. The status is self-defined, but it has to be shared by others in the community in order to be functional. Such concepts define the new-elite families and are shared by others including the old-elite families.

The "old elite" draw their importance from another realm. Traditional names, knowledge of family history, right to use ritual privileges and property, spirit dancer initiation, and similar traditional criteria determine who are members of the old elite. Such criteria are not particularly visible except at ritual gatherings, and therefore are shared more among the old-elite families themselves and not by the community as a whole. In a few cases only do the ascriptions overlap. For example, one member of Council in 1969 was a spirit dancer and the Band Manager's daughter became an initiated dancer during his tenure. In addition, both he and his wife had claim to "big" names. In neither case was the Council member one of the major participants in the smokehouse. Within the smokehouse, the old-elite families have varying status and continue to pass names, information, and property through the generations. Within the reserve community, however, they suffer generally from low income, poor housing, political powerlessness, and limited contacts with whites on their own terms.

Each group uses its own cluster of families as a reference group set in opposition, in many instances, to the other group. The sense of importance does not cross the boundaries established by the different reference groups and therefore is not generally reinforced, rather it is often threatened. Each group accuses the other of inappropriate behavior toward important people.

The data were collected in several ways: (1) initial entry into households was obtained through a health survey; (2) I spent a minimum of two hours a week in each household which agreed to participate in interviews and child observations; and (3) I had contact with members of the extended family as they came in and out of the household in which I was visiting. Some of these led to interviews with grandparents or with parents' siblings, and (4) I attended most ritual and recreational events held on the reserve which members of the study households attended. I was able to observe children at these as well as mother-father, mother-child, and father-child behavior. In addition, many relatives attended such events so it was possible to see the child with several members of his extended family simultaneously; (5) I was sometimes invited to specific family gatherings and these afforded special opportunities to observe relationships and behavior of adults and children, and (6) I spent some time in bars with friends and was able to talk to the men in such circumstances.[3]

New-elite family socialization[4]

A baby born into a new elite family comes into a relatively large and well-furnished home. He arrives from hospital with new clothes, new blankets, and often in a plastic baby carrier. Sometimes he is nursed. If so, he is weaned usually in the first year to a bottle. Often he is on the bottle when he leaves the hospital. He and his mother are picked up at the hospital by the father in a good car of this year's vintage. The house, husband, and other children, have been looked after by a girl (of Indian ancestry) hired for the week of the mother's absence. The girl may stay on for an extra week or two until the mother recuperates. Grandmother may have come with her son to pick up the baby also. If not, she visits on the day of his arrival. Aunts and cousins also come by to drink tea, discuss the birth, and catch mother up on the gossip. When darkness falls, the baby is placed in a bassinet or crib in his parents' room and is tended from there throughout the nights. Often mother will have time-saving devices to help her, i.e., a night light, a bottle warmer, disposable diapers or diaper service.

Father does not help with infant care. He sleeps through the night. Sometimes, if the baby is too noisy, he will sleep elsewhere from time to time — at his mother's, sister's, brother's, or with friends in town. The time of pregnancy and the few weeks after delivery are occasionally the periods in which husbands choose to seek other female companionship. This increases his wife's emotional load and she may express resentment toward the baby. Two mothers informed me that the reason that one of their children was sickly, or difficult to manage, was because they had been angry and resentful toward them and did not give them the "proper" love and attention when they were small infants. The crisis passes in most cases and father returns to see his new family member. As the baby grows he may play with him or hold him from time to time.

The boy keeps to his own rhythm. He sleeps, eats, and wakes to his internal timer and is gratified to find his needs met as he demands. He begins to stay awake longer and to respond to his parents, siblings, and other relatives. The latter begin to comment on his appearance, his manner, and his proclivities. Will he be like uncle or like a cousin? The speculations begin with the first signs of socialization — a trust and an outwardness that includes the adult world.

The boy does not lack for anything. He has good clothes, good food and constant company. He may, by four or six months, share an older sibling's room. He is in his crib by now. He has toys. He sometimes has a yard or balcony to play on, sleep on, or from which to watch the world. He is never alone except when he himself slips away in sleep.

When he is a toddler his mother begins to toilet train him. He is put on the pot from time to time. If he wets, nothing is said, or a mild statement is made that he might have used his pot. He can eat when he likes and often what he likes. He shares the chips and pop of the older children, and may even go to the corner store with them to return bottles and spend the pennies. He visits his grandmother and his aunts, and he may eat or sleep there. He is a person now, consulted about his wishes, free to be wherever and whatever he chooses. The philosophy of autonomy is in full sway.

As the child wanders from household to household within his extended family, he may establish a special relationship with one of his relatives. That individual will do special things with him — tell a story, take a walk, go to town, go shopping and indulge the boy with a gift or treat. This relationship will remain stable over the years, and the boy will be the favored child of that family constellation. This may result in bestowal of privileges later in life in the form of a job, a house, a trip, or whatever. Often such relationships evolve because the youngster reminds the adult of one of his children when he was younger, or of a lost relative, or a close friend. With the selection of a favorite household, the child may decrease his visits to other kin. In these ways, he becomes subject to the socializing influence of a variety of kin, both adults and peers.

As soon as the child begins to walk and talk, he is regarded as a person capable of making certain decisions regarding his own activities. At the same time, parents begin to decrease the degree of indulgence and make some demands on the child. He is expected to be obedient, to come when he is called, to help with small tasks, to find his own sweater if going out, and to do a variety of things which are appropriate to his age. It is anticipated that he will fight with his siblings but be constrained in his manner of attack. He is expected to be polite to his elders but not necessarily to his parents. His toys are facsimiles of his older siblings' activities — miniature hockey sticks, lacrosse sticks, and baseballs. He begins early to imitate his older siblings and to separate the tasks which are male and female. He goes out to play the rough games with his brothers and cousins. His sister stays in with her mother or plays quietly in another area. Sex-typed behavior is well-established by the time the child reaches four and should he divert into less masculine activities, he is quickly informed by older siblings, or teased by parents for "acting like a girl. Boys don't do that".

By the time a boy is four he has also established a more active relationship with his father. They will roughhouse together, they will go to games and other male activities together, leaving mother and female siblings at home. Sometimes they will just ride in the new car, or go to the liquor store, or go to a relative's household such as father's brother's or his cousin's. The male bond begins to solidify at this time and the separation from mother begins. This is not to say that his affection for mother ceases. It does begin to change, however, and as a result as the male bond increases, so does mother's treatment of him change. By the time he is six, mother will cater to him as though he were a man and he will be subject to little, if any, maternal control. Influence is another matter. Mothers retain their influence over sons in an affective way even though it may not be expressed behaviorally. Grown men speak of the gentle and the accommodating mothers they had when they were small, and they maintain considerable respect and affection for them as adults. It is as though the parental relationship were bifurcated in those early years separating into distinct realms of relationships which seldom overlap. Since the early years of marriage often include many volatile encounters between parents and long separations from each other, it is not surprising that children view parents as belonging to separate realms. Criticism of parents by relatives also tends to separate the categories of people seen as mother and father. Statements like "how can the child know what to do when his mother comes from *that* family?" can only leave the child with the impression that mother is very separate from father, not only biologically but culturally and socially.

The enculturation of children continues in a more verbal way as the child increases in age. Deviant toddler behavior is controlled with threats of repercussions from projective agents — "the police will get you, or the ghosts will take you away". As the child's verbal ability increases, threats are translated into more recognizable form and children are spoken to, spoken at, and spoken about. In addition, they are privy to all the gossip which takes place in their house and in the other households to which they have access. This means that they have ample opportunity to determine what is acceptable behavior under given circumstances, and what is not. The new-elite mothers also are quite directive in their methods of socialization, and children are frequently told what they can or cannot do. The incidence of intervention is also high so that children are stopped from continuing or starting activities which are seen as inappropriate. For example, a new-elite mother seeing her child, or a neighbor's child, throwing stones at a house or another child will go outside and yell at them to stop. If the activity continues, she will go out and physically remove her child into the house. Inside, she will scold him and may inflict a punishment such as confining him to his room for the afternoon, or saying that he may not go to an outing that evening. She may also threaten him with projected punishment from his father when he comes home. Seldom are such punishments or threats followed through. A child confined to his room for the afternoon is usually outside again within a few minutes. Seldom do mothers report to fathers the misdemeanors of the children.

By the time the child reaches six years of

age, he is well-informed about his kin. He has developed certain expectations with regard to benefits derivable from them. He knows some of his responsibilities toward them. He has accomplished some of the major tasks of early childhood — weaning, sphincter control, walking, talking, responsibility and identification with an extended family. He has become a member of a peer group and has a high degree of autonomy and independence. He also has some defined concepts about the social order of which he is a member and he shares some adult expectations attached to political and economic status. His view is set toward becoming like his male relatives and the male bonding has already altered his perception of and relationship with females, especially his mother and sisters. Aggression is still expressed physically, but teasing is becoming a predominant form. He is acquiring more verbal skills to deal with a variety of people and situations. Shouting insults across the street to nonkin children is a favorite pastime of children and one which is a good measure of the child's concepts of kinship, the most socially repugnant status others can have, and an understanding of their role and status in the social order. The statements shouted across the playing field are seldom random but have a telling significance. An example of such behavior occurred one day as I was walking toward a house. The children were coming home from school and as I reached the door simultaneously with the six-year-old boy, he and his four-year-old brother began to shout at six-year-old and nine-year-old boys from the other family. The latter were walking across the lawn and were told, "get off our lawn. You're nothing but dirty whites. We don't even know you". The response came immediately. The six-

year-old started hitting the four-year-old while the nine-year-old shouted, "we're more Indian than you. We don't have red hair and we know how to behave. We've got names and you don't. You don't know nothing and your father is always drunk. You're a bunch of nobodies".

The exchange tells us what the children have learned from adults in their own homes. It tells us that being white rather than Indian is perceived as highly negative, and that one important way to hurt someone is to call him white. It also tells us that certain categories of people do not "know" each other socially even though they may not understand the reasons fully. It also tells us that the process of identification is strong and well-ingrained by this age as is evidenced by the references to names, nobodies, and drunkenness as measures of status and appropriate knowledge and behavior. Such insights, commitments, and loyalties will increase within the children as they grow older. They contribute inevitably to the maintenance of the social and political divisions characteristic of the reserve.

At six the child enters school. He may have attended kindergarten in the city but he will not have attended the one held in the old federal school on the reserve. New-elite parents do not believe in segregated education, and feel that the sooner the children "learn how the whites live, the better off they will be. They have to work and live with them so they may as well start now". Children from new-elite homes arrive at school on time, in clean clothes, and with the expectation that they will be in daily attendance and will learn what the school wants them to learn.

The members of the parent and grandparent generation of new elite families have higher levels of formal education than do those in the old-elite families. Most of the men, for example, have sufficient education to have entered the union and trained in the use of highly complex machinery for loading and unloading at the docks. Some hold executive positions with the union, and some have important positions on Council involving administration of large sums of money. Such responsibilities bring good wages as well as prestige. As a result, sons and sons of sons, internalize goals to work with their fathers, cousins, uncles and grandfathers. Education is stressed as one means to that end.

Mothers in the new-elite group also tend to be emphatic about the value of education. Some have finished Grades X or XII, and recognize that they would have to get additional education or training were they to seek employment. Since some wives express the desire to leave their husbands from time to time, they feel encumbered by their lack of formal education. They recognize that they are ''trapped on the reserve unless I get some training so I could support myself and the children''. They tend to project their own desires onto the children, therefore, and assist them by ensuring that the children are properly clothed, fed, and get to bed on time so they can get up in the mornings. Children in the new-elite homes lose some of their autonomy, therefore, when they start school. Their bedtimes become restricted, their time to come in from play is set, and they do not have the choice of attending school or not.

The school emphasizes such things as cleanliness, orderliness, promptness and regularity of attendance. In addition, it requires competitiveness, attentiveness and politeness. To the degree that Indian children meet these demands, it accepts them. To the degree that they do not, it rejects them and becomes punitive toward them. Tardy children are sent to the principal. Dirty children are sent home. Irregular attendance is a matter for criticism. Reluctance to compete results in the child's being ignored and sometimes being classified as dull. To the extent that the new-elite children meet the demands of the school and the old-elite do not, the school serves as a reinforcer of the perceived value and superiority of the children from new-elite families and the negative rejection of the value of children from other families. As a result, the children of the new elite do succeed at a better rate and are more accepted within the school culture.

Although the children are in contact with whites for the first time, their attitudes are not especially negative toward whites and the process of socialization which follows their admission to school is not entirely discordant with their primary socialization at home. In other words, the goals set by parents and shared by children are obtainable in major part through schooling. The schooling process becomes one which is convergent with the primary one and not in opposition to it. It is a continuation of many of the things already stressed at home and reinforced by the image of highly paid fathers, uncles and grandfathers from work in a white world. It is not a secondary process of socialization, therefore, it is a supplementary primary process which broadens the child's experience and purview without in any way disrupting his initial learning.

It is important to note too that when teachers criticize other children from the reserve, or send them home for being dirty, that the children from new-elite families do not equate statements about those children with statements about themselves. They have always viewed themselves as different from those other children, and the school merely confirms those differences. Attacks by school personnel on "Indianness" do not penetrate the Indian children from new-elite homes. They consider themselves separate from the objects of attack. Such attitudes also make the children more amenable to learning the skills and characteristics valued by the school and shared by the home. There is little conflict for the children of the new-elite in school.

The days of the school-age child are taken up with schooling. Most children from the reserve eat their lunch at school, returning home in the late afternoon. They do not go to the homes of their white schoolmates, nor do those children come to the reserve to play. Occasionally, they may walk towards home together but the groups break up at the boundary of the reserve. At that eastern boundary there is a park, and occasionally Indian and white children mingle there for a while after school. Seldom is the period a long one. The Squamish child is subjected only to the socialization influence of the school, therefore, not to that of white mothers and peers. At the elementary level no Squamish children participate in school games or teams after school hours.

The minimal contact with whites serves several purposes. It does not disrupt the Indian socializing influence of the home. It reinforces the intensity of family relationships consolidated by peer groups consisting of relatives rather than strangers. It emphasizes "Indianness" and its separateness without necessarily making an issue of it. At the same time, the school contact reinforces those characteristics which parents see as important to the achievement of occupational goals.

The socialization process continues at home. Peer groups assume more importance

for the prepubertal child and are broadened through various activities to include nonkin. For example, most Squamish boys start playing lacrosse and junior hockey just prior to school entry. Such activities involve team effort, and teams cannot be made up only of kin. These activities also broaden the perception of ethnic identity and of cohesiveness among children from the reserve. At four, one was a member of a particular family and all others were strangers. At six, whites are strangers and while one is still a member of a privileged and superior group — this family rather than that one — one also is a member of a broader group — a team which plays in opposition to white teams. The first fading of the many divisive lines of identity is experienced at this age. The self-identification as a member of a Squamish reserve becomes more important than the identity as a member of a particular family. Such flexibility in definitions of membership become increasingly important as the individual grows older and his affiliations with a variety of groups become more complex. Such flexibility is also the forerunner of the ability to define and redefine situations as they occur. Although ascription of status appears rigid, its behavioral component is often amazingly flexible.

The elementary school years bring no new elements into the socialization process. Rather, it is a period of growth and development which broadens the individual's experience and perception. Considerable learning takes place in social skills. The ascription of status to self and others becomes a major preoccupation for as the child approaches puberty it becomes essential that he know with whom he may properly associate and whom he may or may not regard as a potential mate.

During the later elementary school years there is a return to the indulgence and autonomy afforded the infant and toddler. Parents still insist on school attendance but bedtime hours are not so rigidly enforced. Absenteeism is permitted on various occasions and not particularly questioned. For males, drinking often begins around ten to twelve years, and while this behavior is not approved of by mothers, it is not overtly curtailed or disapproved unless it results in drunkenness. Part of the culturally accepted male image is involvement in drinking. Since male identification begins early, it is also completed early, and "boys" of ten to twelve are viewed as entering manhood, i.e., "*young* men". It is not extraordinary that they should act as men, therefore. In several homes, children drink with parents and participate with adults at social gatherings in a variety of homes. Use of drugs is not acceptable culturally, however, and this difference offsets the Squamish youngster from his white peers. At the time that white students become involved with drugs as an option to alcohol, Squamish children are becoming increasingly involved with alcohol. In a period of four years in which records were kept, I noted only one incident of nonmedical use of drugs. This case was exceptional, distressed many people, and was blamed on his association "with those white kids. He always hung around with them instead of his cousins. We told him he'd get into trouble with them but he didn't believe us". On the other hand, it was not exceptional to have a beer with families where youngsters joined the group, or to hear of some of the older youths having beer parties in one or another household.

When Squamish children finish elementary school they enter the local junior high. Here the schooling process differs markedly from the elementary system. Timetables are worked out individually and students need only be at school when they have classes scheduled. This leaves them considerable free time and also places the responsibility on them for working out their schedules and study periods. In contrast to elementary school, there are more social and sports activities in which students may join. As well, the school services a larger area and thus has a more diverse social and economic group from which students may choose friends. Also, relatives from other reserves attend the same school now, and the number of Indian students in the school is significantly increased. The atmosphere is different, therefore, the controls are fewer, and the opportunities for diverse social experiences are greater. Such factors alter the socialization of Squamish children significantly.

The children of the new-elite families remain in a top position at this educational level. They have the money to buy clothes which are modish for the peer group at any particular time. They have the money to participate in after-school gatherings at malt shops, and to buy their lunches rather than bring them. They can afford to go to shows and to take a date. It is at this social level that meaningful relationships between Squamish and white students occur. Some result in marriages. These are not always approved but neither are they entirely disapproved.

Peer relationships evolve into a variety of activities and groups. Some groups are entirely male or female, others are heterosexual. Some are mixed Indian and white, others are segregated. Squamish students participate in several school teams and activities. They may give up participating in the all-Indian lacrosse team or baseball or hockey and play on a school team, or they may play on both. More time is spent away from home and from the homes of relatives. Youths come and go as they wish at home and demand meals at their convenience. Uniforms for teams are maintained by mothers. Transportation is expected from fathers or mothers. Indulgence continues. At the same time, some responsibilities are met — care of younger siblings, help with packages, errands to the store or to a relative's, care of the lawn, and similar things. The individual is also expected to maintain a passing average in school in spite of his increasing social activities. Fathers and uncles and grandfathers begin to discuss how and when he will start his employment on the docks, who will sponsor him for membership in the union and related concerns. Political awareness also increases after elementary school. The child is privy to innumerable conversations involving Band politics but such conversations become more meaningful as he realizes the effect that such conversations and informal decisions have on his or the family's welfare. The youth begins to develop expectations attached to his perceived privileged status. He expects help in obtaining a job. He expects to get a house if he marries. He expects to be financially maintained until these things transpire. He expects to be treated deferentially within his family groups, and in general. He selects his friends, carefully avoiding those categories of people he has learned not to know. He does not involve himself with smokehouse activities and, like his parents, decries their regressiveness. He looks to the white society for his social contacts, his pleasures, and his job.

The child has become an adult. In the process he has been reared in an indulgent and autonomous way. At the same time, he has been provided ample direction and instruction so that he has acquired the knowledge of

kin necessary for day to day encounters. He has had the experience of being a member of an in-group (the extended family) and a larger Indian group (the Squamish). He has also been exposed to "strangers" some of whom have been Indian and most of whom have been white. With the latter he has formed some ties restricted only by cultural boundaries, and he has shared goals of continuing education, sports activities, and occupational goals. As well, he has been able to establish social relationships with peers who were relatives in preschool days, and with peers who were nonkin, and some who were white in school days. As a young man, social relationships have also been established with a heterosexual group. Now, as a young adult, he looks once again to the support of kin to enlist him in the longshoring union or some other occupation of choice. Since his senior male kin have positions of power within the unions, and within the Band, it is likely that his expectations will be met. As well, such senior kinsmen will continue to socialize him in ways amenable to the group, and to the maintenance of their power within the group. He is fully socialized now. Unless he diverges in a major way from the life-style in which he has been raised, he will not undergo any further process of socialization but rather he will experience continuing socialization as an adult into additional roles of husband, father, foreman, and friend in the same cultural context.

Socialization in old-elite families

Many of the characteristics of atmosphere and procedure vis-à-vis an infant found in the new-elite homes are also found in the old-elite homes. Therefore, this section will be a discussion of the situations and practices which vary rather than a repetition of the total situation. Some differences start at birth. Old-elite families tend to be less wealthy and less well-housed than the new-elite families. As a result, the child and mother arrive home to an overcrowded house, filled with members of two generations, and sometimes with the children of a sibling as well. The baby may have new clothes for the occasion but it is more likely that he is wearing hand-me-downs from an older sibling. It is also unlikely that he will have a new carrier or furniture of his own. He will sleep with his mother until the next child comes, or until he is old enough to move into an older brother's bed. Most of his siblings will be sharing beds as well as rooms. No domestic help will have been hired in the absence of his mother. Rather, the child's grandmother, or an aunt, will have cared for his older siblings, and will help his mother out in the first few weeks of his arrival. His kin surround him from birth and he shares their household. If he is fortunate, he may become his grandparents' favorite, and he may continue to live with them even if his parents should move. In any event, he will maintain closer ties with his immediate kin than does his new-elite counterpart. This is a function not only of his residence but also of his later participation in ritual activities.

The rhythm of his days is similar to that of the other child. He is permitted to grow, develop, and mature in his own way. Likewise, he is highly indulged in infancy and gradually expected to share in tasks and responsibilities. He sees little of his father initially, and does not form any active relationship with him until he is walking and talking. At that time, he begins his male bonding with father, brothers and cousins.

Since the Squamish share most beliefs about rearing children with indulgence, in-dependence and autonomy, his rate of progress in childhood tasks such as walking, talking, weaning, and toilet training are accomplished at about the same rate as that of the new-elite children. On the other hand he learns different things as well. Aggression is not tolerated with such complacency for one thing, and for another he sees a greater part of adult life since playing and sleeping space is also eating and talking space. His bedtime hours are more casual and he can eat constantly or not at all. He has a heavier load of chores also because his mother may be working and his grandmother may need help with laundry and bringing groceries home. In any event, he accompanies her to the laundromat and to shopping on foot. If it is very far, and things are very heavy, he may get to ride home in a taxi. Few, if any, of his relatives own cars. Those who do, drive old models.

Methods of control are similar between households but the old-elite families tend to be less directive and to intervene less in children's activities. As a result, the child in the old-elite family has a less contained situation than that of the new-elite child. However, greater emphasis is placed on his learning who his kin are and restricting himself to that group. His mobility may, in fact, be more circumscribed than his freedom of action would indicate. In general, most of the old-elite children I observed played inside their grandparents' house or yard or that of an uncle. In controlling the child, a different range of projective agents are used, and more emphasis is placed on the importance of not bringing shame to the family name. For example, the two are sometimes combined when the presence of a deceased relative is made real in the statement, "you'd better be careful how you behave or aunt . . . will get after you. She can see you, you know, and she might get mad at what you're doing. She doesn't want to be ashamed of you''. As in the other home, the child is early exposed to gossip about the inappropriate behavior of other children. A typical statement reprimanding a child would be to accuse him of behaving like the A's. Gossip would then continue about the A's, and their uninformed behavior, and what shame it would bring to his family, the B's, were he to behave in that way. The harshness of such statements increases as the child grows older so that a rebuke stated in this manner and in an offensive or derisive tone can be extremely hurtful.

Teasing as a form of control is much more noticeable among the old elite than among the new. The focus of discipline in the old-elite homes is primarily preventive rather than corrective. The issue then is to impress upon the child the inappropriateness of his behavior so he will not repeat it. A child who hears his deviant behavior discussed with anyone who enters the house over a period of a week seldom engages in that behavior again. Not only does he get the feedback directly but it can haunt him into adulthood. Some of these accounts turn into myth-like tales offering great amusement to the listeners. As the child grows older, he learns to cope with such teasing and even to reciprocate with tales about the teller in a way which unites the generations in a recognition of human fallibility. Such moments can be warm and loving as well as derisive.

Shaming as a form of control is always negative and always punitive. When an adult shames a child it is usually for behavior which the family feels will bring shame to all members, and which will need to be resolved as a group. Few young children are shamed but older children and youths sometimes get into difficulties which the family feels are shameful. Old-elite families emphasize kindness, generosity and honesty among other qualities which are desirable in an adult. An older child who will not share something, or who lies, or who is caught stealing, would bring shame to the family. Such instances are not frequent but they do occur. Usually, the statement of the reprimand is put in terms of shaming the family name rather than in any terms of breaking the law or similar broader terms of reference.

Additionally, the child from the old-elite family has claim to a name. He will usually be informed of this name, or people will refer to the fact that he will receive it formally when he is old enough to "live up to it". Not only does this give the child some sense of pride, it also helps him to become more aware of what constitutes "proper" behavior for his family. His grandparents will tell him stories relating family origin and will also talk to him about the "big times" when all the "important" Salish people gather and honor each other. He will be reminded at the end of such stories about his responsibility to keep his name "proud" and to pay suitable homage to relatives and senior people with bigger names.

The child in the old-elite home also has the opportunity to learn traditional hospitality at an early age. In contrast to the new-elite homes where even young relatives are sent to their own homes to eat if dinner time arrives, old-elite families will serve whomever is in the house at the time the food is ready. As a result, cousins often eat in one household and, if adults are present, they will also stay. Reciprocity is high so that people eating in one household two or three times a week may appear at a later time with groceries for the household head, or a gift of some sort. Alternatively, some service will be provided such as babysitting, or laundry, or shopping, or a drive to a doctor, etc. Although the new-elite child has entrée to a number of households in his extended family, he does not live in an extended family situation but rather moves from one nuclear household to another. This is different from the experience of the old-elite child who is surrounded by kin of adjacent generations who eat and sleep with him and who use his home as theirs and vice versa.

By the time the child from the old-elite family reaches six, he is more socially and culturally developed than the child from the new-elite family. He is more socially apt because he has had a broader array of continuing exposure to a large number of people within one household. He knows how to share more and he has developed a full responsibility for day to day tasks, and sibling care. He is more culturally developed because he has had greater exposure to legends, folktales, family histories, references to the spirit world, family name and responsibility, and the like. His contacts with whites and with the city and other places have been more restricted. He is less oriented to going to school because the topic of education or of employment has not been a major one debated within his household. He may not have had any exposure to educated models within his own family.

As a result of these differences, the old-elite child enters school with a different experience and perspective from his new-elite classmate. He may have attended the reserve kindergarten where the staff were people he knew and where all the children were Indian. This does not necessarily prepare him to meet the white school and its personnel. Some of the Squamish children are as much

strangers to him as the white children because he has not been permitted to play with them. Their presence may be of little comfort to him. In addition, the old-elite child may not have adequate clothing by school standards nor may the clothing be clean enough to be acceptable to school personnel. Unlike his new-elite friends, he may be sent home to clean up in the first week of school.

The school starts a second socialization process for the children of the old elite. It is not a continuation of the primary process as it is for those children from new-elite families. The type of English spoken in his home may be dissimilar to that the teacher uses. The method of instruction certainly is dissimilar. In school it is directive and interventionistic. He is not able to observe and then act. He must follow verbal commands. He is not allowed to make a mistake and find his way back; instead, he is corrected in midstream so that he cannot learn through his errors.

The old-elite families do not oppose education but sometimes the pattern of their lives prevent children from attending school. If the family has been at a smokehouse function, and arrives home in the early morning hours, no one will rise to get the children off to school. So he may miss school often. Or he may have to babysit a younger sibling if an adult relative is not available. Funds are not so prevalent that sitters can be paid. In addition, it is an important part of his learning to become a "good" Squamish for him to help with vital chores rather than attend solely to his own needs. For similar reasons he may be tardy. As a result, the school personnel begin to view him as "Indian." This perception devalues him as a person and lowers the teachers' expectations for him. The result is that he lowers his own level of aspiration and never develops the interest and motivation he might were he treated like the more acceptable children of the new elite, or like his white classmates. Just as his living situation is corporate, so are some of his experiences. His cousins begin to empathize with him. They begin to share the resentment and the disinterest too. They turn their energies elsewhere. The pattern of negative reinforcement strengthens.

As his primary socialization continues at home, and his secondary one begins at school, he may also be introduced to ritual activities which one might term as his "anticipatory" socialization. The latter experience does not culminate until he is an adult but he becomes familiar with smokehouse activities and may get involved in helping or attending on a regular basis. It is about the time that he reaches his upper elementary or early junior high school years that he will have his name installed. Such an event is the end result of many years of socializing within the family setting. With the public installation of his name, he publicly takes on ritual responsibilities. He must now attend certain functions, help on behalf of the family and learn more specifically how to "live up to his name". Not only do such activities require time, they also require psychic energy. Both of these withdraw the individual from the active pursuit of studies. As a result, he may have to repeat upper elementary and early high school years. With each grade repetition he becomes a candidate for withdrawal from school before completing Grade XII.

Anticipatory and actual socialization into the smokehouse involves youths in the dilemma of determining their identity. Having an Indian name, and being a participant in ritual activity, heightens an individual's

sense of "Indianness". It also separates him from those who do not participate and especially from the white world. The young Squamish child from the old-elite family learns early not to discuss his ritual activities with peers. Part of this reticence is appropriate to the nature of ritual. Only the initiated share the understandings attached to the significance of ritual events. On the other hand, if an individual is dependent on his ritual status for his identity and sense of worth within a group, then some of the information about that status must be shared publicly. Unlike the new-elite youths who can draw on public knowledge of their family status and use it to impress peers, youths who are learning to be "important" people in another realm have little to share. For some this creates a dilemma, but if they have been well socialized, it simply turns them back to their immediate family and their extended kin for affirmation.

The individual then faces an additional choice — he can become bicultural and continue to pursue both his primary and secondary socialization, or he can reject his secondary process and become more involved in the primary one. For those who choose the bicultural path, the process is not easy because of the conflicting values expressed between the two reference groups and because of the demands each makes on his own time. Naturally, the primary group has more strength because it is in that group that the individual is accepted, cherished, and needed. Such emotional gratification is less easy to find in the secondary group, although it is not impossible. In addition, the youth has to face the reality of recognizing that he needs a modicum of formal education if he hopes to obtain employment. Such conflicts are not easily resolved, especially when the timing of the two major processes is temporally conjoint rather than sequential. Some individuals founder, becoming well-socialized in neither system. Others make a choice. In either case, the degree of conscious conflict is high for the youths of old-elite families, especially the males. The new-elite youths have a smoother process because they are not subjected to secondary socialization processes until the primary one has been completed. Some never go through a secondary process at all in new-elite families.

Socialization of females: old and new patterns

The socialization of females does not differ essentially from that of the males except in role orientation. Female infants are treated with the same respect and concern as are males. The level of nurturance and indulgence does not vary along sex lines. The rate of independence and autonomy does not vary ideologically. However, in some instances it does differ in practice since male children tend to wander farther from home while female children stay close to their mothers or grandmothers. As with all children, the play activities of girls are less rough than those of boys. Body sports do not constitute a major activity for girls in the way that lacrosse and hockey do for boys. Female children spend more time with adult females and less with peers in their first ten years of life. There is a tendency for female groups to have broader ranges in age than comparable male groups. The same patterns prevail, however. Cousins and siblings constitute the peer group. The play group bifur-cates very early, with males and females forming their own groups about ages three and four.

A female child shares many of the same tasks that young males do. She fetches things, she helps carry out things, she helps an elder to a car, and similar activities. About age four, female roles begin to emerge more clearly. Help with food, help with laundry, and similar female responsibilities begin to be shared by the adult woman and the young girl. Infant care is still the responsibility of the oldest siblings, including males, but as the male approaches ages ten to twelve his responsibilities decrease and that of the older female sibling increases. Thus, in a family with ten-year-old boy and an eight-year-old girl, the girl will be charged with the major caretaking of an infant sibling. In the same way, if a meal is needed, she rather than the older boy will prepare it in the absence of an adult. Such patterning is a result of the division of labor along sex lines. It is also a reflection of generally prevailing attitudes that evolve from a predominantly patrilineal system. Women are viewed as the people who accommodate men and help them to achieve their goals. This is not a statement implying superiority-inferiority of one sex. Rather, it is a statement which clearly defines roles and which places an important value on women's services. Women draw satisfaction from being in a position to help men. Men in turn contribute to the status of women by doing ''important'' things which bring the family honor, or good income, or whatever. Even when the system does not appear to work, and men abuse women or women fail to accommodate men, women can still draw their status from being able to keep their households running in the face of adverse economic and emotional conditions.

Young girls learn at an early age that one of the aspects of being ''good'' Squamish women is not only to be able to run a house efficiently, to know family history properly, and to have similar skills, but also to be able to maintain an adequate level of performance in the face of adversity. In fact, women who have not faced such difficulties are not considered ''proven'' by senior women and peers. Thus, should father come home drunk, the young female must stay with her mother, help with the younger children, and run messages and information between households. In this process, she is learning how to be a ''good'' Squamish woman in the face of adversity. In contrast, her brother's appropriate behavior must be to turn his back against the women and help his father, or at least not leave him alone.

Young girls assume responsibilities early, releasing their mothers to attend to their fathers in many instances. For example, one of the problems associated with abusive drinking (especially among the new-elite families who have the income to pursue such activities and the cars to drive) is that men lose their drivers' licenses on drinking charges. In several new-elite households, wives rise at 5:30 A.M. to make their husbands' breakfasts and to drive them to work because they do not have valid drivers' licenses. In such cases, older female children are assigned the tasks of getting breakfast and getting children ready for school. In the same way, young girls will prepare dinner for the family while mother drives male children to the lacrosse or hockey game. Many other activities involving services to males take mothers away from home, leaving young girls in charge of younger siblings.

Summary

I have presented the development of two young boys in two different systems. Some of the beliefs, cultural demands, and individual practices overlap. Several lead to different perceptions and commitments. The children of the old elite and the new elite share some common characteristics, but in general, they begin to separate interests and orientations about the time they reach school entry. Both have shared, to that time, a well-nurtured and somewhat indulgent environment in which their early developmental tasks have been accomplished. As well, they have evolved some special and continuing relationships with kin. Nevertheless, they have a few different perceptions already because of their varying exposure to nonkin and to patterns of behavior and schedules within their households which diverge.

For the new-elite child, who physically and temporally meshes with school expectations, the path is set in a continuing and nurturant pattern of socialization. For the child from the old-elite home, the path falls away into a forest of unlinked and unfamiliar expectations and concerns, many of which conflict with his on-going process of enculturation. The dilemmas begin to emerge. Soon he will be faced with conscious decisions about his identity, his continuing socialization, his involvement in ritual matters, and his life goals. No one will be able to help him make these decisions but he will continue to receive the support and affection of kin. Similarly, his new-elite friend will have to make decisions affecting occupation and life goals but for him the task will be easier because of the strong male bonding and the availability of help from senior kinsmen who have positions of authority in the occupations he wishes to pursue. They act as models, and help him complete his socialization into the working world.

At school, female children perform in much the same way as males, although they tend generally to miss more school because of the family responsibilities mentioned above. In general, girls from the new-elite homes persist longer in school than do old-elite family females. One reason for this is that females in old-elite homes get involved in more tasks associated with ritual events than do males. If it is a gathering in which the family is helping, all females will be expected to help in the kitchen, with distribution, etc. Men do not work in food preparation nor at serving. As well, some females are asked by families to help with a new dancer, to be a "sitter". If the girl assigned is also in school, the rate of absenteeism soars and failure in certain grades is almost ensured during the winter ritual session.

The nature of the female bonding, the clarity of roles ascribed to females, and the cultural support for females not working outside the home all contribute to less conflict for the female in determining her sense of identity and worth. The value of a woman's service is immediately visible. The importance of her presence in keeping a household going is equally easily perceived. It is not the same for the male for he may earn the money in a nonvisible way, i.e., out of the community. He may also spend his cheque, or a major portion of it, before he gets home. He may also be absent from home for a period, living with someone else. His presence is often viewed as neither helpful nor desirable on the part of the female.[5] Such behavior and lack of visibility makes men's roles appear less important than those of women. In any event women perceive that their roles are clearer and that they are culturally, not individually, determined. The identity crisis comes only if women reject their prescribed roles. I met no Squamish women who actively did so.

Female socialization differs from that of the male in content but not in process. The division of the sexes is accomplished long before puberty. As noted, girls receive the same nurturance as boys but their life-styles diverge early. They are expected to help men, and to learn to be "good" women and wives. Towards this end they become "mothers", at least in role behavior, by the time they are ten years of age. Although females stay in school longer than males, only one Squamish woman had a job outside her home during the time of the study. Female models are lacking for roles other than wife, mother, aunt, and friend. Such roles emphasize female bonding in the same way for girls as the male bonding does for men. The groups are not in opposition but serve the same function — personal support during crises and company during good times. As in other cultures, the Squamish female matures long before the male. At fifteen years of age most Squamish females are women capable of establishing sound relationships, capable of running a household, and capable of coping with adversity. Men await their twenties before settling, and even then the culture allows them greater freedom, if not license. Men work hard but have considerable freedom from family responsibility. Women work hard and have little freedom from responsibility. The meeting of this responsibility is viewed as an achievement and the "good" Squamish woman proves her mettle by meeting all demands placed upon her.

NOTES

1 I am grateful to the many Squamish people who welcomed us and who helped me to prepare this paper. Special thanks are due to the Charlie family who took us into their group in the Squamish way. Without such kind help, this work could never have been completed.

2 At the time of the study, only one family allowed their child to visit school friends off the reserve. No white children were seen on the reserve during the same period.

3 The data collected have some inherent biases. The most notable one is the female bias. Approximately 90 per cent of my time was spent with women and their children. Male views and observations of male behavior are therefore lacking. This may not be entirely negative since women are primarily responsible for children in any society. However, such a bias leaves certain questions unanswered, for example, the question of whether men are excluded actively from the socialization process in the early years or whether they simply are not there by their own choice. It also raises the question as to when the identification process of small boys begins, and what models are available to them in the absence of fathers. These questions can only be partially answered with the data I have.

4 The reader must remember that the categories of "new" and "old" elite are analytic terms which have some inherent reality but which fail to represent the many overlapping and complex areas.

5 Some females claim they flourish when their husbands are gone, and that it is the only time they have enough money and food, i.e., when they are on welfare.

7

Family and kinship relationships

There exists an American kin family system with complicated matrices of aid and service activities which link together the component units into a functioning network. . . . Understanding of the family as a functioning social system interrelated with other social systems in society is possible *only by rejection of the isolated nuclear family concept.*

. . . we take these findings as indicating a relatively high degree of isolation for the contemporary nuclear family compared with both the existing literature and other marital statuses and family types. Indeed, so great is the disparity between nuclear families and other family types that in applying our criteria for 'systemness' we conclude that whereas for nuclear families the household is the relevant family system, for those living alone and the single, widowed, or divorced the extended kin network may indeed be the basic family system.

The relative importance and character of kinship influence in society was discussed in some detail in Chapter three. It was demonstrated that most individuals, upon birth, acquire a specific group of relatives and a concomitant set of systematic rights and duties concerning their relationships with kin and non-kin. The parent-child bond not uncommonly spans four generations and permeates the relationships created by marriage. Kinship patterns may be numerous or few, general or specific, enmeshed or casual, binding or unimportant, depending on the society. This chapter focuses on the role of kinship in Western society. As will be seen below, this issue remains controversial among social scientists.

Kinship patterns in Western society

Cross-cultural comparisons of kinship systems reveal substantive differences, because of varying cultural traditions, responses to social change, and social structures. Several basic characteristics of kinship in Western and traditional societal settings are defined in the descriptive profile below.

Traditional kinship systems	*Western kinship systems*
kin as society	kin as networks
unilineal	bilateral
hierarchical kin patterns	egalitarian kin patterns
major functions	minor functions
obligation behavior	choice behavior
kinship control	kinship criticism

Traditionally, kinship relations were all-embracing. To be born into a kinship group was not unlike being born into a ''society'' with clear specifications on how to relate to all of one's relatives, whether primary, secondary, or tertiary. These duties and rights didn't change much during the life cycle of the individual, except as new statuses were acquired. Western kinship, in contrast, is more fluid. Kin networks are formed which cross over the standard boundaries between primary and secondary relatives somewhat selectively, depending on the reasons for the relationship. Some networks, for example, reflect strong affectional ties, regular visiting, and regular contacts by telephone and letter. Other kin networks, however, may emphasize financial interdependence or merely patterns of mutual aid. Adams (1968), in his study of nearly 800 urban residents in North Carolina, found very different reasons for the maintenance of kin networks which emphasized parents and those which emphasized siblings. Ongoing relations with parents typically involved considerable concern, as expressed in frequent contact, readiness to help, and strong feelings of affection and obligation. Sibling networks, however, were maintained because of similarity of interests and a psychological need to compare notes on ''how things were going''. Relations with uncles, aunts, and cousins were generally seen as inconsequential and incidental. It should be apparent that these networks are modified by geographical distance, educational, occupational, and religious differences, and related matters defined by life style.

While traditional societies tend to have a unilineal kinship pattern, Western society is bilateral. No single set of kin have any essential priority or superordinate status. A couple may interact with both the husband's kin and the wife's kin equally. Parsons (1959) terms this pattern as multilineal. A bilateral system can have its disadvantages when, for example, both families demand "equal time", or to be home on Christmas day.

Most kinship systems of the past emphasized the superiority of the older generations and of males over females. Power is seldom exercised in Western kinship. If power exists, it is not based on one's status in the kinship structure but on statuses acquired in other sectors of society. A younger brother and his family, for example, may have a leadership role in a kin system because of unusual financial resources or prestigious achievements. Typically, however, the nuclear families of brothers and sisters are defined as equals regardless of age, birth order, generation, or sex.

One of the more apparent differences between traditional and Western kinship is in the functions performed by kin. Traditional kin were commonly involved in major political, religious, and economic activities. The production and distribution of goods and services took place within the kin structure. Western kin emphasize "soft" functions such as companionship, financial aid, babysitting and counseling. Indeed, the empirical evidence of kinship helps is consistent and profuse. The basic findings are briefly summarized below.[1]

1. Mutual aid, including the exchange of services, gifts, advice and financial assistance, is widespread within kin networks. Financial assistance is most apparent during the early years of marriage (e.g., Sussman, 1953; Adams, 1968). Osterreich (1965), in her study of English Canadians in Montreal, found that mutual aid was maintained in spite of geographical mobility (see also Irving, 1972).
2. Visiting among kin living in the same urban area outranks visiting among friends, co-workers, or neighbors (e.g., Bell and Boat, 1957). Irving's study in Toronto (1972) found that 75 percent of those whose parents lived in the same neighborhood visited them weekly.
3. Babysitting and taking children "out on the town" are common activities of grandparents (e.g., Sussman, 1953).
4. Caring for aged persons during illness, providing a home for a widowed parent, shopping and housekeeping are common tasks performed by children for their parents and parents-in-law (e.g., Bott, 1971; Streib, 1958).
5. Kin members moving to new areas or simply traveling are regularly assisted by the kin network. Aid varies from providing a "place to stay" to help in finding a job (e.g., Schwarzweller, 1964; Rossi, 1955). Kohl and Bennett's study of rural-urban migration in Canada (1965) documents the important role of kin in helping the migrant "make it".

The distinction between traditional and Western kinship systems is not as clear for obligation and choice behavior as for the other patterns. In traditional societies, the

---

1 Students interested in studying this literature further will want to consult Sussman, 1970.

expectations concerning residence, mate choice, assistance, kinship rituals, and related kin behaviors are learned early and remain predictable throughout life. The average individual has little choice. In Western society, obligation behavior is of a different order. There are advantages, or payoffs, in making kin-approved choices. When an individual acts in conjunction with the wishes of kin, systems of reciprocities develop between and among kin. Members of kin networks come to share both rights and duties. There are two key distinctions between the Western system of obligation behavior and the traditional system. Individuals may choose to enter into these reciprocities, and thus define the degree and extent of kin involvement; and these relationships are based on feelings of affection. Whatever the system of kinship reciprocity, however, kin remain the primary source of social comment (kinship criticism rather than overt control) for the individual. Kin, of as many as four generations past, are the carriers of the traditions and values of the present and recent past. As such, they provide an on-going critique of changing patterns of thought and behavior. The individual confronted with the future cannot readily ignore the counsel and ongoing social comment of kin.

Blood (1970) argues that all kinship systems the world over are changing toward the Western model described above. Current research on kinship patterns in other cultures appears to confirm this point of view (cf. Hill and Konig, 1970).

Isolated or kin-integrated family system

Though the evidence of kinship ties in Western society seems compelling, there continues to be controversy among social scientists, as illustrated in the quotations at the beginning of this chapter, concerning the appropriate family model to be used in describing Western society. Parsons (1959) has distinctly preferred the usage, "the isolated nuclear family". Others consider this term inappropriate and prefer "the modified extended family" (Litwak, 1965). As early as 1943 Parsons developed the position that the American family is a conjugal system, structurally isolated from kin and essentially free from the influence of kin, because of the open, multilineal character of the nuclear family and its binding dependence on the occupational system.[2] By 1962, Sussman and Burchinal had amassed sufficient empirical evidence contrary to their understanding of this position to fully reject the isolated nuclear family concept. For the most part, this posture has prevailed, as subsequent research has either continued to demonstrate the salient role of kinship, or has simply proceeded on the assumption that the nuclear family concept is dead (Adams, 1968;

2 Parsons' argument is treated in more detail in Chapter eight.

Schneider, 1968; Farber, 1971; Irving, 1972; Schneider and Smith, 1973). A recent paper, however, has reopened the issue (Gibson, 1972). It raises several questions which merit consideration.

In the first place, Gibson demonstrates that the influence of kin in Western society has been grossly exaggerated. It is commonly assumed, for example, that visiting with kin exceeds the amount of visiting with non-kin. A study by Bell and Boat (1957), among others, is often identified as offering supporting evidence for this "fact". However, a closer look at the actual results shows that visits with friends in a given month exceeded visits with relatives in three out of the four neighborhoods studied. Visiting with relatives is for many people, of course, a primary activity, as is visiting with friends. However, it is not uncommon to ignore those who spend more time with friends as merely exceptions to the rule, even though they are usually a large part of the sample.[3]

Second, it is well to establish exactly how much inter-house activity among kin needs to exist before the isolated nuclear family concept can be dropped in favor of a modified extended kin pattern. Gibson argues that the degree of interaction between related households should be greater than the interaction within a nuclear household, before the isolated nuclear family concept can be dropped. This borders on the ridiculous, but Gibson is right in demanding more explicit criteria before accepting the nuclear family myth. In this regard, it should be noted that Parsons thought of the nuclear family as only relatively isolated, not totally isolated, as is commonly assumed. Indeed, Parsons first introduced the phrase "interlocking conjugal families".

Third, the so-called functions of the kinship system in Western society, described in some detail earlier in this chapter, may not be comparable with other kinship systems. In fact, these "soft" functions are predominantly interchanges between parents and their married children. Apart from ties with grandchildren, other kin ties are generally only cursory and incidental and seldom affectionate. These functions, though different in kind, are quite simplistic compared to the highly intricate and complex functions performed within "society-like" kin groups. It is these grand and visible distinctions that led Parsons to the comparisons he made. In other words, Parsons employed an inter-cultural or cross-cultural frame of reference in his analysis, while Sussman and others have tended toward an intra-cultural frame of reference.

Gibson's study (1969, 1970, 1972) is based on 486 disabled men and their families. His findings are interesting because these are families in which the need for

---

3 Irving (1972) in his Canadian study, ignored the fact that over half of his respondents saw their friends more often than relatives. See his article later in this chapter.

external resources, i.e. kin, is maximized. It was found that 51 percent of accessible kin (living in the same area) were seen at least monthly, but 49 percent of the families received no kin services of any kind. Only 17 percent of the available kin provided a service to the disabled families. Data reported in Gibson's earlier papers showed that ministers, priests and doctors were seen as a more important source of support than siblings or parents. Friends and neighbors were three times more likely to be identified as sources of help than parents.

In a sense, these findings are unique and should be interpreted as a modest exception to the large body of contrary evidence. However, there is ample reason to suspect that many important questions haven't been asked in much of the kin research to date and that the *analysis* of typical findings tends to emphasize kin-integration rather than kin-isolation. It is likely that both types of families exist side by side in Western society. Indeed, there are types and degrees of both kin-isolated and kin-integrated families yet to be identified and explored. Further research must avoid the "prove it" mentality and rather seek to understand and explain both the how and why of the nuclear family-kin network relationship as well as the numerous other kin exchanges involving single-parent families, unmarried liaisons, and single persons.

SUMMARY

Although kin are important in the lives of individuals in all societies, the type and degree of kin influence varies widely both cross-culturally and sub-culturally. In general, traditional kinship systems are characterized by "society-like" organization, unilineal and hierarchical authority patterns, major functions such as economic production, and behavior regulations which tend to be obligatory and uncompromising. In essence, one's kin are in control of one's destiny. Western kinship systems, in contrast, are characterized by relatively small networks of relationships involving both blood and affinal relatives. Nuclear families are generally defined as equals regardless of age, birth order, generation or sex. Although kin relationships are chosen partly out of a "sense of" obligation, the relationships typically include feelings of affection, mutual aid, and frequent contact. Parent ties are the most active and emotionally based, while sibling ties, where active, are maintained because of common interests. Western kin are seen as persistent social critics throughout the life span of the individual.

Social scientists are still undecided as to the meaning of kin influence in Western society, compared to other societies. Though most prefer the "modified extended family" model in describing the Western system, several social scientists continue to advocate greater emphasis on the relative autonomy of the nuclear family. The evidence suggests that there are types and degrees of both kin-isolated and kin-integrated families which must be identified and studied before we are able to understand or explain Western kinship influence.

The remainder of this chapter includes two articles describing kin relations among French Canadians (Garigue, 1956) and working class English Canadians in Toronto (Irving, 1972). Relevant Canadian research is discussed in the introduction to each article.

French-Canadian kinship and urban life

It is commonly assumed that urbanism has a negative influence on kinship exchange. In this paper, Garigue demonstrates "that the critical factors in diminishing kinship recognition are the cultural values of the society, not its degree of urbanization". Utilizing data collected from forty-three French Canadian households in Montreal in 1955, he found that French Canadians maintain kinship ties partly out of obligation and partly by preference. It is argued that socialization in large families and an emphasis on the French Canadian identity leads to a preference for maintaining traditional ideal values and multi-kin ties.

A study of mobility and kinship contact among French Canadians in western Canada (the community of St. Jean Baptiste, Manitoba) by Piddington (1961) provides further support for the pervasiveness of the kinship bond among French Canadians. These bonds facilitate the maintenance of an identity outside Quebec in such French settlements as the one in Los Angeles. The maintenance and renewal of the French Canadian identity is also enhanced by the influx of immigrants who are very often related to those who have already migrated. Most of Piddington's informants were able to provide extensive information about both local and distant kinsmen.

Studies of rural French Canadian family life also illustrate an intricate kinship structure relative to mate choice, relations between affinal and consanguineal kin, and the dispersement of property. This structure is not unlike kinship structures in many of the traditional societies of the world (see Lamarre, 1973). The internal dynamics of the nuclear family unit, as well, tend to reflect many of the traditional principles. Garigue (1962), for example, found a strong division of labor between husband and wife. Authority is attributed to the husband as provider, an authority which is also recognized in the conduct of the wife's responsibilities. The mother is the center of affection in the family and has the main responsibility for the welfare of the family. Relationships between siblings are defined by their differences in age and sex.

However, this view of the French Canadian family may be somewhat stereotypical. There is evidence of change. Rioux (1959) argues that urbanization and industrialization have had a profound impact on the kinship system among French Canadians in Quebec. He argues that kinship recognition has decreased considerably in Montreal as compared to rural areas. Tremblay (1966) suggests that the nuclear family is becoming more important than the kinship system, women are achieving more equal roles in society as well as in the family, and parent-child relationships are becoming more democratic, as reflected in greater permissiveness, value differences between parents and children, and the decreasing role of the father. Other studies (e.g., Carisse, 1972, 1975; Hobart, 1973) offer clear support for certain of these trends. Even so, it is likely that French Canadian culture will continue to influence the family system, at least relative to kinship exchange.

French-Canadian kinship and urban life

Philippe Garigue

The present study is aimed at describing the importance and character of kinship among French Canadians of Montreal. It is directed at the problem raised by Wirth[1] and numerous other sociologists, who have assumed that kin ties lose significance in an urban setting. The data were collected between September 1954 and February 1955, from 52 persons in 43 households. As the study was specifically directed at assessing the influence of urbanism on kinship, only informants of urban background were selected, though some households included persons who were born outside Montreal. No significant difference seems to appear between those households whose members were all born in Montreal, and those with members born elsewhere. Thirty genealogical tables were collected from persons whose background was urban from birth. We believe it can safely be assumed that the sample conforms to the dominant urban behavior among French Canadians, even though the extensiveness of interviews and the consequent restriction on the number of people who could be visited in the five months of the fieldwork prevented the taking of random sample.

All interviews were conducted in French,

Philippe Garigue, Ph.D, is Dean of the Faculty of Social Sciences at the University of Montreal.

Reproduced by permission of the American Anthropological Association from the *American Anthropologist*, Vol. 58, No. 6, 1956 (pp. 1090–1101).

and took place in the homes of the informants. The informants are mostly of medium income; only three were of high income, and five of definitely low income. The study is not intended as an analysis of the total effect of urban life on the kinship system of all Montreal French Canadians — for instance, no attempt was made to study the ''pathology'' of urban life — but enough data were collected to answer the more limited question as to the general influence of urbanism upon kinship.

The urban French-Canadian kinship system is a variant of that generally reported for Western societies. It is a patronymic bilateral structure, with two major dimensions of lateral range and generation depth. While awareness of descent and pride in the history of a family name is shown by the majority of informants, frequency of contact is highest between members of the same generation, and cuts across consanguineal and affinal ties. These lateral and generation dimensions involve different patterns of behaviour: a formal pattern of expected obligations operates between the generations; a more informal choice according to personality preference operates between members of the same generation. The nuclei of the kinship system are the parent-child and sibling relationships of the domestic family, which is held to be an autonomous unit. The expected roles of the members of the broader kin group vary according to their position in the formal and informal patterns, and their closeness to Ego's domestic family. These roles separate the total kin into a number of subgroups having special functions. The total kin group is expected to come into action only for very formal occasions, such as a funeral; in most situations, only the subgroups are involved. Women are more active within the kinship

system than men, and this fact, combined with their primary role as wives and mothers, gives them a great deal of influence and supplies the continuity of the kin group. While all informants showed a high degree of conformity to kinship obligations, they also reported factors which they believed were causing segmentation. The most important of these were said to be social mobility and cultural differentiation, which resulted in a decrease or even loss of contact between members of a kin group.

The Structure of Kinship Knowledge

Thirty of the 52 informants were asked for the range of their genealogical knowledge. The maximum limit of this range was determined by knowledge of the sex of a person, in addition to his family name. For instance, children of lateral kin were included if the informant was aware of their sex in addition to their proper genealogical link. The mean of such knowledge is a range of 215 persons. The smallest range was 75; the ten with least knowledge ranged from this to 120. The next ten ranged from 126 to 243; the highest ten from 252 to a maximum of 484 known kin. These known kin were distributed in a wide lateral range rather than extensive depth of generations. Including Ego's generation, one informant reported three generations, ten informants reported a range of four generations, thirteen informants reported five generations, and six informants claimed knowledge of six generations. The three cases with the lowest range of knowledge can be regarded as abnormal. In one instance, the mother's line was not known, and in two more the true bilateralism was distorted by ignorance of the second ascending generation.

The most extensive knowledge of kin was usually concentrated into the generations of Ego and his parents, which together included from one-half to two-thirds of the total persons known. Knowledge of the second ascending generation was often reduced to from one to eight known ancestors. In the third and fourth ascending generations, knowledge was restricted in most instances to a single ancestor. Variations in the lateral range, total size, depth of generations, etc., were linked to the age, sex, and marital status of the informants.

The age of the informants varied from 19 to 72, with an average of 30.5 years. There was a definite tendency for depth and breadth of range to increase with age. The controlling factor in the ratio of increase seems to be the size of the informant's kin group during adolescence. Among informants up to about 40 years of age, their own and their first ascending generation were most important. Among older informants, descending generations became increasingly important. The largest kin knowledge was reported by married persons.

The sex of the informants seemed to be an important factor in kin recognition; only two of the informants who reported the fifteen largest kin groups (186 to 484) were men. All of the ten largest kin groups were reported by women. Sex is also a major factor in determining the stress placed by the informant on the father's or the mother's line. Just over half of the men had a greater knowledge of their father's line; women knew more of their mother's line than their father's by a ratio of three to one. If knowledge of Christian names is taken as a sign of greater kinship awareness, a second and more limited range can be distinguished, which runs from a minimum of 54 to a maximum of 288. The proportion of kin whose Christian names are also known, to those known only by family name and sex, varied from one-half to nine-tenths. These ratios do not correlate with the extremes of the first range, and there was only a slight increase in the largest ranges. Ignorance of Christian names was always greatest in the descending generations of the domestic families with which there was little contact.

If kinship ties are graded in order of their importance as foci of activities, the first among them is the sibling tie. This seems to relate to the size of the sibling groups, and to the maintenance of sibling unity after marriage. The average size of the informant's sibling groups was 5, with one instance of an informant who was one of 16 siblings. There is an over-all correlation between total knowledge of kin and the size of the sibling groups closest to the informant: his own, his father's, and his mother's. The larger the number of persons in these groups, the greater the total kinship range. Moreover, the scope of lateral kin is increased through marriage of siblings, since these in-law ties tend to be rather firm. Thus, the "core" of the kinship system is formed by domestic families linked by sibling and parent-child ties, and by lateral ties arising through the marriage of siblings. Recognition outside that core operates according to lines of descent. In this instance, only some of the members of the sibling groups involved will be known. Some qualification must be introduced between the recognition arising from membership in the core, and through descent. Because of the frequency of cousin marriages among French Canadians, both modes of recognition can operate at the same time. While it is not possible to say whether the importance given to affinal ties through sibling marriages may not be due to the frequency of cousin marriages, there is no doubt that many kinship ties created through the marriage of a sibling are as important as those of cousinship.

Another characteristic of the urban French Canadians is the wide geographical scattering of their kin groups. While all had kin within Montreal, proportions running as high as three-fourths were reported scattered not only within the province of Quebec, but further afield in Canada and in the United States.

Important Aspects of Kinship Behavior

Urban French Canadian men and women not only give different stress to kinship, but also have different roles. Men, for instance, reported that they usually thought of their kin group in terms of their male relatives; their knowledge of their female relatives was more restricted. In all instances, however, their attitudes towards their mothers, wives, or sisters, gave these female relatives great influence not only over household matters, but also in many outside affairs. Women seemed to have a greater awareness of the kin group as composed of both sexes. Not only was their knowledge of the total kin group greater so that in a number of instances wives knew more of their husbands' kin than the husbands themselves did, but they also had a much greater knowledge of the affairs of the kin group. While men reported their kin contacts as being largely for leisure-time activities, the women reported their reasons for contact as mostly "family affairs" such as children, births, marriages,

or illness. A marriage or a funeral was the occasion for intense activity by the women, and it was they who took the initiative in organizing the gathering of relatives, who suggested visits to each other's homes, and who wrote letters or telephoned news to relatives. They also spent more time with their kin than did the majority of men.

While there are individual variations in behaviour, this sex differentiation was a formalized expectation. A number of wives reported that while they were intimate with only a limited number of kin in their husband's line, they were expected by most to keep them informed of family affairs by letters or telephone calls. The wife, not the husband, would have been blamed for failure to do this. All informants, male and female, stressed the fact that it was the women who acted as links between the various households of the kin group.

It is beyond the scope of this paper to explore the reasons for this sex differentiation. It may have a close relationship to the fact that, as domestic families are generally large and servants beyond the means of most French Canadians, the women are essentially housewives and only work outside before having children, or because of great economic necessity. It would be wrong, however, to take this predominantly domestic role of women as a sign of their inferior status in the kin group. On the contrary, the continuity of the kinship system over time may be attributed to their dominant position in it. This influence of the women in the kin group is distinct from the authority role of men within each domestic family. The domestic family is headed by the husband, in whom the Civil Code of the province of Quebec vests a great deal of authority; it is an autonomous unit, with a sole legal representative. Within each household, however, the exercise of this authority is qualified by consultation with one's wife, and outside the domestic family by consultation with one's mother or sisters. But even then, the use of authority is held to be a male prerogative. Within a sibling group it may also happen that the eldest brother, especially at the death of the father, will acquire a position of authority over all the other siblings. Similarly, a grandfather has a great deal of authority. The pattern of authority, even apart from the legal definitions given to it by the Civil Code of Quebec, is therefore male, and relates to age and descent.

The equalitarian relationship between father and children or between persons of a different age, reported for the United States, is not present among the French Canadians. While a father allows his children a certain latitude of behaviour, it is not marked by any feeling of emotional closeness. Emotional ties are more usually directed toward the mother or the wife, or located within the sibling group. Thus, while a woman's legal status is subordinate, her roles as a mother or wife or sister make her the focus of most of the emotional life of the kin group. While the men determine the status position of their domestic families or of the whole kin group, the women are the "integrators" of the kin group, and as such its effective leaders. This female leadership role is different from the role of older men, who act as symbols of kinship continuity, but who are not the active agents of the life of the group. The foci of kin links are thus the women, and particular women can actually be regarded as leaders of the kin group. In the case of a grandmother of one of the informants, this leadership role had become a benign dictatorship, and practically all formal kin activities took place at

her home.

For both men and women, the frequency of contact with relatives was the result of a number of factors. For instance, while only 16 of the 43 households reported relatives in the same parish, all informants reported their highest frequency of contact with their fathers and mothers and with their siblings, even if these lived in distant parishes of Montreal. Only when the degree of kinship was more remote did informants remark that geographical distance influenced contacts. Besides degree of kinship and geographical location, personal preference was an important factor in contact. Personal preference for kin was reported as a factor outside Ego's family of orientation and, if married, his household and his spouse's family of orientation. We may distinguish formal recognition from personal preference in kin relationships. While overlap between these two was reported, the formal dimension operates predominantly between generations, especially upward, while personal preference was especially strong in the selection of contacts with affinals or cousins.

This can best be illustrated by describing the frequency of contact reported by a married man, aged 34, who was a skilled worker in a Montreal factory. He has been chosen as an example because he is about average in the range of kinship recognition, with a total of 233 kin, 203 of whom were alive at the time of the survey. Of these, 93 lived in Montreal, scattered in a number of parishes; 72 were reported living in various parts of the province of Quebec, and 38 more were reported in Ontario and in the United States. During each week the informant frequently met members of his two brothers' households, who also lived in Montreal. Contacts with one of these households were more frequent, as they lived in the same parish. There were few weekends in which the brothers did not meet. He also visited his wife's parents some weekends, but his wife went more often, taking along their three children. He was very friendly with his wife's brothers, and the husband of one of his wife's sisters; he sometimes went out with either his brothers or his wife's brothers, or with his wife's sister's husband. It was rare, however that they all came together as a group. Several times a month he met various uncles and cousins who also lived in Montreal, either through a chance meeting or because they were visiting the same household. He saw members of the household of one of his uncles more frequently, as they owned a grocery store where the family sometimes shopped. He reported that he met an average of 40 to 45 relatives each month, including those of generations older and younger than himself. He met far more of them in certain seasons of the year such as Christmas, and during Christmas 1954 he thinks that he must have seen nearly all of the 93 relatives who live in Montreal. He also went regularly, about once a month, to see his own parents who lived a few miles outside Montreal. He usually went with one of his brothers who owned a car, and they took their families with them. During the summer his wife and children generally went there for about a fortnight. Each time he visited his parents he usually met one of his married sisters who lived near their parents' home. He would also meet members of another sister's household when they came from the Eastern Townships to Montreal. About every other year, another of his brothers would come up from the United States where he lived with his family, and they would gather for a family reunion,

either in Montreal or at their parents' home. The relatives he did not meet he heard about, either through letters, or through conversations. Altogether, he had seen 115 of his relatives during 1954, and had heard from another 57. He admitted that he wasn't always as interested in family affairs as he should be, and that his wife knew more of his own relatives than he did. By way of an excuse, he said that he was a junior executive in his local trade union branch, and had very little time to spare between his work and his union duties.

What seems interesting in this informant's report about his frequency of contact, which was quite different from that of his wife, was that he recognized a strict obligation to see only a certain number of relatives. Outside of this range, frequency of contact and the sense of formal obligation were much less important. However, because all his siblings were married, the range of formal obligation comprised the core of the kinship system and totalled over 50 persons. Yet, since some of these persons were located outside Montreal and were seen less often, the informant reported himself as lax in his kin duties. Informants also made a distinction between obligations to meet relatives who were very close and obligations to meet kin of ascending generations. They reported that while they were expected by older relatives, other than their father and mother, to fulfil certain kinship obligations, this expectation was satisfied by a low frequency of contact, usually limited to visits at Christmas or the gathering for a family reunion. The frequency of these reunions varied, and most informants reported them as taking place about once a year. They had no fixed dates and usually took place at the home of one of the relatives who acted as a focal point for the activities of the kin group. A very good excuse had to be given for not going, but most informants stated that they went willingly. Sometimes as many as 40 or more persons would get together, depending on the size of the home or the economic resources of the persons involved.

The highest frequency of contact took place between relatives of the same generation and, apart from sibling contact, were mostly based on personal preference. This personal preference was recognized as the major factor in the contact, and informants verbalized it in the statement that such meetings were the result of "just liking to get together." It can thus be suggested that all the various modes of kinship recognition which have been described operate according to different criteria. Certain kin, such as Ego's parents, siblings, spouse's parents, or siblings' spouses, are held to have special claims and are given priority over all others. Recognition of these claims keeps the legally defined autonomy of the domestic family, as well as its life as a unit, at a low threshold, since its members will readily adjust their own lives to the needs of such kin. With other persons, a formal recognition will exist but this recognition can be satisfied by more limited actions, such as attendance at a funeral or a wedding, or by letter-writing, so that the autonomy of the domestic family with regard to them is much greater.

The criteria which give rise to these different modes of recognition, and which govern frequency of contact, cannot be presented as clear-cut categories. Involved in the idea of kinship recognition are factors which informants characterize as differences in "family spirit," or "family unity," so that there are extensive variations as to who is included in those having "priority," or

just a "formal" recognition. Many informants, for example, held that cousins were persons who involved some formal recognition, while others would regard close affines as more important to them than cousins. Difficulties in trying to determine the range of each category were often linked to the frequency of cousin marriages. Cousin marriages among the 30 informants who gave their genealogical knowledge varied from one instance of a second-cousin marriage, to two first-cousin and four second-cousin marriages in one kinship group. Altogether, 11 of the 30 informants reported such marriages. In another case, three brothers had married three sisters, and the two kin groups, which had not been previously related, had developed multiple ties which cross-cut the various dimensions of the kin group.

Closely related to the frequency of contact is the frequency of services between relatives. It could be offered as an unverified generalization that those kin who are held by close kinship links, and who see each other most frequently, help each other most frequently. These services included the loan of needed objects, baby-sitting, shopping, taking care of the household during the mother's illness, gift giving, the making of extensive loans, or the giving of general economic help. A young mother reported that she was receiving help from her mother, sisters, and female cousins. Less frequently, she would also turn to her husband's female relatives.

The pattern of services revealed even more clearly than did the frequency of contact that the kin group of birth is preferred to the kin group of marriage. Not only would there be a preference for one's own line, but also a preference for help from members of one's own sex, within each kin group. However, occasions were reported in which the distinction between the lines was blurred. All the adult females of a kin group, consanguineal and affinal, would help in preparing the family reunion. The buying, preparing and serving of the food, as well as the clearing up, would be the joint task of all the women who came. Another instance of overlap was given by a lawyer, who reported that his relatives, both consanguineal and affinal, came to him for legal advice, for which he charged a fee according to the economic status of the relative. Relatives in the medical profession are also reported as having their services requested by kin. Persons who sell things required by relatives, such as groceries and household utensils, were reported to have their kin as customers. This does not mean that all goods and services were obtained through relatives, but there is a certain degree of economic reciprocity holding the kin group together. Moral problems as well as economic were referred to relatives, especially to those in Holy Orders. Twenty-six of the 30 informants reported relatives in Holy Orders. One informant had 11 such relatives, both priests and nuns. One of these, a priest who was met during one interview, said that he was usually asked to officiate at the baptisms, weddings, and funerals of his relatives. Occasionally, they also came to him for advice. The only religious service he did not wish to perform for them was to act as their confessor.

All informants reported that they had received important services from relatives at some time during their lives. One stated that she would not think of going to a place where she had no relatives. Another informant reported that the problem of childrearing in a city was minimized if a mother could have the help of female relatives. One male informant stated that life in Montreal would have been impossible for him and his own domestic family during the depression of the 1930's if his relatives had not helped him. He not only received loans and other economic help, but went to live with his in-laws, and was able to find work through cousins. Of the 43 households visited, nine either comprised three generations or included other relatives outside the consanguineal unit. Working for a relative was frequently reported, and most informants stated that they knew of kin who were in this position. Certain economic enterprises are operated by persons who are related to each other in various degrees. Instances of this were given for a garage, a hotel, a grocery store, and a small industrial plant. Services are sometimes also requested of relatives who are marginal to the frequency of contact. Distant kin who, because of their status and general social position, can give important recommendations or introductions, are sometimes asked to exert their influence. If these relatives are also political figures, their politics will be supported as well as their help sought. The kinship system of urban French Canadians is an important mechanism for manipulating the social environment, and what might be called nepotism, but is referred to by French Canadians as "family solidarity," is a daily practice.

One of the marked characteristics of French-Canadian urban kinship is its high degree of elasticity. Outside the range of "priority" claims, narrow formal recognition is balanced by selective contact according to personality preference, and the resulting kin group is as much linked to personality preference as to institutionalized formal recognition. This elasticity also permits it to adapt itself to the elements which operate against its continuity in time. Among such elements is the process of social differentiation caused by social mobility. There is, in fact, a close correlation between social status and frequency of contact, and informants who were upwardly mobile were those who reported the greatest loss of contact with their lateral kin. Social mobility therefore tends to dislocate the lateral range in which personal preference is so important, but it does not seem to separate a person completely from the kin group. Certain formal ties are still recognized, and informants reported instances of a person helping his entire sibling group to move upward. Furthermore, a new kin group forms rapidly at the higher level. Social mobility does not seem to imply a complete loss of the recognition of kin obligations, but merely the movement from a kin group at one level to another kin group at a different level. Cases were quoted in which the acceptance of a spouse into the kin group at the higher social level was conditioned by the possibility of having to accept a number of the spouse's relatives. If the spouse was rejected, there would be a gradual loss of contact with the person who had married "beneath" him. In this instance, there would be a regrouping with the kin at the lower social level.

Segmentation of the kin group is caused not only by social mobility, but also by the development of cultural differences. Informants quoted instances of relatives who had "gone English," and with whom little contact was maintained. Cultural differentiation usually arose through marriage with a non-French Canadian. While the majority of marriages reported in the informants' kin groups were with French Canadians, each informant could also list marriages outside, but never more than three for a single kin group. They were to be found at all social levels. Informants stressed that such marriages usually meant a loss of contact unless the spouse was a Catholic, spoke French, and accepted the assigned kin role. Again, the lateral kin ties were more vulnerable in such situations; the "priority" relatives generally kept their association. While parents and siblings usually came to accept these marriages, it was the more distant relatives, with whom personal choice was most important, who showed disapproval and dropped the couple, so that their children grew up with a restricted kin knowledge.

Conclusions

The collected evidence indicates no trend toward transformation of the present French-Canadian urban kinship system into the more restricted system reported for the United States. While difficulties were reported in maintaining a united domestic family or an integrated kin group, there is no reason to suppose that these difficulties were caused primarily by urban living. Moreover, many cases were reported where the kin group re-formed after a period of disunity. There are many reasons for believing that the present system will continue. Far from being incompatible, kinship and urbanism among French Canadians seem to have become functionally related. Each urban domestic family, each household, each person, is normally part of a system of obligations arising from the recognition of kinship ties.

The present system is elastic, and can readily adapt itself to different situations. This is due largely to the limitations placed upon kinship recognition by French Canadians. The "priority" kin are limited in number compared to the total recognition. The formal extension between generations is satisfied by a low frequency of contact. The wide lateral range offers the greatest freedom of choice through the operation of personal preference. Lastly, because the "priority" claims are related to a small number of large sibling groups, kinship contact and awareness of kinship obligations must always be multiple. The fact that a French Canadian is normally socialized in a large household conditions him at an early age to multiple kinship obligations. The socialization is carried out in a kinship world in which authority is male and narrowly defined, and emotional needs are satisfied through sibling, cousin, mother-child, grandmother, and aunt relationships. The pattern is continued in adult life, but with a greater freedom since each person can have a wide range of personal preference. The fact that personal preference will bring together persons of roughly the same age, status, and background, makes for a great deal of unity in these subgroups. These peer groups not only serve as leisure-activity groups, but after marriage are often the kinship group into which the children of a new couple will become socialized.

It is beyond the scope of this paper to go into the psychological implications of this type of socialization, and the possibility of avoiding the constraint usually attributed to extensive formal kin obligations by manipulating them to suit personal preference. While the whole kinship range cannot be thus manipulated, and a "priority" core remains unchanged to give continuity, enough elasticity is obtained to suit a wide range of situations. Furthermore, because the women are most active in kinship affairs, and yet not identified with the legal formal authority structure, kinship is not conceived of as a pattern of strict "patriarchal" obligations but as a reciprocal relationship from which much pride, pleasure, and security can be derived. Lastly, as sibling groups are large, selection according to personal preference does not unduly decrease the size of the kin group, but allows emotional ties to unite a large number of kin according to the emphasis placed on emotional preference. The resulting personality type seems to be that of an individual who, while he recognizes many kinds of kinship obligations, actually satisfies these obligations by selecting kin with whom he has the best relationships.

These characteristics of urban French Canadian kinship are no new development, but seem to have been in existence since the period of New France.[2] It can be suggested that one of the reasons for this continuity is its elasticity, already referred to. All informants agreed that there was a French-Canadian family ideal. While not aware of all its implications, they would verbalize about it and criticize variations from this ideal on the basis that to cease to behave like a French Canadian was to become "English". These ideals about family and kinship were not isolated but were part of a cultural complex which included the French language as spoken in Quebec, a specific system of education, membership in the Catholic Church, and various political theories about the status of French Canadians in Canada. To be a member of a French-Canadian kinship group implied attitudes and beliefs about some or all of these.

In conclusion, some of the theoretical implications of the research can be pointed out. One of these is the relationship between the size of sibling groups and kinship behaviour.

The hypothesis is offered that socialization in a family of many full siblings results in special perceptions of kinship obligations. It was found that the size of sibling groups tends to run in families, and that children raised in large families accepted as normal the fact of having many children and the implications of multiple kinship recognition. French Canadians, one of the most prolific groups in the Western world, have made the tradition of a large sibling group one of the ideals of family life. This raises the problem of assessing the influence of urbanism on French-Canadian kinship. One of the most widely accepted generalizations about kinship is the proposition that the greater the urbanization, the smaller the kinship range, and that this apparent result of city life is everywhere the same. A number of writers believe that the invariable result of urbanization is to reduce the kinship range to the domestic family. Wirth[3] gave this statement its classical formulation, and it has been reiterated by more recent authors such as Burgess and Locke,[4] Cavan,[5] and Kirkpatrick.[6] While it is to be accepted that there will be a difference in birth-rate between rural and urban areas, this does not necessarily imply that urban kinship is doomed to universal disappearance.

Against this hypothesis of universal similarity, recent studies carried out in London[7] have shown that kinship recognition is compatible with urban life. While there may be a world trend toward urbanization and industrialization, there is little evidence for the disappearance of kinship awareness. The cluster of social characteristics by which urbanism is usually defined, such as population density, specialized functions, and a distinct pattern of social relationship, may exist in a variety of cultures. There is apparently a basic cultural difference in the description of kinship as reported in London and in the United States.[8] Perhaps this difference does not arise from fundamental variations in urbanization but from variations in concepts about the family and kinship.

One recent study[9] suggested a great deal of uniformity between the rural and urban kinship systems in the United States. While some societies are undoubtedly more urbanized than others, it seems that the critical factors in diminishing kinship recognition are the cultural values of the society, not its degree of urbanization. For instance, French Canadians share what might be called the techniques of the American way of life. Yet the kinship system of the French Canadians of Montreal seems to be fundamentally different from that reported for the United States. These differences, furthermore, are not due to more extensive rural survivals among the French Canadians, or to longer urban conditioning in the United States, but in each instance seem to be part of the established urban way of life, with its cultural values.

Many writers seem to have identified the effects of urbanization as a world-wide process with the effects of the cultural values to be found in the United States. This is understandable, since most studies of urbanization have been carried out in the United States. However, this study of the French Canadians suggests that the relative influences of urbanization and cultural values on kinship must be seen as distinct.

NOTES

1 Louis Wirth, "Urbanism as a Way of Life," *American Journal of Sociology*, XLIV, 1 (1938), 1–24.

2 See Philippe Garigue, "The French-Canadian Family," in Mason Wade (ed.), *Canadian Dualism – La dualité canadienne* (Toronto: University of Toronto Press; Québec: Les Presses Universitaires Laval, 1960), pp. 181-200.

3 Op. cit.

4 E. W. Burgess and H. J. Locke, *The Family* (New York: American Book Company, 2nd edition, 1953).

5 R. S. Cavan, *The American Family* (New York: Crowell, 1953).

6 Clifford Kirkpatrick, *The Family* (New York: Ronald, 1955).

7 R. F. Firth, "Studies of Kinship in London" (MS., to be published by the London School of Economics); Michael Young, "Kinship and the Family in East London," *Man*, LIV, 210 (1954), 137-39: L.A. Shaw, "Impression of Family Life in a London Suburb," *The Sociological Review*, II, 2 (1954), 179-94; Peter Townsend, "The Family Life of Old People," *The Sociological Review*, III, 2 (1955), 179-95.

8 Helen Codere, "A Genealogical Study of Kinship in the United States," *Psychiatry*, XVIII (1955), 65-79.

9 D. M. Schneider and G. C. Homans, "Kinship Terminology and the American Kinship System," *American Anthropologist*, LVII (1955), 1194-208.

Patterns of kinship interaction

This article is Chapter four from a book which presents the results of a study of relationships between fifty-four married couples and their parents and parents-in-law. The data was obtained from a purposive sample drawn from the caseload of the Family Service Association of Toronto. The criteria used in defining the sample led to the selection of Canadian-born, English, white, Protestant, lower-middle class, first-married couples together fifteen years or less and involved in marital difficulties, both of whom agreed to participate in the research project.

The findings are typical of most studies dealing with the structure and process of kinship exchange in North American society. The majority of married couples visited and telephoned their parents and parents-in-law regularly and defined these exchanges as positive experiences. Helping patterns in the form of financial aid, care during illness, and emotional support were found to be widespread. Kinship exchange was more frequent and satisfying between married couples and the wife's parents and conflict was most pronounced between wives and their mothers-in-law.

This study has made an important contribution to literature on kinship in Canada in two ways. First, the author interviewed both husbands and wives, a practice which remains uncommon in family research. Second, the analysis illustrates the importance of system and subsystem characteristics of kinship interaction, and structural and symbolic influence. These concepts have been neglected in other kinship studies.

One should, however, call the reader's attention to several unexplored questions in the results discussed below. It is reported that 45 percent of those with parents living in a distant city managed to see them at least several times a year, leading to the conclusion "that geographic proximity is not a necessary condition of extended family relationships". The fact that 55 percent of this group seldom or never visited their parents is ignored. Similarly, over half the respondents saw friends more often than parents, compared to about 30 percent who saw parents and parents-in-law more often than friends. These two quite different groups of married couples are not discussed.

The data does not, in my view, provide strong support for the assumption that the isolated nuclear family is a myth, as the author concludes in his book. One of the more important findings is that the respondents desire to control the frequency of interaction with their parents. Although the married couples wanted their parents to live in the same geographical area, they were concerned about the invasion of their nuclear-family boundaries. Parents and parents-in-law did not drop in on their married children as frequently as married children did on their parents, indicating "a less permeable boundary" in the nuclear family. In addition, telephone calls were more often initiated by married children, not their parents. Considerable research remains to be done to demonstrate that the myth is, in fact, dead.

Other studies of kinship in English Canada tend to show similar results. Pineo (1968) found frequent inter-kin visiting, more often with the husband's parents than the wife's, in his study of 327 working class families in Hamilton, Ontario. A related study of a working class district in Toronto (Crysdale, 1968) found few differences between blue-collar and white-collar patterns of involvement in organizations and participation in primary relations with others. Contact with relatives differed little by social class. Education, however, had a significant impact on degree of closeness to relatives. Persons with less than grade eight education interacted equally with relatives and a variety of others. Persons with some high school or post high school education, however, were not as close to their relatives (28 and 12 percent, respectively) as they were to a variety of non-relatives (63 and 72 percent, respectively). Osterreich (1965), in her study of Anglo-Saxon families in Montreal of lower and middle class background, found that attitudes toward relatives and the nature of contact differed little even if one's kin lived outside the city. While frequency of contact and mutual aid were related to physical proximity, the assumption of potential help and a strong sense of primary ties prevailed across geographical distance. These studies, however, are in apparent contrast to the findings of a study by Seeley, Sim and Loosley (1956) of upper middle class families in

Toronto. Kin relationships occurred on ritual occasions, and kinship bonds were weak and little different from friendships based on individual preference. The wife maintained kin contact symbolically through letter-writing, sending gifts and cards, and related obligations. Kin seldom lived in the same community or city.

It would seem from these four studies, and the more recent study of Irving, that kin ties are systematic and important for working class and middle class English Canadians, but perhaps symbolic and casual for upper middle class English Canadians.

Patterns of kinship interaction

Howard H. Irving

Researchers (for example, Homans, 1950; Robins and Tomanec, 1962) have consistently used the *frequency of interaction* as one indicator (and often the chief one) of the degree of intimacy or interpersonal involvement in a social relationship. To study this important index of relationship, it is necessary first to examine the sample from the perspective of geographic proximity or distance from parents and parents-in-law, since a reasonable degree of proximity is required to permit frequent face-to-face interaction.

Geographic proximity

The respondents were asked whether or not their parents lived in Metropolitan Toronto, and the actual distance in mileage was recorded. This automatically supplied the same information about in-laws, as both husband and wife were asked the same ques-

tions. It was decided for the sake of clarity of analysis that the reported distances would be organized into four categories: (a) from 0 to 3 miles was considered the "same neighbourhood"; (b) more than 3, but less than 25 miles, was considered the "same metropolitan area"; (c) more than 25, but less than 100 miles, was considered a "nearby city"; (d) over 100 miles was considered a "distant city".

In this study, 72.2 per cent of the respondents had parents living within the Metropolitan Toronto area. Of the remaining 27.8 per cent with parents living outside of Metro, 13.9 per cent had parents-in-law living in Toronto. Thus, 86.1 per cent of the sample had parents and/or parents-in-law in the metropolitan area.

There are many possible reasons for this very high percentage. More than 70 per cent of the respondents had been born in Toronto. The city tends to be a fairly stable commun-

Howard Irving, Ph.D., is Assistant Professor, School of Social Work, University of Toronto.

Chapter four in Howard H. Irving, *The Family Myth: A Study of the Relationship between Married Couples and their Parents* (Toronto: Copp-Clark, 1972), pp. 41 — 61. Reprinted by permission of the author and Copp-Clark Publishing Co.

ity for people born here, as it is a highly industrialized area and offers many job opportunities. This characteristic would be especially important for this working-class sample. Another possible reason for the stability of the sample may have been that the respondents were of British background, for Toronto is one of the centres of Anglo-Saxon life in Canada. The 1961 Census of Canada indicated that 61 per cent of the population of Metropolitan Toronto was of British ethnic origin.

Despite the possible reasons, the percentage of respondents with parents and/or parents-in-law residing in the city was still striking. Although the respondents may not have chosen to live in Toronto specifically because their parents were there, the fact remains that they were far from isolated from them. Even more striking was the fact that 40.7 per cent of the total sample lived in the same neighbourhood as their parents.

The study most comparable to the present one is Komarovsky's *Blue-Collar Marriage* (1964). Her sample consisted of white Anglo-Saxon Protestants not over 40 years of age, and she interviewed husbands and wives who were married to each other. The major difference was that her sample was a non-clinical one. Komarovsky found that 68 per cent of her total sample lived within the same community as their parents, compared with 72 per cent of the present sample. The similarity of these findings indicates very little difference between the clinical and nonclinical samples with regard to geographic proximity. Although the other major empirical studies reviewed were not directly comparable because of the wide variations in respondent characteristics, they usually found that approximately 50 per cent resided in the same metropolitan area as their parents

(Adams, 1968; Reiss, 1960; Aiken, 1964).

The societal ideal of bilateral symmetry (referred to in Chapter II) was upheld within this sample in relation to proximity to parents. There was no significant difference between the number of husbands and the number of wives with parents living within the metropolitan area (75.0 per cent of the wives and 70.4 per cent of the husbands). Part of the reason for this bilateral symmetry may have been that about an equal number of husbands and wives (approximately 70 per cent) had been born in Metropolitan Toronto, and their parents had evidently remained there.

An attempt was made to find out whether the respondents lived near their parents only because their parents happened to live in the area that was most desirable to the respondents, or whether they lived near parents because of a specific preference to do so. It was recognized that this may not have been an either/or proposition. The respondents were asked where they would prefer that their parents and parents-in-law reside. The choices were: in their own home; in the same neighbourhood; in the same metropolitan area; in a nearby city; in a distant city. The results were cross-tabulated with the actual proximity of the respondents to their parents and parents-in-law so that their preferences could be compared with their actual place of residence.

Table 1 indicates that of those with parents living in the same neighbourhood, the greatest percentage preferred that they live in the same metropolitan area, but not necessarily in the same neighbourhood. It is interesting to note, however, that the next largest percentage preferred that their parents live within the same neighbourhood rather than in a nearby or distant city. Of those with

Table 1   Respondents' Preference for Parents' Residential Proximity by Actual Proximity to Parents

Actual Proximity to Parents	Preference for Proximity to Parents (in per cent)				Total	Per Cent
	Same Neighbour-hood	*Same Metro-politan Area*	*Nearby City*	*Distant City*	*N*	
Same Neighbourhood	25.0	65.9	4.5	4.5	44	40.7
Same Metro-politan Area	23.5	55.9	2.9	17.6	34	31.5
Nearby City	8.3	41.7	41.7	8.3	12	11.1
Distant City	11.1	27.8	33.3	27.8	18	16.7
Total N	22	58	14	14	108	
Per Cent	20.4	53.7	13.0	13.0		100.0

$X^2 = 30.723$ $P<.01$
Gamma = 0.430
All totals do not add up to 100.0% because of rounding.

parents living in the metropolitan area, but not the same neighbourhood, the greatest number preferred that they live where they were actually living. The next largest percentage preferred that they live in the same neighbourhood. Of those with parents living in a nearby city, all except one preferred that they live either where they were or closer. Of those with parents living in a distant city, the majority of respondents preferred that they live closer than they did.

The same trends which emerged with regard to parents also appeared for parents-in-law. Of those with parents-in-law in the same neighbourhood, most wanted them to live within the same metropolitan area. This is certainly contrary to the popular belief about antipathy and avoidance in relation to parents-in-law. In fact, the second largest percentage wanted them to live in the same neighbourhood. It should be noted, however, that slightly more selected "nearby city" or "distant city" for parents-in-law than for parents.

The data seem to indicate that when parents lived in the same neighbourhood, the respondents preferred their parents to live close to them, but not as close as they actually did. This might imply some concern on the part of the young married couples about invasion of their family boundaries by parents and/or parents-in-law, or by their own doing when parents and/or in-laws were so close. However, if this was so, there was no obvious backlash reaction, as the respondents still wanted their parents and parents-in-law to live close to them. About half of the sample preferred that their parents and parents-in-law live within the same metropolitan area and an additional 29 per cent

wanted them to live in the same neighbourhood.

It is interesting to note that husbands and
wives had the same preferences as to where
they preferred their parents and parents-in-
law to reside. Although many studies have
indicated that women are closer to their
mothers than husbands to *their* mothers
(e.g., Komarovsky, 1950; Bronfenbrenner,
1961; McKinley, 1964), in the present sample the husbands wanted to live just as close
to their parents as did the wives.

In an attempt to explore further the modal
tendency for the respondents to want their
parents and parents-in-law to live in the same
metropolitan area as they did themselves,
they were asked as an open-ended question
why they had these preferences. The answers
consistently revealed the respondents' desire
to control the frequency of interaction with
parents. They wanted parents and parents-
in-law close enough so that if and when they
chose to visit them (and they did so quite
frequently, as will be discussed), they would
be readily available. The data revealed that
when parents lived very close, the choice
factor did not exist; even when the young
couples in the sample simply chose not to
visit, the parents initiated the contact.

Frequency of visiting

The frequency of visiting has been considered by most researchers to be one of the
most sensitive indices of interaction. The respondents were asked how often they visited
their mothers, their fathers, their mothers-
in-law, and their fathers-in-law. Few other
studies have asked about each member individually. The purpose in doing this in the
present study was to discover whether there

were differences in the frequency with which
the respondents interacted in their various
role relationships.

It is interesting that no significant difference was revealed for either husbands or
wives in the frequency with which they visited each parent. In other words, they reported visiting their mothers as frequently as
their fathers, their mothers-in-law as frequently as their fathers-in-law. In view of
this finding, the analysis and reporting of the
data were simplified by using the responses
to questions about "mother" and "mother-
in-law" as the baseline for discussion about
the frequency of interaction with parents and
parents-in-law respectively.

To discuss the frequency of visiting, the
sample must be placed in perspective regarding geographic proximity to parents and
parents-in-law, as distance is a prime limiting factor of interaction. Although geographic proximity *per se* does not necessarily
determine who interacts on a face-to-face
basis, it does determine who *may* interact in
terms of availability and practicality (Bott,
1957).

Table 2 reveals that, as had been expected, there was a strong, direct relationship between geographic proximity and the
frequency of visiting. The gamma (ordinal)
was high (.685), and the Chi Square was
significant at the .01 level.

Contrary to the theories of isolation from
parents after marriage (discussed in Chapter
2), this study revealed a very high frequency
of interaction with them. As indicated in the
table, 75 per cent of the respondents whose
parents lived in the same neighbourhood visited them weekly or more often. Of those
with parents living in the same metropolitan
area, but not the same neighbourhood, 73.6
per cent visited them weekly or more often.

Table 2   Frequency of Face-to-Face Interaction with Parents by Residential Proximity

| Proximity of Parents | Frequency of Interaction (in per cent) | | | | | Total N | Per Cent |
	More than once a week	Weekly	Monthly	Several times a year	Never		
Same Neighbourhood	47.7	27.3	20.5	4.5		44	40.7
Same Metropolitan Area	11.8	61.8	11.8	14.7		34	31.5
Nearby City	8.3	8.3	66.7	16.7		12	11.1
Distant City		11.1	5.6	27.8	55.6	18	16.7
Total N	26	36	22	14	10	108	
Per cent	24.1	33.3	20.4	13.0	9.3		100.0

$X^2 = 103.042$ $P<.01$
Gamma = .685
All totals do not add up to 100.0% because of rounding.

Two-thirds (or 66.7 per cent) of those with parents living in a nearby city visited about once a month. Approximately 45 per cent of those with parents living in a distant city managed to see them at least several times a year. This seems to support Litwak's finding (1960a) that geographic proximity is not a necessary condition of extended family relationships.

Feelings of emotional closeness did not seem to affect the frequency of interaction. There was no difference in the frequency of visiting parents between those who claimed to be very close in their feelings towards their mothers and those who were somewhat close or not very close. There was a significant difference, however, between those who said they relied on their mothers for emotional support and those who said they did not. Table 3 shows that respondents who relied on parents for emotional support interacted with them more frequently than those who did not.

It is interesting to compare this study with others regarding the frequency with which respondents visited their parents. The research reported in Table 4 is not directly comparable with the present study because of the wide variations in the samples. However, the pattern of findings is interesting. The wives' interaction was used as the basis of the Table, as most studies did not include interviews with husbands as well. All the studies revealed that at least two-thirds of the respondents who had parents living in the same metropolitan area visited them weekly or more often, as compared with about three-fourths of the present sample.

Table 3   Frequency of Face-to-Face Interaction with Parents by Emotional Reliance

Emotional Reliance	Frequency of Interaction (in per cent)							Total N
	Daily	More than once a week	Weekly	Monthly	Several times a year	Few times a year	Never	
Yes	11.5	17.3	40.4	21.2	5.8		3.8	52
No	3.6	16.1	26.8	19.6	19.6	10.7	3.6	56
Total N	8	18	36	22	14	6	4	108
Per Cent	7.4	16.7	33.3	20.4	13.0	5.6	3.7	

$X^2 = 13.442$ $P < .04$
Gamma $= .357$

Table 4   Frequency of Face-to-Face Interaction Between Respondents and Parents as Reported in Related Studies

City	Sample Description	Percentage seeing parents weekly or more often who reside within the Metropolitan Area
Boston	161 families in total sample — mostly urban middle class (Reiss, 1960)	66.3
Glenton	58 married couples of stable blue-collar marriage. All respondents under 44 years of age. White Anglo-Saxon Protestants (Komarovsky, 1964)	66
Greensboro	799 married respondents, young to middle age. White Anglo-Saxon Protestants. Includes total socio-economic range (Adams, 1968)	88
Hamilton	327 respondents of which 86% are blue collar (Pineo, 1965)	77
Minneapolis	237 respondents comprising 79 grandparent-parent-married child lineages. White and blue collar (Aldous, 1967)	69

In the present study the frequency of visiting was less in relation to parents-in-law than to parents. For example, while 75 per cent of those with parents living in the same neighbourhood visited them weekly or more often, only 59 per cent of those with parents-in-law in the same neighbourhood visited their in-laws that frequently. When asked the reason for the greater frequency of contact with parents than with parents-in-law, the overwhelming response was that parents were seen because of affection and parents-in-law

Table 5   Frequency and Direction of Face-to-Face Interaction Between Respondents and Their Parents

	Frequency of Interaction (in per cent)						
	Daily	*More than once a week*	*Weekly*	*Monthly*	*Few times a year*	*Several times a year*	*Never*
Respondents Visit Parents	7.4	16.7	33.3	20.4	13.0	5.6	3.7
Parents Visit Respondents	3.7	3.7	10.2	21.3	43.5	6.5	11.1

$X^2 = 131.081$ $P < .01$

because of obligation.

Whereas other studies have simply asked how often the respondents had seen their parents, the present study inquired as to the *direction* of the interaction as well, that is, who initiated the contact. This was sought by asking how often the respondent visited his parents and parents-in-law and how often they visited him.

Table 5 shows that the young married couples visited their parents and parents-in-law much more frequently than the parental generation visited them. This would seem to contradict the popular belief that parents and parents-in-law try to interfere with or break into the family boundaries of the young married couple. It seems especially significant that despite presumably greater difficulty in mobility (because of small children in the majority of cases), it was the young married couples who made visits to their parents and parents-in-law. While 57.4 per cent of the respondents visited their parents weekly or more frequently, only 17.6 per cent of the parents visited them as often. Although the visiting of in-laws was not as frequent, the pattern was the same for them as for parents.

As a further examination of the direction

of parental contact, the respondents were asked whether they dropped in on their parents and/or parents-in-law unannounced and whether their parents and/or parents-in-law dropped in on them unannounced. The data revealed that significantly more of the young married couples dropped in unannounced on their parents and parents-in-law than their parents and parents-in-law did on them. This implies greater informality on the part of the married children towards their parents, than on the part of their parents; that the parents do not drop in unannounced as frequently indicates a less permeable boundary in that direction.

When the respondents were asked whether they felt that they saw parents and parents-in-law just about enough, or whether they would prefer to see them more or less often, about half answered that they saw them just about enough. Nearly 40 per cent wished they could see their parents more often, and almost 18 per cent wished to see their parents-in-law more often. Only 8.4 per cent, or nine of the 108 respondents, preferred to see their parents less often. As would be expected, about twice as many wished to see their in-laws less often.

The respondents were asked whom they saw most often socially — parents and parents-in-law, friends, or other relatives. Although over half (52.8 per cent) saw friends most often, close to one-third (30.6 per cent) saw their parents and parents-in-law more often socially than anyone else. If one accepts the proposition that the social environment must necessarily have some effect upon the functioning of the young married couple, it would seem to follow that parents and parents-in-law, at least in that third of the sample which reported interacting with them more often socially than with anyone else, must have a significant impact upon the respondents.

The kind and frequency of activities which the respondents shared with their parents and parents-in-law were also of interest to this study. About half of the respondents engaged occasionally in social activities such as visiting or going to movies or parties with parents and parents-in-law. The most frequently shared social activities were ritual occasions such as holidays, birthdays, and anniversaries. Nearly 68 per cent of the respondents regularly spent these occasions with parents and parents-in-law.

Telephoning and letter writing

Face-to-face contact alone cannot be the total measure of the frequency of interaction in today's world of rapid communication. Telephoning and letter writing, frequently mentioned in previous research as areas which needed investigation, were subjects of inquiry in this study.

Telephoning is an ubiquitous form of communication in Toronto. Leichter and Mitchell (1967) pointed out that "The use of the telephone not only mitigates against di-minished contact through distance, it may actually intensify contact" (p. 103). The present study lent a good deal of support to Leichter and Mitchell's statement. A total of 62.9 per cent of the sample telephoned their parents weekly or more often, 23.1 per cent calling daily, and an additional 23.1 per cent phoning more than once a week.

Of those whose parents lived in Metro, 78.4 per cent phoned weekly or more often. Close to one-third (32.4 per cent) called daily. Of the respondents whose parents lived in a nearby city to which telephone calls would be long-distance, 58.3 per cent phoned weekly or more often. Of those with parents living in a distant city, almost 90 per cent (or all but two respondents) called several times a year.

Inquiries regarding the direction of the telephoning revealed that although not skewed as much as the direction of face-to-face interaction, the trend of the young married couples' initiating the contact with parents rather than vice versa was apparent here as well. The fact that parents were evidently more relaxed about initiating telephone contact than visits may well have been due to their feeling that the young couple's privacy was invaded less by a phone call, again indicating their sensitivity to their children's family boundaries.

Young married couples called their parents-in-law as often as their parents-in-law called them. The total amount of telephoning was much less than in relation to parents. In fact, the difference between the frequency of contact by phone with parents and with parents-in-law was striking. Only 15.9 per cent of the respondents whose parents-in-law lived in the same neighbourhood telephoned them more than once a week, as compared with 63.6 per cent calling their parents that much. Of those with parents-in-law in the same metropolitan area, 65.5 per cent *never* telephoned them, while only 10 per cent with parents living in the same area never phoned. This finding would seem to lend support to the theory that young husbands and wives both interact less with parents-in-law than with parents.

A similar trend appeared in relation to letter writing: there was less written correspondence to parents-in-law than to parents. As would be expected, there was an inverse relationship between the frequency of letter writing and the geographic proximity to parents. The further away the parents were, the more frequent was the letter writing. Nearly three-fourths of those with parents living in a distant city wrote monthly or more often, and 44.4 per cent of these wrote weekly or more often. There was no significant difference in the direction of this type of communication; parents and married children wrote to each other with about the same frequency.

All of the above data indicates a clear and direct relationship between proximity and the frequency of contact. Distance is a necessary but not sufficient condition of interaction, determining who *may* interact, but not necessarily who *will* (Bott, 1957). As has been discussed above, the data revealed that parents-in-law were seen less, called less, and written to less than were parents, indicating that the closeness of the relationship, in terms of blood ties, had something to do with the frequency of interaction.

The sex variable

There are other major factors involved as well, an important one being the sex of the respondent. Many studies have been done in this area, and most have revealed that women are closer to their mothers than men to their mothers and therefore would be expected to interact more with them. (This is discussed in detail in Chapter 2.) Contrary to the findings of other studies, there was no significant difference between husbands and wives in the frequency of face-to-face contact with parents in the total sample. However, when geographic proximity was controlled for, a difference was noted. Table 6 shows that of those with parents living in Metro, 39.5 per cent of the wives and 27.8 per cent of the husbands visited daily or more than once a week. The other categories were almost identical except for those who had not seen their parents in the last year: this total was 7.4 per cent of the husbands but none of the wives.

Perhaps the main reason for the rather unusual finding of minimal differences between husbands and wives with regard to the frequency of visiting was that, as has been mentioned previously in another context, the societal ideal of bilateral symmetry was realized in this sample in relation to proximity to parents. There was no significant difference in the number of husbands and wives who had parents living in the Metropolitan Toronto area, and husbands preferred to live just as close to their parents as wives did to theirs.

An interesting difference emerged between husbands and wives with regard to the total amount of time spent with parents-in-law. Although not statistically significant, the trend seems worthy of noting: husbands reported spending more time with their parents-in-law than wives did with theirs. One reason for this was that the wives' mothers visited more frequently than the husbands' mothers, thereby increasing the probability of the husbands seeing their mothers-in-law more often than their own

Table 6   Frequency of Face-to-Face Interaction with Parents by Sex; Parents Residing Within the Metropolitan Area

Sex	Frequency of Interaction (in per cent)							Total N	Per Cent
	Daily	More than once a week	Weekly	Monthly	Several times a year	Few times a year	Never		
Husbands	5.6	22.2	41.7	22.2	8.3			36	48.6
Wives	15.8	23.7	39.5	10.5	10.5			38	51.4
Total N	8	17	30	12	7			74	
Per Cent	10.8	23.0	40.5	16.2	9.5				100.0

$X^2 = 3.484$ Not significant
Gamma $= -0.212$

mothers.

The data revealed a statistically significant difference between husbands and wives with regard to the direction of contact with parents. While 25.9 per cent of the wives' mothers visited their daughters weekly or more often, only 9.3 per cent of the husbands' mothers visited their sons that frequently. This would seem to indicate that mothers were more reluctant to visit their sons because they felt hesitant to intrude upon the domain of their daughters-in-law. This finding offers empirical support to the theory of many researchers that parents are closer to married daughters than to married sons. A significant finding indicating how important it obviously was for wives to see their mothers, was that although 52 per cent of the wives in the sample worked, there was no significant difference between them and the non-working wives in the frequency of visiting their mothers. (Of those wives who worked, 83.3 per cent were employed full time and 16.7 per cent part time.)

The most striking difference between the sexes was with regard to respondents telephoning their parents. Table 7 indicates that while 42.6 per cent of the wives called their parents daily, only 3.7 per cent of the husbands did so. Although a much larger proportion of husbands phoned their mothers more often than once a week, there were still over twice as many wives who did so (63 per cent of wives as compared with 29.6 per cent of husbands). Likewise, 9.3 per cent of the husbands had no telephone contact at all with their parents, compared with only 1.9 per cent of the wives.

The direction of telephoning followed the same pattern. Whereas half of the mothers telephoned their daughters more than once a week, less than one-quarter of the mothers called their sons that frequently. It is interesting that 38.9 per cent of the mothers-in-law called their daughters-in-law weekly or more often, while only 11.2 per cent telephoned their sons-in-law that often. Furthermore, 44.5 per cent of the wives called their

Table 7   Frequency of Telephoning Parents by Sex of Respondent

Sex	Frequency of Telephoning (in per cent)							Total N	Per Cent
	Daily	More than once a week	Weekly	Monthly	Several times a year	Few times a year	Never		
Husbands	3.7	25.9	24.1	13.0	24.1		9.3	54	50.0
Wives	42.6	20.4	9.3	22.2	3.7		1.9	54	50.0
Total N	25	25	18	19	15		6	108	
Per Cent	23.1	23.1	16.7	17.6	13.9		5.6		100.0

X² = 33.605 P<.01
Gamma = −0.550
All totals do not add up to 100.0% because of rounding.

mothers-in-law, whereas only 9.3 per cent of the husbands phoned their in-laws.

The pattern which emerged quite clearly was that women — wives, mothers, and mothers-in-law — were in touch much more frequently by telephone than were men. This was true to the extent that mothers-in-law spoke to daughters-in-law rather than to sons, and daughters-in-law phoned mothers-in-law.

It should be noted that although the mothers and mothers-in-law were usually the ones who were actually telephoned, most of the respondents made it clear that when they themselves called, they were inquiring about their fathers and fathers-in-law as well.

There was no significant difference between husbands and wives in the frequency with which they wrote to their parents and with which their parents wrote to them. The same pattern of sexual differences discussed above emerged again in relation to letter writing in that of those writing to parents-in-law, 18.6 per cent were wives, and only 3.6 per cent were husbands. In other words,

here, too, women were most often the ones who kept in touch, even with in-laws. It seems that wives represent the emotional or expressive element in the family and are therefore expected to be the locus for interaction with parents and parents-in-law.

Another area in which some interesting patterns emerged with regard to sexual differences was the structure of visiting, that is, whether the respondent went visiting alone, with just his spouse, with just his children, or with the whole family. The greatest percentage of the sample (65 per cent of the wives and 61.1 per cent of the husbands) visited their parents most often with the whole family. Only 11.1 per cent of the wives visited their parents alone as compared with 27.8 per cent of the husbands. It could be (as suggested by Peter Townsend, 1957) that the husbands visited on their way home from work. The reason for the small number of wives visiting alone was that 16.7 per cent of them (as compared with 2 per cent of the husbands) visited with their children. When they did not visit with the whole family, very few men brought their children with them. Thus it would follow that the mothers and fathers of married daughters saw their grandchildren somewhat more frequently than the parents of married sons. Although the husbands' parents were not visited as frequently, they generally saw the whole family at once when they were visited.

Years married

Another variable besides proximity and sex which was studied in relation to the frequency of interaction was the number of years the couple had been married. A few researchers (notably Leichter and Mitchell, 1967; Komarovsky, 1964; and Reiss, 1960) have studied life cycle stage as one variable of familial interaction. The limited number in this sample did not permit a study of this variable; it was therefore controlled for by limiting the respondents to those married fifteen years or less. For purposes of analysis, the sample was divided into those married for "less than five years" and those married for "five years or more," as this was the median point in the distribution categories of years married.

Twenty-four respondent couples, or 44.4 per cent of the sample, had been married for less than five years, and 30 couples, or 55.6 per cent, had been married for five years or more. It had been expected that, despite the limited sample size, some significant differences might appear between those more recently married and those married longer, with respect to the frequency of interaction with parents and parents-in-law. It had been thought that the younger marrieds (and their parents as well) might still have been working through some separation feelings and thus might have interacted more frequently. However, the findings did not bear this out. There was no significant difference between those married less than five years and those married five years or more with respect to the frequency with which they visited parents and parents-in-law, or with which the parental generation visited them. When all the categories of years married were cross-tabulated with other variables of interaction, no differences were found, even at the extreme ends.

When the number of years married was studied in relation to proximity, very little difference was revealed between the two groups. Cross-tabulations were done on the number of years married against the frequency of face-to-face interaction, telephoning, and letter writing. There was no significant difference, although there was a slight trend toward greater frequency with those married for less than five years.

The "years married" variable proved to be statistically significant in relation to the frequency of interaction in one instance only. This was with regard to the people within their social network with whom the respondents had most social interaction. Table 8 illustrates that a significantly higher number of those married for more than five years saw friends most often socially, while those married for less than five years saw their parents most often socially. In discussion with the respondents it was learned that the younger married couples spent more time with parents because many of their friends were still single, and the young couples had less in common with them now that they were married. It could also be that the younger marrieds were in a more dependent position, as some had started out their marriages living with parents. They were thus

Table 8   People Seen Most Often Socially by Number of Years Married

Number of Years Married	Social Network (in per cent)			Total N	Per Cent
	Friends	Siblings	Parents		
Less than 5 years	37.5	12.5	50.0	48	44.4
Five years or more	65.0	20.0	15.0	60	55.6
Total N	57	18	33	108	
Per Cent	52.8	16.7	30.6		100.0

$X^2 = 15.412$ $P<.01$

financially as well as emotionally dependent upon them. The older marrieds seemed to have made friends who lived the same kind of life as they did; thus they did not need their parents for their social life as did the younger marrieds. It should be noted, however, that although they did not see their parents most often socially, the couples married five years or more still interacted a good deal with them. In fact, they saw their parents as often as did those married less than five years, but they saw friends more often.

In summary, this study revealed that even in a sample of people of British background, an ethnic group which allegedly has relatively little family orientation, there was a great deal of interaction between the married couples and their parents and parents-in-law. About three-fourths of the respondents who had parents living in Metropolitan Toronto both visited and telephoned weekly or more often. The amount of interaction becomes even more striking when one realizes that the parents were phoning and visiting the married children as well.

Part Three

The Family
and Social Change

8

The family
in industrial society

Like most stereotypes, that of the classical family of Western nostalgia leads us astray . . .
Grandma's farm was not economically self sufficient. Few families stayed together as large
aggregations of kinfolk. Most houses were small, not large . . . . divorce was rare, but we have no
evidence that families were generally happy. Indeed, we find, as in so many other pictures of the
glowing past, that in each past generation people write of a period *still* more remote, *their*
grandparents' generation, when things really were much better.

William Goode, World Revolution and Family Patterns *(New York:*
The Free Press, 1963), p. 7. Copyright © 1963 by The Free
Press of Glencoe, a Division of The Macmillan Company.

The family institution in all societies has a rich and diverse heritage. To fully
understand the present family forms, functions, and behaviors, it would be necessary to systematically identify the family-society linkages through history. A
number of scholars have attempted this task (e.g., Morgan, 1877; Westermarck,
1903; Zimmerman, 1947), with only limited success. Others have traced the basic
features of ancient civilization family patterns, the impact of the early Christian
period, feudalism, the renaissance and reformation, relevant family patterns among
the Celtic, Anglo-Saxon and French peoples, and the influence of the early Colonial
period in North America (e.g., Bardos, 1969; Queen and Habenstein, 1974). Limited information is available concerning marriage and family patterns during the
colonizing period in Canada (Glazenbrook, 1950; Clark, 1942). This material is
very interesting and informative. It is difficult, however, to demonstrate precisely
how our present family is connected to these historical patterns. Vestiges of the past
do appear to exist; there are certain recurrent themes, and some generalizations seem
reasonable, such as that marriage and family law is strongly connected to our
Judeo-Christian heritage. Nevertheless, it is generally preferable to emphasize our
more recent past and family-change issues in comparative context.

This chapter focuses on the relationships between industrial and industrializing
society and changes in marriage and family life. It is argued that industrialization
and urbanization affect family form and function in every society. It should be

noted, however, that these effects have been grossly exaggerated and that they vary from society to society.

Characteristics of industrial society

The literature concerning the nature of industrial society (e.g., Goode, 1963; Wilensky and Lebeaux, 1958; Ogburn and Nimkoff, 1955) seems agreed on several general principles. Organizations and institutions are interdependent with societal needs and objectives relative to the production and consumption of goods and services. Jobs and careers in industrial societies tend to be specialized, requiring specific training, and geographical mobility (rural-urban in particular, but also from city to city) is widespread in response to job demands and opportunities. Vertical mobility (''climbing the social ladder'') is open to well-trained, acceptable, and successful specialists — an emphasis on achievement rather than ascription. Technological innovation is fundamental to industrial growth (e.g., computers, birth control pills, space exploration, innovations in transportation, communication, housing).

Durkheim (1960), Toonies (1963), Wirth (1938), and others emphasize the impersonal, mechanistic, rule and work ethic orientation of the industrial society. In an interesting and provocative work by Slater (1970), industrial society is described as giving preference to property rights over personal rights, technological requirements over human needs, competition over cooperation, violence over sexuality, concentration of goods and power over distribution, the producer over the consumer, means over ends, secrecy over openness, social reforms over personal expression, striving over gratification, and Oedipal love over communal love. These principles are said to become more evident as societies become more industrialized.

The controversy

The proposition that these characteristics destroy or significantly alter traditional marriage and family structure and process is widely accepted. It is commonly assumed, for example, that industrialization, urbanization and modernization weaken kinship ties, facilitate the emergence of the nuclear family household, remove family functions, and encourage romanticism, sexual freedom, illegitimacy, juvenile delinquency, crime and divorce. The work of Ogburn (1955) on *Technology and the Changing Family* illustrates these points. Ogburn saw the family as a passive ''victim'' of the forces of industrialization. The family, suffering from culture lag (changes in values are unable to keep pace with changes in the technological sector) is forced to adapt to changing societal demands. Ogburn attempted to show how seven major functions of the family system were radically changed as a result of rapid advances in technology. Six functions (economic, protective, religious, recreational, educational, and status-conferring) were largely taken over by non-family institutions. The remaining function (meeting the intimacy needs of adults and children) of the family became more intensive and demanding, but more satisfying. Ogburn also emphasized the dysfunctional influence of changing values (e.g., the development and acceptance of birth control techniques) on family stability.

Parsons (1959) has emphasized the structural isolation and segregation of the kinship unit. He argues that kin ties and the extended family household do not "fit" with industrial society. The family unit must be integrated with the realities of occupational demands. These include areas such as how employees use their time, the priority of job ties over family and kin ties, and the relative freedom to be geographically and socially mobile if duty or opportunity knocks. In consequence, Parsons argues, kin ties tend to be "multilineal" and based on friendship rather than obligation. Marriage itself, rather than kinship, is the basic structural keystone. Similarly, the family unit must be small and readily mobile to adequately cope with job demands. Therefore the "isolated" (from kin) nuclear family household with fewer children becomes the predominant family form.

These assumptions were accepted by many family sociologists. It now appears, however, that industrialization cannot be "blamed" for family change. Most would agree that industrialization is a sufficient but not a necessary causal agent in family change. Goode's (1963) monumental analysis of world revolution and family patterns in Africa, India, China, Japan and the West led him to conclude that: (a) before industrialization takes place, there are frequently indigenous sources of change in family systems; (b) family characteristics that are supposedly a result of industrialization existed before industrialization ever occurred; (c) in some societies, the family institution itself may have facilitated the movement toward industrialization; and (d) the causal relationship between industrialization and the family, regardless of the direction of this influence, is sufficiently unclear and complex to justify caution in drawing any conclusions.

Furstenberg (1966), in his study of the reports of foreign travelers who visited North America before the industrial revolution (1800–1850), found evidence of common stress points with regard to the domesticity of women and discipline of children. Free mate choice and romanticism were found to be widespread in another study of early North American patterns (Lantz, et al., 1968). It is now widely established that the nuclear family household was the predominant family form in New England (e.g., Demos, 1970), England (Laslett, 1973), and most of Northern France and Europe (Parish and Schwartz, 1972) prior to industrialization. One recent paper has demonstrated that social class, economic, legal, and political differences within and among societies in Western Europe are more useful in explaining family change than industrialization processes (Berkner, 1973). Even household size has remained relatively stable in spite of industrialization in some societies (e.g., India — Orenstein, 1961).

In addition, there is no evidence that kinship ties are automatically or necessarily weakened, let alone severed, because of geographical and social mobility. Braun (1960), for example, in his study of Sweden, found that kinship ties were strengthened. Either industry tended to locate closer to kinship-near communities or kin tended to move together to the same area. Furthermore, our review of research in Chapter six clearly documents the pervasiveness of kin relationships in Western society.

Linkages between family and society?

The controversy described above has yet to be resolved. The issues largely rest on the degree to which one can generalize to most societies, the extent to which particular family structures and processes did or did not exist prior to, or as a result of, industrialization-urbanization processes; and whether one could ever *prove* that there is a causal relationship between technological and value change and family change. The work of Goode (1963), though cautious, asserts that industrialization does have "crucial points of pressure" (p. 369) on the traditional family. These pressures include the usual necessity of physical mobility, which is a *sufficient* condition for decreasing the frequency and intimacy of contact with kin. Goode recognizes that these effects are partly counteracted by greater ease of contact through communication and transportation advances in industrialized economies. He also asserts that industrialization creates differential opportunity among social class levels. Certain individuals, among siblings and kindred, are able to advance rapidly while others do not, thus creating a sufficient condition for discrepancies in life styles. Goode further argues that industrialization creates a value structure which recognizes achievement more than birth. The individual alone is responsible for success, whereas kin in general are able to exercise little influence. Goode does, however, give credence to the role of upper-class elders in creating and maintaining jobs. Because of this, upper-class kin have retained control long after kin in other social classes have lost any significant influence.

Perhaps the most valid and universal consequence of industrialization identified by Goode is the independent employment of women (Goode, 1963; 372-374). As the woman (particularly the married woman) moves into the labor force, she gains financial autonomy and is less dependent on others. The woman thus achieves a solid bargaining position and is better able to realize her own rights and wishes in the family system. As suggested in Chapter two, there are a number of other changes which seem related to industrialization. These include, but are not limited to, increased divorce rates, a decrease in household size and size of the family, decreased mortality rates, increased educational levels for larger portions of the population, a decrease in age at marriage (this appears to be leveling off), and increasing problems for the adolescent. Blood (1970) argues that while the relationship between industrialization and the role of kinship in society is not determinate, kinship patterns do change in common directions. Certain of these were discussed in Chapter seven.

Even so, it should be emphasized that industrialization-urbanization processes are sufficient but not necessary conditions for family change. The family does not inevitably change in similar ways in all societies. It appears that the cultural milieu must be supportive of the relative gains of technological innovation before its institutions will be responsive to or initiate change.

SUMMARY

The characteristics of industrial and industrializing society, including job specialization, geographical and social mobility, and technological innovation, pose both significant problems and opportunities for marriage and family structure and process. Family patterns, however, do not always change as a result of these societal pressures; industrialization is a sufficient but not a necessary causal agent in family change. Commonly accepted consequences such as the nuclear family household, loss of family functions, romanticism, and divorce have been found to be prevalent patterns in pre-industrial societies. There are, even so, "crucial points of pressure" which appear to encourage change, including the independent (outside the home) employment of married women, decreased family size, decreased mortality, increased divorce rates, and more pronounced adolescent turmoil. The effects of industrialization and urbanization processes, however, seem to be subject to supportive sources of change in the family institution and the cultural milieu.

Three articles are included in this chapter to illustrate certain of the issues raised. The first paper provides insight into the theoretical issues underlying the role of the family itself in social change. The other two papers deal more directly with family change in Canada. The paper on the Hutterites shows the continuous struggle between family priorities and the communal life throughout their history. The last paper discusses and illustrates generational changes in Ukrainian family patterns. Changes in the middle class, more typical, Canadian family are considered in some detail in Chapter nine.

Family organization and problem solving ability in relation to societal modernization

In this short paper, Professor Straus offers an alternative way of conceptualizing the relationship between the family and social change in modernizing societies. He emphasizes the fundamental impact of modernization processes on the family in terms of the creation of decision-making or problem-solving situations. This is equivalent to saying that industrialization is a sufficient but not necessary influence for change on the family. By redefining the role of kinship in terms of problem-solving ability and family-kinship structures in terms of the number of functions they perform, Straus provides a useful means of interpreting the different ways in which the family responds to technological change.

While the model is easy to understand and is a pronounced improvement over the more traditional concept of the family in industrial society as a passive victim, it also oversimplifies the issues. For example, both problem-solving ability and functionality of families would seem to vary relative to the socio-cultural milieu of the society, as well as the class or caste structure of the society. In other words, the problem-solving abilities of the family may well be regulated by the class structure in which the family finds itself.

Straus's model may be convenient for theoretical purposes, but the fact that certain problems don't "go away" suggests that further work is needed.

Family organization and problem solving ability in relation to societal modernization

Murray A. Straus

In this paper "modernity" is assumed to be a variable which can apply not only to whole societies, but also to individuals (Inkeles, 1969) and families (Young and Young, 1968). It is further assumed that the modernization of one or more elements of the macro social structure influences both individual personality and family structure. Similarly, the presence of men with the social-psychological characteristics of modernity and the modernization of a key institution such as the family will influence many other aspects of society, probably in the direction of modernity. Thus, Figure 1 shows

Murray A. Straus, Ph.D., is Professor of Sociology, University of New Hampshire, Durham, New Hampshire.

From *Journal of Comparative Family Studies*, 3 (Spring, 1972), pp. 70-83. Reprinted by permission of the author and the publisher.

Figure 1 Societal, Individual, and Familial Modernity

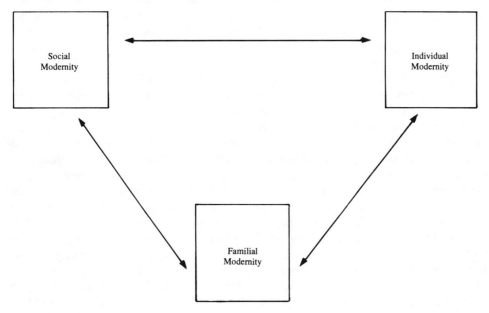

the macro-structure of society, the family system of society, and the personality structure of the population as mutually influencing each other.

At this level of abstraction, there is little disagreement among sociologists. But when we attempt to specify the relationships represented by the arrows in Figure 1, disagreement and confusion become one of the hallmarks of the empirical and theoretical literature. The specific point of contention to which this paper addresses itself is the question of the extent and conditions under which the family system constitutes an impediment and a facilitator of the modernization process.

Following Adams (1968), Horowitz (1966), Levy (1966) and others, a "modern" society is assumed to be monetized and industrialized in both the rural and the urban

sectors of its economy, and to have a highly developed and widely available technology in all sectors of the society, including health, transportation, and communication and mass media. In addition, the structural pressures generated by rapidity of change and the consequent need for flexibility in such a society, together with the need for high educational levels, will push such a society towards a democratic political system (Bennis and Slater, 1968).

Modernization, or the process of change to a society having these characteristics, is a world wide aspiration and, barring a planetary catastrophe, it is unlikely to be halted.[1] Assuming this to be the case, a critical issue is to determine how the process of modernization can be guided so that it is minimally destructive of other human values, including familistic values.

The family and modernization

The perspective on this issue which dominated much of sociology in the forties and fifties is exemplified in the work of Parsons (1949). Analysts such as Parsons hold that the relatively "isolated" nuclear family is the family system best adapted to the modernization process. They base this conclusion on a number of assumptions, including the following: (1) The kin have major responsibility for the transmission and enforcement of social values and norms. (2) The older generation is more likely to be the repository and valuers of traditional behavior patterns (Davis, 1940). (3) To the extent that nuclear units are not in frequent contact with their kin, the effectiveness of the kin in transmitting the traditional culture will decrease. Thus, a newly married daughter living in a different city from her parents cannot readily turn to them for advice or support when her first child is born. Similarly, the grandparents cannot offer information and support if they do not know (because of absence from the scene) when it is needed or appropriate. In such circumstances new parents are more likely to be influenced by the mass media, professionals, and their age and social status peers, and such influence is often likely to be different from that which the grandparents have provided.

One reason why the theory just outlined has been a controversial issue for many years is that the results of empirical studies designed to test the theory are contradictory. On the one hand, Wilkening's (1950) study of North Carolina farmers (a relatively traditional group) found that those most involved in a network of kinship interaction were the slowest to adopt modern farming practices.

Similarly, Fliegel (1956) found a low but significant negative correlation between familism and use of modern farming techniques, and this correlation held up despite numerous controls. Probably the most extensive data are those reported by Kahl for samples in Brazil and Mexico. In both countries, his measure of familistic values was found to be negatively related to a wide range of values indicative of modernity (Kahl, 1968: 36). Stuckert (1962) found that vertical mobility is associated with less visiting with kin, less use of family as a reference group, and less concern for family unity. Finally, Straus (1969a) studied a sample of 448 wives and found a consistent tendency for women high in interaction with their kin to be less modern in values, in role prescriptions for their children, and in their own behavior. On the other hand, Van den Ban (1967) has summarized a series of studies which show *no* relationship between kinship integration and use of improved farm technology, and Litwak's study of Buffalo, New York residents found that kinship solidarity had no deterring effect on social and geographic mobility (Litwak, 1960a, 1960b).

It seems clear then that one cannot either accept or reject the Parsonian theory on the basis of the present empirical evidence because some of this evidence is consistent with the theory and some is contradictory.[2] A situation of this type suggests that rather than simply more empirical studies, there is first a need for a re-examination or specification of the theory. The present paper offers a modest step in this direction.

One specification which seems necessary has to do with the assumption that the kin group is a repository of traditional culture. Parsons' deduction of greater conservatism for those in frequent contact with kin follows only if the assumption concerning the kin group as a repository of traditional culture is correct. But if the society as a whole and its kin groups are "modern", then the culture which the kin transmits and enforces will also tend to be modern (Bennett & Despres, 1960; Coult & Habenstein, 1962; Litwak, 1959-60; Litwak, 1965; Marsh & Coleman, 1954; Marris, 1967; Vincent, 1966).

Another difficulty with the formulation of the kin as "traditional" and therefore a deterrent to modernity is the fact that what is "traditional" is not necessarily opposed to modernity as defined in this paper (Gusfield, 1967) and "non-traditional" may be anti-modern, as in the case of the agrarian romanticism of some alienated American middle class youth (Kavolis, 1970).

In the light of these two difficulties — the fact that the kin may transmit *either* modern or traditional values and behaviors (or both simultaneously) and the fact that "traditional" is not necessarily anti-modern — the utility of this element of the theory becomes questionable. To deal with these difficulties I suggest that we substitute for the "traditional versus modern" continuum a variable which can be called *problem solving ability*. By this is meant the ability to cope with situations or circumstances requiring some sort of group or individual cognitive effort to resolve the situation in a manner commensurate with the actor's values. It is the process of developing a new response to situations for which no existing behavioral pattern is available to achieve the actor's goal. Implicit in this definition is the assumption that the modernization process creates countless situations in which groups or individuals must discover or adopt a new mode of dealing with the situa-

tion, or the values themselves, or the situation itself. The definition eliminates situations which, through familiarity or simplicity, permit the participants to take immediate action based on habits without the mediation of thinking.[3]

A second conceptual clarification is necessary before going on. This is to substitute for the simple dichotomy of "nuclear" versus "extended" family a continuous variable based on the number of functions performed. Following Winch and Blumberg (1968) we will call this the "functionality" of the kin group. This substitution is needed because we assume that only under rare circumstances does one find a truly isolated nuclear family system. The world over, people participate in extended kin networks so that membership in an extended network of kin is not a differentiating factor. But these networks do vary tremendously in the number and importance of the functions they perform. Toward the high functionality end of the continuum are family systems such as that of the high caste Hindu, in which the extended kin is not only a corporate economic and residential unit (through the institutions of family ownership of land or business and the joint household) but also is central to the religious, socialization, status placement, and social interactional functions. In the classic Hindu joint family, the constituent nuclear units are clearly subordinate to the extended kin (Gore, 1968). Toward the low functionality end of the continuum is the urban middle class family system of contemporary USA. Here the extended kin does not constitute a corporate group, has minimal or no religious and socialization functions, and is an optional focus of social interaction and economic aid.

The nuclear units are clearly central and, even when there are extensive economic ties between nuclear units, great care is taken to structure them in a way which preserves the autonomy of the separate units (Litwak, 1959-60).

Family types and modernization

Taking into account the original formulation by Parsons and others of the isolated nuclear family as the type best adapted to a modern industrial society and also the modifications of this theory implicit in the substitution of "problem solving ability" for "traditional versus modern" and "span of functions" for "nuclear versus extended", we are now in a position to summarize the revised theory in propositional form.[4]

AXIOMS

I. The greater the number of *functions* performed by the kin group, the more *dependent* an individual is on the kin.

II. The more *dependent* the individual is on the kin group, the greater the degree of control which the kin can exercise.

III. The more the kin is concerned with transmitting and enforcing a relatively fixed set of values and behaviors, the lower the situational problem solving ability.

IV. The greater the emphasis of the kin on situational problem solving, the more the process of modernization is facilitated.

THEOREM

To the extent that the kin is concerned with transmitting and enforcing a relatively fixed set of values and behaviors, the greater the number of functions performed by the kin, the greater the modernizing *inhibiting* effect of the kin group. Conversely, to the extent that the kin is concerned with situational problem solving, the greater the number of functions performed by the kin, the greater the modernity *facilitating* effect of the kin group.

The key variables in the summary of the theory just presented are the span of functions of the family and the problem solving ability of the family. The span of functions variable importantly affects the social control and socialization effectiveness of the family, and the problem solving ability variable influences whether the social forces of the family will be exerted in directions which facilitate or hinder modernization. Although both of these are continuous variables, for ease of exposition, they will be dichotomized to form a taxonomy with four types, as shown in Figure 2.

Type A. In examining Figure 2, we start with Type A because it is the familiar classical extended family. This type of family has evolved in response to, and is highly functional for adaptation to, a fixed agrarian social order. It is a mode of social organization which has served mankind well for thousands of years. Each member knows his place and has a secure place.

The modernization-inhibiting effect of this type of family is likely to be maximal for several reasons. First, the emphasis on fixity of *place* or position rather than on *problem*, although providing its members with a repertory of behaviors well suited to the premodern social order, lacks the flexibility needed for adaptation to the constant change of a modern and modernizing society. Thus, the family units themselves will be resistant to change and have difficulty adapting to the demands and opportunities of a modern society, for example, in such areas as adoption of new farming techniques (Wilkening, 1950), sanitary and health practices and

Figure 2 A Taxonomy of Families in Relation to Modernization Contribution

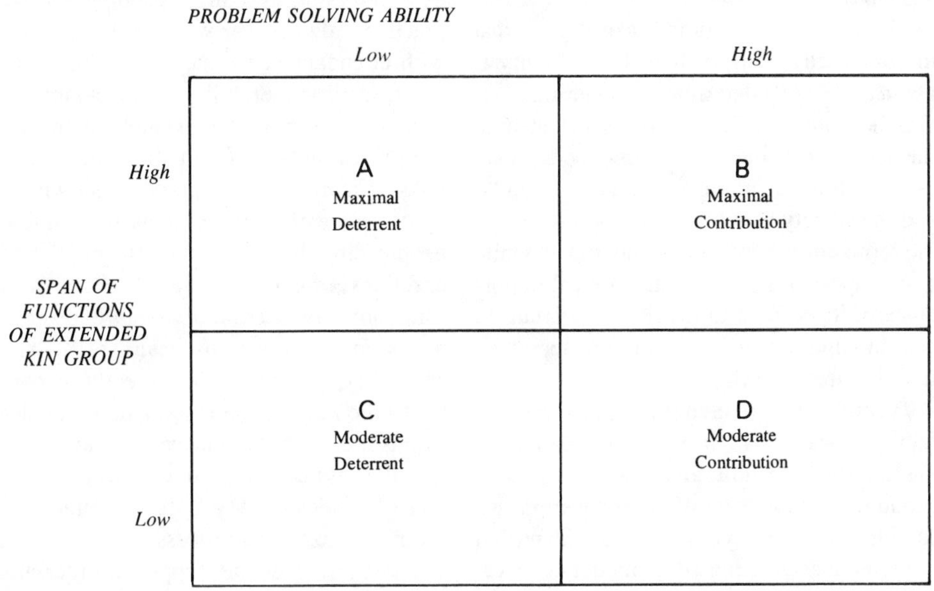

PROBLEM SOLVING ABILITY

	Low	High
High	**A** Maximal Deterrent	**B** Maximal Contribution
Low	**C** Moderate Deterrent	**D** Moderate Contribution

SPAN OF FUNCTIONS OF EXTENDED KIN GROUP

household management (Straus, 1969a), and educational support for their children (Strodtbeck, 1958). Second, individuals born into such families are not socialized into modern psycho-social patterns so that, even when freed from familial social controls, as individuals they tend to experience difficulty in adapting to the demands and opportunities of a modern society. Finally, those individuals who do become modernized tend to experience role strain and psychological tensions because the pattern of behaviors subsumed under the concept of modernity involve deviation from the patterns valued by their kin. Straus (1969b) for example, found that adolescents in Bombay, India who are high in achievement orientation tend to have the highest level of adolescent-parent conflict, whereas the reverse occurred in his parallel study in Minneapolis, USA (see also Douvan and Adelson, 1958; Dynes, Clark, and Dinitz, 1956; Ellis, 1952).[5]

Type B. The criticism which, with considerable justification, has been directed toward theories holding that the extended family of high functionality is a deterrent to individual and societal modernization, is based on the identification of a number of contrary instances. Among the examples which can be cited are the Lebanese, the Japanese, and the Parsees of India. As in the case of Type A, each of these groups has a family system in which the extended kin perform many functions and exert considerable influence. The difference is that (for varying reasons) a substantial part of this influence has been channeled in directions which promote modernization and adaptation to the demands of a modern society. Probably the most dramatic case is that of the Japanese (Goode, 1963: 321-365).

These examples should make it clear that the extended family of high functionality is not *necessarily* a deterrent to modernization. On the contrary, kin networks oriented to the social structure of a modern society may assist individual members or nuclear units, and the society as a whole, in the process of modernization.[6] At the same time, while granting the existence and theoretical importance of Type B families, it is important to bear in mind that at this point in history such families are quite rare.

Types C and D. Having examined the two family types which, in principle, should be maximally deterrent and maximally contributive to the process of modernization, we can turn to the two types which are identified in Figure 2 as exerting either moderate deterrent effects (Type C) or moderate contributive effects (Type D). The deductive reasoning which led to assigning both these types only a "moderate" influence is the same as that which attributes major influence to the other two types: When the extended family is high in functionality, the social control and socialization power of the family are assumed to be the greatest. Conversely, when, as in the case of Types C and D, the extended family has few functions, the effectiveness of the kin as agents of social control are sharply reduced. Thus, although Type C families are low in problem solving ability, the negative effect on modernization is not as great as with the Type A families because the influence of the kin is, on the average, lower in respect to all spheres of life.

This process can be illustrated by imagining the introduction of some new seed variety or cropping practice into two different regions, one characterized by extended families of low functionality and the other by extended families of high functionality. New practices always carry the risk of failure, with attendant economic losses, embarrassment, and vulnerability to criticism. The farmer who is part of a kinship system with a minimal number of functions faces these risks primarily with respect to his own family of procreation. Consequently, with fewer people directly concerned with his farming practices, the psychological costs of the same objective risks are probably lower and he is more likely to assume the risk. Moreover, since he is not directly responsible to the kin in economic matters, the decision is much more exclusively up to him. He is under less constraint to convince his kinsmen of the desirability of the new practice — always a hazardous process.

The same principles apply in other areas of activity, for example, some new element of household technology. Take the case of a wife living with her husband in a fraternal joint-household. Assume that a village development worker is trying to introduce some new practice — a solar cooker, or a pressure cooker — and that the wife in question is educated and inclined to try the new device. But if she is part of a joint household, she is likely to be more hesitant than if she were living only with her husband and children because, even if she does not need to secure permission of others in the household, she knows that they will be watching her closely. In the event of difficulties or failure, she may be subject to ridicule by them as well as by her own husband and children.

Similar reasoning applies to Type D families: those high in problem solving ability and low in functionality of the kin. Parsons and others claim that the relative exclusiveness and intensity of the parent-child bond in families which fall into our "low functionality" category gives parents tremendous power in moulding the socialization process (Parsons, 1959: 254-256) because affective ties are so powerful. On purely deductive grounds, a contrary conclusion is possible. That is, other things being equal, social control and socialization in a context of a high functionality extended kin group might be the *more* powerful process for several reasons including: (1) If the affective relation of the child with his parents is not satisfactory, there are likely to be alternative socializing agents with whom the child does have close affective ties; (2) the simple fact of a greater number of persons teaching and exerting pressure in the same direction; (3) the economic and social reward power of the high functionality extended family.[7]

I know of no empirical research which has tested these two competing theories, although the Japanese case suggests the validity of the above formulation. A more direct test is planned in the next phase of my own research on family group problem solving (Straus, 1968, 1970, 1971). For the sake of the present theoretical discussion, however, we will assume that, other things being equal, the low functionality family setting is less powerful as a socialization agent and that, as a consequence, socialization for individual modernity is less effective when the child is part of a kin group with few functions than would be the case in high functionality families which are oriented to a modern society.

In addition to the assumed lower socialization effectiveness of the low functionality extended family system, such a system has fewer resources to ensure adherence to its norms and values among its constituent nuclear units, i.e. resources such as land or other wealth, sociability, and religious rites and sanctions. Consequently, as a result of its limited span of functions which in turn limits both its social control and socialization power, the Type C family (on the average) is assumed to have less deterrent effect on modernization than the Type A family and the Type D family is posited as having less of a contribution to modernization than the Type B family.

Modernization and the humane society

At the beginning of this paper it was argued that modernization is world-wide and, barring a world wide disaster, it is also a process which is not likely to be halted in the near future. Assuming this to be the case, we turn now to a consideration of how the process of modernization can be guided so that it is minimally destructive of other human values, including familistic values.

The emphasis of this paper has been on instrumental roles, as indicated by the use of "problem solving ability" as one of the variables defining our taxonomy of families. But the instrumental functions served by psycho-social modernity are not sufficient by themselves for the maintenance of a social system, much less a humane society. Both the nuclear family and also the network of extended kin fulfill important expressive, integrative, and tension management functions. Such functions are documented by the studies reported in Shanas and Streib (1965) and in the recent study by Schwarzweller and Seggar of rural to urban migrants (1967) which showed that the greater the migrant's involvement with kin in the community to which they had migrated, the greater the feeling of personal stability and freedom from psychological tension. Thus, although the two family types which make up the bulk of the world's population are deterrent to the rapid adoption of modern psycho-social characteristics, it does not follow that interaction with the extended kin can or should be eliminated, even in societies desperately needing to modernize. Instead, what does follow is the need to include the family in the developmental process. The potential benefits of such an inclusion are twofold. First, the socialization, social control, and economic resources of the family can aid the modernization process. This would, of course, be valuable. But there is ample evidence that it is not necessary. Modernization can and does take place with any family system, though perhaps more rapidly with some than others.[8] Rather, the main benefit is to avoid, insofar as possible, the conflicts between nation and family and between individual and family which, in the past, have so often characterized the modernization process.

It is beyond the scope of this paper and the knowledge of this writer to specify in detail the different methods for achieving such an integration of the family system with the process of modernization. Instead, I will simply mention the approach of the research program with which I am associated.[9] This program consists of studies designed to uncover the causes and consequences of variations in the problem solving ability of family groups. These studies, although recognizing the importance of individual characteristics, focus on *group* characteristics such as communication patterns, authority structure, and interpersonal trust. Furthermore, in relation to the question of modernization, the research program assumes that a family structure which maximizes group problem solving ability is at least as important in facilitating modernization as is a population with the cognitive structure capable of dealing with the complexities of modern life. The need for such *individual* competence has long been recognized (Anderson and Bowman, 1966; Hagen, 1962; McClelland and Winter, 1969) and is reflected in the priority typically given to education in national development plans. But only the communist countries have paid much attention to the organization of the family as a factor in modernization, and in the past their approach has tended to assume that the family is the enemy of the state and hence must be weakened (Geiger, 1968; Goode, 1963: 270-320). Both the purely individual approach and the enemy of the state approach, however, have high human costs. Both, implicitly or explicitly create conflict between the modernized individual and the family, and neither takes advantage of the potential power of high functionality families for promoting modernization. Rather than such approaches, the idea behind our research program suggests that considerable effort should be devoted to enhancing the problem solving ability of family *groups*.[10] In terms of the taxonomy of families presented in this paper, this means steps which will enable Type A families to shift toward the Type B end of the continuum, and Type C families toward the Type D end. That shifts of this type can occur, even within the context of a family system which most highly epitomizes Type A, has been shown by Goode's analysis of the Japanese (1963: 321-365) and by Singer's study of the families of 19 leading industrialists in Madras, India (Singer, 1968).

We hope that the results of our empirical

studies and theoretical formulations will provide at least part of the factual and theoretical basis for such an approach. In addition, there is a need for programatic experiments. An example of such an experiment would be a longitudinal study in which the "experimental" sample of families will be aided in improving their problem solving ability, and their subsequent behavior compared with a control group of families. If the results of this experiment are in the direction we anticipate, it will point the way to at least one of the possible approaches to facilitating modernization with minimal disruption of other human values, and perhaps even with the enhancement of familistic values.

NOTES

1 The critical practical and philosophical question of the ultimate desirability of modernization cannot be covered in this paper except to note that there are many grounds for reservation concerning the ultimate desirability of modernization. But these reservations are not shared by the great mass of humanity in low income countries. The world over, these peoples are demanding higher standards of consumption, health, and physical and economic security, which can only be produced by a modern monetized socio-economic system (Levy, 1966; Moore, 1963). It is beyond the power of intellectual and political elites to decide whether or not a society shall modernize. An answer of "no" will, in my opinion, simply result in the replacement of such an intellectual and political elite by leaders more responsive to the populace.

2 This discussion omits consideration of causal direction. It should be clear that even if the studies were entirely in agreement in finding a negative association between kinship ties and modernity, the causal direction could just as logically be in the opposite direction to that assumed in this discussion. That is, those rejecting modernity may seek out familial relationships.

3 It should be noted that "problem solving ability" refers to a complex process which involves a number of separate but interwoven elements (Kelley and Thibaut, 1969). To deal with such a concept empirically (either for research purposes or to aid families in increasing their problem solving ability) requires a specification of each of these elements. There are a number of approaches to such a process of specification. Litwak, for example, takes as key elements "role flexibility" and "role substitutability" and has specified the conditions which maximize these variables. In the present research program, we have also found it convenient to divide the problem solving process into the following phases: problem identification, information search, decision, implementation, and evaluation. It is not meant to imply that a given family, or even most families, follows the sequence implied in the listing of these five phases. In the first place, the number of phases identified is arbitrary. Other research workers have specified both fewer and more phases. Second, certain of the activities specified can be carried out simultaneously or in different order. In fact, one of the objectives of the research program is to determine the extent to which families actually behave in terms of the type of phases and sequence of phases which analysts of the problem solving process have typically specified. Moreover, even assuming the validity of these phases, each must also be specified both conceptually and operationally.

4 This use of the axiomatic format outlined by Zetterberg (1965) is not intended as a formal proof but only as a convenient device for making the nature of the argument explicit. See Costner and Leik (1964) for some of the limitations of this format as method of proof.

5 This characterization of Type A is, of course, an "ideal" or constructed type. In reality, there are innumerable qualifications and variations, of which three will be mentioned: (1) the severity of conflicts between the modernizing individual and his family and the

presumed psychological stresses involved in modernization appear to have been overestimated by writers such as Mead (1955). Less impressionistic evidence suggests that modernization has no adverse effect on mental health (Inkeles, 1969) and, under some circumstances, may even be anxiety reducing (Straus, 1966). (2) When economic pressures are sufficiently great, even Type A families may be instrumental in the modernization process by supporting the out-migration and hence (indirectly) the modernization of individuals or nuclear units. For example, Eames' study of families in the village of Senapur, India (1967: 170) found ". . . that the joint family system operating in the village enhances rather than hinders the movement of the married male. Knowing that the nuclear family will be taken care of by the joint family in Senapur, or the wife's family in her parental village, is an important factor enabling the individual to leave Senapur without having to take his nuclear family or worry about their well being". Similarly, in the new nations of West Africa, where government cannot provide the welfare services taken for granted in industrial societies, the extended family fills the gap. A number of studies summarized by Aldous (1962) shows that relatives supply places of residence and provide other services for rural to urban migrants. See also Wilkening, Pinto and Pastore, 1968: Young and Young, 1966. (3) The hierarchical power structure of the traditional extended family can theoretically provide freedom of action for those at the top, and can also provide an authority structure for enforcing changes in the direction of modernization. The *head* of an Indian joint family, for example, may be so secure in his position that he is free to innovate. This is illustrated by the "Neo-Buddhist" movement in India, which is certainly a radical (and in a certain sense, a modernizing) innovation. Professor Elinor Zelliot has pointed out to me that a number of key supporters of Ambedkar were in such a position. They operated from a secure base and could violate the norms of the kin group with relative impunity. Similarly, the head of a joint family might try out some new farming practice without being fearful of

the reactions of his kin should it fail because they dare not criticize him.

6 Nevertheless, the revisionist critics of Parsons' "isolated nuclear family" theory may have gone too far. The "modified extended family" described by Litwak (1959-60), and shown by him not to restrict geographic and social mobility (Litwak, 1960), fits the Type B family as described in this paper. But, such families can still exercise restrictive and non-adaptive social controls in other spheres of life. Indeed, theorists such as Kingsley Davis (1940) and Barrington Moore (1958) hold that, in a society characterized by rapid social change, such a conservative role is almost inevitable because the rapidity of change produces age-cohorts with different cultures. These generationally-linked cultural differences, when coupled with the socialization and conformity enforcing functions expected of families in most societies, may make the family an *inherently* conservative group. Thus, even among subcultures in which the kin group is for the most part an agency for transmitting and encouraging the type of traits which fall under the general heading of "modernity" it is still a force for social stability rather than social change in many important areas of life. For example, two religious groups in American society noted for both the strength of their extended kin ties and for their contributions and adaptation to modernity are the Jews and Mormons. Yet it takes no great stretch of the imagination for Americans to guess the reaction of typical upper middle class American Jews or Mormons to the discovery that their son, grandson, or nephew intended to marry a Negro, and from there to appreciate the essentially conservative nature of the kin group and the mechanisms by which it enforces its norms. In most instances these norms can only be evaded by physical absence — in short by withdrawal from the family.

7 See in this connection, Sweetser (1966) for evidence on the relationship between succession in instrumental roles and intergenerational solidarity, including sociability and affective ties, and Goode's

discussion of the Japanese case (1963: 325). Goode argues that Japanese fathers were able to maintain control over their sons during the modernization period because the father was the channel through which operated a *network* of patronage on which the son was dependent for status placement.

8 In addition, as Safilios-Rothschild (1969) has recently shown, familial modernization does not have a necessary direct linkage with

societal modernization in other spheres, particularly political and industrial.

9 Co-investigators in the program are Joan Aldous, Reuben Hill, and Irving Tallman of the University of Minnesota. The program is supported by NIMH grant number 15521.

10 See in this connection Etzioni's discussion of the "Modernization of Collectivities" (Etzioni, 1968: 436) and Litwak and Szeleny (1969).

REFERENCES

Adams, B. N., Kinship Systems and Adaptation to Modernization, in: Studies in Comparative International Development 4 (1968), pp. 47-60.

Aldous, Joan, Urbanization, The Extended Family, and Kinship Ties in West Africa, in Social Forces 45 (1962), pp. 6-12.

Anderson, C. A. and Mary Jean Bowman, Education and Economic Development, Chicago 1966.

Bendix, R., Tradition and Modernity Reconsidered, in: Comparative Studies of Society and History 9 (1966-67).

Bennett, J. W. and L. A. Despres, Kinship and Instrumental Activities: A Theoretical Inquiry, in: American Anthropologist 2 (1960), pp. 254-267.

Bennis, W. G. and P. E. Slater, The Temporary Society, New York 1968.

Costner, H. L. and R. K. Leik, Deductions From "Axiomatic Theory", in: American Sociological Review 29 (1964), pp. 819-835.

Coult, A. D. and R. W. Habenstein, The Study of Extended Kinship in Urban Society, in: Sociological Quarterly 3 (1962), pp. 141-145.

Davis, K., The Sociology of Parent-Youth Conflict, in: American Sociological Review 5 (1940), pp. 523-535.

Douvan, Elizabeth and J. Adelson, The Psychodynamics of Social Mobility in Adolescent Boys, in: Journal of Abnormal and Social Psychology 56 (1958), pp. 31-44.

Dynes, R. R., A. C. Clarke, and S. Dinitz, Levels of Occupational Aspiration: Some Aspects of Family Experience As a Variable, in: American Sociological Review 21 (1956), pp. 212-215.

Eames, E., Urban Migration and the Joint Family

In a North Indian Village, in: The Journal of Developing Areas 1 (1967), pp. 163-178.

Eisenstadt, S. N., Modernization: Protest and Change, Englewood Cliffs, New Jersey 1966.

Etzioni, A., The Active Society: A Theory of Societal and Political Processes, New York 1968.

Ellis, Evelyn, Social Psychological Correlates of Upward Social Mobility Among Unmarried Career Women, in: American Sociological Review 17 (1952), pp. 558-563.

Geiger, H. K., The Family in Soviet Russia, Cambridge, Massachusetts 1968.

Goode, W. J., World Revolution and Family Patterns, New York 1963.

Gore, M. S., Urbanization and Family Change, Bombay 1968.

Gusfield, J. R., Tradition and Modernity: Misplaced Polarities in the Study of Social Change, in: American Journal of Sociology 72 (1967), pp. 351-362.

Hagen, E. E., On the Theory of Social Change, Homewood, Illinois 1962.

Horowitz, I. L., Three Worlds of Development, New York 1966.

Inkeles, A., Making Men Modern: On the Causes and Consequences of Individual Change in Six Developing Countries, in: The American Journal of Sociology 75 (1969), pp. 208-225.

Kavolis, Vytautas, 1970. "Post-Modern Man: Psychocultural Responses to Social Trends." Social Problems 17 (Spring): 435-448.

Kelley, H. H. and J. W. Thibaut, Group Problem Solving, in: G. L. Lindzey and E. Aronson, Editors, The Handbook of Social Psychology (2nd edition), Reading, Massachusetts 1969.

Levy, M. J., Jr., Modernization and the Structure of Societies, A Setting for International

Affairs, Princeton, New Jersey 1966.

Litwak, E., The Use of Extended Family Groups in the Achievement of Social Goals: Some Policy Implications, in: Social Problems 7 (1959-60).

——, Geographic Mobility and Extended Family Cohesion, in: American Sociological Review 25 (1960), pp. 385-394.

——, Extended Kin Relations in an Industrial Democratic Society, in: Ethel Shanas and G. F. Streib, Editors, Structure and the Family: Generational Relations, Englewood Cliffs, New Jersey 1965.

Litwak, E. and I. Szeleny, Primary Group Structures and Their Functions: Kin, Neighbors, and Friends, in: American Sociological Review 34 (1969), pp. 465-481.

Marris, P., Individual Achievement and Family Ties: Some International Comparisons, in: Journal of Marriage and the Family 29 (1967), pp. 763-771.

Marsh, P. C. and A. L. Colemen, The Relation of Kinship, Exchanging Work, and Visiting to the Adoption of Recommended Farm Practices, in: Rural Sociology 19 (1954), pp. 291-293.

McClelland, D. C., The Achieving Society, New York 1961.

McClelland, D. C. and D. G. Winter, Motivating Economic Achievement, New York 1969.

Mead, Margaret, Editor, Cultural Patterns and Technical Change, New York 1955.

Moore, B., Political Power and Social Theory, in: B. Moore, Thoughts on the Future of the Family, Cambridge, Massachusetts 1958.

Moore, W., Social Change, Englewood Cliffs, New Jersey 1963.

Parsons, T., The Social Structure of the Family, in: Ruth N. Asnhen (ed.), The Family: Its Functions and Destiny, New York 1959.

Safilios-Rothschild, Constantina, Quelques Aspects de la Modernisation Sociale Aux Etats-Unis et en Grece, in: Sociologie et Societes 1 (1969): pp. 23-37.

Schwarzweller, H. K. and J. F. Seggar, Kinship Involvement: A Factor in the Adjustment of Rural Migrants, in: Journal of Marriage and the Family 29 (1967), pp. 662-671.

Shanas, Ethel and G. F. Streib (eds.), Social Structure and the Family: Generational Relations, Englewood Cliffs, New Jersey 1965.

Singer, M., The Indian Joint Family in Modern Industry, in: M. Singer and B. S. Cohn (eds.), Structure and Change in Indian Society, Chicago 1968.

Smelzer, N., The Modernization of Social Relations, in: M. Weiner (ed.), Modernization, New York 1966.

Straus, M. A., Westernization, Insecurity, and Sinhalese Social Structure, in: International Journal of Social Psychiatry 12 (1966), pp. 130-138.

——, Communication, Creativity, and Problem Solving Ability of Middle- and Working-Class Families in Three Societies, in: American Journal of Sociology 73 (1968), pp. 417-430. Reprinted in M. B. Sussman (ed.), Sourcebook in Marriage and the Family, Third Edition, Boston 1968.

——, Social Class and Farm-City Differences in Interaction with Kin in Relation to Societal Modernization, in: Rural Sociology 34 (1969a), pp. 476-495.

——, Adolescent-Parent Conflict in Bombay and Minneapolis in Relation to Social Class and Family Roles, Paper presented at the annual meeting of the American Sociological Association, San Francisco 1969b.

——, Methodology of a Laboratory Experimental Study of Families in Three Societies, in: R. Hill and René König (eds.), Families East and West, Paris 1970.

——, Social Class and Sex Differences in Socialization for Problem Solving in Bombay, San Juan, and Minneapolis, pp. 282-301 in Joan Aldous et al. (eds.), Family Problem Solving. Hindsdale, Illinois: Dryden Press, 1971.

Strodtbeck, F. L., Family Interaction, Values, and Achievement, in: D. C. McClelland et al., Talent and Society, New York 1958.

Stuckert, R. P., Occupational Mobility and Family Relationships, in: Social Forces 41 (1962), pp. 301-307. Also reprinted in N. W. Bell and E. F. Vogel (eds.), A Modern Introduction to the Family, New York 1968.

Sweetser, D. A., The Effect of Industrialization on Intergenerational Solidarity, in: Rural Sociology 31 (1966), 156-170.

Van Den Ban, A. W., Family Structure and Modernization, in: Journal of Marriage and the Family 29 (1967), pp. 771-773.

Vincent, C. E., Familia Spongia: The Adaptive Function, in: Journal of Marriage and the Family 28 (1966), pp. 29-36. Also reprinted in J. N. Edwards, Editor, The Family and Change, New York 1969.

Wilkening, E. A., A sociopsychological Approach to the Study of the Acceptance of Innovations in Farming, in: Rural Sociology 4 (1950), pp. 352-364.

Wilkening, E. A., J. B. Pinto, and J. Pastore, Role of the Extended Family in Migration and Adaptation in Brazil, in: Journal of Marriage and the Family 30 (1968), pp. 689-695.

Winch, R. F. and Rae Lesser Blumberg, Societal Complexity and Familial Organization, in: R. F. Winch and Louise Wolf Goodman (eds.), Selected Studies in Marriage and the Family, New York 1968.

Young, F. W. and Ruth C. Young, Individual Commitment to Industrialization in Rural Mexico, in: American Journal of Sociology 71 (1966), pp. 373-383.

——, The Differentiation of Family Structure in Rural Mexico, in: Journal of Marriage and the Family 30 (1968), pp. 154-161.

Zetterberg, H. L., On Theory and Verification in Sociology, Totowa, New Jersey 1965.

The dialectic of family and community in the social history of Hutterites

The Hutterites are frequently seen as a uniquely cohesive community with few, if any, conflicts. Peter's paper explores the credibility of this assumption and rejects it. Through the use of historical documents on the Hutterite colonies, he demonstrates the existence of conflict between community principles and family commitments. Five historical periods illustrative of the relative dominance of the community of goods over family priorities, and vice versa, are discussed in considerable detail. This conflict, in Peter's description, is an excellent example of the struggles of a relatively homogeneous and traditional subculture with the "external" forces of modernization. These external forces, however, do not explain the basic internal conflict of family versus community ties, and the cyclical nature of these ties. Internal changes are associated instead with the degree of commitment to the Hutterite religious ideology. When this commitment recedes, identification with the family and its autonomous functions increases. As the commitment to the religious ideology increases, community principles once again dominate colony life.

The relative success of Hutterite communes compared to other communal experiments through history, not to mention the relative stability and change of subcultures in general, is of considerable interest. It has been argued that the success of the Hutterites is due to several factors, including ideological commitment, elected rather than charismatic leadership, financial stability, insulation and isolation from external influence (if necessary, the Hutterites fled from the country if opposition became oppressive), explicit goals in the socialization of children, and the regulation of the size of each colony. Peter has emphasized the fundamental role of ideological commitment. Other factors, however, are obviously also important.

It may be noted that Peter has not made clear how he identified the community and family historical periods. However, upon reading the manuscript it becomes apparent that he relies on the general conditions dominant in the Hutterite colony during the period. Without further evidence, it is difficult to trace the transition to a particular year.

The relative persistence of subcultural, contracultural (groups which reject the values of larger society) and utopian family forms within North American society will be considered in greater detail in Chapter nine.

The dialectic of family and community in the social history of Hutterites

Karl Peter

The Problem

The common sociological assessment of the Hutterite community is that of a highly integrated Gemeinschaft (community of goods) having great cohesive powers, exemplified in its religious-ideological system, its monolithic social and economic structure, its economic independence, and its ability to maintain social and cultural distance from its host society.

Considering the visible structural unity of a Hutterite community, supplemented by the highly effective social controls which induce members to remain in their communities, and considering further the seemingly successful resistance of Hutterites against forces of acculturation throughout their history, the conclusion that the Hutterite communities are structurally, functionally and ideologi-cally highly integrated seems to be inescapable. Shu-Ching Lee (1970), Deets (1939), Peters (1965), Gross (1965), and Eaton and Weil (1953) each emphasize the cohesion among the Hutterites.

Hostetler and Huntington (1967) identify external disruptive forces affecting Hutterite communities, such as war and persecution, neighboring practices, land restrictions, public education and competing religious revival or renewal groups. Internal disruptive forces include leadership failure and defection. Their origins are said to lie in individual inadequacies, in "poor" leaders or "weak" family lines. Although the authors recognize that communities which appear "to be cohesive and well-managed to the outside may actually be suffering from chronic internal troubles" (Hostetler and Huntington, 1967: 91–105) they fail to offer any systematic

Karl Peter, Ph.D., is Associate Professor of Sociology, Simon Fraser University, Vancouver, British Columbia.
This article was specially written for this book.

social structural or dynamic source of such internal conflict, apart from the observation that cleavages in communities tend to run along family lines.

In an earlier paper (Peter, 1971), I argued that what appears to be a smoothly integrated, highly cohesive Hutterite community is in fact a highly dynamic constellation of social forces and counterforces resting on a precarious basis of continuous success in order to survive. The unrelenting and enormous population increase of Hutterites, the pressing need for adequate means of motivation and successful reward of its membership, the maximization of production and the changing division of labor, the maintenance of restrictions on consumption, and the continuous pressure to finance its fantastic growth patterns are suggestive of the dynamic system of interaction in Hutterite communities.

Researchers able to probe beyond the mere appearance of Hutterite unity and cohesion are able to see recurrent manifestations of strife and conflict generated within the system. The existence of communities which have broken away from the Hutterite church and the existence of groups who were excommunicated, or sought court settlements for the termination of internal struggles, provide the raw data for the hypothesis that social cohesion among Hutterites is problematic. While there is little disagreement among informed students of Hutterite communities concerning the existence of conflict and strife, there is disagreement as to whether the origin of conflict can be attributed to individual inadequacies, as Hostetler and Huntington (1967) suggest, or whether this conflict is of a social structural nature. This paper suggests that permanent and inherent sources of conflict may be attributed to the dialectical relationship between the Hutterite community of goods and the Hutterite family.

A preliminary look at historical data shows the following: from 1535, when the Hutterite sect was founded, to the present time, a total span of 437 years, the Hutterite community moved through five phases, alternating between the dominance of the family by the community and the dominance of the community by the family. A graphic presentation of these phases is found in figure 1.

In its first phase, which lasted for about 150 years, the Guetergemeinschaft (community of goods) dominated the family. For the next eighty-five years the family became the dominant structure. In the year 1761 the community of goods was revived, lasting for only fifty-six years. From 1819 to 1860 the family again dominated, only to be replaced by a second revival of the community of goods in 1861, lasting up to the present time.

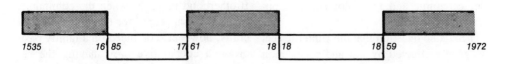

1535   16 85   17 61   18 18   18 59   1972

Figure 1 The alternation of the Hutterite community of goods and the Hutterite family. Shaded periods designate the dominance of the community of goods. Light periods designate the dominance of the family.

These preliminary observations on the alternation of community and family in the Hutterite social system point to some recurrent and persistent social processes operating within the system independent of time, physical environment and the host society. It is the specific aim of this paper to analyze these processes and to formulate their principles in dynamic forms.

The terms "Hutterite community of goods" and "Hutterite family" are used in this paper to stand for primary groups which are engaged in a struggle over the control of property and labor relations, consumption and production, child socialization and mate selection. The actual and recurrent forms of struggle between the Hutterite community and the Hutterite family are denoted by the term "dialectic". The Hutterite "religious ideology" refers to a set of legitimate ideas favoring the communal control of the above-mentioned practices.

The elimination of spurious factors

To demonstrate that a dialectical relationship between the Hutterite community and the Hutterite family can in fact account for the successive historical change in dominance of one by the other depends first on the elimination of alternate factors of explanation. The following inquiry concerns itself with those factors most often associated with patterns of change in sectarian groups: war, persecution, economic and technological development and growth.

There is no question that the Hutterite sect was greatly affected by war and persecution throughout its history. The migratory route from Germany to Moravia, Hungary, Romania, Russia, the United States and finally Canada was initiated in every case by warfare or persecution or both. Some historians have suggested that the disappearance of the community of goods in 1685 might have been due to the incessant warfare raging in the countryside at that time, which made it impossible for Hutterites to keep their communal storage places and eating facilities. While this is true to some extent, Hutterites in the years following 1547 survived much more extensive and more cruel forms of warfare and persecution than those which prevailed about 1685. Moreover when the sect gave up its community of goods a second time, about 1818, warfare and persecution were not in evidence. If the disappearance of the community of goods at one time is associated with war and persecution and at another time it is not, and if severe forms of persecution and warfare at a third period of time are associated with the retention of the community of goods, it would seem that war and persecution are neither necessary nor sufficient conditions to account for the phenomenon in question. At best they are contributory factors.

Economic and technological changes occurring throughout Europe also had a great impact on Hutterite communities. The Industrial Revolution eliminated a great variety of crafts from the communities. Changing tastes and changing techniques in pottery, for example, one of the main crafts of Hutterites, had a noticeable effect on the entire Brotherhood in 1685, when the community of goods disappeared for the first time. The crafts, however, continued on a family basis or on a cooperative basis having the extended family at its core for the next eighty-five years. In 1817, when the community of goods disappeared for a second time, economic pressures again were not in evidence. The sect had a limited number of flourishing crafts capable of adequately supporting the entire community.

One of the more remarkable features of Hutterite history is the fact that during the dominance of the family from 1818 to 1859, most crafts died out. The communal experiments which began in 1859 took place within the framework of a community entirely oriented toward agriculture. Although there were agricultural precedents, because the sect had always maintained an agricultural base sufficient to fulfill its own material needs, the successful revival of the community of goods on the basis of agriculture demonstrates the adaptive qualities of the sect toward changing economic and technological conditions. If this is the case, the failure to adapt to changing economic and technological factors cannot be taken as a source of the alternative patterns between community and family.

Growth patterns followed by the restructuring of a group, as exemplified in a more complex hierarchy, and accompanied by centralization and specialization in structure and functions, cannot be taken as the source of the changes and fluctuations observed in Hutterite history because Hutterites never tried to form social structures beyond Gemeinschaft relations. Nor did they ever insist on territorial consolidation or on one particular host society. While growth, both in population and in wealth, has occurred and is particularly evident at the present time, such growth patterns did not lead to the emergence of more complex structures. As a matter of fact the division of labor in Hutterite communities today is much simpler than it was 450 years ago when Hutterites maintained a great variety of crafts. Those social structures beyond the boundaries of the individual communities, such as the "bishop's convention of preachers", were also kept structurally simple by dividing the whole population into three largely autonomous groups. The bishop's convention of each of these groups was able to maintain primary and face-to-face interaction of all preachers.

In summary, population growth was channelled into the multiplication of identical community structures, preventing the emergence of higher differentiated and specialized structures. War, persecution, technological changes and growth, singly or in combination, accordingly cannot be taken as causes of recurrent changes. Instead, they must be considered contributory factors which facilitated or inhibited the unfolding of contradictions internal to the structure of Hutterite communities.

The dialectic of community and family

Given the nature of German culture at the beginning of the sixteenth century, and given the selectively constructed religious ideology of Hutterites, only one social structure of a primary nature — the community — was of interest to Hutterites. Since their religious ideology strongly favored the communal living arrangement under general cultural conditions in which the family exercised authority over property ownership, child socialization and mate selection, Hutterites insisted on having these properties transferred in practice to the community. Notwithstanding their convictions, these relations in fact continued to be a prerogative of the family in all societies which played host to the Hutterite sect. In practice, therefore, there always was and there continues to be a visible alternative to the primary relations of the Hutterite community. The controversy between the family-oriented Mennonites and Amish on the one hand, and the community-oriented Hutterites on the other hand, emphasizes precisely this alternative. These sectarian groups, whose overall religious-ideological systems are so similar, are split on the question of whether the family or the community ought to control property, socialization and mate selection.

In the face of this historical controversy, Mennonites and Amish, supported by a family-oriented ideology, in fact always maintained family prerogatives of property, socialization and mate selection, while Hutterites, supported by a community-oriented ideology, alternated between family and community. It seems that the family-oriented ideology of Mennonites and Amish provided stability of relations in practice, while the community-oriented ideology proved to be inherently unstable in practice. It is therefore reasonable to assume at this time that the Hutterite community of goods depends to a high degree on the existence of a strong commitment to its religious ideology, which reinforces its communal characteristics, because the alternative of the family is always available. If this religious ideology is weakened and loses its grip on the members of the sect, the alternate structure of the community of goods, the family, becomes a practical possibility. Mennonites and Amish, in contrast, do not suffer from similar structural contradictions because their family-supporting religious ideology does not create tensions toward the creation of communal structures. It is also reasonable to assume that Hutterites living under family arrangements but having a communally-oriented re-

ligious ideology and undergoing experiences which strengthen the initially weak religious ideology attempt to move from their family arrangement to the creation of new communal structures. The dialectic between the Hutterite community and family, therefore, can be summarized in two more precisely defined hypotheses:

1) Hutterites having a communally-oriented religious ideology and living under communal arrangements have a tendency to transform their communal living into family living arrangements when the religious ideology loses its central significance and weakens.
2) Hutterites having a communally oriented religious ideology but living under family living arrangements, tend to transform their family living arrangements into communal living arrangements when the religious ideology attains greater significance.

A look at the data will explicate the conditions under which these contradictions will occur.

The first dialectic phase, 1535–1685.

Because the Hutterite community assumed the right to control property relations, production and consumption, child socialization and mate selection, the family was never mentioned in Hutterite writings nor in primary historical data. Hutterites spoke of marriage, not the family. Marriage was first a union of God with man and woman and secondly a union between man and woman. Marriages were arranged twice a year by the local preacher, who took great care that such worldly characteristics as love and affection did not interfere with the divine nature of marriage. Children were handed over to community nurses soon after birth and the mother was required only to nurse the child when necessary. Later, when the child was weaned, for which a definite time was set community-wide, the child was educated and cared for entirely by the community kindergarten or the school until it reached the age when it could enter the labor force of the community. No private property of any kind was allowed, neither for the individual nor the marriage partners. Man and wife throughout the day participated in work groups separated by sex. They were allowed to sleep together at night. These practices indicate that the control of the sex urge and procreation were the only functions granted to marriage partners. In addition, these communal practices in fact denied the emergence of parent-child relations other than adult-child relations characteristic of the community as a whole.

The sum total of these practices was the result of an overwhelming religious conversion-experience which originally propelled the founding members of the Hutterite sect. So strong were their convictions that nothing but an extreme type of the community of goods would save their souls that they practically abolished all family relations and allowed only the most primary husband-wife relations, something for which there is no biblical reference at all. Those parts of the Bible which provided the Hutterites with a communal model are extremely vague and refer only to a community of consumption. But the community of goods first instituted by Hutterites included an extreme form of a community of production, a community of consumption, and a community of primary social relations.

It is most interesting to note that with the passing of the founding generation, several

processes made themselves felt which began to contradict the early model considerably. In the first instance, the enormous level of conviction and sense of sacrifice which characterized the first generation could not be maintained when people were born into and socialized by the communities. Extensive recruitment of new members on other than religious criteria weakened the faith even further. Simultaneously with the weakening of religious convictions, family relations began to acquire more significance. The new emphasis on family relations occurred principally in three areas. Those masters of crafts or managers who had access to or control over the resources of the communities began to appropriate goods, materials or money for themselves, making their families the principal beneficiaries. By 1650 such practices had diffused to all individuals in the communities so that common consumption through redistribution became increasingly impossible, because goods were appropriated by individual families before they could reach the communal pool.

Coinciding with this trend was an ever-increasing readiness of parents to circumvent the austere environment of the kindergarten and the school. Parents would take their children home for longer periods and spoil them, so that on their return the school would experience difficulties with them. As the school replied to such deviant behavior with harsher and harsher measures, parents searched for ways and means to keep their children out of the school altogether. Those parents having authority in the communities were the first to use their power and influence to do so, only to initiate a trend which soon spread to all members, rendering the Hutterite school ineffective.

Mate selection posed an even greater problem. The preachers who were supposed to match marriage partners according to divine criteria found themselves unable to do so for their own sons and daughters, whose affections for certain partners were well known. Increasingly they were unable to deny to others what they could not deny to their own offspring. The matching ceremony, therefore, became a meaningless ritual justifying mate selections which were in reality made on the basis of affection.

The social dynamics created by a declining religious commitment to the community of goods, accompanied by an increasing family appropriation of goods and coinciding with an undermining of the socializing system, led to a progressive erosion of the community of goods and an increased reassertion of the family, which eventually absorbed all these functions when the last community of goods broke up in 1685.

To be sure, the community of goods did not disappear without a heroic struggle. Bishop Andreas Ehrenpreis fought for twenty years against the trend with all his powers of persuasion and exhortation. Earlier in the period the Hutterite bishops were strong enough to impose some sort of compulsory savings plan on all communities intended to protect the Brotherhood against war, plunder and famine. Severe restrictions of consumption were necessary to fulfill the saving goals. Since equality of access to common resources is easier to maintain under conditions of scarcity than of affluence, and since the savings plan absorbed the accumulated wealth of the communities entirely (except for working capital and capital needed for expansion), the absorption of profits by families was kept in check. After the exodus of Hutterites from Moravia to Hungary in 1622, the savings were spent in re-

building new communities and no new savings plan could be instituted after the rebuilding period ended. The final outcome, therefore, proved to be inescapable. War and persecution provided only the challenges, acting like snares for the spiritually and socially weakened communities and bringing them to fall.

It seems that these data do in fact support our first hypothesis. The structural design of the Hutterite community of goods by the over-zealous founding fathers was psychologically too demanding of parents and children alike. When the religious convictions moderated, as they had to moderate once children were born and raised in the communities, Hutterite parents and children were left in a state of psychological tension which drove them to reassert the traditional family prerogatives. The reassertion of the family could only be attained by weakening the community of goods, and while there is no evidence at all that the Hutterite membership willfully weakened their communities, the trend became irreversible when the economically and socially weakened communities failed to overcome the external challenges of the time.

The second dialectic phase, 1685–1761

Of the Hutterite communities in Hungary and Transylvania which discarded the community of goods in 1685, only five communities were able to maintain their religious ideology and consequently survived for the next seventy-five years. These communities were organized around the family as a basic unit, but maintained a number of community functions for which the families assumed responsibility. Each family had its private home and economic pursuits were a private affair. Property was held in the name of the family. The preacher was elected from the male population and his upkeep was provided by contributions from the various families. Schools were maintained on the same basis as the church. Welfare measures for widows and orphans likewise were provided by contributions of families. The individuals grew up in families and early as well as later socialization, apart from schooling, was predominately a family affair and certainly a family responsibility. Mate selection took place on the basis of individual choices channelled and modified by family preferences. All in all, none of the far-reaching and strict community prerogatives characteristic of the first phase were maintained during the second phase.

The simultaneous occurrence of two processes led to the re-establishment of the community of goods. First, religious persecution of these remaining Hutterite communities led to the conversion of most but not all Hutterites to the Catholic faith. Secondly, while this conversion progressed among Hutterites, the religious ideology of these same Hutterites was adopted by some recent Lutheran migrants from Carinthia. These people had been deported to Transylvania because of their Lutheran convictions. The key to the understanding of why the community of goods was revived by these former Lutherans and some of the original Hutterites lies in the self-selective mechanism by which an active, goal-oriented group was formed.

All of these Lutherans were converted and had voluntarily chosen the hardship of forced migration rather than religious acquiescence. They had lost all their friends, relatives and belongings in Carinthia. The Catholic authorities had given them ample time to make up their minds. They were kept in prison for four months and a simple recantation would have freed them and restored their property to them. While some did recant, those who were finally shipped off to Transylvania formed a group of strong-willed religious converts ready to suffer for their convictions. A further selection took place when the Lutheran officials in Transylvania (where the Lutheran religion was tolerated) demanded that the migrants take the oath of loyalty to the Austrian Crown. A small group refused to do so. They were punished and forcefully dispersed over the countryside.

Some of these Lutherans found work among the persecuted Hutterites and consequently came in contact with Hutterite religious ideas, to which they became strongly attracted. After a short while they consolidated into a group which was joined by some Hutterites who were ready to defy the authorities, and together they spontaneously reinstated a community of goods among themselves.

This self-selective mechanism distilled from a larger group of Lutheran converts and persecuted Hutterites those personality types which were the most committed religiously and most extreme. Or, in other words, the religious ideology of the newly-formed group was strengthened through a shrinking membership of two larger groups to their most orthodox members. For this orthodox membership, the community of goods as it had existed two hundred years earlier was the right model in the religious-psychological sense, and they proceeded to copy rigorously the old structures and the old customs. It is for this group of orthodox members that the processes in our second hypothesis seem to hold true.

The third dialectic phase, 1761–1818

In order to escape persecution the newly formed community of goods, which again called itself the Hutterian Brethren, first migrated to Wallachia and finally settled in Russia, northeast of Kiev. The community of goods began to flourish after the group reached Russia in 1770. Within a few years goods and monies lent to them were repaid. The various crafts proved to be extremely productive and profitable. The community became a showcase of success for peasants and nobility in the area and the members of the community earned a reputation for honesty, good work, cleanliness and morals.

In 1801 they were able to acquire Crown land and consequently set themselves up on even more favorable economic terms. This remarkable trend toward prosperity and independence, however, suddenly reversed itself. Within the next eighteen years the community of goods collapsed.

The assistant of the office of trustees for foreign settlers, Fadjeew, who was ordered to investigate the difficulties of the Hutterite community, reported in March 1818:

I noticed already at the beginning of my investigation that the root of the disunity of the Mennonites [the group was officially called Mennonites] was to be found in the contradiction between the principles that were supposed to govern this group and the real concrete social conditions characterized by the corruption of the brethren . . .
. . . I found that the rules of ethics and indestructible single-mindedness which the founders of the community regarded as a duty were not observed anymore. These duties were in full force and produced a rare example of unity between several dozen families as long as their

number was smaller, as long as they did not have their own land and as long as they had to divert some of their earnings to pay their local nobleman.
However, when the brethren began to occupy their present location which put them into possession of . . . good land and produced several other advantages for them, surplus was created within the group. Under conditions of an increasing population, several persons began to discover that it was possible to live by the work of others. Among the 50 families several began to neglect their duties and lived on the products of the diligent. At this time the tendency emerged to obtain private property and secure earnings of one's work to the advantage of one's own family . . . .

Another contemporary observer reported:

The masters which headed the various economic branches of the community demanded independence. Each of them withdrew from the common treasury and opened businesses of their own. They bought raw materials and sold the goods independently. Instead of handing over the revenues to the community, they just presented the invoices . . . the tendency to enjoy the good life . . . brought apathy, hostility, envy and dissatisfaction into the Gemeinschaft and step-by-step caused the disintegration of the group.

Hutterite reports written during this time indicate that the last founding fathers of the community of goods in 1761 died between 1800 and 1810. When the leadership of the community was transferred to members born and socialized in the system, "they had neither the loyalty, integrity nor the diligence to conduct the offices and duties with which they were entrusted."

The processes of disintegration which took 150 years to develop during the first phase were crammed into 57 years during the third phase. The loss of religious strength and conviction led to the weakening of community values and norms, and made it possible for the family to reassert itself.

The failure of the community to absorb accumulated wealth and allocate it for community purposes played a major role in the disintegrating processes, as it did during the first phase. When families were given the opportunity to compete for such wealth under conditions where they felt no religious restrictions to do so, the disappearance of the community of goods became inevitable again.

The fourth dialectic phase, 1818–1859

For several decades those Hutterite families who had abolished their community of goods in 1818 lived in considerable poverty and social disorganization, until in 1842 the Russian authorities allowed all Hutterite families to resettle close to some Mennonite villages, assigning about 175 acres of land to each family and providing some capital for a new start. The settlement quickly flourished, and three years later was able to repay the loan it had received. In 1846 the first group of families asked for permission to form a community of goods. When such permission was finally given in 1856 a complicated series of communal trials, some failures, some successful, began. Employing the same self-selective mechanism already observed among the persecuted "old" Hutterites, as well as the converted Lutherans in 1761, one group of Hutterite families after another got together, pooled their resources and instituted the community of goods. Those groups which failed eliminated those

members who socially, psychologically and religiously were unable to adapt to the conditions in the community of goods. As more communal trials followed, the whole population sorted itself out in such a way that only those people were left to carry on the community of goods who possessed the required dedication, enthusiasm and conviction to endure the restraints which the community of goods imposed on them. Three such groups distilled themselves out by such self-selective processes: the Dariusleut, the Lehrerleut and the Schmiedenleut. Those which failed, and those who never tried, came to be known as Praerieleut. When all four of these groups migrated to the United States between 1874 and 1879, the three former groups formed the nucleus of all North American Hutterite communities, while the Praerieleut were culturally and religiously absorbed by the larger society. Again a weakened religious ideology was strengthened and made central through the elimination of members until the orthodox remained. When only orthodox members were left in the group, the religious-psychological strains toward the retention of the community of goods was great enough to overcome their family attachments. This phase, therefore, shows a variation of the same fundamental processes outlined in our second hypothesis already found to be supported by the data of the first reestablishment of the community of goods in 1761.

The fifth dialectic phase, 1859 to the present

Before going into the analysis of the fifth dialectic phase between the Hutterite community and family, it is helpful to offer a tentative theory by which the alternation between the community of goods and the Hutterite family might be explained. At the same time, this theory can be applied to evaluate the community-family relations as they exist at the present time, allowing us to make an analysis of the structural sources of conflict in Hutterite communities.

The change from the community of goods to the family is characterized by the following conditions and processes:

1) The initial existence of a body of extremely committed converts to the Hutterite faith, or a body of orthodox members, creating a community of goods (in terms of consumption, production, property relations, education, socialization and mate selection) congruent with their religious convictions.
2) Extreme convictions are difficult to maintain after the first generation, leading to a contradiction between a moderate level of conviction and an extreme type of the community of goods.
3) With the further weakening of the religious ideology facilitated by the loss of charismatic leaders, incoming converts with weak commitments, or the increasing inadequacy of the socialization process, the contradictions between the religious convictions and communal structures and practices increase to a point at which family relations are more congruent with the real religious convictions of the membership than are communal relations.
4) The changeover from communal practices to family practices is facilitated by the absence of community goals (escape from persecution, growth, migrations, etc.) and is equally facilitated by the presence of economic surpluses, over which families increasingly gain control, until the community of goods is impossible to maintain.

The change from the family to the community of goods is characterized by the following conditions and processes:

1) The communal orientation of the Hutterite religious ideology accounts for a latent psychological contradiction for some members when these members live under family practices.
2) It is, however, impossible to induce group action in response to these psychological contradictions unless the membership shrinks through self-selective processes:
   a) from a heterogeneous membership (in attitudes, strength of religious convictions, etc.) to a homogeneous membership;
   b) corresponding with this development toward a homogeneous membership, social disunity changes into unity. The contradiction of religious convictions and social structure (communal ideology but family living arrangements) is removed when a sufficiently homogeneous group finally has the strength to act on its convictions and re-establish a community of goods.

If the first four points of this tentative theory are applied to an analysis of the present community of goods, the following picture emerges. The community of goods in force at the present time does not conform to the extreme models of 1535 and 1761, but is in fact much more sophisticated and balanced. The socialization of children is a responsibility divided between community and the family, thus avoiding the severe psychological effects of the early socialization practices. Mate selection is largely left to the individual, channelled by family preferences. The role of the community is confined to providing opportunities for meeting potential mates rather than determining the choice of the mate, as formerly practised. The restrictions on property ownership are somewhat relaxed, allowing for private possessions in the form of clothing, furniture, dishes, books and other personal belongings. This less extreme type of the community of goods largely avoids the contradictions from which the former extreme community of goods suffered, after the death of the first generation of orthodox believers.

In today's Hutterite community, a relatively low commitment to its communal religious ideology is congruent with a relatively moderate type of the community of goods. Furthermore, most Hutterite communities are extremely goal-oriented in terms of financing their expansion, necessitated by their enormous population increase. Such goals are of course considered legitimate. The financing of these new communities entirely absorbs the surplus created, and consequently inhibits families from gaining access to the surplus. A relatively simple division of labor aids the control of production and the collection of surplus by the community authorities.

The dialectic between family and community, however, has taken different forms. With less emphasis on the religious ideology as motivation to participate in the community, the motivational focus of the participating invidiual has shifted to social motivation, and social rewards in the form of status and role attainments in the community. The importance of the hierarchical order in Hutterite communities, the emphasis on even very small status differentiations, and the significance of the behavioral validations of status attainments in all aspects of the daily life of the communities, demonstrate the existence and the extent of this motivational system.

The Hutterite community and the Hutterite family participate in this motivational system by assuming the following functions. In the first instance, the community raises certain concrete status aspirations in Hutterite individuals as part of its general cultural motivation. In the second instance, the community proceeds to fulfill these status aspirations through a promotional system based on increased age and differentiated by sex. Since, however, the number of status positions in each community is limited, and since the high population increase always provides a surplus of status applicants, the communities must "branch out" to create new status positions with which to reward status applicants who come of age.

On the other hand, the nature of the status and role aspirations and the realization of these aspirations for any Hutterite individual depends largely on the size and the position of the individual's extended family. Status positions are distributed by the vote of all baptized male members, and since family members tend to vote for each other, families with the most votes can favor their members to the exclusion of other families. There are only sixteen family lines among Hutterites and most communities are composed of members from one to five families. Various voting blocks are therefore possible, raising the possibility of an unequal status distribution for different families.

As long as a community is able to "branch out" on schedule and thus create new status positions for all applicants, regardless of family origin, conflicts will be restricted to minor squabbles. If, on the other hand, a community cannot branch out for any reason, status competition becomes intense. The respective families become the agents and focus of such competition. It is at this point that community interests and family interests begin to contradict each other.

It is of course possible that status competition leaves the community of goods intact for a long time, thus giving the outward appearance of unity and cohesion, when in effect intense family rivalries for status exist. However, when family conflicts reach a point where communication breaks down permanently, and renders the central authority in the organization and co-ordination of production and consumption ineffective because of lack of communication and compliance, the community enters a process of progressive disintegration. By this time, it usually is in considerable financial difficulties, and if Hutterite bishops and other communities do not interfere financially and organizationally, the community of goods might break up. Up until the present time, however, the financial and organizational trusteeship of a troubled community by the bishop and his advisors has prevented the total breakup of a community. There are nevertheless a few communities which have reached a chronic state of disintegration.

In summary, the dialectic fifth phase between the Hutterite community and Hutterite family is characterized by a more balanced model of the community of goods, which successfully avoids the contradictions of the former community models. At the same time, the Hutterite family is projected into a powerful position never before attained. This powerful position came about as the result of a shift in motivation from the religious-ideological to social roles and statuses, the attainment of which are largely controlled by the family in proportion to its own position of influence in the community.

The failure of communities to create an adequate supply of roles and statuses for that part of the population which comes of age intensifies family rivalries over such roles and statuses, and eventually leads families to undermine, sabotage or ignore the co-ordinating authority of the community, thus initiating a trend toward community disintegration, very much in the same way as disintegration has occurred during phases one and three of Hutterite social history.[1]

NOTES

1 A more elaborate treatment of these historical fluctuations may be found in Peter (1967).

REFERENCES

Deets, Lee E.
   1939 The Hutterites: A Study in Social Cohesion. Gettysburg, Pennsylvania: Time and News Publishing Co.
Eaton, Joseph W. and Robert J. Weil
   1953 Culture and Mental Disorder. New York: Free Press of Glencoe.
Gross, Paul
   1965 The Hutterite Way. Saskatoon: Freeman Publishing Co.
Hostetler, John A. and Gertrude Ender Huntington

   1967 The Hutterites in North America. New York: Holt, Rinehart, and Winston.
Lee, Shu-Ching
   1970 "Group Cohesion and the Hutterian Colony" in Tamotsu Shibutani (editor), Human Nature and Collective Behavior. Englewood Cliffs, New Jersey: Prentice-Hall.
Peter, Karl
   1967 Factors of Social Change and Social Dynamics in the Communal Settlements of Hutterites, 1527-1967. Unpublished

Doctoral Dissertation, University of
Alberta, Edmonton, Alberta.
1971 "The dynamics of open social systems",
in James A. Gallagher and Ronald D.
Lambert (editors), Social Process and

Institution: The Canadian Case, Toronto:
Holt, Rinehart and Winston.
Peters, Victor
1965 All Things Common. Minneapolis:
University of Minnesota Press.

Changing family patterns among Ukrainian-Canadians in Alberta

In Chapter three, some fifteen ethnic groups were identified, four of which were discussed in detail. It was suggested that the ideal-typical family life style among English Canadians may well be the modal family life style among other ethnic groups as well (except among French Canadians). Even so, existing differences are relatively visible dimensions of community life (eg., Jewish and Ukrainian holidays). There is considerable support, governmental and otherwise, for the maintenance of multi-culturalism. The melting pot hypothesis generally assumed to be applicable to the United States is less appropriate for the Canadian scene because of the emphasis in this country on ethnic celebrations and gatherings, food and diet traditions, certain ritualistic practices in the home, and certain ceremonies. Many Canadians participate in these celebrations and have come to enjoy several "ethnic" foods. In essence, these practices reinforce multi-culturalism. The vitality of these differences, of course, depends on their continued social support.

Nevertheless, there is marked change in marriage and family life over time within many ethnic groups in Canada. These changes are fundamentally associated with culture contact among people with different values and practices. Children of first generation parents are systematically exposed to values and practices that differ widely from those of their parents. In view of the identity struggles of youth and the need for peer group support, some degree of cultural assimilation is inevitable. These processes are particularly intense where there are very visible majority patterns. Generational change can be expected in industrializing society; urbanism and the industrial complex seem to promote a convergent and standardizing trend in both urban and rural areas — gross diversity is minimized. Some have argued that the technological characteristics of Western society lead to the development of age cohort world views which are distinct in content and commitment from those of the cohort born only one year before. Whether these views are so distinct remains undemonstrated. It is clear, however, that differences in family life style can be expected over time.

In this particular study of Ukrainian-Canadians, Hobart compares marriage and family patterns among first and third generation Ukrainians in Alberta. The patterns of the first generation closely reflect those of their native country. Those of the third generation, in contrast, closely approximate those of the ideal-typical English Canadian family: small families, maternal employment, egalitarianism in marital and parent-child relationships, values supportive of divorce and intermarriage, and weaker kin orientation. Hobart found that these patterns occur regardless of whether one lives in rural or urban areas. In order to reduce the length of this paper, the tables have been removed.

Though this study is extremely interesting and offers insight into the values of three generations, a number of questions should be kept in mind by the reader. First, without comparing these results with those of other studies of ethnic groups, it is impossible to conclude that Ukrainian-Canadians have unique characteristics. Perhaps all immigrant groups have changed in similar ways. Second, the findings are frequently confusing and attempts to explain the ambiguities are inadequate. The discussion of intermarriage, for example, cannot be definitive without a specific test of the assumptions made by Hobart. The same is true of the discussion of family roles. The findings are not expected and indeed remain confusing, Hobart's explanations notwithstanding. The responses to two measures of familism are perhaps the most confusing part of the study. Third generation respondents gave a clearly more traditional response than did first generation respondents.

Therefore, even though the general trends are as expected, the study does not provide adequate insight into the relative persistence of certain traditional Ukrainian values. Further research is necessary.

Changing family patterns among Ukrainian-Canadians in Alberta

Charles W. Hobart

This paper presents information on the family life of a sample of Ukrainian-Canadians in Alberta. The concern is primarily with the size of families, their living arrangements, the respective roles of husbands and wives, and the ways in which children are raised in these families. These data are further analyzed in terms of various sub-groupings of the sample: by sex, generation, social class, education, assimilation to Canadian life, and rural-urban residence. In each case the pattern for the sample as a

Charles W. Hobart, Ph.D., is Professor of Sociology, University of Alberta, Edmonton, Alberta.
This paper was specially written for this book.

whole is described and then broken down into the individual patterns characteristic of the various sub-groupings.

Review of literature on Ukrainian family patterns in Canada

Numerous publications are to be found dealing with Ukrainians in Canada; however, only a minute portion of this literature is relevant to this paper. Most of the literature is published in Ukrainian, much of it in the form of social histories, and much of it predictably glorifies the Ukrainian Homeland and Ukrainian contributions to Canadian Society.

The literature in English falls into four broad categories. There are collections of bibliographies of Ukrainian pioneers (Editorial Committee in Edmonton, 1970), accounts of pioneer settlements in various districts (Panchuk, 1971), autobiographies (Romaniuk, 1954), summaries of Canadian Census data (Hunchak, 1945), and social histories of Ukrainians in Canada, some of which include discussion of assimilation processes (Lysenko, 1954; Marunchak, 1970; Young, 1931; Yuzyk, 1953, 1967). Only the Young and Lysenko works merit further mention.

Young's work, which is entitled *A Study in Assimilation*, has a number of scattered references to high birth rates, high urban juvenile delinquency rates, breakdown in parental authority and the marginality of children among Ukrainian Canadians. His data was derived primarily from informal interviewing of "leaders" in various communities having substantial Ukrainian populations and a small number of questionnaire returns obtained through a non-random sampling process.

The Lysenko volume includes a chapter on "Assimilation in Family Life Through the Generations". As in the Young volume, data were obtained from informal leaders and informed observers in a few communities having large Ukrainian settlements. The bulk of the discussion deals with various aspects of parent-child differences, disagreements, and conflicts. There is material on differences in the experiences between these generations, differences in values, differences in philosophy (the old were essentially pessimistic, believing that optimism invited retribution from fate; the young were optimistic and hopeful of the future).

There have been no other studies, either prior to the 1964 year in which the data herein reported were collected or in the eight years since then, based on comprehensive survey research data which provided a detailed statistical picture of changing family patterns of Ukrainian-Canadians in Alberta.

The sample

The sample consisted of 809 adults of Ukrainian ethnic origin who were interviewed in Alberta between June, 1963, and October, 1964. Forty-nine percent of the sample are men and 51 percent are women. Sixty-four percent of those interviewed are from three small rural communities and farms in the vicinity of these communities. The remainder of the sample lived in Edmonton. The Edmonton sample was drawn from six voter registration districts selected to include a cross-section of the Ukrainian population in terms of density of Ukrainians, social class, age of the district, etc. This was a systematic sample of those on the voter lists having Ukrainian (or shortened Ukrainian) names. There was a certain amount of error resulting from this procedure — Poles and Russians were occasionally misidentified as Ukrainians. However, it was the most feasible procedure available since there exists no list of Ukrainians in Edmonton, and the size of the research budget did not permit recourse to more precise area probability sampling procedures. The adequacy of the sampling procedure may also be questioned because a certain proportion of those on the sample list had moved without leaving a forwarding address, and because of more frequent refusals to be interviewed by the sample members in Edmonton.

The interview schedule was lengthy, consisting of over 200 items. Accordingly, it is not possible to describe it in detail here. Many aspects of family and personal history, participation attitudes and value identifications were explored. Each interview took between an hour and a half and three or more hours. The rapport with interviewees was generally quite good, though somewhat better in rural areas than it was in Edmonton. Interviewers were usually invited to share refreshments by their subjects. One lonely elderly lady insisted that the interviewer accept a gift as an expression of her gratitude for the conversation. Well over half of the interviews were conducted in the Ukrainian language, and a standard translation was provided to each of the interviewers. They were instructed to refrain from modifying this translation except as necessary to clarify the meaning of questions to the interviewees. Modifications were necessary rather often because of the dialect and educational differences in sample members.

The interviewing was done by five Ukrainian-Canadian university students, three females and two males, all of whom were fluent in their mother tongue. After each interview was completed it was checked twice, to make sure that there were no inadvertent omissions. The information in the schedule was then coded for punching on IBM cards, and subsequent computer analysis.

Results

Family size and residential patterns

Most respondents came from large families. Fourteen percent, for example, came from families with ten or more children. There are sizable differences between different age groups. Respondents from families of seven or more children constituted 37 percent of those under thirty-five years of age, 45 percent of those thirty-five to forty-nine years old, and nearly 50 percent of those over fifty years of age. The largest families were reported by respondents born in Canada rather than the Ukraine.

In families of six or more children 36 percent come from families born in the Ukraine, compared to 52 percent of those born in Canada of Ukrainian-born parents, and only 12 percent of those born in Canada to Canadian-born parents. This pattern makes sense. In comparison with the homeland areas, the manpower needs of the new settlement areas were large and the conditions for raising large families were favorable, since plenty of good land was rather easy to obtain. The result was that the first generation of settlers had many children, significantly more than those who had lived most of their lives in the old country. The third generation, of course, came from families in which Canadian influences have been strong, resulting in a sharp decline in family size. The data also shows that city residence and a high level of education and employment were associated with coming from small families.

Seventy-five percent of the sample members (604 out of 809) were married, 13 percent (106 subjects) were single, 10 percent were widowed, and 2 percent were separated or divorced. There is little point in reporting in detail the number of children born to the married respondents, since at least one third may well have more children before their families reach maximum size. The modal number of children reported was four, and only twenty-one subjects reported having ten or more children. The ideal number of children reported by the sample members is a more significant figure, since it is probably less likely to change than is the actual number of children in the family. The most frequent ideal number, mentioned by 40 percent of the respondents, was four children. Women preferred more children than men, regardless of age, mentioning one child more, on the average, than men. Among persons preferring five or more children, 37 percent are fifty years of age or more, whereas only 14 percent of those under the age of thirty-five want this many children. The difference is greater for women than for men.

When subjects are grouped by generation the same pattern is found. Thirty-five percent of those born in the Ukraine preferred five or more children, as compared with 30 percent of those born in Canada of Ukrainian-born parents, and 11 percent of those born here of Canadian-born parents.

Among other characteristics of subjects, the two which are most strongly associated with family size preferences are rural-urban residence and the occupation of the husband.

Forty-one percent of the subjects who lived in Edmonton said three or less was the ideal number of children, whereas only 18 percent of those living outside of the city did so. One reason for this pattern is that two thirds of those over sixty years of age lived outside of the city, and elderly people prefer more children, as we have seen.

Subjects were divided into four categories in terms of husband's occupation: executives, proprietors, and major and minor professionals; clerical, sales and skilled manual workers; semi-skilled and unskilled workers; and farmers. The latter two groups were somewhat older than average, but the first two were quite comparable, and the first was in fact the youngest in composition. Accordingly it is surprising to find that 45 percent of the men in executive and professional occupations preferred five or more children, as compared with 43 percent of the farmers, 18 percent of the white collar and skilled workers, and 12 percent of the semi-skilled and unskilled workers. The wives of the professional men did not share their husbands' enthusiasm for many children: only 14 percent of the wives, as compared with 45 percent of their husbands, wanted five or more children. Wives of the farmers were in closest agreement with their husbands, since 41 percent of this group wanted large families. Twenty-seven percent of the middle class women and 14 percent of the lower class women wanted five or more children.

Educated women wanted fewer children, but for men there is no significant relationship. Both husbands and wives in upwardly mobile families wanted fewer children than those not upwardly mobile. This finding is not in contradiction with that discussed in the preceding paragraph, because very few of these families had moved into the professional occupations in which men hoped for large families. Wishing for large families is negatively associated with assimilation to Canadian society (defined as favorability toward intermarriage, name changing, and discarding traditional Ukrainian customs).

When subjects were asked to respond to the statement, "In my marriage I want my children to be planned with the aid of birth control devices," about one fourth failed to respond. Most non-respondents were over fifty years of age (73 percent) and they were divided equally by sex. Of those who did respond, 45 percent agreed (8 percent "agreed strongly"). There were no sex differences in those favoring birth control. However, there were sizable differences by age. Contraception was favored by 58 percent of those under thirty-five, 44 percent of those aged thirty-five to fifty, and 30 percent of those aged fifty or more. These differentials are more extreme when the sample members are classified by generation of Canadian residence. Use of birth control devices was favored by 25 percent of those Ukrainian-born, 49 percent of the second generation, and 57 percent of the third generation immigrants.

The data on home ownership reveal that three out of every four owned the homes in which they lived. An equal number lived with their mates (74 percent) and 11 percent lived alone. Most of the latter were women over fifty years of age. Renting was found to be more characteristic of third generation than of first or second generation Ukrainians, of urban than of rural and village residents, of those favoring assimilation to Canadian society rather than non-assimilation, of those caring little about the perpetuation of Ukrainian traditions, of those with higher educational attainments, and of non-farmers. The only major exception is

that ownership is more characteristic of the highest occupational class than of the other two (non-farm) occupational classes.

Intermarriage

Four items in the interview schedule concern intermarriage between Ukrainians and non-Ukrainians. One relates to intermarriage of the respondent himself, one to intermarriage among his brothers or sisters, one to intermarriage among his offspring, and one to his attitudes toward intermarriage. Twelve percent of the sample were married to non-Ukrainians. Slightly over one third of the sample (36 percent) had intermarried siblings and one third had children who had intermarried, assuming that only those aged forty and over may have married offspring. In response to the question, "Do you think that intermarriage between Ukrainians and non-Ukrainians should be discouraged?" 30 percent of the sample said yes and 70 percent of the sample said no.

Those items dealing with intermarriage were cross tabulated with eleven other characteristics. Most of the relationships which were found are consistent and clear. Age, farming occupation, favoring Ukrainian culture, and political chauvinism are all inversely associated with being intermarried and with favoring intermarriage. Education, generation of Canadian residence, and social mobility, in contrast, are directly associated with being intermarried and favoring intermarriage. Urban residents are more often intermarried but more often oppose intermarriage, and both their siblings and their offspring are less often intermarried. The only explanation for this curious pattern appears to be that Ukrainian nationalistic sentiments are stronger in the city than in the country. Social class, indexed by education and occupation, is another curious variable since, contrary to expectation, the highest class men are *less* frequently intermarried than are the other non-farming classes, but they *favor* intermarriage more than lower class men. Age, involvement in farming, and absence of particular ideological involvement are inversely associated with sibling intermarriage and directly associated with offspring intermarriage. The oldest subjects less often have siblings who have intermarried than do middle-aged subjects, but they have the highest proportion of married offspring, and accordingly of intermarried offspring.

Many of the inconsistencies in the above patterns of relationships are explainable by the association between age and particular characteristics. The relevant considerations are (1) older subjects have more brothers and sisters (2) who have more often passed marriage age, and (3) they more often have children who have reached marriage age than do younger subjects. These appear to account for the facts that subjects who oppose assimilation, who are politically chauvinistic, and who favor Ukrainian culture, more often have siblings who are intermarried than do subjects who favor assimilation, are not chauvinistic, and are not enthusiasts of Ukrainian culture.

Family roles

Included in the 809 subjects who were interviewed were 106 single people, 99 members of families broken by death or separation, and 604 members of unbroken families. Information was collected on the work experience of the wives in these families, whether it was the husband or the wife in the family who was interviewed.

Most wives did not have paid employment: only 38 percent of the wives in the 362 non-farm families worked, 29 percent full-time and 9 percent part-time. It may be noted that this pattern is similar to the percent of women employed in Canada as a whole. Among the farm families 8 percent of the wives worked full-time at paying jobs and 2 percent worked at part-time jobs. There are interesting variations between social classes in the frequency with which wives work. The higher the social class level of husbands, the more wives work, full or part-time. Over half of the women in the executive-professional families work, 42 percent full-time and 11 percent part-time, compared with one-third of the women in the middle and lower class families (about 23 percent full-time and 10 percent part-time in both cases). A rather high proportion of women work at occupations demanding considerable training and/or providing rather pleasant working conditions. Almost half (43 percent) of the wives work as lesser professionals (36 percent) or operators of small businesses or semi-professionals (7 percent). Twenty percent work as clerical and sales workers, technicians, or skilled manual workers, and only 37 percent work as semi-skilled or unskilled workers. Tabulation of the skill level of the wife's job classified by the class level of her husband's employment shows that the highest proportion of women in the executive-professional jobs are married to men in similar kinds of jobs. Similarly, the highest proportion of women in the second class of jobs are married to second occupation class men. The same pattern is evident in the lower class.

Two items in the interview schedule concerned attitudes toward women working: "Do you think it's a good thing for a woman to have a paying job after she is married? . . . Why?''; and ''In my marriage I want the wife to share in the financial support of the family as much as she is able.'' There is strong agreement that the wife should ''share in the financial support of the family as much as she is able''; 83 percent of the 704 subjects who responded to this item agreed or agreed strongly with it. In response to the more specific second question that it would be a good thing for the wife to have a paying job, only 40 percent of the total sample agreed and 59 percent disagreed. Women more frequently than men believe that women should help in the financial support of the family, and the younger subjects believe this less frequently than the older subjects, for both male and female respondents.

Some interesting patterns in the responses of subjects to these items emerge when they are tabulated by various characteristics of the respondents. More assimilationist and better educated subjects tended to agree that it is a ''good thing for a woman to have a paying job after she is married'' but to disagree with the statement that she should share in the financial support of the family. Similarly there was a tendency for third generation subjects to agree with the first statement and to disagree with the second statement. It appears that some feel there may be values for the woman in working after she is married, but these should not include family support. The latter is apparently felt, increasingly, to be solely the husband's responsibility at the same time that for the wife to work is becoming increasingly acceptable. Upper social class men and upwardly mobile men tended with disproportionate frequency to say that women should not contribute to the financial support of the family, despite the fact that their wives do work with greater frequency

than do wives in any other social class group. Both men and women apparently agree that the money earned by women should be under their own control.

The reasons which subjects gave why women should or should not work are instructive. The most frequent reason for not working, mentioned by half of the sample, was that it was her duty to stay at home and raise the children. Five percent said that it was the husband's sole responsibility to support the family. The most frequent reason given why the wife should work, mentioned by 24 percent of the sample, was that she should help to support the family financially. Women more often tend to emphasize the need to help in the financial support of the family, and the men tend to emphasize her responsibility for raising the children. Younger men tended to emphasize their responsibility for supporting their families, and also to see working wives as posing an unemployment threat.

Some insight into the role relationships of husbands and wives in the sample may be gained from items dealing with the division of labor and authority between husband and wife, and the claims which the family has upon each of them and which they have upon each other. The three items which deal with division of authority or relative dominance of husband and wife include: ''In my marriage I want the husband alone to make the important decisions for his family''; ''In my marriage I want the husband and the wife to have an equal voice in making family decisions''; ''In my marriage I want the wife to gracefully accept whatever money the husband feels he can give her.'' The responses to the first two items are quite consistent: 82 percent of the respondents object to the husband's making the important decisions for his family alone, and 98 percent are in favor of an equal voice in decision-making for the husband and the wife. However, these findings do not fit with the expression of 84 percent of the sample that the wife *should* gracefully accept whatever money the husband feels he can give her. The tradition of male dominance persists in certain respects, despite the relative egalitarianism of Canadian society. It appears that the "equal voice of the wife" is expected to be a discreet voice when financial matters are under discussion.

There are a number of age-sex differences in the responses to these items. With respect to the first item, which stated that the husband alone should make the important decisions, men agreed slightly more often than did women, and older subjects agreed more often than did younger subjects. This pattern is reversed for the second item: younger subjects and female subjects more frequently expressed strong agreement than did older and male subjects. With respect to the third item, dealing with the wife's acceptance of her husband's financial decisions, there were no differences in the pattern of responses of men and women, but there were age differences. Older and younger subjects more frequently expressed agreement than did the middle aged group. These differences were sharper for women than for men.

It appears from these responses that women and young people are somewhat more egalitarian in their sex role conceptions than are men, but the differences are not extreme. Middle aged women — who are characterized neither by the traditional orientation of the older women, nor by what we suggest may be the timidity of the younger women — are more insistent on having a voice in financial affairs. However, about three fourths of this group appear to accept masculine judgement.

An egalitarian approach to these marital role issues is associated with a number of other characteristics of respondents. There are three predominant patterns. Favoring acculturation to Canadian society is associated with wanting an equal voice for husband and wife in making family decisions and with not wanting the husband alone to make the decisions. Third generation respondents, in contrast to others, most often held egalitarian attitudes as indexed by all three items. Level of educational attainment and of occupational placement both serve as rough indices of social class position and show that higher class *men* are more egalitarian than lower class men. However, women who had an average level education and who were married to men in the middle occupational class tended, significantly more often than either the lower or the higher class women, to agree that women should accept gracefully whatever the husband feels he can give her. Thus, there is some tendency for the old patriarchal orientation to be perpetuated somewhat among middle class wives.

We have seen that four fifths of the sample members felt it would be a good thing for wives to "share in the financial support of the family," but only two fifths felt it would be a "good thing for a woman to have a paying job after she is married." About nine tenths of the respondents (88 percent) agreed with the item, "In my marriage I want an equal sharing of housework if both husband and wife have jobs outside the home." Men agreed with the statement only slightly less frequently than did women (86 percent and 90 percent).

Three items in the questionnaire dealt with the relative claims of family and of work on the time and energy of the husband: "In my marriage I want the wife to accept the fact that the husband will devote most of his time to getting ahead and becoming a success"; "I want the kind of marriage in which the family has first claim on the husband's time, even if it interferes with his getting ahead in the world"; and "In my marriage I want the wife to be responsible for training our children so that the husband can concentrate on getting ahead." The responses to these items are not completely consistent. Although 85 percent wanted the husband to devote most of his time to getting ahead, 53 percent wanted him to share child training responsibility with his wife, and 44 percent wanted the family to have first claim on the husband's time, even at the price of interference with his advancement. Clearly, some 30 percent of the sample wanted both success at the price of family life *and* close family life at the price of success.

The responses to each of these items show important age-sex differences. There were no sex differences between the responses of subjects to the first item (husband will devote most of his time to getting ahead), but younger subjects of both sexes were more likely to disagree with the item. Older women agreed with the second item (family has first claim on the husband's time) almost twice as often (62 percent and 34 percent) as the younger women, and they also agreed with it more often than the older men. Younger women, on the other hand, disagreed with it more frequently than did younger men, the proportions being 66 percent and 56 percent. There were no differences in responses by sex to the third item (wife responsible for training children) but among both men and women older subjects agreed with the statement more than twice as

often as did the younger subjects, the proportions being 74 and 31 percent. What this pattern of responses suggests is an increase in the importance of familism among younger subjects, seen especially in the first and third items. The second item shows that the contradictory responses are most characteristic of older women and least characteristic of younger women. Younger people of both sexes are least eager to have the husband devote himself solely to getting ahead, and they seem most aware of the costs to family solidarity which a success emphasis must exact.

The pattern of relationships between these items and other characteristics of respondents is inconsistent. Generally, there is a consistent relationship between the indicators of integration and acculturation — education, social class, mobility, assimilation, and membership in the third generation — and rejection of the item that the wife alone should train the children. However, there is also an inverse relationship between many of these same indicators and wanting the family to have first claim on the husband's time. Still, the former set of relationships is consistently stronger. It appears that both ambition for success and familistic egalitarianism tend to increase with acculturation, and the strain of contradiction between these two values is felt in more acculturated Ukrainian origin families just as it is felt in other middle class Canadian families.

Familism and family solidarity

Four items in the schedule dealt with various aspects of familism, which was broadly conceived as an emphasis on family solidarity and giving precedence to the claims of the family over those of the individual. The first dealt with the conflict which a woman may experience between family obligations and social life: "I want the kind of marriage in which the family has first claim on the wife's time, though it may interfere with her social life." This issue is not a major one among members of the sample: over three-fourths of the sample (72 percent) agreed with the statement. However, there was less unanimity among the younger subjects than among the older ones. Agreement was expressed by 67 percent of those under thirty-five years of age, by 71 percent of those aged thirty-five to fifty, and by 82 percent of those over fifty years of age. It is perhaps remarkable that these differences are not more distinct. Tabulation of this item by generation shows that it is not age, but generation, which accounts for the differences in distributions: 86 percent of those born in the Ukraine agreed with the statement, as did 68 percent of those Canadian-born of Ukrainian-born parents and 70 percent of those born to Canadian-born parents. There are no differences between men and women, and few of the other characteristics of respondents are associated significantly with certain responses. Disagreement with the item is associated with the assimilation index, with high educational attainment, and, for women only, with higher social class membership. Thus, the kind of egalitarian attitude which tends to deny that the woman should be always at the disposal of her husband and children is characteristic of the more assimilated, better educated respondents.

An item which dealt with another aspect of familism, relationships with in-laws, stated: "I would object to long and frequent visits from the husband's or the wife's parents after marriage." Half of the sample said they would object, and the other half said they would not. There are insignificant sex differences but sizable age differences. Sixty-four percent of the subjects under thirty-five years of age said that they would object, while 35 percent of those fifty years of age and over said that they would object. When the subjects are grouped by generation the differences are sharpened further. Those saying they would object included 67 percent of the third generation subjects, but only 35 percent and 30 percent of the second and the first generation subjects respectively. Indicators of integration and acculturation are positively associated with objecting to long visits, as are upward social mobility, and higher social class membership. Urban residence, however, is associated with acceptance of long visits, which is clearly contrary to the general pattern, since urban residence involves residential integration. The explanation may be that many urban residents, having originated in these predominantly Ukrainian rural areas, miss their relatives and so welcome visits from them.

The other two familism items dealt with tendencies toward the erosion of strong family solidarity: "In my marriage I want the husband and wife to have freedom to have their own interests and freedom to go on separate vacations"; and "I would be opposed to divorce even if my children suffered from my unhappy marriage." Only 7 percent of the sample expressed agreement with the first statement, and 36 percent expressed strong disagreement. There were no sex differences. Third generation subjects strongly disagreed far more often (54 percent) than did second generation (39 percent) or first generation subjects (21 percent). Thus, younger and more Canadianized subjects were more committed to family solidarity than were older, Ukrainian-born subjects.

Correspondingly, higher class subjects and those upwardly mobile, and pro-assimilation strongly disagreed significantly more frequently than those with opposite characteristics. These data suggest that this item differentiates not so much between subjects who are high and low in familism as between those high and low in egalitarianism. The former apparently want the wife to share with the husband in activities, whereas the latter care less about the pursuit of common interests.

Divorce was opposed even though children suffered from an unhappy marriage, by one fourth of the sample, and was acceptable to the remaining three fourths. There were very few differences between those accepting and those rejecting the statement. First generation immigrants rejected the statement less (5 percent strongly disagreed) than did second generation (10 percent) and third generation subjects (15 percent). Urban residents and those with higher educational attainments also disagreed slightly more frequently than did rural and less well educated subjects. Acculturation and integration into Canadian society do not appear to be associated with a more favorable attitude toward divorce.

Child rearing attitudes

We have seen that there are significant differences between various segments of the sample in the number of children felt to be ideal. We would expect that there would also be significant differences in attitudes toward child rearing. Since the old country, peasant tradition was a strongly patriarchal one we would expect first generation Ukrainians and those less exposed to Canadianizing influences to have a somewhat more authoritarian approach to child rearing. Those more accul-

turated should prefer a more permissive approach.

The information on this subject consists of nine items selected from the Parental Dominance sub-scale of the Shoben Parental Attitude Survey. These items deal with the tendency in parents to assign to the child a distinctly inferior role and to demand unquestioning submission from him under penalty of severe punishment. Sample items include: "A child should fear his parents to some degree"; "It is wicked for children to disobey their parents"; and "Parents should never enter a child's room without his permission."

These items were scored to obtain a child dominance score. The possible range of scores is from nine to thirty-six and the actual range was from twelve through thirty. A high score is indicative of a domineering orientation.

Mean dominance scores are available for the sample and for an English Canadian comparison group, composed of 301 subects, drawn from farmers and other rural residents in the parkland district of central Alberta and from residents of Edmonton. In age, sex, and proportion residing in rural areas it was precisely comparable with the Ukrainian sample. The mean score for the Ukrainian sample is 21.67, while the mean score for the comparison group is 20.56. The dominance score of the Ukrainians is thus only slightly higher than that of the comparison group.

Among the Ukrainians, women have somewhat higher mean scores (22.2) than do men (21.6), and older subjects have somewhat higher mean scores (22.8) than do younger subjects (20.8). Although the differences here are in the direction that we predicted — anticipating that female and older interviewees would be more conservative than male and younger subjects — they are slight.

There are strong relationships between the dominance scores and all of the independent variables which have been dealt with in this section except rural-urban residence: surprisingly, rural residents showed no more patriarchal attitudes in child rearing than did urban residents. Low dominance scores were more characteristic of men, younger people, second and third generation Canadian, higher class people who are upwardly mobile and are better integrated into Canadian society. The respondent characteristics which are most powerfully associated with the dominance scores are generation, age, education, and occupation level. Age and generation both measure the same thing, since most of the first generation subjects are elderly, and education and occupation both index social class. Tabulation of dominance scores by generation and by education level shows that education is more powerfully associated with the dominance variables than is generation. Almost half (45 percent) of those with at least a high school diploma fell in the lowest dominance score grouping, whereas only 12 percent of those with less than a grade nine education had scores in this grouping. Correspondingly, about a third of the third generation subjects' scores fell in the lowest grouping, but only 13 percent of the first generation subjects' scores fell in this grouping.

A more detailed picture of subjects' attitudes toward various child rearing issues is obtained by looking at the subjects' responses to the individual items. The items may be grouped into three categories. The first group deals with obedience (child must always consult his parents, disobedience to parents is wicked, and children should not be often allowed to have their own way). About

20 percent of the respondents agreed with these items. The second group relates to the parent-child relationship (child should fear parents), privacy of the child, and dominance (child should always accept parent's decision), and about 10 percent agreed with these items. The last three items deal with control of occupational choice, discipline technique, and parental image, and emphasize the superordination of the parent and the subordination of the child. Only about 3 percent of the sample agreed with these items.

There are interesting subgroup differences in the responses to these items. Women emphasize that children should consult their parents, should fear their parents, and should not be allowed to have their own way, more than do men, no doubt because they bear most of the responsibility for supervising children. The most striking differences between subgroups are generational differences, which vary widely between different items. Despite the more patriarchal orientation of the older subjects, the third generation respondents — who most frequently have small children — emphasized obedience more than first generation subjects. Third generation subjects were noticeably more liberal than first generation subjects only in their disapproval of shaming as a discipline technique.

There were also sizable differences in responses to these items between respondents by level of education. Those better educated (who tended to be younger) more often denied that a child should have his own way or that the parent should obtain the child's permission before entering his room. On most of the other items, however, the better educated subjects were more permissive in their responses than were the less well educated.

In general, the data show no general tendency toward greater patriarchalism on the part of some subgroups and greater egalitarianism on the part of other subgroups. Older subjects are generally more authoritarian than younger subjects. Those in direct contact with young children — i.e., women, younger people — tend to emphasize that the child should not be permitted to have his own way, and should consult his parents before acting. Well educated Ukrainians tend toward permissiveness in their dealings with children.

Summary

This paper has presented information on changes in family life which are associated with increased integration into Canadian society in a sample of Ukrainian-Canadians.

In general, we found characteristic differences between two groups: one was composed of younger, third generation, well educated and occupationally well placed subjects who were oriented toward integration into Canadian society and who tended to be little interested in traditional Ukrainian ways. The other was composed of older, first generation, less educated subjects, who were farmers or laborers, who were isolated from the rest of Canadian society and who were strongly identified with traditional Ukrainian practices. The first group tended to come from smaller parental families, and they specified a smaller number of children as ideal. They had lower rates of home ownership than did the latter, although their rates were yet high. They were more often intermarried and more often favored intermarriage. Wives in this group more often worked, and they felt an obligation to contribute to family support, but their husbands tended rather vigorously to reject the suggestion that this contribution *should* be made. Both sexes in this group advocated a more egalitarian relationship between husband and wife, especially in regard to deciding upon expenditures, and responsibility for child raising, than did those in the second group, but they also identified more strongly with the success value as well. Thus there was evidence of conflict between the claims that occupational advancement and family egalitarianism made on the time of the father, in this group.

Members of the first group were far less concerned about familism and maintaining close relationships with relatives than the latter, and they were *slightly* more willing to consider divorce where children appear to suffer from an unhappy marriage. The former group consistently advocated less domineering attitudes in dealing with children, but *there is evidence that* in some areas young women were more domineering than older subjects, no doubt because they were actually dealing with small children in the home.

These data thus demonstrate clearly the impact of acculturation into Canadian ways on the home and family life as sample members. There is no evidence of a trend toward family disintegration, but the tendencies toward a smaller, more mobile, and more egalitarian family, as seen in both husband-wife and parent-child relations, are undeniable. The independent variables most associated with this trend are generation, education, and pro-Canadian cultural orientation. Women tend to be in some ways more conservative than men, but they are not consistently so. The influence of the urban environment is less pronounced than we had expected.

NOTES

1 E. J. Shoben, Jr., "The Assessment of Parental Attitudes in Relation to Child Adjustment," *Genetic Psychological Monographs*, Vol. 39, (1949), pp. 103-148.

REFERENCES

1970 The Editorial Committee in Edmonton. *The Ukrainian Pioneers in Alberta: A Series of Biographical Sketches of Ukrainian Pioneers*. Edmonton, 1970.

1945 Hunchak, N. D. *Canadians of Ukrainian Origin*. Ukrainian Canadian Committee, 1945.

1947 Lysenko, Vera. *Men in Sheepskin Coats: A Study in Assimilation*. Toronto: Ryerson Press, 1947.

1970 Marunchak, Mykhailo H. *The Ukrainian Canadians: A History*. Ukrainian Free Academy of Sciences, 1970.

1934 Paluk, William. *Canadian Cossacks*. Canadian Ukrainian Review Publishing Co., 1934.

1971 Panchuk, John. *Bukowinian Settlements in Southern Manitoba Gardenton Area*. Battle Creek, Michigan, 1971.

1954 Romaniuk, Gus. *Taking Root in Canada*. Winnipeg, Manitoba: Columbia Press Ltd., 1954.

1968 Vousenki, Ol'a. *The Ukrainians in Canada*. Ottawa: Trident Press, 1968.

1931 Young, Charles H. *The Ukrainian Canadians: A Study in Assimilation*. Toronto: Nelson Press, 1931.

1953 Yuzyk, Paul. *The Ukrainians in Manitoba: A Social History*. Toronto: University of Toronto Press, 1953.

1967 Yuzyk, Paul. *Ukrainian Canadians: Their Place and Role in Canadian Life*. Toronto: Ukrainian Canadian Business and Professional Federation, 1967.

9

The family
in post-industrial society

Marriage and the nuclear family constitute a failing institution, a failing way of life. No one would argue that these have been highly successful. We need laboratories, experiments, attempts to avoid repeating past failures, exploration into new approaches. . . . Unheralded and unsung, explorations, experiments, new ways of relating, new kinds of partnerships are being tried out, people are learning from mistakes and profiting from successes. They are inventing alternatives, new futures, for our most sharply failing institutions, marriage and the nuclear family. . . . Can we accept the fact that . . . . the name of the game is change, and that we are desperately in need of just such a revolution in the area of living partnerships and family life as has taken place in industry, agriculture, flight, space, and all the other aspects of life?

Carl R. Rogers, Becoming Partners: Marriage and Its Alternatives
(New York: Delacorte Press, 1972), pp. 212 – 213.
Reprinted by permission.

This final chapter discusses the ways in which marital and family forms and practices are changing and resisting change in North American society. It is suggested that the characteristics of post-industrial society pose unique and significant challenges for the family. These characteristics are briefly identified in the first section. The implications for values and behavior in general, and for marriage and family life in particular, are discussed in the next section. The last part of the chapter explores some of the reasons why most individuals choose the predominant family options, while an increasing minority are opting for alternative life styles such as communes or group marriage. The relative success of these alternative life styles is considered.

Characteristics of post-industrial society

The post-modern (Etzioni, 1968) or post-industrial (Bell, 1973) society is said to have begun after World War II. It is generally agreed that this term applies to significant changes in social structure relative to at least three sectors of North American society: the economy, the occupational system, and science and technology. According to Bell (1973), these changes are reflected in several features of modern society which constitute important departures from industrial society.

First, there has been a change from a goods-producing to a service economy.

Most of the labor force is no longer engaged in agriculture or manufacturing, as is the case in the majority of the world's societies, but in services such as trade, finance, transportation, health, recreation, research, education and government. The most pronounced growth in the service professions has been in health, education, research and government.

Second, the occupational system has changed from an emphasis on semi-skilled and skilled labor to the preeminence of the professional and technical class. The number of white-collar workers now exceeds blue-collar workers by a ratio of five to four. The growth of the professional and technical class has been double that of the average labor force. The growth rate of engineers and scientists is three times the growth rate of other occupational groups.[1]

Third, perhaps the fundamental principle of post-industrial society is the centrality of knowledge as a source of innovation and policy formation. While industrial society is concerned with the coordination of workers and machines for production, post-industrial society emphasizes the use of knowledge in social control, directing innovation, and forecasting. The intellectual institutions play an ever-increasing role in societal management and political affairs. Post-industrial society is characterized by a "future orientation" in the interest of controlling and planning technological innovation.

Fourth, while industrial society focused on inventions, post-industrial society is concerned with the management of organized complexity. Bell refers to this principle as "intellectual technology". Problem-solving rules are substituted for intuitive judgments, and the computer organizes multitudinous variables (Bell, 1973: 28–29).

Bell's arguments are fully developed in his monumental work, *The Coming of Post-Industrial Society: A Venture in Social Forecasting* (1973). In most respects, the changes found in post-industrial society could be thought of as progressive. More people are officially involved in helping others and in solving problems. The availability of knowledge and ways to use it are at an all-time high. The future seems distinctly optimistic; the tools exist to create a better world. However, as Bell points out, these principles also pose serious questions. First, can society handle such a marked reorganization of its role structure? Can the expectations associated with the positions that people occupy be modified and redefined as quickly as positions are created and destroyed? Second, the relationship between politicians and the knowledge sector (scientists, technocrats, engineers) has always been one of superordinate-subordinate. Will politicians and intellectuals be able to marshal their respective resources cooperatively? Third, culture is unprepared, and due to its

---

1 The statistics reported are based on U.S. data as reported by Bell (1973). Canadian statistics show similar trends (cf. Kubat and Thornton, 1973: 110 – 173).

traditions and values unable, to cope with the radical changes in the technocratic and knowledge spheres of post-industrial society. Culture will tend to splinter or fragment.[2] Bell's book is largely devoted to the development of the post-industrial thesis and to forecasting the probable changes in social structure. The implications of these patterns for individuals, sexuality, marriage and family life, however, are not fully drawn. These matters are considered below.

In the most general sense, modern society represents several conditions which are favorable to diversity and experimentation with alternative life styles. These same conditions, however, are also favorable to the maintenance of traditional life styles. The most fundamental of these conditions or principles is obviously the emphasis on heterogeneity itself. Multiculturalism is not only accepted but encouraged in Canadian society. Differences in behavior and values are expected and tolerated even in small communities, though they aren't always approved. As reported earlier, many students know of unmarried couples living together, though few are doing so themselves; many approve of trial marriage, though considerably fewer are even willing to try it; and many believe in multiple loving, though few have experienced it (see Hobart, 1974b; Whitehurst, 1973a).

The emphasis on heterogeneity may be reflected in several different ways. The range of expectations applicable to particular positions in our society tends to be relatively broad. In some societies, however, positions are very clearly defined and deviations from this "narrow" standard are not permitted. In Canada, the expectations for a given position vary widely among subcultures, and the range of expectations in a given subculture tend to be relatively broad; in this sense, there are many acceptable behaviors that lie between what one must do and what one must not do. This range includes the ideal and most valued behavior as well as the many "shoulds" and "should nots". This condition of latitude permits individual behavior to vary from the ideal but still be tolerated.

Laws in our society tend to be sufficiently ambiguous to support a large legal profession. Many behaviors thought to be illegal can be shown to be legal. Illegal behavior is frequently ignored due to the absence of an official complaint and a general preference not to enforce certain laws. In addition, lawyers are often able to contest fines and sentences for illegal behaviors on technical grounds. This is not to say, of course, that the law is ineffective in response to criminal behavior; rather, that domestic law is uniquely subject to variable definition and enforcement. Canada and the United States have long emphasized the *freedom* to pursue religious or ideological beliefs and practices without the interference of the government. Though

2 Reviews of Bell's book by the "intellectual community" have been favorable to the general theme of the argument (see for example Bendix, 1974). There is considerable agreement that North American society has entered the post-industrial era.

the majority may disagree with the values of those men and women occupying a communal house in the neighborhood, they will probably tolerate, if not respect, their right to "do their thing". Geographical mobility (the possibility of moving away from friends and family), social mobility (the possibility of moving up the social ladder and away from the values of one's lower status), and geographical isolation (the extent to which there is unexplored or uninhabited space where one can "hide") each provide an opportunity for marriage and family options. Finally, the emphasis on secondary role relationships and impersonal ties in post-industrial society enables individuals to lead their own lives behind closed doors and "in front of disinterested and uninvolved" neighbors.[3]

Implications of post-industrial society for values and behavior

Recent literature emphasizes the unprecedented problems and opportunities of post-industrial society. Etzioni (1968), for example, discusses the unique potential of post-modern societies to follow a path of self-guidance and self-enhancement. His book provides insight into how this might occur. Similarly, Slater (1970), while recognizing the more elaborate structure of modern society and the intense struggle of man for meaning and identity, describes the emergent "new" culture as giving preference to personal rights, human needs, cooperation, sexuality, openness, personal expression, gratification, communal love, the consumer over the producer, distribution over concentration, and ends over means. Post-industrial society is said to offer a variety of opportunities and life styles without precedence in human history, because of widespread leisure and affluence (Galbraith, 1962) and global mobility that is both rapid and inexpensive (Bennis and Slater, 1968).

Others, however, see life in modern society as considerably more confusing and demeaning. Toffler (1970), for example, in his book *Future Shock* describes the "temporary society": material goods and products are designed for a throw-away culture; organizations are here today and gone tomorrow; rentalism has led to a culture of new nomads in a concrete jungle; man is described as modular (prefabricated and artificial) and mobicentric (selfhood linked to transience and movement) which necessitates temporary friends, relationships, and families; the information explosion is seen as too much for the sifting and sorting capacities of man; and overspecialization of jobs and interests is seen to lead to multiple subcults splitting both society and man into competing subparts. Several other writers have concluded that these conditions facilitate the emergence of the counterculture among youth

3 These arguments are commonly identified in introductory sociology textbooks and reflect assumptions concerning the nature of mass society.

(Roszak, 1968), a "hang loose" ethic or lack of commitment to anything (Kenniston, 1965), the return to rural areas and the increasing politicization of the rural population (Reich, 1970), and the marked interest in human potential movements (Howard, 1970). Roszak (1968) argues that modern society is failing to meet the relatedness needs of people. In consequence, people "naturally" turn to alternative ways of satisfying these needs.

Implications of post-industrial society for marriage and the family

As I have emphasized throughout this book, marriage and family life can only be understood in sociocultural context. Sociocultural conditions represent a sufficient influence for change on family life; whether change actually occurs in response to these conditions, however, will vary from society to society. The characteristics of post-industrial society are seen to pose significant questions for the individual and his relationships with others.

The literature which deals directly with marriage and the family in post-industrial society is both profuse and diffuse. It is not unusual to see contradictory materials on the family, published within days of each other, focusing on the struggle of the family to survive in a hostile environment or attempting to identify ways for the family to find a future. The "future oriented" literature tends to emphasize the creative aspects of innovations such as trial marriage, swinging, homosexual marriage, adultery, polygamous households, and communal relationships. The "survival" literature, in contrast, tends to focus on the decline of parental authority, marital and family problems, divorce, abortion, and changing sex roles.

The research evidence, drawn largely from United States data, does seem to indicate that marriage and parenthood are becoming more problematic. Each of these subjects is briefly discussed below.

Marriage Enduring heterosexual satisfaction appears to be an increasingly scarce commodity. In the last decade, the majority of studies indicate decreased satisfaction with length of marriage (e.g., Pineo, 1961). Satisfaction within marriage is found to be at a particularly low ebb during the parenting years (Rollins and Feldman, 1970). Marital adjustment, where it occurs, tends to be sex biased — wives tend to adjust more than their husbands (e.g., Luckey, 1960). Wives are increasingly asking for equal and just treatment (equitable rights and duties) in both the home and workplace, in a social context in which males are inadequately socialized to cope with changing sex roles. Sexual adjustment remains a central problem in marital interaction because of the socialization of males and females (Clark and Wallin, 1965; Mitchell, Bullard and Mudd, 1962). One of the more provocative studies of this decade documents the dependence of marital satisfaction on economic success (Scanzoni, 1970). It is evident, therefore, that economic instability, decreasing purchasing power, and occupational achievement cannot be ignored in attempting to understand modern marriage. Similarly, dual career marriage poses new and increasingly difficult problems for marriage in a society that requires geographical mobility, is hesitant about hiring couples, and finds it difficult to organize its economic system around couples rather than individuals (Bebbington, 1973; Holmstrom, 1972).

Parenthood There seems to be an unambiguous trend toward a lower valuation of childbearing and parenting, partly because parenthood is a threat to human survival (the population explosion), but primarily because children tie women to the household (Gavron, 1966; Friedan, 1963). This devaluation of parenthood also reflects the confusion and guilt of contemporary parents (Bronfenbrenner, 1970; LeMasters, 1974) and the increasing preference for childless marriage (e.g., Veevers, 1973). Rossi (1968) has concluded that the problems of motherhood are threefold: (a) there is a concerted pressure on the married woman to be a mother — the greater this pressure, the more negative the woman's attitude toward the role, whether she is aware of it or not; (b) parenthood is typically an involuntary act — once started it is difficult to stop, short of abortion — accordingly, there are more unwanted pregnancies than unwanted marriages; and (c) parenthood is irrevocable — it is possible to have ex-jobs, ex-spouses, but not ex-children — which leads to psychological withdrawal tactics on the part of mothers. The use of leisure time in families tends to be individual or couple oriented rather than family oriented (Larson, 1971a). Furthermore, *family* use of leisure time is subjected to severe competition from alternative responsibilities and opportunities. The contacts and requirements of professional opportunism require "extra work" during "non-work" time which militates against family activities. Should work-related competitive pressures be absent, the demands of the community also solicit the undivided attentions of family members. Under these conditions, the responsibilities and opportunities of family life may become *options* in a field of options, the nurturant and relatedness needs of children notwithstanding.

The choice of alternative life styles

From the preceding discussion it becomes evident that the structural changes in post-industrial society, the visible struggle for meaning or purpose in life in a culture emphasizing transience, and the increasing problems within traditional marriage and family forms and practices, together would facilitate experimentation with alternative life styles. The relative freedom to do so is probably conducive to the development of an ideological commitment to non-traditional and innovative ways of meeting one's relatedness needs. What proportion of our population will actually attempt radical alternatives, remain strongly committed to the traditional monogamous and nuclear family life styles, or progressively adjust to new ideas and practices depends on many factors. Certain of these factors can be readily identified. Figure 9.1 provides a detailed illustration of an overall perspective of the conditions which support the relative stability of marriage and family values and practices, and those conditions which increase the likelihood of choosing or experimenting with alternative marriage and family life styles.

Before briefly discussing figure 9.1, it should be noted that there is little agreement among family sociologists on these matters. There has been very little theoretical work on alternative life styles,[4] and current research has provided very little insight into the reasons why people choose alternative life styles.[5] This model is presented to facilitate consideration of the issues in choice and experimentation. Hopefully, discussion of these suggestions will improve our understanding of the family and social change in post-industrial society.

In figure 9.1 a basic set of assumptions is first presented. These assumptions focus on the typical ways in which an individual comes to hold particular values and to behave in particular ways. Pre-industrial and post-industrial society are compared. In general, most individuals in pre-industrial society will share the same values and behave in much the same way because alternative ways of thinking and doing simply do not exist. Children will be trained to fit into a society that is only modestly different from the society of their parents and grandparents. Sanctions will usually be quite effective because they need not be excessively punitive (i.e., the rewards are well worth the costs) and the individual is not exposed to any alternatives which might lead him to question "the way things are". Post-industrial society is a very different situation. The individual is exposed early to a vast array of different values and practices through interaction with children at school, watching television, going to movies, listening to music and reading. It is decidedly more complicated to adopt values and behaviors similar to those of one's parents or grandparents. It would be neither simple nor natural for an individual to grow up unchanged from those who

4 There have, however, been several attempts to define and categorize various life style alternatives (see Ramey, 1972). Even so, there is considerable disagreement about the best or appropriate ways of describing what is happening and why.

5 The papers included in this chapter deal directly with these matters; the reader is encouraged to be critical of them. The "experts" may be little better than the average layman at either predicting or understanding the changes occurring in the family.

reared him. The application of sanctions such as "don't or else" or "if you do, then . . ." are typically met with reactions such as "but why, that's not the way it is for . . .". Scott (1971) demonstrates that as values and behavior become more heterogeneous, sanctions tend to become more rigid and harsh in order to keep things as they are. It is ironic that the increased use of sanctions typically facilitates more rapid and more radical change (see 6b in figure 9.1).

The other section of figure 9.1 deals directly with the conditions which influence choice in post-industrial society. In other words, it is *not* true that all individuals automatically reject the values and behaviors of their parents and grandparents. The majority of people in Canadian society continue to be monogamous, obtain a license when they marry, maintain a separate residence from parents and others, bear and rear their own children, and continue to live with their first or second spouse until death do them part. Even so, an increasing minority are choosing to live the single and swinging life style, to live with a potential spouse before marriage, and if they marry, to not have children. Experimentation with mate swapping, group marriage, communal life, and group sex appears to be increasingly approved and practised in certain sectors of society. The basic question is why most continue in the traditional modes while others choose or experiment with life style alternatives.

The basic conditions which influence choice are organized into those which affect a child's acquisition of values and those which affect adults in the "switching" of values. It was suggested earlier that post-industrial society does tend to undermine satisfying parent-child relationships and traditional ways of meeting the relatedness needs of the individual (see figure 9.1, 8a and 12a). Thus, these are *sufficient* conditions to influence the choice of alternative life styles. In the case of children, parents may still choose how they will rear them. The excessive use of sanctions (11a) facilitates opposition to the values of parents. In contrast, disinterest in the experiences of children encourages them to search for their values in other relationships (9a). Encouraging children to consider or try alternatives, in a sufficient environment for change, is obviously supportive of the adoption of new values (10a). Similarly, when adults see their own relationships as basically unsatisfying, they will be more readily induced to try alternatives because there is little to lose and everything to gain (14a). In general, these conditions are highly congruent with the sufficient conditions of post-industrial society.

Choosing to remain monogamous or faithful to one's spouse, however, is also possible in post-industrial society, even though conditions such as 8b and 12b do not exist. Children may still be reared to prefer monogamy if their parents effectively illustrate the virtues of this relationship, do not force this system "down their

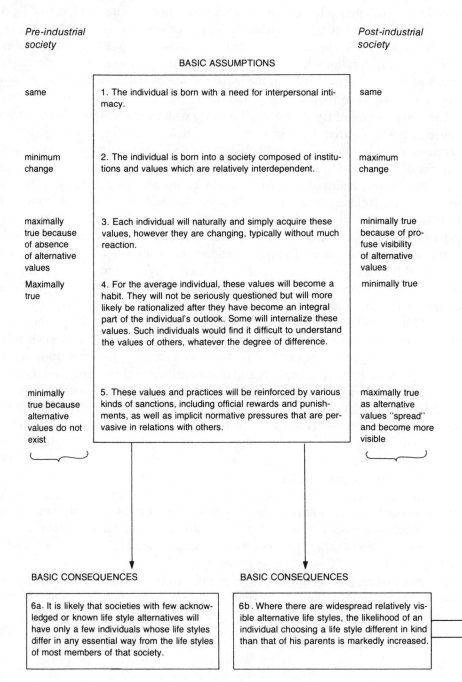

Figure 9-1 Why Alternative Life Styles are chosen

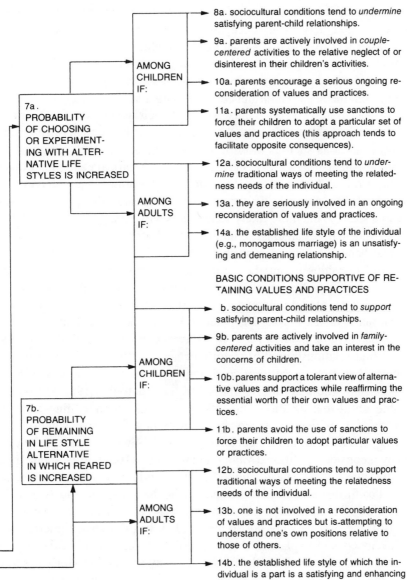

BASIC CONDITIONS REGULATING CHOICE
OF ALTERNATIVES

7a.
PROBABILITY
OF CHOOSING
OR EXPERIMENT-
ING WITH ALTER-
NATIVE LIFE
STYLES IS INCREASED

AMONG
CHILDREN
IF:

8a. sociocultural conditions tend to *undermine* satisfying parent-child relationships.

9a. parents are actively involved in *couple-centered* activities to the relative neglect of or disinterest in their children's activities.

10a. parents encourage a serious ongoing re-consideration of values and practices.

11a. parents systematically use sanctions to force their children to adopt a particular set of values and practices (this approach tends to facilitate opposite consequences).

AMONG
ADULTS
IF:

12a. sociocultural conditions tend to *undermine* traditional ways of meeting the related-ness needs of the individual.

13a. they are seriously involved in an ongoing reconsideration of values and practices.

14a. the established life style of the individual (e.g., monogamous marriage) is an unsatisfy-ing and demeaning relationship.

BASIC CONDITIONS SUPPORTIVE OF RE-
TAINING VALUES AND PRACTICES

7b.
PROBABILITY
OF REMAINING
IN LIFE STYLE
ALTERNATIVE
IN WHICH REARED
IS INCREASED

AMONG
CHILDREN
IF:

b. sociocultural conditions tend to *support* satisfying parent-child relationships.

9b. parents are actively involved in *family-centered* activities and take an interest in the concerns of children.

10b. parents support a tolerant view of alterna-tive values and practices while reaffirming the essential worth of their own values and prac-tices.

11b. parents avoid the use of sanctions to force their children to adopt particular values or practices.

AMONG
ADULTS
IF:

12b. sociocultural conditions tend to support traditional ways of meeting the relatedness needs of the individual.

13b. one is not involved in a reconsideration of values and practices but is attempting to understand one's own positions relative to those of others.

14b. the established life style of which the in-dividual is a part is a satisfying and enhancing relationship.

throats'', and are acceptant of other values while reaffirming in word and deed their own values. Adults satisfied with their relationship but willing to consider the advantages and disadvantages of alternatives will be less likely to choose an alternative life style.

There is also an important sense in which conditions such as 8b and 12b do exist in post-industrial society. In essence, the greater the diversity in values and practices, the easier it is to "do one's own thing", including retaining the values of the group of which one is a part. The Hutterites, for example, have effectively maintained their values and practices in post-industrial society by isolating and insulating their young from the negative influences of the larger society. Many religious groups are able to successfully keep themselves and their young on the "straight and narrow" even though they regularly come in contact with alternative values, primarily because conditions such as those in the model (see 9b, 10b, 13b, and 14b) are possible in post-industrial society. Perhaps the best empirical example of this principle is in the work of Christensen (1969) on sexual attitudes and behaviors in Denmark and Utah. In general, he found that the greater the permissiveness and diversity in a society, the more likely subcultures will persist. Variables such as age, education, residence, social class, ethnicity, and church attendance explained sexual attitudes and behaviors considerably better in Denmark than in Utah.

The interrelationships among the basic conditions regulating choice of alternatives or the retention of a particular life style are complex. Figure 9.1 does not identify these factors, as the model is intended to be suggestive rather than comprehensive, and general rather than specific. The reader will note, however, that certain relationships are apparent. For example, if socio-cultural conditions tend to support satisfying parent-child relationships (8b), family-centered activities (9b) will be easier to participate in than if socio-cultural conditions tend to undermine satisfying parent-child relationships (8a). Similarly, couple-centered activities (9a) will be easier in unfavorable child-rearing environments (8a), while both couple-centered and family-centered activities are acceptable choices in a favorable parent-child environment. Obviously also, family-centered parents (9b) who encourage their children to seriously reconsider traditional values and practices (10a) will facilitate the choice of alternative life styles. The likelihood of their children choosing alternatives, of course, will be further enhanced if the parents themselves are seriously involved in a reconsideration of their own values and practices (13a), while the opposite effect would exist if the parents were not so involved (13b). Many such interrelationships can be developed and explained through further development of the model. The reader is encouraged to evaluate the model critically in searching for ways to further our understanding of changing marriage and family forms and practices.

Stability within life style alternatives

Once an individual has chosen to become part of a group marriage or a commune,[6] the following questions arise. How long will it last? Will this experience be any more satisfying or demeaning than other relatedness experiences? The most general answer to both of these questions is that the model just presented is equally relevant to non-traditional and innovative family forms *if these forms are as generally accepted within the society as a whole as the traditional forms*. In view of the fact that this is usually not the case and that the majority of individuals are not reared in non-traditional family settings, there are additional considerations.

Traditional forms of marriage and child rearing are "supposed" to work and to endure. The fact that marriages break down and children sometimes have to be put up for adoption is "just one of those things". Non-traditional marital and family forms are not supposed to work, however, and when they don't few are surprised. After an exhaustive study of communes (both historical and contemporary), Kanter (1972) demonstrated that utopian experiments have not been very successful. The more successful historical communes are characterized by several dimensions of commitment, including the willingness of members to stay in the system, the ability of members to stick together, the readiness of members to obey the demands of the system, the contribution of resources and energy, a willingness to share the social costs of membership, and the capacity to reduce one's interest in other life styles (pp. 59–162). Those utopian experiments which reflected all six of these dimensions of commitment were the most successful. Kanter describes contemporary communes as encompassing fewer visions of social reconstruction, fewer hopes for permanence, fewer people, fewer demands, and fewer regulations (p. 166). Contemporary communes which are formed for reasons of retreat dissolve quickly, whereas those which have a sense of mission are seen to last longer. The Constantines' recent book on the results of their study of group marriage (Constantine and Constantine, 1973) describes the advantages and disadvantages in considerable detail. Most participants anticipated that the relationship would be permanent and did not think of it as experimental. Children seemed to thrive on the extra attention and affection provided by several parents. Even so, group marriage is difficult for most people because of the more complex relationships involved. Most are unable to make the necessary adjustments. The Constantines conclude that group marriage would likely be a growth experience for only a limited few. Even so, the essential difficulties of

6 It may be noted that this statement may be turned around to read "Once an individual has chosen to become part of a conjugal marriage after having lived in a group marriage. . . ."

alternative life styles should not be overemphasized — utopian communities are possible. The following quotation from Kanter makes this point clearly.

> In any human group there is a gap between what works or has functional or organizational value, and what is desirable or has personal or social value. Utopian communities attempt to narrow this gap between the practical and the ideal, but they are not always successful. . . . The life of communes . . . has its limits and costs as well as its benefits and advantages. Utopian communities are not the answer to everything. They are difficult to create, even more difficult to sustain. They exact a dedication and an involvement that many people find unappealing. They sometimes have shortcomings that make them fail of the perfection they promise. But . . . they do supply partial answers. . . . The importance of considering the potential for utopias . . . transcends whether or not . . . communes work.[7]

SUMMARY

Post-industrial society appears to be characterized by an emphasis on services rather than production of goods, the preeminence of the professional and technical class, and the primacy of knowledge rather than tradition. Attitudinal and behavioral differences resulting from permissive standards, ambiguous or conflicting regulations, freedom of beliefs, geographical and social mobility, geographical isolation, and impersonal relationships are emphasized. The unique opportunities for self-enhancement and societal improvement in post-industrial society are as prominent as the problems of individual adjustment, strain in interpersonal relationships, and societal disorganization. There is, indeed, increasing research evidence of significant problems in traditional marriage and parenthood patterns.

In response to these problems, a minority of Canadians are turning to alternative life styles. It appears that changes are inevitable. What these changes will be, and how widespread they will be, however, depends on many factors. A model of the conditions which support the relative stability of marriage and family values and practices, and those conditions which increase the likelihood of choosing or experimenting with alternative marriage and family life styles, was presented to facilitate consideration of the basic issues. In general, it is argued that individuals in post-industrial society do not simply or naturally acquire the values and behaviors of parents or friends, because of the vast array of different values and practices to

---

7 Rosabeth M. Kanter, *Commitment and Community: Communes and Utopias in Sociological Perspective* (Cambridge, Mass.: Harvard University Press, 1973), pp. 235 – 236. Reprinted by permission of the publisher.

which they are exposed. Rather, the *kinds* of conditions to which they are exposed will increase the probability either of adopting alternative life styles *or* of retaining the life style (or some modified or improved version of the basic theme) in which the individuals were reared. It is also suggested that this model is applicable to the relative stability of innovative life style alternatives.

Although a more determinate relationship between marriage and family patterns and society has been suggested in this chapter than in chapter eight, it must be emphasized that post-industrial society, as well as industrial society, represents *sufficient* rather than necessary conditions for family change. Whether the impact of post-industrial society is as great as has been implicitly suggested, is difficult at present to test empirically, and must be subjected to considered critical analysis.

The remainder of the chapter consists of articles on the values of innovative women, childless marriage, innovative marriage, and a forecast of future marriage and family relationships.

Life plans of innovative women: a strategy for living the feminine role

There is now an abundance of literature on the roles and statuses of women. Books, anthologies, special issues of professional journals, and articles on women historically and cross-culturally are readily available. A newsletter of research on women has been published in Canada since 1972 (Eichler and Stephenson, 1972). Those interested in reading further may wish to consult the following selected references: Bart, 1971; Bardwick, 1971; Huber, 1973; C. Epstein, 1971; Reeves, 1971; Theodore, 1971. Canadian references include, among others: Report of the Royal Commission on the Status of Women in Canada, 1970; Stephenson, 1973.

In this provocative essay Carisse reflects on the masculine bias in the conceptualization of careers and develops an alternative approach which articulates four career sectors: work, family, organizational involvement and education. Based on a careful analysis of bibliographical data and personal interviews, Carisse analyzes the career dilemmas of the married woman in these four career sectors. Other than the unmarried woman, three types of life plans are identified and described in some detail: the dual career woman, the cyclical career woman, and the latecomer. This paper represents a significant contribution to an understanding of the problems of both the single and married woman in Canadian society.

Life plans of innovative women: a strategy for living the feminine role

Colette Carisse

For thirty years she was Emile Durkheim's companion. . . . She protected him from all material care, from all frivolities and she assumed on his behalf the education of Marie and André Durkheim. . . . To the very end she afforded her husband the most favorable working conditions. Well-educated, she was able to collaborate in his work. For many years, she copied certain manuscripts and did all his proofreading. She always participated, not only in all the material tasks such as managing, administering, keeping up the correspondence, reading and distributing proofs, but also she contributed to the drafting of texts and often, discreetly yet firmly, she even made corrections.

(In memoriam, *L'Année Sociologique*, 1927.)

This paper is based on a content analysis of biographical data. I have charted the career profile of 149 French-Canadian women who have made outstanding contributions in various fields chosen to cover different life sectors: production of goods, production and distribution of knowledge, participation in political, religious, social and familial activities.[1] The qualification of outstanding is characterized not only in terms of excellence, but more specifically in terms of innovativeness, which is defined as follows: a new pattern of behavior which is deviant with regard to the dominant norm of a social group, but which is positive with regard to the prevalent situation of that group.[2] These women have been successful most often in a professional career, and also through active participation in society. In studying their biographical data, gathered through interviews, we want to see what has led to a "successful career".

Background materials relevant to the present study deal with factors influencing occupational choice, career choice and career development. A critical, though cursory, review of the literature is presented first, in order to justify our own approach in assessing the steps leading to a successful feminine career.

Critical review of the literature

The basic concepts in research findings on occupational or career choice are generally related either to characteristics of the person or to social circumstances beyond the control of the individual.[3] The critical agents are usually parents, acting as mothers or fathers or as members of a social class with specific life chances.

For the theorists with a psychoanalytical perspective (cf. Brill, 1949), an individual's personality and impulses lead him to choose a career in which he may satisfy, through sublimation, his basic life impulse. The meaning given to work activity is the basis of

Colette Carisse, Ph.D., is Associate Professor of Sociology, University of Montreal, Quebec.

This paper was specially written for this book.

different theories. For some Freudians, ability to work is an indicator of normalcy; for others, work activity is the extension of the libidinal energy; and for still others, it is related to the instinct to master one's environment. When choice is not related to these dimensions, it is often explained by the identification principle. For example, a boy with a sadistic impulse could sublimate it by choosing to become a butcher, a surgeon or a "hired killer". Similarly, in another case study, a girl who had chosen to be a mathematician was found to identify with her father's sexual characteristics and to reject her mother's femininity. (Sommers, 1956).

The personality theorists typically combine the principle of expending psychic energy with various genetic factors and childhood experiences which influence the general style an individual develops to satisfy his needs (cf. Roe, 1953; Holland, 1966). For example, a major discriminatory factor in vocational orientation is the interest one manifests toward persons or objects, these attitudes being in turn related to modes of socialization within the family. Some social psychologists, following Maslow and Rogers, have added the notion of congruence between different images of the self and images of the occupational reality or images that significant others have both of the self and of the occupational world. Normal development toward maturity will lead to a realistic appraisal of the self's capacities and attitudes in relation to vocational demands. For Ginzberg et al. (1951), vocational choice process occurs along with adolescent development. Ginzberg has defined a series of steps having irreversible choices that lead to a narrowing range of alternatives and a final choice. In the formulation of most research concepts and theories, the choice of a career is actually the finalization of a process. Only one theory, the "developmental self concept theory" (Super, et al., 1957) postulates that development through life stages is a never-ending process. The self of a well-integrated individual is perceived as a continuously developing entity, shifting somewhat through life, as experience indicates that changes are necessary to cope with reality. A career is a field for self-expression and choices are part of the individual's technique of adjusting to a changing reality.

A third type of explanation of career choices comes from sociologists who have tried to understand the social forces which affect individual decisions. Choice of occupation, for example, is often related to the life chances and values determined by the social characteristics of the family and social class. Kohn (1969), in a well-articulated comparative research study, has shown that there is a coherence between social class perceived as an environment, values defined as constructs of reality and parental socialization behavior. In the values they stress and in the methods they use to teach them, parents prepare their children for the type of social roles and occupations they are likely to fulfill. Middle-class occupations characteristically deal more with the manipulation of interpersonal relations, ideas and symbols. Accordingly, middle-class parents expect self-directed behavior in their children. Bronfenbrenner (1958) had also found that middle-class parents are more egalitarian and rely more on reasoning and appeals to guilt. Lower-class jobs, in contrast, usually require that the individual conform to rules and procedures established by authority. Lower-class parents, likewise, are known to be more authoritarian, consistent with the necessity of maintaining order, obedience and conformity.

The family also shapes not only general values but also the educational aspirations of the children, and in turn, the school system teaches the proper values that will bring about the reproduction of the economic system through, precisely, occupational choices. It is Bourdieu's argument (1969) that class dominance is assured through this mechanism. The implications of the education system for occupational choice are predictable. Children from the lower class start school with the same mixture of fear and aspirations as children from the middle class. They soon learn that, according to the middle-class standard, they do not perform well. They soon learn to adjust and develop aspirations that are "realistic". They learn to "keep their place"; some social critics would say it is the main thing they learn from school. This process of adaptation is reflected in the fact that mobility is small from one generation to another. Using the same line of reasoning, we could add that male dominance in certain careers is also self-reproducing through the choice of courses at school and the job selection practices at work. Even if father-son succession into a specific occupation is relatively rare in an urban setting, the range of possible alternatives is relatively small. However, both the family and school system function within a specific socio-cultural environment which varies according to geography, climate, economic conditions. The debate is open as range of alternatives objectively available depends largely on the stage of technological development already attained in a given society. The individual characteristics explored by psychologists and social psychologists affect choices within a range determined, to a large degree, by social, cultural and economic conditions. The debate is open as to the degree of determinism and the relative chances for subjective "life plans" to materialize.

In an examination of these theories, the first objection is that they are built mostly upon data gathered from a male, middle class, high school or college population in the urban settings of highly developed countries (United States or Britain). Their applicability may not be universal. When they are tested on feminine or underprivileged populations, the data lead to circular or negative statements, e.g., women are not work-oriented or underprivileged boys are passive (Ginzberg, et al., 1951). These masculine-based theories and batteries of tests should be looked upon with caution, especially when one reads such conclusions as these: career women score higher on needs achievement and intraception, while homemakers have higher needs on heterosexuality and endurance, therefore a career girl is seeking to prove her worth and uses her career to avoid the sexual demands that marriage would impose upon her (Hoyt and Kennedy, 1958, as reported by Osipov, 1968: 188–189).

Secondly, the postulate that once a choice is made, life-long work is taken for granted is questionable. It is generally assumed that all men want to work, that it is the center of their life plans, and that a vocational activity is most desirable. For Brill (1949), to quote an extreme position, vacations are even a neurotic fad. . . . These approaches (with the exception of the development of the self-concept) cannot incorporate the new thinking on permanent education, the third age or the four-day week. But they certainly justify the "moonlighting" (second job) option. A mother who retreats from the labor force while children are under three years of age will be categorized as unemployed, in this work perspective. If she changes jobs to one that is more compatible with family involvement, she again will be "unstable" from a career point of view. Ideally, a career is a "succession of related jobs, arranged in a hierarchy of prestige, through which persons move in an orderly sequence" (Wilensky, 1961: 523). This definition persists as an ideal type even if "most men never experience the joys of a life plan because most work situations do not afford the necessary stable progression over the work-life" (Wilensky, 1961: 523). A fortiori, this last statement applies to female workers.

The third difficulty is a consequence of the previous approach. Work is seldom considered as a life sector that is closely related to other life sectors, namely family and community, and their interconnectedness is rarely explored when male workers are studied. Yet the findings of a recent study show clearly that unmarried men have a different level and content of work aspirations than married men. Their preference and involvement are similar to those of married women, while unmarried women have work attitudes similar to those of married men (Fogarty, Rapoport and Rapoport, 1970: 231). To our knowledge, only one study (Wilensky, 1961) has systematically linked work participation of male workers with community participation. The findings suggest a causal sequence among education, an orderly career and community participation, while a chaotic experience in the economic order fosters retreat from both work and the larger communal life. Sussman and Cogswell (1971) have questioned the assumption that decisions are made on a one-to-one basis

between the worker and the work system. They propose the notion that men plan their lives within the intricate web of primary group relationships and environment opportunity for leisure activities.

The fourth criticism, which stems from a social critic's point of view, is that the concept of "career", which is limited to the work setting, should be broadened to a life plan perspective. If we consider the consequences of the contemporary explosion of knowledge and its mass diffusion, we cannot continue to plan for an occupation and then enter a lifelong career. Instead, we will have to envisage the allocation of resources for further education, both to update job performance and to improve personal life style. If we also take seriously the need for being active in formulating society's goals, active participation will compete with career needs in the allocation of resources.

Thus the assumption is made that, in view of these modern values, *a study of life plans for both men and women should include all four sectors to which individual resources have to be allocated, namely, work, family, social participation and educational projects* either for personal development or job performance.

The postulates which I have criticized, however, are perfectly coherent with the normative patterns prescribing complementary roles for men and women, both inside and outside the family system. The differentiation of sex roles to facilitate a smooth-running modern industrial society has been raised to the status of a theory by Parsons. An industrial society based on production of goods and services requires from its personnel certain imperatives: high mobility, performance geared to competence, and a high level of education. In their drive to meet work role expectations and to surpass the average, men will get reinforcement from family systems. While men will be instrumental in giving their family a social status and a standard of living, the wife should give support and affection as part of her specialized duty within the family.[4] Scanzoni has given this theory a new glamour by formulating it in an exchange theory model. We knew that money is exchanged for power in the transactions between the economy and the polity. We now learn that it is also exchanged for love in the transactions between economy and family systems (Scanzoni, 1970).

This description largely fits reality, and for the silent majority who do not question the goals of our industrial society (i.e., mass production for high profits) and for those who take for granted the incompatibility of instrumental and affective roles, it corresponds to generally accepted role prescriptions. Some enlightened men are protesting against this social division of labor but we have yet to see a men's liberation movement contesting this rigid definition of their place in society.

In this research, I have dealt with women who are exceptions to this ideal cultural model: deviant alternatives to this model are typically chosen. The data are analysed from two perspectives. The first perspective is grounded on well-known theory. In his societal pursuits, man gets reinforcement from the household and family systems. Since women do not receive similar reinforcements and since they are still responsible for carrying on their prescribed roles as mother and wife, a strategic re-allocation of their personal resources is necessary. The second perspective stems from the critical approach adopted in this paper: a reality that is positively deviant is studied in order to

find new patterns, thus showing that a requisite variety is emerging in our society (Buckley, 1968). In order to be highly adaptable, a society must be morphogenic, in other words create new patterns of behavior in answer to new situations. These behaviors become new alternatives. It is part of our task as sociologists to uncover these new patterns, thus making them "visible". In this sense, deviation from the norm can be positively valued.[5]

Strategic choices

It would have been fascinating to compare life plans of significant men to life plans of significant women. But a first assignment remains to find out empirically the multiple answer patterns developed by women who succeeded in being creative outside of their home activities. From what we know of prescribed sexual roles, it is assumed that men will have few conflictual choices to make and that women will likely have many.

Successful and creative men
- Will have a high level of initial schooling
- Do not have to choose between family and career because of normative conflict of roles
- Have a high level of social participation if career is successful
- Will have a conflict between the need for permanent education and the responsibility to earn a living

Successful and creative women
- Will have a high level of initial schooling
- May have to choose between family and career because of normative conflict of roles
- May have to choose between a high level of social participation or a successful career

- Will have resources available for educational pursuit if negative choices have been made for work or family alternatives

Through a study of biographical data of 149 innovative women in Quebec, the paths that have led to successful involvements have been retraced, in order to assess strategic deviations. The assessment is made by comparing these choices to the modal choices of the female population.

1) *Initial schooling*: Innovators usually come from a milieu with higher than average material and intellectual resources; they are also better educated themselves (Berelson, 1964). Women in our sample are no exception. Seventy-five percent have more than a secondary school education, as compared to 5.5 percent of women in Montreal and 2.3 percent of women in the province of Quebec (1961). Half of them have seventeen years or more of schooling. This is a first deviation from the norm, especially for the women who are now forty.

2) *Getting married*: For men, marriage is not normally in conflict with the pursuit of a career. But a woman can ask herself if, in order to succeed in making a social contribution, she should ever get married in the first place. In fact, women in the group under study are more often single than women in the general population. Thirty-four percent of them have never been married, as compared to 20 percent in the total population (Province of Quebec, 1968). A sub-hypothesis is that women with a career uninterrupted by marriage will adapt to the situation by having fewer children than those with a cyclical career. This appears clearly in table 2.

3) *Gainful employment*: Eighty-six percent of the women interviewed were employed full time, compared to 36 percent in Montreal and 40 percent in the province. However, while the breadwinner role prescribes continuous employment for men, only 60 percent of the sample had an uninterrupted career.

4) *Social participation*: While only 18 percent of the women in Quebec belong to some social-political organization (Dépatie), 58 percent of the innovative women were involved in different community activities, usually in a position of leadership and intensive participation. We know that philanthropic activities help the career of the organization man, and conversely an orderly career favors social participation (Wilensky, 1961) but it is doubtful that the proportion would be higher for men than the one observed in the sample. The hypothesis is thus confirmed.

5) *Continued education*: Nearly half of the women in the group went back to school to get a higher degree or to update their academic knowledge. This is less often the choice of married women with continuous professional activity (30 percent). There is no comparative data for a male population, but only a small proportion of men already engaged in a career return to school. In a society experiencing an explosion in the production and distribution of knowledge, choices of innovative women in updating knowledge can be qualified as very modern. But in the perspective adopted here, another interpretation is warranted: lacking group reinforcement, women have to count on additional personal resources in order to do better than average. This behavior, even if we

Table 1   Profiles of Positive and Negative Choices Between Four Dichotomous Alternatives

Choices	Number of women in each profile	Alternative 1: getting married	Alternative 2: uninterrupted career	Alternative 3: further education	Alternative 4: social participation
FOUR positive choices	6	+	+	+	+
THREE positive choices	18	−	+	+	+
	22	+	−	+	+
	13	+	+	−	+
	6	+	+	+	−
TWO positive choices	15	+	+	−	−
	18	+	−	−	+
	8	+	−	+	−
	12	−	+	+	−
	11	−	+	−	+
	0	−	−	+	+
ONE positive choice	11	+	−	−	−
	9	−	+	−	−
	0	−	−	+	−
	0	−	−	−	+

Alternatives are defined as follows. *Further education:* an academic pursuit full time or part time of at least one year's duration, leading or not to a degree. *Community participation:* active membership in at least one association either as member of the executive, founding member or responsible for special activities. *Married:* legal or common-law marriage. *Continuous professional activity:* continuity means lack of interruption, total or partial, usually at the occasion of marriage or family responsibility. This activity is usually full-time gainful employment; however, in one case for unmarried women and in two cases for married women, this continuous full-time activity is unpaid. We have considered these activities as "professional" even though their work might be considered as unproductive because it was not included in the national product.

qualify it as modern, is also in line with my general hypothesis.

Additional insight can now be gained by combining the four different alternatives facing an adult woman. (The initial action of the teen-ager in pursuing a higher education is not considered here.) Four outcomes are possible, from a logical point of view. Positive actions can be taken in all four alternatives, namely getting married, pursuing an uninterrupted professional activity, participating in community activities and getting more education.

Only six women were successful in pursuing all four alternatives. However, it should be noted that all of them have small families or no children at all, and four have experienced a broken marriage. The point is not that they were too ambitious, but that society does not supply enough resources for women. The majority of women (sixty-four) chose only two alternatives, the discriminating factor being marriage versus uninterrupted career. Fifty-nine women succeeded in making three positive choices, the one negative choice again being marriage versus an uninterrupted career. Twenty women channelled their energy in one major direction, either priority to marriage with late involvement in outside activities, or a continuous professional activity, in the case of single women.

This first analysis of the material confirms the hypothesis that breaking the prescribed feminine role implies a strategy in the allocation of scarce resources. From a further analysis of the material, a typology of four different life plans, representing a cluster of meaningful behaviors, is derived.

Types of life plans

When we first look at the profiles in table 1, the diversity of actual combinations of options is striking. But after closer examination it becomes obvious that the choice between marriage and a continuous career is the most important discriminating factor in the pursuit of activities which lead to innovation. There are four career types: the never-married career girl, the dual-career woman, the cyclical career woman (those who had a career before marriage and retreat temporarily), and the "latecomer" (those who were never involved before their marriage in a specific activity). Table 2 shows clearly that these four types have characteristics of their own.

Type I: *The career girl* No one would dare call her an "old maid" for not being married. Half of them have completed graduate studies and half of those with at least an M.A. went back to school later to get a Ph.D. or to take further specialization in their field; most of those who had not completed college went back to school. They also participated in community activities, but most of their time was devoted to their work. One fifth of the innovative career girls were selected because of their activities in sports, politics, program implementations and other non-income-producing activities. Two of them also have children of their own. In both cases, this was a deliberate choice. A majority (thirty-five) have careers comparable to the careers of men having the same initial level of schooling; their careers are made up of periods of stability with moves leading to positions of higher responsibility. They are to be found mostly in the academic field or in liberal professions in bureaucratic settings.

Type II: *The dual career woman* It was assumed that at marriage — or at least when they have a child — women have to make a strategic decision: to work or not to work. Forty percent of the married women had a continuous career, probably a typical male career.[6] Most of these women, however, reported in the interview a certain restraint in the time and energy they allocated to their work achievement. But if they accommodate at work they also accommodated at home: most of them have a small family of one or two children. For women of their age group, who were raised in a society where fertility is among the highest in developed countries, family size is uniquely low (Carisse, 1964). A second cost to their continuous career is that they go back to school less often than the three other groups, even if 40 percent is a very high proportion compared to the general population of married women who took further schooling after marriage. Their community involvement, while high compared to the general population, is the lowest (both in proportion and intensity) of all four groups. Obviously, "you can't have your cake and eat it too." The decision to have a dual career (at home and at work) in the early stage of the life cycle leaves less resources for other investments in the family, in the community and for the development of the

Table 2   Types of Life Plans and Specific Characteristics of Each Type

Types of Life Plans	Age Group				Initial Schooling				Innovative Activity in Full Time Employment			
	20-29	30-39	40-49	50+	11 years or less	12-14	15-17	18+	Full time employment	Part time employment	Social parti.	Other
Unmarried with continuous professional activity n=51	16	14	8	13	6	5	14	26	40	1	8	2
	31.4%	27.5%	15.7%	25.5%	11.8%	9.8%	27.5%	51.0%	78.4%	2.0%	15.7%	3.9%
Married with continuous professional activity n=41	11	11	11	8	7	8	13	13	30	4	3	4
	26.8	26.8	26.8	19.5	17.1	19.5	31.7	31.7	73.2	9.8	7.3	9.8
Married with discontinuous professional activity n=33	4	12	11	6	3	7	9	14	16	6	7	4
	12.1	36.4	33.3	18.2	9.1	21.2	27.3	42.4	48.5	18.2	21.2	12.1
Married with late career or "recyclage" n=24	3	2	10	9	10	9	3	2	8	4	10	2
	13.0	8.7	43.5	34.8	41.6	37.5	12.5	8.4	33.3	16.6	41.2	8.3
TOTAL N=149	34	39	40	36	26	29	39	55	94	15	28	12
100%	22.8	26.2	26.8	24.2	17.4	19.5	26.2	36.9	63.1	10.1	18.8	8.0

self through further education. If we take a closer look at the content of their work activity, we also see that few of them have careers in liberal or scientific professions. Most of the women with dual careers work in fields with built-in flexibility: arts (performance or teaching), journalism, teaching. In general, they are not as highly professionalized through schooling as their unmarried colleagues, but neither do they have more schooling than those women who choose to have a cyclical career. Some of them have a semi-professional career and their more significant contributions lie in activities outside of their regular work. However, 75 percent of the innovative contributions were made in their work situation.

Type III: *The cyclical career woman* These women had a professional activity before their marriage; they presently have an activity that is similar to what they had done previously. However, they are not always gainfully employed in full-time work. Some have resumed professional activity in voluntary associations, political parties, etc.[7] A closer look at the biographical data gives us an interesting insight into the way qualified women accommodate to life. The temporary retreat at the occasion of marriage or motherhood takes all possible forms. If retreat from activity is total, it seldom exceeds five years. Two women completed their Ph.D. after marriage, worked part time when their children were under four years of age,

Table 2   Types of Life Plans and Specific Characteristics of Each Type (continued)

Types of Life Plans	Back to School		Community Participation			Size of Family	
	Yes	No	Intense	Presence	Not mentioned	Small 012	Large 3+
Unmarried with continuous professional activity n=51	29	22	15	15	21		
	56.9%	43.1%	29.4%	29.4%	41.2%		
Married with continuous professional activity n=41	14	27	3	15	23	29	12
	34.1	65.9	7.3	36.6	56.1	70.7	29.3
Married with discontinuous professional activity n=33	16	17	5	17	11	13	20
	48.5	51.5	15.2	51.5	33.3	39.4	60.6
Married with late career or "recyclage" n=24	13	11	8	9	7	5	19
	54.1	45.9	33.3	37.5	29.1	20.8	79.2
TOTAL N=149	72	77	62	56	31	47	51
100%	48.3	51.7	41.6	37.6	20.8	48	52

and then assumed full careers.

But women do not simply go back to work as the literature says. The comeback itself is most diversified. Some women take time to go back to school; half of them did. Much of their energy has also been devoted to community work; their rate of participation is higher than that of women who choose to have a continuous career, married or not. Very often, this participation led directly to paid work in a similar type of professional activity, but a few gave a sustained contribution to some movement or organization without going back to "regular employment". In fact, we have to emphasize that half of the women in this group were interviewed because of their contributions in movements or voluntary associations.

The energy that was not devoted to a continuous career was thus used for personal development through further studies, for community service through intense social participation, and also for family involvement reflected by a higher number of children. Half of them have three or more children. This is a halfway position between the dual-career families and the latecomers to an active social life.

Type IV: *The Latecomer* This is a very special group indeed; it accounts for one woman in six in the total number of subjects. It is thus probable that this path leads less easily to innovation as defined here. They are differentiated from the previous group by the fact that they did not get involved in a professional activity (paid or benevolent) before their marriage. In the first place, the majority of these women did not have access to college education. Six out of twenty-five did not even complete secondary school. However, they seem to have discovered "permanent education" before the word became fashionable; 60 percent went back to school either to get a degree and specialized training, or for their own personal satisfaction. But their main energy, for a longer period of time than the previous group, has been devoted to a large family. It is certainly a commitment to family life, since all of them have three or more children. Their participation in community affairs is usually outstanding.

The "latecomers" are persons who are involved in their society as much as in their family; two thirds of them have come to our attention because of their significant contribution in religious, social or consumer sectors, family or humanitarian movements. This involvement is also very intense: one third of them have participated in two or three associations at a high level of responsibility. However, some women in this group became active in the labor force, either by chance or because of particular circumstances that forced them to go "out" and earn a living.

This group is also older than the three previous groups: their activity could very well represent a type of "benevolence" that is fading out. This is the "good deeds" type of work. However, when we look more closely at what they are doing, we see that the majority are involved in the new type of pressure groups that either work for ideas and reform or attempt to influence the expression of collective needs and objectives. In modern parlance this is participation rather than old-fashioned charity work: none of these women distribute food baskets at Christmas time.

On the question of whether new patterns are emerging, the following observations can now be made.

1. The points of impact in society measured by the number of positive choices can be more or less numerous. The majority of women choose two or three alternatives from those selected for analysis.

2. There are no irreversible choices, but certain patterns do emerge.

   a. Only the unmarried women succeed in achieving an orderly career along with a high level of community participation and personal development through permanent education.

   b. Combining a continuous career with family activity is quite possible. The family versus work dilemma is thus a false one. However, a price has to be paid if these two alternatives are chosen. No resources are left to be allocated to some or all of the following: community participation, permanent education or a large family (three or more children).

   c. Some women have a highly flexible life: they do not have a continuous career but invest in a middle-size family, adult education, community participation, and eventually go back to work, seeking employment or picking up a chance when it comes by. Their contribution can be made either in community work or gainful employment.

3. There seems to be a division of feminine labor which corresponds to different life

plans.

a. Those who want a fully active life can choose not to get married, a choice consciously made by some of the subjects.

b. Having a large or middle-size family seems to be a specialized activity in opposition to a continuous career.

c. Social participation, if we remove from it the negative connotations attached to ''volunteer work'', could also be a positive choice made by married women, where it is accepted that the husbands earn the family living.

Conclusions

The coherence between the definition of sex roles, the separation of public and private life (work versus family), and the predominance given to work activities in a society geared to production has resulted in a social organization whereby man is motivated to meet work expectations, receives reinforcement from household and family systems, and thus has access to societal resources. If he does not himself contest the societal goals, he lives in a world that is coherent, and thus has few conflictual choices to make. Woman, because her sex role is defined as complementary (a latent postulate being that it is opposed to and incompatible with the male social role), will live in a conflictual situation whenever she outsteps her affective role within the family. In order to adapt to this situation, she will have to invent a strategy, thus creating new models. It is my contention that this is a morphogenic process, in as much as these behaviors become new alternatives for choice, thus increasing variety in the social system.

In order to avoid suffering from meaninglessness and ennui, human beings need to be engaged in activities that are goal-directed and to participate in the cultural definition of self and society. This ideal cannot be realized even on a small scale if roles are highly segregated around the home for women and around work for men. The high level of specialization which is concomitant with advanced technology favors the creation of alternatives. Multiple answers can be developed offering a variety of life plans for *both* men and women. This paper has presented actual choices of 149 women who have not only departed from the traditional role segregation, but have also succeeded in creating meaning, both for themselves and for society.

The models they have created are alternatives for both men and women, in as much as trends indicate a desire for desegregation of sex roles. Which combinations of choices will be preferred depends, on the one hand, on the work needs of society, and on the other hand, on a possible change in the positive evaluation of active leisure and quality of life generally.

Society appears to offer the educated woman the option of working or not working. While working is prescribed for men, it is still elective, even deviant, for women. Women are likely to decide positively if work values continue to be dominant in a culture which defines success in terms of mobility in professional or managerial rank, with increased status and power. But decisions will also be influenced by job opportunities linked in turn to technological innovations, a positive valuation of consumption, and the creation of new societal desiderata such as medical care and help to underdeveloped countries. Women may well decide negatively if the quality of life is culturally redefined in terms of personal development through permanent education that broadens knowledge and understanding of the world we live in, and also through creative activities for the purpose of self-expression. They may also decide to engage in community activities if our society succeeds in inventing structures of participation that will be effective in defining the goals we will be committed to. This civic model may very well offer greater intellectual and social stimulus in nonwork associations than the work situation, providing imaginative and fresh approaches to problems of the human community.

If men are influenced by the same outcome, they could be companions in the elaboration of life plans, including, for the men, the option to enjoy a personal life based on a new type of relationship. The biographies analysed in this paper are like laboratory trials; they prove that experiments in life plans do exist and can be successful.

NOTES

1. Paper presented at the meetings of the Canadian Sociological and Anthropological Association, St. John's, Newfoundland, June 1971. Translated from French by the Author. I am grateful to John Mogey and Elliott Kraus for a critical review of the paper, which resulted in substantial changes and rewriting. Lyle Larson also reviewed the text carefully for grammar and style.

2 This research project has been financed by a Canada Council Grant; it is part of a broader research project under the direction of the present author and J. Dumazedier (C.N.R.S. France). The basis of our choice and selection of subjects to be studied has been elaborated in a previous communication, ''Family Values of Innovative Women'', presented at the seventh World Congress of Sociology, Varna 1970 and published in *Sociologie et Sociétés*, vol. 2, pp. 265 — 281, 1970, and translated in M. Sussman, ed., *Cross National Family Research*, (Leiden: F.J. Brill, 1972).

3. This survey of the literature is largely based on a recent analysis of career theories by Samuel H. Osipov, *Theories of Career Development*, (New York: Appleton-Century Crofts, 1968).

4. What sociology professor wouldn't like to have a wife as devoted as Louise Durkheim was to her famous husband? (see excerpt)

5. Low frequencies in a distribution cannot obviously be drawn from a representative sample of the general population. In order to get a sample of innovative women, we relied on the following procedure. We made a list of names of women mentioned in the mass media during the year 1969, in relation to something they had accomplished. Two newspapers *(Le Devoir* and *La Presse)*, and TV and radio broadcasts were used. We are grateful to the people who gave us access to their files. We thus made a list of some 2,000 names. We asked informants in different fields to add names to the list, and experts to designate whom they considered innovative. Very soon in this process ''prominence'' became apparent and few new names were added. The subjects interviewed were distributed as follows, according to our system of categorization. Producers of cultural models: scientific research (10), artistic creation in arts and theater (35), sports (5). Communication of models: teaching (14), mass communication (17). Economic activities: production (7), distribution (7), syndicalism (6). Societal activities: credit (7), family (13), pressure (13), religious activities (5), political action (5), personal expression (16). In the present analysis only 140 interviews had been transcribed and were ready to be coded on the topics pertinent to this article.

6. Fogarty, Rapoport and Rapoport have coined the expression ''dual career family''. They apply it to families in which both husband and wife have a full time career. This is true for

the families of this group of women, but dual also means two careers for women: homemaking and professional activity.

7. This calls for a timely definition of the concept "professional activity". It could mean simply productive work, i.e., producing goods and services that contribute to the gross national product and consequently appear in the gross national income: that is, in effect, paid work. It usually has this strict sense in the French "activité professionnelle". We prefer, however, to define the concept by the content of the activity. A professional activity calls for: a) exclusive competence derived from a body of systematic knowledge; and b) normative regulation that orients the activity towards service (Wilensky, 1964). One characteristic of skill is its transferability; it can be applied in different fields. It is also linked to a long

prescribed training. From this point of view, the medical doctor working free of charge in a family planning clinic is not less professional than her colleague who has a high-class practice. However, the argument against such "benevolent work" is that women, by this type of activity, are nurturing and patching a society damaged by the men working in the system (E. Sullerot). Besides, being unpaid, this work brings esteem, but not prestige or access to power. On the other hand, many women argue that everything can't be evaluated in terms of money. Leaving these sentiments aside, we can still argue that the president of a citizen's committee is doing work that is just as valuable in an active society as that of a member of parliament, except that one is paid, the other is not.

REFERENCES

BERELSON, Band, and Gary Steiner, *Human Behavior*: *An Inventory of Scientific Findings* (New York: Harcourt Brace World Inc., 1964).

BOURDIEU, Pierre et Jean-Claude Passeron, *La reproduction* (Paris, Editions de Minuit).

BRILL, A.A. *Basic principles of psychoanalysis* (Garden City, N.Y.: Doubleday, 1949).

BUCKLEY, Walter, "Society as a Complex Adaptive System" in *Modern Systems Research for the Behavioral Scientist* (Chicago: Aldine Publishing Co., 1968), pp. 490-514.

CARISSE, C., *Planification des naissances en milieu canadien-français* (Montréal: Presses Universitaires de Montréal, 1964). "Family Values of Innovative Women: Perspective for the Future?", in M. Sussman, ed., *Cross National Family Research* (Leiden: F.J. Brill, 1972), pp. 35-52.

DEPARTIE, Francine, Participation socio-politique des femmes du Québec, no. 10, Etudes préparées par la Commission Royale d'Enquête sur la situation de la femme canadienne, 1971 (Ottawa: Information Canada, 1971).

FOGARTY, Michael, Rhona Rapoport, and Robert Rapoport, *Sex, Career and Family*, (London: George and Allen Unwin Ltd., 1970).

GINZBERG, E., S.W. Ginsburg, S. Adelard,

and J.L. Herma, *Occupational Choice: An Approach to a General Theory* (New York: Columbia University Press, 1951).

GOFFMAN, E., *Asylums* (Chicago: Aldine Publishing Co., 1961).

HAVIGHURST, R.I., "Youth in exploration and man emergent", in H. Borrow, *Man in a world at work* (Boston: Houghton Mifflin, 1964).

HOLLAND, I.L., *The Psychology of Vocational Choice* (Waltham, Mass: Blaisdeel, 1966).

HOLLINGSHEAD, A.B., *Elmtown's Youth* (New York: Wiley, 1949).

KOHN, Melvin, *Class and Conformity: A Study in Values* (Homewood: The Dorsey Press, 1969).

LIPSETT, L., "Social Factors in Vocational Development", *Personnel Guidance Journal*, 1962, (40), pp. 432-437.

MULVEY, Mary Crowley, "Psychological and socio-psychological factors in career prediction of women," *Genet. Psychol. Monogr.*, 1963, 68, pp. 309-386.

OSIPOV, Samuel H., *Theories of Career Development* (New York: Appleton-Century-Crofts, 1968).

ROE, Anne, "A psychological study of eminent psychologists and anthropologists and a comparison with biological and physical scientists", *Psychological monographs*, 1953, 67, no. 2 (Whole no. 352).

ROE, Anne, *The Psychology of Occupations* (New York: Wiley, 1956).

SCANZONI, John H., *Opportunity and the Family: A Study of the Conjugal Family in Relation to the Economic Opportunity Structure* (New York: Free Press, 1970).

SOMMERS, V.S., "Vocational choice as an expression of conflict in identification", *American Journal of Psychotherapy*, 1956, 10, 520-535.

SULLEROT, E., *Demain les femmes* (Paris, Lafont-Gonthier).

SUPER, D.E., et al., *Career development: self-concept theory.* (New York: CEEB Research Monograph, no. 4, 1963).

SUSSMAN, Marvin and Betty Cogswell, "Family influences on job movement", Paper presented at the Eleventh International Family Research Seminar, London, September 1970. Published in *Social Forces*, Fall 1971.

SUPER, D.E., J. Crites, R. Hummel, Helen Moser, Phoebe Overstreet, and C. Warnath, *Vocational development: a frame work for research* (New York: Bureau of Research Teachers College, Columbia University, 1957).

WILENSKY, Harold, "Orderly careers and social participation: the impact of work history on social integration in the middle mass", *American Sociological Review*, Vol. 26 (August 1961) 4, pp. 521-539.

YOUNG, M.D., *The Rise of Meritocracy* (Baltimore: Penguin Books, 1961).

The life style of voluntarily childless couples

Veevers has written extensively on married women who have chosen not to bear or rear children. This article discusses what it means to be a voluntarily childless wife. There is a distinct preference, if not idealization, for the marital bond; role differences between husbands and wives are minimized; learning is preferred to teaching, which leads to an emphasis on intellectual relationships with others; there is a quest for novelty and travel; and there is freedom to aspire realistically for professional success, to choose to work or not to work.

As Veevers indicates, the data is based on a non-random sample of fifty-two married women and should not be generalized to other voluntarily childless women. In an earlier article (Veevers, 1973), the sample is more carefully described. It will be helpful to briefly summarize this information. The average age of the sample is twenty-nine, ranging from twenty-three to seventy-one years. All are Caucasian and live in urban areas (Toronto and London, Ontario) and most are middle class. Most have had some university experience. With the exception of one housewife, all are employed or furthering their education. Most are areligious and inactive in religious circles. Most were reared in stable homes by full-time housewife-mothers. The average length of marriage in the sample is seven years. Though the marriages are basically egalitarian in decision-making activities, most follow the traditional division of labor. Most indicate they would seek an abortion if they became pregnant.

More than half of the wives are on the pill. About one quarter of the husbands have had a vasectomy and another 25 percent are seriously considering it. Nearly one third of the wives entered marriage with a childlessness clause in their marital contracts. The remainder have remained childless as a result of a series of decisions to postpone having children — a future that has never arrived. In the interim, these women have come to reassess their goals and opted for childlessness.

It may be emphasized that voluntary childlessness is only one fourth of the picture. It would be valuable to compare the life style of voluntarily childless couples with the involuntarily childless, those who didn't want children but have them, and those who wanted children and have them. A variation on this theme would include comparisons with those who plan to have children but haven't yet started their families, and those who do not want children but expect to have them anyway (there's "nothing else to do").

The life style of voluntarily childless couples

J. E. Veevers

Most persons in our society spend most of their active adult years in a living situation which revolves, in varying degrees, around the needs and interests of children. Whether or not Canada can be called a child-centered society remains a moot point, but it is undoubtedly true that most adults, especially most women, devote a large proportion of their waking hours to the care, management and amusement of their children. The cohabitation of adults and children necessitates predictable structuring of the daily round of adult activities. Most persons in our society marry at a fairly early age, and most remain married to one or another mate for most of their active adult years. Concur-

rently, most married persons have and want at least one child, who is usually born very soon after marriage.[1] Consequently, with the exception of the very rich, the very indifferent, or the very innovative, most adults structure most of their adult lives in such a way as to take into account the demands of child care. The presence of children, whether they are wanted or accepted or merely tolerated, perforce dictates limitations of life style alternatives.

Contrary to these generalizations, there exists a statistically deviant group of persons who, for a variety of reasons, are not involved in the child-centered life style (Veevers, 1972a). It has been estimated that of all

J. E. Veevers, Ph.D., is Associate Professor, Department of Sociology, University of Western Ontario, London, Ontario.

This article was specially written for this book.

Canadian women who ever marry, approximately 10 percent never become mothers, and of these, approximately half are voluntarily childless (Veevers, 1972b). During the past several years, an on-going study has been concerned with the phenomenon of voluntary childlessness in Canada. Preliminary data are available based on intensive depth interviews with a non-random self-selected volunteer group of fifty-two subjects who have been married for a minimim of five years, and who have remained childless by choice.[2] Although such a sample is small and can in no way be assumed to be representative of childless wives in general, the qualitative richness of the data is suggestive of a number of possible alternatives to the dominant cultural norms. The present paper is part of a series of articles based on these data.[3] Its scope is restricted to just one aspect of the phenomenon of voluntary childlessness, namely the existence and nature of a child-free life style.

The pronatalist biases of both the general public and social scientists are such that, if a query regarding fertility motivation is raised at all, it tends to be phrased in negative terms: why do some deviant persons not want children? Moreover, once the question has been posed, the answers sought also tend to lead to unpleasant definitions of the parental role (Veevers, 1973a; 1973b). While both of these kinds of questions are legitimate strategies of inquiry, they do not exhaust the implications of the available data. In addition to negative factors relating to the rejection of motherhood because of the undesirable aspects of the child-centered life style, there are positive factors relating to the rejection of motherhood because of desirable aspects of the adult-centered life style. The former kinds of factors are primarily *reactive* ones: that is, they involve reactions to the disadvantages of having children. The latter kinds of factors are primarily *attrahent* ones: that is, they involve attractions towards the advantages of the adult-centered life style. Reactive motivations for voluntary childlessness may involve such negative factors as unhappy parental marriages, atypical experiences with siblings, or an absence of strategies for minimizing the financial and emotional costs of parenthood (Veevers, 1973d). Conversely, attrahent motivations for voluntary childlessness may involve such positive factors as intense marital relationships, maximization of occupational opportunities, the quest for novel experiences, and many diverse preoccupations which might be loosely designated as self-actualizing. It is with the latter attrahent properties of the child-free life style that the present paper will be concerned.

I. Dyadic withdrawal: the idealization of husband-wife relationships

Most women perceive that the roles of wife and of mother are complementary and compatible. They endorse the components of the motherhood mystique which suggest that children do not detract from the man-woman relationship, but rather strengthen and improve it. Others may also perceive that children are necessary for a good marriage, and believe childless marriages to be therefore unhappy. Many voluntarily childless wives, in contrast, reject these assumptions. They remain childless not so much because they are against children as because they are for marriage, and believe that children are a disruptive force which would alter both the intensity and the quality of the husband-wife relationship.

Berger and Kellner (1970:61) suggest that

one dynamic involved in the construction of a new social reality to be shared jointly by a married couple is the gradual exclusion of others, who are relegated to positions of less and less significance in the social world, and who are eventually either disregarded entirely or given only a minor role. Such processes are not necessarily either deliberate or recognized, but they constitute a necessary step if the marital relationship is not to be endangered. In the child-free life style, such processes are carried to their logical extreme, and the childless couple see in each other "a reference group of one". A dominant component is commitment to the ideal that a married couple should be a self-sufficient unit, who look to each other for the satisfaction of most (and perhaps all) of their social and psychological needs. Such couples approximate the pattern of total involvement outlined by Cuber and Haroff (1966). They relate to each other not only as man and wife, but also as lover and mistress and as "best friends". The presence of children makes such dyadic withdrawal difficult if not impossible.

A shift from a dyadic relationship to one involving children involves quantitative and qualitative changes in the nature of the man-woman relationship.[4] The childless, perhaps more than their parental counterparts, recognize and anticipate such changes. They consider that the presence of a third person would lessen the intensity of their dyadic commitment, and their contentment with the marital situation is high enough that they seek mechanisms to maintain the status quo, rather than to alter it in any way. For example, one wife comments:

A child would come between us. I wouldn't be able to be as close to my husband if I had a child because a child is so helpless and needs so much attention. And then I don't know if I want to share him.

A less extreme statement of the same viewpoint, and one more frequently expressed, is the explanation of the postponement of children because "we wanted to enjoy each other first". There is a clear if unspoken implication that a couple cannot really enjoy each other if they have children.

Unilateral commitment to a strong and exclusive dyad is perceived to be dangerous, in the sense that one's emotional vulnerability to the existence and concern of the spouse is very great. Although such danger is recognized, the rewards of such an intense and exclusive relationship are perceived as worth the risk. For example, one woman comments that "you have all your emotional eggs in one basket", but this exclusive commitment is viewed as a positive thing with which children would interfere, rather than as a frightening thing. She goes on to comment that "if you have children, then not all of your emotional involvement would be with each other anymore and you would have lost something".

In discussing the causes of divorce, Berger and Kellner (1970:69) contend that:

Typically, individuals in our society do not divorce because marriage has become unimportant to them, but because it has become so important they have no tolerance for the less than completely satisfactory marital arrangement they have contracted with the particular individual in question.

In the same way, some individuals in our society may avoid parenthood not because they consider marriage unimportant, but because they consider it of such primary importance that nothing else should be allowed to interfere with it. The purpose of marriage has become marriage as an end in itself, the quality of the dyad being something to be preserved at all cost.

It is sometimes suggested that one impetus to parenthood is the perception that a problem exists, and that having a child might constitute to some degree a solution to that problem. For example, there are frequent allusions to the idea that childbearing may solve or at least diminish husband-wife tensions, or that motherhood may provide fulfillment where other sources of fulfillment for the woman, such as marriage and/or a career, have failed (LeMasters, 1970:28; Udry, 1971:444). One characteristic which distinguishes some childless couples from some parental couples may be that they do not perceive serious problems in their lives, and so do not seek parenthood as a solution to them. Satisfaction with the present is associated with a desire to preserve the status quo.[5] As long as the child-free life style is rewarding, there may be serious hesitation to introduce any change and hence possibly to threaten that desirable state. Many of the wives interviewed would agree with Michels (1970:14) when she explains: "Life is so good right now that we hesitate to change it in any way."

The desire to maintain the intensity of commitment to the man-woman relationship by avoiding distractions and deflections from the dyad is not considered a credible motive for avoiding parenthood, and is generally interpreted by others as the immature inability of one of the marital partners to compete with a baby and to become resigned to sharing the spouse with someone else (Popenoe, 1936; LeMasters, 1957:531). It is widely believed that the marriages of childless couples are less happy and less fulfilling than the marriages of parents.

One of the paradoxes associated with the child-free life style is that it appears that those childless couples who have the "best" marriages are the most likely to encounter hostile responses from others. If a childless husband and wife are hostile towards each other, and apparently have an unsatisfactory relationship, the observation of their interaction simply confirms the belief of parents that such is to be expected among those without the benefits of children. Moreover, since the mutual involvement of the husband and wife is minimal, their potential for involvement with the community at large is still high, whether or not they share others' concern with children. However, if a childless husband and wife have a close and intense relationship, their apparently successful marriage represents a double threat. On the one hand, their very existence challenges the folk-wisdom that children are necessary for a happy marriage; on the other hand, their preoccupation and satisfaction with each other minimizes their interest in the community at large and lowers the probability of their involvement with it. Although it is always hazardous to generalize from small samples, our data indicate that the childless couple who are least likely to be greeted with hostility are the couple who have a mediocre or even a poor relationship, and who maintain extensive interests in and involvements with the greater community.

II: Occupational commitment

1. *Mobility and Security*   Although with one exception, all of the childless wives work and intend to go on working indefinitely, not all have a sense of occupational or professional commitment. Approximately

half of the wives interviewed are dedicated to their work and take a large part of their identity from it; in contrast, the remaining half work mainly for extrinsic rewards, such as money and the satisfactions of interacting with others in the job situation. This is not to imply that the latter group are necessarily dissatisfied, since most report that they like their work, but only that their occupation is not a significant source of identity or intrinsic fulfillment.

For those who are not intrinsically involved in their work, the important component of the child-free life style is the fact that they are (or feel) free to move from one job to another, or even to quit work altogether. The "trap" involved in having children is the possibility of being "trapped" in a job which one no longer likes, but which is necessary because of one's responsibilities. The child-free life style allows one the freedom to change jobs, to take a more interesting job for less pay, to go back to school, or in other ways to remain mobile inside or outside of the occupational structure.

Social, occupational and geographical mobility are all greatly facilitated by the simple fact of the relative affluence of childless couples. As noted elsewhere (Veevers, 1973d:193), if couples were to be matched in terms of the husband's income, the childless would be shown to have many times more resources than their parental counterparts. Compared with mothers, childless wives are much more likely to work outside the home[6], and if they do work, they are more likely to work continuously and to be relatively successful. In addition, they "profit" more from their incomes because of the lesser need to hire household help. Even more importantly, the childless avoid the direct and indirect costs of child-rearing, which have

been estimated to range from \$20,000 to \$60,000 per child.[7]

2. *Professional Aspirations*   There can be little doubt that being a mother adversely affects the probability that a woman will achieve marked success in her professional and occupational endeavours. Whether or not motherhood significantly affects a woman's general competence and ability at the average level is a question for debate, but there is clear evidence that it significantly affects the probability of extraordinary achievements. Many case histories are available of remarkable women who have managed to have very successful careers while being married and raising large families. However, while such examples do suggest that a combination of many roles is possible for some exceptional women, they do not alter the fact that a woman's potential for professional success is greatly enhanced by avoiding the motherhood role.[8] For example, in a still unpublished study, Sells (1972) examined the rates of completion of degrees among Woodrow-Wilson fellows in the United States, controlling for sex, marital status and child-bearing. Among this very select group of exceptional students, drop-out rates ranged from 26 to 66 percent, depending on the field of study and a number of personal factors. In the humanities, the difference in drop-out rates for those with and without children is only two percent for men and 13 percent for women, a pattern not markedly different from that in the social sciences, where the difference is three percent for men and 11 percent for women. However, in the physical sciences quite a different pattern emerges. In this field of study, having a child decreases a man's chances of completing his degree by only one percent, but re-

duces a woman's chances by 31 percent. Whatever the explanations for this discrepancy, the perception on the part of female graduate students in the physical sciences that having a baby will significantly lower their chances of career success seems to be well-founded. If motherhood makes such a significant difference among a group of women known to have exceptional ability and high motivation, it might be assumed to make even more difference in the professional careers of women of average or below average ability who are not as highly motivated in the first place. It is not surprising that approximately 40 percent of the women in *Who's Who* are childless (Frank and Kiser, 1965: 69).

The childless wives interviewed have not yet made what might be considered "outstanding contributions" in their different fields of activities, and except for their decision to be childless are not innovative.[9] However, their average age of twenty-seven is still too young to have made "outstanding achievements" and their life plans and degree of expressed motivation would indicate that their potential for innovation is relatively high. For example, one wife is doing original research as a post-doctoral fellow in biochemistry; two are completing doctorates in the physical sciences; and one novelist and one artist are just beginning to achieve some professional recognition after years of apprenticeship.

Many voluntarily childless wives perceive that their varied career and professional interests occupy much the same place in their lives that children occupy in the lives of mothers. However, the question of who is compensating for what is open to a variety of interpretations. The relationship between childlessness and career achievements is complex and probably reciprocal. As childless women become more successful in their careers and are increasingly rewarded for their achievements, they become more committed to remaining in their careers. A number of childless wives are seriously concerned with the extent to which having children would disrupt otherwise promising career prospects — a concern well justified by the fact that children do in many cases constitute a major disruption of professional development, much more so for women than for men. Conversely, it seems probable that when women are not experiencing success in their careers and are not finding them rewarding, becoming pregnant may be a convenient and an acceptable way out of an unpleasant situation. If some women do not achieve professional recognition and success because they become mothers, it is also possible that others become mothers because they do not achieve professional recognition and success. In the world view associated with the parental life style, the high achievements of childless women are considered to be attempts to compensate (usually unsatisfactorily) for their "failure" to achieve motherhood. In the world view associated with the child-free life style, motherhood is designated as neither a significant achievement nor an especially creative act. It is contended that it is equally plausible that for some women a baby may compensate for the book they never wrote, the picture they never painted, or the degree they never finished. Several voluntarily childless wives reported that the only times they had seriously considered having children was when they had suffered some substantial career set-back, such as failing a major examination, conducting an expensive but useless scientific experiment, or being unable to find suitable employment.

III. The quest for experience

In the child-free style, a recurrent theme is the value of new experience: on seeing new places, feeling new sensations, performing new tasks, coping with new situations. The experiences are considered valuable in two respects. First, they are considered necessary for the development of one's full potential, for growth or progress or what might be called self-actualization. Second, they are valued as ends in themselves, for the sake of their newness and their disruption of routines. Kirkpatrick (1963:513) suggests that, assuming adequate birth control, childless couples are probably less adventurous than married couples who choose to be parents. Our experience with the present sample suggests that, if anything, the opposite may be the case. The desire to sample life is variously interpreted, and some childless couples are very adventurous but have chosen to be venturesome in ways other than parenthood. The quest for new experience has several manifestations: the search for novelty, the desire to travel, and the absence of "generativity".

1. *Novelty, Newness and the Avoidance of Routine*   For some childless wives, the search for new experience involves deliberate attempts to be innovative, and to avoid predictable routines. A first requirement to achieve these ends is to minimize the number of familiar and predictable tasks with which one must be involved, thereby gaining a considerable amount of free time. Again and again, the childless wives refer to the fact that full time housewives with children had

so much of their time pre-empted by the necessity of performing daily and repetitive tasks that they had no opportunity to seek out novelty, to have new experiences, or to develop themselves as persons.

In the world view of the voluntarily childless, being child-free is defined as having the potential for new experience. It is the potential itself that is of central importance for their construction of reality, not whether or not they have managed to take full advantage of unique opportunities. Childlessness means the freedom to go on seeking new experience. Such freedom may never be used, or may be used only very seldom in very mundane and very conventional and non-creative ways. As an extreme example, one wife comments:

I think that it would be very much of a shock to him if we were to have a child now, because he is just the type of guy who wants to pick up and go down to the Dairy Dell for an ice cream when he wants to go. He likes to be organized but he does not like to have to go through the rigamarole all the time of getting things ready.

When this woman talks about the joys of being free to travel, she means free to drive fifty miles out of town for a picnic. What is important is not the nature of the experience in objective terms, but the potential for taking advantage of opportunities for new experiences should they ever arise.

A minority of wives had made a point of seeking new experiences which, although not exactly unique, are not entirely typical of suburban routines of middle-class couples. For two wives, the search for new experience involved joining a nudist camp and tentative experiments with swinging. Two others were involved with the drug culture, and their quest for new experience involved the extensive use of a wide variety of drugs. A number of other wives reported transitory experiments with drugs, mostly marijuana, to see what it was like and whether or not it would produce a new experience. Some who had no drug experience explained that it was due to lack of opportunity, and that given a chance they would like to try marijuana or other drugs at least once.[10]

Positive values on the quest for experience may lead to some ambivalence about the processes of pregnancy and birth. Women may wonder what being pregnant would feel like, and be fascinated by natural childbirth as a wondrous and miraculous experience, while considering the child produced to be of somewhat secondary importance.

With the exception of some women who are intensely involved in demanding careers, most childless women report that they have a considerable amount of leisure time, and that this is an important aspect of their lives. A wide range of leisure time interests are pursued. These include some typically feminine pursuits, such as gourmet cooking, sewing and needlework, as well as typically masculine pursuits, such as woodwork, hiking and competitive track and field. Many are involved in activities not typically associated with either sex, such as reading, and passive entertainments such as concerts and movies. There is no apparent pattern in these activities, other than the discrepancies to be expected with wide differences in income. Two possible exceptions to this generalization are the relatively small amount of leisure time devoted to formal organizations and the relatively large amount of leisure time devoted to pets.

Very few of the women interviewed are involved in many formal organizations. By and large, they are not "joiners", and express little interest in clubs, lodges, study groups or recreational associations. A major objection appears to be the extent to which formal organizations violate values of spontaneity and freedom. Even when the theme of the formal organization is of special interest, as for example, Zero Population Growth, woman's liberation or a political party, their attendance is only sporadic.

All childless wives are aware of the stereotype that childless people are inordinately fond of pets of various kinds, and tend to treat animals like humans. Of the wives interviewed, about one third had no pets at all, about one third had one pet, and about one third had two or more pets. It is difficult to estimate whether or not this distribution is comparable to the distribution of pet ownership in the general population, since appropriate statistics are predictably difficult to obtain. However, what data are available suggest that about 60 percent of all parents own pets.[11] The presence of pets in a home has, in some respects, some similar consequences to the presence of children. To the extent that pets act as child surrogates, their presence may be a direct factor in facilitating postponement of childbearing or in eliminating it altogether. Two kinds of processes are involved: in some instances, the existence of a pet obviates the perceived "need" for a child by fulfilling the same functions. Of the childless wives with pets, about half openly admitted that animals served as child surrogates, and argued that in fact animals were more satisfactory. However, for many of the childless wives without pets, experiences with the problems associated with pet care directly reinforced the decision not to have children. To some extent, the presence of a dependent animal interferes with the adult life style in the same way as does the presence of a dependent child.

2. Wanderlust: the importance of traveling. Most childless wives express great enthusiasm for traveling, and perceive that one of the major advantages of being childless is being able to enjoy longer and more frequent trips than they could otherwise manage. A considerable part of their conversation is concerned with recapitulating past travels, and with planning future ones.

Some childless wives have managed to do a considerable amount of traveling, avoiding the short and superficial tours offered to the usual tourist. For example, one young wife recently returned from a hitch-hiking trip with her husband around Canada and the United States. The previous year, they had spent some time on a walking tour of Morocco, and were making plans and saving money to return to Africa the next fall, where they hoped to take a month-long trip by camel caravan across the Sahara. An older couple spend at least two months a year traveling in Europe or in the West Indies, and during the rest of the year make many week-end trips to New York, Boston or other large centers in the north-eastern states. One young wife accompanied her geologist husband on excursions to the Arctic, and another frequently managed to be included in zoological field trips. Several wives spoke of the possibility of saving enough money to both stop work for six months or a year and travel around the world, and had saved enough money and made enough arrange-

ments to make such large scale plans plausible. All reiterated the impossibility of even considering such adventures if children had to be included in the plans.

Although some childless couples do manage long and exotic trips, in most cases the travel plans must be arranged in terms of the requirements of two jobs, leaving the childless with not much more holiday time than parental couples. However, an important characteristic of the child-free life style is that travel is less likely to be restricted to one or two weeks a year formally designated as vacation time (Veevers, 1973d:194). In comparing childless and parental couples, the discrepancy in amount of traveling is probably greater for the wives than for the husbands. Typically, mothers remain with their children while fathers travel as their occupations dictate. In contrast, childless wives are more free either to travel with their husbands, or to seek deliberately the kind of work which involves extensive traveling.

IV.   The absence of "generativity"

Erikson introduces the concept of "generativity", which he defines as "the interest in establishing and guiding the next generation" (1963:276). One component of the child-free life style is a distinct lack of generativity, which is manifest in two related forms: a preference for learning versus teaching, and a dislike of or disinterest in childish things.

Some childless wives lack generativity, in that of the complementary roles of teaching and learning they consistently prefer learning and tend to gravitate to people whom they define as either peers or superiors.[12] Within this perspective, the wives express concern with being competent, and with utilizing oneself and one's abilities to full capacity. Their lack of interest in children is the same as their lack of interest in other people they consider to be their intellectual inferiors, and who they therefore do not find challenging, stimulating, or helpful. What holds their interest is not reviewing things they already know, but learning new things. One wife expresses this directly:

Child-raising is a bore, because you are always going over the same things. I do not have any teaching instincts at all. I don't like to deal with people who know less than I do. I like to deal with people who know more than I do.[13]

In keeping with their preference for learning rather than teaching, many childless wives make consistent and deliberate efforts at developing their skills and potential. They tend to view education as a life-long process rather than an end state. Many are in school, or are taking night courses, or are planning to return to school some day. Others are concerned with developing their facility for self-expression by writing, painting, drawing, sculpting, or even arranging flowers! A general orientation regarding competence makes them strive to maximize their own competence, while expressing considerable impatience for the incompetence of others. In fact, their levels of competence and ability vary considerably, but many have in common a value on self-improvement and on the learning situation.

In the opinion of many voluntarily childless wives, "the main trouble with children is that they are so immature". Although this comment and others like it are offered facetiously, they reflect an important component of the child-free life style relating to a

dislike of childish things, or at least a disinterest in them. Although there is a general positive orientation towards children in our culture, the adjective "childish" which means "being like or befitting a child" also means "puerile, weak and silly". "Childish" has a negative connotation and "childlike" a positive one, but both adjectives refer to the same objective behavior.

Leisure time activities which are designated as "family entertainment" are by implication wholesome and moral; in contrast, activities which are designated as "for adults only" are those which are of at least questionable morality, such as smoking, drinking, drug use, and vicarious and direct sexual experience. One of the significant aspects of the child-free life style is that one can evaluate recreations and entertainments by some other standard than whether or not they are "good for" or "suitable for" children. One can select a place to live by other criteria than that it is a "great place to raise children", which by implication means safe, conventional, predictable and dull. As long as parents are committed to the idea that they should do all or most things with their children, and committed to the idea that only certain kinds of activities are possible or suitable for children, their opportunities for new experience are drastically limited.

It is commonly believed that "parents should be more moral than non-parents" (Goode, 1968:339), a perspective often shared by the childless. A disadvantage of having children may be the feeling that as a parent one is obligated to give up a number of minor vices which, although not seriously wrong in and of themselves, are not a "good example" for the moral development of one's children. Parenthood may be defined as precluding slightly immoral, naughty or unacceptable activities. Among people who marry very young and have children very soon thereafter, the moral constraints imposed by their parents because they were "too young" for adult pleasures may be almost immediately replaced by constraints imposed by their image of the necessity of parents to set a good example for their children. In the process, they are only peripherally involved if at all in adult pleasures and recreations. Once the life style of adults who are accountable only to each other is observed and enjoyed, there may be a real reluctance to return to the child-centered world of wholesome movies, polite vocabulary, and safe and educational pursuits, all of which are already excessively familiar from one's own safe and wholesome childhood.

V. Egalitarian role relationships: minimizing husband-wife differences

Most of the childless wives interviewed report that their marriages are characterized by very egalitarian sex roles, with an orientation in which the husband and wife are considered to be of equal value to the relationship, with equal levels of authority and equal levels of competence. Kirkpatrick (1963: 527–531) suggests that with the birth of the first child, sex differences are accentuated, and existing sex roles are more clearly defined and differentiated. Whether or not this is so, most childless wives believe it to be so. They perceive that the present state of sharing which they have with their husband would be disrupted by the necessity of caring for children, and by implication by the necessity of staying home full time. Egalitarian role relationships may be both a consequence and a cause of childlessness.

For example, Carr (1963:559) compared the marital adjustment of a matched sample of infertile and fertile marriages and found that "the dominance pattern reported by the infertile couples was more likely to show a democratic pattern and less likely to display disagreement than that of the fertile couples."

Egalitarian role relationships are often perceived, both by laymen and by social scientists, as having come about as a result of a power struggle between husband and wife, in which the wife "won" in her desire to become more emancipated, and the husband, having "lost", reluctantly extended additional privileges to her. However, in a number of the marriages studied, the initial impetus for the wife's emancipation appears to have originated with the husband, who not only tolerated her outside interests but actively encouraged them.

VI. Some interpretations and implications

The child-free life style incorporates and integrates a number of related themes. One significant aspect is the emphasis on spontaneity. The childless can utilize their copious leisure time to take advantage of opportunities or impulses with a minimum amount of arranging, maintaining flexibility and variety in their daily round of activities. Compared with parental couples, they need to take into account fewer contingencies involving other people's desires and needs: the life style combines the maximum opportunity to plan with the minimum necessity of doing so.

A second related theme is the emphasis on options: on maintaining as many alternatives for the future as possible. There is a value on preserving as many choices as possible regarding the course of one's potential development and the nature of one's future experiences. As LeMasters (1970) has repeatedly observed, parenthood is one of the few roles from which one may not honorably withdraw. The sense of responsibility for the welfare of children may be defined as precluding the option of terminating reciprocal role relationships with one's spouse or one's employer. Children also dramatically limit one's future options by simply dramatically limiting one's future affluence. The financial limitations they impose, both in terms of direct costs and in terms of the loss of the mother's income, preclude a number of kinds of experiences. The folk-wisdom that money cannot buy happiness may very well be correct, but there is no doubt that money can and does increase the range of one's alternatives: in the child-free life style, the maximization of present and future alternatives is considered crucial. Although the child-free life style does not necessarily involve a preference or a demand for unstructured situations, the childless enjoy the belief that they could change the structure of their lives if they so desired.

The essence of the child-free life style comes down to an emphasis on the "free". Minor themes like spontaneity and options relate to the major orientation: the maintenance of a sense of autonomy. It is not suggested that in any ultimate sense the childless are necessarily any more free than people with children. Like parents, they are constrained by their early socialization, by conventional social expectations, by the requirements of earning a living, by the limitations of their abilities and resources, and by a host of other factors. However, what is important for the life style is that they *feel* autonomous.

The opportunities which are open to a childless wife are clearly different from those open to a mother, especially a mother with pre-school-age children. However, the fact of being childless is not in itself sufficient to ensure participation in the child-free life style. Before that can occur, the woman must learn to define the differences associated with being childless as worthwhile opportunities. Not all childless women learn to do so. For example, Blood and Wolfe (1960:137) asked childless women in the Detroit area to list some of the good things about not having children, and found that over a third were not able to think of any advantages at all. The fact of being and/or feeling relatively free is of course of little consequence if one shares the opinion expressed in Janis Joplin's aphorism: "Freedom's just another word for nothing left to lose!" The voluntarily childless not only feel free, but define freedom as a major advantage of non-parenthood.

Almost all of the childless wives interviewed considered the child-free life style to be a highly satisfactory alternative. However, not all of the major themes which have been described were considered to be equally important by all of the women. Some of the women interviewed would heartily concur with all of the themes; others would consider only several of them to be significant. For example, the quality of marriages ranges from total husband-wife involvement to indifference to hostility, and only those wives involved in total relationships are concerned with the theme of dyadic withdrawal. The model presented constitutes an ideal type, which particular couples will approximate in varying degrees.

It is difficult to determine the extent to which the advantages of the child-free life style are significant factors in the decision never to have children. About a third of the wives in the present sample decided before marriage to be permanently childless: essentially, they had a childlessness clause in their marriage "contract". The other two-thirds decided to remain childless after a series of postponements of childbearing (Veevers, 1973c). Given the limitations of the present data and the dangers of generalizing from a small non-representative sample, it is tentatively hypothesized that those voluntarily childless wives who decided at a very young age never to have children tended to be primarily influenced by negative reactions against the motherhood role. Conversely, it is tentatively hypothesized that those voluntarily childless wives who followed the postponement model tended to be primarily influenced by positive reactions towards the child-free life style. It is probable that although all cases may involve a combination of both reactive and attrahent factors, the relative significance of negative and positive motives varies. For involvement in the child-free life style to constitute a significant contingency in the development of childless careers, non-mothers must not only observe that their lives are better than the lives of their childbearing peers, but that their lives are better *because* they do not have children. Mothers may be observed to suffer many deleterious effects from having children, but such consequences may be attributed to their own incompetence or neuroses, rather than to the fact of motherhood per se. Alternatively, the "problem" may be defined as an inappropriate interpretation of the motherhood role, such as having too many children or having them too closely spaced. Any person may be involved in the concerns of the child-free life style: for that involvement to become significant for the development of permanent childlessness, there must be the added definition that its many benefits are directly due to the absence of children, as a necessary if not a sufficient condition.

NOTES

A preliminary version of this paper was presented to the National Council on Family Relations at their Annual Meeting in St. Louis, Missouri, October, 1974. The author is deeply indebted to Professor Norman W. Bell of the Department of Sociology of the University of Toronto for his thoughtful guidance and for his many helpful suggestions at all stages of the research. The author also wishes to thank Professor Douglas F. Cousineau of the Department of Sociology of Glendon College for his critical evaluation of the manuscript.

1 Leslie (1967) estimates that of all women getting married for the first time, approximately 50 percent have a child within two years. This figure is not surprising when one considers that of all brides getting married for the first time, approximately one in five is pregnant at the time of her wedding. Of all such brides who are teenagers, approximately

one in three is pregnant, and of those weddings in which both bride and groom are teenagers, more than half of the brides have already conceived (Christensen, 1958:206; Burchinal, 1960; LeBarre, 1968:47; Udry, 1971:142). Data from the 1961 Canadian census indicate that of all wives who become mothers, the average interval from marriage to the birth of the first child is less than two years. The group of women who postpone motherhood for the longest time are those who marry very young and who have relatively small families: even under these unusual circumstances, the interval from marriage to the birth of the first child averages less than four years (Harrington, 1969:17).

2   For descriptions of the methodology and differentiations among kinds of childless couples, see "Voluntary Childless Wives: An Exploratory Study" (Veevers, 1973c).

3   For the presentation and discussion of additional findings, see "The Child-Free Alternative: Rejection of the Motherhood Mystique" (Veevers, 1973d) and "The Moral Career of Voluntarily Childless Wives: Notes on the Construction and Defense of a Deviant World View" (Veevers, 1974).

4   In discussing dyadic withdrawal, Slater (1963:469) observes that:

> The advent of the first child in itself tends to weaken the exclusive intimacy of the dyad, first by providing an important alternative (and narcissistic) object of cathexis for each member, and second, by creating responsibilities and obligations which are partly societal in nature, and through which bonds between the dyad and community are thereby generated.

5   Strong (1967:2246) studied over 300 childless Negro couples in Washington, and reports two types of voluntarily childless couples: the tradition-oriented who had had negative family experiences, and the upward-striving who had enjoyed positive family experiences. Strong suggests different central concerns of these two groups. "The tradition-oriented group desired economic security and freedom from the impoverished and unstable background that many of them had known, while the upward-striving group emphasized maintaining the status quo which they had

achieved".

6   This generalization holds for both white and non-white women of all ages from fifteen to forty-nine, with the largest discrepancy being found among white wives aged twenty-five to thirty-four (Sklar, 1971).

7   Christensen (1958:470) cites a 1944 study by the Metropolitan Life Insurance Company which estimated that for families with an income of between $5,000 and $10,000 a year, the total cost of raising a child to the age of 18 would be over $20,000. Considering the progressive decline of the dollar, he suggests that a more realistic figure in 1958 would be about $30,000. Kirkpatrick (1963:512) estimates that in 1962 the cost at the $5,000 to $10,000 income level would be about $30,000. The Institute of Life Insurance focused attention on the variability of cost by basic family income, and concluded that:

> Adequate provisions for bringing up a child for 18 years were estimated to cost over three times the family's annual earnings in 1969. This figure was derived from an income of a four member family in which earnings were between $7,500 and $10,000 after taxes in 1961. . . . For 1969, the cost of raising a child ranged from 290 percent to 360 percent of the annual family income. . . . For moderate budget families, the total cost of bringing a child into the world and raising him to the age of eighteen emerged, with many assumptions and limitations, as about $30,000. *This figure completely discounts the dollar worth of the mother's time and effort* (Sohn, 1971:1–7, emphasis mine).

Pennock (1971) presents data taking into account the dimensions of rural urban variations, regional differences, and total family size. The recent *Report of the Commission on Population Growth and the American Future* (1972) estimates that it costs the average family about $60,000 to raise one child and to send it to college: about $20,000 in direct costs and about $40,000 in indirect costs. The cost of a second child is obviously lower, being estimated at only about $29,000. Similar estimates of the high cost of raising a child are beginning to have legal implications and credibility. *The Windsor Star* (November

25, 1971) carried the following news item:
A drug firm that filed a faulty birth control prescription for a woman will have to pay $42,000 in expenses to raise her unexpected child. The decision was handed down by a Superior Court in Los Angeles to a 46-year-old who was given sleeping pills instead of the requested birth control pills, became pregnant, and gave birth to a son who is now 6. The money is that which should cover the cost of raising him until he is 21.
Occasionally, even higher costs are suggested. Rosenthal (1972) estimates that: "For a mother with grade school education, two children would cost about $120,000. For a mother with a year of graduate study, the figure would be about $200,000."

8 For example, in a study of women scientists and engineers, Perrucci (1970) found that childlessness was more common among the career-oriented and the successful than among the non-career oriented and the less successful.

9 Our usage of the term "innovative" is in the sense suggested by Carisse, (1976) who defines it as:
. . . a new pattern of behavior which is deviant with regard to the dominant norm of a social group but which is also positive with regard to a prevalent situation of that group . . . this positiveness is assessed by two criteria: participation in an active society and self-development of the individual.

10 Although marijuana use is illegal and is still socially defined as deviant behavior, it is not unusual and in many groups it is considered acceptable. In 1971, the Alcoholism and Drug Addiction Research Foundation surveyed a random sample of 1,200 adults living in Toronto. They report that of adults aged twenty to twenty-five, 28 percent had used marijuana at least once during the past twelve months; and that of adults aged twenty-six to thirty, 13 percent had done so. Of those persons who used marijuana, more than half had done so at least seven times in the past year (Smart and Fejer, 1972).

11 The U.S. National Center for Health Statistics (1971:39) reports information on a national probability sample of over 7,000 noninstitutional children in the United States aged six to eleven years. Of these, 60 percent are reported by their parents to own a pet. The actual proportion of all parental couples who have animals in the home may be expected to be somewhat higher than this, as some pets may be perceived as belonging to the parents and so not reported in questions concerning children. It is possible that the probability of pet ownership is somewhat different for the parents of very young children, or of teen-age children, that it is for the parents of children aged six to eleven. No statistics are given on the kinds or number of pets, but some information on responsibility for pet care indicates predictably that in most cases (about 80 percent) the pet owned by the child is usually cared for by the parent.

12 The preference for learning over teaching is obviously not characteristic of all childless wives, for some of them have chosen teaching as a profession and appear to be performing the role competently and with reasonable satisfaction. However, their interest in generativity and in teaching is adequately fulfilled by their work five days a week with other people's children.

13 In response to the question of whether or not she liked children, another like-minded wife replied:
Look, let's face it, nobody ever says it but children are stupid. When a six-year-old has an I.Q. of 120 that means he is very smart *for a six-year-old*. But compared to even a slow grown-up person he is stupid. I guess I like kids as well as I like other stupid people. I mean — I know it's not their fault, but all the same I don't want to spend much time talking with them. And even bright people may be ignorant. Teenagers are as smart as adults, but they haven't lived long enough to know much. They are smart, but they are not informed. I like people who are both — and I guess that always means adults. I've always preferred people older than me.

REFERENCES

Berger, Peter, and Hansfried Kellner
  1970 "Marriage and the construction of
    reality." Pp. 50-73 in H.Q. Drietzel
    (ed.), *Recent Sociology* No. 2. London:
    Macmillan.
Blood, Robert O. Jr. and Donald M. Wolfe
  1960 *Husbands and Wives: The Dynamics of
    Married Living*. New York: Macmillan.
Burchinal, Lee G.
  1960 "Research on young marriage:
    implications for family life education."
    Family Life Coordinator 9:6-21.
Carisse, Colette
  1976 "Life plans of innovative women: a
    strategy for living the feminine role."
    See pp. 379-394 in this book.
Carr, Genevieve Delta
  1963 "A psychosociological study of fertile
    and infertile marriages." Dissertation
    Abstracts 24:5598.
Christensen, Harold T.
  1958 *Marriage Analysis*. New York: Ronald
    Press.
Commission on Population Growth and the
    American Future
  1972 Report. Washington, D.C.: Commission
    on Population Growth and the American
    Future, 726 Jackson Place N.W.
Cuber, John F., and Peggy B. Haroff.
  1966 *Sex and the Significant Americans: A
    Study of Sexual Behavior Among the
    Affluent*. Baltimore, Maryland: Penguin
    Books.
Erikson, Erik K.
  1963 Childhood and Society. New York:
    W.W. Norton.
Frank, Myrna E., and Clyde V. Kiser
  1965 "Changes in the social and demographic
    attributes of women in 'Who's Who'."
    The Milbank Memorial Fund Quarterly
    43:55-75.
Goode, William J.
  1968 "Pressures to remarry: institutionalized
    patterns affecting the divorced." Pp.
    331-341 in Norman W. Bell and Erza F.
    Vogel (editors) *A Modern Introduction to
    the Family*. New York: Free Press.

Harrington, Judith A.
  1969 Childlessness in Canada 1961. Master's
    Thesis, Department of Sociology, The
    University of Western Ontario, London,
    Ontario.
Kirkpatrick, Clifford
  1963 *The Family as Process and Institution*.
    New York: Ronald Press.
LeBarre, M.
  1968 "Pregnancy experiences among married
    adolescents." *American Journal of
    Orthopsychiatry* 38:47-55.
LeMasters, E. E.
  1957 "Parenthood as crisis." *Marriage and
    Family Living* 19:352-355.
  1970 *Parents in Modern America*.
    Homewood, Illinois: The Dorsey Press.
Leslie, Gerald R.
  1967 *The Family in Social Context*. New
    York: Oxford University Press.
Michels, Lynnell
  1970 "Why we don't want children."
    Redbook Magazine (January):10-14.
Peck, Ellen
  1971 *The Baby Trap*. New York: Bernard Geis
    Associates.
Pennock, Jean L.
  1970 "Cost of raising a child." Paper
    presented at the 47th Annual Agricultural
    Outlook Conference, Washington, D.C.
Perrucci, Carolyn Cummings
  1970 "Minority Status and the Pursuit of
    professional careers: women in science
    and engineering." *Social Forces*
    49:245-259.
Pohlman, Edward
  1970 "Childlessness, intentional and
    unintentional: psychological and social
    aspects." *The Journal of Nervous and
    Mental Disease* 151:2-12.
Popenoe, Paul
  1936 "Motivation in Childless Marriages."
    Journal of Heredity 27:469-472.
Rosenthal, Jack
  1972 "Two children, from birth to B.A.,
    estimated to cost $80,000 up." *New York
    Times*, December 30.

Sells, Lucy
1972 "Disciplinary and sex differences in doctoral completion." Unpublished manuscript. Berkeley: University of California, Department of Sociology.

Sklar, June
1971 "Childless women." Paper presented at the Annual Meeting of the Population Association of America, Washington, D.C.

Silverman, Arnold and Anna
1971 *The Case Against Having Children*. New York: David McKay.

Slater, Philip E.
1963 "On social regression." *American Sociological Review* 28:339-358.

Smart, Reginald G. and Dianne Fejer
1972 Marijuana Use Among Adults in Toronto. Toronto: Addiction Research Foundation.

Sohn, Sara A.
1971 "The cost of raising a child." Unpublished mimeograph. New York: Institute of Life Insurance.

Strong, Ethelyn Ratcliff
1967 "The meaning of childlessness to childless negro couples." Dissertation Abstracts 28:2346.

Udry, J. Richard
1971 *The Social Context of Marriage* (second edition) New York: J. B. Lippincott.

United States National Center for Health Statistics
1971 "Parent ratings of behavioral patterns of children: United States." Vital and Health Statistics, Series 11, Number 108.

Veevers, J. E.
1972a "The violation of fertility mores: voluntary childlessness as deviant behavior," Pp. 571-592 in Craig Boydell, Carl Grindstaff and Paul Whitehead (editors), *Deviant Behavior and Societal Reaction*. Toronto: Holt, Rinehart and Winston.

1972b "Factors in the incidence of childlessness in Canada: an analysis of census data," *Social Biology* 19:266-274.

1973a "Voluntary childlessness: a neglected area of family study." *The Family Coordinator* 23:199-205.

1973b "The social meanings of parenthood." *Psychiatry: Journal for the Study of Interpersonal Processes* (in press)

1973c "Voluntarily childless wives: an exploratory study." *Sociology and Social Research* 57:356-366.

1973d "The child-free alternative: rejection of the motherhood mystique." Pp. 183-199 in Marylee Stephenson (editor), *Women in Canada*. Toronto: New Press.

1975 "The moral career of voluntarily childless wives: notes on the construction and maintainence of a deviant world view." *The Family Coordinator* (forthcoming).

Communes, group marriage, and the upper-middle class

This study reports on a three-year consideration of communal living and group marriage by eighty couples. Sixty-two of the couples were interested in the possibilities of these life styles, while eighteen were either already living in communes or group marriages or had had previous experience. The results are based on interviews, questionnaires, discussion group notes, correspondence, and anecdotal records. The major reasons for the wives' involvement included isolation with children, over-dependence on husband for adult contact, or underutilization of talents and training. Husbands were more concerned about the "rat race" or a desire for higher living standards. Both husbands and wives were concerned about child-rearing and training issues, the need to expand their sexual intimacies, and the processes of change and its implications. As a result of the study experience, three group marriages and three communes have been formed.

It may be emphasized that this is *not* a study of group marriage itself (its successes and problems), but rather a study of a group of people interested in considering the issues and implications of entering alternative life styles. It is also a select group, as fifty-five people who wanted to join the group were rejected.

In view of our earlier discussion of stability within alternative marriage forms, it is appropriate at this point to briefly discuss the general advantages and disadvantages of group marriage from both a societal and an individual perspective. Students interested in further study of group marriage in particular will find the following references helpful: Constantine and Constantine, 1973; Kilgo, 1972; Bartell, 1971. No attempt is made in the following discussion to deal with life styles other than group marriage. The list is intended to be illustrative rather than exhaustive.

Advantages to society
1. There are economic advantages. Collective consumption will reduce waste and permit communal purchase of items now purchased separately by nuclear households. The pooling of resources will reduce the necessity of high individual income and permit a more systematic response to unemployment (e.g., one member of the six), job fluctuation, and related problems.
2. Group marriage could facilitate the more efficient management of human resources. Household and child-rearing responsibilities could be handled by specialists. Those most interested and best trained in child care, for example, could assume these tasks, permitting those more interested and skilled in other areas such as cooking to specialize.

3. Educational possibilities are enhanced. An efficiently run household will release individuals for more educational time with children and greater participation in extra-marriage learning experiences.

4. By providing more adults with an opportunity for intimate relationships with children, even though there are fewer children (e.g., six adults and two children), the need for each couple to have their "own" will be reduced. Space will also be more efficiently utilized. Many, if not most, nuclear families occupy far more space than is needed in a society suffering from increasing population density problems.

5. Extramarital sexual variety (swinging and adultery) which now tends to create serious marital problems, would most likely be reduced because of increased variety within the marital group.

Advantages to the individual

1. The undue emphasis on individualism and egoism in Western society seems to have become a central problem in satisfactory marital adjustment. As individuals share themselves with several others, group pressures will facilitate greater cooperation and the development of a group-centered personality, as found among the Kibbutzniks and the Hutterites.

2. Finances are a fundamental sore point in monogamous marriage. Inadequate financial success decreases conjugal satisfaction (Scanzoni, 1970). Financial cooperation within the group marriage will reduce the seriousness of this problem for the individual.

3. Group marriage would seem to provide a regularized opportunity for the development of human potential through small group participation (similar in kind to sensitivity experiences).

4. Assuming rational mate choice, individuals with particular interests or needs could develop and practise these interests (e.g., mothering needs).

5. The satisfaction of an individual's sexual drives may be optimized in a group marriage setting because of multiple legitimate opportunities.

Disadvantages to society

1. Widespread group marriage would require radical changes in the present economic system. The purchasing power of the group marriage, with volume buying (some group marriages incorporate), would markedly increase while the actual consumption of many goods (e.g., lawn-mowers) would be reduced.

2. Family units headed by a larger number of employed adults could not be as responsive to social and geographical mobility as the nuclear family. The present economic structure poses severe problems for the dual-career marital unit, let alone a quad-career marital unit.

3. Quad-marriage is more complicated legally. It would involve more complicated licensing procedures and divorce procedures. The rights of individual members (both adults and children) relative to inheritance and related matters are more complicated than in the nuclear family, given the increase in multi-lineal kin.

Disadvantages to individual
1. One of the common assumptions of Western society is the need for privacy. The opportunity and freedom to seek privacy is reduced in group marriage.
2. The goals of the individual (career, acquisition of goods, interests) must be set aside in deference to the needs and goals of the group.
3. Mate choice becomes a group decision because ultimately the group must approve the new member(s) even though one of the members has strong positive feelings toward the person.
4. Few people are currently socialized for complex psychological intimacy. Most persons married monogamously have difficulty understanding and communicating with their spouses. This problem would be intensified in group marriage.
5. Sexual gratification is closely linked to psychological intimacy. Given the complexities of multi-lateral intimacy, sexual gratification will be more problematic. Pair-bonds will probably form out of necessity.

These suggestions are intended to provoke discussion and critical assessment. Along with the Ramey paper, there is considerable food for thought.

Communes, group marriage, and the upper-middle class

James W. Ramey

Most current articles and discussions about communes and group marriage begin with the assumption that these phenomena are generally associated with youthful dropouts from society, or religious fanatics. There would appear to be, however, a much more significant group, largely made up of upper-middle class, thoughtful, successful, committed individuals, that is also involved in or exploring the possibility of setting up communes or group marriages. There are at least three reasons why this movement is relatively unknown. First, sensational reporting sells newspapers, and "dropouts" in colorful clothing and unwashed beards tilling the soil are sensational. Second, most of us

James W. Ramey, Ph.D., is Director, Center for the Study of Innovative Life Styles, New City, New York.

From *Journal of Marriage and the Family*, Nov. 1972, pp. 647-655. Copyright 1972 by National Council on Family Relations. Reprinted by permission.

would prefer to think of such unusual life styles as aberrant or deviate practices that would only be associated with inexperienced disaffected youth, or religious "kooks." Finally, the people who set up communes or group marriages *without* dropping out of society take great care to remain unnoticed by their neighbors and associates.

In this report on almost three years of activity among a sample of eighty couples, *both* husbands and wives are from the two top occupational classifications, that is, they are almost all in academic, professional, or managerial positions, if they are employed at all. These individuals believe that a commune or group marriage might provide a framework in which they could do better what they are already doing well. In order to function optimally within the present social and economic structure; they seek to organize family units on a more complex basis than the nuclear family structure can accommodate.

What is a commune? Structure and modus operandi among communes can differ to such a degree that the following working definition is suggested:

When individuals agree to make life
commitments as members of one particular
group, rather than through many different groups,
they *may* constitute a commune. The number of
common commitments will vary from commune
to commune, the critical number having been
reached at the point at which the group sees itself
as a commune, rather than at some absolute
number.

What, then, is a group marriage? The critical factor in group marriage is that *each* of the three or more participants considers himself to be married to at least two other members of the group. Actually, in today's world

we should say "pair-bonded" instead of married since some pair-bonded couples may not be legally married. Constantine (1971) has coined the term "multilateral marriage" as a substitute for group marriage since, according to him, group marriage has traditionally involved two pairs, and thus the term would not accommodate a triad group. I prefer to retain the more familiar term, which I believe is self-explanatory, whereas multilateral marriage is not.

This paper concerns both group marriage *and* "evolutionary" communes because the eighty couples in the study were curious about both forms of complex living. Although only eighteen of these couples had any previous experience with group marriage or communal living, they were all initially attracted to the group by advertisements in *Saturday Review, New York Review of Books*, and similar places, inviting couples interested in exploring the pros and cons of various forms of expanded family to meet with the group. The few couples who initiated this activity were open-minded as to the degree of complexity they were willing to consider, ranging from intimate friendship to group marriage, but they were not willing to accept everyone who answered their ad.

They devised a questionnaire as a preliminary screening device which was to be answered by respondents, along with a short essay indicating why they wanted to join the group. The avowed purpose of this screening was to eliminate "swingers" and others whose interest was considered "not serious." Upon receipt of the questionnaire and essay, couples deemed tentatively acceptable were interviewed by telephone and a decision was made to either suggest that they forget about this group or invite them to an orientation session. In our three-year follow-up study, we hope to interview the fifty-five couples who were not invited to join the group as well as the eighty couples who "passed" to see if we can find any real differences between the "accepted" and "rejected."

We have reported elsewhere (Ramey, 1972) the logarithmic increase in the degree of complexity in relationships as one moves from monogamous dyadic marriage through open marriage, intimate friendship, and communal living, to group marriage. It should be recognized that the degree of intensity also increases as one moves up this scale in the complexity of marriage alternatives. Intensity might be called one of the distinguishing characteristics of the subjects of this report. In addition to ability to deal with more complex relationships there must be willingness to take on such a task.

In dyadic marriage the commitment is to the individual. Kanter (1968) calls this cathectic commitment. I would call it "willingness to accept unlimited liability for." A commune is held together by a different kind of commitment, a group commitment rather than commitment to an individual. A group marriage combines these different types of commitment. In Kanter's terms, the addition of cognitive and evaluative commitment to cathectic commitment.

The subjects of this study saw these differences in concrete terms. They were aware that dyadic marriage has become institutionalized in our society and internalized by each of us as we grow up, so that the decisions facing a newly married couple are relatively minor ones (how many children?) within a well-defined formal structure. No such formal structure exists for intimate friendship, communes, or group marriage, however. The participants must evolve their own structure.

This group, then, expended considerable energies on working through cognitive commitment (was the group making sufficient progress to justify continuing to invest energy that could be directed elsewhere?) and evaluative commitment (were the perceived goals and aims of the group worthy of continued support?). These two types of commitment have long since been institutionalized for dyadic marriage.

It was not necessarily the intent of these eighty couples to form communes or group marriages, although several did result from their activities. They seemed more intent on "hashing out" the actual ground rules and decision structure required for setting up alternatives to marriage at varying levels of complexity. Some couples were content to stop at the level of developing intimate friendships. Others were willing to take the additional step of adding propinquity to this relationship and forming some kind of "commune," while a few found other couples with whom they were willing to take the final step of cathectic commitment, *i.e.*, actually establishing multiple pair-bonds. Many couples found that they were either uncomfortable with the level of complexity required or "were still looking for the right people" with whom to become involved in some type of relationship more complex than dyadic marriage.

This paper indicates the kind of people involved in this activity, explicates the concerns that led them to this action, and reports the kinds of problems they discussed and the various activities in which they engaged as a part of the exploration process. Both communes and group marriages have emerged from this group and it is expected that others will emerge. This paper is based on the in-

Table 1 Age of Participants

	Talkers		Doers	
	Male	Female	Male	Female
Youngest	21	21	24	23
First Quartile	28	26	29	26
Median	33	28.5	33.5	28
Third Quartile	42	38	38	37.5
Oldest	56	55	52	47
Mean	35.2	30.7	34.7	29.8
SD	8.66	6.48	3.89	3.87

itial questionnaires, anecdotal information, correspondence files, and observation of group activities.

A few portions of the demographic data will be presented in comparative fashion, contrasting the eighteen couples who have actually lived or are living in communes or group marriages with the sixty-two couples who have expressed active interest in doing so, although it should be understood that the samples are so small that statistical significance cannot be attached to the numbers. For the sake of brevity, the 18 experienced couples will be called Doers and the 62 inexperienced couples will be called Talkers.

Only six couples in the total sample live *outside* a major metropolitan area. New York City, Boston, and Philadelphia metropolitan areas together account for 63 per cent of the Talkers and 79 per cent of the Doers. The age range in the two groups is indicated in Table 1.

Most of these couples have at least one child, and the age ranges of the children in the two groups are comparable. Over two-thirds of each group have at least one child and 50 per cent have at least two, with comparable figures for three, four, and five, and insignificantly small numbers above five.

Standard Census Bureau Occupational Classification categories were collapsed together to arrive at the distribution shown in Table 2. The national percentage distribution is included for comparative purposes. An additional category has been added to account for students, retired individuals, and housewives. The only statistically significant difference between the two groups shows up in this Table, *i.e.*, the percentage of housewives in the two groups is significant at the .05 level.

Academic level is in line with occupational classification. About 90 percent of the men and 42 per cent of the women have completed four or more years of college and 22 per cent of the men and 9 per cent of the women hold the Ph.D.

The original impetus for this group came from several couples who were curious to see if there were others who shared their interest in complex marriage. They decided to run the aforementioned ad in *Saturday Review* and to install an unlisted phone for receiving calls from prospective members. The couple who agreed to answer the phone also accepted the responsibility for maintaining correspondence files and doing much of the "secretarial" work. At first the entire group screened prospects, but once general criteria had been established, this task was turned over to a volunteer committee. The questionnaire used for initial screening is reproduced in Table 3, with the composite answers of the eighty couples. The original intent of these questions was said to be to indicate the degree of "openness" in the marriages of applicants to the group. The answers to questions two and twelve suggest that this group was unusual along the sexual dimension as well as in other ways previously indicated.

Table 2   Occuptational Classification

Classification	Males			Females		
	U.S.	Talkers	Doers	U.S.	Talkers	Doers
	%	%	%	%	%	%
Professional, Scientific, and kindred workers	11.9	72.4	81.3	13.0	44.1	61.1
Managers, Officials, Proprietors, etc.	13.2	19.0	18.7	4.4	6.8	22.2
Clerical, Sales, and kindred workers.	13.0	1.7	—	38.7	6.8	—
Craftsmen, Foremen, and Skilled workers.	19.0	1.7	—	1.1	—	—
Operatives, Services, Farmers, and Laborers.	42.9	—	—	42.8	—	—
Graduate Students, Retired, and Housewives.	—	5.2	—	—	42.3	16.7

What concerns led these couples to spend as many as three nights a week in the various activities of this group? Predictably, certain problems weighed more heavily for the women, others for their husbands, while a few seemed to be of equal concern to both. I have distilled these basic issues from many hours of interviews, discussions, and reading anecdotal records and correspondence.

Wives seemed most concerned about (1) the sense of isolation that comes with raising children, (2) overdependence on the husband for adult contact, and (3) less than optimal development and use of their talents and training.

The first problem occurs over a surprisingly large age span. Many wives feel it even more severely because they waited until their late twenties to start families. Leaving budding careers made them feel even more isolated by the children. These families move more often than the general population. They seldom have a group of ready-made relatives and friends to fall back on. Many who live in

the city are afraid to venture out at all unless absolutely necessary. Those who live in the suburbs complain of a lack of any real community of interest with their neighbors, apart from the children, and even this is lacking unless the children are in the same age group.

Interwoven with the first problem is the tendency toward overdependence on the husband for adult contact. Without support from kinship, friendship, and neighbor groups, husband and wife share isolation in the home, and, as Slater (1968) has put it, they must be lovers, friends, and mutual therapists. What with moving every couple of years, these couples do not have time to develop many friends. The husband satisfies his need for outside contact at the office, but the wife who is not employed outside the home faces a barren prospect indeed. Not that she has no neighbors. She may have many acquaintances but one looks for one's friends among peers, and neighbors frequently seem not to provide peers from

Table 3 Group-Designed Questionnaire for Applicants*

Question	Talkers		Doers	
	YES	NO	YES	NO
	%	%	%	%
We have formed close emotional ties with other families in the past.	69	31	83	17
We have formed close ties with other families that involved sexual intimacy.	47	53	72	28
Our ideal is to link up closely with other families, each retaining its own home & privacy but with much emotional sharing.	90	10	81	19
Our ideal is to form a commune.	43	57	53	47
Our ideal is to form a group marriage.	44	56	53	47
We've had experience in a commune or group marriage.	—	100	100	—
We have a professional background in the behavioral sciences.	50	50	67	33
We have participated in therapy, group therapy, sensitivity training, or encounter groups.	69	31	83	17
Children require firmness and consistency to guide them until they can determine their own attitudes	71	29	81	19
Children should be given as much freedom as possible so long as they don't harm themselves or inconvenience others.	100	—	100	—
We take care that our children don't observe us in a sexual situation.	50	50	43	57
We would expect to be sexually free with any couple with whom we related really well.	76	24	88	12
We can enjoy sex with others without requiring an emotional involvement.	37	63	28	72

*Composite answers for the eighty couples in the study.

whom to choose.

Most of the women in this sample are college educated and trained in a career specialty, but a substantial minority have not had the opportunity to develop a career that optimally utilizes this training. Either they have dropped out of the job market while the children are small or they have been forced to make willy-nilly job changes when their husband's career moves the family to a new location. Others have been unable to make *any* use of their training and ability because their families have been so large as to require their full-time presence in the home.

The men are particularly concerned about two problems that are probably universal among men in our society. They seek a means of freeing themselves from financial insecurity and the rat-race. They also would like to achieve higher living standards.

The first of these concerns is often linked to the need of the wife to pursue her career goals. What do you do when a career opportunity for the husband necessitates a move to Oshkosh, Wisconsin, which will blast the wife's career? Family financial security may be an overwhelming factor in the decision, as when the husband's current job is being phased out. Will the family's financial resources permit them to stay put while he tries to match the Oshkosh offer locally? For many upper-middle-class families the answer is "Not for very long!" Aside from this kind of bind, most males must constantly evaluate and re-evaluate the nature of "opportunity." Is it fair to themselves and to their families to turn down an opportunity to move up the career ladder? Will the career be blighted if the "opportunity" is turned down? How many pounds of flesh does one owe to Mammon (or to increasing family income) anyway?

The second male concern is related to the first. Although they explore the idea cautiously, the notion of sharing at least some capital expenditures, perhaps a summer home or a houseboat or hobby equipment, is an appealing partial solution to the problem of raising the family standard of living — one that men are as eager to explore as the problem of increasing financial security. Not only is it economically sound, if done with the proper safeguards, it is even ecologically desirable to conserve natural resources (this sounds "tongue-in-cheek" but has been a matter of serious discussion in the framework of having to start somewhere, so why not where it is more personally rewarding). While initially concerned about stretching family resources, many of these men have gone on to realize that an enlarged family with multiple incomes and reduced expenses would be very advantageous insofar as all family economic functions in our quasi-capitalistic society are concerned.

As long as the basic economic unit is a nuclear family that must survive on one or at the most two adult incomes, the family is hard put just to stay even with the ever-mounting cost of living. More and more families are tempting bankruptcy just putting their children through college, now that the cost of a year of college is ranging as high as $5,000 with no end in sight. Setting aside money for investment seems far removed from the reality of trying to break even. The

opportunities to share in the joys of capitalism are real enough — they abound at every turn — but without a stake they are unattainable. Conversations about pooling resources to buy big ticket or luxury items almost invariably shift to consideration of the competitive advantages, within our societal structure, of a commune or group marriage. Setting up a rainy day fund to weather a period of unemployment or a Clifford trust for educating the kids are exciting possibilities, but they pale in the wake of the tax and income-producing advantages of, for example, incorporating a group marriage or a small commune as a subchapter S corporation, or using the condominium approach in order to swing the financing of an apartment building.

Childbearing and training are a major concern for both parents and nonparents among our sample. There is common concern for providing the growing child with a variety of adult relationships. Both the commune and group marriage seem to promise the kind of flexibility that would not only provide more adult models, but provide a better male/female mix since there would presumably be more frequent male presence in the home. There is also an expressed need to raise children among adults with compatible life styles so that the children will feel more secure with respect to differences in the life style of their own family and their friends' families, especially after they reach school age. Many respondents are vitally interested in the training of the new generation, whether they have children of their own or not. They hope to establish free schools or to at least explore the possibility of supplementary training.

A major concern of these couples is freedom to include sexual intimacy among the joys of friendship when appropriate. Forty-one couples have formed ties with other families that included sexual intimacy and indicate that they would expect to be sexually free with any couple with whom they related really well. Although the other 39 couples in the sample have not yet had such experience, only 14 of these couples indicated that they would *not* expect to be sexually free with any couple with whom they related really well. One out of three couples in the first group indicated that they also could enjoy casual sexual contacts. Only one out of five couples in the second group so indicated.

This desire to be free to establish intimate friendships appears to reflect both the need to broaden and deepen adult contact outside the dyadic marriage and the belief that such activity measurably strengthens the couple's own marriage. As noted above, there can be little doubt that the stress here is on person-to-person rather than genital-to-genital relationships. These individuals simply do not want to exclude the possibility of intimacy as a part of friendship where and when appropriate. They deny emphatically that intimate friendship is another term for swinging and this distinction would seem to be substantiated by their responses with regard to casual sexual contacts. As I have noted elsewhere (Ramey, 1972), there is a well-developed transitional pattern between swinging with minimal emotional involvement and "matured swinging groups," which Stoller (1970) calls "intimate family networks." I believe the term "intimate friendship" delineates this type of group or network in a more meaningful way, because it applies equally well to friendship with a single individual or couple and such a friendship should not be excluded by terminology

from our understanding of the kind of relationship we are discussing, *i.e.*, one in which the emphasis is on the friendship rather than on the intimacy.

The final major theme that brings these couples together is a shared concern for what is happening. In every age there are a few individuals, often academic or professional people, at the growing edge of society, questioning, examining new social issues before most people know they are issues, looking for new ways to maximize their potential, opportunities, and pleasure within current social structures. Many people seem to believe that youth has a corner on the market of challenging the accepted responses to problems of living and that the older generation simply follows where youth leads. History tells us otherwise. The couples in this sample are among the "life style leaders" of today. By way of example, while social scientists are just now discussing seriously the possibilities inherent in consensual extramarital and comarital relationships, a preponderance of these eighty couples have already been involved in intimate friendships, some of them for over two decades, or since the new generation was in rompers!

How are these couples approaching the task of seriously considering group marriage or communal living? The array of interaction has covered a wide range of activities. Nearly every day at least one group was meeting and on weekends there were usually several, such as regular Saturday afternoon children's activities, a music group, an ongoing encounter group, or the meeting for newcomers.

This latter activity is especially noteworthy because it set the tone for newcomer participation in other activities. Although there was no formal structure or organization

among these couples (individuals simply initiated activities that interested them), several individuals volunteered to screen newcomers for the group. First the new couple
sent in the questionnaire form on which the
screening committee passed judgment. Assuming the new family was found acceptable, they were invited to an orientation meeting, where the emphasis was on drawing out
the newcomers, ascertaining their interests
more specifically, and telling them about the
various study groups, experimental groups,
discussion groups and other activities currently under way, so that they might find
their way into the various activities that interested them most. These initial sessions
with newcomers achieved a level of candor
seldom encountered in any but old established friendships. When asked about this,
newcomers cited both their anticipation,
based on the screening they had survived,
and the emphasis at the meeting on openness, feedback, acceptance of differences in
perception and opinion, and willingness to
dispense with taboo subjects. This atmosphere of permissiveness and understanding
in which feelings and attitudes could be
freely and nonjudgmentally expressed and in
which males and females tended to be treated
as peers appeared to be characteristic of all
of the activities of these eighty couples.

Some of their activities involved only a
few intensely interested people while a few,
such as family day outings, involved almost
the entire group. A few activities were almost exclusively female while a few attracted no wives, but most tended to be couple projects. Some discussions or activities
were short-lived, for example, putting together a complete listing of all families in the
group, with addresses, phone numbers, and
a 100-word statement of their interests. The

first time this was attempted it took six
weeks or so and two or three people were
involved in the project. When it was attempted a second time, after the first listing was
out of date, there wasn't enough interest
among the group as a whole to get the project
off the ground, even though several people
were willing to do the work.

Some activities were longer-term in nature. Study groups tackled a number of potential projects, for example, setting up a
free school, converting a brownstone, running encounter groups, discussing the ins
and outs of a subchapter S corporation, setting up a babysitting co-op, building a boat,
food co-ops, investment pools, condominiums, building co-ops, buying co-ops,
nonprofit corporation and foundation structure, art and drama groups for the kids, or
setting up a home-exchange program.

One of several experimental projects centered around a three-couple group marriage
that was the focus of a discussion group that
provided a sounding board for the problems
of the group marriage, which in turn was the
guinea pig for the group. This group met as
often as the group marriage felt the need, and
the discussion group survived the group marriage, which broke up after six months. The
feedback was invaluable for all members of
the group as well as for the six participants in
the group marriage, who at this writing still
maintain an intimate friendship circle, but do
not feel ready to make a second attempt at
establishing a group marriage.

While it is clearly understood by all members of the sample that their involvement in
discussions and activities associated with determining just what their interest might be in
group marriage and communes is *not* a
commitment to actually undertake living in a
commune or group marriage, it is neverthe-

less of interest to those investigating this area that three group marriages and several communes have developed as offshoots from this group of eighty families so far, and others may reasonably be expected to develop.

Other experimental projects have included joint vacations, renting summer property together, and weekend living together. Another experimental activity was the partial exchange of predominantly male and female family roles between husband and wife or between several adults during periods of experimental living together.

One of the important ongoing discussion themes was the working through of expectations that each couple brings to any consideration of communal living or group marriage, going through the give-and-take process of shaping the nature of the commitments involved and determining the kinds of decision making and ground rules that would be acceptable. This is a difficult but rewarding task and one that inevitably gives rise to splinter groups as like-minded couples find each other.

A representative list of typical problem areas discussed will indicate the complexity of this undertaking. This list is *not* definitive, nor are the decision areas listed in order of importance, since rank order depended on who was involved in the discussion. Those primarily interested in group marriage had to consider many more personal issues dealing with the nature of marital interaction, in addition to these more general questions. Most groups were concerned about decision-making procedures, group goals, ground rules, prohibitions, intra- and extra-group sexual relationships, privacy, division of labor, role relationships, careers, relationship with outsiders, degree of visibility, legal jeopardy, dissolution of the group, personal responsibilities outside the group (such as parental support), geographic location, type of shelter, children, childrearing practices, education of children, group member career education, taxes, pooling assets, income, legal structure, trial period, investment policy, sequential steps in establishing the group, and prerequisites for membership.

One of the impressive aspects of this group is its lack of formal organization. In the beginning a decision was apparently made to charge a $3.00 minimum application fee (a larger donation was acceptable) and to charge a $3.00 refreshment and financing fee to each couple attending any meeting of the group. This custom was very informally observed. Sometimes the host at a particular meeting would waive the fee and at other times some couples might throw an extra twenty-dollar bill in the pot. In this manner the group was able to finance an occasional newsletter, a membership register which involved a 100-word description of each member family, frequent mailings of the "calendar" of coming meetings, and extensive correspondence with individuals, groups, organizations, and publishers interested in communes and group marriage.

The typical meeting would be hosted by a couple interested in a particular group activity or discussion topic on a rotating basis, although some activities were always associated with a particular couple and place. The convention was to notify the hostess at least 48 hours ahead of time of intent to attend. Several different couples acted as clearinghouses for certain activities. They could always be called for the next dates, times, and locations of a particular activity. Except for family activities, there were few times when the entire group was involved in a specific meeting. Groups tended to limit themselves to a number small enough to involve all those who wished to become involved, generally about four to ten couples. Larger groups soon split up in order to achieve greater participation. Each group acted autonomously and sometimes it was impossible to decide who was the leader of a given group. Some groups operated by consensus, others voted, and a few appeared to simply acquiesce to the decisions of one or two individuals within the group. Consensus was far and away the most common means of reaching decisions when decisions were required. The second most frequent pattern was delegation to one couple who were trusted to understand the "sense" of the group and act accordingly.

One of the anomalies of the group was its inability to handle single-parent families or single adults. Since the avowed purpose of the group was to explore the possibilities for building complex family relationships with deliberately chosen members to "replace" the extended family few, if any, of these couples had personally experienced, one could reasonably expect that single-parent families and selected single adults would have been welcomed. To the contrary, such individuals were systematically and almost invariably turned down by the screening committee. The weeding out was not 100 per cent however. Occasionally a single female or a female single-parent family was admitted to the group. No single males or single-parent (male) families were ever admitted. The reasons for the exceptions could not be satisfactorily ascertained, but the reason for the exclusions appeared to be fear of their "unsettling" influence.

In some cases extensive correspondence and/or phone conversation with one of these applicants would transpire before the decision was finally reached. Discussion with both the screening committee and the accepted singles failed to elicit the reasons why some were accepted and others rejected. This remains an area in which the group has not reached consensus, and as long as a large minority feel threatened by the possibility that singles pose some sort of "take-over" or "free-loader" threat, the policy is unlikely to change.

The implementation of decisions by various activity groups within the total sample depended on both the level of interest and the ingenuity of the individuals involved. The same individuals could be observed behaving very differently depending on the group one was observing. One group, becoming concerned about the personal qualities regarded as essential for self and others in a group marriage or commune, decided to take a poll. They circulated a questionnaire to all members who wished to participate (about forty couples), with the profile shown in Figure 1.

This figure suggests value differences as well as differences in standards set for Self and Others. In the main, the highest values are placed on internal, or "feeling" qualities rather than on such external factors as education or appearance. The fact that in every instance these couples set higher standards for Self than for Others is consistent with Self-Other reports in a number of other studies, e.g., Ramey (1958). There appears to be a consistent tendency to set "ideal" standards for Self while appraising Others in more realistic terms. Birkman, Ward, and the present author, working with executives in 1952, found that under stress, the individual was likely to revert to the type of behavior he predicted for Others, even though under normal circumstances he made every

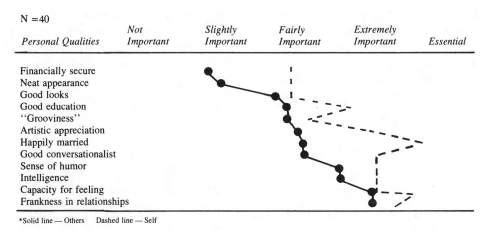

Figure 1 Group Profile: Qualities Valued in Self and Others*

effort to maintain his "ideal" pattern. We believe "Other" to be an expression of minimum role norms and expectations, whereas standards for "Self" represent optimum behavior.

One other example of group decision leading to action should suffice. A small splinter group consisting of three couples, two with small children and one with grown children, and a single female with teenage children, were intensely interested in pooling resources and setting up a commune in an urban setting for the purpose of owning and operating a free school. As the nucleus of an action group, they took the initial step of jointly renting a summer residence together, so that they could actually share living quarters on an experimental basis. Next they began a systematic survey of private schools in the metropolitan area that might be available for purchase, since they reasoned that it was more realistic and simpler to start with an existing school than to start from scratch. They located several schools that could be purchased for approximately $250,000 and

began preparing budget projections and studies of the relationship of type of curriculum to expense, enrollment projections, etc. They also began expanding the group on a carefully selective basis, taking into account the skills that would be needed as well as the simple desire of other couples to become involved. At each step of this process the group acted as a committee of the whole with respect to major decisions but delegated many decision functions to individuals within the group who had special competencies in the relevant decision area.

A major asset of the transactional process among these eighty couples was the fluidity of the group. The fact that it was loose-knit led to an ebb and flow of interaction patterns that was definitely enhanced by input from outside contacts of the member couples. Some were involved in various activities of the group for the entire three-year period. Some moved in and out depending on their interests, and what was happening at a given time. Others were involved only long enough to find like-minded people with whom they then entered into a communal or group marriage arrangement at a distant location, so that their further interaction became spasmodic.

The planned follow-up study should provide some interesting insights with respect to changes in attitude, interests, and life style among these seekers of more complex forms of interrelationship than are possible within the confines of monogamous dyadic marriage.

REFERENCES

Constantine, Larry and Joan Constantine
1971 "Multilateral marriage: alternate family structure in practice." In Robert H. Rimmer (ed.), You and I searching for Tomorrow. New York:New American Library.
Kanter, Rosabeth M.
1968 "Commitment and social organization: a study of commitment mechanisms in utopian communities." American Sociological Review 33 (August).
Ramey, James W.
1958 "The relationship of peer group rating to certain individual perceptions of personality." Journal of Experimental Education 27 (Spring).
1972 "Emerging patterns of behavior in marriage: deviations or innovations?" Journal of Sex Research 8 (February).
Slater, Philip E.
1968 "Some social consequences of temporary systems." In W. G. Bennis and P. E. Slater. The Temporary Society, New York:Harper and Row.
Stroller, Frederick H.
1970 "The intimate network of families as a new structure." In Herbert Otto (ed.), The Family in Search of a Future. New York:Appleton-Century-Crofts.

North American marriage: 1990

The following article is an exercise in forecasting, not prediction. As Bell (1973) indicates, we can perceive the general shape of things to come, but the actuality will depend on our political creativity. In other words, our destiny is subject to our response to the forecast.

Forecasts of this type are based on several different kinds of evidence. Surveys of the attitudes and behaviors of innovative people (the leaders of today), college students (the leaders of tomorrow), and the ordinary layman (the heartland of societal attitudes and behaviors) concerning marriage and the family are widely available. In addition, the Delphi technique, which has been widely employed in the study of technological change, has recently been used by social science experts. In the first wave, questionnaires are mailed to experts in a field (e.g., family sociologists), asking them to forecast the future. The results are collated and returned in the second wave, to indicate to the experts what their fellow experts are forecasting. Based on this information, each expert is asked to revise his forecast and to indicate his evidence. The third and final wave presents the results to each expert and asks for time projections (when each forecast is likely to occur). The apparent significance of this procedure is that experts seldom agree. When agreement is widespread, the legitimacy of the forecast cannot be taken lightly.

In general terms, family sociologists tend to agree with the type of forecast made by Professor Davids. Disagreement tends to center around issues such as how widespread the phenomena will be, whether a given forecast is as probable as others, whether unmentioned forecasts should or should not be included, and when the events will actually materialize.

The reader should not accept these forecasts as truth but should rather be critical, inquire of the evidence, and consider the implications. Even so, it is well to remember that the twentieth century has enabled the science fiction writer to be a prophet almost before the printer's ink is dry.

North American marriage: 1990

Leo Davids

As a preamble for this attempt to predict the options and regulations defining marriage and family life in North America a generation from now, let us consider some of the powerful long-term trends in this area which can be discerned either at work already, or coming very soon. These provide the causal principles that will be extrapolated here to provide a scientific indication of what the mating and parenthood situation is going to look like in another two decades. The remainder of the paper is essentially a working-out of this prediction exercise so that an account of the new situation is built up, which is the best way we have to predict the nature of marriage in 1990.

"Parenthood is fun" myth will die

1. The foundation of almost everything else that is occurring in the sphere of marriage and family life today is a process which will go right ahead in the next decade or two, and will continue to have a vast effect on people's thinking and their behavior. This process is what Max Weber called the *entzäuberung*, the "demystification" or "disenchantment" of human life, which is a hallmark of the modern orientation. Young people, especially, are continually becoming more sophisticated — due to television, modern education, peergroup frankness about all spheres of life, etc. — and they are

Leo Davids, Ph.D., is Associate Professor, Department of Sociology, York University, Toronto, Ontario.

From *The Futurist*, published by the World Future Society, P.O. Box 30369 (Bethesda), Washington, D.C. 20014. Reprinted by permission.

no longer accepting the myths, the conventional folklore, upon which ordinary social interaction has been based during the past few decades. Thus, for instance, young people are gradually rejecting the myth of "parenthood is fun," realizing that parenthood is a very serious business and one which ought to be undertaken only when people are ready to plunge in and do a good job.

Another grand complex of myths that is gradually being rejected is that of romantic love, under which it is perfectly acceptable to meet a person, form a sudden emotional attachment to that person without any logic or contemplation, and to marry that person on no other basis than the existence of this cathexis. Similarly, the whole institution of "shot-gun weddings," in which an unwanted, unintended pregnancy (usually occurring with a lower class girl) leads to what is called "necessary" marriage, is going to become a quaint piece of history which will be considered with the same glee that modern readers feel when they read about "bundling" in Colonial America. With young men and women who are all fully-informed about reproduction and what can be done to prevent it, such things will occur very rarely; romantic mate-selection, likewise, is going to continue only among the impoverished and marginally-educated segment of society.

Insofar as family life remains almost the only area of modern behavior that has not yet become rational and calculated but is approached with unexamined, time-honored myths, we can expect that this area is "ripe" for fundamental change. When serious, critical examination of all this really gets moving, very great changes will come about in quite a short time.

Procreation can be subject to communal control

2. The second independent variable leading to the developments that we are discussing is the total control of human fertility which advances in medical technique have made possible. There is no need here to discuss the pill, intra-uterine device (IUD), and the many other ways that are in use already to separate sex from reproduction, and therefore to free relations between men and women from the fear or risk of begetting children who would be a by-product, an unintended side-effect of fulfilling quite other needs. This control of human fertility means that what procreation does occur in the future is going to be by choice, not by accident. Both illegitimacy and venereal disease will be almost extinct, too, in 20 years. It also means that reproduction and child rearing can henceforth be subjected to communal control, will be potentially regulable by society at large. Without contraception, all the rest of these trends and changes would not be occurring at all.

Husband-wife equalization is "inevitable"

3. Women's Liberation, I believe, is not a fad or a current mass hysteria but is here to stay. Once the schools had instituted coeducation, male dominance was doomed. Let us rephrase that term for present purposes, calling it Husband-Wife Equalization, as a general name for certain tendencies that have been evident for many years and are continuing today. We all know that marriage has shifted, to borrow a phrase, from institution to companionship. Indeed, through the

demystification-sophistication of young women, their employment in full-status work, and because of the control over reproduction that has now become a reality, the equalization (in regard to decision-making) of wives with their husbands has become inevitable. The implications of this are already being voiced, to some extent, in the platforms and proposals of women's rights organizations, and some points will be touched upon herein.

It must be remembered that there will remain in the foreseeable future, a traditionalist minority even in the most advanced and change-prone societies. This segment will expend much effort to maintain patterns of marriage and family living that they feel are right, and which are consistent with the patterns they experienced when they were children. This traditionalist minority will certainly not be gone, or vanished to insignificant numbers, in the short span of one generation; therefore, any predictions we make must take into account not only what the "new wave" pattern is going to be, but also the fact that there will be a considerable number of people who elect to maintain the familiar value system that they were socialized with, and to which they are deeply commited.

Law will accept abortion and new forms of marriage

4. Another trend which is already at work and which, we may assume, is going to accelerate in the future is that legislatures no longer attempt to shape or create family behavior by statute, but are, and increasingly will be, prepared to adapt the law to actual practice, so that it accepts the general viewpoint that public opinion has consensus on. I think that ever since Prohibition, legislators have been forced to agree that sooner or later legal reform must narrow the gap between law on the books and what is really happening in society. It is likely that this reforming and correlation is going to be speeded up in the next few decades, so that the extent to which there is an uncomfortable and problematic contradiction between the law in force and what people are really doing will be virtually eliminated. Thus, all of the ongoing changes with regard to contraception, abortion, new types of marriage contract, etc., will — it is here assumed — be accepted and in a sense ratified by the Law, as the old-style moralists who can still be found in our agencies of social control cease to fight a rear-guard action against the new norms that are, whether they like them or not, emerging. All modes of birth control will become medical problems, free of any statutory limitation.

5. An important consequence of widespread social-science knowledge among young people today, which is coupled with a greater use of principles drawn from sociology and anthropology in the process of law reform, will be the recognition that continuity or consistency for each person or married couple is necessary, in regard to the larger questions at least, for a particular marriage system to work well in the long run. If the agreements entered into, whatever their content, involve major inconsistency, if people seem to be changing the fundamental norms between them in midstream or giving much more than they receive, then obviously the community has unwisely allowed these people to enter a situation which must lead to disorganization and conflict sooner or later. This realization from our functionalist un-

derstanding of how marriage — or any continuing relationship — operates, will lead to acceptance of the clear necessity for such predictability and fairness in every particular case.

So much for the preamble. What are the consequences? Two major principles underlying our model of marriage in 1990 emerge from the forces and trends listed above. They are: (a) the freedom to personally and explicitly contract the type of marriage one wishes; and (b) formal public or communal control over parenthood.

What is meant by the word "marriage," here? To include the newer forms, we require a looser, broader definition than would suffice in the 1950s. Marriage should therefore be understood to refer to a publicly-registered, lasting commitment to a particular person, which generally includes certain sexual or other rights and obligations between these people (that would not be recognized by their community without such married status).

Free choice of the sort of marriage one wishes does not mean that a man and woman (or two men or two women?) will write their own original contract incorporating any combination of rules and arrangements that they like. The reason that such freedom would be beyond that envisioned in our thinking, as argued above, is that they would be able to invent a contract that has severe internal inconsistencies or flights of self-delusion, and which therefore sets up strains for their relationship from the outset. The sophistication which anthropological functionalism has brought to us will lead society to channel the choice of marriage into a selection from among a number of recognized types, each of which has been carefully thought through so that it is tenable in the long run. Thus, people will select from among various ways of being married, each of which makes sense by itself and will enable them to function on a long-run basis once they have had this choice. Neither monogamy nor indefinite permanence are important in this respect, so they will not be required. However, the agreed-upon choice will be explicit and recorded so there's no question of deception or misunderstanding, as well as to provide statistical information, and official registration of this choice is an element of marriage which will remain a matter of public concern.

People unfit to be parents will be screened out

The right of society to control parenthood is something that can be predicted from a number of things we already know. For one thing, the rising incidence of battered and neglected children, and our almost total inability to really cope with the battered child's problem except after the fact, will certainly lead legislators to planning how those people who can be discovered, in advance, to be unfit for parenthood may be screened out and prevented from begetting offspring who will be the wretched target of their parents' emotional inadequacies. Furthermore, increasing awareness of the early-childhood roots of serious crime and delinquency will also lead to an attempt to prevent major deviance by seeing to it that early socialization occurs under favorable circumstances. It does not appear that there will be many other really effective ways in which rising crime rates could eventually be reversed. This, however, will again mean that those who raise children will have to be evaluated for this purpose in some way, so that only those parents who are likely to do a respectable job of early socialization will be licensed to release new members of society into the open community. If such testing and selection is not done, we have no way to protect ourselves from large numbers of young people who have been raised in a way that almost inevitably will have them providing the murderers, rapists and robbers of the next generation. Since we now begin to have the technology and the knowledge to prevent this, we may confidently expect that parent-licensing is going to come into force soon.

One other trend, perhaps phrased from the negative side, must also be mentioned here as we try to describe the norms that will probably circumscribe marriage in another generation. This trend is the decline of informal, personal social control over married couples which was formerly exercised by kinsmen and neighbours. It would not make sense to anticipate massive changes in the law and explicit contractual entry into marriage as the normal way to shape married life, if mate selection and the interactions between husband and wife were still under the regulation of custom, vigilantly enforced by aunts, grandfathers or brothers-in-law. It is precisely because the vast mobility of modern living has led, along with other factors, to the isolation of the nuclear family — which is the source of so many problems in the family sphere today — that this new kind of regulation will be called into force and accepted as necessary and proper. The recognition that marriage has left the sphere of *Gemeinschaft* will help to bring about a consensus that the regulation of this area of life will have to be handled like any other kind of socially-important interpersonal behavior in today's *Gesellschaft* civilization.

Courtship may be "Dutch treat"

What will courtship be like in about twenty years? We can assume that courtship will, as it does currently, serve as a testing ground for the kind of marriage that people have in their minds, perhaps even dimly or unconsciously. Thus, insofar as particular young men or women may have begun to feel that the type of marriage they would like is Type A rather than Type B, their courtship would be of the sort that normally leads to Type A, and in a sense tests their readiness to build their relationship along those lines. Only the traditionalist couples will keep up such classic patriarchal customs as the male holding doors, assisting with a coat, or paying for both meals when a couple dines out together. The egalitarians would go "Dutch treat," i.e., each paying for himself, during this spouse research period. Thus, courtship will be of several kinds corresponding to the kinds of marriage that we are about to describe, with the conventional acts and phases in the courtship signalling the present intention of the parties involved to head toward that kind of marriage. Thus, pre-marriage and marriage will exhibit a psycho-social continuity, the early marriage centering on the basic interpersonal stance that is already represented in courtship.

Of course, courtship will serve this testing and assessing function after people have been approximately matched through computer mate-finding methods. Random dating and hopeless courtships will have been largely prevented through the provision of basic categoric information which people can use to screen possible spouses, such as total years of schooling completed, aptitude and IQ scores, major subjects (which are related to intellectual interests in a very direct way), religiosity, leisure and recreation preferences, and similar things.

For remarriage suitors, data on wealth or credit and occupation would also be used, along with some indication of attitudes concerning home life and procreation. Since homogamy (similarity between spouses) is recognized as an important indicator of marital success, such information will be systematically gathered and made available to cut down on the wasteful chance element in mate selection. It is only when people are continuing their search for a spouse within the appropriate "pool," defined in terms of those who are at the right point with regard to these variables, that courtship as a series of informal but direct experiments in relationship-building will come into play.

Celibacy will be legitimized

Explicit choice of the kind of marriage one enters into is, of course, an effect not only of the emancipation of women but of men as well. What will some of the major options be? With the insurance functions that were formerly secured by having children (who would provide during one's old age) being completely taken over by the government (assisted by unions, pension funds and the like), there will be little reason to warn those who choose childlessness against this course. With celibacy no bar to sexual satisfaction, society will accept the idea that some segments of the population can obtain whatever intimate satisfactions they require in a series of casual, short-term "affairs" (as we call them today), and will never enter any publicly-registered marriage. With celibacy or spinsterhood fully legitimized, and with no fear of destitution when one has retired

from the labor force, there will undoubtedly be a sizeable number of people who decide not to enter into a marriage of any sort on any terms.

Trial marriage for three or five years

Another not-unfamiliar option in this regard will be the renewable trial marriage, in which people explicitly contract for a childless union which is to be comprehensively evaluated after three years or five years, at which point either a completely new decision can be reached or the same arrangement can be renewed for another term of three or five years. This would not be, then, a question of divorce; it is simply a matter of a definite arrangement having expired. The contract having been for a limited term, both parties are perfectly free to decide not to renew it when that term is over. This would be a normal, perhaps minor, part of one's "marital career".

A third option, which introduces very few complications, is the permanent childless marriage; the arrangment between the two adults is of indefinite duration, but they have agreed in advance that there will be no offspring, and of course, there is no question but that medical technology will make it possible for them to live up to that part of the arrangement. Some will choose sterilization, others will use contraceptive methods which can be abandoned if one changes his mind and is authorized to procreate.

Compound marriages will also be allowed, whether they be polygamous, polyandrous or group marriages. However, these communes will not be free of the same obligations that any marriage entails, such as formally registering the terms of the agreement among the members; any significant change in the arrangements among members of such a familial commune will have to be recorded in the appropriate public place in the same way as marriages and divorces which involve only one husband and one wife. There will be great freedom with regard to the number of people in the commune, but internal consistency concerning the give-and-take among the members, their privileges and obligations, will be required. The functional, pragmatic ethics emerging in today's youth culture will be strictly adhered to, some years hence, not as moral absolutes, not because people have come to the belief that these represent the true right and wrong, but in order to prevent serious conflict.

Less than third of marriages will produce children

With the majority of young people in society choosing one of the foregoing patterns, the number of marriages in which children are expected will be relatively small; perhaps 25% to 30% of the population will be so serious about having children that they will be prepared to undergo the rigorous training and careful evaluation that will be necessary for them to obtain the requisite licenses. The marriages intended to produce children will usually be classic familistic marriages, in which the general pattern of interaction between husband and wife, as well as the relationship between parent and child, may be fairly similar to the contemporary upper middle-class marriage that we know in 1970. However, three-generation households will probably increase. I see no reason to believe that all of child rearing will be done in a collective way, as in an Israeli kibbutz or in the communes which have been set up in some Communist countries; infant care may gravitate in the direction of day nurseries, however, while school children will live at home, as now.

Would-be parents will have to prove their suitability

The familial pattern, then, explicitly chosen by some men and women to perpetuate the classic familistic marriage, will be intended to provide a home atmosphere approximately similar to that which can be found in those middle class families of today's society that have the best socio-emotional climate. The community will be assured that this home atmosphere is, in fact, most probable, since it has been prepared for, rather than left to an accident of kind fate and to happenstance talents that people bring to parenthood nowadays. All those who desire to become parents, and therefore to exercise a public responsibility in an extremely important and sensitive area of personal functioning, will have to prove that they are indeed the right people to serve as society's agents of socialization. Just as those who wish to adopt a child, nowadays, are subjected to intensive interviewing which aims at discovering the healthiness of the relationship between husband and wife and of the motivation for parenthood, the suitability that the man or woman displays for coping with the stresses of parenthood, as well as the physical and material conditions that the adopted child will be enjoying, the evaluation of mother and father applicants in future will be done by a team of professionals who have to reach the judgement that this particular individual or couple have the background to become professionals themselves: that is, recognized and certified parents.

Parent-training will be intense

The course of study for parenthood will include such subjects as: human reproduction and gestation; infant care; developmental physiology and psychology; theories of socialization; and educational psychology. Starting with a foundation of systematic but abstract scientific knowledge, the practical and applied courses in hygienic, nutritional, emotional and perceptual-aesthetic care of children will follow, in the same way as training for medicine and other professions. In addition to the subject matter referred to above, prospective parents will be required to achieve some clarity concerning values and philosophy of life, in which they will be guided by humanistic scholars, and will also be required to attain a clear understanding of the mass media, their impact on children, and how to manage mass media consumption as an important part of socialization in the modern urban environment. One side effect of such parent training may be a sharp drop in the power of the peer group, as parents do more and with greater self-confidence.

Suitable examinations will be devised, and only those who achieve adequate grades in these areas will be given a parenthood license. Some young men and women are likely to take the parenthood curriculum "just in case"; that is, although they have not yet thought through the type of marriage that they desire or the kind of spouse they are looking for, they may continue their education by entering parenthood studies and obtaining the diploma, should it turn out that they elect a classic, child-rearing marriage later on. Possibly, fathers will be prohibited from full-time employment outside the home while they have pre-school children, or if their children have extra needs shown by poor conduct or other symptoms of psychic distress.

One of the more striking areas of change, which can serve as an indicator of how different things will be then from what they are now, is age. Age of marriage now is in the early 20's, and child bearing typically occurs when women are in their middle twenties. Also, husbands today are usually about three to four years older than their wives. In another generation, the age of child bearing will probably be considerably advanced, as people who have decided upon parenthood will either be enjoying themselves during an extended childless period before they undertake the burdens and responsibilities of child rearing, or completing the course of study for certification to undertake parenthood. It is probable that women will bear children when they are in their middle and late thirties, so that they will have enjoyed a decade or a decade and a half of companionate marriage in which there was full opportunity to travel, to read, or just to relax before they have to spend 24 hours a day caring for a small child. As to the age difference between husbands and wives, which is essentially based on the patriarchal tradition that the man is the "senior" in the home, it will probably disappear in the case of all forms of marriage other than the classic familistic one; there, where people have explicitly decided that the kind of marriage they want is the same as their parents had back in the medievaloid 1970s, or the ancient 1960s, the husband will continue to be a few years older than his wife.

This picture of the marriage situation in 1990 leaves open various questions and problems, which should be touched upon briefly in conclusion. One of the difficulties in this scenario is the question of what authority will make the necessary decisions: What sorts of committees will be in charge of devising the various internally-consistent kinds of marriage, working out the parent education courses, and, certifying people for parenthood? There are, after all, political implications to controlling marriage and parenthood in this way, and the general public will have to be satisfied that those who exercise authority in this area are, in fact, competent as well as impartial.

Another problem is that of securing complete and valid information: (a) for those who are preparing to locate suitable mates through computer matching, or who are preparing to make a commitment in some specific form of marriage; and (b) concerning those who apply for the parenthood course and later for the license to practice parenthood. Unless we can be sure that the inputs used for making such judgements contain information which is adequate in quantity and true as well, these new systems will not be able to function without a great deal of deviance, and might easily engender prob-

lems which are worse than those which we confront today.

Will childlessness lead to less long-range investment?

A third issue is that of parenthood having tied people to the community, and given them a commitment to the environment: What will childlessness do to one's motivation for planning/preserving; will it demotivate all long-range investment? Research on this could start now, comparing parents with the childless.

Finally, we have assumed that marriage is going to continue, in some way. That is based on the belief that people will continue to desire a secure partnership with another person or small group, and that youth will feel it is better to institutionally buttress their sharing of life, in general, by setting up a marriage of some kind. This depends, in fact, on the interpersonal climate in communities, and the extent to which people feel isolation and unmet needs that marriage will solve. When marriage is not desired, then we will have discovered new forms of warm, dependable primary association replacing the old institution which has supplied psychological support to people through the millennia.

Bibliography[1]

*Abell, Helen C.
  1971 *Rural Families and Their Homes—A Longitudinal Study of Ontario Rural Families*. School of Urban and Regional Planning, University of Waterloo, Waterloo, Ontario.

Aberle, D.F., D.R. Miller, U. Bronfenbrenner, E.H. Hess, D.M. Schneider and J.M. Spuhler
  1963 "The Incest Taboo and the Mating Patterns of Animals", *American Anthropologist* 65: pp. 253-65.

*Abu-Laban, Sharon M.
  1965 "Reference Relationships and Women's Role Preference". Unpublished M.A. thesis, University of Alberta, Edmonton, Alberta.

Adams, Bert N.
  1968 *Kinship in an Urban Setting*. Chicago: Markham.

*Alberta Department of Health
  1968 *Annual Report*. Edmonton, Alberta.

Aldous, Joan
  1970 "Strategies for Developing Family Theory", *Journal of Marriage and the Family* 32:2 (May), 250-7.
  1972 "The Making of Family Roles and Family Change". Unpublished manuscript.

Aldous, Joan, et al., eds.
  1971 *Family Problem Solving*. New York: Dryden Press.

*Allingham, J.D.
  1967 *The Demographic Background to Change in the Number and Composition of Female Wage-Earners in Canada*. Ottawa: Statistics Canada.

*Allingham, J.D., and B.G. Spencer
  1967 *Women Who Work*. Ottawa: Statistics Canada Special Labour Force Studies.
  1968 *Women Who Work*. Ottawa: Statistics Canada Special Labour Force Studies.

Anshen, Ruth N., ed.
  1949 *The Family: Its Function and Destiny*. New York: Harper.

Aoi, Kasuo, Kyjomi Morioka, Kenji Tamura, Yasuhiko Yuzawa and Takeo Shinohara
  1970 "Comparative Study of Home Discipline: Rural-Urban, Sex and Age Differences", pp. 12-38 in Reuben Hill and Rene Konig, *Families in East and West: Socialization Process and Kinship Ties*. The Hague: Mouton.

Ariès, Philippe
  1962 *Centuries of Childhood: A Social History of Family Life*. New York: Vintage Books.

Athanasiou, Robert, Phillip Shaver and Carol Tavris
  1970 "Sex", *Psychology Today* (July), 39-52.

*Atwell, Phyllis H.
  1969 "Kinship and Migration Among Calgarian Residents of Indian Origin". Unpublished M.A. thesis, University of Calgary, Calgary, Alberta.

Bales, Robert F.
  1970 *Personality and Interpersonal Behavior*. New York: Holt, Rinehart and Winston.

*Balikci, Asen
  1959 "Two Attempts at Community Organization among the Eastern Hudson Bay Eskimos", *Anthropologica* 1: 125ff.
  1960 "Some Acculturative Trends among Canadian Eskimos", *Anthropologica* 2: 149ff.

[1] All references with an asterisk * are Canadian.

437

Barash, Meyer, and Alice Scourby, eds.
1970 *Marriage and the Family: A Comparative Analysis of Contemporary Problems*. New York: Random House.

*Barclay, Harold B.
1968 "An Arab Community in the Canadian Northwest: A Preliminary Discussion of the Lebanese Community in Lac La Biche, Alberta", *Anthropologica* N.S. 10:2, pp. 143-56.
1971 "The Lebanese Muslim Family", pp. 342-54 in K. Ishwaran, ed., *The Canadian Family*. Toronto: Holt, Rinehart and Winston.

*Bardal, M.S., E.R. Rogerson and B.D. Dick
1956 "The Married Woman in Employment: An Exploratory Study of How Her Employment Affects the Woman and Her Relationship with her Family and the Community". Unpublished M.S.W. thesis, University of British Columbia, Vancouver, British Columbia.

Bardos, Panos D.
1969 *The Family in Changing Civilizations*, 2nd ed. New York: Selected Academic Readings.

Bardwick, Judith M.
1971 *Psychology of Women*. New York: Harper and Row.

Barsch, R.H.
1969 *Parent of the Handicapped Child*. Chicago: Charles C. Thomas.

Bart, Pauline B.
1971 "Sexism and Social Science: From the Gilded Cage to the Iron Cage: Or, the Perils of Pauline", *Journal of Marriage and the Family* 33:4 (November), 734-45.

Bartell, Gilbert D.
1971 *Group Sex: A Scientist's Eyewitness Report on the American Way of Swinging*. New York: Peter H. Wyden.

Bebbington, A.C.
1973 "The Function of Stress in the Establishment of the Dual-Career Family", *Journal of Marriage and the Family* 33:3 (August), 530-7.

Becker, Wesley
1964 "Consequences of Parental Discipline", pp. 169-209 in W. Hoffman and M. Hoffman, eds., *Review of Child Development Research*, Vol. 1. New York: Russell Sage Foundation.

*Beckstead, A.
1971 "The Greek Family in Toronto", *Journal of the Ontario Association of Children's Aid Societies* (December), 5-8.

Bell, Daniel
1973 *The Coming of Post-Industrial Society: A Venture in Social Forecasting*. New York: Basic Books.

Bell, Norman, and Ezra F. Vogel, eds.
1968 *A Modern Introduction to the Family*, rev. ed. New York: Free Press.

Bell, Robert R.
1966 *Premarital Sex in a Changing Society*. Englewood Cliffs, New Jersey: Prentice-Hall.

Bell, W., and M.D. Boat
1957 "Urban Neighborhoods and Informal Social Relations", *American Journal of Sociology* 62 (January), 391-8.

Bem, S.L., and D.J. Bem
1970 "Case Study of a Nonconscious Ideology: Training the Woman to Know Her Place", pp. 88-99 in D.J. Bem, ed., *Beliefs, Attitudes and Human Affairs*. California: Cole Publishing Co.

Bendix, Reinhard
1974 "Review of 'The Coming of Post-Industrial Society: A Venture in Social Forecasting'", *Contemporary Sociology* 3:2 (March), 99-101.

*Bennett, John W., and Seena Kohl
1964 "Two Memoranda on Social Organization and Adaptive Selection in a Northern Plains Region", *Plains Anthropologist*, 8:22.

Bennis, Warren G., and Philip E. Slater
1968 *The Temporary Society*. New York: Harper and Row.

Benson, Leonard
1968 *Fatherhood: A Sociological Perspective*.

New York: Random House.

*Berg, Dale

1973 "Sexual Subcultures and Interaction". Unpublished Ph.D. thesis, University of Alberta, Edmonton, Alberta.

Berger, Milton M., ed.

1970 "Sexism in Family Studies", Special issue of the *Journal of Marriage and the Family* 33: 3-4 (August-November).

Berkner, Lutz K.

1973 "Recent Research on the History of the Family in Western Europe", *Journal of Marriage and the Family* 35:3 (August), 395-406.

Bernard, Jessie

1956 *Remarriage: The Study of Marriage*. New York: Dryden Press.

1964 "The Adjustments of Married Mates", pp. 675-740 in H.T. Christensen, ed., *Handbook of Marriage and the Family*. Chicago: Rand McNally.

1966 *Marriage and Family Among Negroes*. Englewood Cliffs, New Jersey: Prentice-Hall.

1968 *The Sex Game*. Englewood Cliffs, New Jersey: Prentice-Hall.

1972 *The Future of Marriage*. New York: World.

*Bernhardt, David, ed.

1970 *Being a Parent: Unchanging Values in a Changing World*. Toronto: University of Toronto Press.

*Berry, J.W., and G.J.S. Wilde, eds.

1972 *Social Psychology: The Canadian Context*. Toronto: McClelland and Stewart.

Bettelheim, B.

1969 *The Children of the Dream*. New York: Macmillan.

Billingsley, Andrew

1968 *Black Families in White America*. Englewood Cliffs, New Jersey: Prentice-Hall.

*Birket-Smith, Kaj

1929 "The Caribou Eskimos", in *Report of the Fifth Thule Expedition*, Vol. 5 No. 1.

Copenhagen: Gyldendalske Boghandel.

1953 *The Chugach Eskimo*. Copenhagen: Nationalmuseets Skrifter.

1959 *The Eskimos*, rev. ed. London: Methuen.

Bitterman, Catherine M.

1968 "The Multimarriage Family", *Social Casework* 49 (April), 218-21.

Black, K. Dean

1972 "Systems Theory and the Development of the Marital Relationship". Unpublished manuscript.

Black, K. Dean, and Carlfred B. Broderick

1972 "Systems Theory vs. Reality". Unpublished manuscript.

Blake, Judith, et al.

1961 *Family Structure in Jamaica: The Social Context of Reproduction*. New York: Free Press of Glencoe.

*Blishen, Bernard R.

1958 "The Construction and Use of Occupational Class Scale", *Canadian Journal of Economics and Political Science* 24:4, pp. 519-31.

1967 "A Socio-Economic Index for Occupations in Canada", *The Canadian Review of Sociology and Anthropology* 4:1 (February), 41-53.

Blitstein, Dorothy R.

1963 *The World of the Family: A Comparative Study of Family Organization in Their Social and Cultural Settings*. New York: Random House.

Blood, Robert O., Jr.

1967 *Love Match and Arranged Marriage: A Tokyo-Detroit Comparison*. New York: The Free Press.

1969 *Marriage*, 2nd ed. New York: Free Press.

1970 "Social Change and Kinship Patterns", Ch. 11 in Reuben Hill and Rene Konig, eds., *Families in East and West: Socialization Process and Kinship Ties*. The Hague: Mouton.

Blood, Robert O., Jr., and Donald M. Wolfe

1960 *Husbands and Wives: The Dynamics of Married Living*. New York: Free Press.

*Bock, Philip K.
1966 *The Micmac Indians of Restigouche: History and Contemporary Description*. Bulletin No. 213, Anthropology Series No. 77, National Museum of Canada. Ottawa: Department of the Secretary of State.

*Boldt, Edward D.
1966 "Conformity and Deviance: The Hutterites of Alberta". Unpublished M.A. thesis, University of Alberta, Edmonton, Alberta.
1968 "Acquiescence and Conventionality in a Communal Society". Unpublished Ph.D. thesis, University of Alberta, Edmonton, Alberta.

Bolton, Charles D.
1961 "Mate Selection as the Development of a Relationship", *Marriage and Family Living* 23:3 (August), 234-40.

Bossard, James H., and Eleanor S. Boll
1966 *The Sociology of Child Development*, 4th ed. New York: Harper and Row.

Bott, Elizabeth J.
1949 "A Comparison of the Social Organization of the Emo and Ponemah Bands of Ojibwa Indians". Unpublished M.A. thesis, University of Chicago, Chicago, Illinois.
1971 *Family and Social Network: Roles, Norms and External Relationships in Ordinary Urban Families*, 2nd ed. London: Tavistock.

*Bouvier, Leon
1968 "The Spacing of Births Among French Canadian Families: An Historical Approach", *The Canadian Review of Sociology and Anthropology* 5:1 (February), 17-26.

*Boyd, Monica
1974 "Family Size Ideals of Canadians: A Methodological Note", *Canadian Review of Sociology and Anthropology* 11:4 (November), 360-70.

*Boyer, L. Bruce, Ruth M. Boyer and Arthur E. Hippler
1974 "Ecology, Socialization and Personality Development among Athabascans", *Journal of Comparative Family Studies* 5:1 (Spring), 61-73.

Braun, R.
1960 *Industrialisierung und Volksleben*. Erlenbach-Zurich.

*Breton, Raymond, and John E. Macdonald
1971 "Aspects of Parent-Adolescent Relationships: The Perceptions of Secondary School Students", pp. 151-168 in K. Ishwaran, ed., *The Canadian Family*. Toronto: Holt, Rinehart and Winston.

Broderick, Carlfred B., ed.
1971 *A Decade of Family Research and Action*. Minneapolis: National Council on Family Relations.

Bronfenbrenner, Urie
1970 *Two Worlds of Childhood*. New York: Russell Sage.

Buckley, W.
1967 *Sociology and Modern Systems Theory*. Englewood Cliffs, New Jersey: Prentice-Hall.
1968 *Modern Systems Research for the Behavioral Scientist*. Chicago: Aldine Publishing Co.

Burgess, Ernest W., Harvey J. Locke and Mary M. Thomes
1963 *The Family: From Institution to Companionship*. New York: American Book Co.

*Burshtyn, Roslyn, ed.
1970 *Day Care: A Resource for the Contemporary Family*. Ottawa: Vanier Institute of the Family.

*Byles, John
1969 *Alienation, Deviance and Social Control: A Study of Adolescents in Metropolitan Toronto*. Toronto: Social Planning Council of Metro Toronto.

Calhoun, A.W.
1945 *A Social History of the American Family*. New York: Barnes and Noble.

Campisi, Paul J.
1948 "Ethnic Family Patterns: The Italian Family in the United States", *American*

Journal of Sociology 53: pp. 443-9.

*Canada Department of Labour, Women's Bureau
  1957 *Why and Wherefores: An Inquiry into Women's Occupational Choices*. Ottawa: Information Canada.
  1958 *Married Women Working for Pay in Eight Canadian Cities*. Ottawa: Information Canada.
  1960 *Occupational Histories of Married Women Working For Pay in Eight Canadian Cities*. Ottawa: Information Canada.
  1968 "Women in the Labour Force", *The Labour Gazette* 68:5 (May), 258-312.
  1969 *Women's Bureau '69*. Ottawa: Information Canada.
  1970a *Report of the Royal Commission on the Status of Women*. Ottawa: Information Canada.
  1970b *Facts & Figures—Women and the Labour Force—1969*. Ottawa: Information Canada.
  1970c *Working Mothers and Their Child Care Arrangements*. Ottawa: Information Canada.
  1970d *Women's Bureau '70*. Ottawa: Information Canada.
  1971 *Sex Role Imagery in Children: Social Origins of Mind*, Studies of The Royal Commission of the Status of Women in Employment. Ottawa: Information Canada.
  1974 *Women in the Labour Force: Facts and Figures*, 1973 ed. Ottawa: Information Canada.
*Canadian Citizenship Branch
  1967 *The Canadian Family Tree*. Ottawa: Information Canada.
*Canadian Council on Social Development
  1965 *Urban Need in Canada: A Case Study of the Problems of Families in Four Canadian Cities*. Ottawa: Information Canada.
  1971 *The One-Parent Family*. Ottawa: Information Canada.

Caplow, Theodore
  1968 *Two Against One: Coalitions in Triads*. Englewood Cliffs, New Jersey: Prentice-Hall.
*Card, B.Y.
  1968 *Trends and Change in Canadian Society: Their Challenge to Canadian Youth*. Toronto: Macmillan Co. of Canada.
*Card, B.Y., et al.
  1963 *The Métis in Alberta Society*. Edmonton: Alberta Tuberculosis Association.
  1966 *School Achievement in Rural Alberta*. Edmonton: Alberta Advisory Committee on Educational Research.
*Carisse, Collette
  1966 "Accommodation conjugale et réseau social des mariages bi-ethniques au Canada", *Revue française de sociologie* 7: pp. 472-84.
  1969 "Orientations culturelles dans les mariages entre Canadiens français et Canadiens anglais", *Sociologie et Sociétés 1:1 (May), 39-52*.
  1970 Valeurs familiales de sujets feminins novateurs: perspectives d'avenir", *Sociologie et Sociétés* 2.2 (November), 265-81.
  1972 "The Family as a Mediating Structure in the Circulation of Information: A Systems Approach". Unpublished manuscript.
  1976 "Life Plans of Innovative Women: A Strategy for Living the Femine Role", see Ch. 9 in this book.
*Carisse, Collette, and Norman Bell
  1971 *Family Research in Canada*. Ottawa: Vanier Institute of the Family.
*Carr, Gwen B.
  1972 *Marriage and Family in a Decade of Change*. Don Mills, Ontario: Addison-Wesley.
Caudill, William
  1962 "Patterns of Emotion in Modern Japan", in R.J. Smith and R.K. Beardsley, eds., *Japanese Culture: Its Development and Characteristics*. New York: Johnson Reprint Corporation.

Caudill, William, and H. Scarr
  1962 "Japanese Value Orientations and Culture Change", *Ethnology* 1 (January), 53-91.
Caudill, William, and Helen Weinstein
  1970 "Maternal Care and Infant Behavior in Japanese and American Urban Middle Class Families", pp. 39-71 in Reuben Hill and Rene Konig, eds., *Families in East and West: Socialization Process and Kinship Ties*. The Hague: Mouton.
*Chance, Norman A.
  1966 *The Eskimo of North Alaska*. Toronto: Holt, Rinehart and Winston.
  1968 *Developmental Change Among the Cree Indians of Quebec: Summary Report, The McGill Cree Project, ARDA Project 34002*. Ottawa: Department of Forestry and Rural Development.
*Chapman, F.A.R.
  1968 *Law and Marriage*. Toronto: McGraw-Hill.
*Chatterjee, P., E. Cameron, E. Edminson, J. Robinson and M.J. Sharpe
  1962 "Two Generation Families". Unpublished M.A. thesis, School of Social Work, University of Toronto, Toronto, Ontario.
Christensen, Harold T.
  1964 *Handbook of Marriage and the Family*. Chicago: Rand McNally and Co.
  1969 "Normative Theory Derived from Cross-Cultural Research", *Journal of Marriage and the Family* 31:2 (May), 209-22.
Clark, A.L., and P. Wallin
  1965 "Women's Sexual Responsiveness and the Duration and Quality of Their Marriage", *American Journal of Sociology* 71:2, pp. 187-96.
*Clark, S.D.
  1942 *Social Development of Canada*. Toronto: University of Toronto Press.
Clausen, John A., et al., eds.
  1968 *Socialization and Society*. Boston: Little, Brown and Company.

*Cleverdon, Catherine L.
  1950 *The Woman Sufferage Movement in Canada*. Toronto: University of Toronto Press.
Cohen, Y.A.
  1964 *The Transition from Childhood to Adolescence: Cross-cultural Studies of Initiation Ceremonies, Legal Systems and Incest Taboos*. Chicago: Aldine.
Constantine, Larry L., and Joan M. Constantine
  1973 *Group Marriage: A Study of Contemporary Mulitilateral Group Marriage*. New York: Collier-Macmillan.
Cooper, David
  1971 *The Death of the Family*. London: The Penguin Press.
*Cormier, B., et al.
  1961 "Family Conflicts and Criminal Behavior", *Canadian Journal of Corrections* 3:1 (January), 18-37.
Cox, Frank D.
  1967 *Youth, Marriage and the Seductive Society*. Dubuque, Iowa: Wm. C. Brown.
  1972 *American Marriage: A Change Scene?* Dubuque, Iowa: Wm. C. Brown.
Cox, Harvey
  1965 *The Secular City*. New York: The Macmillan Co.
*Coyne, C.D.
  1965 "Working Mothers and Private Day Nurseries in Metropolitan Toronto: An Exploratory Study of Working Mothers and their Families, Who Have Placed Their Children in Private Day Nurseries with Emphasis on the Effects of the Children". Unpublished M.S.W. thesis, University of Toronto, Toronto, Ontario.
*Cruikshank, Julie
  1971 "Matrifocal Families in the Canadian North", pp. 39-53 in K. Ishwaran, ed., *The Canadian Family*. Toronto: Holt, Rinehart and Winston.
*Crysdale, Stewart
  1968 "Family and Kinship in Canada", pp. 106-15 in W.E. Mann, ed., *Canada: A*

Sociological Profile. Toronto: Copp Clark.

1971 "Worker's Families and Education in a Downtown Community", pp. 265-81 in K. Ishwaran, ed., *The Canadian Family*. Toronto: Holt, Rinehart and Winston.

Cuber, John F., and Peggy B. Harroff

1963 "The More Total View: Relationships Among Men and Women of the Upper Middle Class", *Marriage and Family Living* 25:2 (May), 140-45.

1965 *The Significant Americans*. New York: Appleton-Century.

Dahl, Nancy S.

1970 *Index 1963-1969, Journal of Marriage and the Family*. Minneapolis: National Council on Family Relations.

*Damas, David

1964 "The Patterning of the Iglulingmiut Kinship System", *Ethnology 3* (October), 377-88.

1971 "The Problem of the Eskimo Family", pp. 54-78 in K. Ishwaran, ed., *The Canadian Family*. Toronto: Holt, Rinehart and Winston.

*David, Gerson

1967 *Patterns of Social Functioning in Families With Marital and Parent-Child Problems*. Toronto: University of Toronto Press.

*Davidson, D., et al.

1959 "Factors and Kinship in Riverdale", pp. 105-15 in W.E. Mann, ed., *Canada: A Sociological Profile*. Toronto: Copp Clark.

*Davies, D.I., and Kathleen Herman, eds.

1971 *Social Space: Canadian Perspectives*. Toronto: New Press.

*Davis, Arthur K.

1971 "Canadian Society and History as Hinterland versus Metropolis", pp. 6-32 in Richard J. Ossenberg, ed., *Canadian Society: Pluralism, Change and Conflict*. Scarborough, Ontario: Prentice-Hall of Canada.

*Davis, Carroll

1966 *Room to Grow: A Study of Parent-Child Relationships*. Toronto: University of Toronto Press.

*Davison, Anne M.

1952 An Analysis of the Significant Factors in the Patterns of Toronto Chinese Family Life as a Result of the Recent Changes in Immigration Laws". Unpublished M.A. thesis, School of Social Work, University of Toronto, Toronto, Ontario.

Delora, Joann S., and Jack R. Delora

1972 *Intimate Life Styles: Marriage and its Alternatives*. Pacific Palisades, California: Goodyear Publishing.

Demos, John

1970 *A Little Commonwealth*. New York: Oxford Press.

Devereux, Edward C.

1970 "Socialization in Cross-cultural Perspective: Comparative Study of England, Germany and the United States", pp. 72-106 in Reuben Hill and Rene Konig, eds., *Families in East and West: Socialization Process and Kinship Ties*. The Hague: Mouton

*Dunning, R.W.

1959a *Social and Economic Change among the Northern Ojibwa*. Toronto: University of Toronto Press.

1959b "Rules of Residence and Ecology among the Northern Ojibwa", *American Anthropologist* 61:1, pp. 806-16.

1971 "Changes in Marriage and the Family Among the Northern Ojibwa", pp. 355-67 in K. Ishwaran, ed., *The Canadian Family*. Toronto: Holt, Rinehart and Winston.

*Dupuis, Monique, et al.

1957 "Caractéristiques socio-culturelles et attitudes parentales". Unpublished M.A. thesis, School of Social Work, University of Montreal, Montreal, Quebec.

Durkheim, Emile

1960 *The Division of Labor in Society*. Glencoe, Ill.: The Free Press. (Originally published in 1893.)

Duvall, Evelyn Millis
  1962 *Family Development*, 2nd ed. Philadelphia: J.B. Lippincott.
  1971 *Family Development*, 4th ed. New York: J.B. Lippincott.
*Dyck, Harold J.
  1970 *Social Futures Alberta 1970-2005*. Edmonton: Human Resources Research Council.
*Eastham, K.
  1971 *Working Women in Ontario*. Toronto: Ministry of Labour, Women's Bureau.
Edwards, John N.
  1969 *The Family and Change*. New York: Alfred A. Knopf.
Ehrmann, Winston H.
  1959 *Premarital Dating Behavior*. New York: Holt, Rinehart and Winston.
*Eichler, Margrit and Marylee Stephenson
  1972 *Canadian Newsletter of Research on Women*. Published at the Department of Sociology, University of Waterloo, Waterloo, Ontario.
*Elkin, Frederick
  1964 *The Family in Canada*. Ottawa: Vanier Institute of the Family.
  1967 *The Child and Society*. New York: Random House.
  1970 "Family Life Education in the Media of Mass Communication", *Family Life Education Survey, Part I*. Ottawa: Vanier Institute of the Family.
  1971 "Family Life Education in the Schools", *Family Life Education Survey, Part II*. Ottawa: Vanier Institute of the Family.
Elkin, Fred, and Gerald Handel
  1972 *The Child and Society: The Process of Socialization*, 2nd ed. New York: Random House.
Epstein, Cynthia F.
  1971 *Woman's Place: Options and Limits in Professional Careers*. Berkeley: University of Californa Press.
*Epstein, Nathan
  1971 "Mental Illness and Mental Health: Focus on the Family", pp. 471-86 in K. Ishwaran, ed., *The Canadian Family*. Toronto: Holt, Rinehart and Winston.
Erikson, Erik
  1963 *Childhood and Society*, 2nd ed. New York: W.W. Norton.
Etzioni, Amitai
  1968 *The Active Society*. New York: The Free Press.
Fairfield, Richard
  1972 *Communes USA*. Baltimore: Penguin Books.
Farber, Bernard
  1964 *Family: Organization and Interaction*. San Francisco: Chandler Press.
  1968 *Comparative Family Systems: A Method of Analysis*. New York: John Wiley.
  1971 *Kinship and Class: A Midwestern Study*. New York: Basic Books.
  1973 *Family and Kinship in Modern Society*. Glenview, Illinois: Scott, Foresman and Company.
Farber, Bernard, and William C. Jenne
  1963 "Family Organization and Parent-Child Communication: Parents and Siblings of a Retarded Child". *Monographs of the Society for Research in Child Development* 28:7.
*Farley, Reginald P.
  1969 "Investigation of Social Integration and Aspirations in Two Relatively Deprived Communities". Unpublished M.A. thesis, University of Calgary, Calgary, Alberta.
Farson, Richard E., et al.
  1969 *The Future of the Family*. New York: Family Service Association.
*Fearn, Gordon
  1973 *Canadian Social Organization*. Toronto: Holt, Rinehart and Winston.
*Ferguson, Jack
  1971 "Eskimos in a Satellite Society", pp. 15-29 in Jean Leonard Elliot, ed., *Minority Canadians: Native Peoples*. Scarborough, Ontario: Prentice-Hall of Canada.

Firth, Raymond
1936 *We, The Tikopia*. London: George Allen and Unwin.

Firth, Raymond, Jane Hubert and Anthony Forge
1969 *Families and their Relatives*. London: Routledge and Kegan Paul.

*Forcese, Dennis P., and Leonard B. Siemens
1965 *School-Related Factors and the Aspiration Levels of Manitoba Senior High School Students*. Winnipeg: Faculty of Agriculture and Home Economics of the University of Manitoba.

Ford, Clellan S., and Frank A. Beach
1951 *Patterns of Sexual Behavior*. New York: Harper and Row.

Fox, Lorene K., ed.
1967 *East African Childhood: Three Versions*. New York: Oxford University Press.

Fox, Robin
1967 *Kinship and Marriage*. Middlesex, England: Penguin Books.

Francoeur, Robert T.
1972 *Eve's New Rib*. New York: Harcourt, Brace, Jovanovich.

*Fretz, J.W.
1967 *The Mennonites in Ontario*. Waterloo: The Mennonite Historial Society of Ontario.

Friedan, Betty
1963 *The Feminine Mystique*. New York: Dell Publishing Co.

Furstenberg, Frank F.
1966 "Industrialization and the American Family: A Look Backward", *American Sociological Review* 31 (June), 326-37.

*Gagnon, Nicole
1968 "Un nouveau type de relations familiales", *Recherches Sociographiques*, 9 (January-April), 59-66.

*Gajda, Roman T.
1960 "The Canadian Ecumene: Inhabited and Uninhabited Areas", *Geographical Bulletin* 15: pp. 5-18.

Galbraith, John Kenneth
1962 *The Affluent Society*. Middlesex, England: Penguin Books.

Gallup, George H.
1972 *The Gallup Poll: Public Opinion 1935-1971*, Vol. III. New York: Random House.

Gans, Herbert J.
1962 *The Urban Villagers*. New York: The Free Press.

*Garigue, Philippe
1956 "French-Canadian Kinship and Urban Life", *American Anthropologist* 58 (December), 1090-101.

1958 *Etudes sur le Canada Français*. Montréal: Faculté des Sciences Sociales, Economiques et Politiques, Université de Montréal.

1962 *La Vie Familiale des Canadiens Français*. Montréal: Presses de l'Université de Montréal.

1967 *Analyse du comportement familial*. Montréal: Presses de l'Université de Montréal.

1968 "The French Canadian Family", pp. 151-66 in Bernard R. Blishen, et al., eds., *Canadian Society*. Toronto: Macmillan Co. of Canada.

Gavron, Hannah
1966 *The Captive Wife: Conflicts of Housebound Mothers*. Middlesex, England: Penguin Books.

Geiger, H. Kent, ed.
1968 *Comparative Perspectives on Marriage and the Family*. Boston: Little, Brown, and Co.

*Gerson, David
1967 *Patterns of Social Functioning in Families*. Toronto: University of Toronto Press.

Getzels, J.W., and E.G. Guba
1954 "Role, Role Conflict and Effectiveness: An Empirical Study", *American Sociological Review* 19: pp. 164-75.

Gibson, Geoffrey
1969 "Kinship interaction and conjugal role relations". Unpublished paper.

1970 "Kinship interaction with parents, children, and siblings". Unpublished paper.

1972 "Kin family network: Overheralded Structure in Past Conceptualizations of Family Functioning", *Journal of Marriage and the Family* 34:2 (February), 13-23.

Gilmartin, B.G., and Dave V. Kusisto
1973 "Some Personal and Social Characteristics of Mate-Sharing Swingers", pp. 146-65 in Roger W. Libby and Robert N. Whitehurst, eds., *Renovating Marriage*. Danville, California: Consensus Publishers.

Glasse, R.M., and M.J. Meggitt, eds.
1969 *Pigs, Pearlshells and Women*. Englewood Cliffs, New Jersey: Prentice-Hall.

*Glazenbrook, G.
1950 *A Short History of Canada*. London: Oxford University Press.

Goode, William J.
1956 *Women in Divorce*. New York: Macmillan.
1959 "The Theoretical Importance of Love", *American Sociological Review* 24:1 (February), 38-47.
1963 *World Revolution and Family Patterns*. Glencoe, Ill.: The Free Press.
1971 *Family Research: A Propositional Inventory*. Indianapolis: Bobbs-Merrill.

Goodsell, Willystine
1934 *A History of Marriage and the Family*. New York: The Macmillan Company.

Gordon, Michael
1972 *The Nuclear Family in Crisis: The Search for an Alternative*. New York: Harper and Row.

Gore, M.S.
1965 "The Traditional Indian Family", pp. 209-32 in M.F. Nimkoff, ed., *Comparative Family Systems*. Boston: Houghton Mifflin.

Goslin, David A., ed.
1969 *Handbook of Socialization Theory and Research*. Chicago: Rand McNally.

Gottlieb, David, Jon Reeves and Warren D. TenHouten

1966 *The Emergence of Youth Societies: A Cross-Cultural Approach*. New York: The Free Press.

Gough, E.K.
1952 "Changing Kinship Usages in the Setting of Political and Economic Change Among the Nayars of Malabar", *Journal of the Royal Anthropological Institute*, 82:1, pp. 71-88.
1959 "The Nayars and the Definition of Marriage", *Journal of the Royal Anthropological Institute* 89: pp. 23-4.

Gouldner, Alvin W.
1960 "The Norms of Reciprocity: A Preliminary Statement", *American Sociological Review* 25 (April).

Greeley, Andrew M.
1974 *Ethnicity in the United States: A Preliminary Reconnaissance*. New York: Wiley-Interscience.

Green, Arnold W.
1941 "The 'Cult of Personality' and Sexual Relations", *Psychiatry* 4:3 (August), 343-48.

Greenfield, S.M.
1961 "Industrialization and the Family in Sociological Theory", *American Journal of Sociology* 67: pp. 312-22.
1965 "Love and Marriage in Modern America: A Functional Analysis" *The Sociologist Quarterly* 6:3 (Summer), 361-77.

*Greenglass, Esther
1971 "Italian Mothers in Canada", *Journal of the Ontario Association of Children's Aid Societies* (December) 1-4.

*Guilbault, Jocelyne, Marie-Thérèse Lacharité and Andrée Lafontaine
1956 "La femme mariée en emploi rémunéré". Unpublished M.A. thesis, School of Social Work, University of Montreal, Montreal, Quebec.

*Guyatt, Doris
1971 *One-Parent Family in Canada*. Ottawa: Vanier Institute of the Family.

Haley, Jay
1959 "The Family of the Schizophrenic: A

Model System'', *Journal of Nervous and Mental Disease* 129:4 pp. 357-74.

Handel, Gerald, ed.
1972 *The Psychosocial Interior of the Family: A Sourcebook for the Study of Whole Families*, rev. ed. Chicago: Aldine.

*Hatt, Judith
1969 ''The Rights and Duties of the Métis Preschool Child''. Unpublished M.A. thesis, University of Alberta, Edmonton, Alberta.

*Hawthorn, H.B.
1955 *The Doukhobors of British Columbia*. Vancouver: University of British Columbia Press.

*Hawthorn, H.B., ed.
1967 *Survey of the Contemporary Indians of Canada*, Part 2. Ottawa: Information Canada.
1968 *Family Roles and Interaction: An Anthology*. Chicago: Rand McNally.

Hayghe, Howard
1974 ''Marital and Family Characteristics of the Labor Force in March, 1973'', *Monthly Labor Review* 97:4 (April), 21-7.

*Heer, David M.
1962 ''The Trend of Interfaith Marriages in Canada: 1922-1957'', *American Sociological Review* 27: pp. 245-50.

*Heinrich, Albert
1972 ''Divorce as an Integrative Social Factor'', *Journal of Comparative Family Studies* 3 (Autumn), 265-72.

Heiss, Jerold
1962 ''Degree of Intimacy and Male-Female Interaction'', *Sociometry* 25 (June), 197-208.
1968 *Family Roles and Interaction: An Anthology*. Chicago: Rand McNally.

*Henripin, Jacques
1968 *Le coût de la croissance demographique*. Montreal: University of Montreal Press.

Henry, Jules
1964 *Jungle People*. New York: Vintage Books.

*Henshel, A.M.
1973 *Sex Structure*. Toronto: Longman Canada.

Hess, Robert, and Gerald Handel
1959 *Family Worlds*. Chicago: University of Chicago Press.

*Hickerson, Harold
1970 *The Chippewa and their Neighbors: A Study in Ethnohistory*. Toronto: Holt, Rinehart and Winston.

Hill, Reuben
1955 ''Courtship in Puerto Rico: An Institution in Transition'', *Marriage and Family Living* 17:1 (February), 26-35.

Hill, Reuben, and D.A. Hansen
1960 ''The Identification of Conceptual Frameworks Utilized in Family Study'', *Marriage and Family Living* 22:4 (November), 299-311.

Hill, Reuben, and Rene Konig, eds.
1970 *Families in East and West: Socialization Process and Kinship Ties*. The Hague: Mouton.

Hill, R., and Roy H. Rodgers
1964 ''The Developmental Approach'', pp. 171-211 in Harold T. Christensen, ed., *Handbook of Marriage and the Family*. Chicago: Rand McNally.

*Hobart, C.W.
1966 *Italian Immigrants in Edmonton: Adjustment and Integration*. A research report for the Royal Commission on Bilingualism and Biculturalism. Ottawa: Information Canada.
1972 ''Orientations to Marriage Among Young Canadians'', *Journal of Comparative Family Studies* (Autumn), 171-93.
1973 ''Attitudes toward Parenthood among Canadian Young People'', *Journal of Marriage and the Family* 35:1 (February), 93-101.
1974a ''Standards of Sexual Morality, a Study of Young French and English Speaking Canadians''. Unpublished paper.
1974b ''Trial Marriage among Students: A Study of Attitudes and Experience''. Unpublished paper.
1974c ''The Social Context of Morality Standards among Anglophone Canadian Students'', *Journal of Comparative Family Studies* 5:1 (Spring), 26-40.

*Hobart, C.W., et al.
1963 *Persistence and Change: A Study of Ukrainians in Alberta*. Edmonton: Ukrainian Canadian Research Foundation.

*Hobel, E. Adamson
1960 *The Cheyennes: Indians of the Great Plains*. Toronto: Holt, Rinehart and Winston.

Hochschild, A.R.
1973 "A Review of Sex Role Research", *American Journal of Sociology* 78 (January), 1011-29.

Holmstrom, L.L.
1972 *The Two-Career Family*. Cambridge, Mass.: Schenkman Publishing Co.

*Honigmann, John, and Irma Honigmann
1971 "The Eskimo of Frobisher Bay", pp. 55-75 in Jean Leonard Elliot, ed., *Minority Canadians: Native Peoples*. Scarborough, Ontario: Prentice-Hall of Canada.

*Horowitz, Gad
1966a "Mosaics and Identity", *Canadian Dimension* 3 (January-February), 14-23.

1966b "Conservatism, Liberalism, and Socialism in Canada: an Interpretation", *Canadian Journal of Economics and Political Science* 32:2 (May), 143-71.

Hostetler, John A.
1963 *Amish Society*. Baltimore: John Hopkins Press.

*Hostetler, John A., and Gertrude E. Huntington
1967 *The Hutterites in North America*. Toronto: Holt, Rinehart and Winston.

Howard, Jane
1970 *Please Touch: A Guided Tour of the Human Potential Movement*. New York: McGraw-Hill Book Co.

Huber, Joan, Guest ed.
1973 "Changing Women in a Changing Society", Special issue of the *American Journal of Sociology* 78:4 (January).

*Hughes, Everett C.
1948 "The Study of Ethnic Relations", *Dalhousie Review* 27: p. 477.

1954 *French Canada in Transition*. Chicago: University of Chicago Press.

*Hughes, Robert H.
1968 *A Study of High School Dropouts in Alberta*. Edmonton: Department of Youth.

Humphreys, Alexander J.
1965 "The Family in Ireland", pp. 232-59 in M.F. Nimkoff, ed., *Comparative Family Systems*. Boston: Houghton-Mifflin.

Hunt, Morton
1969 *The Affair*. New York: World Publishing Co.

Inkles, Alex
1968 "Society, Social Structure, and Child Socialization", pp. 73-130 in John A. Clausen, ed., *Socialization and Society*. Boston: Little, Brown and Co.

*Irving, Howard H.
1972 *The Family Myth*. Toronto: Copp Clark.

*Ishwaran, K.
1971a "The Canadian Family: An Overview", pp. 3-20 in K. Ishwaran, ed., *The Canadian Family*. Toronto: Holt, Rinehart and Winston.

1971b "Calvinism and Social Behavior in a Dutch-Canadian Community", pp. 297-314 in K. Ishwaran, ed., *the Canadian Family*. Toronto: Holt, Rinehart and Winston.

1971c "Family and Community among the Dutch Canadians", pp. 225-47 in K. Ishwaran, ed., *The Canadian Family*. Toronto: Holt, Rinehart and Winston.

1971d "The Canadian Family: Variations and Uniformities", pp. 372-96 in James E. Gallagher and Ronald Lambert, eds., *Social Processes and Institutions: The Canadian Case*. Toronto: Holt, Rinehart and Winston.

*Ishwaran, K., ed.
1971 *The Canadian Family*. Toronto: Holt, Rinehart and Winston.

*Jacobson, Helga
1971 "The Family in Canada: Some Problems

and Questions", pp. 23-38 in K. Ishwaran, ed., *The Canadian Family*. Toronto: Holt, Rinehart and Winston.

*Jenness, Diamond
1922 *The Life of the Copper Eskimos*. Report of the Canadian Arctic Expedition, Vol. 12. Ottawa: F.A. Acland.
1935 "The Ojibwa Indians of Parry Island: Their Social and Religious Life". Canadian Department of Mines, Bulletin 78.

Jennings, Eugene E.
1970 "Mobicentric Man", *Psychology Today* 4: 34ff.

Jocano, F. Landa
1969 *Growing Up in a Philippine Barrio*. New York: Holt, Rinehart and Winston.

Johnson, Ralph E.
1970 "Some Correlates of Extramarital Coitus", *Journal of Marriage and the Family* (August), 449-56.

*Joy, Richard J.
1972 *Languages in Conflict: The Canadian Experience*. Toronto: McClelland and Stewart.

*Kalbach, Warren E., and Wayne W. McVey
1971 *The Demographic Bases of Canadian Society*. Toronto: McGraw-Hill.

Kandel, Denise B., and Gerald B. Lesser
1972 *Youth in Two Worlds: United States and Denmark*. San Francisco: Jossey-Bass.

Kanter, Rosabeth Moss
1972 *Commitment and Community: Communes and Utopias in Sociological Perspective*. Cambridge, Mass.: Harvard University Press.

*Kappel, B.E.
1972 "Self-Esteem Among the Children of Working Mothers". Unpublished M.A. thesis, University of Waterloo, Waterloo, Ontario.

Keniston, Kenneth
1965 *The Uncommitted: Alienated Youth in American Society*. New York: Harcourt, Brace, Jovanovich.

*Kieran, S.
1970 *The Working Wife: A Canadian Handbook*. Toronto: Macmillan Co. of Canada.
1970 *The Non-Deductible Woman*. Toronto: Macmillan Co. of Canada.

*Kilbourn, William, ed.
1970 *Canada: A Guide to the Peaceable Kingdom*. Toronto: Macmillan Co. of Canada.

Kilgo, Reese Danley
1972 "Can Group Marriage Work", *Sexual Behavior* (March), 8-14.

Kinsey, A.C., et al.
1948 *Sexual Behavior in the Human Male*. Philadelphia: W.B. Saunders Company.
1953 *Sexual Behavior in the Human Female*. Philadelphia: W.B. Saunders Company.

Kirkendall, L.A.
1961 *Premarital Intercourse and Interpersonal Relationships*. New York: Julian Press.

Kirkendall, Lester A., and Robert N. Whitehurst
1971 *The New Sexual Revolution*. New York: Donald W. Brown Co.

Kirkpatrick, C., and C. Hobart
1954 "Disagreement, Disagreement Estimate and Nonemphathic Imputations for Intimacy Groups Varying from Favorite Date to Married", *American Sociological Review* 19:1 (February), 10-20.

*Kohl, Seena
1971 "The Family in a Postfrontier Society", pp. 79-93 in K. Ishwaran, ed., *The Canadian Family*. Toronto: Holt, Rinehart and Winston.

*Kohl, Seena, and John W. Bennett
1965 "Kinship, Succession and the Migration of Young People in a Canadian Agricultural Community", *International Journal of Comparative Sociology* 6 (March) 95-116.

Komarovsky, Mirra
1964 *Blue Collar Marriage*. New York: Random House.

*Kosa, John
1957 *Land of Choice: The Hungarians in Canada*. Toronto: University of Toronto Press.

1968 "Marriage and Family Among Hungarians in Canada", pp. 167-83 in B.R. Blishen, et al., eds., *Canadian Society*. Toronto: Macmillan Co. of Canada.

*Kubat, David, and David Thornton
1974 *A Statistical Profile of Canadian Society*. Toronto: McGraw-Hill Ryerson.

*Kupfer, George
1966 "Middle Class Delinquency in a Canadian City". Unpublished Ph.D. thesis, University of Washington, Seattle, Washington.

Kurian, George
1961 *The Indian Family in Transition: A Case Study of Kerala Syrian Christians*. The Hague: Mouton.

*Kurokawa, Minako
1969 "Psycho-Social Roles of Mennonite Children in a Changing Society", *The Canadian Review of Sociology and Anthropology* 6:1 (February), 15-35.

*Kuzel, Paul, and P. Krishnan
1973 "Changing Patterns of Remarriage in Canada, 1961-1966", *Journal of Comparative Family Studies* 4:2, pp. 215-24.

*Laberge, M.W.
1971 "The Cultural Tradition of Canadian Women: The Historical Background", in *Cultural Tradition of Women in Canada*, Studies of the Royal Commission on the Status of Women in Canada. Ottawa: Information Canada.

*Lacasse, F.D.
1971 *Women at Home: The Cost to the Canadian Economy of the Withdrawal from the Labour Force of a Major Proportion of the Female Population*. Studies of the Royal Commission on the Status of Women in Canada. Ottawa: Information Canada.

Lalli, Michael
1969 "The Italian-American Family: Assimilation and Change, 1900-1965", *The Family Coordinator* 18 (January), 44-8.

*Lamarre, Nicole
1973 "Kinship and Inheritance Patterns in a French Newfoundland Village", pp. 142-53 in Gerald L. Gold and Marc-Adelard Tremblay, eds., *Communities and Culture in French Canada*. New York: Holt, Rinehart and Winston. (Translated and taken from *Recherches sociographiques* 12:3, 1971, pp. 345-59).

*Lambert, W.E., A. Yackley and R.N. Hein
1971 "Child Training Values of English Canadian and French Canadian Parents", *Canadian Journal of Behavioral Science* 3 (July), 217-36.

*Landes, R.
1937 *Ojibwa Society*. New York: Columbia University Press.

*Langevin, James M.
1970 "The Traditional Blackfoot Family". Unpublished paper.

*Lantis, Margaret
1946 "The Social Culture of the Nunivak Eskimo", *Transactions of the American Philosophical Society*. Philadelphia.

Lantz, Herman R., Margaret Britton, Raymond Schmitt and Eloise C. Snyder
1968 "Pre-Industrial Patterns in the Colonial Family in America: A Content Analysis of Colonial Magazines", *American Sociological Review* 33 (June), 413-26.

*Larson, Lyle E.
1969 "The Structure and Process of Social Influence during Adolescence: An Examination of the Salience Hierarchy". Unpublished Ph.D. thesis, University of Oregon, Eugene, Oregon.

*1970 "The Family in Contemporary Society and Emerging Family Patterns", pp. 25-41 in Roslyn Burshtyn, ed., *Day Care: A Resource for the Canadian Family*. Ottawa: Vanier Institute of the Family.

*1971a "The Family and Leisure in Post-Industrial Society", in S. Hameed, ed., *Proceedings of the Work and Leisure Conference*, Faculty of Business Administration, University of Alberta.

*1971b *The Family in Alberta*. Edmonton: Human Resources Research Council.

1972a "The Relative Influence of Parent-Adolescent Affect in Predicting the Salience Hierarchy among Youth", *Pacific Sociological Review* 15:1 (January), 83-102.

1972b "The Application and Integration of Developmental, Interaction, and Systems Theory to the Study of Family Reality. Unpublished manuscript.

*1973 "The Influence of the Compressed Work Week on the Family System", pp. 192-215 in S. Hameed and G. Paul, *Three and Four Day Work Week*. Edmonton: University of Alberta Press.

1974a "Systems and Subsystem Perception of Family Roles", *Journal of Marriage and the Family* 36:1 (February).

1974b "An Examination of the Salience Hierarchy during Adolescence: The Influence of the Family". *Adolescence* 9:35 (Fall), 317-32.

Laslett, Barbara
1973 "The Family as a Public and Private Institution: An Historical Perspective", *Journal of Marriage and the Family*. 35:3 (August), 480-95.

*Latowsky, Evelyn
1971 "Family Life Styles and Jewish Culture", pp. 94-110 in K. Ishwaran, ed., *The Canadian Family*. Toronto: Holt, Rinehart and Winston.

Laumann, Edward O.
1973 *Bonds of Pluralism: The Form and Substance of Urban Social Networks*. New York: Wiley-Interscience.

*Légaré, Jacques
1974 "Demographic Highlights on Fertility Decline in Canadian Marriage Cohorts", *Canadian Review of Sociology and Anthropology* 11:4 (November), 287-307.

LeMasters, E.E.
1974 *Parents in Modern America*, rev. ed. Homewood, Illinois: The Dorsey Press.

Lennard, Henry L., and Arnold Bernstein
1969 *Patterns in Human Interaction: An Introduction to Clinical Sociology*. San Francisco: Jossey-Bass.

*Leonard, A.H.
1966 "Employment Trends for Women in British Columbia". Unpublished M.A. thesis, University of British Columbia, Vancouver, British Columbia.

Leonard, George B.
1970 *The Man and Woman Thing*. New York: Dell Publishing.

Leslie, Gerald
1973 *The Family in Social Context*. New York: Oxford University Press.

Levey, Marion J., Jr.
1949 *The Family Revolution in Modern China*. Cambridge, Mass.: Harvard University Press.

Levinger, George
1965 "Marital Cohesiveness and Dissolution: An Integrative Review", *Journal of Marriage and the Family* 27 (February), 19-28.

Lewinsohn, Richard
1958 *A History of Sexual Customs*. New York: Harper.

*Lewis, Claudia
1952 "Doukhobor Children and Family Life". pp. 97-121 in H.B. Hawthorn, ed., *The Doukhobors of British Columbia*. Vancouver: University of British Columbia.

Lewis, Oscar
1959 *Five Families*. New York: Basic Books.
1961 *The Children of Sanchez*. New York: Random House.
1965 *La Vida: A Puerto Rican Family in the Culture of Poverty*. New York: Vintage.

Lewis, Robert A.
1973 "A Longitudinal Test of a Developmental Framework for Premarital Dyadic Formation", *Journal of Marriage and the Family* 35:1 (February), 16-25.

Libby, Roger W., and Robert N. Whitehurst
1973 *Renovating Marriage*. Danville, California: Consensus Publishers.

Liebman, Carol S.
1960 "Family Type and Child's Perception of His Mother's Satisfaction with his Behavior". Unpublished M.A. thesis, Department of Sociology, University of Illinois, Urbana, Illinois.

Linton, Ralph
1936 *The Study of Man*. New York: Appleton-Century-Crofts.

*Lipset, Seymour Martin
1964 "Canada and the United States: A Comparative View", *The Canadian Review of Sociology and Anthropology* (November), 173-85.
1968 *Revolution and Counterrevolution: Change and Persistence in Social Structure*. New York: Basic Books.

*Little, W.T.
1968 "The Domestic Illness Profile Seen in a Family Court Setting", pp. 310-18 in W.E. Mann, ed., *Deviant Behavior in Canada*. Willowdale, Ont.: Social Science Publishers.

Litwak, Eugene
1960a "Geographic Mobility and Extended Family Cohesion", *American Sociological Review* 25: pp. 386-94.
1960b "Occupational Mobility and Extended Family Cohesion", *American Sociological Review* 25: pp. 9-21.
1965 "Extended Kin Relations in an Industrial Society", in Ethel Shanas and Gordon Streib, eds., *Social Structure and the Family: Generation Relations*. Englewood Cliffs, New Jersey: Prentice-Hall.

*Locke, Keith
1969 "The Social Context of Educational Aspirations and Expectations: An Exploratory Study of Edmonton Junior High School Students". Unpublished M.A. thesis, University of Alberta, Edmonton, Alberta.

Lopada, H.Z.
1971 *Occupation: Housewife*. New York: Oxford University Press.

Luckey, Eleanor B.
1960 "Marital Satisfaction and Congruent Self Spouse Concepts". *Social Forces* 39: pp. 153-6.

Lupri, Eugen, and Gunther Luschen, Guest eds.
1972 "Comparative Perspectives on Marriage and the Family". Special issue of the *Journal of Comparative Family Studies* 3:1 (Spring).

Lyness, Judith L., Milton E. Lipetz and Keith E. Davis
1972 "Living Together: An Alternative to Marriage", *Journal of Marriage and the Family* 24 (May), 305-11.

Mace, David, and Vera Mace
1960 *Marriage: East and West*. Garden City, New York: Doubleday and Company.
1963 *The Soviet Family*. Garden City, New York: Doubleday and Company.

MacKenzie, L.T.
1969 "Working Mothers and Marital Happiness: A Study of Women on their Marital Happiness". Unpublished M.S.W. thesis, Acadia University, Wolfeville, N.S.

Mair, Lucy P.
1934 *An African People of the Twentieth Century*. London: George Routledge and Sons.

Makino, Tatsumi, Juzaburo Hashimoto, Kanehiro Hoshino and Yashio Matsumoto
1970 "Juvenile Delinquency and Home Training", pp. 137-51 in Reuben Hill and Rene König, eds., *Families in East and West: Socialization Process and Kinship Ties*. The Hague: Mouton.

Malinowski, B.
1927 *Sex and Repression in Savage Society*. London: Paul.
1929 *The Sexual Life of Savages in Northwestern Melanesia*. New York: Liveright.

*Mann, W.E.
1967 *Canadian Trends in Premarital Behavior*, Bulletin No. 198. Toronto: Anglican Church of Canada.
1968 *Canada: A Sociological Profile*. Toronto: Copp Clark.
1970 "Sex at York University", pp. 158-74 in W.E. Mann, ed., *The Underside of Toronto*.

Masters, William H., and Virginia E. Johnson
  1975 *The Pleasure Bond: A New Look at Sexuality and Commitment*. Boston: Little, Brown & Company.

*Maykovich, Minako Kurokawa
  1969 "Psycho-Social Roles of Mennonite Children in a Changing Society", *The Canadian Review of Sociology and Anthropology* 6 (February), 15-35.
  1971a "The Japanese Family in Tradition and Change", pp. 111-25 in K. Ishwaran, ed., *The Canadian Family*. Toronto: Holt, Rinehart and Winston.
  1971b "Alienation and Mental Health in Waterloo County", pp. 487-500 in K. Ishwaran, ed., *The Canadian Family*. Toronto: Holt, Rinehart and Winston.

Mayo, Katherine
  1927 *Mother India*. New York: Harcourt, Brace and Co.

McCall, George J., and J.L. Simmons
  1966 *Identities and Interactions: An Examination of Human Associations in Everyday Life*. Toronto: Free Press.

*McDonald, Michael
  1964 *Bibliography on the Family from the Fields of Theology and Philosophy*. Ottawa: Vanier Institute of the Family.

*McFeat, Tom, ed.
  1969 *Indians of the North Pacific Coast*. Toronto: McClelland and Stewart.

McIntire, Walter G., Gilbert D. Nass and Albert S. Dreyer
  1972 "A Cross-Cultural Comparison of Adolescent Perception of Parental Roles", *Journal of Marriage and the Family* 34 (November), 735-40.

McKain, Walter C.
  1970 *Retirement Marriage* Storrs, Conn.: University of Connecticut Press.

Mead, George H.
  1934 *Mind, Self, Society*. Chicago: University of Chicago Press.

Mead, Margaret
  1935 *Sex and Temperament*. New York: William Morrow and Company.
  1949 *Male and Female*. New York: William Morrow and Company.
  1963 *Sex and Temperament in Three Primitive Societies*. New York: Dell Publishing Co.

Mencher, Joan P.
  1965 "The Nayars of South Malabar", pp. 163-91 in M.F. Nimkoff, ed., *Comparative Family Systems*. Boston: Houghton Mifflin Co.

Michel, A., ed.
  1971 *Family Issues of Employed Women in Europe and America*. London: E.J. Brill.

Miller, Walter B.
  1958 "Lower-class Culture as a Generating Milieu of Gang Deliquency", *Journal of Social Issues* 14:3 (July), 5-19.

Minturn, Leigh, and William W. Lambert
  1964 *Mothers of Six Cultures: Antecedents of Child Rearing*. New York: John Wiley.

Mitchell, H.E., J.W. Bullard and E.H. Mudd
  1962 "Areas of Marital Conflict in Successfully and Unsuccessfully Functioning Families", *Journal of Health and Human Behavior* 3: pp. 88-93.

Mogey, John
  1971 "Sociology of Marriage and Family Behavior, 1957-1968", *Current Sociology* 17:1/3.

*Moreux, Collette
  1971 "The French Canadian Family", pp. 126-47 in K. Ishwaran, ed., *The Canadian Family*. Toronto: Holt, Rinehart and Winston.

Morgan, L.H.
  1877 *Ancient Society, or Researches in the Lines of Human Progress From Savagery through Barbarism to Civilization*. New York: Holt.

Murdock, George P.
  1949 *Social Structure*. New York: Free Press.
  1957 "World Ethnographic Sample", *American Anthropologist* 59 (August), 664-87.
  1965 *Social Structure*, 2nd ed. New York: Free Press.
  1967 *Ethographic Atlas*. Pittsburgh: University of Pittsburgh Press.

Murstein, Bernard I.
1972 "Person Perception and Courtship Progress among Premarital Couples", *Journal of Marriage and the Family* 34:4 (November), 621ff.

Myrdel, A., and V. Klein
1968 *Women's Two Roles: Home and Work*. London: Routledge & Kegan Paul.

*Naegele, Kaspar D.
1961 "Canadian Society: Some Reflections", pp. 1-53 in Bernard B. Blishen, Frank E. Jones, Kaspar D. Naegele and John Porter, eds., *Canadian Society: Sociological Perspectives*. Toronto: Macmillan Company of Canada.

Narain, Khirendra
1970 "Interpersonal Relationships in the Hindu Family", pp. 454-80 in Reuben Hill and Rene König, eds., *Families in East and West: Socialization Process and Kinship Ties*. The Hague: Mouton.

Neubeck, Gerhard, ed.
1969 *Extra-Marital Relations*. Englewood Cliffs, N.J.: Prentice-Hall.

Newson, John, and Elizabeth Newson
1963 *Patterns of Infant Care in an Urban Community*. Baltimore, Maryland: Penguin.
1968 *Four Years Old in an Urban Community*. Chicago: Aldine.

Niemi, Richard G.
1974 *How Family Members Perceive Each Other*. New Haven: Yale University Press.

Nimkoff, M.F., ed.
1965 *Comparative Family Systems*. Boston: Houghton Mifflin.

Nisbet, Robert
1953 *The Quest for Community*. New York: Oxford University Press.

Norbeck, Edward
1965 *Changing Japan*. New York: Holt, Rinehart and Winston.

Nordhoff, C.
1966 *Communistic Societies of the United States: From Personal Visit and Observation*. New York: Schocken Books.

Norton, Susan L.
1973 "Marital Migration in Essex County, Massachusetts, in the Colonial and Early Federal Periods", *Journal of Marriage and the Family* 34:3 (August), 406-19.

Nye, F. Ivan
1958 *Family Relationships and Delinquent Behavior*. New York: John Wiley and Sons.

Nye, F. Ivan, and Felix M. Berardo, eds.
1966 *Emerging Conceptual Frameworks in Family Analysis*. New York: Macmillan.

Nye, F. Ivan, and Lois W. Hoffman
1963 *The Employed Mother in America*. Chicago: Rand McNally.

Ogburn, W.F., and M.F. Nimkoff
1955 *Technology and the Changing Family*. Boston: Houghton Mifflin Co.

Oliver, Douglas L.
1955 *A Solomon Island Society*. Cambridge, Mass.: Harvard University Press.

Olson, David H., and Carolyn Rabunsky
1972 "Validity of Four Measures of Family Power", *Journal of Marriage and the Family* 24 (May), 224-35.

O'Neill, Nena, and George O'Neill
1972 *Open Marriage*. New York: M. Evans.

Orenstein, H.
1961 "The Recent History of the Extended Family in India", *Social Problems* 8 (Spring), 341-50.

*Ossenberg, Richard J.
1967 "The Conquest Revisited: Another Look at the Canadian Dualism", *The Canadian Review of Sociology and Anthropology* 4:4 (November), 201-18.

*Osterreich, Helgi
1965 "Geographical Mobility and Kinship: A Canadian Example", *International Journal of Comparative Sociology* 6 (March), 131-45.

*Ostry, Sylvia
1967 *The Occupational Composition of the*

Canadian Labour Force, Census Monograph. Ottawa: Information Canada.

1968 *The Female Worker in Canada*, Census Monograph. Ottawa: Information Canada.

1970 *Working Mothers and their Child-Care Arrangements*. Women's Bureau, Canadian Department of Labour. Ottawa: Information Canada.

Otterbein, Keith

1968 "Marquesan Polyandry", in Paul Bohannan and John Middleton, eds., *Marriage, Family, and Residence*. Garden City, New York: The Natural History Press.

Otto, Herbert A., ed.

1970 *The Family in Search of a Future: Alternate Models for Moderns*. New York: Appleton-Century-Crofts.

Parish, William L., and Moshe Schwartz

1972 "Household Complexity in Nineteenth Century France", *American Sociological Review* 37 (April), 154-73.

Parsons, Talcott

1942 "Age and Sex in the Social Structure of the United States", *American Sociological Review* 7: pp. 604-16.

1943 "The Kinship System of the Contemporary United States", *American Anthropologist* 45 (January), 22-38.

1951 *The Social System*. Glencoe, Illinois: The Free Press.

1959 "The Social Structure of the Family", pp. 241-74 in R.N. Anshen, ed., *The Family: Its Function and Destiny*. New York: Harper and Row.

Parsons, Talcott, and Robert F. Bales

1955 *Family, Socialization and Interaction Process*. Glencoe, Illinois: The Free Press.

*Patsula, Philip J.

1969 "Felt Powerlessness as Related to Perceived Parental Behavior". Unpublished Ph.D. thesis, The University of Alberta, Edmonton, Alberta.

*Payne, Julien

1968 "Divorce Reform in Canada", *Buffalo Law Review* 18:1, pp. 119-152.

*Pek, P.W.

1962 "Marital Conflict". Unpublished M.S.W. thesis, University of Toronto, Toronto, Ontario.

Peter, H.R.H. Prince

1965 "The Tibetan Family System", pp. 192-209 in M.F. Nimkoff, ed., *Comparative Family Systems*. Boston: Houghton Mifflin.

*Peter, Karl A.

1967 "Factors of Social Change and Social Dynamics on the Communal Settlements of Hutterites, 1527-1967". Unpublished Ph.D. thesis, University of Alberta, Edmonton, Alberta.

1971 "The Hutterite Family", pp. 248-62 in K. Ishwaran, ed., *The Canadian Family*. Toronto: Holt, Rinehart and Winston.

Peters, E.L.

1965 "Aspects of the Family among the Bedouin of Cyrenaica", pp. 121-47 in M.F. Nimkoff, ed., *Comparative Family Systems*. Boston: Houghton-Mifflin.

*Piddington, Ralph

1961 "A Study of French Canadian Kinship", *International Journal of Comparative Sociology* 2 (March), 3-22.

*Pimm, June

1970 "Research Results on the Effects of Early Childhood Experience", pp. 42-55 in Roslyn Burshtyn, ed., *Day Care: A Resource for the Contemporary Family*. Ottawa: Vanier Institute of the Family.

*Pineo, Peter

1961 "Disenchantment in the Later Years of Marriage", *Marriage and Family Living* 23:1 (February), 1-11.

1968 "The Extended Family in a Working Class Area of Hamilton", pp. 140-50 in B.R. Blishen, et al., eds., *Canadian Society*. Toronto: Macmillan Company of Canada.

*Podoluk, Jenny R.

1968 *Incomes of Canadians*, Census Monograph. Ottawa: Information Canada.

Poloma, M.M.

1972 "Role Conflict and the Married Professional Woman". pp. 187-98 in C. Safilios-Rothschild, ed., *Toward a Sociology of Women*. Toronto: Xerox College Publishing.

Poloma, M.M., and T.N. Garland

1971 "Jobs or Careers? The Case of the Professionally Employed Married Woman", pp. 126-42 in A. Michel, ed., *Family Issues of Employed Women in Europe and America*. Leiden: H.J. Brill.

*Pool, D.I., and M.D. Bracher

1974 "Aspects of Family Formation in Canada", *Canadian Review of Sociology and Anthropology* 11:4 (November), 308-23.

*Porter, John

1965 *The Vertical Mosaic*. Toronto: University of Toronto Press.

1967a *Canadian Social Structure: A Statistical Profile*, Carleton University No. 32. Toronto: McClelland and Stewart.

1967b "Canadian Character in the Twentieth Century", *The Annals of the American Academy of Political and Social Science* 370 (March), 48-56.

*Pryor, Edward, Jr.

1972 "Demographic Data on the Family", *Transition* 2:4 (January).

*Pyke, S.W.

1973 "Children's Literature: Conceptions of Sex Roles", in H. Zurick and R. Pike, eds., *Socialization and Social Values in Canada*. Toronto: New Press.

Queen, S.A., and R.W. Habenstein

1974 *The Family in Various Cultures*, 4th ed. New York: J.B. Lippincott Company.

Radcliffe-Brown, A.R.

1941 "The Study of Kinship Systems", *Journal of the Royal Anthropological Institute* 71:2.

Radcliffe-Brown, Alfred R., and Daryll Forde, eds.

1955 *African Systems of Kinship and Marriage*. New York: Oxford University Press.

Rainwater, Lee

1964 "Marital Sexuality in Four Cultures of Poverty", *Journal of Marriage and the Family* 26 (November), 457-66.

Rainwater, L., R.P. Coleman and G. Hendel

1959 *Workingman's Wife: Her Personality, World and Life Style*. New York: Oceana Publications.

Ramey, James W.

1972 "Emerging Patterns of Innovative Behavior in Marriage", *The Family Coordinator* 34 (October), 67-88.

Rapoport, R., and R. Rapoport

1971 *Dual-Career Families*. Middlesex: Penguin Books.

1972 "The Dual-Career Family: A Variant Pattern and Social Change", pp. 216-244 in C. Safilios-Rothschild, ed., *Toward a Sociology of Women*. Toronto: Xerox College Publishing.

*Rasmussen, Knud

1908 *People of the Polar North*. London: Kegan Paul, Trench, Trubner & Co.

1921 *Greenland by the Polar Sea*. London: Heinemann.

1931 "The Netsilik Eskimos", in *Report of the Fifth Thule Expedition 1921-24*, Vol. 8. Copenhagen: Gyldendalske Boghandel.

Reeves, Nancy

1971 *Womankind: Beyond the Stereotypes*. Chicago: Aldine-Atherton.

Reich, Charles A.

1970 *The Greening of America*. New York: Random House.

Reiss, Ira L.

1960 "Toward a Sociology of the Heterosexual Love Relationship", *Marriage and Family Living* 22:2 (May), 139-45.

1960 *Premarital Sexual Standards in America*. New York: Free Press.

1965 "The Universality of the Family: A Conceptual Analysis", *Journal of Marriage and the Family* 27 (November), 443-53.

1967 *The Social Context of Premarital Sexual Permissiveness*. New York: Holt, Rinehart and Winston.

*Richmond, Anthony
  1967a *Immigrants and Ethnic Groups in Metropolitan Toronto*. Toronto: Institute for Behavioral Research, York University.
  1967b *Post-War Immigration in Canada*. Toronto: University of Toronto Press.
*Rioux, M.
  1959 *Kinship Recognition and Urbanization in French Canada*, Bulletin No. 173. Ottawa: National Museum of Canada.
*Rioux, Marcel, and Yves Martin, eds.
  1964 *French Canadian Society*, Vol. 1, Carleton Library No. 18. Toronto: McClelland and Stewart.
Rivers, W.H.R.
  1906 *The Todas*. New York: The Macmillan Company.
*Roberts, Lance, and P. Kirshnan
  1972 "Age Specific Incidence and Social Correlates of Divorce in Canada". Unpublished paper.
*Robertson, Heather
  1970 *Reservations are for Indians*. Toronto: James Lewis and Samuel.
Rodgers, Roy H.
  1964 "Toward a Theory of Family Development", *Journal of Marriage and the Family* 26 (August), 262-70.
  1973 *Family Interaction and Transaction: The Developmental Approach*. Englewood Cliffs, New Jersey: Prentice-Hall.
Rodman, Hymen
  1966 "Illegitimacy in the Caribbean Social Structure: A Reconsideration", *American Sociological Review* 31:5, pp. 673-83.
Rogers, Carl
  1972 *Becoming Partners: Marriage and its Alternatives*. New York: Delacorte Press.
*Rohner, Ronald R., and Evelyn C. Rohner
  1970 *The Kwakiutl Indians of British Columbia*. New York: Holt, Rinehart and Winston.
Rollins, Boyd C., and Harold Feldman
  1970 "Marital Satisfaction over the Family Life Cycle", *Journal of Marriage and the Family* 32:1 (February), 20ff.

*Rollins, James, and R.E. Du Wors
  1963 "Inter-Ethnic Marriage in Saskatchewan". Unpublished manuscript.
*Romaniuk, A.
  1974 "Modernization and Fertility: The Case of the James Bay Indians", *Canadian Review of Sociology and Anthropology* 11:4 (November), 344-59.
Rose, Arnold M.
  1962 *Human Behavior and Social Processes: An Interactional Approach*. Boston: Houghton Mifflin Co.
*Rosenberg, Louis
  1961 "The Centuries of Jewish Life in Canada: 1760-1960", *American Jewish Year Book* 2. Philadelphia: Jewish Publication Society.
Rossi, Alice S.
  1968 "Transition to Parenthood", *Journal of Marriage and the Family* 30 (February), 26-39.
Rossi, Peter H.
  1955 *Why Families Move*. Glencoe, Illinois: The Free Press.
*Rossignol, M.
  1938 "Cross-Cousin Marriage among the Saskatchewan Cree", *Primitive Man* 11: pp. 26-8.
Roszak, Theodore
  1968 *The Making of a Counter Culture*. New York: Doubleday Books.
Rowe, George P.
  1966 "The Developmental Conceptual Framework to the Study of the Family", pp. 198-22 in F. Ivan Nye and Felix M. Berardo, eds., *Emerging Conceptual Frameworks in Family Analysis*. New York: The Macmillan Co.
*Ryan, Joan
  1976 "The Squamish Family: A Setting for Daily Socialization". See Ch. 6 in this book.
*Ryan, Thomas
  1972 *Poverty and the Child—A Canadian Study*. Toronto: McGraw-Hill-Ryerson Press.

Safilios-Rothschild, Constantina

1970 "The Study of Family Power Structure: A Review 1960-1970", *Journal of Marriage and the Family* 32 (November), 539-52.

1972 *Toward a Sociology of Women*. Toronto: Xerox College Publishing.

Sager, Clifford J., and Helen S. Kaplan

1972 *Progress in Group and Family Therapy*. New York: Brunner/Mazel Publishers.

*Saskatchewan Royal Commission on Agriculture and Rural Life.

1956 *The Home and Family in Rural Saskatchewan*, Report No. 10. Regina, Saskatchewan: Queen's Printer.

Scanzoni, John H.

1970 *Opportunity and the Family: A Study of the Conjugal Family in Relation to the Economic Opportunity Structure*. New York: Free Press.

1972 *Sexual Bargaining: Power Politics in the American Marriage*. Englewood Cliffs, New Jersey: Prentice-Hall.

*Schlesinger, Benjamin

1965 *The Multi-Problem Family*. Toronto: University of Toronto Press.

1966a "The Unmarried Father: The Forgotten Man", *Canada's Health and Welfare* 21 (January), 4-8.

1966b "Parents Without Partners", *Canadian Welfare* 42 (November), 231-6.

1966c "The One-Parent Family: An Overview", *The Family Coordinator* 15:4 (October), 133-8.

1968 "Remarriage — An Inventory of Findings", *The Family Coordinator* 17:4 (October), 248-50.

1968 "Interfaith Marriages — Some Issues", *Social Science* 43:4 (October), 217-20.

1969 *The One-Parent Family: Perspectives and Annotated Bibliography*. Toronto: University of Toronto Press.

1970 "Remarriage as Family Reorganization for Divorced Persons: A Canadian Study", *Journal of Comparative Family Studies* 1:1 (Spring), 101-18.

1971a "The Multi-Problem Family in Canada", pp. 501-13 in K. Ishwaran, ed., *The Canadian Family*. Toronto: Holt, Rinehart and Winston.

1971b "Status of Women in Canada: Summary of Commission Recommendations", *The Family Coordinator* 20:3 (July), 253-8.

1971c "Remarriage as Family Reorganization for Divorced Persons", pp. 377-95 in K. Ishwaran, ed., *The Canadian Family*. Toronto: Holt, Rinehart and Winston.

1971d *The Jewish Family, A Survey and Annotated Bibliography*. Toronto: University of Toronto Press.

1971e *The Multiproblem Family: A Review and Annotated Bibliography*, 3rd ed. Toronto: University of Toronto Press.

1972 *Families: A Canadian Perspective*. Toronto: McGraw-Hill Ryerson.

*Schlesinger, Benjamin, and Alex Macrae

1970 "Remarriages in Canada: Statistical Trends", *Journal of Marriage and the Family* 32:2 (May), 300-3.

Schneider, David M.

1968 *American Kinship: A Cultural Account*. Englewood Cliffs, New Jersey: Prentice-Hall.

Schneider, D.M., and E.K. Gough, eds.

1961 *Matrilineal Kinship*. Berkeley: University of California Press.

Schneider, D.M., and G.C. Homans

1955 "Kinship Terminology and the American Kinship System", *American Anthropologist* 57: pp. 1194-1208.

Schneider, D.M., and Raymond T. Smith

1973 *Class Differences and Sex Roles in American Kinship and Family Structure*. Englewood Cliffs, New Jersey: Prentice-Hall.

Schultz, David A.

1972 *The Changing Family: Its Function and Future*. Englewood Cliffs, New Jersey: Prentice-Hall.

Schvaneveldt, Jay D.

1966 "The Interactional Framework in the Study of the Family", pp. 97-130 in F.

Ivan Nye and Felix M. Berardo, eds., *Emerging Conceptual Frameworks in Family Analysis*. New York: The Macmillan Co.

*Schwartz, Mildred A.

1967 *Public Opinion and Canadian Identity*. Scarborough, Ontario: Fitzhenry and Whiteside.

Schwarzweller, H.R.

1964 "Parental Family Ties and Social Integration of Rural to Urban Migrants", *Marriage and Family Living* 26 (November), 410-16.

Scott, John F.

1971 *Internalization of Norms: A Sociological Theory of Moral Commitment*. Englewood Cliffs, New Jersey: Prentice-Hall.

*Seeley, John, Alexander Sim and Elizabeth Loosley

1956 *Crestwood Heights: A Study of the Culture of Suburban Life*. Toronto: University of Toronto Press.

Shan-Lam, Wong

1970 "Social Change and Parent-Child Relations in Hong Kong", pp. 167-74 in Reuben Hill and Rene König, eds., *Families in East and West: Socialization Process and Kinship Ties*. The Hague: Mouton.

*Siemens, Leonard B., and J.W. Winston Jackson

1965 *Educational Plans and their Fulfillment: A Study of Selected High School Students in Manitoba*. Winnipeg: Faculty of Agriculture and Home Economics, University of Manitoba.

Skipper, James K., and Gilbert Nass

1966 "Dating Behavior: A Framework for Analysis and an Illustration", *Journal of Marriage and the Family* 28:4 (November), 412-20.

Skolnick, Arlene S., and Jerome H. Skolnick

1971 *Family in Transition: Rethinking Marriage, Sexuality, Child Rearing, and Family Organization*. Boston: Little, Brown and Co.

Slater, Philip

1970 *The Pursuit of Loneliness*. Boston: Beacon Press.

Smelser, Neil

1959 *Social Change in the Industrial Revolution*. Chicago: University of Chicago Press.

Smith, James, and Lynn Smith

1970 "Co-marital Sex and the Sexual Freedom Movement", *Journal of Sex Research* 6:2, pp. 131-42.

Smith, M.G.

1966 *West Indian Family Structure*. Seattle: University of Washington.

*Spencer, John C.

1966 *Emerging Family Patterns in Canada*. Toronto: Anglican Church of Canada.

*Spencer, John, ed.

1967 *An Inventory of Family Research and Studies in Canada: 1963-1967*. Ottawa: Vanier Institute of the Family.

Spiro, Melford E.

1963 *Kibbutz: Venture in Utopia*. New York: Schocken Books.

1965 *Children of the Kibbutz: A Study in Child Training and Personality*. New York: Schocken Books.

Sprey, Jetse

1969 "The Family as a System in Conflict", *Journal of Marriage and the Family* 31:4 (November), 699-705.

*Statistics Canada

1967 *Women Who Work*, Special Labour Force Studies, Cat. No. 71-509. Ottawa: Information Canada.

Vital Statistics, Cat. No. 84-201, published annually to 1971. Ottawa: Information Canada.

The following census publications, published in Ottawa by Information Canada, have been used in this book.

1966 Census of Canada, Households and Families, Vol. 2, "Household Composition".

1966 Census of Canada, Households and Families, Vol. 2, "Families by Type".

Cat. No. 99-526 *General Review: Canadian Families*

Cat. No. 92-717 *Marital Status*

Cat. No. 92-723 *Ethnic Groups*

Cat. No. 92-734 *Marital Status by Ethnic Groups*

Cat. No. 92-735 *Religious Denominations by Ethnic Groups*

Cat. No. 93-712 *Household and Family Status of Individuals*

Cat. No. 93-714 *Families by Size and Type*

Cat. No. 93-730 *Number of Persons Per Room*

1974 *Perspective Canada*, Cat. No. 11-507. Ottawa: Information Canada.

*Stefansson, Vilhjalmus

1913 *My Life with the Eskimo*. New York: Macmillan.

Stephens, William N.

1962 *The Oedipus Complex: Cross-Cultural Evidence*. New York: Free Press of Glencoe.

1963 *The Family in Cross-Cultural Perspective*. New York: Holt, Rinehart and Winston.

*Stephenson, M.

1973 *Women in Canada*. Toronto: New Press.

Stolte-Heiskanen, Veronica

1972 "Contextual Analysis and Theory Construction in Cross-Cultural Family Research", *Journal of Comparative Family Studies* 3:1 (Spring), 33-50.

Straus, Murray A.

1969 *Family Measurement Techniques: Abstracts of Published Instruments, 1935-1965*. Minneapolis: University of Minnesota Press.

1972 "A General Systems Theory Approach to the Development of a Theory of Violence between Family Members". Unpublished manuscript.

Straus, M.A., and Susanne C. Graham

1964 *Index 1939-1962, Marriage and Family Living*. Minneapolis: National Council on Family Relations.

Streib, G.F.

1958 "Family Patterns in Retirement", *Journal of Social Issues* 14:2, pp. 46-60.

Strodtbeck, Fred L.

1954 "The Family as a Three-Person Group", *American Sociological Review* 19: pp. 23-9.

Stroup, Atlee L.

1966 *Marriage and Family: A Developmental Approach*. New York: Appleton-Century-Crofts.

Stryker, Sheldon

1964 "The Interactional and Situational Approaches", pp. 126-70 in Harold T. Christensen, ed., *Handbook of Marriage and the Family*. Chicago: Rand McNally.

Sussman, Marvin B.

1953 "The Help Pattern in the Middle Class Family", *American Sociological Review* 18 (February), 22-8.

1968 *Sourcebook in Marriage and the Family*, 3rd ed. Boston: Houghton Mifflin.

1970 "The Urban Kin Networks in the Formulation of Family Theory", pp. 481-503 in Reuben Hill and Rene König, eds., *Families in East and West: Socialization Process and Kinship Ties*. The Hague: Mouton.

1971 "Family Themes for the 1970's", pp. 517-31 in K. Ishwaran, ed., *The Canadian Family*. Toronto: Holt, Rinehart and Winston.

Sussman, Marvin B., and L.G. Burchinal

1962 "Kin Family Network: Unheralded Structure in Current Conceptualizations of Family Functioning", *Marriage and Family Living* 24 (August), 231-40.

Sussman, Marvin B., and Betty E. Cogswell

1972 *Cross-National Family Research*. Leiden: E.J. Brill.

*Szwed, John

1966 *Private Cultures and Public Imagery: Interpersonal Relations in a Newfoundland Peasant Society*, Newfoundland Social and Economic Studies No. 2. Institute of Social and Economic Research, Memorial

University, St. John's, Newfoundland.

Talmon, Yonina

1972 *Family and Community in the Kibbutz.* Cambridge, Mass.: Harvard University Press.

*Taylor, Donald M., Lise M. Simard and Frances E. About

1972 "Ethnic Identification in Canada: A Cross-Cultural Investigation", *Canadian Journal of Behavioural Science* 4 (January), 13-20.

*Taylor, J. Garth

1965 "Social Organization of the Eighteenth Century Labrador Eskimo". Unpublished M.A. thesis, University of Toronto, Toronto, Ontario.

*Tepperman, Lorne

1974 "Ethnic Variations in Marriage and Fertility: Canada 1871", *Canadian Review of Sociology and Anthropology* 11:4 (November), 324-43.

Theodore, Athena, ed.

1971 *The Professional Women.* Cambridge, Mass: Schenkman.

Theodorson, George A.

1965 "Romanticism and Motivation to Marry in the United States, Singapore, Burma, and India", *Social Forces* 44 (September), 17-27.

*Thiessen, I.

1966 "Values and Personality Characteristics of Mennonites in Manitoba", *Mennonite Quarterly Review* 49: pp. 48-61.

*Thomson, Georgina H.

1963 *Crocus and Meadowlark Country: A Story of an Alberta Family.* Edmonton: Institute of Applied Art.

Toffler, Alvin

1970 *Future Shock.* New York: Random House.

Tonnies, Ferdinand

1963 *Community and Society*, translated and edited by Charles P. Loomis. New York: Harper Torchbooks. (Originally published in 1887).

*Tremblay, M.A.

1973 "Authority Models in the French-Canadian Family", pp. 109-119 in Gerald L. Gold and Marc-Adelard Tremblay, *Communities and Culture in French Canada.* New York: Holt, Rinehart and Winston. (Translated and taken from Recherches sociographiques 7:1-2, 1966, pp. 215-30.)

*Turk, James Leonard

1970 "The Measurement of Intra-Familial Power". Unpublished Ph.D. thesis, University of Toronto, Toronto, Ontario.

*Turk, James L., and Norman W. Bell

1972 "Measuring Power in Families", *Journal of Marriage and the Family* 24 (May), 215-22.

Turner, E.S.

1955 *A History of Courting.* New York: E.P. Button and Co.

Turner, Ralph H.

1970 *Family Interaction.* New York: John Wiley.

*Tysko, L.

1959 "Family Life and Family Stability of Negro Families in Halifax". Unpublished M.A. thesis, School of Social Work, Dalhousie University, Halifax.

Udry, J. Richard

1971 *The Social Context of Marriage*, 2nd ed. Philadelphia: J.B. Lippincott Company.

Udyanin, Kasem, and Prasert Yamklinfung

1970 "Family Status and Parent-Youth Relations", pp. 152-86 in Reuben Hill and Rene König, eds., *Families in East and West: Socialization Process and Kinship Ties.* The Hague: Mouton.

United States Bureau of the Census

1970a Census of the Population, Detailed Characteristics, Final Report PC(1)-D1, United States Summary. Washington, D.C.: U.S. Government Printing Office.

1970b Census of Housing, Part I, Detailed Housing Characteristics, United Status Summary, HC (1)-B1. Washington, D.C.: U.S. Government Printing Office.

United States Department of Health, Education and Welfare

1973a *Statistical Abstract of the United States*. National Center for Health Statistics. Rockville, Maryland: Health Resources Administration.

1973b *Monthly Vital Statistics Report*, (HRA) 75-1120, National Center for Health Statistics. Rockville, Maryland: Health Resources Administration.

*Valentine, Victor F., and Frank G. Valee, eds.

1968 *Eskimo of the Canadian Arctic*. Toronto: McClelland and Stewart.

*Vallee, Frank G.

1967 *Kabloona and Eskimo in the Central Keewatin*. Ottawa: Canadian Research Centre for Anthropology, St. Paul's University.

1971 "Kinship, the Family and Marriage in the Central Keewatin", K. Ishwaran, ed., *The Canadian Family*. Toronto: Holt, Rinehart and Winston.

van den Berghe, Pierre L.

1964 "Toward a Sociology of Africa", *Social Forces* 43:1 (October).

*Vanier Institute of the Family

1964 *The Canadian Conference on the Family*. Ottawa.

1967 *An Inventory of Family Research and Studies in Canada, 1963-1967*. Ottawa.

1968 *The Family in the Evolution of Agriculture*. Ottawa.

*Van Stelk, M.

1968 *Man and Woman*. Toronto: McClelland and Stewart.

Varni, Charles

1972 "An Exploratory Study of Spouse Swapping", *Pacific Sociological Review* 15:4, pp. 507-22.

*Vaz, Edmund

1968 "Delinquency Among Middle Class Boys", pp. 773-781 in B.R. Blishen, et al., eds., *Canadian Society*. Toronto: Macmillan Co. of Canada.

1968 "Middle Class Adolescents: Youth Culture Activities", pp. 223-33 in B.R.

Blishen et al., eds., *Canadian Society*. Toronto: Macmillan Co. of Canada.

*Veevers, J.E.

1973 "Voluntary Childlessness: A Neglected Area of Family Study", *The Family Coordinator* 23: pp. 199-205.

von Bertalanffy, Ludwig

1950 *General Systems Theory*. New York: George Braziller.

*Vranas, George J., and Margaret Stephens

1971 "The Eskimos of Churchill, Manitoba", pp. 29-55 in Jean L. Elliot, ed., *Minority Canadians: Native Peoples*. Scarborough, Ontario: Prentice-Hall of Canada.

*Wade, Mason

1950 *The French Canadians, 1760-1945*. London: Macmillan.

1968 *Canadian Dualism*. Toronto: University of Toronto Press.

*Wade, Mason, ed.

1960 *Canadian Dualism – La Dualité Canadienne*. Toronto: University of Toronto Press. Quebec: Les Presses Universitaires Laval.

*Wakil, Parvez

1971 "Marriage and Family in Canada. A Demographic-Cultural Profile", pp. 317-41 in K. Ishwaran, ed., *The Canadian Family*. Toronto: Holt, Rinehart and Winston.

1973 "Campus Mate Selection Preferences: A Cross-National Comparison", *Social Forces* 51:4 (June), 471-77.

Waldman, Elizabeth, and Kathryn R. Gover

1972 "Marital and Family Characteristics of the Labor Force", *Monthly Labor Review* 95:4 (April), 4-8.

*Wargon, Sylvia T.

1974 "Census Data and Social Analysis: A Canadian Example", *Journal of Comparative Family Studies* 5:1 (Spring), 125-33.

Webber, E.

1959 *Escape to Utopia: The Communal Movement in America*. New York: Hastings House.

Weigert, Andrew J., and Darwin L. Thomas
1971 "Family as a Conditional Universal", *Journal of Marriage and the Family* 33:1 (February), 188ff.

*Welfare Council of Ottawa
1961 *Multi-Problem Families*. Ottawa: Information Canada.

Westermarck, E.A.
1903 *The History of Human Marriage*. London: Macmillan.
1930 *A Short History of Marriage*. New York: The Macmillan Company.

*Westley, W.A., and N.B. Epstein
1969 *Silent Majority*. San Francisco: Jossey Boss.

*Weyer, Edward M.
1933 *The Eskimos*. New Haven: Yale University Press.

*Whitehurst, Robert N.
1971 "Violence Potential in Extramarital Sexual Responses", *Journal of Marriage and the Family* 33:4 (November), 683-91.
1973a "Youth Views Marriage: Some Comparisons of Two Generation Attitudes of University Students", pp. 269-79 in Roger W. Libbey and Robert N. Whitehurst, eds., *Renovating Marriage: Toward New Sexual Life Styles*. Danville, California: Consensus Publishers.
1973b "Comparisons of Ideal Spouse Conceptions of American and Canadian University Students". Unpublished paper.

*Whitehurst, Robert N., and Barbara Plant
1971 "A Comparison of Canadian and American University Students' Reference Groups, Alienation and Attitudes Toward Marriage", *International Journal of Sociology of the Family* 1:1 (March), 1-8.

Whiting, John W.M., and Irving L. Child
1953 *Child Training and Personality*. New Haven: Yale University Press.

Wilensky, Harold L., and Charles N. Lebeaux
1958 *Industrial Society and Social Welfare*. New York: Russell Sage Foundation.

Williams, Thomas Rhys
1969 *A Borneo Childhood: Enculturation in Dusun Society*. New York: Holt, Rinehart and Winston.

Winter, W.D., and Antonio J. Ferreira
1969 *Research in Family Interaction: Readings and Commentary*. Palo Alto: Science and Behavior Books.

Wirth, Louis
1938 "Urbanism as a Way of Life", *American Journal of Sociology* 44.

*Wohlstein, Ronald T.
1970 "Premarital Sexual Permissiveness: A Replication". Unpublished M.A. thesis, University of Alberta, Edmonton.

*Woodcock, George
1968 *The Doukhobors*. New York: Oxford University Press.

*Wrong, Dennis H.
1955 *American and Canadian Viewpoints*, prepared for the Canadian-United States Committee on Education. Washington: American Council on Education.

Yang, Martin C.
1945 *A Chinese Village: Taitou, Shantung Province*. New York: Columbia University Press.

Young, Anne
1974 "Work Experience of the Population in 1972", *Monthly Labor Review* 97:2 (February), 48-56.

Young, Michael, and Peter Willmott
1957 *Family and Kinship in East London*. Baltimore: Penguin Books.

Zelditch, Morris
1955 "Role Differentiation in the Nuclear Family: A Comparative Study", pp. 307-53 in T. Parsons and R. Bales, eds., *Family, Socialization and Interaction Process*. Glencoe, Illinois: The Free Press.

Zimmerman, Carl C.
1947 *Family and Civilization*. New York: Harper.
1949 *The Family of Tomorrow*. New York: Harper.

Index